THE BEST OF CHEYENNE BIRD BANTER

25 Years of Bird Stories from the High Plains

BARB GORGES

YUCCA ROAD PRESS

CHEYENNE, WYOMING
2025

Other books by Barb Gorges:

Quilt Care, Construction and Use Advice

Cheyenne Birds by the Month (with photographer Pete Arnold)

Dear Book: The 1916-1920 Diary of Gertrude Oehler Witte

Cheyenne Garden Gossip: Locals Share Secrets for High Plains
Gardening Success

Cheyenne Bird Banter: 25 Years of Bird and Birdwatching News

Except as noted, all essays were previously published in the Wyoming
Tribune Eagle between 1999 and 2024.

Published by Yucca Road Press
3417 Yucca Road
Cheyenne, Wyoming 82001

Printed by IngramSpark, USA

Book design by Chris Hoffmeister, Western Sky Design

Cover photo *Western Meadowlark* by Pete Arnold

ISBN 978-0-9992945-8-1

To the birds and birdwatchers of the High Plains.

Table of Contents

Introduction   **Page xi**

1999   **Page 1**

Article	Title
1	Birding the Colorado coast
2	No headline (bird atlas)
3	No headline (Cats Indoors)
4	Cheyenne birders count 153 individual species
5	Life, death in the backyard
6	Birding know-how a matter of degree
7	Time is here for young to leave nest
8	'Native species' is convoluted concept
9	Songbirds: Sunflower seed is sure to satisfy
10	Blustery days challenge birders, send birds packing
11	Juncos add variety to backyard bird feeder visitors
12	Project FeederWatch relies on citizen scientists
13	Stand up and be counted – by counting

2000   **Page 19**

14	Great Backyard Bird Count needs you
15	Night birding offers unique experience on quiet evenings
16	Birds are now on the move
17	Home on the Prairie
18	Making birds at home in our 'urban forest'
19	Songs tell of habitat, breeding
20	Humans a hazard to navigation
21	Go Birding!
22	'Backyard birding' varies by the yard
23	Ears as important as eyes in early morning bird survey
24	Hummingbirds making their colorful migrations
25	Birds congregating, fattening up to prepare for winter
26	Birds make windy hunt bearable
27	A visit to Lucy's garden creek

2001   **Page 40**

28	Nighttime right time for fauna to frolic
29	Backyard beckons bevy of birds
30	Putting off yard work helps wildlife
31	Robins fledge, face cruel world

Article	Title
32	Don't poison your yard to save it
33	Don't rely on color for bird ID
34	Bird travel plans show variety
35	Pool parties popular with winter birds
36	Close encounters of the bird kind

2002   Page 54

37	Bird count identifies second state record for hermit thrush
38	Some birds aren't crowing about neighbor
39	Immigrant or visitor, red-bellied woodpecker finds food here
40	Finding out where the birds are
41	Birders use cyberspace to advantage
42	Birders flock to observe crane migration
43	Backyards going to the birds
44	Bluebird housing makes a difference
45	Learn to appreciate birds from a distance
46	Brown bird mix-up worth unraveling
47	Records request ruffles feathers
48	Rescuing baby birds not always necessary
49	Local park receives IBA designation
50	Do the Thanksgiving Bird Count without leaving home

2003   Page 77

51	Thanks to awareness, birds now visible on range
52	With birds at feeders, cats are sure to follow
53	Now's the perfect time to identify ducks
54	Cheyenne gaining reputation among warbler watchers
55	Avian guests make themselves at home
56	Dead blackbird tells no tale about West Nile virus
57	Bird of backcountry moves closer to town
58	Birding not just a springtime joy anymore
59	Trumpeter performs for crowd at Holliday Park
60	How to keep up with birding news

2004   Page 94

61	Snow diminishes results of Christmas Bird Count
62	Birders don't always flock together
63	Starlings aren't the darlings of the bird world
64	First sign of spring arrives
65	Prairie Partners provides for plains birds
66	Young chickadees may be changing age-old songs
67	Companions, field guides help with bird identification

Article	Title
68	West Nile virus frightens letter writer
69	Mountain mud bothers birders, but not birds
70	Brown-capped birds cause cracked ribs
71	Windmills safer for birds than other structures
72	Warblers winging their way through on migration path
73	Duck days attract birders to local lakes
74	FeederWatch returns
75	Going where the gulls are adds species to life list

2005   Page 120

Article	Title
76	Resolution produces list of field trip destinations
77	Bird Seed bandits, How hard can it be to outsmart squirrels?
78	Fox squirrels pose ethical, biological problems
79	Are condors coming closer to home?
80	New doves coming to a feeder near you
81	Callers: Give a hoot, Birders need to know etiquette of calling
82	Sharp-tail trip seeks out the other grouse
83	UW researchers seek hummingbird secrets
84	Local bird checklist makes its debut
85	Flamm Fest finds record number

2006   Page 138

Article	Title
86	Woodpeckers find silver lining in devastation done by insects
87	Bird flu and you, so far, so good
88	Research station is, should be for the birds
89	Pup retrieves backyard of wonders
90	Woodpecker visits might bring home improvements
91	A summer of mountain birding
92	The last to go: Warblers put on a late season show
93	Grouse losing ground fast

2007   Page 152

Article	Title
94	This spring watch for 'TVs' soaring above the area
95	Visiting cedar waxwings learn lesson
96	Duck diversity
97	They look helpless, but they probably don't need rescuing
98	Professor sheds light on crossbills
99	'Prairie Ghost' / The 'Where's Waldo' of the wilderness
100	The early birder gets the bird in hand
101	Rosy-finch survey provides bird's eye view
102	Going by the book doesn't prove bird's existence

Article	Title

2008   **Page 170**

103	Birds stay warm, despite cold
104	Doves continue territory expansion, including here
105	On tail of secretive goshawk
106	How to get energy and save our sage grouse
107	12 practical ways you can help keep birds safe
108	Birding naked / It's not nearly as fun as it sounds
109	Nesting season a time for activity
110	Public can chime in on plans for Belvoir Ranch

2009   **Page 185**

111	Wolves in Yellowstone
112	Wyoming has 48 places that are important to birds
113	Young birds stage a summer drama series
114	To feed or not to feed?

2010   **Page 191**

115	Meditation on pine beetles: Is there life after tree death?
116	Listening for birds doesn't get easier with age
117	Spotting nests isn't easy, but here's an idea of where to look
118	New order, new names and new species
119	Bird IDs can be tricky, so a photo is always welcomed
120	Holliday Park summer bird counts total 43 species

2011   **Page 200**

121	Patchwork birding benefits birds
122	Bird feeder quarantine
123	Pelicans at Holliday Park: Why do they stop here?
124	Killer kitchen window adds to national bird death toll
125	Crows come home to roost
126	Deliberate littering leaves local citizens wondering
127	Plan to refresh Lake Minnehaha would benefit park visitors
128	A hawk ate my songbird!

2012   **Page 210**

129	Robins take up year-round residence
130	Snowy owls' visit a sight to behold
131	It's quite clear – birds losing war on the windows
132	Peregrines back with a little help from friends
133	Gardener reports from backyard
134	Colorado black swift wintering grounds are found in Brazil

Article	Title
135	Celebrity field guide author visits Cheyenne
136	Goose population success is messy problem for parks

2013   Page 222

137	Winter is good time to spot unusual birds
138	Game and Fish needs our help
139	Wyoming Birding Bonanza strikes again
140	Early birds yield clues
141	Encourage birding as a lifelong addiction
142	Fall migration kicks up kites, but not the kind found on strings
143	Curiosity, generosity rewarded by UW's Biodiversity Institute

2014   Page 233

144	Owls are among us
145	The great migration, sandhill cranes
146	Let's rethink mega windfarm on behalf of birds, efficiency
147	The bird migration picture gets animation
148	Owl family draws visitors to Lions Park
149	Wyoming refuge is a treasure hidden in plain sight
150	Mind your manners to reduce bird stress
151	6 reasons why you should go to "Bird-day"
152	Can birds save the world?
153	Feral cat policy will fail
154	Risking nice Wyoming weather, grebes, loons get caught

2015   Page 250

155	Archiving bird columns shows changes
156	"Habitat Heroes" wanted to grow native plants
157	Are you a bird expert?
158	Birds are always around to fascinate the young
159	Many mountain birds mean summer of no regrets
160	Feed winter birds for fun

2016   Page 260

161	New camera technology can help birders get perfect shot
162	UW songbird brain studies shed light
163	Bird count day gives us big picture
164	New bird singing, maybe breeding
165	Kids explore nature of the Belvoir Ranch
166	Pondering how much eagles can take in life
167	Collaboration could keep eagles safe
168	Winter raptor marvels, mystery

Article	Title

2017   **Page 272**

169	Birding by app: New adventures in tech
170	Citizen science meets the test of making a difference
171	Bird by ear to identify the unseen
172	Bird-finding betters from generation to generation
173	Kitchen window like a TV peering into lives of birds
174	Project FeederWatch tells us a lot about juncos
175	Wyoming's greater sage-grouse conservation plan

2018   **Page 283**

176	How well do birds tolerate people?
177	Keep birds safe this time of year
178	Bird counting
179	Burrowing owls materialize on SE Wyoming grasslands
180	Condor visits Wyoming
181	Cheyenne bird book coming in late October

2019   **Page 294**

182	Wind development on the Belvoir Ranch has its downsides
183	BirdCast improving birding – and bird safety
184	What the Roundhouse Wind Energy Project application tells us
185	Participating at the Roundhouse hearing
186	Bird families expand in summer
187	Audubon Photography Awards feature Pinedale photographer
188	Nestling ID benefits from crowd sourced help
189	How 3 billion breeding birds disappeared in past 48 years
190	Conservation ranching is for the birds – and for the cows

2020   **Page 308**

191	Be a Citizen Scientist in your backyard
192	Wyobirds and Wyoming Master Naturalists
193	High capacity water wells
194	How to become a birdwatcher
195	2020 Big Day Bird Count best in 18 years
196	Cheyenne Audubon tries a new field trip strategy
197	Summertime is family time for birds
198	Migratory Bird Treaty Act back in full force
199	Project FeederWatch brightens winter with backyard birds
200	First Cassin's finch visits Gorges backyard

Article	Title

2021   page 325

201	Mullen Fire changes forest habitats
202	Close encounters of the robin kind found in backyard
203	Neighborhood Swainson's hawks fledge three
204	Dry Creek restoration to improve hydrology, habitat
205	Fall reservoir birding is a leisurely affair
206	Bird feeding safety: cleaning, cat fencing, glass obstruction

2022   Page 335

207	Ghosts of Christmas Bird Counts past visit local birdwatcher
208	How to keep prairie birds, and us, safe
209	Raptors entice birdwatchers to follow the "The Nunn Guy"
210	WGFD bird farm pheasants; sage grouse farming
211	How power production underlies bird problems
212	Cheyenne Big Day Bird Count catches Arctic visitor
213	Fledge week observations entertain local birdwatcher
214	Merlin's "Sound ID" uncovers hidden birds
215	Audubon Rockies' Hutchinson discusses community science
216	Unusual birds "on the road" this fall in southeastern Wyoming

2023   Page 353

217	Habitat leasing to provide new tool for Wyoming conservation
218	Birders get look behind the scenes, find more eBird perks
219	Longspurs animate local shortgrass prairie
220	House sparrow effect demonstrated in backyard
221	Crow loses life but aids researchers for years to come
222	Not all of Wyoming's birds have been here forever
223	Bird strikes, bird movements interest UW students
224	Biologist on flyway council protecting migratory birds

2024   Page 365

225	Christmas Bird Count looks a bit different from 1956's

Acknowledgements   page 368

Index of Topics   page 370

Index of People, Places, Books,   page 372
Agencies, Organizations, Etc.

Introduction

This book, "The Best of Cheyenne Bird Banter," is from the trove of pieces I wrote for Cheyenne's newspaper, the Wyoming Tribune Eagle, February 1999 through January 2024. The topics of bird feeding, bird identification, bird behavior, bird safety and conservation stay surprisingly green. However, some topics have not, such as the technology for reporting birds.

The pieces that did not make the cut for this book, such as bird book reviews, birding travelogs from beyond the High Plains, Wyoming Roadside Attractions shorts, many bird count reports, pigeon racing stories, redundant columns on bird feeding, and a sprinkling of stories about scouting, quilting and moose hunting, can be found at https://CheyenneBirdBanter.wordpress.com and have also been archived in a book with very limited distribution, "Cheyenne Bird Banter."

I've been the Cheyenne-High Plains Audubon Society's program chair often since 1990, writing some Bird Banter columns about chapter programs or field trips. It was because of the Audubon news releases I was writing that in 1999 Bill Gruber, the Wyoming Tribune Eagle's Outdoors editor, proposed that I write a column he dubbed "Bird Banter." I was hesitant to accept since there were people in town with more expertise, even academic training, in ornithology.

But I did have a minor in writing along with my degree in natural resource management from the University of Wisconsin – Stevens Point, plus three years on the weekly campus newspaper, first in production, then as a reporter and finally as the Environmental section editor. But most importantly, in 1999 I was then a stay-at-home mom taking classes at the community college, and I had time. The internet was just getting started, putting all sorts of resources and people within reach, in addition to my birding friends.

Back then, the Outdoors section was four pages every Wednesday with a lot of information from the Wyoming Game and Fish Department and Bill's weekly column and usually his front page, full-color feature story on his participation in some hearty outdoor recreational activity. Occasionally, my column made the Outdoors front page, too.

Writing for the WTE means using the WTE version of AP Style. It means no bird names are capitalized except the parts that are a proper noun, like Townsend's solitaire. It does make for smoother reading unless you want to talk about how yellow yellow warblers are. Also, when I started, there were "Web sites" and the "Internet." But over time, they morphed into "website" and "internet," the style I decided to use throughout this collection of columns.

There are a lot of word pairs that go through phases of hyphenation and amalgamation, and I've tried to stick with one usage, for instance, "birdwatching" instead of "bird watching" or "bird-watching."

This collection of columns is in chronological order. In the background, Jeffrey and Bryan grow up and get married and have kids, Mark retires, pets come and go, and we find new birds and adventures.

There are recurring themes such as the annual iterations of the Great Backyard Bird Count, Big Day Bird Count, Thanksgiving Bird Count, Christmas Bird Count and Project FeederWatch—just as many birds have their own recurring annual patterns: spring migration, breeding, nesting, fledging, fall migration.

Then there is the bird conservation news: declining numbers of sage grouse and other birds continent-wide, the negative impact of wind and solar energy on birds, other wildlife and people, despite the benefits of changing over from fossil fuels. And who knew that windows and loose cats could also have a terrible impact on birds?

The metamorphosis of technology over 25 years has been tremendous. The Cornell Lab of Ornithology keeps coming up with new ways for eBird to make collecting data enticing for us citizen/community scientists. Artificial intelligence like CLO's free Merlin app keeps getting better at identifying birds in the field. Technology for tracking wildlife keeps shrinking and ornithologists quickly adopt it. Social media keeps birders in touch and helps recruit new members to our ranks.

The push to turn lawns into habitat for birds, bats, bees and butterflies has been gathering momentum over the last 15 years, seeping into both my bird and garden columns and publications everywhere.

I don't know how influential I've been in Cheyenne. When the sky at night is still full of unnecessary and harmful outdoor lighting, or people tell me their cat simply can't stand to be kept indoors, or someone else replaces their lawn with gravel instead of low-maintenance native plants, my contribution feels insubstantial. But then someone tells me they enjoy my columns.

I appreciate having a role in my community out here on the High Plains of southeastern Wyoming. I appreciate being allowed to educate readers about nature through birds, and to say a word on their behalf.

Barb Gorges
Cheyenne, Wyoming
January 2025

1999

1

Birding the Colorado coast

There is a section of the Golden Guides' "Birds of North America" I never expected to use unless I became wealthy enough to take ocean cruises.

The section on sea ducks lists species spending winters along the Pacific and Atlantic coasts and summers on the shores of Hudson's Bay. Perhaps by the time I'm old and retired, I thought, I'll have the funds to travel there.

Then I went on a field trip 20 miles south of Cheyenne a couple of winters ago and saw my first oldsquaw [name changed to long-tailed duck in 2000]. This is a sea duck that spends summers on the North American tundra and winters far out in the ocean. But it also has a habit of hanging out on large inland lakes. Our nearest large lake is the reservoir at the Rawhide power plant just off I-25, not far into Colorado. The water remains open at about 65 degrees all winter, unless the plant must go offline temporarily, said Dr. Ron Ryder, Colorado State University wildlife professor emeritus. Ryder has been studying the ecology of the reservoir for 14 years.

The oldsquaw sighting was somewhat unusual and hasn't been repeated yet this season. However, a red-necked grebe, another coastal-wintering waterfowl species was spotted. Birder Gloria Lawrence says the oldsquaw is a visitor nine out of 10 years on the North Platte River and Gray Rocks Reservoir, probably because these waters are farther north and closer to the duck's normal range.

To look for sea ducks, you may accompany Ron and the Cheyenne High Plains Audubon Society to Rawhide Reservoir on Saturday, February 20. The trip is free and open to the public. The group will meet at the Cheyenne Botanic Gardens in Lions Park by 7 a.m. Call Dave Felley for details.

Ron will be able to take us behind the locked gates, but if you miss the field trip, you can still scope out the bird action from the public observation area. Take I-25 south to Exit 288 (Buckeye) and head toward the mountains for about three miles. You'll need a spotting scope or strong binoculars to appreciate the diverse bird life.

To find out about or to report unusual bird sightings in Wyoming, call the toll-free hotline maintained by the Murie Audubon Society in Casper.

When I checked recently, Gloria had listed canvasback, dipper and northern shrike. Last month the hotline had Eurasian wigeon, Lapland longspur and glaucous gull sightings. Many of the birds listed are in the Casper area, but the hotline serves the whole state.

For those of us who like birding best at our kitchen windows, don't forget the

Second Annual Great Backyard Bird Count sponsored by Bird Source, a joint venture between National Audubon and the Cornell Lab of Ornithology. It is scheduled for this weekend, Feb. 19-21. Just observe the species occurring in your yard or neighborhood for half an hour or so, and then go on-line to report. You may want to explore the website in advance; last year's data is an interesting snapshot of where birds were wintering. [See www.birds.cornell.edu.]

2 Bird Banter

Atlas was the Greek god whose job for eternity was holding the world up on his shoulders. Putting together the new Colorado Breeding Bird Atlas took 1,295 volunteers a relative eternity. Following 73,000 hours of fieldwork over nine years beginning in 1987, it took another few years to turn all that data into the 636-page book that just came out.

Colorado's atlas is a snapshot of avian breeding activity for 264 species in the state. The protocol called for studying a sampling of 1,760 blocks of land out of a total of 10,000. Each measured 10 square miles and needed to be visited at least four times for at least a half day, perhaps at night if owls or other nocturnal species are involved.

Besides volunteers, the atlas project depended on the good will of hundreds of landowners who allowed fieldworkers access.

Wyoming hasn't done a breeding bird atlas yet. Do we have the dedicated volunteers to accomplish a survey within the recommended 10 years?

One of the authors of the Colorado atlas, Ron Ryder, will speak at the next Cheyenne Audubon meeting about the rigors of undertaking such a project.

Birders accompanying Ron to look for seabirds at the Rawhide power plant reservoir late last month did find one species. The red-necked grebe normally winters on either the Atlantic or Pacific coasts. More common species such as common merganser, ruddy duck, and lesser scaup were also seen.

The highlight of the field trip was a stop to see a golden-crowned sparrow that's been wintering at a feeder north of Fort Collins. Closely resembling our usual white-crowned sparrow, it was a long way from its usual winter home in California or its summer range in Alaska.

I had a poor showing at our birdfeeder to report for the Second Annual Great Backyard Bird Count in February. Just a few house finches, house sparrows and juncos showed up. People from about 30 localities in Wyoming counted a total of 61 species. Most often seen was the black-capped chickadee (49 reports), followed by the black-billed magpie (35) and the house finch (35).

The species with the most individuals counted was the gray-crowned rosy finch (756), followed by the house sparrow (619) and the house finch (473).

Nationally, out of 39,000 reports, the top three most frequently reported birds were mourning dove, northern cardinal and dark-eyed junco.

The Favorite Bird Survey had 15,000 participants whose top three favorites were black-capped chickadee, northern cardinal and ruby-throated hummingbird. My favorite, the mountain bluebird, didn't make the top 10. It isn't cute or bright red. While I admire its unearthly blue color, the reason I like it is that it's my favorite harbinger of spring. This is the time of year to see

it migrating to the mountains. Cheyenne Audubon plans a field trip to Pole
Mountain to look for bluebirds March
27. As usual, the field trip is free and
open to the public. Double-check with

Dave Felley about plans to leave the
Cheyenne Botanic Gardens parking
lot at 9 a.m.

Spring migration is underway
in Wyoming.

3 Bird Banter

Thursday, April 8, 1999, Outdoors, page C3

There are hazards to having no
window screens. Eighteen years ago,
my open windows let in the fresh spring
breezes - and a stray kitten.

I formally adopted the kitten, and
in gratitude, Willy brought me trea-
sures that first summer: an earthworm,
a sparrow, a mouse and a tail-less
dead squirrel.

As an active member of Audubon,
I identified his bird kills and marveled
that he was more likely to kill interesting songbirds visiting our backyard than
the abundant resident house sparrows.
Willy had a connoisseur's tastes.

I allowed Willy to be an indoor/out-
door cat for eight years, which was longer than the two- to five-year lifespan
predicted for the average outdoor cat.

When Willy appeared to be aging, I
decided to make him an indoor cat.

This also took care of the hypocrisy
of being a bird-killing cat owner and
president of an Audubon chapter.

In retrospect, I'm not sure why I let
Willy run loose, having myself grown
up with two indoor cats. The outdoor
life is hazardous – I heard tires squeal
and saw cars miss Willy. And loose cats
are more likely to be injured in fights
and pick up lethal diseases.

Scientific studies show that domestic
cats take a huge toll on bird life. Putting
bells on cats doesn't save birds because
either the cat learns not to make the bell
ring or the birds hear it and don't associate it with danger.

A well-fed cat is just as likely to kill

birds. Willy was proof of that.

And so are all the uneaten bird bodies
neighborhood cats leave in my yard.

I also knew I had no justification for
letting Willy run loose on the grounds
that a cat needs his freedom. After all,
my dog was fenced in.

Livestock are fenced in. At least
Willy was neutered and not contributing
kittens to the millions that must be euthanized by animal shelters every year.

I wonder now why I put myself
through the emotional drain of nights
Willy didn't make it home. So many
hazards await a cat: nasty dogs, malicious drivers, thugs with guns, cruel
children and poisons and traps unintentional and otherwise.

Willy spent his second eight years at
home. He became an ardent bird watcher, hiding in the house plants as birds
ate sunflower seeds from the windowsill. It was the diseases of old age that
claimed Willy's life at age 16.

People who know my Audubon connection have been surprised to learn that
my family and I adopted two kittens last
spring, for reasons only other cat lovers
can appreciate.

Henry and Joey are strictly indoor
cats. They've discovered the joys of bird
and squirrel watching. The boys invent
new cat toys and exercise equipment for
them, and I've discovered deodorizing,
clumping cat litter that really works.

This spring my conscience is clear.
My cats will not be killing helpless nestlings of songbird species with declining

population problems. How about you?

For information to share with your cat-owning neighbors and tips for keeping your indoor cat content, contact: Cats Indoors!, American Bird Conservancy.

4

Thursday, May 27, 1999, Outdoors, page C4

Cheyenne birders count 153 individual species

CHEYENNE - Authors of bird identification guides like to split North America in half. They make two volumes, each close to field-jacket pocket-size.

But if the only field guide in your pocket on May 15 was the western version of Peterson's, Audubon's or Stokes', you would never have identified the most interesting bird to show up in Cheyenne on the Big Day Count.

To find the hooded warbler, you need a field guide for the whole continent, such as National Geographic's or the Golden Guide. Range maps show these small, olive-backed, yellow-bellied, black-hooded birds summering east of the Missouri River, where they are common in swamps and moist woodlands.

And that's where we found the hooded warbler: in a temporary, tree-filled swamp at the Hereford Ranch, where it flitted about catching insects.

These warblers are categorized as rare migrants, according to Jane Dorn, records compiler for the Cheyenne High Plains Audubon Society chapter. This year's sighting was not the first record for Cheyenne; they seem to occur at 5-year intervals.

"We're on a minor flyway that comes up the Front Range," Dorn explained.

"We act a little like a migrant trap."

Birds would rather follow the mountains than cross them, and then Cheyenne appears below like an oasis.

Many species, Dorn said, migrate at night, probably to avoid predators. By sunrise they're ready to spend the day resting and feeding.

Within the Cheyenne area, Lions Park is probably the busiest during migration. Birders from Casper, Riverton and Douglas met the Cheyenne contingent there at 6 a.m. the day of the count, and we discovered 55 species in the following two to three hours.

Our best find at the park was the sora, a small, chicken-like bird from the rail family. I saw it first four days earlier with my class of sixth-graders on a bird watching field trip.

Strutting and pecking in a thin cover of willows next to the lake, only 20 feet from us, the bird obligingly showed his bright yellow bill, chicken-like feet, and short, perpendicular tail.

By Saturday, however, he'd retreated to thicker cover at the other end of the lake. That's when birders were forced to use piecemeal identification tactics: recognizing parts of the bird as they are glimpsed and assembling them like a mental jigsaw puzzle for positive identification.

A first record for Cheyenne was a black-throated sparrow seen by Bob Dorn. Ironically, the Dorns were just back from a trip to the Arizona desert, where the sparrows are supposed to be. Perhaps this one got a little excited about migration and overshot his destination!

Besides unusual species, the spring bird count documents changes in populations. Crow populations in

Cheyenne are exploding. The black-crowned night-heron is pioneering new nesting sites.

How many species are counted on the Big Day really depends on how well the Saturday in the middle of May coincides with the migration wave.

This year the weather was fairly cooperative. The wind from the south may have pushed birds into Cheyenne. On the other hand, as Dorn put it,

"Birds don't sit to get looked at when it's windy."

This year's count, at 153 species, was one of Cheyenne's best ever.

Dorn envisions Cheyenne birders someday increasing the count by 20 species, assembling in slightly competitive teams and spreading out at dawn to every known birding hotspot. Who knows what misplaced warblers we'd find then?

Species Spotted in the Bird Count

Pied-billed Grebe
Eared Grebe
Western Grebe
American White Pelican
Double-crested Cormorant
Great Blue Heron
Snowy Egret
Black-crowned Night-Heron
White-faced Ibis
Snow Goose
Canada Goose
Green-winged Teal
Mallard
Northern Pintail
Blue-winged Teal
Cinnamon Teal
Northern Shoveler
Gadwall
American Wigeon
Redhead
Ring-necked Duck
Lesser Scaup

Bufflehead
Common Merganser
Ruddy Duck
Turkey Vulture
Northern Harrier
Cooper's Hawk
Broad-winged Hawk
Swainson's Hawk
Red-tailed Hawk
American Kestrel
Sora
American Coot
Black-bellied Plover
Semipalmated Plover
Killdeer
American Avocet
Greater Yellowlegs
Willet
Spotted Sandpiper
Upland Sandpiper
Marbled Godwit
Western Sandpiper

Least Sandpiper
Long-billed Dowitcher
Common Snipe
Wilson's Phalarope
Franklin's Gull
Ring-billed Gull
California Gull
Rock Dove
Mourning Dove
Great Horned Owl
Burrowing Owl
Chimney Swift
Belted Kingfisher
Lewis's Woodpecker
Downy Woodpecker
Hairy Woodpecker
Northern Flicker
Olive-sided Flycatcher
Western Wood-Pewee

5

Thursday, July 22, 1999, Outdoors, page C4

Life, death in the backyard

I love a good murder mystery – in book form – not in my back yard.

I found the first body under a tree in late June, a young blue jay with feathers just beginning to emerge. Looking straight up through the branches above the body, I could see a pile of sticks in a crotch. Falling out of the nest onto hard-packed earth seemed to be a logical cause of death.

Then I remembered the feud our whole family witnessed from the kitchen window. This could be a case of squirrel retribution.

There's some kind of Saturday morning cartoon humor watching a flying blue jay poke a running squirrel in the posterior. But the possibility that both blue jay and squirrel could be responsible for raiding each other's nests reminds the viewer that this isn't Barney and friends.

This is that old life and death struggle for food and shelter. Blue jays and squirrels compete for nearly the same kinds of foods and trees. And blue jays are known to be omnivorous, eating insects and small rodents as well as the sunflower seeds I put out.

My husband, Mark, found the second blue jay body early in July. Circumstances didn't seem to point to the usual suspects. The body was unmolested by neighborhood cats. The neck didn't seem broken (Bird safety is a good reason for saying you don't do windows – clean ones mislead birds into thinking they can fly through your house.). And there were no outward signs of disease or poisons. Also, a vigorous flock of jays remains in the neighborhood.

It's nice Ziploc makes bird-sized body bags and the morgue is as close as my freezer. Mark and I hope to get friends at the Fish and Wildlife Service to act as coroners and also, for educational use, to act as taxidermists, since they have permits for possessing dead birds.

A couple of years ago, we had a call from a nearly hysterical bird watcher who had found 30 or 40 dead house finches in her yard. Autopsies proved the killer was an outbreak of salmonella passed from finch to finch at infected feeders.

Feeders cause unnatural crowding and need to be cleaned every few weeks, especially if they're up during the summer. Be sure to rinse all the soap off and get them dry before refilling.

This spring another epidemic hit, leaving bodies on lawns all over Cheyenne. As trees greened up in May, it was with dismay I observed my favorite birches would not be returning from their seasonal somnolence.

Randy Overstreet, assistant city forester, explained to me that the murderers are known but only apprehended with strong chemicals. Bronze birch borers are rice-grain-sized insects laying eggs on trunks and limbs of birches. After hatching, the young bore through the bark and feast on the living tissue just underneath. Younger trees, vigorously growing in the birch's native climate, may be able to grow around the damage, but older trees cannot. Trees here are under stress already, trying to survive in Cheyenne's harsh, alien climate.

I'm a weird person. Even if a tree isn't mine and it's the one in the neighbor's yard I observe every day from my window, losing it is a mournful experience for me. What if these boreal skeletons could be thought of as sculpture and left upright? For over half the year living trees are bare, too. In the wild, dead trees provide hollows for cavity nesting birds such as woodpeckers and house wrens.

Birches don't have large limbs that would be dangerous as they decay and drop off. Even cut back to a 12- or 20-foot stump, they could become decorative posts for bird houses or feeders. I like the vine-covered cottonwood trunk at 28th and Evans. It wouldn't be surprising to find a bird nest wedged in the foliage.

The best backyards for birds are full of diversity and seem a little unkempt. I believe every dead tree does not have to be recycled into wood chips or wood smoke. They can continue to serve the avian population – and a few squirrels too.

Not all mysteries are on the

bookshelf. You too can be an outdoor detective. Just keep your eyes open. But I can't guarantee you'll find out whodunit at the end of the 29th chapter!

6 Birding know-how a matter of degree

The phone rings. "Is this the Audubon Society?" I say yes and introduce myself to the caller.

"There's this bird in my yard. It's brown with red on its face."

This is where I offer up my best guess, the house finch. Usually, I can tell by the way callers word the question whether they are, in my mental hierarchy, working on their "first degree" of bird watching or working on accomplishing a higher degree of proficiency.

Some of our bird knowledge seems to be genetic. I have yet to give a talk at a school where the children didn't correctly name the robin. But after that the names seem to be generic categories: "blackbirds," "seagulls" or "ducks."

The ordinary person does not look for birds. He only notices that some bird hits his windshield, the cat dragged in some feathers or some bird has left berry droppings on the front steps.

The first degree of bird watching begins when a person notices some black birds have iridescent heads (grackles), parking lot sparrows come in two styles (male and female house sparrows), and not all birds swimming at Lions Park are ducks (coots and grebes).

To meet the requirement for this first degree, one must find a way to cross paths with birds intentionally. This usually means throwing seed or bread crumbs on the deck or patio. At our house we put up a bird feeder.

This naturally leads to trying to figure out which birds are visiting.

Bird watching isn't just about identification of course. It's also about observing behavior: a flock of goldfinches plays king of the hill on the thistle feeder; the mourning doves have a very peculiar walk; and blue jays grip sunflower seeds with their feet and hammer them with their bills.

Bird watchers attempting the second degree are ready to look beyond their backyards. Birding with other people is the easiest. I started showing up for Audubon field trips. It's so handy to point and ask, "What's that?" And it's even more fun when other people point out a bird and tell me facts not in the field guide.

But perhaps Audubon field trips aren't scheduled as often as the budding birder would like. Here's the first step of the third degree: He decides to plan his own field trip to some of the places he's been before.

However, to really accomplish the third degree in my hierarchy, the birder must intentionally decide to explore a new place. It's finally time to invest in a bird finding book like Oliver Scott's "A Birder's Guide to Wyoming" or, fresh out this spring, the second edition of "Wyoming Birds" by Jane L. Dorn and Robert D. Dorn of Cheyenne. For those of you with the first edition, this one is worth getting. It has easier to read typeface, a water-resistant cover, new introduction with helpful subheadings and more maps and information.

The Dorns have written up 437 Wyoming species, drawing on more than 30 years of personal observation and records going back 150 years. They have charted each species' seasonal occurrence around the state using the latilong system, which divides Wyoming into 28 rectangles and have listed sites where each species has the best chance of being seen.

So, if a birder were to examine her life list for Wyoming and discover she's missing *Amphispiza belli*, the sage sparrow, the entry in "Wyoming Birds" would tell her to look in medium to tall sagebrush between May and September. The best places to look would be 5 to 35 miles west of Baggs, 5 to 10 miles south of Rock Springs, the Fontenelle Dam area in Lincoln County and the Gebo area west of Kirby in Hot Springs County.

The Dorns' book can also be used in reverse. At the back is a list of 124 birding hotspots listed by county. Each entry notes directions for getting there, expected species, best season for visiting and available amenities such as restrooms or campgrounds. Several maps help those of us who do better visualizing directions than reading them.

New to this edition is a section devoted to directions for day tours that link the most notable birding spots.

Just remember to be prepared for Wyoming weather and road conditions so that a day tour doesn't become a week of winter camping.

The further degrees of my bird watching hierarchy pertain to how far one travels and how much time is spent birding. Even further up are the birders who volunteer to collect information for scientific studies or get involved in habitat conservation. Somewhere beyond are the people who share their knowledge, leading field trips or writing books. That's where I find the Dorns, helping us all to reach the Nth degree.

7

Time is here for young to leave nest

August is the time for kids to leave home, avian as well as human, although for college students and kindergartners it's only on a trial basis.

Nevertheless, getting the young to move out of their nest is a perennial parental problem.

Ruth Keto watched a family drama take place in her Sun Valley backyard.

A Swainson's hawk was berating its two young about it being time to hit the road (or the thermals maybe). The young complained loudly, and one continued to cling to the power pole for nearly an hour, as if it were a life raft. As of this writing, the young hawks are still to be seen hanging out around the neighborhood.

Not only do these immature hawks have to leave their nest, they have to flee the country. Swainson's spend the winter in Argentina.

And I worried about sending the boys six blocks to school. Imagine what Swainson's parents think about sending their progeny off to another continent. Of course, birds are supposed to be operating on instinct. If they were capable of agonizing over the perils of a 7,000-mile trip, every winter we'd be finding nests stuffed with the frozen bodies of the timid.

So why don't Swainson's hawks stick around and eat rodents all winter like other hawks? It seems when they don't have to succor nestlings with mice or rabbits, they prefer large, live insects, which are not available here in the winter. A few years ago, farmers in Argentina inadvertently caused thousands of Swainson's hawks to die when they poisoned an outbreak of grasshoppers.

Parents every generation worry they've forgotten to tell the children some essential ingredient for a successful life. I don't suppose all those noisy feeding episodes at the nest are parents imparting words of wisdom such as "Don't forget to preen behind your ears; follow the flock; and don't talk to strange cats."

Despite the desire to empty the nest, it's hard for parents to give up the urge to feed the young. A couple weeks ago we were fishing in the Sierra Madres when I heard a flock's worth of faint but familiar bird song all around me. Having neglected to bring the binoculars (I was using polarized sunglasses to look for fish instead), I had to wait until two birds lighted on a dead branch.

Silhouettes showing crests on their heads reminded me the sounds they made were the same as those from the waxwings raiding the fruit of my neighbor's mountain ash in the winter. Closer inspection proved them to be cedar waxwings rather than Bohemians waxwings.

One waxwing was feeding the other. As it wasn't mating season, I assumed this was a parent feeding a nearly adult-sized juvenile. There were ripe berries everywhere, so why was the parent still feeding it? It might be tough for young hawks to chase down prey but even a youngster unsteady on its wings can bag a raspberry.

Maybe it still wasn't an efficient forager and needed help getting enough calories to put on weight for the winter. Waxwings around here don't migrate so much as spend the winter as itinerant berry-seekers.

Being married to a fisherman takes me places I might not otherwise go, such as the riparian zone where I saw the waxwings. At least, being already mid-August, the mosquitoes on Battle Creek, elevation 7,500 feet, had called it quits. However, the jungle of willow and alder was still cooking in the midday heat.

As we made our way along the banks from fishing spot to fishing spot, I smelled crushed mint and mud. And I felt scratchy. That is, every branch, thistle and nettle tried to leave its mark on my skin. Unidentifiable little brown bird shadows flitted through the dappled leaf light.

Luckily, even this jungle had openings where scattered wild sunflowers grew more than head high, and it was possible to see the sky again and see a belted kingfisher pass by.

In my back yard this past week I heard another familiar bird song. This time it was a goldfinch and one of its young.

The American goldfinch nests late compared to everyone else.

That these seed eaters wait so long makes sense when you realize it takes that long for the new weed and seed crop to mature so they'll have abundant food for their young.

Do goldfinches really drop dry, pointy seeds down the tender gullets of their babies? No. Instead, the experts say they partially digest food and regurgitate. Guess I should have watched those goldfinches more carefully to see if it's true, but I didn't think to wear binoculars while hanging out the wash.

Successful Bird Watching Rule Number 1: Birds are everywhere.

Rule Number 2: Wear binoculars everywhere.

8 'Native species' is convoluted concept

A woman researching a fourth-grade statistics and probability question for the WyCAS (Wyoming Comprehensive Assessment System) called me the other day and asked how many native species of birds and fish are in Wyoming.

Math test question writers like to use local color.

At first glance, this question has a straightforward answer, at least for fish, but I soon realized why the Wyoming Game and Fish Department passed the buck to me (besides non-game biologist Andrea Cerovski being out in the field all week).

There are two variables in this simple question: What is meant by native? And what is a species? Biologists are still debating the answers.

First, the word "species." The most accepted definition is, if two organisms can produce viable (fertile) offspring, they are of the same species.

It can take a while to determine this with creatures as elusive as birds.

For instance, the 1961 edition of "Peterson's Field Guide to Western Birds" lists red-shafted, yellow-shafted and gilded flickers living in different parts of the country. However, people living where the species overlapped noticed hybridizations, so the American Ornithologists' Union (AOU) investigated and changed flicker nomenclature.

The 1983 "Golden Guide to Birds of North America" lists all three species under "Common Flicker." But the 1983 National Geographic guide lists all three under "Northern Flicker." Somebody seemed to have missed an AOU update.

However, the 1996 Stokes guide uses the AOU's 6th edition checklist and has the gilded flicker listed separately and the other two as "Northern."

In the 1999 edition of "Wyoming Birds," the Dorns have the good sense to list the information for the red-shafted and yellow-shafted separately (the gildeds are in southern Arizona and Mexico), just in case further investigation changes the AOU's ruling again.

It's important to remember that God did not invent species nomenclature. Linnaeus did, in the 1700s. Like all classification systems, his taxonomy was invented for human convenience, giving us means for naming organisms as well as showing relationships – possibly evolutionary relationships – between them.

For a fascinating perspective on species and evolution, read "Dinosaur Lives," by John R. Horner, curator of paleontology at the Museum of the Rockies, in Bozeman, Mont.

Besides changes in nomenclature, the number of bird or fish species in Wyoming can change because species become extinct, new species are discovered, species are introduced (especially game fish) or species move to Wyoming of their own accord.

Which brings us to the definition of "native." I called Dr. Ron Ryder, a retired Colorado State University wildlife professor, to refresh my memory. He chuckled and said (the now politically incorrect) definition of native is those species present before the white man came.

So "Wyoming Native" as seen on bumper stickers wouldn't mean the same thing for birds. Being born here isn't enough.

In bird watching circles we quickly

dismiss domesticated birds and escaped exotics, though if the Eurasian collared dove begins breeding in the wild, it will be classified as an introduced species, like starlings and house sparrows, which are native to Europe.

What about birds that are native to other parts of North America but move to Wyoming on their own, like the blue jay? It's been years since farmers planting Great Plains shelterbelts inadvertently provided blue jays with stepping stones to the Rockies. For most purposes, they seem to be lumped with our native species.

We can't classify as native the birds migrating through Wyoming. That would be like census takers counting tourists. But what about birds that spend the summer with us? Some spend the majority of the year in Central and South America.

The latest research points to the idea that our migrants are really tropical birds that discovered they could breed more successfully if they made use of the North's seasonally available resources.

Maybe we should ask Mexican migrants working sugar beets or retired "snowbirds" heading for Arizona where they feel they are native to. And let's not forget the skiers who spend the winters in Jackson. They also have counterparts – birds here only in the winter.

I don't think Lisa Colvin, the researcher in Louisville, expected an essay answer for her math question about how many native bird and fish species we have.

According to my in-house fisheries biologist, Wyoming has 76 species of fish, 54 of which are native.

For birds, I used the Dorns as my authority. Of the 437 species they list as having been observed in Wyoming, one is extinct (the passenger pigeon), 61 are accidentals (off-course migrants like the Arctic tern seen in 1997 or escapees like the Egyptian goose seen in 1962); 18 are visitors (meaning they show up every few years, like your cousin Al the elk hunter); and 86 are migrants (like tourists pausing to refuel at truck stops).

That leaves 271 resident species. Of those, 154 are here only in the summer and nine are here only in the winter. That leaves 108 year-round resident species, but six were introduced: the two mentioned previously, plus other Asian and Eurasian species: the ring-necked pheasant, gray partridge, chukkar (all game species) and rock doves, commonly known as pigeons.

So, after all that math, only 102 species of birds are hardy enough to be year-long Wyoming resident natives.

Those fourth graders are in for one heck of a math problem.

9

Thursday, October 14, 1999, Outdoors, page C4

Songbirds: Sunflower seed is sure to satisfy

It's mid-October, and no one seems particularly interested in my bird feeders.

The cats are falling asleep at the window waiting for some feathered action. I wonder, where is everyone?

It turns out the goldfinches and their friends have been having a weed seed bash nearby, where construction left a huge pile of dirt last summer.

The hill sprouted wild sunflowers, mustards and other opportunistic plants now going to seed.

"You birds'll be back," I muse. "As soon as it gets really cold, you'll be back for my premium black-oil sunflower seed instead of this 'cheep' stuff."

My feeders only carry the finest seed, grown over near Carpenter by Jim Dolan.

The Rubbermaid barrel in the garage is just about empty, though, and I'm looking forward to offering this year's vintage: Mycogen Plant Sciences varieties 83-10 and 83-72.

There's a lot of sunflower seed being grown this year, due to low wheat prices and farmers switching to a three-year rotation system. But Jim's seed stands out because of the quaint customs associated with it.

First, seed is planted between mid-May and mid-June. No irrigation is necessary and no cultivation is used since the fields are pre-treated.

About mid-September the plants mature and begin to dry out.

Ripening sunflowers attract birds. Jim says birds will hit hard if the field is near trees and water. But despite daily predation by birds, farmers have to wait until the plants reach about 10 percent moisture. Otherwise, the seeds will spoil in the storage bins.

A good hard freeze hastens the drying. Then it's time to combine. If conditions are right, just the heads can be cut, and the combine will separate out most of the trash.

Jim funnels the seed through a piece of equipment called a scalper, a whirling metal mesh cylinder that leaves less than two percent trash before shooting seed into the bins.

Now here's the quaint part: Every year since about 1992, Jim's barn has been the scene of the bagging ritual. About mid-November, 20 or 30 Cheyenne Audubon members show up with shovels, scales and sacks. The seed is sent through the scalper once more and Auduboners, standing in a trough reminiscent of grape stompings, shovel it into 25- or 50-pound bags and tie them shut with twine.

Within an hour or two, a couple tons of pre-paid seed orders are bagged and loaded into a convoy of pickups, Toyotas and minivans heading back to the Gorgeses' garage, where the less fortunate pick up their orders.

Those of us able to help bag have an inner sense of harmony with our agricultural ancestors. I'm not sure what my great-grandfather – the Wisconsin dairy farmer who built a round barn – would think of these steel-sided pole barns on the plains, however.

This year's sunflower vintage will be special because Jim plans to retire from farming. Audubon will hardly make a dent in his estimated 240,000-pound harvest, most of which will be commercially bagged for birds or crushed for oil.

In the tradition of Paul Newman giving his salad dressing profits to charities, Audubon profits go to a good cause. They help fund the Audubon Adventures program offered to local fourth through sixth grade classrooms, as well as buying more seed to give to nursing homes and schools with bird feeders.

How much seed should a bird-feeding person buy? Audubon offers its bulk-rate bargain only once a year. Underestimating means buying seed grown who-knows-where, Kansas or Nebraska or someplace. Buying too much means feeding birds into the summer (no problem) or sowing it in the alley.

Storing seed for a year or so is all right if it's kept clean and dry. At our house, a 33-gallon garbage can does the job.

How fast the birds eat seed depends on how well known the feeding location is, how many feeders are in the neighborhood, whether squirrels and aggressive birds like grackles and blue jays raid feeders, and how many times a day the feeders are filled.

It also matters how prolific the natural seed sources are, how deep the snow gets, how many cats "put birds off their feed" and whether the feeders have been exposed to the contagious disease killing finches.

To avoid this last variable, clean feeders every few weeks with soap and water.

According to a publication put out by "Birder's World" magazine, black-oil sunflower seed attracts the most kinds of birds. It's the best buy, unlike many packaged mixes that have a lot of undesirable seed types the birds ignore and let turn to mush under the feeder. Black-oil is also more nutritious than striped sunflower seeds.

When bird watchers reach the addictive stage of this hobby, they experiment with Niger, corn, proso millet, peanuts, suet, oranges and other fruit. After black-oil sunflower seed, however, the next best thing to offer birds is water.

Yep, our avian pals are just out looking for a good time at a good watering hole.

That weed-seed eating bunch I observed was holding their bash on the banks of a tributary of Crow Creek.

10 Blustery days challenge birders, send birds packing

Thursday, October 28, 1999, Outdoors, page C4

Call me a fair-weather birder, but our mid-October snowstorm was not good for binoculars, spotting scopes or field guides.

Of course, the biggest reason for cancelling Audubon's field trip to Glendo Reservoir was poor road conditions.

There were birds to watch at home. Bad weather brought a mob of finches.

The cats sat at the window transfixed as the birds played musical perches on the tube of Niger thistle. Though they show just a slight wash of yellow this time of year, goldfinches still have their distinctive black wings with white wing-bars.

Two days before the storm, Fred Lebsack of the Cheyenne High Plains Audubon Society, Steven Roseberry of the Laramie County Conservation District and I met with Eleanor Grinnell's Community Based Occupational Education (CBOE) science class at the Airport Golf Course.

It was one of those fiercely bright, ferociously windy days. The high school students were to do their monthly water sampling and bird observations at selected points as part of the Audubon Cooperative Sanctuary System program. They document improvements as the golf course adopts environmentally friendly grounds maintenance practices.

Although it too is named for John James Audubon, this program is not related to the National Audubon Society or its chapters. That doesn't stop Fred and me from taking any excuse for bird watching, however, especially for an educational and scientific cause.

But we were disappointed this day. The wind had every bird sitting tight. A few juncos tittered in the brush. Mallards collected along the shore. A pied-billed grebe (not a duck) and a redhead (a duck) didn't let the wind bother them. Both were underwater most of the time, diving frequently after small aquatic animals to eat.

But mostly at each of the eight bird-watching stations, we waited the procedural five minutes, straining in vain for sights or sounds avian, wanting to say "a-ha!" at each falling leaf.

Anyone who's withstood a few falls in Cheyenne recognizes the blustery, sunny weather that precedes a weather front. Lingering migratory birds recognize their flight south is ready for boarding.

Though I will miss them, how can I blame the birds for wanting to double their mileage with a stiff tailwind? Just how many miles does a one-ounce warbler get per insect anyway?

Having struck out bird-wise twice within three days, I decided the day after the storm I would visit a reservoir close to home. Early in the morning Jeffrey and I pulled out our winter clothes and the spotting scope and drove out.

It was as cold as any Christmas Bird Count. The brisk breeze and sunshine conspired to make my eyes water. At age ten, Jeffrey is still a good sport, but he soon climbed back in the solar-heated van. He didn't need higher powered optics to appreciate the lone white pelican out on the water.

Scoping the far shore I was able to identify coots and ring-billed gulls. Even with a field guide in hand, I had to let the only two sandpipers remain nameless, which may save their reputation. They can't be too bright sticking around here this late.

The ducks had to remain nameless too. It takes a better birder than I to identify lumps of brown feathers huddled on the far shore or to identify duck butts, which is all there is to see when puddle-type ducks tip to feed.

Had I disclosed my identification difficulties to May Hanesworth, the doyenne of Cheyenne birding, she would have given me unequivocal IDs. Although she had already given up field trips when I first met her in 1989, May had decades of birding experience to draw from.

May was famous in many Cheyenne circles, [including music, music education, Cheyenne Frontier Days and local bridge clubs] but local Audubon members will remember her as charter member and especially as bird report compiler, a job she did with elegance, accuracy and reliability for decades, until she asked to pass it on to someone else three or four years ago.

May died October 5, just five months short of her one-hundredth birthday.

11 Juncos add variety to backyard bird feeder visitors

Thursday, November 11, 1999, Outdoors, page C4

This time of year brings early darkness, candles at the dinner table, Boy Scout popcorn orders in the living room and Audubon sunflower seed orders in our garage (Don't forget to pick up your orders Saturday.).

A more subtle portent of winter is the arrival of the juncos, starting this year with the one I saw at our feeder two weeks ago.

Actually, juncos never appear at feeders as much as they appear under feeders, picking through spilled seed, some of which I spill on purpose.

Now there are half a dozen juncos searching the ground anytime there are any other birds in the yard.

Perhaps it seems like all you get at your feeder are house sparrows and house finches. But if you look closely, you might recognize the varieties of juncos.

In Wisconsin, where I identified my first junco, and the Midwest and most points east, they are what used to be known as the "slate-colored junco." Later, the American Ornithologist's Union changed the name to "dark-eyed junco."

I thought that a picky distinction until I met the western juncos. At one time they were considered three separate species and one variation, but now they are merely races of the dark-eyed junco, versus the yellow-eyed junco of southern Arizona and Mexico.

Any given winter day, my backyard may host the Oregon, pink-sided or gray-headed forms of junco. I might even be lucky enough to see a white-winged or slate-colored.

Differentiating is difficult, with the best delineation given in the National Geographic field guide. Here's the basic breakdown.

All dark-eyed juncos are sparrow-sized, but plain-colored, unlike the streaky looking sparrows. They all have white bellies, "belly" being a technical term to describe part of a bird's topography.

They twitter and flash their white outer tail feathers as they fly away from you.

The slate-colored form is pure gray, though the female is brownish-gray. They are uncommon in the West.

The Oregon male has a very dark gray, almost black hood, brown back and orangish sides. The female is a lighter version. They are common in the West.

The pink-sided variation of the Oregon has a blue-gray hood, pinkish sides and breeds in the central Rockies.

The gray-headed, of the southern Rockies, has a pale gray hood and body, but a bright rufous-colored back.

The white-winged breeds in the Black Hills. It is all blue-gray, with two white wing bars on each wing.

To add to the fun, realize that these races are considered one species because they can crossbreed and produce fertile, if confusingly colored, offspring.

If you look at the field guide range maps for juncos, it shows juncos year round in Wyoming. But they aren't year round in my Cheyenne backyard.

At one inch square, the range map showing the whole North American continent can't show individual Wyoming mountain ranges. If it could, the mountains would be colored to indicate breeding and year round residency, with the plains colored as additional wintering grounds.

Migration is much more complex than the simple maxim we learn as children: south for the winter and north with the spring. After meeting New Jersey ornithologist Paul Kerlinger [director of the Cape May Bird Observatory] in September and reading his book "How Birds Migrate," it seems every species has its own strategy for dealing with the cold season.

For some it's complete migration – all individuals head south, although perhaps the males leave first or don't go as far south as the females.

Many species, like our western juncos, use the partial migration pattern. Not everyone leaves the breeding grounds. Or perhaps some of the individuals breeding northernmost spend the winter in the breeding grounds of the centrally located individuals of the same species. Or the northernmost leapfrog over everyone and winter the farthest south.

After all this hair splitting (or is it feather splitting?), it's a relief to consider the other new seasonal visitor to my backyard: the red-breasted nuthatch.

It looks the same anywhere it is seen on this continent. Its bold black and white striped head reminds me of a miniature badger.

The bird I've been observing swoops up to the feeder in a bossy, efficient way, making everyone else look like they're in slow motion.

No slave to ancestral migration patterns, the red-breasted nuthatch is what is called an "irruptive migrant." It goes where the food is; wherever its favorite food source – coniferous trees – produced the best crop of seed.

Evidently, however, black-oil sunflower will do for right now.

12 Project FeederWatch relies on citizen scientists

Thursday, December 9, 1999, Outdoors, page C4

This winter I am one of over 13,000 "citizen scientists" across North America.

What that means is, although I hold only a bachelor's of science degree and have never worn a white lab coat, I, too, can contribute to scientific research. So can you – if you learn to identify and count birds at your bird feeder.

Bird watchers have a propensity to quantify their hobby. Some people keep life lists and some people keep backyard lists of the birds they see.

This winter I'll be keeping track of the birds visiting my feeders.

I heard about Project FeederWatch (PFW), which depends on citizen scientists, a few years ago when the National Audubon Society and the famous (in bird circles anyway) Cornell Lab of Ornithology started a new venture called BirdSource.

BirdSource sponsors several kinds of bird studies including PFW. What I didn't know was that PFW started in Ontario in the 1970s and continues as an international effort.

Those long Canadian winters must force people to find exotic entertainment like this.

From November through March,

PFW participants document the ebb and flow of bird species that use feeders. I missed the first reporting period, but that's OK. It's even all right to miss some others if I have a schedule conflict.

If I were to submit my data in the traditional data entry, computer-readable booklet at the end of the season, I would be choosing two consecutive days to count in each two-week period. But I decided to go the on-line route, which allows me to report every week by computer.

Picking two consecutive days at least five days apart from the last two leaves, in my case, weekend count days.

To sign up, I could have mailed in my $15 registration fee or sent it via the internet. But I chose to call in with my credit card number.

In return I got a poster, handbook, data entry book and an identification number. The fee may defray costs as much as it makes people more apt to carry through. Who wants to waste money already invested?

Besides entering information about the birds I see in my backyard, I also describe my feeding setup. At the end of the season I'll describe what and how much I fed the birds. All my data gets compiled with everyone else's.

On the web I can look up animated maps (really!) that show sightings of each feeder species from month to month or year to year starting in 1992.

I begin to realize that in some years the fickle pine siskins weren't personally boycotting me but were wintering in another part of the country.

Ornithologists can't possibly collect as much data by themselves as we citizen scientists can. But they have been able to use our data in published studies about the movement of feeder birds in winter, overall population changes and food and habitat preferences.

An offshoot study was done on the spread of feeder bird diseases. The handbook and website give descriptions of various diseases, mainly those that afflict house finches. Don't read these right after eating.

Of course, every ardent birder's favorite aspect of their hobby is the chance to report rare birds. It's too bad the tundra swan Jim and Carol Hecker saw at Lions Park two days before Thanksgiving doesn't count. I wonder, if someone put out cracked corn at the lake regularly, could it be claimed as a feeder site? Looks like waterfowl have to be write-in species.

Much of the interesting information about PFW contained in the handbook also is available at the website. The site, though, has bird pictures and descriptions and the maps. If you don't own a computer, use a friend's or one at the library. It isn't too late to sign up to be a FeederWatcher, and I hope you will.

13

Stand up and be counted – by counting

The 100th Christmas Bird Count

The National Audubon Society wants YOU! -- to count birds for the 100th annual Christmas Bird Count.

The CBC is the annual celebration of a small group's ability to aid bird conservation by changing long-held tradition. Back before 1900 there was a traditional competition on Christmas to go afield to see who could shoot the most birds. Most of the pile of bodies collected weren't eaten or used for scientific purposes.

Around 1900, optics weren't what they are today, and bird watchers frequently shot birds so they could identify them in the hand.

Fortunately, bird watching wasn't as popular back then as it is today. Even so, ornithologist and Audubon Society officer Frank M. Chapman and 26 of his friends thought the Christmas hunt caused unnecessary depletion.

Twenty-five counts were held the first year, mostly in the Northeast – except for five in the Midwest, one in California and one in Pueblo, Colorado. A total of 18,000 birds of 90 species were counted.

The idea of counting birds without guns continued to grow. In 1998, about 50,000 people in 1,800 count areas documented around 58 million birds.

In North America, 659 species were represented. The non-North American counts, in Central and South America and Pacific islands, reached 1,650 species.

CBC data has always been collected for scientific analysis of bird population trends. The annual report of any one of the recent counts is a book larger than the Cheyenne telephone directory.

But if you have web access, www.birdsource.org/cbc, gives you a century's worth of data.

The CBC isn't just for the leisure class anymore, and it isn't always held on Christmas Day. In Cheyenne, we pick a Saturday within the given three-week window. Even if you have to work, just stick your head outside a minute and count how many starlings are congregating on the power line.

If you aren't ready to tramp around in the cold, be a feeder watcher and count the birds in your own backyard.

As a scientific study, the CBC has a couple constraints. Every count area is limited to a 7.5-mile radius. Ours is centered on the State Capitol Building. If you go out on your own, keep track of your mileage by foot or vehicle and note approximately where and what time you see the birds you count.

One major misconception about counting is you have to be an expert ornithologist. Not true. It helps to go with someone knowledgeable, however. Just be sure to wear warm clothes.

On my first CBC, the 83rd count, an Arctic air mass had settled in over the Yellowstone and Tongue River valleys in southeastern Montana. Because I was a novice, Mark, my husband of three months, graciously allowed me to be the recorder. Luckily, birds hunker down in sub-zero temperatures, and there wasn't much besides a tiny flock of horned larks to unsheathe my gloved and mittened fingers for writing the numbers.

The Cheyenne tradition is to get a warm start by meeting at 7:30 a.m. in the lobby of the Post Office on Capitol Ave. and then tour birding "hot spots." It's perfectly all right to drop out when you're ready to go back to your warm and cozy home and check out the birds at your feeder.

With this year's count scheduled for Jan. 1, you may not be ready to join us so early. Remember, there are no rules about what time you have to start or how long you have to be out. If you'd like, pick up the official count form and map from me ahead of time.

You may call your results in to our CBC count compiler. But it's much more fun to heat up your favorite hot dish or buy your favorite hot salsa and chips and come to the tally party.

After the potluck, we review the winter bird checklist species by species, about 50 or so, and share stories about our day. One year we were able to figure out that two parties of observers counted the same flock of geese because the geese moved between Holliday Park and Lions Park.

Years later, I can look up the first counts I did in Miles City. There in the CBC editions of American Birds are recorded Mark's and my names, names of our hardy bird watching friends, the day's weather and the birds we saw, including all of those ravenous robins we saw in the Russian olives along the rivers.

2000

14 Great Backyard Bird Count needs you

Thursday, February 17, 2000, Outdoors, page C4

Compared to the venerable Christmas Bird Count which celebrated its 100th anniversary in December, the Great Backyard Bird Count is just a flash in the pan of data.

Beginning Friday and continuing through Monday, this year's count will be only the third annual Great Backyard Bird Count (GBBC).

Born of a need for data rather than an update of previous traditions, it is a computer project.

The institutional sponsors, the National Audubon Society and the Cornell Lab of Ornithology, want to track patterns of bird abundance and distribution. They decided to call on the 60 million bird watchers around the country for help collecting data, whatever their level of expertise in bird identification and even if they only count for half an hour.

Over time, the data will show if some species are declining in population like the red-headed woodpecker or, for species like the bald eagle, how fast they are making a comeback.

To take part in this count you need access to the internet; at home, work, a friend's, the public library, or by calling me (see the accompanying information box).

For this modern count there are no Audubon chapter count compilers, no paper maps of count circles and no potlucks at the end of the day. Instead, it's just you and the birds in your own backyard, and then you and the computer as you submit a count for any or each of the four days.

But your bird watching doesn't have to be solitary. The GBBC is so young we can make up our own traditions with family or friends. We could invite our neighbors over to observe our bird feeders over lunch one day and observe their birds the next.

Or we could take a little stroll around the neighborhood together. I know there are flickers on my street. They just never show up in my back yard.

Classrooms around the country are also participating. At the GBBC website, under "Let's Learn About Birds" there are excellent teachers' tips and a six-page bibliography of birding books and media, including juvenile fiction/nonfiction and a glossary of terms.

Other pages on the website – tips on using binoculars and a guide to 50 common backyard birds, including sound clips, range maps and interesting info about each – will improve everyone's level of expertise.

Participation in the GBBC has grown about as fast as personal computer ownership. According to statistics provided by Jackie Cerretani of the Cornell Lab, Wyoming's participation was only 118 counts of the 42,000 submitted nationally last year, but it was up from 19 counts in 1998.

The beauty of computer data collection is that it's compiled so quickly that even the first day of the count you will be able to see results posted on the website.

And then we'll know just where our usual Cheyenne winter birds are hiding out during this mild excuse for a winter.

15 Night birding offers unique experience on quiet evenings

Thursday, March 2, 2000, Outdoors, page C4

[I no longer suggest owling, except for scientific purposes.]

Have you ever tried night birding? The term "bird watching" doesn't really apply, though "bird listening" might.

It wasn't exactly a scene from "Owl Moon," the Caldecott-winning picture book by Jane Yolen, but a nearly full moon was glistening on patches of snow on the mid-February owling expedition.

Members of the Cheyenne High Plains Audubon Society who planned the outing were surprised by the number of people interested in tromping around in the dark and cold on a weeknight.

Kelly Johnson had her Girl Scouts bundled up and Catherine Symchych, a raptor rehabilitator, came all the way over from Laramie.

Owling means listening for owls. Unfortunately, the wind was still going strong, which meant "low audibility" as well as night's normal low visibility.

During the mating season in late February and March, owls hoot a challenge to territorial trespassers. Researchers improve their odds of hearing owls by speaking up first. And just to make sure the accent is right, they use tape-recorded owl calls.

There are a variety of owls that can occur in Wyoming, so it's important to start with the calls of the smallest owls first. Once the bigger owls, like the great horned, are played, everyone else in the vicinity stays mute for fear of being eaten.

It's easy enough to copy for your own use specific calls from one of the commercially available bird song tapes.

Get the "Wyoming Bird Checklist" available from Wyoming Game and Fish Department, to decide which of the 15 owl species to use.

When playing the tape, it's important to be in a woodsy area, have warm batteries in the tape player, and allow for quiet between calls so you can listen for responses.

The night we were out on the road by Lummis Reservoir [I probably mean Wyoming Hereford Ranch Reservoir #1], the taped calls were carried far downwind, but responses couldn't be heard because we were standing upwind by the tape player. At the second stop, outside Lakeview Cemetery, the wind was less boisterous.

Still no owls.

Windless early spring nights are uncommon here, so I'll just have to get up and go owling the next time I notice one.

I did hear birds at night once this winter. Low clouds and a thick fall of snowflakes trapped the streetlights' orange glow and spread it everywhere so bright I could have read the paper.

It was windless and very quiet, no traffic. And then I heard birds twittering in the bushes across the street. Later I heard more somewhere in the back yard.

I've heard that songbirds will huddle together at night to keep warm.

Was I hearing the equivalent of snoring birds, birds trying to get comfortable, or birds confused by the unnatural bright light at 10 p.m.?

If birding in snow and dark doesn't appeal to you, try morning. Check the recording of the night's activities left in the snow.

In the forest I've found rabbit tracks that suddenly stop between two large owl wing imprints and have been surprised by a late awakening grouse exploding from its snow cave.

Early one morning recently, a scant quarter of an inch of snow covered the sidewalks. Whereas in deeper snow footprints are just dark holes, this time even the juncos left prints on the patio so clean, toe joints were visible.

Cottontails left tracks to show where they'd congregated in the middle of the street. A single-minded cat left a single-file string of pawprints down the sidewalk. Down by the ditch, tiny mouse-sized prints emerged from under the concrete barriers and circled back under again.

Every snow print was as if what dogs smell was suddenly made visible.

I'm not sure Lincoln, our dog, is very good at reading smells though. For some reason he got most excited on the way home sniffing the tracks he left when we started out.

Note: Anyone seen their first mountain bluebird yet?

16 Birds are now on the move

As we turned off Happy Jack Road and onto the gravel road to North Crow Reservoir recently, I asked my husband, Mark, if he'd seen his first bluebird of the season yet.

He had barely answered when, on cue, an azure-colored male mountain bluebird crossed our path, stage left to stage right.

The first bluebird report I heard came last month. Robin Groose, president of Laramie Audubon Society, said his wife, Pat, had seen one down near Walden.

Wintering in southern Colorado and points south, mountain bluebirds come back as early as mid-February. You just won't see them downtown. They are a bird of higher, open grass and shrubland country.

What does an insectivorous species that likes its meals on the wing find to eat in February? Snow fleas?

It appears, according to the bird books, that bluebirds are willing to settle for frozen berries.

Since it was too mushy to ice fish at North Crow, we hiked up a creek into the national forest, into a landscape hardly distinguishable from November's. Same dead-tan grass, same leafless branches, same snowdrifts hidden in the shade of evergreens and rock outcrops.

Same birds too – the resident, year round species – junco, nuthatch, flicker, chickadee.

Then suddenly we were surrounded by unfamiliar bird song from the tops of the ponderosas.

Trying my new skills in Zen and the art of seeing birds with binoculars, I sought out a bird shape on a branch with my naked eyes. Then, without changing my gaze, I lifted the binoculars to my face.

Magic! There she was, a motley, streaky, olivish-yellowish colored red crossbill. As usual, the color part of the name comes from the color of the male. Both sexes, though, have the peculiar upper and lower bills that cross at the tips. All the better for extracting seeds from cones.

Not a predictable species to find in the forest, crossbills are nomadic, pitching their tents wherever pines or spruce have produced a good crop.

Later, my Zen method gave me an excellent look at a white-breasted nuthatch. All the resident species are primarily seed and nut eaters, but less fussy than crossbills. For them, going south or peregrinating to other patches of forest would just put them in competition with the locals.

Back here in town, people are reporting their first robins of the year. I gently break the news that we have robins year round, just not as many in the winter.

No, they don't hide a cache of frozen worms. Instead, robins seek out fruit, hanging out in riparian areas where they can find wrinkled rosehips on wild rose bushes or the produce of other moisture-loving plants.

The redheads are back. The duck species, that is. Take a good look at those ducks down in Lions Park. At first glance it may appear that a drake mallard's green head is not catching the sun right. If it appears a rich auburn color, you're looking at a redhead.

Across the country, birds are on the move. Sandhill cranes, having started out in Texas, are stopping over in Nebraska on the Platte River, taking a breather. Some head as far north as the Siberian tundra.

Other kinds of birds that spent the winter in the Caribbean or as far south as Argentina also are loading up on calories and heading north.

Though the peak for Cheyenne is still two months away, the early birds are arriving daily, in search of the proverbial worm.

17 Home on the Prairie

Thursday, April 13, 2000, Outdoors, page C1

What can you do to help prairie wildlife thrive in its native home? The best advice: Don't do anything.

CHEYENNE – On first acquaintance, people from lusher parts of the country believe our shortgrass prairie is in desperate need of improvement.

Not so.

It has developed its own way of dealing with only 15 to 17 inches of annual precipitation from rain and snowfall. Some prairie species won't even thrive in wetter conditions.

The first piece of advice for wildlife lovers contemplating a move to the prairie is, "Don't," said Reg Rothwell,

Wyoming Game and Fish Department supervisor of biological services.

Or at least, he said, "Resist the temptation to bring the English countryside with you."

Rothwell finds that many property owners become disillusioned when confronted with badgers hissing warnings, rabbits munching gardens or stripping bark off saplings, ground squirrels tunneling through the lawn and hawks or other predators eyeing their small pets as snacks.

The solution to these wildlife conflicts is for humans to "create as small a footprint as possible," rather like leave-no-trace camping in the back country, Rothwell said.

The benefits of low-impact living mean less work and cost for property owners as well. Unlike standard Kentucky bluegrass lawns, native prairie needs no irrigation, no mowing and no fertilizer or pesticide.

Plus, it makes a much more interesting view compared to monoculture lawn because its variety of grasses and wildflowers attract wildlife.

Don't even bother with the effort of planting trees, said Andrea Cerovski, Game and Fish nongame bird biologist stationed in Lander. Native prairie bird species are ground nesters.

"Trees encourage predation by birds like crows and nest parasitism by cowbirds."

The prairie, a complex ecosystem, doesn't stand up to fragmentation.

Said Cerovski, if a road or other disturbance subdivides the prairie into less than 125- to 250-acre tracts, some native birds will refuse to breed. It's the visibility problem in an area of scarce vegetation. Put yourself in the bird's nest and imagine living in a glass-walled house. How far away would you want neighbors and passersby?

To nest, most prairie birds scrape a slight depression in the dirt, perhaps lining it with some dried vegetation. Some, like the ferruginous hawk and long-billed curlew, like to incorporate a little cow dung, perhaps for the heat it generates as it decomposes.

Obviously, free roaming cats and dogs are much more of a problem for ground nesting birds than for the tree-nesting species in town.

Grazing, at proper stocking rates, is compatible with most prairie bird species.

Some, like the mountain plover, proposed for listing as a threatened species, demand nearly bare ground before they'll consider nesting.

Others, like sharptailed grouse, prefer a screen of ungrazed vegetation, such as they find in acreage registered in the Conservation Reserve Program.

For the owners of small acreages contemplating grazing horses or other livestock, the best bet is to confer with the experts at the Laramie County Conservation District.

Martin Hicks, wildlife and range specialist with the district, recently advised one landowner how he could safely stock two horses on 11 acres by cross-fencing it into eight pastures and moving the animals every several days. Still, for six months of the year, the horses will require supplemental feeding.

But, Hicks warns, every situation is different. Typically, one horse will need 15 acres of dryland pasture during the six-month growing period.

An overstocked acre or two in our sea of grass isn't a big problem by itself, but as Rothwell points out, the cumulative effect of everyone in a development confining their horses can cause enough bare ground to make it susceptible to appreciable amounts of wind erosion and adds Hicks, wind-borne weed seeds.

Cerovski, in her other capacity as Wyoming coordinator for Partners in Flight, an international partnership of agencies and organizations devoted to the protection of neotropical migrant songbirds, has been working on the Wyoming Bird Conservation Plan.

The plan, due out soon, will list for landowners and managers best management practices for various Wyoming habitat types, including the prairie.

While many range improvement methods such as mowing or haying or prescribed burning mimic natural events, Cerovski recommends avoiding using them during the nesting season, mid-June through mid-July, and even allowing a two-week buffer on either end to protect early and late nesters.

"June and July are most critical for nest building, egg laying, hatching, growth and fledging the young," Cerovski said.

Insecticides should also be avoided, she said. After all, "those insects are the main food items for prairie birds. If provided with other habitat components they need, birds will do a really good job of controlling problem insects."

People becoming prairie dwellers have a lot of expertise available to them through the Conservation District and Game and Fish. Those agencies will offer advice on learning how to coexist with the ecosystem.

But it takes personal time and observation to understand the details of what really happens on a particular piece of prairie.

This spring, you can start by training your ear for prairie bird songs. Learn them by using a tape or CD such as those put out by Peterson's Field Guides or the American Birding Association.

Then walk often (with your dog on a leash) and find out who's out there.

As Rothwell put it, "Appreciate the prairie for what it is."

Prairie Birds You'll Want to Meet

Priority* prairie bird species from the draft of the Wyoming Bird Conservation Plan

Ferruginous Hawk	R/3, RI, SH, PR, SF (cliffs)
Mountain Plover	S/3, PR
Upland Sandpiper	S/2, PR, AG (crop residue)
Long-billed Curlew	S/2, SH, PR, ME, AG, SF
Burrowing Owl	S/2, SH, PR, AG
Short-eared Owl	R/3, SH, PR, WL, AG
Dickcissel	S/2, PR
Lark Bunting	S/4, SH, PR, AG
Grasshopper Sparrow	S/3, SH, PR, ME, AG
McCown's Longspur	S/3, PR, SH, AG
Chestnut-collared Longspur	S/2, PR, SH, AG
Bobolink	S/2, SH, PR, AG

*A Wyoming Priority Species may be rated "3" or common, but over the rest of its range, in other states, it may not be thriving.

Other Bird Species Dependent on Prairie and Shrub Habitat

Northern Harrier	S/2, SH, PR, WL
Swainson's Hawk	S/3, PR, ME, SH, AG, SF (cliff/tree)
Rough-legged Hawk	W/3, SH, PR, AG
Sharp-tailed Grouse	R/3, PR, SH, AG
Say's Phoebe	S/3, SH, PR
Western Kingbird	S/3, SH, PR, AG, FO, RI
Eastern Kingbird	S/3, SH, PR, AG, FO, RI
Horned Lark	R/4, SH, PR
Vesper Sparrow	S/3, SH, PR, AG
Baird's Sparrow	S/2, PR

| Lapland Longspur | W/3, PR, AG |
| Western Meadowlark | S/4, SH, PR, AG |

Species inhabiting Wyoming: S – summer only, W – winter only, R – year-round (resident)
Abundance: 1 – Rare, 2 – Uncommon, 3 – Common, 4 – Abundant
Habitat types, listed for each species in order of where species is most likely to be seen:
PR – Prairie – open expanses of grassland.
SH – Shrubland – dominated by sagebrush, bitterbrush or other shrubs.
AG – Agricultural – pasture, cropland, irrigated meadows.
ME – Meadows – wet to moist meadows and grasslands.
RI – Riparian – bordering streams, lakes or rivers.
WL – Wetlands – water present most of the time.
FO – Forest – dominated by coniferous and/or deciduous trees.
SF – Special Features – unique natural or man-made characteristics.

18

Thursday, April 13, 2000, Outdoors, page C1

Making birds at home in our 'urban forest'

CHEYENNE – Over the last hundred years, part of the prairie in Laramie County has been converted to forest by the residents of Cheyenne.

Either to remind ourselves of homes back East or to block the wind, we've planted trees.

The riparian zones along streams, rivers and lakes, naturally irrigated areas on the prairie grow thick sod, cottonwoods and willows. But here in town, our lawns and trees grow with the help of irrigation water piped over the mountains or pumped from the ground water.

When we want to attract birds to our urban yards, we mimic the amenities of the forest. Sometimes the improvements benefit us as well as the birds.

First, we plant more trees and shrubs, especially the hardy native species requiring less water. Dense plantings, coniferous or deciduous, give birds places to nest and good protection from bad weather and predators such as roaming domestic cats. They may provide food as well for berry eaters like robins and waxwings.

Shane Smith, director of the Cheyenne Botanic Gardens, recommends growing Nanking or sand cherry, woodbine, New Mexico privet and juniper. Other recommendations from the gardens' website include serviceberry, chokecherry, sumac, and varieties of currants.

Besides giving us a little protection from wind, plantings protect us from views of unsightly garbage cans or compost piles.

Birds help us maintain trees. In the spring, warblers can be seen gleaning bugs from the new leaves. Woodpeckers, including flickers, and brown creepers search every inch of the tree trunk year-round.

A plain, ordinary lawn can also attract the native pest patrol. Grackles will patiently pace your sward of green, shoulder to shoulder, their yellow eyes gleaming like searchlights as they delve with their long, sharp bills into the turf for miscreant grubs.

Your end of the lawn maintenance deal is to switch from chemical lawn fertilizers to child/pet/

bird-compatible products.

Ken Stevens of Riverbend Nursery recommends "Sustane," a slow-release, balanced fertilizer with microbes that encourage the natural decay and nutrient cycle.

Pesticides? Why use them when you are inviting avian experts? As for weeds, healthy grass will crowd them out.

Occasional dandelion digging is good exercise, and if you miss one, the seeds will be appreciated by goldfinches.

As testimony to 11 years of organic care, infrequent, deep watering, and grass cutting at the highest blade setting, our lawn has never needed de-thatching or aerating and looks much like the rest of our neighbors' lawns.

But why settle for a boring Kentucky bluegrass lawn? For the same amount of water, or even less if you practice xeriscaping, why not convert to native grasses or the visual diversity of gardens providing seeds and berries for birds?

The birds attracted to our urban forest are often cavity nesters. Trees have to be old and decadent enough to get cavities, but when they reach that point, we usually cut them down because they threaten our safety.

So, we provide bird houses for house wrens, house finches, nuthatches and woodpeckers.

When you are perusing bird house plans, make sure you pick those for species that occur here. For instance, we are not in the purple martin's normal range.

Make sure the entrance dimensions exclude pesky non-native species like house sparrows. Let them build their nests in discount store signs. And erect your bird house so marauding cats, squirrels and starlings can't kill nestlings.

For the cavity nesters as well as the branch and bush nesters like goldfinches, provide fibrous materials like string and hair from people and pets, but not fishing line, or in lengths longer than six inches. And leave some mud for the robins and swallows to plaster their kind of nests.

Forest birds like water for drinking and bathing, though some prefer dust baths. Realistically, during lawn watering season, there's always some water slopping into gutter streams or sidewalk micro ponds. But what about the rest of the year?

If you want to provide five-star accommodations, offer a pool. It doesn't have to be Olympic-sized – I've noticed birds using the dog's water dish. Heated is nice in the winter.

Moving water is especially attractive, whether a fountain or just a milk jug full of water you hang up and then make leak at the rate of a drip every second or so.

Putting food out is always a popular way to attract birds. It is most successful when water and shelter are also present.

Offering sunflower and Niger thistle seed right through the summer gives a nutritional boost to brooding birds and parents feeding nestlings. But in warmer weather, it's doubly important to keep feeders clean and free of deadly bacteria and diseases.

There are lots of selfish reasons for encouraging wild birds to come and live among us: their songs, their colors, their antics and their utilitarian contributions.

Most importantly, birds are still the "canaries in the coal mine" in our age of continuing industry and development. A forest without birds is cause for trepidation.

19 Songs tell of habitat, breeding

[As of 2022, Franz Ingelfinger is a wildlife biologist with Montana Fish, Wildlife and Parks.]

You have no idea how annoying the otherwise sweet "cheer-i-o" of a robin can be until you've had one sing 10 feet from your head at 4 a.m.

I went with the Boy Scouts on my first Ft. Robinson, Nebraska, tree-plant April 8. Although two layers of nylon tent helped keep me warm, it was no insulation from nature's self-appointed alarm clock.

At last month's Cheyenne High Plains Audubon Society meeting, guest speaker Franz Ingelfinger explained the phenomenon of bird song and how it relates to his research.

Birds, male and female, use short call notes for everyday communication.

Usually only the males sing the longer, musical phrases. Simultaneously they broadcast their land claim to keep other males away and invite females, prospective mates, to stop by and check out the quality of their plumage and future nesting spots.

Birds don't sing any louder than necessary, even if their syrinx, or voice box, is capable of louder songs. Apparently, natural selection has evolved a robin that sings loud enough to be heard in the next territory – but not loud enough to attract the attention of a predator passing through three robin-sized territories away.

Ornithologists have found correlations between the duration and pitch of a particular bird's song and the type of habitat it sings in. Franz mentioned a study of Carolina wrens in which their songs were recorded in one habitat and played back in one with different kinds of vegetation.

The songs didn't carry, or resonate, as well when out of place. For denser brush, the wrens had evolved lower-pitched and purer (less warbling) tones, which don't transmit as well in less-dense brush.

What happens when a bird's habitat is disrupted with human-caused noise?

Franz shared the results of a study in the Netherlands along a busy highway, which showed the density of breeding birds drops dramatically next to the road and gradually recovers with increasing distance away.

The study suggests traffic noises mask bird song so the birds can't successfully find each other and mate. The study proves your best birding won't be from the highway – you need to get out and walk.

Franz, a graduate student with the Fish and Wildlife Cooperative Research Unit at the University of Wyoming, is studying the effects of natural gas development on birds of the sagebrush-grassland south of Pinedale in an area known as the Mesa, above the confluence of the Green and New Fork rivers.

In his first season last summer, Franz surveyed bird life adjacent to roads in the nearby, nearly established Jonah field (400 vehicles per day) and the Mesa, which was in the initial stages of development (10 vehicles per day).

His preliminary findings for the high-traffic roads show a 50 percent reduction in the number of singing, presumably breeding, birds within the first 100 meters (110 yards).

These natural gas fields are being developed at the rate of eight wells per section (square mile). They are connected by a spiderweb of roads.

With about 100 square miles

affected in the Mesa field alone, what will reduced breeding along the roads mean for the populations Franz is studying – sage thrasher, sage sparrow, Brewer's sparrow, vesper sparrow and horned lark?

Franz's study, sponsored by the US Fish and Wildlife Foundation, Wyoming Game and Fish Department and the US Geological Survey, examines the costs of drilling for only one aspect of the sagebrush-grassland ecosystem. What about impacts on large game, or the invasion of noxious weeds that always follows new roads?

When will the costs add up high enough to make directional drilling cost effective? Drilling in many directions diagonally from one site would reduce the number of sites and roads needed.

Meanwhile, I'm not sure if I envy Franz as he heads out this week for his second field season. He has to be up before the birds and the sunrise, only to be shrouded in dust with each passing vehicle. But the songs of the dawn chorus will be lovely as he walks out into the sagebrush.

20 Humans a hazard to navigation

Thursday, May 25, 2000, Outdoors, page C2

The other day, my math students at Johnson Junior High were quick to point out the bird auditing the class from the outside windowsill.

It was a male house finch in his bright-red breeding plumage. His beady stare was making some students uncomfortable as he strutted back and forth.

I laughed and explained that the bird wasn't seeing us at all. The coated window glass acted like a mirror, and the poor bird thought his reflection was an interloper to be challenged.

Occasionally the female came by, and I anticipated the students' next concern.

"Do you think those birds are going to...?"

"Of course!" I beamed, "It's spring!"

Lucky for this particular finch, his run-in with windows was only a territorial problem. Every year windows cause the death of hundreds of thousands of other birds.

The sky and trees reflected in a window make birds think they see a clear flight path. They run into the glass at full-tilt, and if they don't break their necks, a predator may kill them while they lie on the ground, stunned.

Confusing birds is a problem for glass-sided skyscrapers as well as our own homes. Suggestions for protecting birds from this hazard are based on breaking up the reflective surface. Pulling the drapes [might not work] works, of course, but it also negates the reason for having windows.

Netting or window screens in front of the glass helps, and so does the typical dusty coating of most Cheyenne windows.

The popular solution is sticking a hawk silhouette on the glass. This could be more effective if the silhouette flutters in the breeze. Try hanging it from a suction cup.

Windows can be hazardous at night as well. High-rise building managers leaving lights on all night waste energy and reap a fallout of dead, dying and stunned migrating birds on their sidewalks in the morning.

Birds migrating at night use many navigational cues including starlight.

In bad weather, the lights of tall buildings and radio towers attract them, and the birds either smash into the structures or circle hopelessly until falling from exhaustion.

The Fatal Light Awareness Program, FLAP, based in Toronto, has volunteers rescuing stunned birds from around buildings in the financial district. The technique, viable for any stunned bird, is to set it upright in a paper bag, which calms it, insulates it a little and protects it from cats and crows until it recovers and can be released.

FLAP's main goal is to convince managers to turn the lights off during migration season. At www.flap.org, the group lists bird-friendly buildings and manager contact information. FLAP founders hope to see this incentive used in other high-rise cities.

No one used to be aware of the extent of bird migration at night. Radar technicians during World War II referred to the unexplained, ethereal shadows on their screens as "angels." In the early 1960s, Sidney Gauthreaux of Louisiana proved the angels were actually huge flocks of migrating birds.

The latest technology, Next Generation Radar, or NEXRAD, is so sensitive it can track weather by tracking dust particle movement. Birds are detected as so many bags of salt water, just another form of precipitation.

Remember, the human body is 98 percent saltwater.

Using radar to figure out where the birds are is useful to human as well as bird safety when it comes to preventing bird and plane collisions or avoiding poisoning of birds during pesticide applications.

This spring, a cooperative effort called BirdCast, sponsored by the U.S. Environmental Protection Agency, is tracking bird migration in the mid-Atlantic region. Partners in the program are the National Audubon Society, Cornell Lab of Ornithology, the Radar Ornithology Lab at Clemson, the Academy of Natural Science, GeoMarine (a private company) and thousands of bird watchers.

The idea is to match up radar images of bird migration with what bird watchers actually observe, a process known as "ground truthing," and then be able to predict the movement of waves of migration.

For now, we Wyomingites will have to be satisfied with word of mouth for following spring and fall migration across the state.

My bird watching correspondent up in Chugwater would like to start an internet list serve to make it more efficient. Meanwhile, check out www.birdcast.org to see what's going on back East.

Migration is an amazing phenomenon. Millions of birds, some weighing only an ounce, accurately hurtle through the atmosphere for hundreds or thousands of miles using navigation systems we can barely understand. Yet we can mortally confuse them with a few bright lights.

Makes me wonder if we humans are advancing.

21 Go Birding!

Mastering bird-watching basics will enhance your time in the outdoors

CHEYENNE – Bird watching is an all-inclusive hobby that has grown immensely in popularity in recent years.

From young children to the elderly or disabled, almost anyone can pick up a pair of binoculars and a field guide and begin to enjoy watching and learning about birds.

Southeast Wyoming lies along the migratory paths of a wide array of bird species and is the year round home to many birds that are as beautiful as they are fascinating.

From identifying birds at the backyard feeder to becoming a full-blown amateur ornithologist, bird watching can be as simple or as all-consuming as you choose to make it.

So, what steps do experienced birders recommend for the casual backyard observer who wants to fan that initial spark of interest in birds into a bigger flame?

"I would suggest you take a class," said Gloria Lawrence. "Or go birding with a group. Go birding every chance you can with people who know birds. Or fumble through the field guide."

Lawrence, who lives near Casper, keeps the Wyoming Bird Hotline up to date. Her interest in birds was sparked by a northern mockingbird that spent a summer singing from the yard light pole when she was a child growing up on a ranch near Chugwater.

She and her husband, Jim, began feeding backyard birds and they learned to identify them, along with those they saw on outdoor trips.

"The spark turned into a roaring fire when Jim and I took a class from Oliver Scott in 1984," Lawrence said. "The fire is burning out of control. I realize in a lifetime I'll barely scratch the surface of what there is to know about birds."

Cheyenne birder Jane Dorn got the tinder for her "spark" – as birders refer to the beginning passion for birds – as a small child growing up near Rawlins, also on a ranch, with a family that hunted and fished.

Dorn could identify game birds and the songbirds her mother fed before she was old enough to go to school.

"I've always watched birds; it's something I grew up doing. I wasn't intensely interested until after taking a college ornithology class," she said.

Jane and her husband, Robert, are co-authors of "Wyoming Birds," a book documenting the occurrence of bird species throughout the state.

"The more you do, the better you get," she said. "Taking a class or going out with a birder is a huge boost to your bird-watching knowledge and shows you what's what locally."

Can a person be too old or too young to take up bird watching?

No, said Lawrence, who helps teach an annual 12-week bird class offered by the Murie Audubon Society at Casper College.

"Many students are middle-aged or older, and many are retired," she said.

"It's a hobby you can pursue for a lifetime," said Dorn, who helped teach a birding class at Laramie County Community College this year.

Birding is ideal for the disabled, and it's easy to add to other outdoor family activities.

One example Lawrence gave of the birding spark flaming at a young age is Joe Scott, whose grandfather, Oliver Scott, wrote the American Birding Association's "A Birder's Guide to Wyoming."

The young Scott, now in high school, and his father, Stacey, like to make the trek from Casper for the Cheyenne High Plains Audubon Society chapter's annual spring bird count.

Scott recently received a grant from the Governor's Youth Initiative for Wildlife. It and other funds he raised will help him build a new flight cage for Casper bird rehabilitators Lois and Frank Layton.

There are just two pieces of equipment needed to enjoy bird watching: A pair of binoculars and a field guide.

"Get the very best equipment you can afford," Lawrence suggested. "I started out with 7x35 Tasco binoculars. When I got my Bausch and Lombs, it opened up a whole new world. Good optics just make birding more enjoyable."

Dorn recommends a minimum power of 7. Go with 8 or 9 if you can afford it. (See the accompanying article on binoculars for a discussion of magnification.)

"Ideally you want to try as many kinds of binoculars as you can," Dorn said.

Choosing binoculars that fit your style of bird watching is as important as fitting them to your hands and eyes.

"If you'll be doing little walking, you can afford heavier binocs with a wider field of view," Dorn said.

She estimated that $200 would buy an acceptable pair of birding binoculars.

Top birders spend as much as $1000. With improvements in quality in recent years, such as lens coatings that improve the brightness of the image, you can get more capability for the same money now.

As a hobby, bird watching doesn't have to be expensive. "You don't need as much (equipment) as golf," Lawrence said.

And, said Dorn, bigger is not always better. "More magnification is not necessarily better. Anything above a 10 you cannot hold steady enough. You buy a scope (with a tripod) when you get serious about shorebirds and waterfowl."

The most important thing about binoculars is to use them, Lawrence said. "Once you get binoculars, use them and use them," until focusing is fast and automatic. And learn how to use the individual eye focus to adjust for differences between your eyes.

Dorn advises testing binoculars for alignment as well. If the two barrels aren't lined up, you may have a headache by the end of a day of birding.

Field guides are a less expensive tool, running from $15 to $25 apiece.

But, said Dorn, "You'll find you'll want to own more than one."

Lawrence will attest to that. "Jim and I have six bookcases. One is entirely filled with bird reference books, floor to ceiling, probably 250 books," she said.

Both women recommended the newest edition of the National Geographic field guide because it's the most up to date, and it covers bird species for the entire United States as well as exotic species that may show up accidently.

"Peterson's (guides) are still excellent, but you need both the Eastern and the Western guides," said Dorn. "The old Golden (guide) is good, but the nomenclature is sort of out of date."

After the initial investment in binoculars and field guides, you can enjoy bird watching from home.

"You don't have to live any place special to bird watch," Dorn said.

You may enhance home bird watching by making your yard attractive to birds, providing food, water and shelter. On a day too rainy to go out last month, just before the peak of spring migration, Lawrence and her husband counted 38 species from their window.

It is possible to spend a lot of money on the hobby. Birding magazines advertise eco-tours to all kinds of international, bird-rich destinations. And the number of bird festivals around the country, usually celebrating particular species, continues to grow.

There's even one in Wyoming, held in Lander each May.

There's always more to learn about birds, even when you're the teacher. "I learned as much as the students," Lawrence said of her experience. "When you try to describe (an ordinary bird) for someone else, you become more aware of what really looks unique about it."

And there's no limit to how much time some people put into bird watching. Lawrence, who goes birding all the time, related a typical story. "It's a habit. I was coming up the stairs with a load of laundry when I saw a painted bunting."

This type of bunting shows up accidentally in Wyoming, with only three documented sightings listed in the Dorns' book. After documenting it with photographs, Lawrence added it to the bird hot line report.

[The bird hot line has given way to the Wyobirds Google Group.]

22 'Backyard birding' varies by the yard

Thursday, June 29, 2000, Outdoors, page C3

I believe that one's own backyard is sufficient for nature observation and enjoyment. Even the plainest of places has stories when scrutinized over the seasons.

But there is something to be said for travel. Earlier in June our family spent a few days in Lander, where the mountains loom close, and three creeks flow through town.

Our room's door in the unpromising 1950s motel facade opened to reveal a panoramic second-story view of one of the forks of the Popo Agie (Po-po'-zha) River and beyond. What a great backyard.

The treetops appeared to be swarming with grackles. One of many robins swooped straight toward us, disappearing between the roof overhang and the top of our window. By craning our necks, we could see some parental tail feathers sticking over the edge of a nest on a ledge.

The next day my son, Jeffrey, and I went to visit a friend [Marta Amundson]. Her house, sitting on a knoll overlooking Ocean Lake, is that of a poet and artist, where even the lowliest household item or task receives thoughtful consideration.

Over tea on the glassed-in porch, we watched orioles and kingbirds squabble and feed on insects, their bright feathers a welcome contrast to the pedestrian house finches at home.

Later Marta sent Jeffrey and me down the path, through the gate and over the stile to the lake itself. As we carefully tippy-toed over a white alkaline crust covering sticky, stinky mud, Jeffrey said, "You know Mom, you look like, well, you look weird, like a soccer mom or something."

Or something, all right: the epitome of the old lady wearing sneakers and binoculars. I am as old as some grandmothers, but I think it was my floppy old green hat that embarrassed Jeffrey.

Luckily for him there were no other people to see him walking with the lady in the weird hat – or to observe him building sandcastles like a 6-year-old.

Ocean Lake fills with return irrigation flows from the Riverton Reclamation Project built in the 1920s. Much of its shoreline is managed by the Wyoming Game and Fish Department as the Ocean Lake Wildlife Habitat Area.

On a nearby spit of land I could see several habitat improvements, goose nesting platforms and even an occasional goose, plus a few avocets.

Next to us some kind of shorebird was poking its bill in the wet sand between waves. Shorebirds are difficult to identify, most having brownish backs, whitish bellies, long skinny legs and bills. I looked hard for some notable feature on these birds, finding only a wash of color on either side of

their long necks.

On the 14th page of shorebirds in my field guide, I recognized the shape of Wilson's phalarope, but mine didn't have the bright neck color.

Perhaps they were young and that's why they weren't doing the phalarope thing yet, swimming in tight circles to stir up food from the lake bottom.

A hazy, cloudy sky acted as camouflage for the terns and gulls flying far out over the lake.

Then, from behind a low hill emerged a squadron of large, light-colored birds. Their necks stretched out (not crooked like herons), their long legs following (not short like geese), the sandhill cranes advanced on me until I could see their red crowns. Then they were past, continuing on their mission to banish hunger.

All back yards are not created equal.

23

Thursday, June 29, 2000, Outdoors, page C1

Ears as important as eyes in early morning bird survey

LINGLE – It is not quiet before the dawn when it's a summer morning [in June] in Wyoming.

Thirty minutes before sunrise June 8, where a gravel road crosses a canal a few miles west of Lingle, Dave Felley listened intently to distinguish the songs of western kingbirds, western meadowlarks and blue grosbeaks.

It was as if members of an avian orchestra were trying to outdo each other.

Felley's job was to not only recognize the different bird songs but to count how many of each kind.

In the dim light by the side of newly sprouted corn fields, Felley used his ears more than his eyes to count the breeding birds at the first

of 50 three-minute stops he would make on this 24.5-mile Breeding Bird Survey route.

Many species of birds have been well studied and counted, especially game birds and birds that pass through migration bottlenecks, such as shorebirds and hawks, said Felley.

In 1966, ornithologist Chandler Robbins devised the BBS to monitor breeding bird population trends across North America.

"What it's best at is counting territorial adults," Felley said. "Songbirds advertise their territory, so every singing bird is a breeding bird."

About 2,500 professional biologists and skilled amateur birders across the country drive one or more of the nearly 3,000 BBS routes once every year.

The Lingle route is one of two Felley, a biologist for the U.S. Fish and Wildlife Service's Ecological Services Field Office in Cheyenne, took on four years ago.

This year, for the first time, he joins the 25 percent of participants who conduct a survey as part of their job. Before, Felley did the surveys on his weekends.

He still has to review bird songs on his own time. "I did that last night," he said. "I went through my CD (of bird songs) for the real tough ones."

More than 90 bird species have been identified on the Lingle route in the 20 years since it was established, according to the BBS database. About 20 of those species show up every year.

How can someone distinguish that many songs? Felley's philosophy is, "If you can remember the melody of a song, you can remember bird song."

National-level BBS coordinators at the U.S. Geologic Survey's Patuxent Wildlife Research Center in Maryland provided Felley with field data sheets giving start and stop times, a list of birds and a map of the route.

Route 92091 must begin by 4:50 a.m. For Felley, that means leaving Cheyenne at 3:30 a.m.

If the weather is too rainy or windy by BBS standards, Felley has to bag it and try another day. The BBS asks that wind not exceed 12 mph, "except in those prairie states and provinces (like Wyoming) where winds normally exceed Beaufort 3: Leaves and small twigs in constant motion, light flag extended."

Every effort is made to keep survey conditions exactly the same from year to year so that the number of birds is the only variable. The BBS works best if the same observer works the same route from year to year.

Humans and their activities are unpredictable, however. Felley's pre-dawn stops were interrupted by several passing pickup trucks that potentially drowned out some bird songs.

Later, trains, tractors and highway traffic echoed through the North Platte River valley. Bawling calves competed with the less-than-bucolic sounds of center pivot irrigation and screaming domestic peacocks.

From year to year there are other changes: New fields plowed, different crops planted, more houses built, road realigned.

At stop number 34, Felley carefully checked out a lone cottonwood. Last year it held a Lawrence's goldfinch, a vagrant from the Southwest.

Next year, Felley will remember stop number 41, where a northern bobwhite obligingly trotted down a roadside ditch as he pulled up and it stayed to be counted.

The BBS is not a census. Rather, it is an index using breeding birds as indicators of population shifts, declines or increases.

By going online at www.mp2-pwrc. usgs.gov/bbs, researchers and curious bird watchers can find a list of scientific articles written using BBS data, as well as the raw data itself, including data from the 80-plus routes in Wyoming.

Birders interested in running a BBS route may check with Wyoming's coordinator.

By about the 25th stop, with the sun well up, you realize this is field work, not a bird-watching field day. But for volunteers, the compensation comes in the enjoyment of birding on an early summer morning.

Felley's last stop was east of Torrington where the land is still native prairie, too sandy and hilly to farm. On a fence post sat a grasshopper sparrow, hardly bigger than its namesake. It threw back its head with such abandon for every buzzy trill it gave. It was easy to believe birds too appreciate summer mornings.

24 Hummingbirds making their colorful migrations

Thursday, August 17, 2000, Outdoors, page C2

The broad-tailed and the rufous are the most common hummingbirds in the Cheyenne area.

Go anywhere in Wyoming's mountains in summer and you're bound to hear the ringing sound of the broad-tailed hummingbird's wings as it skims your hat or nearby flowers. Every mountain cabin seems to be festooned in hummingbird feeders.

A few broad-tailed hummingbirds may be seen in Cheyenne during spring migration, but a hummingbird feeder set out here for the summer is more likely to be emptied by the wind, yellow jackets and house finches.

However, around about August, especially when drought diminishes wildflowers blooming in the mountains as it has this year, we may see hummingbirds hanging out in town around our bountiful, irrigated gardens.

A few years ago, during another dry summer, I saw something hovering over my marigolds which I thought at first was an insect. Now that we're better at spotting them, this August we've had a couple more glimpses of hummingbirds, as have several callers. Maybe it's time to put up our feeder.

To approximate natural nectar for hummers, dissolve one part white table sugar to four parts boiling water. Don't use other kinds of sugar or increase the proportion. Adding red dye is unnecessary. The red on the feeders is enough. If yours has faded, paint the ports with red nail polish.

Be sure to keep your feeders clean. Bill Thompson, author of "Bird Watching for Dummies" recommends cleaning the feeder with hot soapy water before refilling it. During particularly hot weather it may take only a couple days for the solution to sprout mold.

His recommendations of where to put the feeders include where they can be seen easily by you and the hummers, where they are out of direct sunlight, which introduces mold growth, and where they are easy to reach for cleaning and refilling.

There are two species of hummingbirds you may see in Cheyenne. The most likely is the broad-tailed, which is known to summer here but usually breeds in the mountains.

The rufous hummingbird is less common here. It winters in Mexico and migrates north along the Pacific coast as far as Alaska to nest. By June it is heading back southeast through the Rocky Mountains.

According to Jane and Robert Dorn's records in "Wyoming Birds," the rufous has been merely a migrant in the latilong that includes Cheyenne.

There are other hummers seen in other parts of Wyoming: ruby-throated (northeastern counties, rare migrant but the only hummingbird occurring east of the Mississippi), black-chinned (western Wyoming during migration) and calliope (uncommon summer resident in western Wyoming). We are hardly a hummingbird mecca like southeastern Arizona.

Meanwhile, I plant bright tubular types of flowers for the year the broad-taileds decide to spend the summer: bee balm, columbine, four o'clocks, penstemons, petunias, phlox and snapdragons.

I'll have to think about adding bleeding heart, dahlias, nasturtium, zinnias or vines like morning glory. Other plants recommended in books about hummingbirds are less familiar and may not thrive here. Then again, they didn't mention marigolds.

25 Birds congregating, fattening up to prepare for winter

Thursday, September 14, 2000, Outdoors, page C1

"Birds of a feather flock together," especially this time of year.

Most everyone is finished with quietly raising the young out of earshot of predators and competitors, and the birds are ready to socialize again.

Maybe your yard has been invaded by partiers in black: starlings, grackles and red-winged blackbirds.

Sometimes their ruckus makes me think it's dawn in the heart of the Okefenokee Swamp, like the eco-sounds record I had in the '70s.

Local bird expert Jane Dorn said the birds are fattening up for migration; or for winter if they're year round residents. Jane has noticed that, out in the country, lark sparrows are bunching up as well.

One persistent sound in my yard for the last month has been the red-breasted nuthatch. I haven't seen it yet, but the "ent-ent-ent" is unmistakable.

It's hard to spell bird sounds, so try a recording. Maybe you have one in your yard too and don't know it.

I was worried the nuthatch wouldn't be back after a major pruning job on our two big green ash trees, but it's still around, to be heard at least.

The shaggy branches of the silver maples out front seem possessed as migrating warblers wiggle a leaf here and then a leaf there, looking for scrumptious bugs. I haven't gotten a good look at the yellowish birds yet.

Fred Lebsack spotted Wilson's warblers at the Botanic Gardens. Jane mentioned Townsend's.

I had a call from a reader a couple weeks ago about a bird she thought might be a varied thrush. The range map in my field guide showed it as a species of the Pacific Northwest, no closer to us than western Montana.

Later I mentioned the bird to Jane and she said, "Oh yes, sometimes we get them."

Remember, birds can't read maps. According to Kenn Kaufman in "Lives of North American Birds," varied thrushes have strayed as far as New England.

We took our feeders down in early August when some of the finches looked sick. It's good to break the disease cycle, especially in a season when natural food is available.

Finches and sparrows haven't been seen here since, so when a finch-sized bird perched on the wire the other day, I took a careful look. It was a flycatcher, but which one?

Fred recommended I compare

the western wood-pewee, part of the "tyrant" flycatcher group, with the empidonax flycatchers illustrated in the National Geographic field guide. I did.

We're talking about your average little gray birds here, ones that may be molting into even less remarkable plumage. Or they may be the young of the year, wearing some kind of juvenile plumage. And some of these flycatchers, even in peak breeding plumage, can only be told apart by song.

Well, it is not spring – "at-tract-a-mate-defend-a-territory" – time, so they aren't singing.

Jane mentioned that the reservoirs are full of migrating water birds and shorebirds also wearing confusing feathers. You could be an expert using a high-powered scope and still not be sure of their identification this time of year.

Some, like the Wilson's phalaropes I saw up at Chimney Park at the end of August, at least have an identifiable shape and behavior, sort of like long-necked gourds instead of plastic ducks swirling around a tub of water in some carnival game.

Instead of agonizing over which species of flycatcher I have in my yard, I think I'll just enjoy observing the bird as it sits so upright and attentive, flicking its head right, then left, up, then down, then flying out to intercept an insect before resuming its perch.

On a recent evening it was so still I think I heard its beak snapping on prey on one of those forays.

Jane said to watch for orioles and western tanagers migrating too. My neighbor recently described seeing in his yard what could have been a tanager: a red/orange-faced bird that was other-wise yellowish, rather than the red-faced but brownish-colored house finch.

Keep your bird water supply full and be sure to call me when you get interest-ing avian visitors.

26 Birds make windy hunt bearable

Thursday, October 12, 2000, Outdoors, page C2

I made a date with the antelope in Shirley Basin seven months in advance.

When it snowed the week before instead of the week of the hunt, I con-sidered myself luckier than the little warblers caught in the first storm and at least as lucky as the green-tailed towhee that used our patio for a refuge.

By the time Mark and I reached the basin a week later, the snow had melted off to a few streaks secreted in the ripples of the rim, like Styrofoam trash locked in a hedge.

But the wind was relentless, scouring the earth of all loose material.

Most of the vegetation up there is already barely more than boot-heel high.

We hiked for two hours. At the top of the rim, I could raise my foot to take a step and have it pushed sideways by the wind with the strength and noise of a jet-engine's blast. Think blizzard without snow.

Think I'll ask Santa for an anemom-eter so I can measure the wind speed at which my breath is sucked away.

Such a desolate landscape still has wildlife. A flutter of horned larks greet-ed us as we turned off the highway. That one and every flock I saw later flew up and then blew away east with the wind.

How exactly do small birds travel against the wind? Do they wait for a calm day and fly back west? Are their bodies stacked up against some fence in Iowa? Is there an undocumented east-west migration phenomenon?

Maybe they hop back along the

ground since wind speed decreases the closer you get to ground level. I saw several beetles casually crawling between wind-dwarfed shrubs, and even a few asters blooming within inches of the ground.

You notice these things when looking up can cause your sunglasses to be ripped from your face.

Eagles seem to be strong enough to enjoy the wind. We saw three immature golden eagles bouncing through the air like kids on carnival rides.

Finally, we decided to seek protection down on the North Platte and arrived at dusk. As I checked the wind-worthiness of a campground cottonwood, I realized I was looking up at the bottom end of an owl. It left, soundlessly, but the rest of the evening was punctuated by weird squawks from an animal in the thicket.

In the morning we discovered the river bottom was decked out in red, orange, gold and green. Accents were provided by red wing linings of a flicker, blue vest of a kingfisher, green heads of male mallards and the rich rust brown feathers of a female northern harrier flying reconnaissance along the riverbank.

Back at our hunting area, herds of antelope blew about in the wind, just out of reach. Unlike birds, you know when antelope are watching you. They stop, turn their heads toward you, if not their whole bodies, and stare.

I've often wondered why flies, with the ability to cling to the ceiling, get nailed by cats. So too, I wonder how someone on foot in a bare, endless landscape can bring down an animal which can run more than 60 miles per hour and can see a greater distance than a bullet can accurately travel.

Mark was able to compensate for the wind and bring home one antelope. I, with lesser experience, decided not to try.

As I stood on a hill and looked 360 degrees around me, I saw true open space: All the way to the horizon hardly a sign of man beyond the scratch of dirt two-track in the distance.

Selfishly I hoped there won't be too many people coming here in the future who are interested in battling the wind for a look at the play of light on antelope heaven.

27 A visit to Lucy's garden creek

Thursday, November 9, 2000, Outdoors, page C2

I met Lucy nearly 20 years ago when I lived in Casper and worked as an environmental technician, before I cared very much about bird watching.

When I got married and left for a Montana sojourn, we kept in touch by Christmas cards.

On my first spring bird count in Cheyenne 10 years ago, I was surprised to find Lucy among the contingent from Casper. It's a Murie Audubon tradition to push spring a little by coming south to bird with us on our Big Count, because spring migration peaks here about

a week earlier.

Since then, I've also had chances to visit Lucy in Casper whenever the state Audubon board meets there. Two weeks ago, we even had time to look for birds together.

For a person who speaks of recently attending her 60th high school reunion, Lucy is remarkably fit and agile, I thought as I puffed a bit following her up to take a look at Garden Creek Falls.

This was where she hung out with her high school friends. It's still popular with the partying set, which is why, she said, she doesn't come up alone.

From the shoulder of Casper Mountain, we had a view of the city and a distant magpie.

But it's a downstream stretch of Garden Creek that Lucy regards as her backyard. Running below her house, the creek is a deeply cut, winding channel stuffed with bushes – just perfect for a second ramble this particular afternoon and just perfect for black-capped chickadees, juncos and pine siskins.

We saw occasional flashes of blue jay and red wing linings of flickers as we hiked down one side of the creek through Nancy English Park and back up the other side.

For 20 years Lucy and two friends have surveyed the creek above and below her house four times a year. The reports are faithfully sent to the Wyoming Game and Fish Department's non-game bird biologist.

The reports I looked at are a who's who of birds found in Wyoming's riparian areas, although this one is surrounded by a 40-year-old suburban forest planted by adjacent homeowners.

Only one backyard we passed maintained the original flora. What courage these homeowners have in a sidewalks and gutter kind of neighborhood. Imagine the back of a substantial house: sliding glass doors leading to a large patio abutting a well-tended lawn which fades into dry native grasses and rabbitbrush--still within the city limits.

Walking the creek, with houses backing onto it, is a little like walking an alley with a severe erosion problem down the middle.

As we rounded a bend I caught a glimpse of a small log structure, the kind where the mortar makes stripes almost as wide as the logs. I thought it might be some forgotten ranch building now at the edge of someone's yard.

No, said Lucy. Her brother-in-law built it in his back yard for his kids and their cousins, Lucy's children.

I could have sworn the cabin was a contemporary of buildings at South Pass City, except it wasn't sagging. What a great Thoreau house it would make, to live there simply, without stuff, and observe the creek, pen in hand, for a year or so.

Lucy's Garden Creek reports do not mention the species that eats some of the sunflower seed she puts out.

While we enjoyed a cup of tea at the kitchen table after our walks, a doe mule deer nuzzled the few seeds left at the shelf feeder at the windowsill.

The doe's twin sons, nubbins of antlers barely apparent, were still too short to reach. The doe kept her huge, brown eyes on us as she polished the shelf.

The purveyors of bird feeding equipment have all kinds of anti-squirrel devices. Keeping deer out means hanging them higher – and then figuring out how to reach up and fill them.

Biologists talk about corridors wildlife can use to safely travel from one necessary habitat to another, perhaps from wintering grounds to summer range.

Along Garden Creek the wildlife of the mountain and foothills have a way to travel into the city, although we have to be careful when they cross the streets.

But I think this greenway works in reverse for people, taking our imaginations back to the mountain when circumstances only permit a creekside ramble.

2001

28 Thursday, May 17, 2001, Outdoors, page C2
Nighttime right time
for fauna to frolic

There's wild night life in Cheyenne in the spring.

The other night, on the way home from quilt club, I had to brake for a fox trotting across Converse at Dell Range. You don't suppose we could get him to use the pedestrian bridge, do you?

Another night, after a Cheyenne Little Theater production, we were driving a friend home along Windmill when I noticed an upright animal shape in the borrow pit.

The object was still there on the way back. Since there was no traffic, we stopped to look. An eye glinted in the streetlight and glared back at us. We were interrupting a fisherman: a black-crowned night-heron.

Reminiscent of its cousin, the great blue heron, but with short neck and short legs, this 2-foot-tall bird was stalking the edge of a puddle, looking for unwary frogs to stab with its long, strong, black bill.

It's predictable that the open space east of the airport would become a red-light district – brake lights, I mean. Maybe that's why that section of Windmill was recently festooned with streetlights; so we won't run over the low life – low profile, that is – such as foxes, birds, mice and frogs.

Even in my respectable neighborhood it's common to see a couple of cotton-tails loitering on the lawn by the light of the moon.

Later, in the grayness before sun-rise, they move from damp lawns to the warmth and dryness of the asphalt streets, where they become nearly invis-ible - until the dog and I spook them.

If it weren't for rabbits, walking wouldn't give me the upper-body work-out I get from hanging onto the leash of my 100-pound dog as he lunges after his instinctual prey.

There's a lot going on during day-light hours too. Here are some reports I received the first ten days of May:

--Velma Simpkins, in Pine Bluffs, has been getting unusual doves, possibly domestic escapees or maybe Eurasian collared doves, which are spreading rapidly since being accidentally released in Florida.

--Wayne Neemann reported a rose-breasted grosbeak in his north-side yard. This grosbeak is an eastern bird normally, but some stray out here during migration.

--Beth Easton wanted to know how to keep a robin from building a nest on top of her wall-mounted porch light. I suggested temporarily hanging chick-en wire from the porch ceiling down around the light.

--Belinda and Don Moench were at Twin Buttes Lake on the Laramie Plains when they identified two common loons. The little island in the middle of the lake has a colony of nesting great blue herons. Down at Holliday Park, Belinda saw an eared grebe.

--Eileen Poelma had Canada geese in her yard south of Carpenter.

--Caroline Eggleston described small sparrows with rusty brown caps in her yard in Orchard Valley, probably chipping sparrows.

--Betty Wagner has pine siskins and American goldfinches eating her out of house and home in Sun Valley. Her four feeders have a total of 24 ports, and often each will have a bird.

--Fred Lebsack visited Lions Park May 8 and reported a Tennessee warbler (another eastern stray), a wood duck and a blue-gray gnatcatcher.

--Joanne Mason of Wheatland, one of the students in the "Bird Watching for Fun," class Jane Dorn and I taught this spring at Laramie County Community College, came with the longest list of any of the students of birds she'd seen.

The plantings she did about 12 years ago are beginning to really bring in the birds, including a Bullock's oriole, lesser goldfinch, vesper sparrow and clay-colored sparrow.

Things are still slow in my yard. Perhaps too much of our green ash trees got pruned last fall, or maybe there's a hawk roosting on the TV antenna tower, where we can't see it from the window.

I did see a yellow-rumped warbler of the "Myrtle" race (white throat instead of yellow) on May 9, and the next day two red-breasted nuthatches came in. The nuthatches may be the two that spent several winter months debugging our tree trunks.

I'm looking forward to the Big Count on Saturday. It's a chance to renew acquaintances with spring migrants – and with bird watching friends who come down every year from Casper for the event.

Every year we find some stray warbler, shorebird or gnatcatcher I've never seen before. It's as if, for us homebodies, migrating birds bring us a bit of more exotic lands for a few days.

29 Backyard beckons bevy of birds

It's hard to eat breakfast, lunch or dinner these days without picking up the binoculars to admire the birds on my backyard wall.

When I e-mailed my last column to the Wyoming Tribune-Eagle, mentioning the paucity of birds in my yard and all the sightings in everyone else's, a little bird must have been sitting on the wire listening in.

The next day, May 11, my yard was inundated with pine siskins, goldfinches and chipping sparrows, and accented by a black-headed grosbeak, a Bullock's oriole and a rose-breasted grosbeak.

A lazuli bunting showed up, too, and came back with half a dozen friends. They look like small eastern or western bluebirds, with robin-colored, red breasts.

It turns out the buntings like millet, something I usually don't put out because it attracts house sparrows. Dave Felley gave us half a bag when he moved so we've been spreading it out on the top of our concrete-block wall. The buntings have been lining up shoulder-to-shoulder with the mourning doves every day since.

When I observed a house finch

drinking out of the dog's water dish, I decided it was time to try the Solar Sipper again. It's like a fancy dog dish with a removable, black plastic bowl inside a red plastic bowl.

It comes with a black lid that's supposed to absorb heat and keep the water from freezing in winter. The lid has a hole in it for birds to stick their heads through and get a drink.

The birds never learned to use it, but the dog learned to knock off the lid and drink.

This time I put it on the back wall without the lid, and birds are using it. The grackles threw in some stale bread and hard raisins and retrieved them when they got soggy. But I still caught a grackle using the real dog dish on the back step.

The green-tailed towhee showed up a week after everyone else.

He's between robin and sparrow size, and he holds his tail up at a right angle. His greenish-gray coloring makes him invisible where he hangs out under the bushes, unless you see the flashy white patch under his chin or his rust-colored cap.

I had three people tell me about western tanagers in their yards before I saw one in my neighborhood. He was drinking water puddled in a crack in the street.

These tanagers are so tropical looking – orange head, yellow body and black and white wings.

You might mistake a black-headed grosbeak for a robin, until you look more closely. They are more orange than robin-red, their heads are blacker, and their wings and tails are spotted with white. Their thick "gross" – or big – beaks are for cracking seeds rather than drilling for worms.

The rose-breasted grosbeak looks pretty much the same, but instead of orange it has a white belly with a dark

pink bib. I've now seen one in the yard four days out of 14. Perhaps I wasn't looking hard enough the other days.

Other than mourning doves and robins, I don't expect any of these spring birds to nest here. Most are on their way to the mountains or farther north.

Some birds get a very early start with nesting and breeding.

We've gone out listening for owls in February because that's when owls set up their territories and hoot at their rivals.

Meriden rancher Dave Hansen was out branding May 19 when he noticed two great horned owls toddling around his home pasture. Had they blown out of the nest?

It isn't unusual for these owls to leave the nest by now, even if they aren't ready to fly yet. They are as big as the adults, just sort of fluffy, sort of chubby, like a two-year old wearing cloth diapers and plastic pants.

As soon as they learn to fly [actually, they are quite good using their beaks and claws to climb trees until they can fly], they will return to obscurity in the treetops and spend the summer with their parents learning to hunt rodents.

This is the most important time of year to keep all cats indoors – especially if you live out on the prairie with the ground-nesting grassland birds. It's also important not to mow right now.

Cats, unlike native predators, are more numerous and will kill for fun rather than food.

I hope whoever belongs to the gray cat that visits my yard will keep him home. Otherwise, I have to put my dog on guard duty first thing in the morning, and then the green-tailed towhee won't come.

Two bird watchers from California traveling through Cheyenne made arrangements to meet me down at Lions Park on one of the windy days we had whitecaps on the lake.

Other than the western grebes, mallards, a few yellow-rumped warblers and a tree full of goldfinches, there wasn't much to see, and we decided not to walk around the lake.

On the way back to our cars I mentioned the only other sure-fire bird observation we could make would be the yellow-headed blackbirds over by the cattails.

"Yellow-headed blackbirds?" responded the Californians. "We've seen them only three other places!"

So we headed into the wind and soon were rewarded with a yellow-headed male strolling the path toward us until he was at our feet.

Then he flew up and engaged in aerial shenanigans with a red-winged blackbird a few feet over our heads. The Californians were delighted.

So, one birder's blackbird is another's special species. Should I ever look up the Santa Monica Audubon chapter, I wonder what locally abundant bird they will have that will be my fabulous find?

Thursday, June 14, 2001, Outdoors, page C2

30 Putting off yard work helps wildlife

It's best to delay some chores until young birds have time to hatch and leave the nest as fledglings.

Procrastination can be a good thing. Spring snowstorms will melt off the driveway by midday if I don't shovel, and fancy computers eventually are available at garage sales.

On the north side of my house is a deep, dark and quiet forest.

Sheltered by the next-door neighbor's house, when the wind gets there, it drops in speed – and drops litter.

The junipers probably were cute little shrubs when they were planted along the foundation 40 years ago. Today they are leviathans, reaching over my head, 8 or 10 feet high and as wide and deep.

I keep thinking I should cut a few branches at Christmas – especially ones shading the window by my computer. The evergreen smell would be nice. But then I forget, and it's May or June before I dig out the pruning saw.

Why do I procrastinate gardening and yard work, which I enjoy?

Perhaps because my other obligations are less forgiving of missed deadlines. Other than the lawn, of which the boys

have charge, things grow slowly enough around here there's never a pruning crisis – especially since I cultivate the natural look.

Well, the stars finally lined up right last week, and I found the pruning saw and headed for the woods, intent on bagging a few branches.

Actually, the hunting euphemism doesn't translate here. We don't bag branches. We keep them for yard projects and firewood.

I sawed around the computer window and moved to the next window, but as I grabbed a branch, it squawked.

Mama Robin flew up out of her nest and chastised me from the edge of the neighbor's roof as I hurriedly backed away.

Deep, dark woods may be the epitome of safe bird habitat, but this is the first time the robins have chosen it over the trees out front. In fact, the nest is not deep in the juniper branches, but sort of on top.

By pressing my forehead to the

window from inside the house before Mama Robin settled back in, I could see at least three eggs. When she's on the nest, she sits as stoically as an avian Buddha.

A few days later, I had a call from someone concerned because her family cat had slightly mauled a baby bird that fell out of its nest. What should she do?

Here are some suggestions in order of preference.

First, try putting the nestling back in the nest. Some young, however, will just fling themselves out of the nest again, or the nest may be too high for you to reach safely.

Or, if the baby is fairly well feathered and close to being able to fly, let the parents take care of it on the ground. Keep pets and children away.

Once, I tried making a nest out of a bucket, placing it where the parents would visit and feed the baby, but it evidently wasn't cat-proof.

The next option is to buy worms where fish bait is sold and start feeding the baby yourself.

Kelly, who works at the Cheyenne Pet Clinic, said baby birds only need to be fed once a day.

If you're squeamish about worms, try foods from this list she recommends: brown rice (cooked), frozen corn, cooked pinto beans, crushed dog kibble, soaked millet, lean meat, white cheese, fruit (especially oranges), green vegetables, carrots or squash. For treats, try dabs of yogurt, cottage cheese or dried fruit like raisins – but no nuts.

Kelly also said technicians at The Wildlife Rehabilitation Center, located at the clinic, are happy to feed baby birds for you to get them ready for release.

Let me get on my soapbox here for two ideas.

First, nature doesn't expect every seed to lead to a flower or every bird egg to lead to flight. Some progeny have to become food for others, whether it's baby worms feeding robins or baby robins feeding hawks.

But on the other hand, bird blood on your cat's paws is not part of the natural balance because domestic cats are not native to our area.

Letting your cat play with baby birds, besides doing damage to individual birds and bird species in general, does nothing for the cat that you and a catnip mouse couldn't do better indoors. And it's safer for your cat, which won't be exposed to bird-borne diseases and other outdoor hazards.

You could build a screened porch-type kennel like a friend of mine has for her cats. They still get to go outside, but everyone is safe.

This is a great time of year to procrastinate the right things.

Put off mowing the prairie, where killdeer and meadowlarks nest on the ground. Save the tree pruning and ditch clearing until the young have cleared their nests by June or July. Let the wild tangle at the back provide escape from predators.

According to Kenn Kaufman's write-up on robins in "Lives of North American Birds," I may have to wait 12 to 14 days for Mama Robin's eggs to hatch and another 14 to 16 days for the young to fledge.

While I practice procrastinating pruning, if I open the window and let strains of Mozart float down to Mama Robin's nest while the chicks are still in the shell, will they grow up smarter and survive better than other robins? Or will they emerge from the nest chirping the "Piano Sonata in B Flat Major"?

31 Robins fledge, face cruel world

Wind, rain and pea-sized hail over the last few weeks did not noticeably affect our resident robin family.

Every day that I checked the nest, it was normal to see one of the parents settled down over the eggs.

Then one day neither parent was there, and I couldn't see the turquoise-colored eggs either. I wondered if the nest had been raided and abandoned.

Turns out it's hard to see into the shadows at the bottom of a nest if you're looking sideways through a window screen. So I removed the screen.

The tiny nestlings were there. Their little bodies quivered with rapid breathing as they slept silently in a heap between feedings, eyes shut tight.

In the gloom of the nest their bright yellow gapes glowed.

When robin babies wake for feeding, these bright-yellow edges of their mouths, plus their red mouth linings, give the parents a target for dropping in food. As they mature, their beaks become totally yellow.

After a week, the three nestlings became pudgy little feather balls overflowing the nest. Their breasts were taking on an orange hue, polka-dotted with brown.

When I opened the window to look at them, their eyes sparkled at me like the jet beads on a cape my ancient relative left behind.

On the 10th day after they hatched, I could count only two beaked faces staring at me. Had one already jumped ship?

But when I checked back a few hours later, the third one had reappeared. Evidently its siblings had been standing on it.

As I watched, one climbed over another and flapped its wings. As soon as I shut the window, Momma Robin returned with more groceries.

She has had the same routine each time – landing on the edge of the neighbor's roof, at the ridge, hopping a few feet, stopping, then hopping again until she reaches the edge of the rain gutter. Then she hops across to the nest.

A worm is neatly looped up and held by her beak, yet she can still make her one-note call to her young.

Now the grackle family across the street is quite raucous. They too are nesting in junipers. I can't see into their nest, but all the hullabaloo every time one of the adults flies into the bush alerts me to their location.

Parents, bird or human, have to deal with the unpleasant chore of disposing of baby poop. Baby birds produce "fecal sacs," which the parents either eat or carry off.

These grackles have been departing the nest with the white blobs in their bills, but as they fly up and over our house, they lose their grips and the sacs splat on our front window.

It would be convenient if I were doing fecal analysis to find out what the young are eating. But since I've been digging alongside the grackles in the garden, I'd guess it is mostly pill bugs and worms.

A commune of mourning doves visits our yard every day. I can't tell who is male and who is female or who is mated to whom. I've seen up to eight birds at a time. They're probably nesting in neighborhood spruce trees.

Between the birds and the bat that zoomed by the other morning before dawn (no – zoomed is not the right word, because bats make no noise, even less than a flit), we should have good insect and weed seed control this summer.

When the young leave the nest, the parent robins will still be taking care of them. There are a lot of predators and dangerous situations out there for which they need parental guidance.

A caller the other day brought to my attention the perils of deep window wells, especially the 6-foot ones at new houses. A baby bird died in hers because it couldn't climb out and was too young to fly.

The caller suggested propping a branch against the inside of the window well or installing covers.

This week I feel a little like Momma Robin will soon. The boys have left home temporarily. Will they be safe out there in the world?

Will they know enough to feed themselves properly?

Will some kind soul assist them when needed, like the driver the other day assisted ducklings across Dell Range?

In the time it has taken to write this, the first young robin has fledged, one is sitting on the rim of the nest, and the other is on a nearby branch. An unhatched egg lies at the bottom of the nest.

Ken Kaufmann writes in "Lives of North American Birds" that once the young are fledged, the male will take over parenting while the female prepares the nest for the second brood. At this rate I can procrastinate pruning the bushes at least another month – maybe even till Christmas.

32 Don't poison your yard to save it

Thursday, July 26, 2001, Outdoors, page C2

Which is more hazardous, walking New York City streets or hiking Wyoming's back country? They have muggers; we have bears.

New York got ahead of us last summer with an outbreak of West Nile Virus, which can be fatal to some jays and crows -- and some people.

I was surprised, however, by a news release from the National Audubon Society. According to Ward Stone, chief wildlife pathologist for New York State's Department of Environmental Conservation, among 4,000 dead birds collected and tested for the virus, synthetic chemical pesticides were a contributing factor or cause of death more often than any other agent, including the virus.

Lawn chemicals were among the most common toxins.

About a dozen pesticides approved for backyard use have caused

documented die-offs of birds, author Joel Bourne writes in "The Audubon Guide to Home Pesticides."

Nationally, we use three times more chemical pesticides on our lawns at home, school and the golf course than the total amount used by farmers. That statistic comes from David Pimental, a Cornell University scientist.

More than 100,000 cases of pesticide exposure were documented in 1998 at U.S. regional poison control centers. But the centers do not cover the whole country, and many people do not think to report what just seems like flu symptoms.

What's a conscientious person to do?

Recently Audubon published a poster, "10 Commandments for a Healthy Yard," which helps answer that question. Here are the commandments, with my local interpretation.

--Go Organic. For a quick introduction to organic yard care methods

– which will save you money as well as make your yard safer – pick up an issue of Organic Gardening magazine or visit www.organicgardening.com.

--Make Your Turf Tough. Use grass varieties meant for our climate. Use sharp mower blades and cut high. Water well a couple times a week, rather than watering lightly every day.

--Go Native! Plants native to our area will be less susceptible to pests – and take less water. Check with the folks at the Cheyenne Botanic Gardens for suggestions, or visit their website, www.botanic.org.

--Know Your Enemies. Figure out what bugs you have, whether you have enough of them to make treatment worthwhile and when in their life cycles is best to strike – and with what. Call the University of Wyoming Cooperative Extension horticulturist, Liberty Blain, 633-4383, or bring your bugs and diseased leaves to her (in containers) at the Old Courthouse, 310 W. 19th.

--Treat Only When Necessary. Use nontoxic methods first, picking off insects, pruning affected areas and hosing down plants. For more remedies, look for books such as "The Encyclopedia of Natural Insect & Disease Control," edited by Roger B. Yepsen or "Rodale's All-New Encyclopedia of Organic Gardening" edited by Fern Marshall Bradley.

--Pick Your Pesticides. Don't go for the "shotgun" approach. It will kill beneficial insects as well as pests. Use the least toxic product. The Environmental Protection Agency's rating system is "caution" (least toxic), "warning" and "danger" (most toxic).

--Use Biological Controls or Biopesticides. If you can't borrow a goat to eat your thistle, biological pesticides decompose more rapidly and are better at targeting the pest than chemical pesticides. Check the EPA's biopesticides website, ... (although I don't agree that genetically altered plants should be included in EPA's definition of biopesticides).

--Follow Directions and Protect Yourself. And don't forget to protect other people, pets and wildlife habitat from exposure. Read the label. Less is best.

--Respect Your Neighbor's Right to Know. Ever had your windows open to the light summer breeze – and the chemical drift of whatever your neighbor's lawn care service is spraying? Thank goodness the City of Cheyenne is using modern methods to control mosquitoes instead of spraying malathion everywhere.

--Teach Tolerance and Be Tolerant. As the poster explains, "Create natural yards, with a variety of pests, predators, weeds, wildlife and native plant species."

My favorite: "Enjoy controlled untidiness, not time-consuming lawn maintenance," and "show by doing."

I don't use pesticides in my yard, so had I been writing these commandments, I would have left out numbers 6, 8 and 9.

But if we were all to subscribe to the organic yard care philosophy, just imagine what the birds would think!

33 Don't rely on color for bird ID

Thursday, August 23, 2001, Outdoors, page C3

One useful way to identify a bird is by silhouette, because us bird watchers are always looking up toward a sky that often backlights our quarry, turning it into a colorless shape.

Also, the color of some birds, like

hummingbirds, is produced by iridescence, light refracting within the feather structure, rather than pigment. So, if the sunlight doesn't shine just right, colors won't match the field guide pictures.

Knowing your bird silhouettes can help you distinguish groups of birds, for instance, the ramrod straight posture of a flycatcher perched on a wire, compared to the forward tilt of a finch.

It may even help identify unique-looking individual species. The canvasback can be distinguished from other ducks even in the tricky non-breeding plumage of fall because of its ski slope profile from forehead to bill tip.

I was thinking about silhouettes the other evening on our first-ever Cheyenne High Plains Audubon Society overnight field trip.

The campout had also appealed to Auduboners from Laramie, Casper and Wheatland, and we were sitting companionably by a small campfire along the North Platte.

Above us, the bit of sky between the cottonwoods had been serving as a stage since we'd first arrived late afternoon, when the swallows were performing insect-snatching aerobatics.

During dinner, a common nighthawk, with boomerang-shaped wings, joined in, confusing me with its cry, which I have difficulty distinguishing from the western wood peewee.

Then three American white pelicans drifted by. It was quiet enough and they were low enough that we could hear the sound of their wings creaking as they adjusted to air currents.

Even if the light had not been enough to see their smooth, white bodies, black edged wings and golden orange bills and feet, the pelicans' compact body shape and huge wings make for a prehistoric-looking profile easy to identify.

Later, a skein of Canada geese crossed the sky stage. By then the sunset footlights were too low for markings to be picked out. But the proportions were right, and a few honks dispelled any doubt.

Every summer evening along the North Platte and other rivers there is a magic minute when day gives way to night, when swallows turn into bats.

I can never quite pinpoint it. I look up once and see arrow-shaped swallows darting after airborne food, and the next time I look up, the flying insectivores have scallop-edged bat wings.

The bats, probably little brown bats, swoop much lower than swallows – making silhouettes against the firelight as often as against the starlight. It's a comfort knowing that they may be getting mosquitoes before mosquitoes get me.

In the morning I woke at whatever dark hour it was when the killdeer called. Instead of getting up at the crack of dawn for birdwatching, I laid in our flimsy nylon backpacker's tent "bird listening" – until I heard the sandhill cranes rattle by. Those I wanted to see!

After camp was packed up, Jane Dorn led us back to Saratoga Lake.

It's a hard time of year for bird identification since everyone seems to have molted out of recognizable breeding plumage – or hasn't grown up enough to wear it.

However, the common merganser young were old enough that they had the same strange head shape as their mother, making her difficult to pick out as the eleven youngsters crowded around her.

I could correctly identify the first dark, flying tubular shape I saw as a double-crested cormorant, but on the second dark tubular shape, I missed the difference in bill. When that bird landed on a sandbar, it turned out to be a white-faced ibis (now's a good time to pause and look that up in your field guide!).

The marsh wren doesn't seem to have a silhouette at all. It stays as invisible as its nest, a Baba Yaga affair with legs of bulrush stems – if Baba Yaga were an African native who could weave a conical house of reeds with a hole in the side for a door.

The marsh wren boasts of its secure invisibility by constantly singing, driving to distraction birders trying to see it.

Slow animals are seldom seen against the sky or water as silhouettes. Instead, we need to pick out the pattern of their coloration against the pattern of earth and vegetation.

So, it's surprising that when we field trippers glanced away from the song sparrow we were scoping, we noticed the yellowish, olive brown pattern camouflaging the leopard frog at our feet.

By the end of the day, I was home, back with the familiar silhouettes of doves sitting on the utility lines.

I have to remember though that even the most common birds are worth examining closely, for how else will I notice when I'm looking at the square-tailed silhouette of the rarely seen Eurasian collared-dove instead of the usual pointy-tailed mourning dove?

Note: Thanks to everyone who responded to bird rehabilitator Karin Skinner's request for donations. She expects the cliff swallows to be released in the next couple days.

34 Bird travel plans show variety

Thursday, October 18, 2001, Outdoors, page C2

I grew up with the simplistic notion that birds fly south for the winter.

But any winter day in Cheyenne is filled with birds still here: crows, starlings, sparrows, pigeons, as well as juncos, owls, and kingfishers.

Why do some birds change location? The one-word answer: food.

The birds most likely to leave are insect eaters, like warblers and tanagers, because when it's cold the insects quit reproducing or die.

Birds that eat aquatic animals and vegetation, like ducks and shorebirds, are programmed to leave too, since their food storage units get frozen over in winter.

Birds that can switch over to seeds or eat seeds exclusively (or gleanings from garbage like the crows do) can make it for the winter, as long as they eat fast enough to provide the calories they need to burn to keep warm.

Why do birds bother coming north in the spring? I've heard it's because year round birds can't possibly make use of all the fecundity of northern summers themselves and there's plenty left for the migrants. And migrating birds are looking for a boost in energy for their energy-intensive work of raising young.

Few North American field guides show where migrating birds spend the winter if it's beyond the United States. They may show a little of Mexico, but often stop right at the border.

Imagine my delight when I was told about a website that has range maps including North, Central and South America. Migration is so much more interesting when you can get a bigger picture.

The website, http://wildspace.ec.gc.ca/.html, is sponsored by the Canadian Wildlife Service. You can even choose to read life histories of birds and other animals in French. The western grebe becomes "Grébe élégant."

I found one drawback as I researched

the site for the Wyoming Bird Flashcard project. There is no range map for the broad-tailed hummingbird because it never goes as far north as Canada.

The range maps themselves have some shortcomings. They don't show migration routes.

The Wilson's phalarope is shown to breed in a swath across Canada and the northern United States, wintering in southern South America, but how does it travel back and forth?

Does it funnel down through Central America, or does it fly out over the Pacific, or maybe the Atlantic?

My Golden field guide, which cuts range maps off mid-Mexico, shows the Wilson's apparently starts over land, while the red phalarope, which breeds in the Arctic, prefers transoceanic routes exclusively.

Wish I could ask a Wilson's phalarope about its precise itinerary next spring when I see one swimming in circles on the pond just down the road from the sewage treatment plant.

These range maps also don't tell you the timing of migration.

Bob Dorn, co-author of "Wyoming Birds," told me that some species of shorebirds meet themselves coming and going.

The adults may hurry to their Arctic tundra breeding ground early in the spring. But as soon as egg laying is accomplished, the males head south again, passing northbound teenagers. Not old enough to breed yet, last year's young are in no hurry and take their time arriving.

The range maps will show an area where for some species, the birds can be found all year round, between the summer-only breeding range and the winter-only range. Wyoming is part of year round range for the belted kingfisher, so it breeds here as well as winters.

But do we have the same kingfisher on Crow Creek all year round, or do the locals migrate further south, leaving their niche open for the kingfishers coming from Canada?

Or do kingfishers that summer in Canada just hop right over Wyoming and winter in Mexico? The inquiring mind needs to research sources more scholarly than field guides.

And then it occurs to me that birds that migrate to South America during our winter are actually enjoying the southern hemisphere's summer. So why don't they breed at the tip of Chile in December the way they breed on the Arctic tundra in June?

Stan Anderson, head of the University of Wyoming's Wildlife Co-op Unit, says it would be too physiologically demanding.

Looking at the range maps though, there seems to be at least one bird that's thought of this strategy. The common snipe's range map shows it breeding in Canada and northern U.S. – and southern South America.

But, according to Stan, the southern birds don't migrate.

Author Scott Weidensaul, in his book about migration, "Living on the Wind," said five billion birds migrate back and forth in our hemisphere.

It seems to me each kind has worked out its own migration strategy. Each has a story for us to decipher.

35 Pool parties popular with winter birds

Pigeons and doves are among the few birds with the ability to suck liquids, states author Kenn Kaufman in "Lives of North American Birds."

This is because the parent birds produce a milky substance from a gland in their mouths, "pigeon milk," that the young suck by inserting their bills into the corner of the parents' mouth.

The ability to suck carries over into getting a drink of water.

Other birds can fill their mouths with water, but then have to tip their heads back to let it run down their throats.

I'll have to wait until spring to observe mourning doves again, though I suppose I could go down to one of the bridges over Crow Creek and observe the pigeons.

However, I can observe a house finch getting a drink in my backyard. It sits on the edge of the bowl, leans forward to dip its bill in the water and then leans back before dipping again, see-sawing until it's had enough, or until too many other birds crowd in.

Whether or not you plan to compare bird drinking habits, providing water for your backyard birds is a good idea, especially in the winter when natural water sources may freeze.

My present method uses an over-priced, black plastic bowl, about the size of a large dog dish, which was supposed to absorb solar radiation and keep the water from freezing in cold weather.

The bowl is too small to qualify as a bird bath, though a few grackles splashed around in it this summer. But it's easy to pick up and bring in any morning I need to run hot water over it to release the ice before refilling it.

The system we used years ago in southeastern Montana, where winter temperatures were often subzero, involved a shallow plastic garbage can lid used upside down as a liner for a traditional, pedestal-styled bird bath.

The lid being flexible, we could just pop out the circular ice chunk every morning and refill the lid with a kettleful of boiling water. Sometimes the water froze over in an hour, so I'd repeat the procedure later in the day.

The good thing about these two systems is that they cost nearly nothing and are easy to disassemble and bring in for a soap and water cleaning. However, they don't provide a constant supply of unfrozen water.

There are plenty of bird bath options (water for bathing is as important to birds as water for drinking). Some come with electric heating elements built in, or you can buy the element separately.

The luxury models of heating elements are thermostatically controlled so you don't boil any bird feet or waste electricity unnecessarily. They will also shut off automatically if the bird bath goes dry.

I checked locally and both A & C Feed stores have heating elements with or without the bird bath, as do McIntyre's Garden Center and Oasis Market.

Whatever you use for a bird bath, it should be shallow, with the water not more than 2 inches deep. It's better if the bottom slopes down toward the center.

If your bird bath is just a plastic bowl, you may want to hold it down with a large rock in the middle or mount it somehow to keep the wind from tipping it over. Then again, if your site is too windy all the time, the birds won't visit.

Cornell Lab of Ornithology recommends that the bird bath be out in the open, away from hiding places for predators (i.e. house cats), yet with perches not too far away so the birds have some place to sit while they preen.

Roger Tory Peterson, in his video about creating backyard bird habitat, expounded on how attracted birds are to moving water. Although elaborate spigots are available, one easy method is to hang a plastic jug full of water over the bird bath, with a small hole pricked in the bottom to provide a constant drip.

I wonder, if I painted the jug black, would it drip most winter days?

Meanwhile, we had such warm weather clear through the first week of November, that I had to water my still-blooming snapdragons and rudbeckia.

I let the hose run in the garden, and next thing I knew, the siskins, finches and juncos had abandoned the bird feeders for a raucous water party.

I was extremely lucky last week and had a Townsend's solitaire land in the top of one of our big trees. This time of year they make a one note "bink" call over and over, instead of their spring melody.

Unfortunately, our mountain ash is too young to provide a berry crop this year for a fruit eater like the solitaire.

Or was it looking for one of my wild garden water parties it heard about?

36 Close encounters of the bird kind

It was cold enough to freeze water in the birds' water dish (my friend Marta recommends I get one of those heated dog water dishes), but not so cold a morning I thought I needed shoes just to grab the dish to bring it in when I let the dog out.

However, Lincoln made a beeline for a spot on the patio and I forgot all about the water dish.

Huddled on the concrete was a stunned American goldfinch, a male in winter plumage, just the lightest wash of yellow on his feathers.

Birds thumping into our kitchen window rarely happens anymore.

Between the pair of feline faces nearly always present in the window when the birds are active, and the dust on the glass, few birds think our window reflects a continuation of our backyard.

My first impulse was to rescue the goldfinch from the onslaught of the breath of a 100-pound dog, so I scooped him up and cupped him in my hands, leaving his face free.

His toes were just a tickle on my skin, his black eye, alert and unblinking.

"Oh, I am so sorry about the window," I thought. The bird was so light it was as if I held my imagination.

But my bare feet were standing on cold reality.

Bird feet are engineered differently. A goldfinch weighing less than half an ounce feels less cold. First, bird feet are mostly bone, sinew and scale, with few nerves.

Also, as Bill Thompson, author of "Bird Watching for Dummies" explains it, the arteries carrying warm blood from the heart to the toes are interwoven in the legs and feet with the veins, so the arteries warm the cold returning blood. And because bird feet don't have sweat glands, they don't stick to metal perches when it's cold.

After a few minutes, even after

moving to the doormat, I realized it might take longer for the bird to recover than to frostbite my feet.

By this time, the rising sun was eye level and shining on the bird feeder.

Our sunflower seed tube feeder has a saucer attached to the bottom and a wire cage around it that keeps squirrels out and lets small birds in. So I carefully placed the goldfinch on the feeder, safe from stray cats, close to food, facing the sun.

Twenty or thirty minutes later he was gone, though he may have been back later as one of the flock emptying the thistle feeder.

Of the disciplines available to me in the College of Natural Resources at the University of Wisconsin at Stevens Point where I was getting my degree 25 years ago, studying wildlife was far more popular than measuring trees, digging soil pits or analyzing water samples.

It seems to me most people have an urge to touch an animal (especially furry ones) or interact with it. For some people pets or livestock are good enough. For others, only wild animals will do.

For some of us, observation is fine, but there are always crazy tourists trying to pet the buffalo.

Some of the legitimate ways to handle live wildlife are catching and releasing fish, helping band birds, getting certified for rehabilitation work or becoming a wildlife field biologist.

But sometimes wildlife comes to you. I heard of two incidences this fall where birds chose to interact with people.

The beginning of October I got a call from a friend who'd been sitting on her deck with out-of-town visitors when a blue jay convinced them to feed it by hand.

A few weeks later another friend told me about having a blue jay light on her shoulder as she was carrying seed out to fill the feeder.

Our consensus was that these must have been young birds who didn't know better than to trust humans, but being from a relatively smart species, they'd learned it was possible to manipulate food sources.

I once read how to train chickadees to eat from your hand. It involves sitting as still as a bird feeder until they get used to you.

But I don't get chickadees in my yard very often, and I don't think the most prevalent birds, house finches, are as smart.

We have some sort of relationship anyway. They know when the backdoor opens, they don't need to fly far. Within a few minutes the disturbance is over, more seed's been spread and it's time to get back to eating.

How much more trust could a bird-watcher ask for?

2002

37 Bird count identifies second state record for hermit thrush

Thursday, January 10, 2002, Outdoors, C1

CHEYENNE – A hermit thrush, aptly named for its shy and retiring ways, was the star of the Cheyenne Christmas Bird Count held Dec. 29.

Birder Bob Luce, new to the Cheyenne count, pointed it out, and with help from experienced Cheyenne birders, was able to identify the robin-like bird with the spotted breast.

Jane Dorn, count compiler, said there has been only one other winter record of the thrush in Wyoming, which is otherwise a somewhat common bird in summer in the state's coniferous forests.

Normally the hermit thrush winters no farther north than central Arizona and New Mexico.

Total number of birds counted, 4,138, and total number of species counted, 36, were down from last year's 5,686 birds and 43 species despite 24 observers, which was nearly double the number for previous counts.

The weather was colder than last year, with a high of 29 degrees, and a low of 11 degrees.

There was no precipitation and only a trace of snow on the ground.

The wind was out of the northeast and fairly calm, with gusts reaching only 18 mph.

Though the 1,536 Canada geese counted were not as many as last year, only one other CBC has recorded over 1,000 geese. In the 1980s, geese were sometimes not observed on the CBC at all.

Crows also seem to be following the same pattern. While 97 were seen this year compared to 109 last year, crows used to be scarce. Only by the 1994 CBC did numbers counted exceed 10.

The pine siskin was reported only during the week of the count (the three days either before or after the count) and not on the count day. However, their winter populations are irruptive, meaning they go where the food is. So apparently some other location had a better seed crop.

Neither white-winged nor red crossbills, other irruptive species, were seen on the count this year.

Rough-legged hawks, as expected, continued to be the most numerous raptors in winter.

To compare this year's results with previous years or other locations, go to www.audubon.org/bird/cbc.

Cheyenne Christmas Bird Count, Dec. 29, 2001

36 species, plus one other species seen week of the count. 4138 birds counted. 24 observers.

Canada Goose 1536	Red-breasted Nuthatch 6
Mallard 574	Brown Creeper 10
Green-winged Teal 3	Golden-crowned Kinglet 14
Common Goldeneye 12	Townsend's Solitaire 29
Northern Harrier 2	American Robin 24
Red-tailed Hawk 2	Hermit Thrush 1
Rough-legged Hawk 18	European Starling 792
Golden Eagle 2	American Tree Sparrow 14
American Kestrel 1	Song Sparrow 5
Common Snipe 1	White-crowned Sparrow 1
Rock Dove (pigeon) 376	Dark-eyed Junco (total: 78)
Great Horned Owl 1	Gray-headed 3
Belted Kingfisher 5	Oregon 14
Downy Woodpecker 12	Pink-sided 20
Northern Flicker 11	Slate-colored 8
Blue Jay 4	unspecified 33
Black-billed Magpie 41	Red-winged Blackbird 42
American Crow 97	House Finch 41
Horned Lark 21	Pine Siskin (week of the count only)
Black-capped Chickadee 3	American Goldfinch 19
Mountain Chickadee 10	House Sparrow 330

38 Some birds aren't crowing about neighbor

Thursday, January 24, 2002, Outdoors, page C2

As I turned off the hairdryer a little after 7 a.m. one morning recently, I heard the end of a ring. Hoping it wasn't the last, I grabbed the phone. It was my neighbor across the alley, Sue.

"That owl is in the tree again, just west of you and the crows are picking on it."

Naturally, I immediately abandoned my comb, grabbed binoculars and headed for the alley.

Sue was there and coached me until I was able to see the great horned owl myself, ensconced in spruce branches.

One cawing crow flew at the owl, waggling its claws in its face, but the owl didn't budge.

The crow returned to a safe perch on the powerline, flaring its fan-shaped tail. Ravens have wedge-shaped tails and haven't, apparently, moved into our neighborhood yet.

Sue's neighbor across the street thinks this might be the owl they had hanging around for a couple years. Sue thought maybe it liked our alley because there's a yard light that can illuminate scurrying rodents, though a nocturnal hunter like the owl is well adapted for working in the dark.

Great horned owls prey on wildlife as large as Sue's small dog, but she was more concerned about the owl's welfare and us disturbing it. So after another good look at the avian Buddha, I returned to my yard and morning chores.

Meanwhile, the lone crow had succeeded in attracting at least five others to its cause (get the pun?).

Two were in my tree, heckling from the back row. Two swayed on the cable TV line, trying to catch their balance and dignity without missing their timing for hurling invectives.

I couldn't see the spruce anymore, but it sounded like two more crows were in there with the owl. They carried on for at least another half hour.

A few weeks before, before Christmas, Sue had left an owl message for me about 7:15 a.m., which I didn't pick up until much later, but I could remember hearing a mob of crows right about then.

The best part of this owl experience has been to find someone happily excited about having a natural predator in the neighborhood, though the crows are not.

Often enough I get calls from people concerned that hawks are eating the birds at their feeder. Isn't that what sharp-shinned hawks are supposed to do? Isn't a hawk a bird too?

I just figure, when I put out seed, I'm feeding herbivores directly and indirectly feeding carnivores, whether they come to my yard or not.

Great horned owls prefer bigger prey than finches and sparrows. Cornell Lab of Ornithology's on-line field guide mentions they especially like hares and rabbits.

I know we have plenty of cottontails hopping around the neighborhood at 5 a.m. The dog is always trying to drag me along after one whenever we get to do the paper route.

Squirrels are on the list too. We have plenty of those. Five of them come by every morning to sample our sunflower seed.

"....and the occasional domestic cat," reports the CLO. With my luck, it would be my cat on her annual accidental outdoor foray whose bones and hair get turned into owl pellets, instead of the loose cats that defile neighborhood gardens and terrorize wildlife.

Mammals make up three-quarters of the average great horned owl's diet, though 50 species of birds have been recorded as prey, from songbirds to grouse, herons, ducks, geese, hawks, and even other owls.

I wonder if the owl I saw was house-hunting as well. Mid-winter is when owls announce their territories and some may begin nesting in February. They have to start early because incubation takes a month and getting the young airborne takes another two and a half to three months.

However, great horned owls are lazy. They prefer to use old hawk nests in big trees, and I haven't noticed any around here. Otherwise, they are comfortable in a greater variety of habitats than any other owl.

Wouldn't it be fun to have owls for neighbors? It would mean our 50-year-old suburbanized neighborhood has an original piece of the natural mosaic, even though the prairie and its creek-side cottonwood fringe have been swapped for lawns and evergreens.

39 Immigrant or visitor, red-bellied woodpecker finds food here

Birds are illiterate, at least in the usual sense. However, the most successful, longest-lived birds are very good at reading signs in their environment to avoid danger and locate food, shelter and the opposite sex.

Birds do not read field guides.

A red-bellied woodpecker was seen in January in Cheyenne several times by three different people.

I was a little skeptical when I got the first call. I've never seen a red-bellied woodpecker, which, despite its name, is recognized by its black and white striped back and the red on the top of its head (male only) and back of its neck.

Jane and Bob Dorn, authors of "Wyoming Birds," list only two records of the species in the state. One was January 1993 in the latilong that contains Douglas and the other May 1992 in the Cheyenne latilong.

For the purposes of bird records, the state is divided into 28 latilongs, each measuring one degree of latitude by one degree of longitude.

Red-bellieds are birds of the southeastern United States that have gradually increased their range to the north, and now, apparently, to the west.

In the 1961 edition of his western bird guide, Roger Tory Peterson mentions red-bellieds are casual to Colorado, meaning a few records, but they don't merit an illustration. The Stokes' 1996 western edition doesn't mention them at all.

"The Sibley Guide to Birds," 2000 edition, shows the westernmost boundary of the red-bellied's range approximately at the 100th Meridian, that magical line of longitude marking the difference between eastern and western species of biota in North America.

The 100th Meridian slices vertically through the middle of Nebraska, a mere 250 miles east of Cheyenne. What's that distance to an eastern bird with a decent set of wings?

This winter's visitor could be here by some accident of weather – and that would have to be some accident to get the wind to blow out of the east long enough.

It's more likely the intervening Great Plains, thanks to all the mature windbreaks, can now host a species dependent on large trees full of bugs and seeds and fruit.

How many other red-bellieds have visited Cheyenne birdfeeders without being recognized as unusual? How many have met disaster shortly after arriving, such as plate glass windows, storms, loose cats and natural predators, and are never seen by bird watchers?

Chances are we'll have more reports of red-bellied woodpeckers, if only because the number of bird watchers continues to increase.

In this month's issue, National Geographic used the estimate of 63 million bird watchers in this country alone to justify launching its own birding magazine.

What will happen to our red-bellied visitor? We must assume, until proven otherwise, that there's only one, since only one female has been seen each time.

It could survive the winter quite well using the three well-stocked backyard feeding stations it has already found.

It's not a seasonal migratory

species, and it may not be inclined to move in the spring, so it could become a resident.

And, compared to its stronghold in the southeastern U.S., it doesn't have as many species of woodpecker competitors out here.

However, a few observations of red-bellied woodpeckers in Wyoming won't change the "accidental" status of the species until there are breeding records.

If the conditions that allowed one member of the species to find its way here stay constant, chances are more will follow and then breeding could happen.

Birds are opportunists. Short of being dropped here by the wind, a bird wouldn't travel to Cheyenne if it hadn't read signs along the way for favorable conditions for survival.

Whether it becomes a resident depends on finding enough of the habitat it is used to, or adapting to what is available.

It's about the same for the rest of us coming to Wyoming from elsewhere. Except, we people have the ability to make things more like our old homes, so we tend to plant trees, diminishing the grasslands and their species.

40 Finding out where the birds are

Where can teachers take children bird watching, and what birds could they expect to see? I asked that question a couple months ago while preparing a section on field trips for the Wyoming Bird Flashcards CD project.

Next time I write a grant, remind me to figure in field research. It would have been fun traveling the state looking up good bird watching locations.

But even had I visited extensively, there's nothing like a report from someone on site, someone who has intimate knowledge from observations made over time.

I was wondering how I could find people willing to help when I realized the list of Wyoming Christmas Bird Count coordinators was the key. Since then, over a dozen coordinators have generously shared information.

So, where do you take children, or any novice bird watcher? Responses included the Laramie River Greenbelt in Laramie, Burlington Lake in Gillette, Dry Lake outside Lander, Clear Creek in Buffalo, several parks in Casper

along Garden Creek and the North Platte River, Gray Reef Reservoir south of Casper, Clarks Fork River up by Cody, Hume Draw in Sheridan and the elk feeding grounds along the Snake River up by Jackson.

Do you see a pattern – river, lake, draw, creek, reservoir? With the exception of recommendations to visit the cemeteries in Sheridan and Casper and a few notes to look for horned larks on the uplands, water is where the birds are, in Wyoming, or anywhere else.

Some birds, such as waterfowl, depend on aquatic animals and vegetation for food. Others like the protection from land predators while they float in a lake. Some like to hide or nest in bushes and trees which grow thanks to their proximity to water.

Some birds eat the other animals attracted to aquatic environments, and of course, nearly all birds need water for drinking and bathing.

Wet spots are not equally rich in bird species. Should a field trip leader or teacher take children to the local park, or to some really spectacular hotspot a couple hours away? Luckily for us, some of the best birding around Cheyenne is Sloans Lake and the area around it in Lions Park.

If you are a teacher trying to spark an interest in birds in your students, do you give them a long term, close-up look at birds at the feeder outside the classroom window, or do you take them for a day to where multi-colored birds are flitting from branch to branch and blanketing the surface of the lake?

If you are a birder intent on adding species to your life list and choose to dash from place to place, you'll never know what a hotspot your own backyard might be. A friend of mine is discovering bird by bird how interesting her own backyard is.

She works at her computer at a window overlooking a well-developed feeding station with all the usual bird foods, plus dog chow. It seems the most unusual visitor this winter, the red-bellied woodpecker, is attracted to the dog's food (see Feb. 7's Bird Banter for more about the red-bellied woodpecker).

Already she's developing some sense of the time of day the birds prefer to visit and which bird doesn't seem to be just another house finch. Her backyard list has over 30 species so far.

It is this kind of intimate knowledge of a place I was after when I contacted the CBC coordinators. I, a mere reader of lists, might predict certain species in certain habitats, but every spot on earth is unique.

Only the local observer knows which lake has trumpeter swans and what time of year, unless of course the local observer is Terry McEneaney and he has written the book, "Birds of Yellowstone."

Meanwhile, it's my hope Wyoming's teachers and children will go out and watch birds, and through their observations, write books for their own local hotspots.

41 Birders use cyberspace to advantage

Thursday, March 7, 2002, Outdoors, page C2

Ever have the feeling you live in a parallel universe? Once in a while you find a metaphorical door open and discover, for instance, that people you talk to regularly are having a whole other conversation among themselves via e-mail.

Some months ago, a birding friend held a door open for me, but I put off stepping through until a couple weeks ago when I finally signed up for the Wyoming Bird Discussion Group and Bird Alert listserv known as Wyobirds.

Some of you savvy internet users know all about listservs, and now I'm convinced they are the greatest thing since spotting scopes.

Serious birders have always had a communications system. When Gloria Lawrence saw a pale-phase gyrfalcon in her backyard on the banks of the North Platte River west of Casper Feb. 26, she knew exactly which birding friends would want a phone call. She also posted her sighting for all the Wyobirders.

Now that I've subscribed to the Wyobirds listserv, reports from a network of nearly 50 members around the state (plus a few northern Coloradoans who occasionally bird Wyoming) come right to my computer as e-mail messages.

Some of you will cringe at the idea of

even more e-mail. One option is not to subscribe, but to just go to the website and peruse the archives at your leisure. However, if you want to post any replies or reports for the edification of the group, you need to subscribe, which costs nothing except the time it takes to send an initial e-mail.

Wyobirds was started last May by Will Cornell of Rock Springs. A recent transplant from Kansas, Cornell modeled his listserv after one for that state, managed by his friend and birding mentor, Chuck Otte.

Starting with only five members, the first few postings were Will's reports from birding trips. Then other birders from Rock Springs, and then Green River and Casper, began sharing their observations and answering each other's questions about where to find birds.

The summer months were slow, except for an announcement in July from a member in Laramie that the fall shorebird migration was underway. By September the first sighting of a rough-legged hawk was reported. That's the Arctic-nesting hawk that thinks Wyoming is a balmy place to spend the winter.

Migration is a good time for finding birds rare for Wyoming. Last fall there was a red knot near Casper, a surf scoter near Lake Hattie and a little gull (that's its official name) at the sewage ponds in Green River.

Spring migration is already astir, with reports of mountain bluebirds north of Cheyenne Feb. 19 and eastern bluebirds Feb. 21 at Bessemer Bend.

For serious birders able to chase after rarities, the listserv makes an excellent, low-cost alert system. Meanwhile, the rest of us enjoy knowing there's more out there than the house sparrows in our backyards.

But some discussions and reports are of interest to backyard birders too, such as where blue jays are nesting, or that a Townsend's solitaire was heard singing somewhat prematurely Feb. 21 in Green River, or that someone has rosy finches at their feeders.

I saw one example of political lobbying in the archives, but it was quite forgivable. It was against a proposed law allowing falconers to remove wild peregrine falcon chicks from nests and raise them for their sport.

Wyobirds is a good place to pose a bird question. What is the name for a female swan? The young are cygnets, the male is a cob and the female is called a pen.

If you are a grad student studying the mountain plover, this is the group to ask if they've sighted any. Or if you are travelling across Wyoming on Christmas break, Wyobirders will gladly help you find rosy finches.

Late fall there was a flurry of messages about dates and contacts for various Christmas Bird Counts, and already there's increasing discussion of spring birding trips. But unlike members of listservs for indoor hobbies, there's a chance when Wyobirders go outside we'll see each other.

42 Birders flock to observe crane migration

Common wisdom has it birds fly north in the spring and people on spring break either head south to warm up or head west to ski. More than a dozen Cheyenne bird watchers recently headed east instead to see a bit of the sandhill crane migration.

Lots of birds migrate, but few are as dramatic about it as the sandhill cranes. They come from their various wintering grounds in New Mexico and Texas to a 100-mile stretch of the Platte River where they all lay over, eat waste grain and fatten up for the rest of their trip and the breeding season. Some continue north as far as Alaska and Siberia.

In March and early April, it isn't hard to find sandhills between North Platte and Grand Island, Neb., even at 75 miles per hour. Cranes, their nearly four-foot lengths bent double to feed, show as gray lumps moving through old cornstalks.

An individual crane is a graceful, elegant bird to study, small flocks are interesting, but the spectacular part comes at twilight. Thousands of cranes gather in the shallow reaches of the river to spend the night.

They like best where the river has been scoured clean of vegetation so no predators can hide. Before all the dams, the river scoured itself with frequent floods. Now crane conservationists take heavy equipment to the brush.

Cheyenne High Plains Audubon Society president Art Anderson organized our 300-mile expedition east. Friends of his have blinds just downriver from the Rowe Sanctuary run by Audubon Nebraska near Gibbon, where Mark and I visited eight or nine years before.

In that time, Kearney, Nebraska, has become the crane capital: more motels, crane information at the rest area and messages on business marquees welcoming crane watchers. I didn't stop to shop, but undoubtedly there's crane stuff for sale.

At the sanctuary, a whole building is now dedicated to crane souvenirs and several people were available to answer questions. I overheard visitors discussing the likely location of a lone whooping crane.

There was a happy delay when we arrived at the gate to our destination. Right alongside the long dirt driveway was a flock of sandhills—and the whooper.

There are few whooping cranes worldwide, a few hundred, but at least they are easy to pick out because they stand taller than the sandhills and they gleam bright white. We set up spotting scopes and studied the whooper's bright yellow eye and red and black facial markings. The evening breeze was ruffling its plumy feathers.

By show time, we were ensconced in a really swank duck blind. Line after line of sandhills came in from upriver. Some from nearby fields flew right over our heads, close enough we saw their bills open as they made their creaky calls to each other. In near dark their slow wingbeats and the way their long legs extend well past their bodies make them easy to sort out from ducks and geese, small flocks of which were flapping furiously in staccato counterpoint.

A lot of the cranes headed for the big flock around the bend from us. The noise of those thousands of voices reminded me of the roar of fans at Oakie Blanchard Stadium I can hear from my house on a fall evening.

When we left, tardy geese were still coming in, crossing in front of the nearly full moon as if to recreate the artwork hanging in a hunting lodge.

The other show is when the cranes lift off around sunrise. However, the next morning a stolid sky, promising precipitation, squelched the exact moment of dawn. As the day brightened by imperceptible degrees, I became aware that the gray-colored sandbar was really a mass of cranes.

Though we'd pried ourselves out of our sleeping bags before 6 a.m., the cranes in front of the blind were reluctant risers. A lot of other cranes passed by, enticing a few strings to lift off and peel away, but most appeared to still have their heads under their wings.

Finally we gave up and went indoors where a picture window gave us a view of a really nice bird feeding station. There were gobs of goldfinches, several cardinals, nuthatches, chickadees, downy woodpeckers, juncos and, drumroll please: a pair of red-bellied woodpeckers. So now I don't have to wait until I see the one that's been reported in Cheyenne in order to add this species to my life list.

The red-bellieds and the whooper were the perfect souvenirs of my chance to escape routine for a couple days outside in a different landscape – my chance to take a spring break.

43 Backyards going to the birds

Habitat can also be pleasant for people

When Sue and Chuck Seniawski moved to the Monterey Heights neighborhood about 13 years ago, their backyard was not fit for man or beast.

"The backyard was absolutely bare when I got started – just grass, with a couple trees in front of the house," Chuck said.

The Seniawskis worked out a landscape plan through Tom's Garden Spot, a nursery no longer in business, and now those trees and shrubs provide a sanctuary for them and a variety of birds. In one hour on an April afternoon, about 10 species were observed.

Any grade-school child can point out the three major needs of wildlife the Seniawskis have provided: food, water and shelter. As it turns out, what's good for wildlife is good for people.

Reg Rothwell, author of Wyoming Game and Fish Department's free publication, "Wildscape," said good landscaping will increase property value, "but it will also provide auditory and visual screening, protection from wind and excess solar energy and give privacy for the home. Wildlife habitat comes with it."

Shelter

Though the term "birdhouse" implies birds may seek shelter from weather in them, only a few species use natural or man-made cavities, and then usually only for nesting. Most look for shelter in vegetation.

Publications about creating backyard bird or wildlife habitat start with planning for and planting trees. However, most are written with the eastern U.S. in mind and recommend kinds of trees that cannot live long in Cheyenne's environment or need a lot of water to survive.

Rothwell champions native species

for their suitability. "If I can't get natives, I want something like natives," he said.

At the Cheyenne Botanic Gardens, director Shane Smith estimates 80 percent of the plant species recommended for Cheyenne on their website are identified and growing in Lions Park, so people can visit and find out what they look like.

The website lists both local and area nurseries, but Smith recommends checking local nurseries first.

"Take the compass into account," said Smith, giving his general planting rule of thumb. Plant coniferous trees on the north and west side of the house to insulate it from winter wind.

Plant deciduous trees on the south side so that their leaves shade the house in summer, but when their leaves drop in the fall, solar rays will warm the house.

Rothwell, Smith and University of Wyoming Laramie County Cooperative Extension horticultural agent Catherine Wissner warn against planting aspen because it is short-lived, and a longer-lived tree would be a better investment in time and money. Also, one aspen will send out suckers all over the yard, attempting to turn it into a forest.

Wissner said landscaping advice is also available through her office, especially through the master gardener program. Two of the current master gardeners specialize in trees and may be available to come out and look at potential planting sites.

Shrubs are perhaps more valuable than trees for providing shelter for some birds, said Smith. However, one book on gardening for birds pointed out that rigorous pruning may cause growth too dense for birds to navigate easily.

Food

Trees and shrubs can be selected to do double duty as both shelter and food sources if they produce flowers, berries, cones, seeds or other kinds of fruit.

Fruits of chokecherry and Nanking cherry make good syrup and jelly, but the birds will want their share. If your goal is backyard wildlife habitat though, there will be plenty for everyone.

Flowers, whether in the garden or on trees and shrubs, will attract birds. It's the flower nectar attracting hummingbirds and orioles, flower petals for evening grosbeaks, and the insects attracted to the flowers for insect-eating birds.

Bird feeders are not an essential element of a backyard habitat, but they do add to enjoyment. A sunflower seed or niger thistle feeder like the Seniawskis have, covered with cheery-voiced goldfinches, is hard to resist.

Water

Birds visiting the Seniawskis' yard drink and bathe all winter in the heated bird bath located up on the deck. Down below is a pedestal-style bird bath. Birds will appreciate a simple pan of water on the ground as much as an elaborate waterfall or pond, especially if you clean it regularly to avoid the spread of disease.

Nest boxes

Only certain bird species are interested in nesting in a structure or cavity. Some of the swallows prefer to build their own with mud.

Backyard birds in our area that might be interested in your handiwork include downy woodpecker, northern flicker, black-capped and mountain chickadees, red-breasted nuthatch, house wren and house finch. The mountain bluebird, wood duck, common merganser and American kestrel will also use nest boxes but have habitat requirements beyond Cheyenne's average backyard.

The size of the entrance hole determines if the intended species will be able to use it without aggressive species not native to our area, starlings and house sparrows, taking it over. Nest box specifications are available from the U.S. Fish and Wildlife Service's free pamphlet, "For the Birds," and from The Birdhouse Network.

Hazards

Just as visitors to your home should be protected from injury, so should your avian visitors.

Keep your own cat indoors, or build a "cat haven" as Pat and Paul Becker have done. Make sure shrubbery that might hide a loose cat is far enough away from water and feeders so that birds, especially ground feeders like juncos, have a chance to see the cat coming and to escape. A dog installed in the yard makes a great cat repellant.

Pesticides poison insects and seed-producing plants, the very things that attract birds to your yard. If a bird eats enough poisoned insects, it will die.

High amounts of lawn care chemicals were found in birds succumbing to West Nile virus on the East Coast.

The National Audubon Society website offers alternatives, though you can consider the birds themselves as part of your pest management strategy.

Housekeeping

Nature is not tidy.

She doesn't rake up dead leaves and bag them. Instead, decomposing leaves offer sustenance for insects, slugs and worms – and the birds that eat them, before completely breaking down and nourishing the soil. Chuck Seniawski allows leaves to remain under shrubs because leaf litter and its denizens attracts green-tailed and spotted towhees.

The Seniawskis' Backyard Plant List

Remember, trees in neighbors' yards contribute to bird habitat.

Broadleaf trees
Aspen
Flowering Almond
Flowering Crabapple
Locust
Narrowleaf Cottonwood, N
Seedless Mountain Ash

Broadleaf shrubs
Alpine Currant, N
Canada Red Cherry
Cotoneaster
Saskatoon Serviceberry

Spirea (white, pink, blue)
Sumac

Evergreens
Austrian Pine, D
Bristlecone Pine, D, N
Colorado Blue Spruce, D, N
Ponderosa Pine, D, N
Juniper shrubs, D, N

Designation from Cheyenne Botanic Gardens list:
N – native
D – drought resistant after establishment

Tree Planting Disclaimer

Not all birds appreciate trees. Birds, such as the western meadowlark, grasshopper sparrow, killdeer and bobolink nest on the ground in wide-open spaces.

If wide open describes your property, consider allowing it to continue as grassland bird habitat rather than transforming it into forest.

Avoid mowing during nesting season, now through July. Keep dogs and cats confined or on a leash so they won't harm eggs and young.

Be aware that a pole or tree may provide avian predators such as crows with a watch tower and launching pad to use in their quest for prey.

Birds Observed in the Seniawskis' Backyard, 1990-2001

Bluebird, Mountain
Chickadee, Mountain
Crossbill, Red
Crow, American
Dove, Mourning
Falcon, Prairie
Finch, House
Flicker, Northern (Red-shafted)
Flycatcher, Hammond's
Flycatcher, Western
Goldfinch, American
Goldfinch, Lesser
Grackle, Bronzed
Grosbeak, Black-headed
Grosbeak, Rose-breasted
Hawk, Sharp-shinned
Jay, Blue
Jay, Steller's
Junco, Gray-headed
Junco, Oregon
Junco, Pink-sided
Junco, Slate-colored
Junco, White-winged
Kinglet, Ruby-crowned
Longspur, Lapland
Merlin
Nuthatch, Red-breasted
Owl, Great Horned

Peewee, Western Wood
Redpoll, Common
Robin
Siskin, Pine
Solitaire, Townsend's
Sparrow, Chipping
Sparrow, Harris'
Sparrow, House
Sparrow, Lincoln's
Sparrow, Song
Sparrow, Tree
Sparrow, White-crowned
Sparrow, White-throated
Starling, European
Tanager, Western
Thrush, Swainson's
Towhee, Green-tailed
Towhee, Spotted
Vireo, Red-eyed
Warbler, Nashville
Warbler, Orange-crowned
Warbler, Townsend's
Warbler, Wilson's
Warbler, Yellow
Waxwing, Cedar
Woodpecker, Downy
Wren, Rock

44

Thursday, May 2, 2002, Outdoors, page C2

Bluebird housing makes a difference

I didn't grow up with bluebirds. First, because I was a suburban kid. Second, I didn't look much at birds; and mostly, it was a period of time during which bluebird populations in the Midwest had decreased due to pesticides and loss of cavity nesting places like hollow trees and wooden fence posts.

Notes in my old field guide indicate my first eastern bluebird was July 1975, when I rode my bike out into the countryside between split shifts for the food

service at the University of Wisconsin-Stevens Point.

Then, in 1978, I reported for the campus paper on a talk by Vincent Bauldry of Green Bay, Wisconsin, who had built a better bluebird nest box. He had 21 years of experience showing that a hole in the roof (screened to keep out predators) had greatly improved nesting success. By the end of the year, Bauldry's design got national coverage when I sold the story to Organic

Gardening magazine.

Bauldry claimed his design imitated rotting wooden fence posts where eastern bluebirds liked to nest. Added moisture from rain helped the eggs stay hydrated and excluded competing species, such as starlings.

When I mention this "skylight" concept to bluebird box experts out here, they think I'm crazy, maybe because few cedar fence posts on western rangeland rot in the dry climate.

There are, however, other modifications Bauldry used that can be seen in modern bluebird nest box plans today.

A traditional bird house, the kind people now paint decoratively and display in their living rooms, is often cube-shaped with a peaked roof. Bauldry made his with a flat roof and made it more than twice as deep so eggs or nestlings were beyond reach of a marauding racoon's arm.

The increased depth, he said, would also keep the young in the nest longer, so they would be stronger when they fledged. He added horizontal saw cuts on the inside of the front wall to help the babies climb the greater distance to the entrance hole.

Bauldry eliminated any kind of twig-like perch sticking out by the entrance, making it more difficult for nuisance birds to find a vantage point from which to harass the bluebirds.

His nest box design is clearly utilitarian, with one side swinging open so old nesting material can be cleaned out between broods, a feature of most modern nest boxes for any species.

I don't know if it's Bauldry's innovation, but his box and several modern boxes usually have the back wall extend either below the floor and/or above the roof so there's something to nail to the fence post or other support. Bluebirds evidently don't care for the rock-a-bye-baby effect of hanging bird houses in trees.

When Alison Lyon [Holloran] of Audubon Wyoming gave a presentation on mountain bluebirds at the Wyoming State Museum in conjunction with the opening of the Wyoming Conservation Stamp Art Competition, Show and Sale last month, someone in the audience wanted to know how to attract mountain bluebirds to Cheyenne.

Unless the city expands its limits halfway to Laramie and dedicates the land to open range, and also raises the elevation from the present 6,100 feet to something over 7,000, the mountain bluebird's preference, it's unlikely they will ever do more than pass through during migration.

The most dependable place to see mountain bluebirds close to town is Curt Gowdy State Park, where several Eagle Scout candidates have installed nest boxes and a little further up Happy Jack Road, at North Crow Reservoir.

Reports of mountain bluebirds begin in the last half of February, making them a harbinger of spring for me. I once made a quilt and re-colored the Flying Swallows pattern to represent them and commemorate this annual event.

It turns out my favorite sign of spring, the spot of sky blue in a gloomy landscape, can be found all winter as close as southern Colorado, though many more head south into Mexico.

By summer, mountain bluebirds can be found from Arizona and New Mexico north to eastern Alaska.

Catching a glimpse of a mountain bluebird is always a treat. I double check to make sure what I'm looking at isn't a western or eastern bluebird. Much less abundant in Wyoming than the mountain, their ranges extend into western and eastern Wyoming, respectively, overlapping the mountain's range.

With red on their breasts, I always

think of these two as the blue-coated versions of the closely related robin, since they are the same general shape, though smaller.

Mountain bluebird males are blue all over, and the females are less bright, more gray.

Besides dressing up the landscape, bluebirds eat insects. That is one reason why so many smart people encourage bluebird nesting around their property by installing a series of nest boxes along a "bluebird trail." Providing nest boxes makes a difference to the birds too, especially for the eastern bluebird, whose population has made progress in recovering.

If you like bluebirds or are serious about building a bluebird nest box or trail, the ultimate resource for information and specifications, such as using a 1 and 9/16 inch entrance hole, is the North American Bluebird Society website, www.nabluebirdsociety.org.

45 Learn to appreciate birds from a distance

Thursday, May 16, 2002, Outdoors, page C2

Most birdwatchers never have a close encounter with their quarry.

Identification of birds in the field is based on patterns: color, shape, behavior, location, and voice, because even with binoculars, an impression is all we get.

The skillful birder knows just what to key in on for each kind of bird. To distinguish two of the large, soaring birds around Cheyenne this summer, key in on the black and white pattern on the underside of the wings.

Swainson's hawks have the forward half or leading edge of the wing and the body light and the trailing edge of the wing dark. Turkey vultures, which seem to be sticking around instead of migrating through Cheyenne, are just the opposite. In addition, their wings tilt upward in a shallow "v."

The sparrows I like best are the ones with distinct markings. Half a dozen white-crowned sparrows, their heads marked with alternating black and white stripes, were in our backyard the last week of April and first week of May, singing non-stop all day until they continued their migration to spend summer in the mountains.

Some birds are so distinct, a silhouette is enough. Such is the case for the white-faced ibis, several of which have been reported the last couple weeks at reservoirs around southeastern Wyoming. I glimpsed one wading in Crystal Reservoir May 5.

Certainly the white on this ibis species's face is hardly enough to justify its name. You'd think it would be named for that incredible bill. Look up a picture of this exotic-looking shorebird to understand how amazed I am when I see one.

Short of putting bird food on the windowsill or getting trained or licensed to handle live wild birds for research or rehabilitation, birders don't usually get very close to birds, especially to owls.

If you are very lucky, you may notice one imitating a lump of tree trunk as it naps during the day. Otherwise, all you have to go on are signs and sounds: a hoot in the dark, a rabbit leg on the lawn, wing marks in the snow or pellets under the tree.

Andrea Cerovski, Wyoming Game and Fish Department nongame bird biologist, is on tour this year with Jupiter, a great horned owl.

During their appearance at the April Cheyenne High Plains Audubon meeting, Jupiter viewed the room from his position on Andrea's glove.

His eyes were huge and black, and he stared back at the audience. He is new to the lecture circuit and was finding everything to be of interest, especially the Cub Scout den that came in. Perhaps the high voices of young children reminded him of squeaking prey.

Jupiter's feet, with their huge talons, restlessly renewed their grip on the glove. His beak, though short, has to be sharp enough to shred flesh. His soft-edged feathers would, were he to hunt, break the sound of his flight so prey couldn't hear his approach until too late.

Hissy, the resident great horned owl at the Wyoming Children's Museum in Laramie, has had a lot more public exposure and seemed rather bored when introduced at the Audubon Wyoming reception there a few days later.

Because their mottled coloring camouflages the contours of their closed wings, it takes a close look to see why these two birds are not in the wild. Each has a mangled, unusable wing, due to collisions with man-made obstacles.

I'm like many people who wish they could communicate with wild animals. I want them to respond to me, yet when I sat still enough that a mountain bluebird foraged three feet away, as happened recently and unexpectedly, I was as happy to be accepted as nothing but a nonthreatening part of the landscape.

But I'm glad the law bans people from making pets of wild birds. We've interfered enough already, especially by changing many of their habitats.

When identification is especially vexing, I wish I could hold the bird in my hand. But if you've ever taken ornithology and studied bird skins, or "birds on a stick," you know that a bird in hand, out of context, can be just as vexing.

Then there's the occasional dead bird. For any dead bird, anytime of year, bag it. Pull a plastic bread bag over your hand like a glove. Pick up the bird and pull the bag inside out over the bird and tie the bag shut. Then double-bag it and take a close look through the bag at the bird if you like, before disposing of it.

After June 1, the county environmental health department's system will be in place for examining dead birds, especially black birds, for West Nile virus.

Meanwhile, if you'd like to see live wild birds, some preparing to nest and some just passing through in migration, join Audubon members on the Big Count this Saturday. You'll never believe how many kinds of birds there are here unless you see them for yourself.

46 Brown bird mix-up worth unraveling

Thursday, May 30, 2002, Outdoors, page C2

Lazuli bunting, indigo bunting, rose-breasted grosbeak, green-tailed towhee, yellow-rumped warbler, yellow warbler: the birds of spring migration are a colorful bunch.

Less obvious are the "LBJs"

– "Little Brown Jobs," as they are sometimes called.

To appreciate the visiting LBJs, we must first distinguish them from the usual brown riff-raff, so let's review.

First and most prominent in the

cityscape is the house sparrow. They build messy nests in three-dimensional signs or any other cavity, pick miller moths out of car radiators in parking lots and are seen wherever there's urban detritus to peck.

This time of year, the male house sparrow is a rich chestnut brown pattern on the back and wings, with a black goatee and bib and gray crown (top of head). The female has no black markings. Both have pale gray breasts and bellies.

The second most common brown bird in Cheyenne is the house finch. They like big trees and bird feeders stocked with black oil sunflower seed.

Both male and female are about the same size as the house sparrow but appear more slender and have breasts streaked with grayish brown lines.

The male in prime breeding plumage right now has a bright red forehead, red breast and red rump. Lesser males and males at other times of the year have faded pink or even yellowish hues.

As members of the finch family, house finches have big, thick bills for cracking seeds.

House finches and house sparrows are here year round. Once you can reliably distinguish them, male and female, you'll discover there are other brown birds eating at your feeder or flitting through the parks.

The pine siskin is a streaky brown bird easy to mistake for a female house finch. When it flies, a little yellow shows in its wings and tail.

Siskins can show up in Cheyenne any time of year. They are smaller than a house finch by three quarters of an inch and have a smaller bill suited to eating the tiny niger thistle seeds they love.

Some people in town had siskins all winter, but our tube-style thistle feeder was untouched until the beginning of May. Now it's crowded with siskins and the closely related goldfinches, one for each of the eight perches and a dozen waiting for openings. Their cheerful songs get a bit strident as they retreat to the trees while I refill the feeder.

Occasionally I will see one kind of sparrow often enough that I begin to distinguish and remember its unique field markings. Such is the case with the clay-colored sparrows showing up in our backyard this month.

As small as a siskin, the clay-colored sparrow still has to head at least as far north as Montana to nest. It has a very pale gray breast that sort of glows from a distance. The rest of it is a non-descript brown pattern with darker streaks over the head, through the eye and in front of the eye. Luckily it has a unique song, four buzzes in each phrase, like an insect.

There's another petite, nondescript sparrow in my yard, the chipping sparrow.

Chippies have one notable field mark, a rusty brown crown. They will spend the summer here, especially in weedy places, so there is plenty of time to get to know them well.

Sometimes a birdwatcher has to be able to identify parts of a bird because it won't come out for a clear view.

This spring I think Mark and I identified a new (for us) brown bird. As it skulked in the bushes, there was a flash of brown, then an eye and a leg. The pale breast had markings.

The best identification we could make using our field guide was the veery. But there are three or four other thrushes that look similar. I'll have to learn more about them before my next encounter.

So far I've been discussing backyard brown birds. Don't forget the bigger migration picture and the bigger brown birds.

Shorebirds are on their way north to breed and stop briefly at our local reservoirs. Identifying the different species is a real art. For me, it's like trying to distinguish identical triplets.

One must find the slight differences in brown plumage, body shape, length and tilt of bill, length and color of legs. Heaven forbid their legs or bills are discolored by mud from probing the shoreline for edibles.

The problem is, the sandpipers, dowitchers, yellowlegs and the other shorebirds that nest in the far north are never here long enough in one season to become as familiar to me as their relations that nest here, such as the killdeer.

I guess that means at my present rate I'll never run out of obscure brown birds to learn to identify.

47

Records request ruffles feathers

One of the fringe benefits of writing this column is hearing from other people watching birds.

In the last month there have been reports of robins building a nest on a ladder and nesting on a porch light fixture plus one report of a robin attacking what it thought was its rival – its own reflection in a clean window.

The rest of the year the most common calls are requests for help identifying birds.

Luckily there aren't many calls from people with rare bird sightings. If someone were to insist, for instance, that they have a pink flamingo in their garden – and it's not plastic – I would refer them to Jane Dorn, whose training and expertise in birds extends far beyond our local backyards.

Jane compiles the reports for our local Christmas Bird Count, the Big Day spring count and local reports for American Birds, a quarterly journal.

If a species is unusual for Wyoming or for the time of year, Jane will ask the observer for more information because she is also a member of the Wyoming Bird Records Committee.

A photograph of the bird in question is extremely useful, or verification by one or more knowledgeable birders. It boils down to credibility and the honor system, unless Jane gets a chance to run out and see the bird herself.

An observer can send a report directly to the committee, in care of the Wyoming Game and Fish Department nongame bird biologist, but there are advantages to working with Jane for rare bird sightings in our area.

First, she is intimately knowledgeable about the birds here and second, she may be able to vouch for your credibility and birding ability when your report is being reviewed for inclusion in official state records.

Eventually the accepted reports are used to revise new editions of the "Atlas of Birds, Mammals, Reptiles and Amphibians in Wyoming," published by Game and Fish.

Some rare bird observations indicate nothing more than a migrant blown off course, while for other species, reports begin to accumulate, showing they are changing their migration patterns or expanding breeding ranges.

Imagine my surprise and dismay when a request for documentation after last month's Big Day count was met with hostility and suspicion.

The best birding on the Big Day count starts at sunrise, so it helps to have birders in our hottest bird spots simultaneously.

Each year, while Jane and her husband Robert, also an expert birder, are scoping the Grasslands Research Station first thing, birders from Casper and our local Audubon chapter start at Lions Park. We can't wait to see what unusual migrants will turn up.

This year, two out-of-state birders met up with us for a little while and were the first to spot a Connecticut warbler, a first record for the Cheyenne latilong (a latilong is an area one degree of latitude by one degree of longitude). The two enthusiastic birders helped many people get a chance to see it.

Each year, before the Casper birders leave town, I try to record their observations, but with so many people participating this year, I didn't get a chance to check with everyone.

Knowing most of the Casperites and the two out-of-state birders subscribe to the Wyobirds listserv, Jane and I compiled a preliminary list and sent it over the internet with a request for documentation of two rare species, including the warbler (I only saw a few of its feathers).

The responses of the two out-of-state birders, who have evidently birded the Cheyenne area frequently on their own, appeared quickly. One asked, who is Jane Dorn and why should he report anything to her? The other complained that the state records committee had never acknowledged other reports he'd

sent in and he wasn't going to send in any more.

Since then, two Casper birders have sent Jane excellent documentation for the warbler, and one of our local birders may be able to do so for the other bird, a glossy ibis.

This whole episode brings up two points. One, if visitors have the ability to identify rare birds and they take the time to befriend and share their talent with the locals, it is time and expertise that is greatly appreciated. Otherwise, they appear to be roving rare bird baggers.

Second, the all-volunteer records committee needs to figure out how to deal with its backlog of reports. Modern communications technology would benefit the scattered members who find it difficult to meet in person.

There's also a third point to make. As willing as birders are to serve as citizen scientists, there is an increasing amount of data organization and processing needed for wildlife planning and management purposes. The state wildlife agency is the logical institution to handle it.

Game and Fish should consider increasing its nongame bird staff so data can be prepared in a useful and timely way.

48 Rescuing baby birds not always necessary

Thursday, August 8, 2002, Outdoors, page C2

Mid-July I got a call from a member of the staff at the Cheyenne Pet Clinic. Would I know where to find killdeer? Someone had brought in a chick and the staff wanted to release it near other killdeer in hopes they would foster it.

There was no information about

where the chick had come from. Why was it brought in?

"They said it fell out of the nest," replied the staffer. We had to laugh. Killdeer nest on the ground.

In fact, here in the grasslands, most birds nest on the ground, including the western meadowlark, and even hawks such as the northern harrier (formerly named marsh hawk) and ferruginous hawk.

Some grassland birds may nest in the few available bushes, but otherwise, it's an entirely different group of birds adapted to building nests in trees in our yards, along riparian areas (streams and creeks) or in forests.

In other treeless habitats birds also nest on the ground. Think of all the shorebirds, penguins and seabirds.

Just yesterday I was reading one of Christopher (Robin) Milne's autobiographical books in which he describes finding an owlet on the ground near his home in Dartmouth, England, and how he thought he needed to take it home and raise it himself.

Well-informed people in this country know that they need a permit to raise wildlife and besides, owlets walk around on the ground before they learn to fly as a normal part of their development. Burrowing owls even nest underground.

I think there is a default setting in our brains when the phrase "baby bird" is uttered. We automatically envision a tree with a cozy nest of tiny, featherless robins. Their parents take turns perching on the rim, stuffing worms and insects into their gaping mouths.

For many birds, this picture is accurate. When their eggs hatch, the young are helpless, naked and blind creatures that spend a week or two in the nest. They are classified as altricial young and are called nestlings.

Ground nesting bird species tend to have precocial young called chicks. Shortly after hatching, the chicks, covered in downy feathers, are running around after their parents. Think about domestic ducklings and chickens. Though they can't fly right away, falling out of the nest is not one of their problems.

When do baby birds need rescuing? My rule of thumb is when a life-threatening catastrophe is human caused, such as last summer's incident when children tore down swallow nests on the Greenway. Or there are loose pets that may cause injury. I hope you've been too smart and soft-hearted to let your pets roam, especially during the May, June and July nesting season.

There will always be a baby robin that leaves its nest prematurely. Even if you put it back, whatever defect in the nest construction or in its baby brain that caused it to fall or jump the first time will usually cause it to do it again.

It's important to remember that for every year's crop of young animals, a high percentage is meant to be food for other young. Even People for the Ethical Treatment of Animals can't turn carnivores into herbivores. Just make sure the balance of nature isn't upset because your Fluffy or Fido is pretending to be one of the native predators.

Even if people mistakenly rescue a bird, it's still a good sign that they care about the welfare of wildlife. Perhaps they are ready to take other, less direct actions, on behalf of wildlife, such as using organic lawn care products, recycling and supporting organic farming, pollution control and native landscape reclamation.

Though this year's nesting season is nearly finished, except for the goldfinches and a few birds trying to get a second brood in, it's not too soon to make your own small contribution and work on turning your cat into a house pet.

If the part you dislike about house cats is the litter box, let me put in a plug for Arm and Hammer's "Super Scoop" clumping kitty litter. It is more expensive per pound than regular clay, but it lasts longer and works better.

I take a minute a day to scoop tidy,

nearly odor-free litter box lumps into an empty produce bag, bread bag or cereal box liner, and maybe add a little fresh litter to the box if the level is getting low. However, I only dump the entire litter box contents once or twice a year. A 14-pound box of litter lasts my two cats about three weeks.

Think of it, something as minor as fresh-smelling, easy to use cat litter could improve the chances of survival for birds in your neighborhood.

A couple days after receiving the killdeer call, I was at the clinic for my menagerie's annual visit, so I was able to meet the young women who had been on the hunt for a foster home for the chick.

They spent hours hiking over hill and dale before finding likely killdeer parents. Because the chick was not part of a study, it was not banded or fitted with a radio transmitter. No one will ever know its fate.

In the natural world, sometimes it's better to leave well enough alone.

49 Local park receives IBA designation

Thursday, October 31, 2002, Outdoors, page C2

Sloans Lake and the many birds that frequent the area have helped Lions Park become an Important Bird Area

Lions Park is finally an official state Important Bird Area. Those of us who start our annual spring bird count there thought it deserved recognition as soon as we heard the definition of an IBA.

However, it was not easy to convince the technical review committee.

The idea of identifying places important to birds, publicly or privately owned, was started in Europe in the mid-1980s by Birdlife International. The National Audubon Society translated it for the U.S. in 1995.

Audubon Wyoming began soliciting for nominations a few years later and hired an IBA director, Alison Lyon, in 2001 with help from Partners in Flight and other grantors.

Alison, who earned her Master's at the University of Wyoming studying sage grouse, is developing a program that can directly improve the welfare of birds in Wyoming.

When Alison asked Cheyenne High Plains Audubon Society members if we had a site to nominate, we immediately thought of Lions Park.

Art Anderson, chapter president and retired U.S. Fish and Wildlife Service biologist, took charge of the nomination, setting up a meeting in the spring of 2001 with Dave Romero, head of the parks and recreation department, now retired.

Dave and his staff were very enthusiastic about the nomination and provided maps. IBA designations can be touted in civic and tourism advertising, and funding may be available for conservation improvements. There is no regulatory component.

An IBA must meet at least one of four criteria and Lions Park meets numbers one, two and four.

The first criterion includes importance for a species of concern in Wyoming, which in this case would be the western grebe that nests at the lake.

The second criterion, a site important to species of high conservation priority, is met by several of the species on that list that have been seen at the park.

The fourth is the park's strongest suit: a site where significant numbers of birds concentrate for breeding, during migration or in the winter.

Lions Park has a reputation during spring migration for diversity and numbers of birds. I once recorded 60 species in two hours. Migration was also Gloria Lawrence's arguing point in getting the nomination accepted.

Gloria and her husband Jim drive down from Casper every spring to join the chapter in birding the park. She is one of the seven members of the Wyoming IBA technical review group made up of a cross-section of the state's ornithological experts.

The members are Stan Anderson, University of Wyoming, Laramie; Tim Byer, Thunder Basin National Grasslands, Douglas; Andrea Cerovski, Wyoming Game and Fish Department, Lander; John Dahlke, consultant, Pinedale; the Lawrences, Murie Audubon Society, Casper; and Terry McEneaney, Yellowstone National Park.

The nomination originally included all Cheyenne's city parks and the Greenway. However, some technical review group members argued that a city park's intense human use couldn't possibly be compatible with bird use. Maybe, they suggested, Lions Park is more important to bird watchers than to birds.

In reality, the parks are microcosms of the city. Cheyenne is an oasis for migrating birds that funnel along the Front Range.

While Lions Park has gotten a close inspection every year for one day mid-May, turning up all sorts of warblers thought to be unusual for this area, undoubtedly these same warblers can be found in any neighborhood with large trees and many bushes. That was true this spring when a chestnut-sided warbler visited my backyard and a magnolia warbler visited the neighbors'.

Lions Park does have one characteristic that our backyards don't have – a lake. So in addition to neotropical migrants like warblers, it gets a variety of shorebirds and waterbirds.

Funding from Partners-in-Flight, passed through Audubon Wyoming, has become available to our local Audubon chapter for monitoring work.

Many of the previous records are from Christmas Bird Counts and spring Big Day Counts which lump observations from around the city.

Now the chapter needs to plan for making more detailed surveys, training volunteers in survey protocol and compiling databases useful to science. Then we can figure out what conservation projects might be of benefit to both birds and the park.

While Lions Park will never achieve global status like Yellowstone National Park may, the information we collect at least gives us more understanding about where we live.

50

Do the Thanksgiving Bird Count without leaving home

If you are reading this Thanksgiving Day and you have an hour of daylight to spare, you can take part in the Thanksgiving Bird Count. It's as easy as counting the birds at your feeder, which means you probably don't even have to go outside.

Last year, 448 people in 12 western states participated. John Hewston of Arcata, California, has been compiling the results since 1992.

It is OK to surreptitiously peer over Aunt Edith's shoulder at dinner and watch the birds out the dining room window. If you have relatives that have been featured in Dear Abby, maybe birds can provide a better topic of dinner conversation than your cousin's off-color jokes or medical concerns.

Perhaps you are merely a visitor to Cheyenne. There is no residency requirement to take part. Just count where you are and e-mail or call in your results today.

Some people look forward to a little excursion before or after dinner. It would be a great time to visit one of our local parks and select a site for counting.

Here are the directions:

1. Select a circular area on the ground 15 feet in diameter, to include feeders, bird baths, shrubs, etc. – even a body of water. Imagine the circle extending upward as a cylinder.

2. For one hour, count the numbers of birds of each species that come into this circle or cylinder. Count the maximum number of individuals of a species seen at one time. Otherwise, you may be counting the same chickadee every time it comes for another helping.

3. Record the number of birds of each species seen inside the count circle. You can also record birds seen outside the circle, but keep that list separate.

4. Record conditions and location information: location of count circle (address), habitat type (kind of vegetation and amount), number and kinds of feeders and baths, weather, temperature and beginning and ending times.

5. Send your report, your information from steps 3 and 4, as well as your name, mailing address and phone number to me.

In a few months John will send you the compiled results.

If you have an identification question, I'll return your call tomorrow.

Here's a list of the birds I've had at my feeders lately:

--House sparrow – chestnut brown back with plain, pale gray breast.

--House finch – brown bird with streaky brown breast. Males have red head, chest and rump markings.

--American goldfinch – slightly smaller than house sparrow, but unstreaked, grayish-yellowish body and black wings with white wingbars.

--Dark-eyed junco – smaller than house sparrow, various colorations of gray, white and pale reddish brown, but all have white outer tail feathers visible when they fly.

--Red-breasted nuthatch – even smaller than a junco, blue-gray back, pale red breast, black stripe through eye.

--Robin – some of them think Cheyenne is south enough. They are berry eaters this time of year.

--Blue jay – robin-sized, but blue and white with a crest on the top of the head. Stellar's jays have been reported in town, but they are blue and black.

--European starling – robin-sized, brownish black with white speckles (stars) and short, stubby tail.

--Downy woodpecker – slightly larger than a house sparrow, black and white.

--Northern flicker – brownish robin-sized bird with spotted breast, black crescent-shaped "bib" at top of breast, and very long bill. When it flies, look for the white rump patch and red wing linings.

This must have been a good year for flickers. I've had a lot of calls about them. Technically, they are in the woodpecker family, but they are as likely to peck out grubs in lawns as bugs in tree bark.

If you are really lucky, a hawk may visit your feeder too. Usually it's the little sharp-shinned hawk, a forest bird that is willing to negotiate backyard branches.

However, a couple weeks ago, while on our daily morning walk, my neighbor and I saw crows harassing a rough-legged hawk. After nesting on the Arctic tundra, this large raptor winters across the U.S., but usually in open country, not in town.

It's that chance of unpredictability that makes watching even my bird feeder interesting. I can't wait to see what shows up today – in your yard and in mine.

2003

Thursday, February 20, 2003, Outdoors, page C2

51 Thanks to awareness, birds now visible on range

The Society for Range Management held its six-day, annual meeting in Casper earlier this month. In the 23 years I've been a member there have been noticeable changes.

First, a majority of presentations were made with PowerPoint rather than slide or overhead projector. The abstracts were on CD rather than in a book. Fewer people wore ties. More women attended in a professional capacity.

Most amazing to me was the inclusion of three sessions of papers on rangeland birds.

The society began in about 1948 as a group of western public land managers who seceded from the Society of American Foresters to concentrate on rangeland, usually considered to be the naturally treeless regions.

The new society soon attracted producers (ranchers), wildlife biologists (primarily big game) and more recently, folks from the minerals industry concerned with mined land reclamation.

This year a symposium titled "Rangeland Birds and Ecosystems" sponsored by Audubon Wyoming, broadened SRM's perspective even more. It was divided into three sessions: "Birds as Environmental Indicators in Rangeland Ecosystems," "Resources and Management Practices for Healthy Rangeland Ecosystems" and "Partnerships and Funding Opportunities."

For most ranchers and others working on rangeland, birds have merely provided background music, but interest is building. As many as 150 people at one time attended these talks.

How did birds get on the agenda of a society which uses a cowboy, "The Trail Boss," for its logo?

The invitation came from Bob Budd, an extraordinary man who has been building bridges for some time now between livestock producers and the environmental/biology community.

Years ago, he was in Cheyenne as the executive director of the Wyoming Stock Growers Association. Even though I represented Audubon, I found him easy to visit with and open-minded.

I wasn't nearly as shocked as the ranching community was when he took a position with The Nature Conservancy to manage their Red Canyon Ranch property near Lander. He now also directs science stewardship and planning.

Bob has been able to demonstrate ranch management practices that benefit livestock and wildlife. He won't allow ranchers to make "environment" into a four-letter word, or on the other hand, let environmentalist keep old stereotypes of ranching.

Bob's credibility continues to remain high, high enough to be the newly elected president of SRM.

At the bird symposium I was reminded one can never generalize about rangeland. Fire as a management tool may work wonders in one place and create a long-lived disaster in another.

One can't generalize about rangeland bird species either. One prefers bare ground, another prefers a jungle of sagebrush. One species is happy with a couple hundred acres of unfragmented grassland, another needs 50,000 acres including three distinct types of habitat for breeding, nesting and raising young.

One of few generalizations to be made is that bird species present in a rangeland ecosystem can indicate its health – usually taken to mean approximating historical conditions.

Managers have learned to create perfect and uniform pastures with plants livestock need to graze for maximum weight gain. But just a little untidiness, a little bare ground here, a little ungrazed patch of shrubs there, can produce the full historical spectrum of birds.

This sounds suspiciously like advice given to birdwatching homeowners to lay off the pesticides and pruning shears and let at least part of the yard go natural.

Wildlife biologists at the symposium presented best management practices for birds for several types of habitat. I thought, gosh, I've heard this before – 20-some years ago from my range management professors at the University of Wyoming. Maybe what's good for cows can be good for birds.

Rangeland has perpetuated itself for millennia, and we are still figuring out the intricate relationships between climate, soil, plant and animal, and how to take advantage of them.

No one can predict when a tiny facet of scientific understanding will catch the light and shine it on matters of human importance.

Three of my former UW classmates, also still SRM members, study things as obscure as the way mesquite beans weather in Texas. Seems to me the study of rangeland birds has as much beneficial potential.

52

Thursday, April 17, 2003, Outdoors, page C2

With birds at feeders, cats are sure to follow

Last month I complained my backyard feeders were attracting very few birds.

Then a flock of 15 juncos showed up the day before the big storm and some of them are still here, more than a week into April. Evidently, they aren't ready yet to return to the mountains, their summer home.

Birds with more normal migration patterns have been observed. Wilson Selner called last week about a spotted towhee in his yard (formerly named the rufous-sided towhee). This is about a month earlier than I've seen these robin-colored birds in my yard.

The turkey vultures are back too. We'll wait and see whether they are passing through or staying to nest in town.

Twice in the last week I've caught the wispy sound of cedar waxwings while out walking the dog. They can be year-round residents – if they find enough berries and blossoms.

Along with the return of birds to my

feeders is the return of an unwanted visitor, a black cat – definitely bad luck for a bird crossing its path.

I am not too fussy about the demise of a few non-native birds like house sparrows – birds that crowd out the native species. However, it's usually the native birds, especially those passing through on migration, which become victims. Or ground-feeding birds like juncos. Or ground-nesting birds like meadowlarks and other grassland species.

Is it possible to be a cat owner and a bird watcher at the same time? Yes, if you keep your cat indoors.

If you are interested in the conservation of wildlife, remember domestic cats are not predators native to North America. The native fauna have not evolved skills for evading domestic felines. They aren't fair game.

Experts estimate the loss of hundreds of millions of birds each year, not to mention small mammals, amphibians and reptiles. Well-fed cats and belled cats are still successful hunters.

If you value your cat's well-being, the American Veterinary Medical Association reminds you to keep your cat indoors because loose cats are more likely to contract fatal cat diseases and rabies.

Outdoor cats also transmit diseases to humans. Almost all human cases of pneumonic plague have been linked to cats. Cat-scratch fever infects 20,000 people a year and is particularly dangerous to children and people with compromised immune systems. Toxoplasmosis is a problem for pregnant women and their babies.

My bird-watching, cat-owning friends who still allow their cats outdoors unsupervised say their felines are incapable of adapting to the indoors.

As the owner of two indoor cats, I can imagine outdoor cats mean less hair, less furniture scratching and less kitty litter. But on the other hand, I like knowing that my cats are not in danger of being hit by a car, swallowing poison, being abused by people, killed by other animals or caught in a trap.

Besides, what point is there in having a pet cat if it isn't around to pet?

Pet ownership means pet-proofing your house, but it is possible to convert a cat to the indoor lifestyle with minimal impact by following these tips from the American Bird Conservancy's website, www.abcbirds.org/cats.

--Make the change gradually. Slowly limit the time your cat is allowed outdoors.

--When the cat is indoors, pay more attention to it. Invent cat games and toys. Play with your cat instead of watching TV.

--Provide scratching posts and trim your cat's claws every week or two.

--Provide interesting places to lounge, such as by the window overlooking your bird feeder.

--Provide quality, clumping litter. It won't be so hard to make yourself clean it once a day.

--If you are gone a lot, your cat would appreciate a companion. ABC recommends a dog, or another cat, of the opposite sex. My cats are brother and sister and regularly nap and play together.

--Provide fresh greens. The pet stores have kits for growing catnip, etc.

--Take your cat outside once in a while, either on a leash or in a cat-proof enclosure.

Whatever it takes to make your cat an indoor cat, know that bird watchers will thank you.

As for the neighbor's cat in your yard, try explaining to the neighbor the rewards of an indoor cat, keep the bird feeders away from the bushes and let the dog out frequently. If all else fails, borrow a trap from the Cheyenne Animal Shelter, 632-6655.

53 Now's the perfect time to identify ducks

Thursday, May 1, 2003, Outdoors, page C2

A cold, nasty spring day is a good day for ducks. My husband Mark and I laid the spotting scope in the backseat of the car and headed out to check the reservoirs on Crow Creek.

Spring is the easiest time of year to identify ducks: the males have complete breeding plumage; the drab and confusing females are swimming close to their associated males; and there aren't any half-grown young with half adult plumage.

There are difficulties though. The day we went out, cold wind made my eyes water when I tried to look through the scope. Some ducks dive, so when Mark got the scope centered on an individual, by the time I took a look-see, there was only empty water, with the duck reappearing somewhere outside the scope's field of vision.

At our city park lakes, at first glance every duck seems to be a mallard, the males sporting those distinctive green heads. But don't short-change yourself by assuming the ordinary.

Mallards are puddle ducks. When they tip over to feed, only their tails are visible. When one comes back up, look to see if it's a drake mallard with bright green head and yellow bill, or does it have a green head and a big black bill like a spatula (male northern shoveler)?

Or is it pointy-tailed and brownish gray all over except for a white breast ending in a streak up the side of its neck (male northern pintail)?

Or is it completely blah brown and gray, but with a very black butt (male gadwall)?

Or maybe the most noticeable field mark is a white crescent on its cheek (male blue-winged teal). Or the whole duck is a reddish, cinnamon brown (male cinnamon teal).

Or maybe the duck you're looking at keeps diving, completely submerging to feed. Does it have a dark red head and a light-colored bill (male redhead)?

Or are the duck's head and breast black followed by a pale gray back, white sides and black tail (male lesser scaup)? Or perhaps it is patterned black and white with a big white splotch on both sides of its head (male bufflehead).

Or maybe the duck has a white cheek, black cap, red-brown body with a tail held at a jaunty, nearly vertical angle (male ruddy duck).

Or maybe the head seems small for a duck and there are ragged feathers sticking out from the back of the head (some kind of merganser) like the birds we saw at Lions Park and couldn't narrow down to species.

Or maybe the bird floating on the lake isn't a duck at all. The American coot is really a swimming chicken – all black with a white bill and lobed toes instead of webbed feet.

While we saw the above-mentioned birds Easter weekend, this is not a complete list of duck and duck-like possibilities.

It was evidently too early for grebes, non-duck waterbirds easy to spot at Lions Park. The pied-billed (black and white bill) grebe is half the size of a mallard. Even though it's light brown, it reminds me of a rubber duckie the way it bobs and dives.

In contrast, the western grebes that show up every year are large gray birds with long, elegant, white-fronted necks.

While some of the ducks I've listed might have spent the winter here or may spend the summer and nest, others are passing through to higher latitudes.

But even for the ducks that summer here, don't wait too long to try your hand at identification.

By July some ducks begin to molt or the young, soon adult-sized but not adult-colored, start paddling around and then you're stuck trying to use much more subtle field marks such as the shape of the head or the shadow of a facial marking. It's less frustrating to spend time with a field guide and in the field studying the birds while markings are clear.

Ducks, because they are often in the middle or on the other side of a lake, are often out of binocular range and difficult to identify. With a little help from other birders and a spotting scope, you should be able to figure out most of the ducks – males in breeding plumage anyway.

Then you can start on the next challenging group of birds. Where Crow Creek was flooding the day we were out, Mark and I saw the quintessential long-legged, long-billed, mottled gray shorebird.

Oh gosh. Thirty-eight pages of the field guide to pick from. Was it a kind of plover, yellow-legs, willet, sandpiper or dowitcher? Maybe I should take up a different challenge next instead, like warblers or flycatchers.

54 Cheyenne gaining reputation among warbler watchers

Thursday, May 15, 2003, Outdoors, page C2

After a winter of watching seed-eating birds from the windows, it's time to get out and do some weekend warbler watching.

Cheyenne has a reputation for attracting all sorts of unlikely warblers. In the past 10 years the Big Day bird count has produced a cumulative total of 26 species. There are only 55 species in all North America.

The warblers, in turn, attract birders—even from Casper.

The Big Day count is not as formal as the Christmas count and only counts the number of all species observed, not the number of individual birds seen. Cheyenne – High Plains Audubon members choose the date, usually the closest Saturday to the middle of May. We expect that to be the height of spring migration.

Lions Park is a great place to look for warblers because it has the big trees and the bushes, but it really is just a microcosm of all of Cheyenne, a wooded island on the Great Plains for a group of birds technically known as "wood-warblers."

To me, the warbler family resemblance is that all are small busy birds that are, if not all yellow, partly yellow or yellowish, with the exception of a few such as the northern waterthrush - which ornithologists may decide to put in its own family anyway.

The beginning of the warbler wave is the end of April, when yellow-rumped warblers first show up. They are one of the few warbler species that are willing to subsist on berries until it's warm enough to hatch insects – the only food for most warblers.

Last year the wave peaked at 17 species on the Big Day.

The warblers that visit Cheyenne aren't always the ones predicted from studying range maps in field guides

– birds don't read books – so that's what makes warbler watching so much fun.

I have a vivid mental picture from 1996 when Oliver Scott, grand old man of Wyoming birding, heard something in a thicket on the outskirts of Cheyenne and despite his 80 years, jumped a fence and "bagged" the first prairie warbler ever recorded in Wyoming. It was only about 600 miles off its official course.

The prairie warbler was observed again in 2000 and 2001. This might indicate a trend, a range expansion, or maybe we have increasing numbers of better prepared warbler watchers.

Over half the warblers seen in Cheyenne the past 10 years are considered rare migrants, birds thought not to regularly migrate through Cheyenne.

However, in the case of the chestnut-sided warbler, the range map shows its migration route staying east of a line nearly the same as the 100th Meridian, through Kansas, Nebraska and the Dakotas, but its breeding range stretches west across Canada into Alberta. Why would this species not cut kitty-corner through Wyoming?

Twelve of the warbler species observed on Big Days spend the summer and breed in Wyoming, but typically not in Cheyenne. These birds prefer the mountain forest. Some, such as the yellow warbler, provide the background music along willow-choked mountain streams.

Of course, warblers migrate in the fall too, but they aren't as much fun then. They don't come as a wave as they do in the spring. Instead, they slip south over several months.

Plus, the males have lost their distinctive breeding plumage, the young of the year have indistinct juvenile plumage and the females are still confusing. You must be a birder who has run out of other identification challenges to want to take on fall warblers.

I have seen a few warblers from inside. Just last week we had a yellow-rumped flitting 10 feet from the living room window. Another time I saw a Wilson's from a basement window, but generally, most of us wait for the weekend to get outside and do our warbler watching.

The wave will be tapering off over the next few weeks. If you want to try warbler watching, find someplace like Lions Park that has big old cottonwoods. Stand still, watch the treetops and wait for movement to indicate a bird. Then, still with your eyes on the bird, quickly raise your binoculars. Some warblers prefer lower strata, so check smaller trees and bushes too.

You know, nothing's flitted by the window over my computer this morning. Maybe it's time to take a break and hang out some laundry.

Cheyenne Big Day Count -- Warbler species observed, 1993-2002

Species name	Status	'93	'94	'95	'96	'97	'98	'99	'00	'01	'02
Tennessee Warbler	rm							x		x	x
Orange-crowned Warbler	s, unc	x	x	x	x	x	x	x			x
Nashville Warbler	rm					x					
Virginia's Warbler	s, rare	x			x	x	x	x	x	x	x
Northern Parula	rm					x		x	x		x
Yellow Warbler	s, com	x	x	x	x	x	x	x	x	x	x
Chestnut-sided Warbler	rm								x	x	x
Magnolia Warbler	rm								x		
Black-throated Blue Warbler	rm									x	
Yellow-rumped Warbler	s, com	x	x	x	x	x	x	x	x	x	x
Black-throated Green Warbler	rm								x		
Townsend's Warbler	s, rare			x						x	x
Prairie Warbler	rm				x				x	x	
Palm Warbler	rm			x		x				x	x
Blackpoll Warbler	rm	x	x	x	x	x	x	x	x	x	x
Black-and-white Warbler	rm	x			x	x	x	x		x	
American Redstart	s, unc	x	x	x	x	x	x	x		x	x
Prothonotary Warbler	rm					x					
Ovenbird	s, unc			x	x			x	x	x	
Northern Waterthrush	s, rare	x		x	x	x	x	x	x	x	x
Connecticut Warbler	rm										x
MacGillivray's Warbler	s, sc	x		x	x	x	x	x	x	x	x
Common Yellowthroat	s, sc	x	x	x	x	x	x	x	x	x	x
Hooded Warbler	rm		x	x				x			
Wilson's Warbler	s, sc	x	x	x	x	x	x	x	x	x	x
Yellow-breasted Chat	s, unc		x			x		x	x		x
yearly total		**11**	**9**	**13**	**12**	**16**	**11**	**16**	**15**	**17**	**17**

Compiled by Barb Gorges from Cheyenne - High Plains Audubon Society records.
Wyoming seasonal status as listed in "Wyoming Birds" by Jane Dorn and Robert Dorn
rm = rare migrant
s = summer resident
Abundance: **r** = rare, **unc** = uncommon, **sc** = somewhat common, **com** = common

55

Avian guests make themselves at home

In our family, the months of May and June are traditional for family gatherings: weddings, anniversaries, new babies, birthdays and graduations. So, the avian open house in my backyard fits right in.

First, at the beginning of May, the white-crowned sparrows always visit – unobtrusive guests blending in with the usual brown birds hanging out on the ground picking up spilled seed under the feeders – except that they sing.

I could listen all day to white-crowned sparrow singing. After a couple of weeks, in the midst of the commotion of other arrivals, I suddenly realized they'd slipped out without a chance for me to thank them for all the songs. No matter – I'll catch them at their next gig in the mountains this summer.

After a whole winter without so much as stopping by for Sunday dinner, the entire goldfinch contingent descended upon us and have been eating us out of house and home ever since. They gossip constantly and bicker over who gets which of the eight perches on their favorite thistle feeder.

There's a new thistle feeder too, except it's designed with the seed ports below the perches. The goldfinches hang upside down and reach for the seed the way they would on a ripe sunflower head.

The new feeder takes a little getting used to. The neophytes flutter a lot at first before learning to relax and hang by their toes. Two of the goldfinches got so good at it, they tried hanging on the old feeder one day. However, the feeder wasn't designed for this, with the seed ports under the perches further away than on the new feeder, so the birds really had to stretch. They looked like little yellow bats.

Goldfinches are always cheerful and entertaining company, so as far as I'm concerned, they can stay as long as they like.

On the other hand, two blue jays have recently discovered our yard. Like haughty, well-dressed, querulous relations (but not like any one in my human family!) they scare all the other guests into silence. They mostly stay away from the feeders by the house and join the mourning doves on the back wall where we spread millet. Luckily, mourning doves are too pea-brained to realize if they are being snubbed.

One year we had a whole parade of western tanagers on the back wall. However, this year I only saw one flash through the yard. I've been getting reports from other backyard birders though, so this must be the year the tanagers are obligated to visit the other side of the family.

I've also gotten a lot of calls about orioles in Cheyenne's residential neighborhoods. The Bullock's oriole, western counterpart of the Baltimore, prefers to hang its pouch-shaped nest in cottonwoods by a creek. Whether they'll nest in town is something we can only surmise if we observe their unique nests.

The other orange bird has been by, the black-headed grosbeak. The striped-looking female visits most often. She doesn't mind sharing the shelf feeder with the house finches.

I always look forward to a visit from her cousin, the rose-breasted grosbeak. I heard reports and even received a digital photo from another backyard birder, but it was the third week in May before one came here. All black except for a white underside and a hot pink bib or ascot, one male shyly joined the finches. He must have liked the fare we offered because later he was happily singing from a treetop.

Chipping sparrows, spotted towhees, green-tailed towhees and several warblers put in appearances as expected, but why is it some of my favorite guests visit least often? Absence makes the heart grow fonder? I know my annual spring avian open house has reached its zenith when the buntings come. This year it was two lazuli bunting males,

glimpsed only briefly three mornings. They truly are a piece of sky, as their name implies.

Now, at the beginning of June, most of these house guests have moved on to summer homes in the country or the mountains. The goldfinches and doves will stick around, but things will get quiet when everyone goes on nesting duty. And then it won't be long before the robins bring their fledglings out for a worm hunt on the lawn.

Having company is work. We have to fill the feeders every day, sweep the seed hulls and wash off the whitewash, but what's a little housework when my favorite company is visiting? I'm already looking forward to next year.

56 Dead blackbird tells no tale about West Nile virus

Thursday, July 10, 2003, Outdoors, page C2

While I was away over a weekend, my friend Ruth left two phone messages. The first, left Saturday, was, "Call me."

By the time she left the second call Sunday morning, she knew she wouldn't reach me before leaving town herself.

Apparently, she had found a dead blackbird while mowing her neighbor's lawn. Would I find out if it had West Nile virus? Instructions for retrieving the double-bagged body followed.

Well, what are friends for? However, I hoped the neighbors weren't watching as I pulled up in Ruth's driveway late Sunday afternoon, got out of the car, walked to the big black plastic trash can provided by the city, lifted the lid, removed the carefully wrapped package and left with it.

The bird had been gently roasting all day in the solar-heated garbage container, but it only gave off a faint smell.

At home I put it in the refrigerator until appropriate offices would be open on a weekday.

A few weeks before, a neighbor had called about dead blackbirds in her yard, concerned about West Nile virus. I had given her my best guess on who to call. Now it was my turn to find my way through bureaucratic channels.

Turns out the state veterinary lab has a special toll-free West Nile virus hotline, 877-996-9000.

Among other information in its extensive message, it listed the only species of birds accepted for testing: crow, raven, blue jay and magpie.

Based on Ruth's description and its heft, I knew without having to open the package, this dead bird was not one of the four species mentioned. So, I unceremoniously removed it from the fridge and dumped it in my own big black garbage container.

We will never know if Ruth's bird died of West Nile or something else.

Before the coming of the virus, people reported dead birds in their yards for which the cause of death apparently was not a predator or an accidental collision with a window.

There are a host of bird diseases and sometimes the avian amenities we provide in our yards lead to an unnatural concentration of birds and the setting for a mini epidemic.

A few years ago, a woman called me, reporting 30-40 dead blackbirds in her yard. If memory serves, autopsies diagnosed salmonella.

Disease around feeders and bird baths is more likely in summer. So if you notice sick or dead birds in your yard – and you haven't sprayed chemicals lately – put away your feeders for a while.

It breaks up the party and encourages the birds to go after all those annoying bugs hanging around the garden and patio. Otherwise, wash your feeders frequently.

Birds and other animals can be carriers of West Nile virus, and when a mosquito bites one of them before biting humans, there's a slim chance for serious medical problems for the humans.

However, Cheyenne and Wyoming, except for mountain snow melt areas and some streams, are the most mosquito-free places I've ever lived.

Wyoming has other insect diseases of concern besides West Nile. No one this time of year spends the day afield without checking for ticks afterwards to avoid Rocky Mountain spotted fever.

Diseases carried by insects have always been around and have had major impact on civilizations.

It would be nice if we could do away with all creepy-crawlies. Of course, that would mean no more songbirds since so many are dependent on insects for food. Even a lot of the seed-eating species depend on insects and other arthropods to feed their young.

There is worry that West Nile will itself decimate bird populations. Chickadee numbers seem to be declining in the northeast, where West Nile was first diagnosed on this continent (American Birding – The 103rd Christmas Bird Count, National Audubon Society).

And animals recovering from West Nile virus appear to have permanent brain scarring (Smithsonian magazine, July 2003).

My advice is to take recommended precautions. Empty standing water every couple days, use mosquito larvae-eating fish in ponds, dress appropriately for areas with lots of insects and monitor your own patch of terra firma for changes.

A couple blue jays showed up in my yard this spring for a few days and then disappeared. West Nile crossed my mind. But the quiet was, apparently, due to nesting. This morning the racket in the alley turned out to be a young blue jay.

Oh good. Come on over, son – help yourself to some of the bugs in my yard!

57 Bird of backcountry moves closer to town

Two friends and I have a favorite hiking destination in the Pole Mountain area. We're beginning to hike it often enough to notice seasonal and yearly changes in vegetation, stream flow – and our physical fitness.

Our destination is a shaded spot on the bank of a creek from which we have a view down a narrow little canyon [now named Hidden Falls at Curt Gowdy State Park]. We always enjoy a bit of rest there before striking back up the trail to a solar-heated vehicle.

This summer the falling water can be heard, but not seen. When my teenage son, Jeffrey, accompanied us one morning, he scampered up and around the canyon walls and reported that apparently natural debris had shifted most of the flow out of sight.

Whether the change has anything to do with it or not, this summer we've noticed a new bird.

As swallows whipped around and robins called, a quick gray shape determinedly skimmed the surface of the creek, following it to the dark recess made by the rock wall of the formerly visible waterfall.

The first time we saw it, we looked at each other and said, "Dipper?" The second hike it happened we were sure the stubby-winged bird was an American dipper.

Pole Mountain, in my mind, is not high country. I've seen dippers as they dart in and out of waterfalls high in the mountains or dive into rapid mountain rivers, but I wouldn't expect to find one along a tame little stream so close to the plains.

The dippers (there are other species in Europe and South America) are aquatic songbirds. They dive for insect larvae in streams, propelling themselves underwater with their wings or they simply walk the stream bottom. They can stay submerged up to 15 seconds before popping up on a rock midstream where they stand and bob a bit before plunging back in.

Formerly called the water ouzel, this species of the Rocky Mountains builds a domed nest just above streams or behind waterfalls where it will receive continuous spray, according to the field guides. They've also adapted to human construction by building nests under bridges that span mountain streams.

I've never seen a dipper nest. Even if the creek wasn't too cold to wade, I'd be reluctant to follow the Pole Mountain bird for fear of disturbing it.

With some birds you might wait until after nesting season to take a look, but dippers are year-round residents. They stay all winter, as long as the water stays open, and move downstream only if it freezes.

How do dippers react to people? Our hiking destination is in the middle of this dipper's territory, judging from the way it passes us as we sit at the edge of the creek. I don't know how many other people visit. If this is the dipper's first year in this canyon, it may find it to be too populous and have to move on.

However, indirect pressure from people may be more detrimental. Kenn Kaufman states in "Lives of North American Birds" that the dipper has declined or disappeared in some of its former haunts because of declines in water quality affecting its food source.

2003   87

This makes dippers a good indicator of the presence or absence of pollution.

The cause for decline in water quality is usually people, directly or indirectly. All kinds of human activities can pollute mountain streams with additional sediment or unnatural chemicals.

It's ironic that the more we help people to connect with wildlife and the outdoors, the more likely they are to want to work, live and recreate in wild places and the more often wildlife is pushed out.

Maybe, tongue-in-cheek, we proponents of wildlife conservation could be more helpful if we chose to live in urban apartments, spend our vacation at home and enjoy wildlife programs on TV, leaving the outdoors to those sometimes dangerous wildlife species.

Rather than the classic motto of opponents of industrial sitings, "Not in my backyard," our new motto could be "Staying in my backyard!"

The Pole Mountain dipper is now practically in our backyard. We must be doing something right. However, we need to respect our new resident's privacy if we want to encourage it to stay.

I don't suppose we could salt the creek with caddis fly larvae as sort of a neighborhood welcoming committee's plate of cookies, could we?

58 Birding not just a springtime joy anymore

Thursday, October 2, 2003, Outdoors, page C2

The next time Doug Faulkner plans to come up from Colorado to bird Cheyenne, I hope to tag along again.

He's one of those people who, after scanning acres of ducks, can look around and say, "Gee, it'd be nice to see a peregrine," and wham, something nails a duck and seconds later we all get a chance to see a peregrine falcon standing on its prize on a sandbar in the middle of a drought-stricken reservoir, only a mile south of Cheyenne's city limits.

By the way, the colloquial name for the peregrine was duck hawk. Chicken hawk, a name I mentioned in my last column, referred to red-tailed hawks.

For whatever reason, perhaps years of attending children's soccer games on Saturday mornings, I've never done much purposeful birding in the fall. Besides, it didn't seem appealing because many birds are more difficult to identify than in the spring. They've molted out of their distinctive breeding plumage or they are the young of the year and haven't acquired adult feathering.

Fall birding for me has always been just a matter of what crosses my path. So it was interesting to revisit spring birding haunts and see what was flitting. Technically, this excursion was during fall migration, even though it was the last weekend of summer.

Doug, who is a bird specialist for the Rocky Mountain Bird Observatory located at Barr Lake State Park outside Brighton, Colo., gathered up a group of six other birders for a second annual fall foray to Cheyenne.

First stop, where I met the group, was at the Wyoming Hereford Ranch by the horse barn, overlooking the riparian thicket of Crow Creek. I arrived earliest, but the vista was pretty quiet. Two big bird lumps were sitting in the treetops, one a turkey vulture and the other an unidentifiable hawk showing me only a speckled shoulder.

A lone car pulled into the avenue of cottonwoods and then stopped – a birder, of course. It was Gary Lefko, part of Doug's group. He was studying a small bird lump in one of the trees, which in turn studied us. It had a faded red breast, white belly and a face like a bluebird. It hunched like a bluebird, but had its wings tight across its back where we couldn't examine them for blueness.

Was it an eastern or a western bluebird? Mountain bluebirds have no red markings. When Doug came along at last, he pointed out the obvious field mark. Easterns have a red breast that comes up to their chins like a turtleneck sweater while westerns have the equivalent of a v-neck. So, we had an eastern.

"O.K., we can go home now!" Doug said. Eastern bluebirds are rare enough here to be celebrated as the find of the day.

Back at the creek overlook, the turkey vulture took off, the hawk had gone and small birds were jumping. "Western tanager, western wood peewee, Townsend's solitaire, ruby-crowned kinglet, Wilson's warbler!" Everyone was calling something.

Some of these species, such as the tanager and later, the green-tailed towhee we saw by the office, come through my yard in the spring on route to the mountains, but I had never seen them in the fall before.

The Wilson's warblers were the most numerous. At Lions Park, they seemed as thick as butterflies in the garden. Over the course of the morning, we also saw yellow-rumped, orange-crowned, Townsend's and MacGillivray's warblers plus a chestnut-sided warbler

which had none of its chestnut-colored field markings this time of year.

Undoubtedly, any neighborhood in Cheyenne with mature vegetation is hosting these travelers. The week before I'd glimpsed a Townsend's warbler in my own bushes as it fueled up on bugs to continue its trip from breeding grounds somewhere between southeast Alaska and Washington state to wintering grounds stretching from California into Mexico and Central America.

At the reservoir, the coots were easily identifiable, same all-black plumage. Pintails still had pointy tails and gadwalls were still black behind. We'd seen blue-winged and green-winged teal in the creek.

The birds that had lost the most coloring were the phalaropes, those sandpipers that swim in circles to churn up food. In the spring, the Wilson's phalaropes are marked with red and black, but winter plumage is gray and white.

Then it was pointed out that these particular little whirling dervishes were red-necked phalaropes instead. They were just passing through from a summer spent high in the Arctic.

Since my North American bird field guides don't show where these phalaropes winter, I had to do a little more research to discover that they prefer the open ocean, south of the Equator, off western South America. It's amazing the endurance of a 1.2-ounce bird with a wingspan of only 15 inches.

I'm glad the visiting Colorado birders took me along for a bit. Birding in the fall, though challenging, turns out to be just as exciting as in the spring.

59 Trumpeter performs for crowd at Holliday Park

The man walking the circumference of Lake Minnehaha was approaching us when he noticed our binoculars and paused to make a remark about the trumpeter swan we were watching.

"Yeah, there was a flock of them here last week."

"You mean the pelicans?" I asked.

"Oh, no, swans."

We had seen pelicans about then, but we hadn't been at the lake when he was. However, it's unlikely a whole flock of swans would escape notice by the local birding community.

We shrugged, and the man continued on. At least he wasn't mistaking the white domestic geese that sometimes show up on this small lake at Holliday Park in the middle of Cheyenne.

This particular trumpeter swan visited between about Nov. 8 and 12, feeding on submerged vegetation growing from the lake bottom. It was still using the lake as of press time. It may not have attracted much attention from motorists on busy Lincolnway since, with its head and elegant neck underwater much of the time, it mostly resembled a large white, inflated, plastic bag stranded in a raft of Canada geese, dwarfing them and the other waterfowl.

American white pelicans have thick necks about equal the length of their long, orange bills. By contrast, trumpeter swans have long, slender necks and much shorter black bills. Males and females are indistinguishable unless you have them in hand and check under their tails. The more common tundra swans are smaller and their bills are also black, but with large yellow markings up by the eyes.

The mute swan, star of European fairy tales such as "The Ugly Duckling" (my favorite version is told by Marianna Mayer and illustrated by landscape artist Thomas Locker), has a black and orange bill. Like so many other birds introduced to North America for their entertainment value, the mute swan has escaped domesticity and, in the northeast, is becoming a nuisance to people and out competes native waterfowl.

Tundra swans have been common enough to support hunting seasons in some states, however, numbers for the trumpeter continue to improve more slowly.

Originally found across most of North America, by the early 1900s, the trumpeter was nearly completely decimated due to over-hunting for its meat and feathers, loss of breeding and wintering habitats and other effects of increasing human population. Remnant flocks held out in remote places like Yellowstone National Park, where hot springs keep water open in the winter. Red Rock Lakes National Wildlife Refuge in southwestern Montana was devoted to its recovery in 1931.

Ruth Shea, executive director of The Trumpeter Swan Society, told me that today there are about 17,000 trumpeters summering in Alaska, 3,700 in western Canada, 3,000 in the Midwest and about 300 in the greater Yellowstone area, for a total of about 25,000.

In winter the Canadians crowd into the Yellowstone area. Biologists attempt to disperse the birds to keep them from damaging their food source. Also, having all your swans in one basket makes the flock susceptible to die-off from any passing disease.

The problem is that when there were less than 100 trumpeters south of Canada in the thirties, the birds lost a lot of their species memory. With swans, migration routes seem to be less imbedded in their DNA and more likely passed down by example. They still know how to get as far south as Yellowstone, but old routes beyond seem to be lost.

Ruth expects our trumpeter is like the few other lone birds that show up in central and eastern Wyoming during fall migration. It could be a subadult from Canada exploring new wintering areas, but no one knows for sure. David Allen Sibley's range maps show rare observations in states across the country, except for the eastern seaboard where there are none.

How did this one swan find our island of city trees and this speck of a lake? Maybe we will see it again now that we are on its mental map.

But swans have a lot of challenges when they migrate, much like the Ugly Duckling's. First, when flying with a wingspan of six to eight feet at speeds of 40-80 miles per hour, collisions with power lines become deadly. Next, a trumpeter has to find open, shallow water for feeding – all winter long.

Then, in states where the similar-looking tundra swan is hunted, a few trumpeters are always mistakenly shot. Anywhere waterfowl hunting has been permitted, some swans will die from poisoning by picking up old lead shot as they graze submerged vegetation. And,

though the trumpeter is our largest native waterfowl species, standing an imposing four feet tall, coyotes are often successful in bringing it down.

Comparing range maps in old field guides with those published since the 1990s, it is easy to see the results of restoration work. Breeding and wintering ranges in Alaska and Canada have expanded, as has the year-round range in greater Yellowstone.

There's even a dot of purple over western Nebraska and South Dakota indicating the year-round restoration flock there. Ruth mentioned that in nearby northeastern Wyoming, one nesting pair has been documented several years. Other restoration flocks are in Minnesota, Michigan, Wisconsin, Iowa and Ontario, Canada.

Trumpeter swans live 15-25 years in the wild, if we can give them what they need: the right space, natural food and fewer obstacles.

Wouldn't it be great if trumpeters began to visit Lake Minnehaha so regularly that every casual observer became a swan expert?

Trumpeter Swan Society

The Trumpeter Swan Society was established in 1968 to coordinate restoration and research efforts among multiple agencies and organizations. To learn more about trumpeters or to report observations, visit the TTWS website, www.trumpeterswansociety.org.

60 How to keep up with birding news

Thursday, December 11, 2003, Outdoors, page C2

I am an amateur watcher of birds. Other than a college ornithology class, the bird knowledge I have has been gained informally, by observation, by talking to people and by reading.

I've picked up a lot from Audubon chapter members, many of whom are experts on local birds. Some are even formally educated and employed bird biologists.

My library has expanded from a single field guide to about two dozen reference books plus the whole internet – sometimes very useful when local experts aren't available to answer my questions or the questions I get from readers.

But no science is static, so it's important to read the periodicals. My husband, Mark, and I have been reading Audubon magazine for years, but it deals with conservation issues affecting birds more so than birdwatching, which is of high interest to local chapter members.

So, a few years ago I responded to subscription offers from Bird Watcher's Digest and Birder's World. Both magazines are informative as well as entertaining, written so even novice birdwatchers can enjoy articles about attracting birds to backyards or anecdotes from the field.

Then, after several years of participation in Project FeederWatch, I finally joined the Cornell Lab of Ornithology. Now in addition to the quarterly newsletter, Birdscope, I get the quarterly magazine, Living Bird. Both focus on the Lab and its far-ranging research.

And then there's the American Birding Association. Because people who are my fonts of local birding wisdom belong to the ABA, I always figured it was over my head. But when it sent me a membership offer this fall, I reconsidered. After nearly five years of exploring birdwatching topics through this column, I decided I needed to expand my horizons.

As I suspected, the ABA is geared for the serious birdwatcher, though it is still accessible for us aspiring to higher expertise. Shortly after I joined, however, I had an encounter that personified the elitist stereotype I feared. It started with a phone call from an impatient visitor from the Midwest who'd left his directory of ABA contacts at home but got my number from someone at the Cheyenne Botanic Gardens.

I have had many nice people with bird questions referred to me, but this man was in a hurry. He was sure he'd seen a kingbird at Lions Park that had a bill too big to be just a western. Could it be a Couch's or a tropical kingbird?

Having never heard of either of these species, I quickly scrambled through my Sibley's and found that they range from Mexico a little way into Arizona and Texas, and they are almost indistinguishable from our western kingbird, except they lack white outer tail feathers.

My very apparent ignorance made the caller even more snappish. Wasn't there anyone else who could come down immediately and verify his rarity? I gladly passed him off to a more knowledgeable birding friend who went to the park but didn't see the bird.

Later, my friend, who also belongs to the ABA, told me that our western kingbird sometimes loses the white color of the outer tail feathers in the fall before migrating. And he agreed that this particular specimen of ardent birder came off as rather unpleasant.

Luckily for the ABA, the members I know are much kinder and more patient with those of us of lesser experience. Half the members, according to a 1999 ABA survey, can identify over 300 species by sight and 75 species by sound. About 40 percent bird more than 50 times a year, and for half the 20,000 members, birding is their main leisure activity.

The ABA, in addition to promoting birding skills and ornithological knowledge, even for those under 18, also provides volunteer opportunities using birders' expertise. Among its programs is support of a conservation project at the location of each annual convention, plus involvement in issues directly affecting birds.

Too often birdwatchers are reluctant to get involved in the politics of conserving birds. They would rather run out to get a last glimpse of the endangered spotted owl than ask for an alternative to cutting the whole forest.

Birdwatchers can also be consumers of products of which the collection or manufacturing can have negative impacts on birds. How can one lament the effects on wildlife from drilling for oil in the Arctic National Wildlife Refuge, yet purchase a new SUV that gets less than 10 miles to the gallon?

It isn't possible to live without any impact on the world's resources, but it is irresponsible to race after elusive life list birds and ignore the health of those birds and their environment. So I'm glad to find that an organization like the ABA caters to listers, but reminds them of their responsibilities.

Audubon and Cornell, with their partnership on the Christmas Bird Count, Project FeederWatch and other Bird-Source programs, are also making the connection between birdwatching and bird conservation.

But before Ted Williams' latest piece in Audubon magazine can cause too much heartache, or the latest article in the ABA's Birding magazine, describing the feather-length difference between longspurs, gives me a headache, it's not a bad idea to step outdoors and hear the twitter of the plainest juncos and remember why I was attracted to birdwatching in the first place.

Birding publications and organizations:

www.americanbirding.org)
www.audubon.org
www.birdwatchersdigest.com
www.birds.cornell.edu

2004

61 Snow diminishes results of Christmas Bird Count

Thursday, January 8, 2004, Outdoors, page C2

If someone was counting the human population of Cheyenne last Saturday, based on the number of pedestrians observed, they might have come up with only 14 of the 53,011 reported by the Census Bureau – those of us foolish enough to be outside on the annual Christmas Bird Count.

Birds visible in the blowing snow underrepresented actual numbers as well. Most were hunkered down, waiting out the storm. Where one might expect the twitter and movement of juncos and other sparrows in tangles of shrubs, or the rhank-rhank of nuthatches in trees, most often there was only the steady tisp-tisp of tiny snow pellets hitting Gore-tex outerwear. Some years we see more than 50 species. This year it was 35, plus three observed during "week of the count" (the three days before and three days after count day, Jan. 3).

Canada geese, however, were easy to find, bunched up in open water, unwilling to fly out to snow-covered fields to feed as usual. Water in this dry country is easy to pinpoint. Between Hereford Reservoir No. 1, Lake Minnehaha and Sloans Lake, 2,092 geese were counted, up from 1,451 last year.

House sparrows were in great abundance if you knew where to look. At Avenue C-1 and Jefferson Street, a couple hundred swarmed between feed at one house and cozy bushes at another.

Over at the South Fork subdivision west of South Greeley Highway, what at first looked like another flock of house sparrows feeding on the ground between homes turned out to be 40 horned larks. The presence of grassland birds wasn't too surprising since the subdivision was recently carved out of the surrounding prairie.

Lapland longspurs are not found often, but a birder joining us from Ovid, Colo., who has lots of longspur experience from living in Kansas, was able to identify their peculiar call as they flew over with flocks of horned larks.

House sparrows and European starlings don't seem to limit activity during snowy weather, and I would think American crows wouldn't either, but on this count, we were hard put to find them and their close relations, the black-billed magpies. Last year, we counted 250 crows and 48 magpies. This year, we were down to 41 crows and six magpies. Since crows and magpies are among the most noticeable birds to be affected by West Nile virus, this decrease isn't too unexpected after a summer when the first human cases occurred here.

Warblers don't normally show up

on our Christmas count. In 29 years of available data, only twice have they been observed. The yellow-rumpeds seen Saturday are the most likely to winter here since they are one of the few warbler species that can change from a summer insect diet to an after-frost berry diet.

In great contrast was the Guernsey – Ft. Laramie count held Dec. 20. This is a new count designed by the Cheyenne count's former compiler, Jane Dorn, who, with her husband Bob, has retired to the Lingle area.

The center point of this count circle is the Platte-Goshen county line where the railroad tracks cross it. The 7.5-mile radius stretches from the east end of Guernsey State Park to the west side of Ft. Laramie National Historic Site. A map shows no mountain ranges on this far eastern edge of Wyoming, but the land is a wonderful jumble of geology and habitats.

Ten of us met at the main entrance to Guernsey State Park, drove along the reservoir edge and hiked up Fish Canyon. There was snow in the old road tracks in the shade, but otherwise, we were shedding layers as we went. The high for the day was 61 degrees.

After lunch at the Oregon Trail Ruts State Historic Site, we explored Hartville, an old mining town set in a narrow, winding canyon. We parked by the churches for a better look at a downy and a hairy woodpecker in the same tree and were greeted by two locals – two inquisitive black dogs. Further up, we were entranced by a front-yard feeder full of goldfinches.

Lucky for us, the open water at Grayrocks Reservoir was at the lower end, within the count circle. A thousand mallards attracted 31 adult bald eagles and three immatures. Most of the eagles merely stood around on the ice, but one aerialist performed, stooping to slam into, then eat, a duck.

We ended the count at Fort Laramie, the historic site, not the town, hiking the Laramie River in two groups in opposite directions and finding great blue herons.

While the group I was with waited back at the cars for the other, the sunset turned the hills pink, and two bald eagles flew low overhead, along with skeins of geese so high they could have been mistaken for wisps of cloud.

We missed the companionship of Barbara Costopolous of Guernsey, whose husband's funeral and burial was that day. We counted 31 species this year (plus seven week of the count), but with her help next year, who knows?

Cheyenne Christmas Bird Count

Tally taken Jan. 3, 2004
35 species and 4,579 individuals count day
cw – count week only, 3 species
Canada Goose 2092
Mallard 796
Northern Shoveler cw
Green-winged Teal 3
Common Goldeneye 10
Common Merganser 1
Sharp-shinned Hawk 1
Rough-legged Hawk 4
American Kestrel 1

Wilson's Snipe 2
Rock Pigeon 133
Belted Kingfisher 1
Downy Woodpecker 4
Northern Flicker 8
Blue Jay 3
Black-billed Magpie 6
American Crow 41
Horned Lark 305
Red-breasted Nuthatch 9
White-breasted Nuthatch cw
Brown Creeper 5

Golden-crowned Kinglet 6
Ruby-crowned Kinglet 1
Townsend's Solitaire cw
American Robin 60
Brown Thrasher 1
European Starling 369
Yellow-rumped Warbler 2
American Tree Sparrow 16
Song Sparrow 7
Harris's Sparrow 1
White-crowned Sparrow 2
Dark-eyed Junco, race unknown 50

White-winged Junco cw
Slate-colored Junco 35
Gray-headed Junco 8
Oregon Junco 10
Pink-sided Junco 54
Lapland Longspur 2
Common Grackle 1
House Finch 74
Pine Siskin 1
House Sparrow 454

Guernsey – Ft. Laramie Christmas Bird Count

Dec. 20, 2003
31 species and 2,907 individuals count day
cw – count week only, 7 species
Canada Goose 938
Mallard 1528
Green-winged Teal 2
Common Goldeneye 4
Common Merganser 1
Hooded Merganser cw
Wild Turkey 12
Great Blue Heron 2
Bald Eagle, adult 31, imm. 3
Sharp-shinned Hawk 1
Rough-legged Hawk 1
American Kestrel cw
Merlin cw
Killdeer 1
Ring-billed Gull cw
Herring Gull cw
Rock Pigeon 2
Belted Kingfisher 3

Downy Woodpecker 3
Hairy Woodpecker 1
Northern Flicker 3
Northern Shrike 2
Blue Jay 8
Black-billed Magpie 9
American Crow cw
Horned Lark 6
Black-capped Chickadee 9
Townsend's Solitaire 35
American Robin 70
European Starling 131
American Tree Sparrow 20
Song Sparrow cw
Dark-eyed Junco 26
Red-winged Blackbird 13
House Finch 4
Pine Siskin 5
American Goldfinch 26
House Sparrow 7

62

Thursday, February 5, 2004, Outdoors, page C2

Birders don't always flock together

I meet people who, when learning I watch birds, say, "Oh, that's something I'd like to get into someday." Or, "I watch birds at my feeder." Getting them to come out on an organized field trip is another matter.

Having read a lot of novels, I would know what to expect of a weekend at

an English country house: dinners, fox hunting, murder, etc. But not a lot of novels are based on bird watching, so if you've never been on a field trip, let me shed some light, using for example, the recent mid-January joint field trip sponsored by Cheyenne-High Plains and Fort Collins Audubon societies featuring a tour of Cheyenne's birding hotspots.

First, you have to find a field trip. This one was listed in the Wyoming Tribune-Eagle and other media as free and open to the public. You can also call the local Chamber of Commerce, visitor's bureau, library or local bird columnist to find a contact or look up the nearest Audubon chapter through www.audubon.org.

CHPAS welcomes novice birders. There are just a few things novices should know to better blend in with the group. Dress for the weather and for walking. Avoid wearing white or bright colors that can alarm the birds. Leave pets at home, although well-behaved children are welcome. Bring food and water, and if traveling to the boonies, bring a bit of toilet paper and a bag to bring it home in.

Make sure your vehicle is gassed up and ready for the kinds of roads to be driven. The bird watchers' vehicle of choice lately seems to be the small all-wheel-drive wagon – rugged, roomy enough and economical on fuel. If you are new to the group or a novice birder, see if you can carpool – it's much more fun, less polluting and makes it easier for the group to park. Be sure to offer the driver a little something for gas for long trips.

Arrive at the meeting place early or on time. Many field trips peregrinate, moving from place to place like a flock of birds, and unless you know the route, you may not be able to catch up.

Don't be afraid to introduce yourself. This trip, we had 14 folks from Fort Collins, six from Cheyenne and one from Laramie. Next time I think I'll bring nametags for everyone.

We started at the Wyoming Hereford Ranch with admonitions to not cross fences, open gates or point binoculars at windows, since we were guests on private property. With more and more birders visiting, we should also stay out of the brushy side of Crow Creek in the bunk house area.

I was worried that the serious birders might be bored because the reservoirs were mostly frozen and the beginning of spring migration still far off. But they were quite satisfied with identifying blue-winged teal in the creek – unusual, but not unheard of this time of year. A white-winged junco was another nice find.

Over at Wyoming Hereford Ranch Reservoir No. 2, we parked on the road's shoulder, and several folks brought out spotting scopes. Everyone had a chance to see the common goldeneye close up.

At Hereford No. 1, the geese on the far side, near the only open water, turned out to be decoys tended by several hunters. At Holliday Park, the ducks and geese were all crowded around a gentleman ignoring the "do not feed" sign. The visiting birders were impressed by the black-crowned night heron rookery, the nests in the tops of the trees clearly visible without the leaves.

Lions Park produced an American wigeon, several black-capped chickadees and one of the top finds of the day, golden-crowned kinglets playing hide and seek among the cones at the top of an evergreen.

As satisfying as being the first one to identify a bird is being able to help other people see it. Most birders are very generous this way. As a novice, it's instructive to watch which way the binoculars are turning and ask for help to see what everyone's looking at.

But don't hesitate to bring to attention a bird no one else is observing, even if you don't know its name (but be sure to commit to memory early the identification of the too common starling and house sparrow).

One of the less experienced birders was the one to point out the

Townsend's solitaire at the Cheyenne Botanic Gardens.

After lunch at the gardens' picnic tables (it was sunny, windless and in the 40's), we found red-breasted nuthatches and a brown creeper in the spruces by the parking lot at Little America.

By mid-afternoon, most of the local birders had dropped out, but the Fort Collins crew proclaimed that they like to bird till they drop. I wonder how many additional stops they made on their way home.

While it was, with the exception of the birds I've already mentioned, a slow day, much of the fun was meeting other birders. One man from Fort Collins asked if I knew a couple from Casper he met in Alaska at a birding convention. Well of course – I was visiting them at their country house the next weekend (minus foxes and murder).

Many of the Fort Collins birders said they are looking forward to coming up again on their own, now that they know where to go and where to find the public restrooms.

And we've been invited to visit them.

Watch for announcements about the next adventure or call the columnist.

63 Starlings aren't the darlings of the bird world

Thursday, February 19, 2004, Outdoors, page C2

The European starling has done as well as any immigrant left to fend for itself in the middle of New York City. It was introduced in 1890 by Shakespeare aficionado Eugene Scheiffelin (also spelled Scheffland) who, as head of the American Acclimatization Society for settlers from Europe, wanted to bring to his new home all the birds mentioned by the bard.

The starling's legendary success, nearly 200 million individuals in North America and spreading worldwide, has come at the expense of native birds such as bluebirds, nuthatches, swallows and woodpeckers – all species that nest in cavities coveted by aggressive starlings.

Though in Europe, their native land, starlings might be prized as caged pets because of their ability to mimic, or as canned pate de sansonnet, meat pie of starling, I was reminded by recent phone calls that here they can be pests.

Callers want to know how to keep large flocks of starlings from roosting in their trees and buildings and leaving all that whitewash. They have reason to be concerned as starlings can transmit diseases to people and livestock, and their droppings encourage the growth of pathogens. Starlings also eat crops and contaminate livestock feed.

The first step is to determine whether the birds observed are starlings because all birds in the United States are protected by law except for pigeons, house sparrows and starlings.

Starlings are chunky little birds, short-tailed and short-winged, which appear black, somewhat iridescent, though in the fall new feathers are tipped in white, like little stars. By spring, the stars wear off and their bills become bright yellow.

A quick look at a field guide shows that other black-colored birds have easily distinguished differences.

Starlings showed up in Wyoming in the 1930s and are now found in human-modified areas throughout the state. They are classified as predacious birds that can be taken in any manner except as restrictions apply to methods. Catherine Wissner, at the University of Wyoming Cooperative Extension office in Cheyenne, reminded me that it's illegal to use firearms in the city.

Stan McNamee, director of the Laramie County Weed and Pest District, advises against chemicals except where starlings have invaded a contained area such as a barn. It's highly likely that without confinement, other kinds of birds would be poisoned as well. He said the most effective chemical requires licensing.

Non-lethal methods of dealing with starlings are based on making them unwelcome. Wyoming Game and Fish Department biologist Steve Tessmann recommends a publication available at the Cheyenne office, "Homeowner's guide to resolving wildlife conflicts." He said a few nights of sporadically flashing floodlights could disrupt roosting starlings and run them off for good.

Fluttering mylar strips as another deterrent were recommended in a University of Florida Cooperative Extension bulletin. I suppose I should be grateful for the remnants of a plastic bag left by the wind in the top of one of our backyard trees.

Bob Lee, director of Environmental Management for the City of Cheyenne, recommends trying a modern-day scarecrow, a garden hose sprinkler with an electric eye that shoots water whenever it detects movement.

A Nebraska Cooperative Extension publication I found through the website recommends limiting food and water available to starlings. In a livestock operation, that means cleaning up grain spills and feeding pellets larger than a half inch in diameter, which is larger than starlings can swallow.

In your backyard, limiting food means avoiding the starling favorites, bread crusts, milo, millet and platform-style feeders in favor of black oil sunflower seed and tube or hopper feeders that are screened or balanced to keep out bigger birds.

Starlings are always squeezing their messy nests into tight, human-made places in addition to natural cavities, so screening those openings can help. Make sure nest boxes for other birds have no perches in front of the entrances and the entrance holes are sizes that exclude starlings.

It even matters how you prune your trees. Starlings prefer large, densely branched trees compared to more natural, open branching.

You can also find companies that make obstacles to roosting, spikes and coils and generally barbaric looking items, which can be installed on roofs and other problem areas.

Though the Columbia University web page on *Sturnus vulgaris* (Latin for starlike and common) is quite scientific, the author proposed, possibly tongue in cheek, "....maybe combining trapping with a pate production plant would make it (trapping) cost effective."

A weed or pest is only a plant or animal out of place. Isn't someone in Wyoming growing chicory as a crop? Marketing pate to bluebird lovers might work. Just so we won't later mourn the passing of starlings like we have passenger pigeons. But one crafty look from those beady black eyes dismisses that worry.

64 First sign of spring arrives

Late winter in Wyoming means only a few more snowstorms until summer. However, it's still worthwhile looking for signs of spring.

On Washington's real birthday, I saw my favorite sign, my first mountain bluebird, up at Curt Gowdy State Park. At almost 1,500 feet higher than Cheyenne, the advent of spring should be two weeks behind there. But skimming over the brown grassland at about 7,500 feet in elevation in late February is normal for mountain bluebirds. The northern edge of their winter range is only southern Colorado, so they don't have to travel far to be here.

Bluebirds are insect eaters, seen typically perched on a fence post or the tip of a shrub before launching themselves after a flying delicacy, or just hovering like a hawk, waiting to pounce on an unsuspecting caterpillar. Are there any live insects so early? A fly-fisherman, standing on ice on the edge of open water at Granite Reservoir that same day, seemed to think so.

Bluebirds, like their close relatives the Townsend's solitaire and American robin, will eat berries, but as we rambled the nearly snowless open country dotted with pine, the mountain bluebird's favorite terrain, the berries seemed few and far between. The bluebirds were also, so maybe it all works out. By the time the rest of the crew, wintering as far south as Mexico, heads back, insects should be hatching.

Other people may count the robin as their sign of spring. I used to, until I started getting outside more in the winter and realized there are always a few around, especially in riparian thickets with berries. I don't think they really count for spring until they show up on our lawns.

In lower country, too low for mountain bluebirds, I look for western meadowlarks. Maybe it's more precise to say I listen for them, though most of the time they are singing in plain view on a fence post. Perhaps they make a good first sound of spring because it means it's warm enough to have windows open.

You'd think that migrating birds would have some inside information on weather so they wouldn't start back until conditions were perfect. This isn't so. I remember an April a few years ago when we took John Flicker, newly appointed president of National Audubon, on a field trip around Cheyenne. Fresh snow glinted on everything that bright morning, and there, like a drop of frozen sunshine, was a dead meadowlark, yellow belly visible in a snowdrift.

Birds here year round make changes in honor of spring. Some, like the male house finches and goldfinches, get brighter plumage. Others start hanging around in pairs. On our February ramble, up above a rocky outcrop, I saw two ravens fly looping patterns in perfect tandem, as if performing a three-dimensional skating routine. A pair of mallards has been swimming quite cozily in the ditch by my house since mid-February.

The noise level in the neighborhood has changed too, or maybe I'm just not bundling up my ears as much. The house sparrows and house finches are really making a racket. It seems a little early to be defending nesting territories but having experienced spots of warm weather over the last couple months, maybe they are itching for spring as much as anyone.

I know I shouldn't tempt fate by mentioning this, but does it seem to you that in town the ground has been even more brown than white this winter? Though it is nice not to have to shovel often or watch snowbanks turn black and then turn into slushy reservoirs at every curb, are we missing anything, besides recharging the aquifer, by not having a blanket of snow to protect the prairie for the winter?

I hope you were careful about what you wished for on Groundhog Day, especially in the Arctic where aerial photography over 50 years has documented how a warming climate is thawing the permafrost and increasing woody vegetation.

Audubon Alaska executive director Stan Senner (you may remember his visit to Cheyenne years ago when he was director of Birds in the Balance) is quoted in the December 2003 issue of Audubon magazine, "Almost every Arctic nesting bird will be affected in some way by climate change. The northward march of woody vegetation may extend the ranges of birds like the Arctic warbler. But birds that nest in open situations, like the long-tailed jaeger, may be limited by more woody vegetation."

Who knows how a warming climate will play out here? Maybe we'll have mountain bluebirds regularly on the Christmas Bird Count. There is already a report for one in Wyoming as early as February 3 and one as late as January 1. If the bluebird season extends any further, what will I do for a sign of spring?

My cousin (once removed, I think) sent pictures from northern Wisconsin today of snow hip deep. I grew a little wistful – until I remember spring in snow country is mud season. I appreciate again living in what was once known, perhaps only prematurely, as the Great American Desert.

65 Prairie Partners provides for plains birds

Thursday, March 18, 2004, Outdoors, page C2

Say "observatory" and we think of astronomy.

Say "bird observatory" and first thing to come to a birder's mind is Point Reyes Bird Observatory, established in California in 1965. However, an internet search last week gave me 27 more bird observatories in the first 50 hits.

The one closest to home is the Rocky Mountain Bird Observatory (now Bird Conservancy of the Rockies), founded in 1988 and headquartered in Brighton, Colorado, at Barr Lake State Park.

The purpose of a bird observatory is the conservation of birds. Last month, Rocky Mountain Bird Observatory biologist Tammy VerCauteren gave a presentation in Cheyenne about her work as coordinator of the Prairie Partners program which exemplifies the observatory's mission of research, monitoring, partnership, education and outreach.

The shortgrass prairie, the western part of the Great Plains stretching from Canada to Mexico, including eastern Wyoming, was overlooked when concern was raised over the decline of bird populations nationwide – until recently, when it was discovered that prairie species are declining the most rapidly.

Research documenting the decline doesn't in itself help birds. Research that shows what is causing declines still won't help unless the information is passed on to the people who make land use decisions.

In this case, 70 percent of the short-grass prairie is privately owned, so Prairie Partners works not only with state and federal land agencies, but must work to reach farmers, ranchers and other landowners and managers.

Of course, land management suggestions need to be economically feasible to be taken seriously. With funding from various agencies and private foundations, Rocky Mountain Bird Observatory was able to publish "Sharing Your Land with Shortgrass Prairie Birds," a 36-page manual that describes the region's ecology, birds and management recommendations.

Some suggestions are as simple as not mowing at night during the two or three months ground-nesting prairie birds are resting on their nests. Others are more elaborate instructions for grazing strategies depending on whether the birds to be benefited prefer taller grass or no grass.

Mountain plover, a species once petitioned for listing as threatened or endangered, prefers to nest in heavily grazed, nearly bare situations and even in plowed fields. Rocky Mountain Bird Observatory offers to survey and flag plover nests two to three days before farmers cultivate. Advertising the Mountain Plover Number, 877-475-6837 (April 12- July 4), brought a good response last year. Tammy expects even more calls as word gets out. Just lifting machinery or avoiding the nest by a few inches is all that is necessary.

My favorite win-win recommendation is directions for building an escape ladder that allows birds that have fallen into stock tanks to climb out instead of drowning and contaminating the water.

In addition to consulting on bird-friendly practices, Rocky Mountain Bird Observatory knows where the assistance and money is for habitat improvements. While most farmers and ranchers are familiar with the 20 or so Farm Bill programs and working with the Natural Resources Conservation Service, there are also private lands programs through the U.S. Fish and Wildlife Service as well as cost-sharing assistance from the Prairie Partners program itself.

Of course, the most convincing information comes from peers. Tammy has organized workshops hosted by ranchers in which friends and resource professionals meet on the land. In addition to grazing and farming operation suggestions, one might hear about economic diversification, such as tapping into the cultural and wildlife resources.

For instance, getting listed as a site on the Colorado Birding Trail helps make more people aware of the benefit of maintaining land in agricultural production and brings revenue to rural communities offering services to travelers.

Rocky Mountain Bird Observatory's urban workshops, which bring people out to farms and ranches so they will understand where food comes from, have been immensely popular.

Also very popular is another Prairie Partners publication, "Pocket Guide to Prairie Birds." Measuring about three by four inches, it truly is a pocket field guide. Nearly all of 23,000 copies printed so far have been distributed for free, and Tammy is looking for funding to print more. Each of 86 prairie species has a clear photo, a range map covering the prairie states, a few of the most diagnostic markings needed for identification, and most importantly, a description of the species' favorite habitat and feeding practices.

A quick glance at the food icons on the bottom of each page shows that prairie birds are big on insects and rodents – the bane of farmers and ranchers. Perhaps we will be rewriting that song from Oklahoma about farmers and cowmen to read "Oh, the farmer and the plover (or harrier and the cowman)

should be friends."

The folks at the Rocky Mountain Bird Observatory are definitely the friends to make when it comes to doing something for birds on the prairie.

66 Young chickadees may be changing age-old songs

Thursday, April 15, 2004, Outdoors, page C2

Black-capped chickadees were the stars of the storytelling at the Cheyenne-High Plains Audubon lecture last month.

Dave Gammon, a doctoral candidate in the biology department at Colorado State University, was the storyteller. As all graduate students do, Dave had had the opportunity to ask a question and investigate possible answers and was now ready to tell his story.

To begin with, in deference to his major professor's expertise, he chose to study chickadees. While Dave observed a captive specimen in the lab, it proceeded to sing a variation on the standard "fee-bee" tune that they are known for.

Reading the literature regarding black-capped chickadees, Dave discovered a study that showed that all across the country, they have one song that sounds pretty much the same everywhere, except in certain pockets.

Dave discovered in Fort Collins, Colorado, the males have three songs (only males sing). Where others sing the standard fee-bee, these birds have added an introductory syllable for a second song Dave describes as "fa-fee-bee," or sometimes a third, "chick-a-fee-bee."

All up and down the Poudre River corridor, full of trees essential to chickadee habitat, the songs are similar, though there is a noticeable variation

from northwest to southeast. However, out on the prairie, in isolated islands of trees in small towns and on ranches, chickadees have added additional introductory notes to the "fa-fee-bee" song.

A lone bird on a ranch near the Wyoming border, which Dave recorded and nicknamed Ivan, was singing half a dozen introductory notes. To some extent, Dave recorded something similar among the chickadees at Guernsey in eastern Wyoming. Why does this happen and how does it happen? These were the questions Dave set out to answer.

He employed about 50 volunteers, who helped capture songs with dish microphones, and the good will of more than 20 landowners. He was able to incorporate and replay samples of those songs for us in his PowerPoint presentation as well as depicting them graphically as sonograms – lines representing the pitch, depth and length of sounds.

In chickadee culture, Dave said, the males are the first to rise. They sing without much notice of other males until they realize the females are awake. Then they stop abruptly and get directly to the mating business. Later in the day, singing is more a matter of declaring territorial boundaries.

Perhaps having a repertoire of more than one song type helps these chickadees communicate better. Many songbirds have more than one song and scientists seem to think it's an advantage.

Dave tested to see if different songs were reserved for females, the males' way of showing off, but could find no statistical evidence.

Perhaps defending males would match particular songs of aggressors or vice versa, sort of a "Your Mama" insult competition, escalating until fisticuffs – or at least wing beating – occurred. But unlike other bird species, there was no significant statistical difference.

Perhaps, thought Dave, these changes in chickadee song are merely accidental, the result of young birds making mistakes and never being corrected. Does humanizing that idea make parents responsible for the beginning of heavy metal music?

A chickadee nestling, Dave said, is born in a cavity of a tree, insulated from noise. During incubation and after hatching, he is unlikely to hear his father sing near the nest because it would attract predators. After a few weeks, the youngster leaps from the nest, never to return, and moves one or two kilometers away where he stays the rest of his life.

Normally, in prime chickadee habitat, where the woods stretch for miles, wherever the young chickadee lands, he will be surrounded by chickadee mentors. If he makes singing mistakes,

and he will – Dave has recorded juveniles really jazzing things up – he'll learn to conform.

But if any young chickadees ever disperse as far as old Ivan's lonely place, they'll probably wind up sounding much like him. What would their mothers think if they knew!

Apparently, there are other pockets of subversive chickadee song in an example of convergent evolution: Martha's Vineyard, Massachsetts; Puget Sound, Washington; Fort Lupton, Colorado; besides Guernsey. The only Cheyenne chickadees Dave found were mixed pairs of mountains and black-caps – another interesting conundrum.

And then one of the audience members, visiting from Casper, thought maybe her backyard chickadees might also sing "fa-fee-bee." Dave's eyes lit up.

The new questions are: How widespread is this phenomenon? How long ago did these breaks from the standard "fee-bee" occur? Will a multiple song repertoire eventually prove to be advantageous to chickadee survival and population growth? What new variations will this year's hatchlings come up with?

Dave would like to squeeze in one more chickadee field season. We hope wherever he lands his first job after earning his degree, it's in black-capped chickadee habitat.

67

Thursday, April 29, 2004, Outdoors, page C2

Companions, field guides help with bird identification

I am a social bird watcher, either out on an Audubon field trip or with family and friends. If I see a bird by myself, it's usually in relation to some other activity, like the opportunity I had to hike the nature trail at Hynd's Lodge up at Curt Gowdy State Park when I gave

my son a ride for a Scout event a couple weekends ago.

With husband Mark also away, I found myself on my own. So, having heard various glowing reports of waterfowl sightings at Wyoming Hereford Ranch Reservoir Number One, I decided to see for myself, by myself. I didn't even bring the dog who accompanies me on so many rambles.

My first stop at the west end of the reservoir gave me three American white pelicans on the island, surrounded by a flock of small indistinguishable birds standing in the shallow water.

The lighting was bad because the sun isn't very high at 8 a.m. mid-April and was shining in the spotting scope. The wind joggled it too and made my eyes tear. Apparently, the birds were sleeping with their heads tucked in, making identification impossible – for me anyway.

Normally, I would turn to other birders with better optics and more experience and say, "So, what do you think they are?" And then I realized, I hadn't even remembered my field guide. If you identify something fairly unusual on your own and want to report it, everyone else will examine your credibility before accepting it. That's why it's nice to bird in a group – plenty of backup.

It will be too bad if that flock with the pelicans turns out to have been some unusual shorebird. Most likely they were Franklin's gulls, including black-headed adults and a lot of pale-headed immatures – but I wouldn't bet my meager reputation on it. Don't even ask me about the duck silhouettes I saw.

Along the north side of the reservoir, at a better angle to the sun, field marks became useful identification tools again. There were northern shovelers (green heads and bright chestnut brown sides), northern pintail (white neck streak), American wigeon (wide white stripe from bill to crown), green-winged teal (red head with green over the eyes like a pair of fancy shades) and blue-winged teal (white crescent on each side of the face).

The passel of double-crested cormorants flying looked as streamlined as double-barreled shotguns with wings. One American coot flashed its white bill, but with its unique, chicken-like shape, I didn't need that field mark. An American avocet, white with pink and black markings, was stalking prey in the shallows on its long, thin legs.

By the time I got to the dam, more wind was making the water increasingly choppy. I was able to pick out several western grebes even though the gray water and whitecaps nearly camouflaged them. Between glassing the water with binoculars from inside the car and getting out with the scope, I lost sight of a pair of what probably were common mergansers. A window mount for the scope would have been handy, except the car was vibrating too much in the wind.

There were other birds I could confidently identify. Killdeer and red-winged blackbirds were providing background music. Mourning doves were decorating the fence. A belted kingfisher flew a sortie overhead, as did a northern harrier.

Below the dam, more ducks flew up from the creek and Canada geese struck statue poses, only their long black necks visible, appearing like iron pipes jutting up from the thick grass. Several turkey vultures coasted low while two Swainson's hawks held onto their cottonwood perches as the wind buffeted them. No warblers, probably too windy or too early in the season, but most likely because I didn't have the 20 extra pairs of eyeballs we'll have for our Big Count on May 15.

Farther up the road, the pastures were being flooded. Mallards dotted the short grass like rocks. I noticed one, and then another, though also of mallard hen brown color and size, they had extremely long legs – and very long, downcurved bills. Hmm, godwits, willets, yellow legs? Nope. Long-billed curlews. I checked my book when I got home.

I'm certain what I saw wasn't any outlandish species of curlew. The cinnamon brown of the underwings when one of the birds flapped clinched the i.d. If the meadow remains somewhat undisturbed this spring, a curlew nest wouldn't be surprising.

I survived my solo field trip. It was only five miles from home. Of course, my most amazing sighting was while pulling into my own driveway. Two Eurasian collared-doves flitted from the top of one of our front yard trees and over the roof of our house.

Still considered uncommon new immigrants to Cheyenne, I won't tell you how many hours we drove around town looking for them for the last Christmas Bird Count. There's a possibility these birds were similar looking, ringed turtle doves, someone's escaped pets, so I quickly put out some millet on the back wall to see if they would come back for more study.

I'm glad I went out so I could see the doves and all the other birds. Next time though, I'll bring the book.

68 West Nile virus frightens letter writer

Thursday, May 17, 2004, Outdoors, page C2

My bird phone calls this time of year usually concern identification of migrants or the inconvenient nesting of robins. Two weeks ago, however, a caller said she had received an unsigned letter from a neighbor asking her to stop feeding birds. The anonymous writer worried that birds concentrated around a feeder will contribute to the spread of disease, including West Nile virus.

While I abhor unsigned criticism, the letter writer did bring up points worth examining.

First, various bird diseases have been transmitted at feeders, including salmonella, and some of those are deadly for birds and or transmissible to people. That is why it is important to keep feeders clean and to quit feeding for several weeks if any sick birds are observed – whether lethargic or with facial tumors or other growths or sores.

My caller estimated she feeds five pounds of seed a day, so I said she should probably clean once a week. Scrubbing feeders with a solution of one part bleach to nine parts hot water is the usual advice.

Raking up seed hulls and any seed that has been rejected is important too. Buying sunflower seeds already hulled or making or selecting mixes minus unpopular seed such as milo can reduce debris.

Nectar feeders need to be cleaned every few days so that hummingbirds don't succumb to the lethal molds that can grow so fast in sun-warmed sugar water.

Summer bird feeding, as Francis Bergquist points out in an article in the May issue of Wyoming Wildlife magazine, is more for the pleasure of the bird watcher than the needs of the bird. Because birds have plenty of natural food sources available, stopping feeding for the summer is not a problem.

Providing a bird bath instead of food could be beneficial and entertaining, but may further antagonize my caller's neighbor because shallow, stagnant water is where Culex tarsalis, the mosquito responsible for Wyoming's West Nile virus woes, leaves its larvae to hatch.

Dumping out the bird bath water every three or four days will kill the larvae before they hatch, but other scummy organisms may need scrubbing.

At last week's Cheyenne-High Plains Audubon Society meeting, guest speaker Terry Creekmore, vector-borne disease coordinator for Wyoming Department of Health and head of the state's West Nile virus surveillance program, shed additional light on birds and the virus.

He said infected mosquitoes can infect birds, people and other animals when they bite. Birds are bitten on bare skin around their eyes and feet or under their wings. Rarely do human West Nile virus cases come from anything but mosquitoes.

Terry said certain birds, for the few days the virus is active in their bodies, can infect the mosquitoes that bite them. Laboratory studies of 30 bird species show several that can harbor enough of the virus to pass it on to mosquitoes: crow, blue jay, grackle, house sparrow, house finch, robin, red-winged blackbird, mallard and starling. These are some of our most common city birds.

Gus Lopez, director of the Laramie County Health Department, who also attended the meeting, was quick to point out that human infection rates are dependent on numbers of mosquitoes. With Laramie County's BTI-based larvicide spraying program and education efforts, the prevalence of the virus can be kept low, though not eliminated.

There is a slim possibility that West Nile virus, along with other diseases, can infect a person handling a sick or dead bird. To dispose of a dead bird, use a plastic bag like a glove, pick up the bird and then pull the bag over it, tie it shut, seal it in another bag and put it outside with your other refuse.

To find out if the state wants to analyze your dead bird and how to submit it, call 1-877-WYO-BITE. At Wyoming's West Nile virus website, www.badskeeter.org, check out all the statistics and advice.

Basically, the risk of getting seriously ill or dying from West Nile virus decreases with the increase in funds available for spraying in the area, with increasing dryness of the weather and with increasing distance from rivers, creeks and irrigation water. Young and healthy people are least susceptible to the fever and encephalitis that may result from infection. Bird feeding is not listed as a hazard.

In Wyoming, people are at more risk of death or injury from a traffic accident than from death or illness from West Nile virus. In 2003, 165 people died and 6,248 were injured in more than 16,000 traffic accidents. In that same year, only nine people died of West Nile virus out of 392 cases reported.

Just as you buy a car with safety features, wear your seat belt and drive safely, you can look for and eliminate standing water in such places as clogged rain gutters and avoid spending the evening mosquito hours outdoors or wear protective clothing and DEET insect repellent.

What about the birds themselves? Crows, ravens, magpies and the different species of jays seem to have the lowest survival rates. However, in the wild, any evidence of dead birds is quickly eaten, so the total effect of the virus is not usually directly measurable.

However, last summer, radio-collared sage grouse being studied for the impact on their populations of coalbed methane drilling inadvertently became subjects of an impromptu West Nile virus study when researchers found them dead or found their empty radio-collars. This summer, $1 million has been granted to begin a three-year study of the relationship between sage grouse, West Nile virus and the stagnant waters of coalbed methane discharge ponds.

The future looks brighter. The virus first appeared in New York City in 1999 and in Wyoming in 2002, but already there is a horse vaccine, and introduction of a human vaccine is only a couple years away.

Hopefully, birds that survive West Nile virus will be able to pass their antibodies on to their young so that eventually equilibrium will be established as it has in Africa, where the virus was first isolated in 1937. I predict a plethora of wildlife study topics for graduate students for quite some time.

69
Thursday, July 8, 2004, Outdoors, page C2
Mountain mud bothers birders, but not birds

Ever notice how often precipitation in Wyoming is dangerous? When temperatures are cold it forms ice and drifts, stranding people and animals.

When it's warmer, precipitation comes as fog, thunderstorms, hail, tornados and floods. This summer, we've been treated to the unusual – days of gentle drizzle. Drizzle, however, can make a malicious, muddy mess of roads, which it did in the latter part of June, on the eve of our Audubon chapter's fourth annual birdwatching camp out.

Just before Mark and I were due to leave home Friday afternoon for Friend Park Campground on the west side of Laramie Peak in the Medicine Bow National Forest, our boys drove in from the Boy Scout camp on the east side. "Slick roads, Mom!" they reported.

A quick call to the Forest Service district office in Douglas confirmed what we suspected, Friend Park was out of reach, but the Esterbrook campground was possible. That's where the Wyoming Native Plant Society was meeting Saturday morning, and we had already planned to join them later for dinner.

So I called everyone I had a number for and gave them the change in plans and prayed anyone else would be too much of a fair-weather birder or have too much common sense to chance the mud on the road into Friend Park.

Our birdwatching goal was to check out several types of habitat with Bill Munro, the district wildlife biologist, as our guide. We were particularly interested in burn areas that might attract uncommon woodpeckers. Two years ago, when we first tried to schedule the annual camp out at Friend Park, we got smoked out by the Hensel fire.

Our route along Horseshoe Creek was full of birds, including the spotted towhee, green-tailed towhee and lazuli bunting. These are birds I see in my Cheyenne backyard only during spring migration, and they made for bright and enjoyable identification practice for the novice birder in our group.

Two families of pygmy nuthatches scampered around the ponderosa pine branch tips. At only four inches long, it's a wonder these sociable gossips manage to be so voluble while stuffing their bills with insects for their young.

Almost all large soaring birds overhead were turkey vultures – the few others remained unidentified. Flitting in the willows along the creek were yellow warblers, robins, goldfinches, broad-tailed hummingbirds and cedar waxwings.

At a bridge, we found an American dipper working the stream. Scrambling around, we were able to find both its old and new nests stuck to the underside of the bridge. The other bird wading the creek, doing an imitation of a dipper, turned out to be a spotted sandpiper.

Sunshine and a veneer of mud on the roads dogged us all the way to the scout camp at Harris Park where we found a bird-full place for picnic lunch.

Our older son, Bryan, the camp's ecology director this year, showed us a recently deceased bird. Jane Dorn identified it as a western wood-pewee. Yesterday it had been lethargic, Bryan said, and today it was dead. Its lack of fat reserves led us to think that while the previous week's cold weather had kept flying insect levels down, it may also have contributed to the starvation of this particular flycatcher.

However, another kind of flycatcher, the Say's phoebe, its nest stashed under the eaves of the dining hall, seemed no worse for wear. House wrens were acting suspiciously like they had a nest in the tool shed, and the western tanagers, which Bryan said were nesting over the nature lodge, could be seen busily feeding, making up for lost time.

The Hensel fire had crept into the upper end of the camp in 2002, so we followed the Black Mountain road on foot through camp and out into the forest to explore the burn.

Someone earlier in the day had complained that there was no good, leafless, time of year to bird the coniferous forest, but here there was nothing but black trunks and a carpet of green splashed with wildflowers. It still was not easy, especially when the sought-after woodpecker species are mostly black and their white markings would be shining like sunshine on charcoaled bark. We found hairy woodpeckers, but no three-toed or black-backed.

For three of us, the Black Mountain fire lookout became our goal and we concentrated on the ascent rather than birdwatching, but we didn't miss the blue grouse unconcernedly grazing just off the trail. On the way down, it was much easier to observe the treetops and notice a Swainson's thrush singing the cascading melody we'd heard all day.

Evening showers while we shared potluck back at the campground made the trip down to pavement afterwards a bit of a nailbiter. So for next year, we've set our sights on another good birding location but with more gravel on the road: the Sierra Madres, on whatever weekend follows the July 4th holiday.

For those of you managing water supplies during this multi-year drought, we will entertain suggestions to plan a camp out in your area, but we can't guarantee rain, only good birds, good food and good company.

70

Brown-capped birds cause cracked ribs

Bird research can be hazardous to the researcher.

Just ask University of Wyoming zoology professor Dave McDonald's graduate student. She was poised high in the Snowy Range to ascend a crack in a rock with technical climbing gear to photograph a nest of brown-capped rosy-finches. It could possibly be the first such nest documented this far north.

Instead, a variety of emergency

medical technicians and sheriff's deputies became intimately familiar with the nest location because one of the student's pieces of climbing protection came out of the crack and she was dumped onto the jagged boulders several feet below.

Hours later at the hospital, she was diagnosed and treated for a dislocated hip and two cracked ribs.

The trip out was excruciating for her and her rescuers. Getting to the ambulance involved negotiating a snowfield and about a mile of narrow trail, which meant the litter, centered on the trail, left the bearers to scramble over rocky or boggy terrain on either side, huffing and puffing in thin air at over 10,000 feet in elevation.

The adventure actually began the day before, July 10, when the nest was first found.

Dave sent out an invitation to the Wyoming birding community to join him in a search for brown-capped rosy-finches.

To his surprise, about 20 people between the ages of three months and 70 years old showed up that morning at the Forest Service's Centennial visitor center.

About half were wildlife biologists on their days off, but everyone was anxious to see this bird, even if it meant hiking steep trails and terrain.

For many of us, the brown-capped rosy-finch would be a life bird, one we'd never seen before.

The Snowy Range, remnant of higher mountains embedded within the lower but more extensive Medicine Bow Range, has been designated a Wyoming Important Bird Area primarily because of its importance to the brown-capped rosy-finch, which is listed as a declining and rare species in the IBA site description:

"The site is the only area in the state of Wyoming where Brown-capped Rosy-Finches occur and breed. In addition, the species is considered a 'species of local concern' within the Forest Service."

Alison Lyon, IBA coordinator for Audubon Wyoming, devised a survey form which was handed out to all the observers.

Dave made suggestions for areas to search based on his previous observations.

This species of rosy-finch locates its nests in cliffs near snowfields. The melting snow attracts an abundance of hatching insects that make good food for nestlings. Other times of the year, rosy-finches are seed eaters.

Mark and I were lucky enough to observe one brown-capped rosy-finch for 20 minutes as it foraged among the rocks high above Lake Marie.

Imagine a milk-chocolate brown bird with raspberry-flavored sides. It was a life bird for both of us.

One group saw American pipits skylarking but no rosy-finches. Two others had several sightings and a fourth group had only rosy-finch fly-overs, but nearly stepped on a pipit's nest full of eggs.

It was a fifth group lucky enough to come upon the rosy-finch nest that would become infamous. First, they observed several birds fly and twice saw one disappear near a rock face. Getting closer, they were able to determine the bird was flying into a crack, and they were able to hear the chicks peeping. But then a snow cornice above them broke, hurling ice and rocks, and they had to make a run for it.

Brown-capped rosy-finch breeding populations center on the peaks of the Colorado Rockies, ranging north only a little way into Wyoming and south in winter only as far as northern New Mexico.

The black rosy-finch and the gray-crowned rosy-finch have much more extensive ranges across the west. By August, when their nestlings are on their own, all three species begin to gather in mixed flocks, eventually moving south or to lower elevations for the winter.

Banding data is just beginning to unravel the extent and timing of rosy finch travels. For instance, a gray-crowned banded in a yard above Lander one March showed up three days later at a banding station in Jeffrey City. Abandoned swallow nests in highway underpass tunnels near Laramie provide roosts after breeding season.

In addition to another survey next July, Dave is thinking about making a third attempt yet this summer to document the jinxed nest, but it won't be his grad student climbing up there.

She has plenty of rosy-finch literature to read and data to analyze from her field work with the other two species earlier this year, giving her time to heal completely.

71

Thursday, August 5, 2004, Outdoors, page C2

Windmills safer for birds than other structures

Birds and wind farmers think alike when it comes to maximizing the power of wind. Both are attracted to places like rims and passes where wind speed accelerates. Raptors (hawks and eagles) riding thermals and migrating passerines (songbirds) are the most likely species.

Unfortunately, birds may collide with the wind turbines and their towers. However, of the estimated 100 million to one billion birds that die in collisions with man-made objects every year, only one or two of every 10,000 are attributable to wind turbines, as of 2001. Communications towers and windows are much deadlier.

Greg Johnson, a wildlife biologist for Western EcoSystems Technology, Inc., an environmental consulting firm headquartered in Cheyenne, pointed me towards www.west-inc.com, where the studies he and his company have done on wind power and avian mortality are posted.

WEST has done studies in 11 states, but the one most interesting to me was for the Foote Creek Rim Wind Power Project built near Rock River.

In the first building phase, completed in 1998, 69 turbines were installed on 2000 acres of grass and shrub lands. Only 26 acres were disturbed by construction and five miles of road were built. Five meteorological towers were also installed.

Each 600-kilowatt wind turbine tower is 131 feet tall, and the blades have a diameter of 138 feet. Study plots were established at the base of each turbine and meteorological tower. Carcass searches were done every four weeks for all plots and every two weeks for half.

Results had to be adjusted for "removal bias" – how many carcasses were eaten or taken away by scavenging animals, and "searcher efficiency bias" – how proficient people were at finding dead birds or piles of feathers.

The study plots were salted with carcasses of non-protected birds such as pigeons, house sparrows and game farm birds, identified unobtrusively with duct tape, to see how many were found by searchers and scavengers. The searchers were 80 percent proficient. Scavenger success depended on the season.

Over the study's three years, carcasses of 122 birds of 37 species were found. The 69 turbines were responsible for 83, and the five meteorological towers killed 36 (three were unknown). Passerine species accounted for 112 birds (92 percent) and 36 of those were horned larks. Half the birds were probably migrants. Few mortalities occurred in the winter.

Overestimating bias, the average number of avian mortalities calculated was 1.5 per turbine per year. On the other hand, the meteorological towers each averaged 8.09 birds per year.

Mortality rates will obviously vary from site to site because of differences in bird abundance, species composition, landscape features and wind plant features. Right away though, one can see that making meteorological towers free-standing like turbine towers, rather than supported by guy wires, probably would reduce mortality.

In another study at Foote Creek Rim, researchers examined the avian mortality differences between blades manufactured with paint of high ultra-violet reflectivity, 60 percent, and the usual 10 percent of normal paint, but though birds can see UV light, that didn't seem to make a significant difference in this study. What did reduce mortality was larger, slower-moving blades.

One surprising finding of the first study was the number of bat deaths. One would think that bats, equipped with echolocation abilities, would be able to avoid towers and blades.

At Foote Creek Rim, 47 dead bats were found the first year, 18 the second and 14 the third year. Perhaps there is a learning curve. All were found during the summer, most in August. Considering bat hibernation and migration, that timing isn't surprising. But it is surprising that the turbines were responsible for all the deaths—none of the carcasses were found under the meteorological towers.

There's high bat mortality at other wind plants also. One hypothesis is bats send out echolocation signals less frequently while migrating. So how did they avoid the meteorological towers at Foote Creek Rim? Perhaps the explanation will be related to how the rotation of wind turbines befuddles radar.

Another question needing research: as wind plants begin to be developed in sage grouse habitat, will the increase in traffic have the same negative effect on them as it does in oil and gas developments?

Personally, I've been in love with windmills, with their symmetry and kinetics, ever since I spotted my first Chicago Aermotor in a pasture. Wind power has to be better for us and wildlife than bulldozed habitat, tailings piles, evaporation ponds and plumes of particulates.

To look at it another way, one of the Foote Creek Rim turbines can power at least 150 of our houses, according to the American Wind Energy Association calculations (www.awea.org), and probably more with Wyoming's notorious wind. How many more birds are killed by thumping into the windows of those same houses? But that's a topic for another day.

72 Warblers winging their way through on migration path

Early mornings mid-August get a chill snap to them that foreshadows September and indicates warbler weather – warbler migration weather.

A trickle slowly builds through the last week of August. By then, you can stare at almost any deciduous tree and see the flutter of the leaves, branch by branch, as these small passerine birds hunt for insects and other arthropods.

The migration will continue into October. The last warblers to leave will probably be the yellow-rumpeds. They don't mind eating berries when the insects die off. The other warbler species are stricter insectivores.

The best time to look for warblers is early morning. They migrate at night and come to earth by dawn quite ravenous. They flit frantically, as if they've had three cups of coffee on an empty stomach. It makes them hard to track with binoculars, especially since they all seem to be shades of yellow, greenish yellow or olive green – the same colors as leaves losing chlorophyll.

Identifying fall warblers can be tough since the adult males are no longer in their distinctive breeding plumage, the young don't have all their adult feathers, and the females are so subtly marked, they tend to look all alike. But if you identify them as Wilson's warblers around here, you could be right as often as fifty percent of the time.

The last weekend in August, our family attended the Rocky Mountain Bird Observatory (now Bird Conservancy of the Rockies) member's picnic at their headquarters in Barr Lake State Park near Brighton, Colorado. One of the activities was visiting a bird banding station in the park.

With newly banded birds in hand, RMBO staff member Arvind Panjabi was able to compare male Wilson's of different ages. The younger the bird, the more yellow-green feathers are interspersed with the cap of black feathers on the top of its head. For the females, the cap is just a gray-green smudge.

Arvind didn't think the Wilson's warblers being caught in the mist nets that day were the ones that spent the summer in the mountains. He suggested that these were the birds that nested in Alaska and Canada, and the mountain populations migrate later. No one will know for sure until more banded birds begin to be recaptured at other banding stations.

The different populations of Wilson's probably winter in different areas as well. Some go only as far south as the Gulf Coast and Florida, and some are found throughout Central America. Other warbler species spread out into South America.

Another activity at the picnic was a talk by RMBO volunteer Bill Schmoker about learning to recognize bird songs and calls. He claims bird songs aren't any harder to remember than snippets of popular songs, even bird calls of just one note.

It helps to see the bird which is singing or calling when learning new vocalizations. I had that opportunity to make a connection at the banding station when some of the Wilson's chipped loudly while being held. When released, they didn't fly far and continued their one-note chips from cottonwood branches overhead.

Back at home, with a window open one morning, my subconscious identified the same chip and sure enough, there was a Wilson's in the tree outside. However, even if it had never made a sound, I could have found it by following the stares of my two indoor housecats.

Warblers weren't the only species to be caught in the mist net while we visited. A young western wood-peewee modeled its cream-colored wingbars which will turn whiter with age. We were also afforded the treat (well, maybe you have to be a birder to enjoy it) of watching a Hammond's flycatcher, a petite bird, work to swallow a moth.

We have spring migration records for about 25 warbler species in Cheyenne from our Big Day bird counts, but we don't have a comprehensive count like that in the fall, and because there's no guarantee that what flies north will fly the same route south, we can't suppose all the same species will be here now.

However, we do have observations accumulating through e-mail postings to Wyobirds. One e-mail posted last week by Ted Floyd, editor of the

American Birding Association's magazine, after a visit to Cheyenne, listed yellow, yellow-rumped, Townsend's and MacGillivray's warblers and the common yellowthroat. Also, Vicki Herren, a Cheyenne-High Plains Audubon Society member, identified a Nashville warbler, considered a rare migrant here.

September is the height of the warbler season, so it isn't too late to get out and look for activity in the tree branches. By October, the show will be over except for a few stragglers and some of those berry-eating yellow-rumpeds hanging out as late as November.

The Sibley bird books are probably the best at elucidating the different species at this time of year. There's also the Stokes Field Guide to Warblers, though I haven't seen it yet myself.

But like not knowing the name of the driver on a country road who gives you a happy wave of the hand in passing, it isn't necessary to know a bird's name to enjoy that brief moment when it examines you with its bright black eyes before turning to clean another beetle from the branch.

73

Thursday, October 28, 2004, Outdoors, page C2

Duck days attract birders to local lakes

Great minds think alike, certainly the minds of the field trip chairs for Cheyenne-High Plains and Laramie Audubon Societies, Art Anderson and Rhett Good, respectively. Fall is a great time for duck watching and Hutton Lake National Wildlife Refuge is a great place to go. Thus, members of both chapters converged there Oct. 9.

It was a wonderful day to be outside. The dirt track of a road was almost completely dry. The wind was hardly enough

to ripple the water and didn't tear up my eyes when I peered through the spotting scope. Sunlight glinted off the Jelm Mountain observatory.

The refuge, southwest of Laramie, includes several lakes besides its namesake, all within practically a stone's throw of each other. They lie out on the Laramie Plains with hardly a tree in sight.

The refuge lakes are part of a collection spread between the Medicine Bow

Mountains to the west and the Laramie Range to the east. They are hollows blown out by the wind and filled with water naturally or with a little human assistance.

All birds that swim are not ducks, of course. The most abundant bird on the water was the American coot, more closely related to chickens than ducks. Completely black except for white bills, coots are easy to winnow out while searching for more interesting birds, but they can be fun to watch. Several were playing king of the hill on a pile of debris.

Ducks get easier to identify by October and November because they resume the brighter colors of the breeding plumage they discarded in May and June. Their summer feathers, called eclipse plumage, are drab.

Females are never easy to identify. Going by body shape is almost better than sorting through particular arrangements of brown feathers.

The easiest duck for me to pick out on this trip was the American wigeon. The light streak from the top of its bill up and over the top of its head was quite distinctive.

Someone pointed out a ruddy duck. If it hadn't been holding its tail in that diagnostic, peculiar upright position, I'm sure I would have given up. Unlike the other duck species males, its breeding plumage season runs much later, March through August. Right now it is gray instead of ruddy colored.

The male green-winged teal were easier to pick out, sporting a wing-shaped patch of green over each eye. Unless they fly, you may not see the speculum, or patch, of green on each wing.

Other ducks observed included northern shoveler, ring-necked duck, canvasback, gadwall, lesser scaup, redhead and only a couple mallards. Another non-duck waterbird, eared grebe, also made an appearance.

The first birders to arrive at the first lake were able to identify black-bellied plover and a bald eagle before they flew off. When the rest of us arrived, the long-billed dowitchers and American avocets were still probing the shoreline unconcernedly. Someone identified a California gull.

At a second lake, a sharp-eyed birder noticed that the motionless lump sitting on the hillside opposite was a ferruginous hawk. As we moved on, a prairie falcon crossed our path. Later, a red-tailed hawk gave a nice performance. Northern harriers, however, were the most common hawk of the day.

Canada geese aren't hard to identify, but every time a small flock flew over, we had to make sure they weren't the sandhill cranes we kept hearing off in the distance. Finally, when we stopped on a high spot overlooking the last refuge lake, someone was able to scope out four tall, pale gray beings in a distant pasture feeding on insects, rodents, seeds, etc.

While all optic equipment was focused on the lakes, other terrestrial birds were also noted: horned lark, song sparrow and marsh wren.

We left the refuge to check out other Laramie Plains lakes, but one was back lit and by the time we got to Twin Buttes Lake, wind was chopping at the water and only gulls were circling round.

When I got home, the new issue of Wyoming Wildlife had arrived, and perusing it, I came across mention of an online map of duck migration based on reports by hunters, www.ducks.org/migrationmap, on the Ducks Unlimited website.

Now that would be handy. I was thinking it might track migration so that I could find out how much earlier pintails and blue-winged teal migrate. But it isn't very specific, has no archives, and it needs a lot more participants.

So, we'll just have to get out and look for ourselves on local lakes, which I did the very next day, at Sloans Lake in Lions Park. With no one to turn to for authoritative identification, I scrutinized what I determined was a female ruddy. Three days later, birding with Cub Scouts, we scoped a bufflehead and a redhead, both ducks, though they don't use that noun in their official common names.

A week later, Mark and I identified eared grebe, pied-billed grebe and more ruddy ducks.

Lions Park was designated a Wyoming Important Bird Area for a reason. It's not just for mallards begging handouts. I'm looking forward to more trips around Sloans Lake to see what the season brings in.

74 FeederWatch returns

Website is a nest of information

The new Project FeederWatch season begins this Saturday, so if you've considered joining, sign up now and make the most of the yearly $15 membership fee.

This will be my sixth season reporting on the birds in my backyard (and front yard now too). In preparation, I visited the Project FeederWatch website last week to see what was new and to log on and update my information.

The Project FeederWatch home page is the portal to rich resources, even if you don't sign up to submit data. First, there are the headings across the top of the page, "About FeederWatch, Instructions, Data Entry, Explore Data, News, About Birds and Bird Feeding."

I skipped the first two, knowing already that this is a joint research and educational project of Cornell Lab of Ornithology, National Audubon Society, Bird Studies Canada and Nature Canada, attracting 16,000 participants last year who reported, either online or on paper forms, weekly or bi-weekly, over 3.7 million birds at their feeders. Some watch less than an hour each time, like me, and some spend hours at their window.

Project FeederWatch makes it easy for the rankest beginner to take part by sending a poster to help with identification, plus a handbook explaining bird watching, bird feeding and bird counting.

Online, the heading "All About Birds and Bird Feeding" is an even richer source of information. If all of you consulted this section, I may never get another phone call asking about bird feeding, making bird columnist a lonelier job. Topics include feed, feeders, tricky IDs, diseased birds, strange-looking birds, Bird of the Week and a link to an online field guide.

This last is a whole other wonderful website, AllAboutBirds. While this is no substitute for flipping book pages when comparing birds for identification purposes, it has detailed information on each species (not just feeder birds), from sound and video recordings to egg descriptions.

Besides the species accounts are these headings: "Birding 1-2-3, Bird Guide, Gear Guide, Attracting Birds, Conservation, and Studying Birds." This last is information on how to sign up for Cornell's famous Home

Study Course.

I found myself exploring the field guide quite a while before backtracking to the Project FeederWatch home page. Then I went to the "News" heading where vast amounts of data have been distilled into scientific reports and feature articles. But if you are feeling adventurous, try "Explore Data." That's where, among other things, I can access my own data submitted since 1999, neatly charted by year.

Again I got sidetracked. First, I looked up the map showing Feeder-Watcher locations last year – 21 in Wyoming including five of us in Cheyenne. Our state top 25 species list begins with house finch, followed by house sparrow, American goldfinch, dark-eyed junco, northern flicker and starling. Seventy species were reported, but some were one-time wonders such as mountain bluebird late winter. And some, like the bald eagle, hardly fit the definition of feeder bird. The reports of flocks of turkeys and chukars seem more like something from a gamebird farm.

While I was in the Map Room, I checked out mountain chickadees on animated maps of North America showing observation locations month by month and year by year. I also looked up the population trend graph and found fairly consistently over time that these chickadees visit 50 percent of participating feeders in the Northern Rockies, averaging three birds per count.

Back at the Project FeederWatch home page is a series of links down the left side. "FeederCam" will give me a live view of the feeders at Cornell in Ithaca, NY, when my computer decides to be more compatible.

"Participants' Corner" has a lot to offer, including photos and stories. My favorite anecdote was from a woman in Maine covered by a swarm of 30-50 chickadees on her shoulders and arms, and nuthatches on her head, when she stepped outside during an ice storm.

From the "Feeder-bird Quiz" I learned that the most commonly reported bird is the dark-eyed junco. The "Young FeederWatchers" link has charming artwork plus extensive coverage of Monty the (stuffed) Moose's trip to Cornell. His classmates in British Columbia, who participate in the classroom version, were able to observe him filling feeders through the FeederCam.

Along with various news stories on the home page, I noticed there will be a prize, including binoculars, for the FeederWatcher who submits the millionth checklist, expected to occur this season. Let's see, if I'm home for all my weekly counts, that will be 21 chances between now and the end of the season April 8.

Finally, I logged on with my personal password and number and updated my feeder site description so I'm all set for my first count day on Saturday. I'll do the usual, leaving paper and pencil on the table under the window so that any of us in the family can jot down what we see whenever we walk by – if it is a new species or a greater number of any species recorded earlier in the day. Later, I'll enter the data online.

I'm ready, and I know the birds are too. They ignored our feeders until that six-weeks-late frost/snow on Halloween. Maybe I'll put out millet for those Eurasian collared-doves still hanging around our neighborhood.

75 Going where the gulls are adds species to life list

It was obvious, based on time of which day and the location – early morning Saturday near a wetland in Fort Collins, Colorado, – that the flock of four Subaru Outbacks and five other fuel-efficient vehicles gathering belonged to birders, especially since one bore the plate "Skuas," referring to a type of oceanic bird.

Another clue was that about half the vehicles were then left behind in the parking lot.

Birders carpool not only to lessen the necessity of drilling for oil in the Arctic National Wildlife Refuge, but because we're sociable, and it's easier to share sightings while enroute. It's also easier to park where there isn't a lot of room to pull off the road, which was the case at our first stop at the edge of Long Pond.

A local resident stopped to inquire what we were looking for. With nearly a dozen scopes on tripods set up, we were either peering through the windows of the waterfront homes on the far side or checking out the birds on the water.

We were on a gull trip this mid-November day. Our leaders, Doug Faulkner and Tony Leukering, had the expertise and the optics to find something beyond the most common species of the plains, the ring-billed gull.

My expertise lags far behind, but at least I don't refer to them as seagulls. However, I wished I'd studied up the night before. Instead, I had to juggle my notes and my field guide with frozen fingers while gray chill also found my toes.

Squinting through my scope made my eyes water, increasing the difficulty of picking out how much black and gray marked the inside of a wingtip of a floating gull surrounded by a flock of common mergansers.

Birders, sharing observations of particular feathers seen from about 400 yards away, had it slightly easier because of the landmarks on the opposite shore, such as the green canoe, the overturned red canoe and the collection of chaise lounges.

Three gull species, herring, California and Thayer's, were identified. The Thayer's, normally an Arctic breeder wintering on the west coast, is considered rare in Colorado and has not yet made the records in Wyoming. I could add it to my life list, but not to my list of birds I can identify by myself.

Someone also picked out a large gull, white head with marbled brown body, and determined it to be a young great black-backed gull. It certainly was larger than the other gulls, and also far from home, the Atlantic seaboard.

As we wandered from lake to lake, we found a very pale gull normally seen along the northeastern and northwestern coasts of North America. The back of the glaucous gull lives up to its name which is Latin for a silvery, bluish color. I think I can add that species to my self-identifiable list, unless someday I have to compare it to the glaucous-winged gull, which strays much less often to Colorado and Wyoming from the west coast.

If you've only buzzed by Fort Collins on the Interstate admiring the snow on the peaks, or only shopped College Avenue, you might find it incredible that it's a hot spot for rare gulls. However, one look at a map more detailed than a road atlas shows you are in lake country.

The area at the foot of the foothills is pockmarked with ponds. All are man-made. Some reservoirs cover almost a square mile, making lakefront developments common.

Luckily, lakefront has been set aside in the Open Space system. One of our stops, Fossil Creek Reservoir, just west of the Windsor exit, has recently been developed for wildlife viewing.

No rare gulls at Fossil Creek, but I did pick up a new life species. The American Ornithologists' Union has very recently determined that the four smallest of the 11 races of Canada goose are now to be known as a separate species, the cackling goose.

Without DNA testing equipment, birders will have to depend on relative size, color and location for identification. Doug said the geese we were seeing were cackling, migrating through from their tundra breeding grounds. For a long goose discussion, go to www.sibleyguides.com.

I also saw a species that I thought was a genuine life bird for me, only to discover once home that I saw it in New Mexico 10 years ago. The greater white-fronted goose's name refers to its white face. Otherwise, it is blah gray-brown. But it's the orange bill, and orange legs if you can see them, which stand out in a crowd of cackling/Canadas. We counted six of them swimming in a line like the ducks on that pull-along toy I had as a toddler.

Like so many other field trips, this one was open-ended. A couple folks from Casper turned back around noon and a couple more of us from Cheyenne headed home around 2 p.m., the rest disbursing later. No new gulls were added without us, but we missed the trumpeter swan.

Tony said an increase in the sightings of rare gulls is partly due to increasing population and range thanks to people inadvertently providing more food sources, but also because more people are looking for gulls, and more people are capable of picking out the rare species.

To become a gull expert, I should probably invest in that huge book, Gulls of North America, Europe and Asia by Olsen and Larsson. But nothing takes the place of field observation and the patient mentors I've met so far.

2005

76 Resolution produces list of field trip destinations

Wednesday, January 5, 2005, Outdoors, page C2

Here we are at the top of the 2005 calendar, with a total of 53 Saturdays for field trips. This year has a bonus because it starts and ends on Saturdays.

My resolution is to get to know birds better by getting out more often. One of the best ways to do this is on organized field trips.

A week or so ago I was compiling a record of Cheyenne – High Plains Audubon Society field trips for the past 17 years. There is a noticeable, yearly pattern.

Unlike scheduling monthly chapter programs for variety, field trips thrive on return engagements. In bird watching, no matter how many days you visit the same place, any one of them could be the day you see an interesting bird behavior, a bird that's new for you, or rare for the whole birding community.

The field trip year for Cheyenne birders is anchored by two major events, the Christmas Bird Count, usually held the Saturday after Christmas, and the Big Day bird count held on, or the first Saturday after, May 15. Both events concentrate on Cheyenne, especially the two designated state Important Bird Areas, Lions Park and Wyoming Hereford Ranch. Both sites are representative of the city in general, a forested island on the plains, attractive to avian life.

What also attracts birds and makes a good field trip location is water, the centerpiece of both of those IBAs and most of the past destinations.

Time of year is also important. With the exception of the Christmas Count and excursions around town in January, mostly to combat cabin fever, admire chickadees and to see if there is any open water where a lost duck has unexpectedly dropped in, migration is the big draw.

Mountain bluebirds cruise in as early as February, and after that it's a steady stream of visitors. Things settle down briefly in June, but then in July, Arctic-nesting shorebirds have finished their parental duties and start the parade through Wyoming in reverse.

By November, birders are watching for stragglers, wondering if they'll stick around to be counted at Christmas and wondering also if later and later dates for the last observation of a migrating species reflects global warming.

With the advent of spring migration, and again in the fall, the chapter's constellation of field trip destinations is broader. To the west are Hutton Lake National Wildlife Refuge and all the other Laramie Plains Lakes.

To the east are sharp-tailed grouse dancing grounds and further east is the area referred to as Goshen Hole, a collection of public access areas in the vicinity of Hawk Springs Reservoir, such as Wyoming Game and Fish Department's Table Mountain and Springer-Bump Sullivan Wildlife Habitat Management Areas.

To the south are Pawnee National Grassland and the reservoirs along the Colorado Front Range.

The big reservoirs to the north, along the North Platte, Alcova, Pathfinder and Seminoe, are a little far for a day trip, but Murie Audubon members from the Casper area keep close tabs on them.

Though farther, Cheyenne birders are much more likely to make an overnight trek to Nebraska to see the sandhill crane migration sometime during the height of the phenomenon, between mid-March and mid-April. We're there more to enjoy the mass of birdlife rather than the diversity of species, but also cherish the hope we'll glimpse a rare whooping crane.

Come summer, water is still an attraction, but Cheyenne – High Plains Audubon members also begin to head for the mountains, just like the juncos. It looks like the Snowy Range survey for brown-capped rosy-finches will be repeated after last summer's success.

Then there's the annual chapter camp out which over the years has met more weather-induced obstacles than the Christmas Count. We've tried twice to hold it at Friend Park, at the foot of Laramie Peak, but the first time we got smoked out by a forest fire and last year the mud was too deep.

This year, the plan is to schedule the camp out for July 8-10 and headquarter it at Battle Creek in the Sierra Madres. The gathering of birders will be put to work looking for nesting flammulated owls and purple martins.

One of the enjoyable past camp outs was to the Saratoga area. Several Wyoming Game and Fish Department public access areas, Treasure Island, Foote, and Saratoga Lake, are in the North Platte River valley, featured in the annual Platte Valley Festival of the Birds June 5-6.

Other areas with public access administered by Game and Fish are cataloged in their publication, "Access to Wyoming's Wildlife." Reviewing the table of contents is like reading the names of old friends, stirring up memories of many family outings, with or without Audubon.

Bird watching is a classic example of what can be a solo recreational pursuit. But the advantage to an organized field trip is that someone is bound to know something more about birds than I do, which is a much better way to learn than by reading, especially since local knowledge of local birds may best that of a book written for all North America.

I don't know yet how many return engagements will be scheduled by the chapter this year. Each will be a welcome reunion, if not an adventure to some place new.

Wednesday, January 19, 2005, Outdoors, page C1

77 Bird seed bandits

How hard can it be to outsmart squirrels?

Fox squirrels are a by-product of bird feeding in Cheyenne. While they are cute and fuzzy and entertaining, the ones attracted to my yard have also been destructive, crashing bird feeders and stripping tree bark, not to mention stealing food meant for birds.

Originally, Cheyenne had hardly any trees and no tree-type squirrels. Birds had no competition at the feeder until, the story goes, somebody imported a few squirrels from Nebraska.

Much thought by people who feed birds has gone into outwitting squirrels. The problem is they seem to adapt to all our strategies to exclude them. Fighting them off is a bit like fighting an infection with antibiotics. Do you use the lowest level of technology that will do the job for now, or do you use a well-fortified feeder to begin with? It all depends on your means and patience.

Feeding birds in Cheyenne is as simple as throwing black oil sunflower seed on the ground. It's everybody's favorite, and you'll get a wide assortment of seed-eaters including sparrows, juncos, finches, chickadees and nuthatches – and eventually, squirrels.

The first level of advice often given is to offer squirrels their own feeding station stocked with favorite foods, such as dried corn. Many companies offering bird feeders also offer a platform on which to spike a whole ear.

Baffling the wee beasties

However, with five furry and frisky eaters now gnawing on my trees, I'd rather not attract them to my yard at all. Putting sunflower seed in a tube, hopper or platform feeder protects it only somewhat from squirrels.

These kinds of feeders can be set on a pole, especially if you live where the wind tends to dump seed out of hanging feeders, but sooner or later the squirrels learn to shimmy up the pole.

Commercially made baffles are available that mount on the pole below the feeder. Some look like large, upside down, plastic salad bowls, so perhaps you can drill a hole in the bottom of that extra one you got for a wedding present.

Ruth Keto said greasing her feeder pole with canola oil has worked well so far in her Sun Valley neighborhood. It's not certain yet how often the oil needs to be reapplied to keep it slippery, or if it's actually a matter of fastidiousness which the squirrels will eventually overcome and finally get their paws dirty.

In our yard, we tried slipping a 6-inch diameter plastic pipe over our feeder pole before setting it in the ground. The same length as the pole was above ground, it worked because the pipe is too big around for the squirrels to get a grip – until the plastic weathers and the surface becomes rougher.

Lela Allyn has a solution that recycles two-liter pop bottles. She cuts a hole in the bottom of a bottle the diameter of the pole, then slits it all the way up the side. She slips the bottle around the pole and tapes up the slit. It takes several pop bottles, starting at ground level, to bypass the distance squirrels in her Cheyenne backyard have learned to jump.

Pop bottles applied to Lela's clothesline in the same way have protected feeders hanging from it. Any squirrel stepping on a pop bottle will cause it to spin and the little seed burglar will lose its footing.

Feeders hanging from the arm of a pole or tree branch are usually invaded from above. Once again, a dome-shaped baffle, this time hung above your feeder, could solve your problem, whether commercially produced or of your own invention. These also serve a secondary purpose in partially protecting the feeder from snow and wind.

Caging the consumables

Putting your feeder in a cage is another way to keep out squirrels. It also has the benefit of keeping out large birds, such as grackles and blackbirds, which may monopolize feeders.

Our family bought a Duncraft sunflower seed tube feeder in 1993, and it is still in good shape. It came with a plastic-coated wire mesh fence around it, capped by a plastic roof and a plastic tray at the bottom. The wire mesh had big enough openings for a small bird to reach the seed ports, but not a squirrel.

After years on the pole protected by the plastic pipe, we moved it to a tree branch in the front yard. In only a couple weeks, we caught a squirrel wedging itself under the roof and between the tube and the cage.

An inspection of new Duncraft products at a local store showed we could buy the new version with a presumably squirrel-proof locking mechanism on the cap of the tube, plus metal roof and tray securely attached to the mesh.

Instead, we bought a new cage. This is complete with a wire top and bottom, and it will fit most tube feeders. The top opens with a presumably squirrel-proof latch so that you can fill the feeder. The handle of the feeder fits through a slot when the cage is closed. So far, so good. Of course, it's only been a few months.

Small wire cages are sold for holding blocks of suet. Woodpeckers and chickadees, which normally like to eat insects, are attracted, but so are squirrels. We had one of these suet feeders, but the birds never had a chance at it. The squirrels hung from it and nibbled. Finally, they unlatched it so the whole block fell out. I see in a catalog there's now a big cage just for hanging a suet feeder inside.

Platform feeders attract ground-feeding birds that will not tackle a tube feeder. Dark-eyed juncos are ground feeders, though they will use a platform four feet in the air. Cage adaptations are available commercially, but I'm thinking I could fix something over the top of our shelf feeder. It has to be removable so the feeder, like all feeders, can be cleaned every few weeks to avoid spreading bird diseases.

Duncraft has come out with a platform feeder guaranteed squirrel proof, based on the theory that squirrels need both paws to grasp a seed. They claim they have a metal grid with spacing too close together for two paws in one opening, but large enough for bird beaks. The platform is entirely metal so the squirrels won't chew their way in to the booty. How long will it take them to learn to use their paws to scoop seed instead?

For about as long as we've had that sunflower tube feeder, we've had the same brand of tube for niger (also spelled nyger) thistle seed. This seed is very fine and needs ports, or tube openings, that are very small. Luckily, they automatically exclude squirrels and large birds in favor of the thistle-eating species with thin bills such as goldfinches and pine siskins. That's good, because thistle seed is quite a bit more expensive than sunflower seed, and I'd hate to waste it on squirrels.

On the other hand, if you enjoy feeding the increasing numbers of Eurasian collared-doves, and the mourning doves when they come back in the spring, you are out of luck. Cage methods probably won't work well because the doves are about the same size as the squirrels, and the squirrels like the doves' favorite food, white millet.

Springing surprises

One obvious solution to the squirrel problem is to decimate the population. However, without the proper licensing, this may be against the law in the ordinary backyard. Instead, members of the bird feeding community have become quite inventive and several have patented their anti-squirrel technology.

First, there's the Twirl-a-Squirrel Electronic Baffle I saw in a catalog. The weight of the squirrel activates a motor that starts twirling your tube feeder until the squirrel falls off. I think it's only a question of time before one of them figures out how long it has to hold on before the batteries die.

Another battery-operated feeder, by Duncraft, actually zaps squirrels with electric current they say birds can't feel.

Then there's the Yankee Flipper by Droll Yankees. This operates on batteries also, but it flips the squirrel off. For $10 you can buy the action-packed video that shows how effective this feeder is. Recently, the company added the Yankee Dipper, Yankee Tipper and Yankee Whipper, which all use the principle of perches that collapse when a large enough animal lands on them.

Then there is spring technology. Hopper feeders are roofed containers filled with seed that spills out a crack at the bottom where it is caught on a tray, or perhaps the seed is available through a series of ports along the bottom while birds perch on a bar. Barbara Costopoulos of Guernsey loves her spring-loaded hopper feeder. She has it adjusted so that the weight of a squirrel will close the ports.

Another of her feeders is by the Perky-Pet company. It looks like a square tube feeder wrapped in metal fencing and decorative metal leaves.

When a squirrel lands on a perch, the metal fencing, attached by springs, is pulled down and a leaf blocks each seed port, like the portcullis on the entrance to a castle.

Quality counts

If no one has been feeding birds or squirrels in your neighborhood for a long time, you may be able to get away with a lightweight feeder – for a while.

The first time we hung a feeder in our front tree, it was a Mother's Day gift from the boys, bought with their meager allowance. First the squirrels took the cap off the tube and reached in for the seed. Next, when the seed level got too low, they began breaking off chunks of the thin and brittle plastic tube so they could reach farther in. Finally, the feeder was knocked to the ground. Destruction was complete in about two weeks.

Paying for quality is cheaper in the long run. But don't forget to protect your investment. Use eyebolts and snapping clips so your hanging feeders can't be swung loose by squirrels or wind. Save your money for bird seed.

Bird feeding information:

Check out Cornell Lab of Ornithology's Project FeederWatch Web site, and also the book, The FeederWatcher's Guide to Bird Feeding.

78 Fox squirrels pose ethical, biological problems

Wednesday, February 2, 2005, Outdoors, page C2

Just minutes after e-mailing the Jan. 19 Birdseed Bandits story to the Wyoming Tribune-Eagle Outdoors editor, I watched as a squirrel extracted sunflower seed from my tube feeder while it was hanging inside its supposedly squirrel-proof cage.

The squirrel hung from the outside of the top of the cage by its hind feet, stretched full length and reached through with its front paws for one of the tube's lowest seed ports. The squirrel's weight caused the cage to tilt sideways, but the free-hanging tube within remained vertical and the end of it touched the side of the cage. That the squirrel found a weak spot in my defenses does not surprise me.

I'm also not surprised a story about keeping squirrels out of birdfeeders generated several kinds of responses. One reader, in Billings, Montana, reminded me of the red pepper cure. Squirrels hate it and birds can't taste it. However, she said keeping enough on the bird seed is a lot of work.

A Casper reader said he has a 95-percent effective system. He hangs his feeders from a horizontal steel cable with baffles between, above and below feeders.

A reader from Greeley, Colorado, wanted to know why I didn't mention live-trapping. He said he's released problem squirrels as far away as Casper and Cheyenne. Gee, thanks a lot! Obviously, this solution only changes the location of the problem, not to mention moving live wildlife across state lines is illegal.

Wyoming Game and Fish Department warden Mark Nelson, stationed in Cheyenne, encourages anyone wanting to borrow a trap and legally move a squirrel to call him at 638-8354.

Outside city limits, where hunting fox squirrels is legal, one needs a state small game license. Gun and bow season is Sept. 1 through Dec. 31, though for falconers it is year long.

Then a local caller who feeds 12 squirrels a day, without apparent harm to trees, asked why I was so intent on decimating them. Personally, I like the little imps. I just hate seeing the many places on our trees where they've stripped the bark. Lisa Olson, city forester, said squirrels feed on the cambium layer, the layer responsible for tree growth.

According to the American Society of Mammologists, fox squirrels also eat other tree parts: seeds, fruits, buds and some flowers. They are particularly fond of acorns, walnuts, pecans, etc., but since Cheyenne doesn't offer a lot of nut trees, I'm thinking they've latched on to bark instead. On the plus side, they prune my trees nicely while gnawing off twigs for nest building, meaning fewer visits required by an arborist.

The Billings reader reminded me squirrels will also eat baby birds and bird eggs, a fact documented by the mammologists society's paper, and an additional reason to consider the effects on the balance of nature of a species that was brought by people to our city.

The problem with feeding squirrels is that if we supplement their diet, they are likely to produce more than the average three pups per litter and even nest twice a year. Good nutrition equals increased fecundity which can mean increased population and increased tree and bird damage.

There are some people who might point out that Cheyenne's historic vegetation, except along the creeks, was treeless. But for those of us who appreciate trees and are too kind-hearted not to feed the squirrels and won't or can't hunt them, we need to look at their natural predators. Dogs and cats kill them too, but kindhearted people don't allow that to happen.

In the simplified version of the perfect predator-prey relationship, as the prey species population increases, predators move in and/or finding more to eat, are able to produce more young.

Eventually, the effects of their higher numbers outstrip the prey population's ability to reproduce. Normally the predators do not get every last squirrel. Instead, they starve, leave or produce fewer young than average or don't reproduce at all. With less hunting pressure, once again prey numbers begin to climb, and the cycle begins again.

Wildlife managers have learned that a healthy population fluctuates.

Hunting, collisions with cars, power line electrocutions and disease also limit squirrel populations, but at least with natural predators, we have more watchable wildlife. Those species mentioned by the mammologist society I've seen within Cheyenne's city limits are red-tailed, ferruginous and rough-legged hawks, great-horned owls and red foxes.

There's a chance that my squirrel problems are localized. If I keep spilled seed cleaned up and keep squirrels out of the feeders, they might move on. If, however, it is a city-wide problem, we need to look at how to attract more of the natural predators. Besides food, they want a place to nest or den safely. How about adding a crossing guard or tunnel for those foxes that insist on navigating Dell Range Boulevard?

It is unlikely Cheyenne will ever be without fox squirrels. As another of many species affected by human action, intentional and unintentional, will nature find a balance for squirrels which people can live with? Some say bird feeding also presents ethical wildlife problems, but that's a discussion for another day.

79 Are condors coming closer to home?

Wednesday, February 16, 2005, Outdoors, page C2

If seeing is believing, can you believe what someone else is seeing?

In January someone reported seeing a California condor in the Alcova area. The news was reported second hand on the Wyobirds e-list with a follow up of another second-hand report about a second person's observation. As I usually do when confronted with obscure or unusual species, I checked records in Wyoming Birds by Jane and Robert Dorn.

No condors are listed in the Dorns' second edition, or in the 2004 edition of the Atlas of Birds, Mammals, Amphibians and Reptiles in Wyoming available from the Wyoming Game and Fish Department. The Wyobirds posting refers to two Wyoming records, and although I've sent an inquiry about them to the author of the posting, I have yet to receive a reply. When I asked Jane, she thought one of the records referred to was one so very old that it was impossible to establish the credibility of the witness.

Greg Johnson, a local wildlife biologist with a good network of professional contacts, remembered hearing about a condor seen at Flaming Gorge awhile back.

The California condor is an endangered species. Ten thousand years ago it ranged across the southern United States, but by the time of European settlement, it was found only in a coastal strip from British Columbia to Nuevo Leon, Mexico.

By the 1930s it was confined to central California. The last wild condor was trapped in 1987 and joined 26 others in a captive breeding and reintroduction program in California. Some of the condor's survival problems still exist: collisions with power lines, shootings, lead poisoning from feeding on carcasses of animals that have been killed with lead shot as well as the killing of young condors by eagles and coyotes.

However, a reintroduction effort

in northern Arizona back in 1996 has been very successful. Condors released there are courting, nest building and in the last two years, have fledged three young birds.

Apparently, one of the Arizona birds, Condor 19, took a two-week trip north in August 1998 and followed the Green River. In the Peregrine Fund's archives of field notes, researcher Shawn Farry reports being contacted by Loren Casterline, an adult who was with Varsity Scout Troop 1834 at Kingfisher Island in Flaming Gorge Reservoir Aug. 6. The site is in Utah, five miles south of the Wyoming line.

While the scouts swam, the condor left a perch 100 meters away and landed within several meters of Casterline (condors are known to be curious about humans), but then his movement caused the bird to take off over the lake. A Fish and Wildlife Service news release mentions "Flaming Gorge, Wyoming," so perhaps there was another observation.

Condor 19 returned to the Arizona release site seven days later, making a total round trip of at least 600 miles. The U.S. Fish and Wildlife Service agent in Casper, Dominic Domenici, contacted Arizona about the new reports and learned that the whereabouts of two immature condors was unknown.

Condors are fitted with two radio transmitters – one on each wing – but ordinary radio telemetry used for locating wildlife doesn't work for a species capable of ranging as far as the condor. As funding becomes available, one of the radio transmitters on each bird is replaced by a solar-powered, satellite-based one that reports Global Positioning System fixes, or locations.

Locations are transmitted every hour through the day and then the data is e-mailed every evening to researchers, conveniently plotted on a topographic map. Apparently, the missing condors are not wearing the improved technology. How likely is it a condor really has visited the middle of our state? Unlikely, say the Arizona researchers, but not impossible.

The second observer is said to have been able to make a direct comparison with a nearby eagle, but depth of field can play tricks. None of the other Casper birders combing the area saw any condors. Turkey vultures have a wingspan of 5½ feet, eagles are at 6½, while the condors are at 9½ feet. Though condors have a red-skinned head devoid of feathers like a vulture, their bodies are 46 inches long – 20 inches longer than the vulture's.

Adult condors have a black and white pattern under their wings that is the reverse of the silver and black pattern for vultures. Immature golden and bald eagles have white under-wing markings, but an immature condor has none.

The way to make a rare bird report more creditable is to have more people see the bird and to photograph it. At this point, the sightings remain unconfirmed. If a formal report were to be submitted to the Wyoming Bird Records Committee and accepted, what would it mean? It would mean a condor has scouted the neighborhood. Whether or not it leads to return trips and breeding records for a future edition of the Atlas, only the condors can tell.

80 New doves coming to a feeder near you

Pine Bluffs has that clean, scrubbed look of a small town on the treeless Great Plains – the look that comes from the cleansing effect of strong wind.

But on the side of the Lincoln Highway, 40 miles east of Cheyenne, is a small house cozily set in a thicket – a haven for birds.

Velma Simkins said she's lived there since 1933, when she and her husband bought the house as a young married couple. They planted the trees and shrubs.

She called me the other day for help identifying strange doves feeding on the seed she puts out. She's familiar with the Johnny-come-lately species, the Eurasian collared-dove, but thought these were different. Since a traveling birder reported white-winged doves in nearby Burns last year, my husband Mark and I decided it was worth looking into, but by the time we could check a week later, the strange doves were gone. We decided to make the drive anyway and meet Velma.

It wasn't hard to find her house, across from huge steel grain elevators. Sixteen Eurasian collared-doves were perched on nearby utility lines. A few blocks down another dozen of the pale gray doves with black marks across the backs of their necks were perched near another grain storage facility. Not a pigeon in sight. Have the doves run the pigeons off?

Velma said the only pigeon she sees is a pet belonging to the neighbors. There haven't been any pigeons since the old elevators were replaced. I imagine new, tighter facilities probably give pigeons less access to food and means may have been taken to eliminate them entirely, since they are one of three introduced bird species that can be controlled (the others are house sparrow and European starling).

So why are there Eurasian collared-doves in the vicinity? Are they hardier or smarter? We are still learning about this Middle East species that successfully colonized Europe, was later brought to the Bahamas as a caged bird where it escaped in 1974 and soon made its way to Florida and beyond. The similar looking ringed turtle-dove has escaped frequently but has not prospered or expanded its range beyond a few urban areas.

The first Cheyenne record for the Eurasian collared-dove was the Big Day Count in May 1998. Now they can be found regularly. I counted a flock of 20 in my neighborhood last summer, but there seemed to be fewer mourning doves. Perhaps the collared-doves, which are year-round residents, are getting the jump on the native migrating mourning doves when it comes to claiming good nesting habitat.

Eurasian collared-doves first show up on the 87th (1986-87) Christmas Bird Count, but in only two count circles. By the 103rd count they were observed in 263 circles. The earliest observation for Project FeederWatch, an annual, winter-long count, was 1995, but another was not recorded again until 1998, and then every year after that.

The Great Backyard Bird Count held in February 1999 recorded collared-doves in eight southeastern states. This year's map shows the western frontier as a curve stretching from southern California up through Idaho and points east, though it seems to have skipped Nevada.

Kenn Kaufman notes in his book, "Lives of North American Birds," that in Europe, in warm climates, this species raises up to six broods a year. That's only one or two young each, but the young have a habit of dispersing long distances. They feel at home wherever there are large trees and open ground.

What about that other dove, the white-winged dove? It is a bulkier, darker gray bird with large white wing patches that become crescents when the wings are folded. It is a native species expanding its northern most limits, traditionally the southern edge of the southwestern states. Kaufman mentions it as an important pollinator of giant saguaro cactus.

There are a few records for Wyoming, one going back to 1954. But if the observations in northern New Mexico and Colorado are any indication, we'll probably be seeing more of them.

I visited with Ron Ryder, retired Colorado State University wildlife professor, and he said scientists are looking into this explosion of doves. Eurasian collared-doves have been observed in just about every county in his state, even in inhospitably cold places like Gunnison and the San Luis Valley.

They are flocking to grain elevators like pigeons, he said, noting a recent posting on Cobirds, the Colorado bird watchers' e-mail list. It mentioned a flock of 200 Eurasian collared-doves, with a few white-wings in Flagler, Colo. He also mentioned wildlife managers are discussing listing the Eurasian collared-dove as a game bird. As an introduced species, it is not protected by the federal Migratory Bird Treaty Act.

The word "invasive" conjures up rapacious, economically debilitating species like kudzu, zebra mussels and leafy spurge. But other than apparently displacing a few mourning doves and pigeons, no one is sure yet what this wave of immigration will mean if it continues.

Kaufman said in his 1996 book, "If it spreads in North America as it did in Europe, the Eurasian Collared-Dove may soon be among our most familiar backyard birds."

Gosh, what will the robins think?

81 Callers: Give a hoot

Wednesday, March 16, 2005, Outdoors, page C2

Birders need to know etiquette of calling

A windless winter night is a good time to call for owls. Their response is only muffled by traffic, barking dogs, shifting feet and blood rushing in your eardrums.

The February evening the Cheyenne – High Plains Audubon Society sponsored an owl outing attracted a field trip record of 31 local listeners. I'm guessing popularity was due partly to owl mystique and partly because the evening followed an unseasonably warm day.

Calling owls has been immortalized by the children's picture book, "Owl Moon," the story of father and child crunching over the snow on a moonlit night. On our outing, starlight was soon washed out by a huge orange moon just past full, however, snow was hard to come by.

We didn't have anyone willing to imitate an owl, so we used recordings.

First, we played the northern saw-whet owl several times, with pauses in between to listen for responses. We then moved on to long-eared, eastern screech and great horned owls. Starting with the largest would have inhibited smaller owls.

The chapter had another owl outing five years ago, but this time I heard concerns about its effect on the owls.

Calling owls or any other bird is actually a form of avian harassment. It works because birds respond to an intruder on their territory. Songbirds tucked away in leafy shrubbery will respond to the vocal sound birders make, "pish, pish." It sounds like the avian alert signal, so they come out to see what's going on.

You can understand why frequently antagonizing birds into alarm mode is not good. The American Birding Association states in its Code of Birding Ethics, "Limit the use of recordings and other methods of attracting birds, and never use such methods in heavily birded areas or for attracting any species that is threatened, endangered or of special concern, or rare in your local area."

Cheyenne birders hardly ever resort to pishing or recordings, and I was surprised once when a birder from out of state on one of our field trips started playing calls. As a birder friend said, "It seems like a cheesy way to bird," in a recreational situation.

Calling owls is a time-honored way of surveying for them, however. Jennifer Bowers, a local wildlife biologist, told me about her experience listening for Mexican spotted owls in Apache-Sitgreaves National Forest in Arizona.

From the end of April to the end of July, her workday started at 4:30 p.m. with a hike into the backcountry, arriving at the beginning of one of many survey routes about 7 p.m. One kind of survey involved stopping at predetermined intervals and hooting. I can just imagine the interview for this job. Bowers said it's difficult to demonstrate hooting over the phone – it's rather loud.

The other type of survey was to hoot where a pair of owls was known to nest. By the end of the season, the young were noticeable.

The surveys took about an hour or two, depending on the amount of paperwork generated by responding owls. The biologists were usually back at the field camp around midnight, only to get up and do a willow flycatcher survey at 4:30 a.m.

Inconveniencing Cheyenne owls once every few years for the sake of education is worthwhile, I think. But this time we decided to limit our calling to areas we visually survey on the Christmas and spring counts.

Apparently, we weren't disturbing very many owls. We tried calling among the big trees at Lions Park. We tried out Crow Creek where we'd seen great horned owls last year. Nothing. By then some of the neophyte owlers must have thought we were crazy.

We had one more stop to make, the High Plains Grasslands Research Station, where we had written permission to visit that evening. We parked along the road near the entrance and before the last car door closed, people with better hearing than me heard a saw-whet.

We walked along the road until the calls became more distinct. While great horned owls are often seen on our counts on the piney island of the station, Jane Dorn, who has surveyed it for about 25 years, recalls only one other saw-whet. She said this time of year they are migrating through to their preferred nesting habitat in the mountains, so that's why we wouldn't find them on the Christmas count or the spring count in May.

Saw-whets are tiny, only eight inches long and not even three ounces. The great horned owl is 22 inches and three pounds. I can only surmise that an owl that calls constantly as this saw-whet is advertising for a mate and unconcerned with a larger owl making a midnight snack of it.

We had a beautiful moonlit evening outdoors and we gained new information. Also, it will be a long time before any of us forget the northern saw-whet owl's call. Now that we know it, we may start hearing what we would have otherwise missed before we could distinguish it from all the other night sounds.

Wednesday, April 27, 2005, Outdoors, page C2

82 Sharp-tail trip seeks out the other grouse

As the driver of the last car in the caravan, I expected whatever the attraction was that had caused lead driver Bill Gerhart to pull over to the side of the gravel road would be even with or ahead of him.

The goal of our Audubon chapter field trip was finding sharp-tailed grouse north of Hillsdale. In the dimness before sunrise on this calm, mid-April morning, I searched the pasture ahead for any movement on the lek.

Leks are dancing grounds, where males come back every year to congregate, display and compete for females as the females hang out at the periphery. When I finally caught a flash of movement, it was even with my car. How nice for my passengers who had never seen sharp-tails before.

Mention grouse around here lately and most people think immediately of the sage grouse. Technically known as "Greater Sage-Grouse," it is in the news as a declining species in the way of oil and gas drilling.

The image of the sage grouse male in full display appears in wildlife publications regularly. He has two large, yellow-skinned, inflated air sacs embedded in a drooping white neck ruff and a fan of spikey tail feathers.

The sharp-tailed male, on the other hand, has just one spikey point to his tail, and no white ruff, though he does have small purple air sacs on either side of his neck.

Because sharp-tails don't make the news as often as their relatives, I asked Kathleen Erwin, a wildlife biologist with the U.S. Fish and Wildlife Service office in Cheyenne, about them.

Though their population has declined, they are not in as much trouble as sage grouse, she said, except for the Columbian sharp-tail, a sub-species that prefers mountain shrub habitat found in south-central Wyoming and other western states. It is being petitioned for addition to the list of threatened or endangered species.

As so often is the case, the changes to native habitat are a problem. However, sharp-tails will adapt to using cropland more so than sage grouse. We saw two fly over fresh green shoots of winter wheat on our field trip.

Bill, a Wyoming Game and Fish Department wildlife biologist as well as one of our trip leaders, said the Conservation Reserve Program started in 1985 encouraged the reseeding of cropland with grass species for erosion control and provided a good base for sharp-tails to rebound.

Drought is a factor right now,

Kathleen said. The grouse need enough vegetation to hide their eggs from predators. Their nests are mere scrapes on the ground. Drought also cuts down on the number of insects available to feed the young right after hatching, before they grow into the adult diet of mainly seeds, buds and leaves.

The development of native prairie habitat also brings new predator species that the birds aren't used to, said Kathleen. Converting prairie to houses brings domestic cats and more skunks.

And then there's the competition. Ring-necked pheasants brought in by game bird farms will push sharp-tails out, said Kathleen. Later on our trip we had an excellent view of two cocks of this Asian species fighting on the side of the road.

Sharp-tails are a resident species in southeastern Wyoming as well as grasslands extending north into Canada, which means you should be able to see them any time of year. But they are a lot easier to find in spring on leks.

The six or seven sharp-tails we found were completely oblivious to us as we watched from our vehicles.

The males held their pointy tails erect, stretched their stubby wings horizontally and with head down, stepped rapidly in little circles, advanced on their rivals or retreated. The white of the undersides of their tails was the only contrast to the color of the dry grass landscape or the rest of their feathers that are also the color of dry grass.

With our windows open we heard tail feathers rattling and the weird cooing sound as the males deflated their air sacs. When the orange globe of sun slipped over the uncluttered line of the horizon, all the photographers were happy.

This particular morning it was we who left first, rather than the birds, to search out other leks. Often, the shadow of a passing hawk sends all grouse airborne. While a hawk in flight is often favorably compared to a fighter jet, flying grouse are the epitome of short-winged, big-bellied bombers. They prefer to flap and glide, and never far from the ground.

In late April, we are now part way through the pageant of spring migration. The snow geese have come and gone, and the warblers and shorebirds are just now showing up. If we miss the ducks, we'll see most of them again in fall migration. But the grouse show is mostly finished. Many people view sage and sharp-tail leks every year and some, wildlife biologists as well as volunteers, perform surveys.

Every year we hope they find good news. Otherwise, it could forecast the future demise of something more important than just another roadside attraction.

For a copy of Habitat Extension Bulletin 25, "Habitat Needs and Development for Sharp-tailed Grouse," call Wyoming Game and Fish Department, 777-4600.

83 UW researchers seek hummingbird secrets

Wednesday, May 25, 2005, Outdoors, page C1

Hummingbirds are captivating creatures.

Bradley Hartman Bakken, a Ph.D. candidate at the University of Wyoming, can entertain an audience for an hour with his PowerPoint show of fascinating hummingbird facts.

For instance, hummingbirds can flap their wings 30 to 80 times per second and their tiny hearts beat 500 times per minute at rest and 1,200 when active. They are the only birds or vertebrates that can fly backwards.

But Bakken didn't come to the study of hummingbirds through the pursuit of trivia. His interest is in the physiology of kidneys, and he began working with hummingbirds as an undergraduate under the guidance of Carlos Martinez del Rio, a professor in the Zoology and Physiology Department.

Bakken discovered that hummingbirds use – or actually don't use – their kidneys in a unique way.

They live almost entirely on flower nectar, except for the occasional bit of protein from a passing insect.

Because nectar is mostly water and hummingbirds need a lot of sugar, they must expel a lot of water. Bakken said if humans drank as much water as hummingbirds in proportion to their body size, they would die – their kidneys would be overwhelmed.

But hummingbirds and humans are both able to lose water through breathing and evaporation through their skin.

Hummingbirds are just much more efficient. Because they are so small, their proportion of skin surface to body volume is very high. Humans, being bigger, have a much lower ratio so sweating doesn't help us as much.

In fact, hummingbirds give off so much sweat, another hummingbird researcher, Ken Welch, a visitor to UW from the University of California Santa Barbara, said they smell like wet dogs.

The only time hummingbird kidneys kick in is when the birds are feeding, Bakken said. They don't use their kidneys overnight since they can lose as much as 11 percent of their body weight just by evaporation during that time anyway.

If humans lost as much, they'd be in a coma.

Bakken has been working with captive broad-tailed hummingbirds. His next step will be to determine the effect of a lower surface to volume ratio in a larger hummingbird. He travels this fall to Santiago, Chile, for three months to study the giant hummingbird. This larger bird weighs 21 grams and is similar in size to a sparrow – dwarfing Wyoming's broad-tailed hummingbirds that only weigh about 3.5 grams. [Later, he'll look into nectar-feeding bats in Mexico.]

Scott Carleton, another UW doctoral candidate, also works with hummingbirds to explore the physiology of energy use.

"They have the highest mass specific metabolic rate of birds," he said, "and they're easy to study – it's all nectar."

Carleton wanted to know whether hummingbirds operate more on stored energy or on the energy that comes directly from nectar.

Because the sugar from sugar beets has a different carbon isotope signature than cane sugar, the breath of a hummingbird can be analyzed with a mass spectrometer to determine how much of which sugar it is burning.

The hummingbird is fed one kind of sugar and then switched to the other. The first sugar, stored as fat, produces one isotope and the other, burned as it is consumed, shows the other.

Welsh traveled to Wyoming to spend three weeks here this spring to answer a similar question. He demonstrated how his research subject takes a sip of nectar from within a mask that analyzes the carbon dioxide and oxygen in its breath. The results appear instantly on a computer graph.

What fuels a hummingbird when it takes its first sip of the day?

It appears that within five minutes the bird fuels hovering flight totally on the sugar it is ingesting. Humans also make use of sugar quickly when exercising intensely, but still have to get 50 percent from stored energy.

The researchers also found that caged hummingbirds, which are less active than those in the wild, are able to maintain their weight when tempted with a constant source of sugar water. Except twice a year, Bakken said.

Even though day length is controlled and never changes for his hummingbirds in the laboratory, they tend to put on extra weight in the spring and fall as if in preparation for migration.

Bakken said this could be in their genetics and not just a response to day length or temperature.

Hummingbird facts

--331 species of hummingbird are found in North, Central and South America, but fossils of modern-type hummingbirds from 30 million years ago have recently been found in Germany.

--Ecuador has the most species, 163, and the U.S. has 19. Wyoming has black-chinned, calliope, broad-tailed and rufous hummingbirds.

--The rufous migrates farther than any animal when comparing distance to body weight. In spring they migrate from Mexico along the coast of California to Alaska, then return south via the Rocky Mountains in July and August. If a 6-foot man took as long a journey proportionate to his size, he could make 13 trips to the moon and back.

What to feed hummingbirds

Wyoming wildflower nectar is 80 percent water, so make yours four parts water to one part sugar. Use red feeders, but don't dye the nectar. Use only regular table sugar – either cane or beet sugar but not honey since it's too waxy and could carry mold spores.

84 Local bird checklist makes its debut

Wednesday, May 25, 2005, Outdoors, page C2

Trumpets please!

The long-awaited "Checklist of the Birds of Cheyenne, Wyoming and Vicinity" is now available at the Cheyenne Audubon website and at local Audubon events.

The checklist has the names of 324 species seen in the Cheyenne area, including season and abundance information for each.

It's a handy guide for boasting. For instance, in our backyard this spring we've had white-crowned sparrows for several weeks. The checklist shows the species as "C," or common, in spring and fall migration. But it gets an "R" for rare in winter and not observed at all in summer.

A field guide's 1-inch square range map of North America for this species makes it hard to tell specifics for our location. The description may mention that white-crowns spend the summer in the mountains, which explains why they aren't here then. But there's no wow factor for white-crowns in Cheyenne in spring.

On the other hand, the lesser goldfinch that spent an hour at our thistle feeder last week gets a wow. It's marked as rare during spring and fall migration and has not been reported any other season.

A local checklist is an invaluable aid to any birders new to an area or traveling through. It keeps them from calling the state bird hotline for sightings of the yellow-headed blackbird, for instance. It's a common bird here, but rare on either coast.

For us locals, the checklist gives us guidance on which warblers to study before spring migration or which sparrows to pick from when faced with an identification challenge.

It's also a useful way to check off – hence the name 'checklist' – which birds you've seen in Cheyenne. You could have one copy of the list for each year, one for each field trip and one just for your backyard.

If you don't write down every bird you see while peddling the Greenway, reading the list when you get home will jog your memory.

Where, you may wonder, does the information for this checklist come from?

This index to local birding was compiled by three members of the Cheyenne-High Plains Audubon Society. Jane and Robert Dorn, co-authors of "Wyoming Birds," have 25 years of Cheyenne birding experience documented by extensive notes. Co-compiler Greg Johnson is close on their heels in expertise.

Whether to list a bird as abundant, common, uncommon or rare is a judgment call and every checklist has its own definitions.

For this one, expect to observe an "Abundant" species almost every outing with little effort, in appropriate season and habitat. Think house sparrow, house finch, western meadowlark, red-winged blackbird, European starling and American crow.

"Common" means some effort may be required to locate the species – like the American goldfinch, Swainson's hawk, great blue heron, American coot.

"Uncommon" means considerable effort is usually required – or serendipity. These include the ruddy duck, ferruginous hawk, Eurasian collared-dove and belted kingfisher.

"Rare" means that the species is difficult to find because of low numbers and/or secretive habits. I hope that the Laramie County Community College birding class members realized how lucky they were to see a black-necked stilt a couple weeks ago.

There's also the category "I" for introduced species such as northern bobwhite, an escapee from game bird farms. The category "V" stands for vagrant – birds blown off course during migration – like the painted bunting for which we've had one or two sightings in the last 25 years.

In addition to his avian expertise, Greg digitally formatted the checklist. He is also the one who has his phone number on it for receiving updates and additions.

There's a distinct advantage to modern technology when compiling and publishing a checklist.

First, it's easy to update. Greg will never have to re-type any of the 324 bird names unless the American Ornithologists' Union changes them.

The biggest advantage is that no one has to fund the printing of hundreds of copies – and then get stuck with them when they need updating.

While the chapter will have a limited number of printed checklists available, anyone can go to the website to print their own. Portable document files, PDFs, print up cleanly, without any Internet tag lines. And the checklist is formatted for standard paper size.

I was not happy when I tried to piece together a legal-sized checklist for

Juneau, Alaska, I found on the Internet last year.

Of the checklists I've collected from around the country, some are printed on cardstock, some on slick paper with color and some cost a dollar.

But for a sponsoring organization like Audubon for which one of the goals is education, it doesn't make sense to restrict access to a great learning tool like the checklist.

Last year Greg agreed to be chapter compiler and was the one to finally bring the checklist to life. I'll have to ask him if he has any great ideas for the next step. That would be taking all the random bird sightings and getting them into a publicly accessible internet database.

But right now is the height of migration. Time to get out there, checklist in hand.

Wednesday, July 20, 2005, Outdoors, page C2

85 Flamm Fest finds record number

Kim Potter undeniably deserved to be crowned Queen of Flamm Fest earlier this month. Like other queens, she displayed talent – a talent for finding flammulated owl nests.

Having honed her skills in Colorado, Potter was able to find a large aspen with a hole 20 feet above ground. By lightly scratching the bark she got a female flammulated owl to come to the entrance. Because it was the second weekend in July, we were certain that Kim had found the first documented nest in Wyoming.

Flamms are tiny – less than 7 inches long and weigh just over 2 ounces. They are 5 inches shorter and weigh less than half the amount of the northern flickers that make many of the holes the owls nest in. Flamms prey on insects, especially moths, by inspecting infested trees.

Their name probably comes from an old word that means "with flame" as some appear to have a reddish brown color. Flamms are a western mountain species, although they are seen at low elevations during migration. The U.S. Forest Service considers them a sensitive species.

Several years ago, Rocky Mountain Bird Observatory biologists Doug Faulkner and Rich Levad made a list of bird species that had not been documented in Wyoming but which they felt should be here because of the similar habitat the birds use in neighboring states.

With their knowledge of preferred flammulated owl nesting habitat in Colorado, Rich and Doug made an educated guess that other RMBO biologists confirmed when they found a flamm in the Battle Creek area three years ago.

Historically, these owls have been considered rare, but most likely their camouflage coloration, small size and quiet hoots made them easy to overlook.

Thus, we created Flamm Fest, the nickname given to the fifth annual Cheyenne-High Plains Audubon Society campout. Our mission was to spread out and see how many more flamms we could find.

Just about every one of the 31 participants, ages 11 and up, got a good look at one, either the female or, on Friday night, a male responding to Kim's tape. She was demonstrating the survey techniques we would be using the following evening.

We divided into nine teams and each was assigned a route to drive. At half mile intervals the recording was played and surveyors waited for an answering hoot.

The road our group was to travel was closed to vehicles so we set off on foot at twilight, only to discover a culvert was missing over a wide stretch of icy water. Everyone crossed with different degrees of dryness.

On the way back we walked without turning on flashlights and stopped every 500 paces to call for owls. We did have a response from a saw-whet owl, but no flamms.

Five of the teams were luckier and counted a total of 10 flammulated owls. At a lot of the survey points it was too windy or too close to running water to hear return hoots. At some points the habitat was very different. But it is just as important to know where the owls are not as it is to know where they are.

Other owls that responded or were seen were long-eared, eastern screech, great horned and possibly a pygmy.

During daylight on Saturday, we checked out the only known colony of purple martins in Wyoming. They also like old flicker holes in old aspen trees.

The whole grove was aflutter with several other cavity-nesting species: mountain bluebird, red-naped sapsucker, house wren and tree swallow.

Purple martins in the west are a different subspecies than those in the eastern part of the country. The westerners don't use manmade apartment-style bird house complexes – but then no one has ever put one up near where they live in the forest. We looked for other colonies but didn't find any.

One unexpected bird was a bushtit down along the shrubby lowlands of the Little Snake River valley. Both the tiny round bird and the spruce tree it nested in were completely out of their normal forest habitat.

We were also very close to the state line. A GPS reading may show the nest is a latilong breeding record for Colorado. But the bird itself, since it flew over the fence marked "Wyoming State Line," will at least be a Wyoming observation record.

Our Flamm Fest campers were from an unexpected diversity of locations. From Wyoming, 19 people represented Cheyenne, Casper, Lingle, Riverton and Saratoga. We also had birders from the Denver area, western Colorado, Salt Lake City, Rapid City, New York City, Washington, DC and Chicago.

If a simple Cheyenne chapter outing and the lure of flammulated owls can draw this group, who knows whom we'll find on next year's campout to the Bear Lodge in the northeast corner of the state.

Also, what species might we find?

Broad-winged hawk, golden-winged warbler, yellow or black-billed cuckoos and black-backed woodpecker are some of the Black Hills specialties not found elsewhere in Wyoming.

We've got to find another catchy title – and maybe a trophy if Kim joins us again and proves to be Most Valuable Birder.

.

2006

86 Of birds and beetles

Woodpeckers find silver lining in devastation done by insects

Are they the feathered equivalent of American Red Cross volunteers? Or are they just looking to build a home a short commute from where they make a good living?

Whichever best describes them, American three-toed woodpeckers and black-backed woodpeckers show up in forests that are under siege from bark and wood-boring beetles.

Not only do the birds make homes in dead trees, they make meals out of the beetles and their larvae, filling an important niche in the ecosystem there.

Other woodpeckers in Wyoming, including flickers, sapsuckers and downy and hairy woodpeckers, are fairly common, but the three-toeds and black-backeds are quiet and hard to detect.

The three-toed woodpecker can be found in most mountain ranges in the Cowboy State, but the black-backed sticks to the northwest corner of the state and the Black Hills in the northeast.

Outside the state, the range of both species covers forests in much of Canada and interior Alaska plus the Rockies in the northern United States.

Recently, three-toed woodpeckers in North America were split into a species

separate from those ranging from Scandinavia to northern Japan.

The birds are relatively unknown despite pages of references for studies of three-toed and black-backed woodpeckers listed in "Birds of North America."

Many of the three-toed studies were done in Scandinavia; it isn't known if the findings hold true in North America.

A relationship with beetles

The three-toed and black-backed woodpeckers both have three toes that help them rise to the challenge of finding wood-boring and bark beetles.

Other woodpeckers have four toes, two facing front and two facing back.

These three-toed specialists use a different stance and grip on a tree trunk that gives them greater force in drilling than all but the much larger pileated and ivory-billed woodpeckers.

Other general woodpecker-evolved adaptations are: stiff tails used as props; long, sticky tongues; and skulls with built-in shock absorbers to withstand all the hammering.

While they might make huge holes to find beetles deep inside the tree, the woodpeckers also can scale or peel off the bark to find beetle larvae.

The birds put their nests in dead

trees, called snags. This takes them a few weeks, but a pair will do it once a year.

Old nest holes then are snapped up by bluebirds, chickadees and other cavity nesters that don't have the beaks for the job.

In an average forest, there are always a few trees in decline that provide beetles for a few woodpeckers. But then Mother Nature provides a bonanza every so often when wildfire strikes.

Possibly both birds and beetles can smell the smoke. Beetles are on the scene of the fire within a couple of weeks, and black-backed and three-toed woodpeckers are right behind them.

Steve Kozlowski, a U.S. Forest Service wildlife biologist in Laramie, said three-toeds are normally at such a low density that you are lucky to find one on any given day. But after the Gramm fire near Foxpark in 2003, 14 were seen in one day.

Trees in distress

Even in healthy forests, beetles congregate where a single tree is succumbing to disease, lightning strike or windthrow, said Jeff Witcosky, a regional entomologist with the U.S. Forest Service in Golden, Colorado.

Old-growth coniferous forests are more vulnerable to beetle kills because young trees have better defenses against beetles.

One way that beetles might find distressed trees, Witcosky said, is through hydrocarbons known as terpenes that are given off by injured tree tissue. The beetles may be able to sense the compounds with their antennae, he said.

In lodgepole pine forests stressed by drought, mountain pine beetles might randomly land and chew bark before deciding whether to attack or try another tree.

Although there is about one beetle for each species of coniferous forest tree, the different kinds of beetles can be lumped into two main groups.

The bark beetles, favorites of three-toed woodpeckers, lay their eggs just under the bark, where they hatch as rice-grained sized larvae that chew little tunnels in the tree's cambium, or growing layer.

These traceries in the layer that would become the newest tree ring eventually reach all the way around and prevent sap from moving between roots and needles, killing the tree. When the bark falls off, the tunnels look like shallow etchings in the wood.

The other general category includes all the wood-boring beetles. The larvae of the beetles, favorites of black-backed woodpeckers, eat deeper into the wood. Growing as long as 1½ inches, when they reach the adult stage they chew their way out, fly off, mate and deposit eggs under the bark of another tree victim.

These beetle life cycles can last from one to three years, depending on the kind of beetle. All that time, they are at the mercy of chisel-billed birds that like beetle larvae more than any other insect flesh.

Surrounded by acre upon acre of lodgepole, ponderosa pine or spruce, how does a woodpecker search efficiently for hidden food?

Doug Faulkner, University of Wyoming bird biologist, said it would make a good master's thesis project to find out.

Do the birds key in on other signs of a tree's distress? Can they smell the same terpenes that attract beetles?

Jane Dorn, co-author of "Wyoming Birds," said she has heard larvae chewing when she's close enough to an infected tree. Woodpeckers presumably have better hearing than people.

Populations fueled by fire

Arvind Panjabi, a bird biologist with Rocky Mountain Bird Observatory, spent several years studying the effects of the 85,000-acre Jasper fire that burned in the Black Hills National Forest in South Dakota and Wyoming in 2000.

In the areas of ponderosa pine that burned the hottest, black-backed woodpeckers increased tenfold and peaked the second year after the fire.

Because the Hills are isolated, Panjabi guesses the boost was due to an increase in reproduction rather than the unlikely scenario of birds flying in over hundreds of miles of grasslands.

Because the woodpeckers at a burned area are eating well and are at maximum good health, they lay larger clutches of eggs. But the boom lasts only three to five years.

No one is sure what happens to the increased numbers of woodpeckers if another part of the forest isn't burning by then.

The bark beetles eaten by three-toeds seem to prefer singed spruce trees. But within a few years these burns lose their appeal and the beetles also have to leave for blacker pastures.

Panjabi found that in the Black Hills, numbers of Lewis's and red-headed woodpeckers in the burn area continue to slowly increase even as the three-toed and black-backed are decreasing.

Sometimes, black-backeds and three-toeds on a new burn have competition in the form of salvage logging of burned trees. They must be harvested within six months to make good lumber, but without burned trees there are no beetles and no birds.

To share the bounty, wildlife biologists recommend leaving groups of snags standing. Single snags spread out won't support these two species of woodpeckers. Neither will clear cuts.

It is important to be accommodating since without regular woodpecker numbers, normal beetle populations might grow out of hand, forest ecologists say.

Wyoming forests are currently experiencing beetle epidemics too large for woodpeckers or people to control. Beetles are not only attacking sick trees, but apparently healthy ones as well.

The only sure control, Witcosky said, will be a long enough episode of extreme cold which will kill the larvae. Winters have been too warm lately.

87

Wednesday, February 1, 2006, Outdoors, page C2

Bird flu and you, so far, so good

Bird flu is everywhere I look. The virus keeps popping up in the news and has even become the punch line of jokes.

Bird flu is also, literally, everywhere. Wild birds can carry many subtypes of Influenza A without getting sick, but some can be deadly for poultry like chickens, turkeys and ducks. Wild ducks mingling with domestic ducks are thought to have sparked the ongoing bird flu epidemic in Asia and eastern Europe.

Not all bird flu viruses are highly pathogenic, but the subtype making the news, H5N1, is deadly to poultry. Ninety to 100 percent of infected birds die within 48 hours. During the Asian outbreaks in 2003 and 2004, flocks were also killed by farmers and officials to try to control the spread of bird flu. It has not yet spread to birds in the United States.

In 1997, the first cases of humans infected by poultry surfaced in Hong Kong. The risk to people from bird flu is normally low, but of 140 reported cases of people with H5N1 since the beginning of 2004, about half have died. So far, no people have contracted it in North America.

As of Jan. 7, human cases are being reported in Cambodia, China, Indonesia, Thailand, Vietnam, and Turkey.

But it's a good idea to practice poultry hygiene, especially because of all the other avian-transmitted diseases. So don't breath near a sneezing duck, don't wipe a chicken's nose and don't touch your face with your hands after cleaning the chicken coop. The U.S. Centers for Disease Control recommends poultry workers wear protective suits and treat all birds as if they are infected.

Most of us don't come in contact with live chickens, a sad commentary on the disconnect between consumer and food source, but it is possible to contract bird flu from inadequately cooked poultry from countries presently dealing with outbreaks. You'd have to travel to those countries to eat it since the U.S. has embargoed their unprocessed poultry products.

Bird flu vaccines are in the works, but meanwhile people should get regular flu shots, say experts at the CDC. Should bird flu come to the U.S., you have a better chance of survival if you are in good health. Plus, there's a slight chance that if human flu and bird flu come together in the same host, the dreaded evolution may happen – bird flu transmissible from human to human. It has apparently happened only once so far, between a mother and a closely-held child.

We birdwatchers are also concerned with the ramifications of bird flu. Two dozen Asian wild bird species have been reported to have died from H5N1. However, there are no cases yet of the virus being transmitted from wild bird to human.

What does worry us is how migrating birds will spread H5N1. So far, birds from "infected" countries have not spread it along migration routes through Taiwan, the Philippines and Australia.

We backyard birders also want to know if it's safe to continue feeding birds. It is, as long as we follow the precautions we've always had to promote the health of birds and birdwatchers.

Keep bird feeding areas and feeders clean. Disinfect them every few weeks with a mild bleach solution and rinse well.

If you notice a sick bird, stop feeding. A sick bird acts lethargic, has feathers out of place, is fluffed up more than the other similar birds or might have crusts around its eyes. Clean up spilled seed and debris, then disinfect and put away your feeders for a week to encourage healthy birds to stay away.

Take precautions for your own health, remembering that there are other diseases carried by birds, including West Nile Virus and salmonella. Never handle birds, dead or alive – or anything full of bird droppings – without disposable gloves or plastic bags over your hands.

Be careful not to breathe the dust when sweeping up old seed hulls, and keep your hands away from your face until you can wash them well.

Now that I've assured you that you can safely eat chicken and feed birds in our country, that's not to say that new wrinkles in bird flu won't develop while this edition of the Outdoors section is going to press.

Since sound bites can be maddeningly uninformative for people with above average interest in a topic, let me recommend the CDC website, www.cdc.gov/flu/avian. I found it to be informative, clearly written and frequently updated with advice, especially for poultry workers, travelers and people caring for bird flu patients.

For people who work with wild birds or hunt birds or mammals, information from the National Wildlife Health Center's Wildlife Health Bulletin #05-03 is extremely useful. Find it at www.nwhc.usgs.gov/research/WHB/WHB_05_03com.

The media and the experts frequently look back to the 1918 global flu pandemic to try to forecast what will happen when this strain of bird flu evolves the potential to transfer from human to human.

Hopefully, the disadvantages of our modern global mobility will be offset by the advantages of modern science, medicine and communications. Meanwhile, do something to protect yourself. Promote your personal health. Take a walk. Go birding.

88 Research station is, should be for the birds

Wednesday, March 1, 2006, Outdoors, page C2

From a bird's eye view, Cheyenne is an island of trees in a sea of grass.

During migration it makes an ideal place for a layover. More than 150 species of birds were identified in one day mid-May by members of the Cheyenne - High Plains Audubon Society.

We stick to places with public access such as Lions Park and get permission to visit the U.S. Department of Agriculture's High Plains Grasslands Research Station west of town, where 170 bird species have been documented over time by Bob and Jane Dorn.

The station began as a federal horticultural research facility in 1928. Earlier, the city of Cheyenne had acquired a 649-acre section from the state for the Round Top waterworks. It obtained another two sections through trades and sales with local landowners including Zelda Ketcham and Minnie Cox-Brown. It then leased just over 2,000 acres to the federal government for 199 years.

Many of the experimental trees and shrubs there still survive and will become the basis for a future arboretum sponsored by the Cheyenne Botanic Gardens. However, a large part of the station is grassland. This suits the station's mission as of 1974, which is to study rangeland management.

Last November, I learned the city planned to annex their station property with an ordinance stating:

"That the City of Cheyenne is dedicated to keeping all of this land in the public domain as land of community wide significance. Should the USDA see no further use on all or part of the land, the City of Cheyenne will preserve this land for parks and recreation department uses. Cheyenne's urban areas are growing and steadily increasing in population over time. Cheyenne's growth will place further pressure on existing park facilities and require the addition of new areas for parks, recreation and open space for the community of Cheyenne."

From the bird's eye view, this is wonderful.

But the person who gave me the information, station neighbor Bill Cox, was not happy.

Neither was Laramie County Commissioner Jeff Ketcham when I spoke with him a couple weeks ago after the ordinance passed. By the way, Zelda Ketcham was his great-grandmother.

The city, to its credit, took the least intrusive annexation option. The typical annexation requires banning septic systems, firearms discharge and livestock.

It's good the city took the Wyoming Statute 15-1-407 option instead, since there are few toilets at the station, the deer population needs to be controlled to protect the tree and shrub specimens, and experiments call for cattle grazing.

This option also doesn't give the city the usual developmental oversight within one mile of the city boundary, nor does it allow landowners to use this island of city as a basis for more annexations.

So why are the neighbors and the county, in separate lawsuits, trying to get the annexation appealed?

They don't see an ordinance as a very permanent thing. Ketcham knows how little it would take to change it, or even to have the city decide to sell the property. The lease with the USDA is renewed annually.

Perhaps the station's neighbors are watching the county's development of the former Archer agricultural experimental facility east of town. Plans call for a business park along I-80, the relocated fairgrounds, a motocross track and shooting range. Only a third to a quarter of the 800 acres is slated for open space.

When I spoke with Mayor Jack Spiker and Councilman Tom Seagraves who sponsored the ordinance, both assured me of the pureness of their intentions.

Seagraves said annexation would give the city's property protection by city police and city fire departments and would deal with a water issue brought about when the new water treatment facility left Round Top high and dry.

From a bird's eye view, the landscape around the research station has become a checkerboard of new residential development. Ironically, the owners of these new homes want the freedom of the county's less restrictive regulations, but many opt for exclusivity provided by very restrictive covenants that may limit numbers and kinds of livestock and outbuildings.

Studies show here on the high plains this rural development changes the kinds of birds seen from grassland species to urban species.

What kills the native small mammals and ground-nesting birds that have adapted to life without trees are people allowing dogs and cats to prey on them, people mowing during nesting season (June through mid-July) and people planting trees from which avian predators can more successfully search for prey.

Right now the island of city property known as the Grasslands Research Station is a great stopover for migrating birds, and a refuge for our native breeding grassland birds.

I want to believe that annexing the research station really is the farsighted action claimed in the ordinance's language. One hundred years from now citizens will applaud the preservation of open space in what might become the new focus of the city. Maybe it will be known as the Central Park of the West.

From a bird's eye view, something more permanent than a mere city ordinance is needed. This special landscape needs some kind of binding city-county agreement that allows for the continuation of the research station's lease for the next 121 years and a plan for if they decide some year not to renew it.

Conservation easements allow private landowners to preserve land in perpetuity.

Does the station's neighbors' attorney, Gay Woodhouse, know of a legal tool available to cities?

If we are serious about protection – and no one I've talked to disagrees with preserving this open space - let's find a way to show we mean it.

89 Pup retrieves backyard of wonders

We had no idea so much of our backyard was edible. Euell Gibbons, author of "Stalking the Wild Asparagus," would be proud of us. Grass, leaves, sticks, weeds – of course I'm talking about edible from the perspective of a 3-month-old puppy.

Our yard is only about 100 feet wide by 50 feet deep, but it is amazing how many microhabitats it has as examined by the nose of a puppy.

First, there are all the dead leaves under the shrubs. Sally dragged out some really disgusting looking black specimens which turned out to be dried mushrooms. Maybe I should take her to France to look for truffles.

Then, there are the ants which she licks up. I never knew golden retrievers had anteaters in their lineage, but I guess she provides a natural way to control their population.

The pile of composting leaves by the garage is proving irresistible. Sally flings herself on them, like any child, tunneling to dig out choice bits of decaying roughage.

Wind-blown leaves scuttling across the patio also attract her notice. One such leaf took a sudden turn and as it blew closer, it became a little brown mouse intent on making it to its home in the corner of the raised bed only 10 feet from where we sat.

I'm out a lot now supervising Sally, and I've discovered backyard bird life is more interesting from outside than from a window.

The robins are not perturbed by us at all. One fearlessly marched on the bird bath – even though a panting puppy watched from a pounce away. The squirrels, however, seem to be avoiding the yard. This means a respite for the trees they've been gnawing, especially this last dog-less year.

Also, without the squirrels to antagonize them, a pair of blue jays has decided to build a nest in the spruce tree. They don't hesitate to come down into the yard for whatever bits they need while we watch.

Our cats are avid window birders and Sally seems to have the same avian interests. She noticed a flock of noisy gulls sailing over the house, though she hasn't tuned in yet to the whistling wing beats of the occasional mallard.

Walking the backyard with Sally half a dozen times a day lets me observe the changing pattern of sunlight and shade and the chronology of snowmelt. Each day, the ratio of green to brown in the lawn improves, tulips emerge a little more and leaves grow.

The dawn chorus steadily increases. I can pinpoint the day the mourning doves added their calls, April 9. The singing of grackles, house finches, starlings and house sparrows increases in frenzy daily. On the other hand, the juncos seemed to have departed the yard for the mountains April 10, but I won't know if it's for good until we get the next snowstorm.

This year, the Eurasian collared-doves are even more abundant in the neighborhood. There must be some nesting nearby since I can hear their croaky cooing almost every time I'm out.

Will our usual spring visitors be as tolerant of a puppy and still show up in mid-May?

I'm on the lookout for the spotted towhee, green-tailed towhee, white-crowned sparrow, western tanager, rose-breasted grosbeak, lazuli bunting and indigo bunting. I hope to find the yellow birds too, goldfinches and different kinds of warblers.

Our dog before the last one was also a golden retriever which Mark took bird hunting. We'll see if Mark wants to get back into it and if Sally proves adept.

Someone asked me if we could hunt birds and still be members in good standing with the National Audubon Society. Of course. Audubon is not an animal rights group. There is no more honorable way than hunting, short of raising it yourself, to put meat on the table – Vice President Dick Cheney's canned hunts not included.

If all bird species had always been given as much thought, management, study and funding as game birds, Audubon could become a mere birdwatching club. But interest in non-game birds continues to increase so someday there may be parity.

Sally, to her discomfort, has discovered not everything in the yard is safely edible. We were surprised to see juniper and chokecherry on the Cheyenne Pet Clinic list of plants toxic to pets. So we've put the sheep fencing back up.

But even while accompanying a sick dog, there is something beautiful about the backyard in spring at 4:30 a.m. That particular morning, there was only the slightest breeze, and it was warm enough to stand barefoot. The full moon was setting behind the neighbor's trees, and the Big Dipper was visible overhead. Sleepy robins could already be heard.

With Sally's taste for wood products, I'm thinking maybe I can train her to carry my bird field guide.

She can walk next to me as we explore the world beyond the gate.

90 Woodpecker visits might bring home improvements

Wednesday, May 24, 2006, Outdoors, page C2

After receiving half a dozen phone calls this spring from people inquiring what to do about woodpecker damage to their wood-sided houses, I decided to investigate and find the best recommendations available.

The primary culprit in our area is the northern flicker. You can identify it by its size which is about three inches longer than a robin. It is named for its red wing linings that flash as it flies. It has a white rump patch, black necklace, polka-dotted breast and a bill that looks about as long as its head is deep.

It's the bill that is used by the males to drum on reverberating surfaces to proclaim territory ownership and attract mates. Both males and females hammer at wood and even synthetic stucco to excavate a nest cavity.

Wood siding has a nice hollow resonance that reminds the birds of a rotten tree, their natural alternative.

Woodpeckers also drill for insects, but in the case of flickers, they're much more likely to be seen on the ground probing for ants, their favorite food. Cheyenne's dry climate is unlikely to produce siding infested with insects.

The first suggestion for avoiding woodpecker damage is to live in a brick house.

The next suggestion is to scare the flickers away. When they started drumming on his house, Cheyenne resident Chuck Seniawski went to that spot, but from the inside, and hammered the wall with his fist. He said it has worked the last two years.

When I searched for "woodpecker

damage" on the internet, I found a short but comprehensive article put out by Colorado State University Cooperative Extension, www.ext.colostate.edu. Click on Natural Resources and look for woodpeckers. The authors recommend taking immediate action, "because woodpeckers are not easily driven from their territories or pecking sites once they are established."

I also found www.birdcontrolsupplies.com which offers a complete assortment of deterrents, some of which you could make yourself. Starting at $8 there is the windsock approach, with big eyes printed on bright yellow to evoke a scary predator. Its mylar streamers flash in the wind.

Then there's the bucket of wood filler with a chemical deterrent added. Also, for $190 you can get an electronic device that intermittently gives off the sounds of a dying flicker. For $225 you can invest in a 25-foot square net to fence the birds off. You'd only have to keep it up during the courtship and nesting season – beginning about March, based on calls I got, through June.

Then there's the accommodation suggestion. Put up a flicker nest box over the hole the pair has been excavating in your house. The benefit is you get free insect and ant extermination services all summer.

One of the best sources for information on bird houses is the Cornell Lab of Ornithology's monitoring project, The Birdhouse Network.

Whether you build or buy, Cornell says to keep in mind these recommended features for all bird houses:

--Untreated wood at least ¾-inch thick, pine or cedar.

--Extended, sloped roof for protection from predators and weather; it can be fit into a slot on the back board of the nest box so water doesn't run down into the box.

--Rough or grooved interior walls so young can climb out to fledge.

--Recessed floor with drainage holes.

--Ventilation holes at top of sides.

--Easy access for monitoring and cleaning, usually a side panel that swings out but latches closed.

--Galvanized screws or nails.

--No outside perches to aid predators.

--Predator guard if mounted on a pole.

--Hole diameter sized for species, 2.5 inches for flickers.

The latest feature in flicker houses you can buy from places like Wild Birds Unlimited stores is the entrance hole surrounded by slate. It looks like an eighth to a quarter-inch thick square of slate has been drilled with the same 2.5-inch hole as the entrance and then mounted to prevent squirrels from chewing and enlarging the hole and taking over the nest box for themselves.

Cornell has plans for a flicker nest box, though it shows a hinged roof rather than the preferred access through the side. All you need is a 2-inch by 8-inch by 10-foot board cut into these lengths: 32-inch back, 24-inch sides (2), 24-inch front (center of entrance hole drilled 19 inches from the bottom), 4.25-inch floor and 10.75-inch roof or longer. You might want to look at the drawing before assembly.

The key to a successful flicker house is to fill it with wood chips. It helps the flickers think they're excavating a hole in a rotten tree.

Mount the nest box on a pole or the side of your house 6 to 30 feet high with the entrance facing southeast. It would be interesting to know if most damage occurs to that side of people's houses.

Once the birds decide to move in, you can monitor the nest for The Birdhouse Network and viola – the bird problem becomes a home enhancement for both you and the flickers.

91 A summer of mountain birding

Everyone in Wyoming is lucky to live less than two hours from an outcrop of granite, evergreens and mountain birds.

While I frequently visit the Sherman Mountains in the Laramie Range just west of Cheyenne, summer is the time to travel farther.

The Black Hills were the location for Cheyenne – High Plains Audubon Society's annual campout at the end of June. The 25 bird watchers were from seven Wyoming communities and Colorado and included members of three of Wyoming's Audubon chapters.

Our mission was to survey several different timber sale units between Moskee and the Wyoming – South Dakota state line and generate a species list for each.

My group first walked an area that looked as though it might have been thinned 20 years ago. We heard a variety of singing birds and thanks to the expert ears of Chris Michelson of Casper, we were able to put names to them such as western wood pewee, plumbeous vireo, warbling vireo, hairy woodpecker, red crossbill, Townsend's solitaire, mountain bluebird, black-capped chickadee, Mac Gillivray's warbler and red-naped sapsucker.

Our second unit was old growth – or at least any stumps left from logging were no longer visible. It was definitely quieter. The species composition was different, and we picked up our first ruby-crowned kinglets.

Our anecdotal evidence, gathered with a low amount of scientific protocol, supports the theory that there is more bird species diversity in a disturbed forest. On the other hand, the disturbed forest is missing species that prefer old growth.

Several birds that caused excitement were dickcissels, a grassland species we found sitting on fence posts just outside the forest boundary north of Sundance.

Dickcissels flock unpredictably, especially here on the western edge of their range. About the only thing you can say for sure is that their overall population numbers keep dropping as grasslands endure disruption. But conditions were right this spring – they like moisture – and I was finally able to add them to my life list.

Returning to the Hills is to return to my memories of the summer I was on a Forest Service boundary survey crew. If only I had been paying more attention to birds then!

One of my favorite spots was the meadow below Warren Peaks where, having camped alone, I woke the morning of my 22nd birthday to a bright mist hanging over a hillside massed with blue and yellow flowers.

This year, I found I had missed the peak for arrow-leaved balsamroot and lupine. The meadow was still thick and green, but sported a new power line right through the middle.

A power line also decorated the landscape for part of our hike in Yellowstone National Park in July. A teaching commitment took me to Powell, and my husband Mark thought it would make a good excuse for a trip to Yellowstone afterward.

Our hike took us up above Mammoth Hot Springs, starting on the Swan Flats along Glenn Creek, up and over Snow Pass and back by way of the Hoodoos. The hike was nearly seven miles total.

We weren't hiking in an actual Bear Management Area, but I took the precaution of wearing a bear bell on my boot. Grizzly bears are not on my list of mega fauna I want to see – at least not while on foot.

The avifauna, however, was abundant. Every time I stopped and the bell fell silent, the forest was filled with bird song: Vireos, chickadees, robins, juncos, chipping sparrows, a red-tailed hawk and even red-winged blackbirds at the pond at the pass.

None of these were birds we couldn't see in our local forest, but it was special to know we were in Yellowstone, the Mecca for wildlife observation. However, other than birds, we saw only a mule deer, ground squirrels and five other hikers.

On our evening drives, along with great vistas, we saw lots of elk and occasional buffalo.

We got a chuckle when we realized another roadside distraction was a lone pronghorn, an animal easily seen outside Cheyenne. It calmly stood while people illegally approached.

Jeffrey, our son the antelope hunter, wondered aloud why animals in Yellowstone don't run from tourists. Simple. They've never been shot at with anything more than a camera.

One thing Yellowstone has that our local mountain range doesn't is a bird book devoted exclusively to it. "Birds of Yellowstone" by park ornithologist Terry McEneaney is a must if you hope to get the most out of your trip bird-wise. It highlights the characteristic birds of Yellowstone, provides a list of good birding places, and its checklist is the best I've ever seen for indicating what time of year and in what habitat and abundance a bird may be found.

Under "Sandhill Crane," Terry writes that the park sandhills winter in the Rio Grande valley of New Mexico and Mexico. They come back and build their nests in late April and early May. Nests are mounds of vegetation in shallow, wet meadows. There are usually two eggs and the young fledge in late August to mid-September.

A pair of cranes we saw one evening had built a nest on the island in Floating Island Lake.

They were both there, nattering to each other quietly as twilight deepened.

Too far away and too dim to photograph, they will have to remain as part of an image from our travels I can't stick on the page of a photo album.

92 The last to go

Warblers put on a late season show

As the leaves turned yellow-green in late summer, you may have noticed them shaking without benefit of a breeze.

Did you see small, greenish-yellow warblers picking through the foliage for insects?

Since 1993, Cheyenne-High Plains Audubon Society has documented 29 species of warblers on its Big Day counts held mid-May, at the peak of spring migration.

We haven't given the same scrutiny to fall migration since warblers trickle through Cheyenne beginning late August and on into October. In the spring, the timing of their presence is more concentrated.

Most of the reports I've received this fall are for easily recognized warblers: Townsend's with its mask, Wilson's with its black cap and beady black eyes and yellow-rumpeds with their yellow rump in contrast to blue-gray back and wings.

The yellow-rumped warbler stands out in many ways. First, it's just about the most common wood warbler species, which is probably why it has a well-known nickname.

Can't you just hear the ornithologist tracking the quick-flitting unknown bird deep in the bushes and finally exclaiming, "It's just another butter butt!"

The yellow-rumped comes in two forms that were previously two separate species. One, the myrtle warbler, has a white throat and is considered the eastern form. The other, Audubon's warbler, has a yellow throat. It breeds in the Rocky Mountains and winters in the southwestern United States and Mexico.

We see both forms in Cheyenne, so it is always worthwhile to scrutinize this common bird.

The yellow-rumped has odd habits for a warbler. Last month, friends and I hiked up to Emerald Lake in Rocky Mountain National Park, elevation 10,000 feet. Although there was fresh snow on the peaks and aspen in full color lower down, we found yellow-rumpeds busy catching flying insects, and in a most unwarbler way.

They perched on a picturesque dead tree at the lake's edge, then flew out over the water after their prey and circled back to their perches. This activity is called hawking, and flycatchers are the group of birds that use it most often. According to my books, it's a recognized feeding behavior for yellow-rumpeds too, but not for most warbler species.

What also sets the yellow-rumped apart is its wide range of gastronomic preferences. Other warblers have to head south when it is too cold to find live insects, but the yellow-rumped starts picking berries. That's how the myrtle got its name – it likes to eat wax myrtle berries.

Apparently, yellow-rumpeds have a digestive system that can deal with the berries' waxy coating. I don't think around here we have any myrtle, or bayberry, its other favorite food.

But both Audubon's and Myrtle forms stick around Cheyenne quite late, eating other kinds of berries and seeds. Robert and Jane Dorn list records as late as the first week in December.

Other warbler species' latest dates are in mid-October.

Pete Dunne's Essential Field Guide Companion calls yellow-rumpeds "The Swarm Warbler." I have seen this phenomenon myself, in Lions Park.

Warblers migrate at night. By morning they are ready to come to earth and refuel.

As I walked the dog one spring morning, between the new community house and the lake, yellow-rumped warblers tumbled across the path at my feet like wind-blown leaves.

While they may swarm during migration, yellow-rumpeds prefer to spread out for breeding in the coniferous forests of the mountains and the north. Little is known about this part of their lives compared to that of other, more gregarious songbirds.

David Flaspohler, author of the extensive account in Birds of North America, made a lot of observations while completing his dissertation on metapopulation dynamics and reproductive ecology of northern forest songbirds in the upper Great Lakes.

It was already observed that the female is usually the sole nest builder, though the male may sing and keep her company while she works.

Flaspohler was able to watch eight nests in northern Wisconsin in 1996 and documented that incubation is almost entirely done by the female.

"Male often sings in vicinity of nest

during incubation," he wrote.

When it's time to feed the young, the male helps, in between bouts of singing. In other species, parent birds are very quiet near the nest because they don't want to attract predators.

Many other sections of the account, however, state "No information." It looks like aspects of butter butt life history could provide many more topics for theses and dissertations.

For instance, the last time yellow-rumpeds were tested for the effects of spruce budworm pesticides was 1987, in only one place and for only one kind of pesticide.

Or, why was the yellow-rumped the most abundant warbler found in collisions with towers in Florida, but rarely in Pennsylvania?

Yellow-rumped populations are said to be stable or increasing, but standard avian demographic data is lacking.

Another species, the greater sage-grouse, is suffering from rampant oil and gas development in Wyoming today and is finally attracting lots of research funds.

Had more research been done earlier, wildlife biologists may have been able to make better recommendations sooner to stave off the disastrous situation we have now. Then again, sound biological recommendations need to fall on willing White House ears to have any effect.

Meanwhile, enjoy warbler watching.

Consider posting your bird observations on eBird.com. Every little bit helps us figure out the puzzle that is life on Earth.

93 Grouse losing ground fast

Wednesday, November 8, 2006, Outdoors, page C2

Sage grouse have the misfortune of living directly in the path of natural gas development. In Wyoming, we are talking about the bird known by the formal common name, Greater Sage-Grouse.

While some species benefit from human activity – think Norway rat, pigeon, starling, coyote, cockroach – the sage grouse is not one of them.

Matt Holloran spoke at the Cheyenne High Plains Audubon Society meeting last month about his studies on the natural gas fields near Pinedale as a University of Wyoming doctoral candidate. He's now a consultant with Wyoming Wildlife Consultants.

While much of his talk was still couched in the language used to successfully defend his dissertation, accompanied by graphs and charts, Matt's findings are clear enough. No sage grouse, much less anyone else, wants to

live next to a drill rig or producing gas well, whatever the season.

First, there are the dancing grounds, or leks, where males perform on spring mornings, and females come to observe and decide on a mate. Leks have to be open areas with good visibility, but a little thing like a flyover by a predator like a golden eagle is enough to cancel the show for the rest of the morning.

Matt calculated the success of each lek by the number of males that continued to attend.

During five years of study, it was obvious that the negative effect of drill rigs and producing wells on grouse increased as structures got closer to leks. It also increased where the wells were positioned closer together.

Matt even determined that leks downwind from a rig were affected more negatively than leks upwind. Noise was the factor.

The Best of Cheyenne Bird Banter

Also, the closer a road was to a lek and the busier it was, the greater the negative effect. One has to travel more than 5 kilometers away from drilling or wells before leks appear to be unaffected.

Mated female grouse leave the lek to find perfect nesting habitat. They like to lay their eggs under sagebrush where tall grasses also help screen them from predators. They react poorly to drilling, and fewer chicks survive.

Later, when females from disturbed areas share summer habitat with females from undisturbed areas, the former are more likely to die. One of the reasons may be that, having learned to ignore human activity, they are no longer paying close attention to predators.

When leks lose male sage grouse, do the birds leave a disturbed area and move to a new area, or do they just stop reproducing the next generation?

There aren't a lot of places for sage grouse to go.

As a range management student 25 years ago, I learned all the techniques for killing sagebrush to encourage more grass for cattle to graze. Fire is especially effective, retarding sagebrush growth for over 200 years in some cases. Sheep, however, are browsers, and since they nibble shrubs, sagebrush isn't managed the same way for them.

It would be great if we could provide habitat for sage grouse somewhere away from the gas fields. Energy companies are used to thinking in terms of mitigation.

But no one knows yet exactly how to build and connect all the habitats needed for sage grouse, nor does anyone know exactly how other factors, such as West Nile Virus, predators and drought work together to affect numbers of grouse. Their populations have been declining since the 1960s.

Matt said when peregrine falcon numbers were dropping, all it took was a ban on DDT and the population rebounded. In comparison, sage grouse are a puzzle.

He does, however, have several suggestions. One is to increase the distance between gas field activity and leks and nests, as stipulated by the Bureau of Land Management, based on his findings.

Keeping well density to less than one per 699 acres, which is a little larger than one square mile, can be done with directional drilling. Multiple wells could share the same site and access road, pumping gas from pockets up to a mile away in all directions, leaving more land surface to sage grouse.

Something as simple as garbage control on the well sites would quit attracting ravens to the area. They eat sage grouse eggs.

Another key to sage grouse survival that Matt recommends is that "intact sagebrush-dominated habitats be protected and managed for suitable understory conditions."

Natural gas is not a renewable resource. I don't understand the federal government encouraging drilling everything as fast as possible. The resource will just run out faster.

Slower development would give an area of exhausted wells a chance to be reclaimed for sage grouse before new areas are disturbed. And, sage grouse are not the only ones to suffer from high-speed development. Consider our small western Wyoming towns.

Procrastination is a hallmark of being human, so pessimist or realist that I am, I don't think alternative energy will be given the brain power it needs to find the most inspired solutions until it is absolutely necessary.

Let's hope it's not too late for the Greater Sage-Grouse by then.

2007

94 This spring watch for 'TVs' soaring above the area

Wednesday, February 21, 2007, Outdoors, page C2

Do you know where Wyoming turkey vultures spend the winter? It could be Venezuela.

Keith Bildstein, director of the Acopian Center for Conservation Learning at Hawk Mountain Sanctuary in Pennsylvania, is working on a migration study in which turkey vultures wintering in northwestern Venezuela have been tagged. He predicts bird watchers in western North America will see them this spring and report back to him.

Little is known about the migration of the "TV," as birders refer to it, and even though it is a species with a stable population that is increasing northward, it's better to do your research in advance of problems, said Bildstein, when I talked to him recently. Also, sometimes the new information will translate to less fortunate species.

Bildstein studied raptors for his dissertation, so it is quite natural to find him at Hawk Mountain, the famous place where so many hawks pass on migration. What bothered him was that observers would refer to "just another turkey vulture." He thought they deserved more respect than that.

Turkey vultures in eastern North America don't migrate much except to get out of the cold – it is hard to chip meat off frozen carcasses.

Bildstein said satellite studies show TVs travel independently and individual birds may not travel the same route each year. They stop along the way and share roosts and food with the local vultures. Maybe they pick up pointers on great Florida real estate.

Meanwhile, when birds of the western subspecies head south, they travel down through Mexico, Central America and into Columbia and Venezuela, possibly heading as far as Argentina. On the wintering grounds they raise the population of vultures to four times that of the year-round resident subspecies. The residents, being smaller birds, are crowded into marginal habitat, Bildstein said.

Two of the places the "gringo" vultures like to hang out are the zoos in Barquisimeto and Maracay. Last winter, zoo folks told Bildstein about a tagged TV they found that turned out to be part of a study in Saskatchewan, Canada.

Bildstein and Adrian Naveda, a biologist from Maracay, put their heads together and designed the northward migration study, counting on the help of the legions of birdwatchers in North America.

It was easy to gather the visiting vultures. Zoo management cleared out one of the aviaries, stocked it with dead chickens from the market, waited for the vultures to walk in, closed the door and tah-dah, 100 vultures ready for tagging. However, grabbing birds with 67-inch wingspans probably wasn't easy.

Bildstein has had one report of a tagged bird so far. It was found shot 45 miles north of the release site. The rest of the birds should be migrating along the coast. In early morning, the warm ocean creates small thermals near shore, giving the TVs an early start. Then, it's a matter of riding one thermal after another over land all day long, day after day. As many as 2,000,000 turkey vultures have passed by an observation point in one season.

Here in Cheyenne, we may see TVs as early as March and definitely will by April. They have favorite roosting spots in the Avenues and are often seen circling over the cemeteries. Recently, they have been noticed far into the summer, however, the nearest nest is probably near Guernsey, according to Doug Faulkner, who is working on the definitive book about Wyoming birds for the University of Wyoming.

OK, this is where you come in. Let's review TV i.d. The most common large birds flying over Cheyenne in the spring, summer and fall are the turkey vulture and the Swainson's hawk, which, incidentally, spends the winter in Argentina and shares the vultures' migration route.

As they soar overhead, look at the underwing patterns. The leading (front) edge of the Swainson's is light and the trailing edge is dark. Turkey vultures have the reverse: dark on the leading edge and light, actually silvery, on the trailing edge. Seen up close, they have red-skinned, featherless heads.

If you see one of the marked birds, it will have either a red tag with white numbers or a blue tag with black numbers wrapped over the leading edge of the wing, visible from top or bottom.

If you see one of these birds, you need to make note of the date, specific location, color and number of the tag, which wing it is attached (the bird's right or left) and the circumstances of the sighting, whether the bird was alone or in a group of vultures, flying, perched, feeding or roosting. Dead birds should also be reported.

Report sightings to: Keith Bildstein, Hawk Mountain Sanctuary Acopian Center for Conservation Learning. All reports will be recognized and individuals reporting tagged birds will get summary information about the study.

If you would like to print your own copy of the "Wanted" poster, go to www.hawkmountain.org.

The February issue of Smithsonian magazine tells of the demise of millions of vultures in India in just 10 years due to ingestion of a new livestock antibiotic while feeding on dead cattle. It has led to a terrific increase in wild dogs and, in turn, human cases of rabies. Valuable time was lost puzzling it out and there is no guarantee vulture populations will ever recover.

Though turkey vultures are the widest ranging of the vulture species, from Canada to Tierra del Fuego, and probably the most numerous vulture species in this hemisphere, everything that can be learned about them helps keep them that way.

To learn more to marvel over about turkey vultures such as their terrific sense of smell, the way the young protect themselves and the sounds they make, go online to All About Birds, www.birds.cornell.edu/AllAboutBirds/BirdGuide/Turkey_Vulture.

95 Visiting cedar waxwings learn lesson

Driving under the influence is a tragedy waiting to happen. Flying inebriated can also have fatal results as was illustrated in our backyard.

It was Feb. 23, and I was assembling my lunch when I heard two thwunks, one right after the other on different windows facing the backyard. Birds, no doubt.

As I brought my sandwich to the table, I realized one of the cats was looking intently out the window to the patio below. I followed his stare and saw a cedar waxwing lying on the concrete.

In the seconds it took me to run out the back door, it died, the milky-white nictating membranes pulled over its eyes. As I picked it up, the head lolled. Broken neck.

I'd been hearing the flock for the past few days, a faint, wispy, background sound, not to be heard on a regular basis. Waxwings don't migrate predictably so much as they go where the berries are. And the neighbors' juniper bushes are full. Over the winter, berries can sometimes ferment, leading to intoxication and poor flying judgment.

I wonder if drunk birds also smack into natural obstacles?

Windows confuse birds, reflecting landscapes like mirrors. However, half of each of our windows is screened and I hope that breaks the image or allows a bird to bounce off the flexible material rather than hard glass.

Mark and I leave the shiny side of the windows dirty, tape junk CDs shiny side out, and add those static cling window stickers. This time there was even a staring cat.

Waxwings would be easy to carve.

Their pale brown plumage is so fine you don't notice individual feathers, except for the wing tips with their little drops of red "wax," a carotenoid pigment substance.

They have a black mask, a crest on the back of the head and a band of bright yellow on the tip of their tail, as if someone had dipped them in paint.

I couldn't bring myself to bag and toss in the garbage this gorgeous bird so I left it to naturally decay where the dog wouldn't get it.

I forgot all about the second thwunk until I let the dog out but called her back before she noticed the second bird.

It was another cedar waxwing, huddled on the cement, but breathing. Just stunned.

I set it on the back wall to give it a better vantage point to fly from when it recovered. It didn't have the red drips on its wing tips and later I read that birds hatched last year won't have them yet by this spring. One lucky teenager.

It occurred to me to run back in the house and grab my camera. I got one bad photo and while lining up for a second, the bird flew over my head. Good.

Being a sunny, 50-degree day, I decided to eat my neglected sandwich on the back steps, in the company of two dozen waxwings in the tree overhead. They sat still and quiet, blending in with the bare gray-brown branches, except for their pale yellow bellies.

Were they having a moment of silence for their fallen comrade? Or had they decided to sober up before flying again? I couldn't ask them and find out.

When son Jeffrey came in from school he announced there was a dead cedar waxwing on the front step. I checked the wing tips. Another youngster. It left a few tiny feathers stuck to the front window.

It is now March 13 as I write this, three weeks since I first heard the flock. It is still here. We have found no other accident scenes. Evidently, the waxwings have learned to avoid the windows and it seems they learn from each other since we would have noticed if all 30-40 of them had had to bump into our windows to learn the lesson.

Every time I take the dog out, I listen for the waxwings. They are either across the street in the junipers picking berries or resting in our trees. Jeffrey can't wait for them to move on so it will be worth his while to wash the car he parks in the driveway under a tree.

This is the longest cedar waxwings have ever stayed in the neighborhood and I know they will leave at some point. And, just like their larger and even more nomadic counterparts, the Bohemian waxwings, their return will be as unpredictable.

If waxwings were as common as house sparrows and starlings, would I enjoy them as much? Perhaps I should take a closer look at those abundant species. But then, they hardly ever crash into windows.

Spring migration has been going on for a couple months already, imperceptibly if you didn't know to watch the waterfowl. In the last week I've seen robins, heard mourning doves and heard reports of bluebirds, and so the rush begins.

Most migrating birds won't be drunk, but they don't stay long enough to learn the local obstacle course, so I guess we will leave cleaning windows until later. I should hang more deterrents. And then it will be baby bird season, and they fly into everything. And then it's migration season again.

Well, if it looks like we never wash our windows, you'll know why.

Besides, who has time for chores when there are birds coming in?

Wednesday, April 18, 2007, Outdoors, page C2

96 Duck diversity

How to separate those mallards from shovelers

Spring is a wonderful time to learn to identify ducks because all the drakes (males) are in full breeding plumage. No matter how old they are or where you see them, they look just like their pictures in the field guides – which you can't say about many other bird groups.

Plus, ducks are large and easy to see, especially here on Sloans Lake in Lions Park. A spotting scope is handy to have, but the lake is small enough you can see important field marks with binoculars.

First, let's dismiss all the geese, the large gray birds with the black necks and heads that are here all year round.

Be sure to impress your friends that this species is properly named "Canada Goose," not "Canadian Goose."

Next, let's sort out all the brown ducks. These are the females of all duck species. Without inspecting their body shape and particular wing feathers, the best way to identify them is to see with which males they swim.

Then, let's review the field marks of the "Mallard," the most abundant, most recognizable local duck here year round. Many no longer migrate because they've figured out misguided people will feed them.

The mallard drake has the bright, iridescent green head (except when molting in the fall), bright orange legs, bright yellow bill and a tail that curls. There are many other features that could be described, but these field marks distinguish the mallard from other ducks we see locally.

Also, they are the only ones, along with the Canada geese, that will approach you for a handout.

Another duck with a bright green head, the "Northern Shoveler," has an elongated body shape ending in a black bill that looks like a shovel or spatula. Its breast is bright white, and its sides are chestnut brown.

Two species of ducks have plain red heads, as in the bright brown chestnut color of red hair.

One, aptly named "Redhead," has a nice rounded head like the mallard's, with its bill jutting out at about a 90-degree angle to its forehead. The other, the "Canvasback," has a sloping forehead continuous with the slope of its bill, what the field guides like to call a "ski slope."

A third red-headed duck, the "Green-winged Teal," has a section of green feathers that can be seen when it extends its wing, but it also has a green, wing-shaped marking that encircles its eye and extends to the back of its neck.

The "American Wigeon" has the same green wing shape over its eye, but it has a spectacularly wide white stripe from the top of its bill to the back of its head.

A white stripe up either side of its neck distinguishes the "Northern Pintail," an otherwise grayish bird. The stripes are easier to see than the long, pointy tail.

A white crescent on each side of its face, between eye and bill, sets the "Blue-winged Teal" apart, since many other ducks also show a blue speculum (section) on their wings.

If a duck is all chestnut red, and shaped like a mallard, it is the "Cinnamon Teal." If it has a tail that sticks up stiffly, and it sports bright white cheeks and a bright blue bill, it's a "Ruddy Duck."

There are several black and white duck species, two of which we see in winter, "Common Goldeneye," and "Bufflehead." But by spring, you are most likely to see the "Lesser Scaup." Its head and tail ends are black, and its middle is white. The "Ring-necked Duck" looks just like it but with good optics, the black tip on the blue and white bill is noticeable.

The "Gadwall" has the distinction of being the plainest duck, just a sort of fine, tweedy gray, but it is the only duck solidly black under the tail.

It is possible to see mergansers on Sloans Lake. All three species, "Common Merganser" being most likely, have long thin bills for catching fish. They have small heads with feathers that sprout like a bad hair day.

Not all birds that can swim are ducks. The "American Coot" doesn't have webbed feet. It has a compact all-black body like a rubber ducky and a distinctive bright white bill.

The grebes are not ducks either. The "Western Grebe," a larger gray bird with a long, white-fronted neck, will be back soon, entertaining us with its water-dancing mating rituals.

The "Pied-billed Grebe," small, short-necked and brown with a black and white bill, is not as noticeable. Horned and eared grebes are more likely on larger reservoirs.

And then there are the big, dark brown "Double-crested Cormorants" that float low, as if waterlogged, or fly overhead looking like sticks with wings.

There are a couple unidentifiable ducks at Sloans Lake that are the offspring of domestic white ducks mating with mallards. You'll know that's what they are because they have the mallard shape, if not size and colors, and they hang out with the mallards.

Also, there are all those other swimming birds that make surprise visits: pelicans, swans and unusual gulls and terns.

I meant to make this a simple guide to the most common ducks to be seen at Sloans Lake this spring, and already

I've mentioned 16 and referred to a dozen other water birds.

At least it will make it easier for you to decide what birds to study in your field guide.

I know it's hard to believe that so many kinds of ducks can show up on a lake in the middle of town, surrounded by people walking dogs. But that's the magic of migration. All you have to do is look.

97 They look helpless, but they probably don't need rescuing

Wednesday, May 9, 2007, Outdoors, page C1

Everyone wants to be a springtime hero, but is that tiny bird on the ground in dire straits?

Nothing is as appealing as rescuing a helpless baby bird fluttering on the ground. Everyone wants to be a springtime hero. Becoming one appears to be as easy as scooping up the tiny bird, but is that the right thing to do?

Laura Conn, veterinary technician, knows first-hand how many times a year nestlings are rescued because they all seem to end up at the Cheyenne Pet Clinic where she works.

"People find them on the ground or don't see Mom for a while, or they want to remove a nest from the threat of outdoor cats," Conn said.

Last year it was 39 common grackles, a dozen robins and well over 50 house sparrows besides an assortment of other bird species.

"It can be a couple nests a day. Sometimes because of construction, workers will bring them in," said Conn.

The clinic's standard advice is that unless birds are in immediate danger, it is safer to return them to the nest. "But everyone wants to bring them

in," said Conn.

One myth is that a baby bird alone on the ground has been abandoned. However, if it has feathers already, it may have been pushed out of the nest by its parents who are probably nearby, keeping an eye on the youngster as it makes the transition to independence.

This would be especially true of birds that hatch precocial young, the young of meadowlarks, killdeer and other ground nesting birds. The chicks hatch with feathers and can practically run as soon as they depart the shell.

Altricial young are those helpless, naked nestlings like robins and sparrows that need a few weeks for feathers to grow in.

If the nestling is found completely or semi-featherless, the best thing to do is put it back in the nest. If the nest has been destroyed, fashion one from a basket or bucket.

A second myth is that once a human has touched a baby bird, the parents will abandon it. Not true, said Conn.

As for marauding cats, Conn said young birds probably have a better chance of surviving under the protection of an angry parent bird than if they are brought into the clinic.

The rate of survival of young birds transferred to the clinic is one in three.

At the clinic the bird is assessed for damages. Falling may produce injuries, making the bird impossible to rehabilitate. Injuries from cats are seldom seen since there's usually nothing left of the baby bird after a feline encounter, Conn explained.

If the nestling is in good shape, it is popped into the incubator. Then it's time to mix up special mash, either meant for young poultry, or special mixes for wild birds.

A rescued baby bird needs feeding every two hours, at least until 10 p.m., when the last clinic employee goes home. All the employees pitch in at the height of nestling season, even the front desk, said Conn.

The Cheyenne Pet Clinic is the only local facility with the necessary federal permit for handling wild birds. It is not legal to tend wild birds without a permit.

Robert Farr, the clinic's founding veterinarian, said he would be interested in hearing from anyone with previous experience who would like to help by taking orphans home. Volunteers can work under the clinic's permit and the clinic will provide the food.

Conn has been caring for baby birds since she started at the clinic as a volunteer 19 years ago. While injured large wild birds also come in, such as the great horned owl which was recently recovering from tangling with a barbed wire fence, most are sent on to the veterinary hospital in Fort Collins. But small birds are cared for at the clinic until their release.

Ducklings are also brought in occasionally, but said Conn, "We try to find someone to take them quick – they don't do well here."

Some birds that come in are very prone to stress and succumb quickly while others seem hardier, said Conn.

Some summers it seems like all the young survive and other summers they don't. The older the nestling is, the better its chances of surviving. Some birds just seem to be tougher, like robins.

Depending on how old the bird was when it came in, it can take two or three weeks before it is ready for release.

First, it has to be able to eat on its own. "It's hard to train them to eat," said Conn. "We can't do it as well as their mothers. And they have to be able to fly well on their own, too."

Typically, the birds are taken to the park where there are plenty of trees, since most of the rescued young are tree-nesting species. Sometimes employees will release the birds in their own backyards where they can leave food out, but the young birds don't stay around long.

Rescuing a helpless young bird is a noble act, but knowing when a bird needs rescuing is even nobler.

How to best help wild birds

Dazed adult bird on ground

Most likely it has run into a window. Carefully set it on a branch where a cat can't reach it while it recovers. If birds often hit your window, consider applying a shiny decal to the outside of the glass, or hang netting or something shiny in front of it during the spring and early summer.

Injured adult or young bird

The Cheyenne Pet Clinic routinely provides assessment and first aid. Call 635-4121. For hawks and owls and other large species, please consult the staff on how best to transport the bird to avoid further injury to it or injury to you.

Feathered young bird on ground
Most often, the parent birds are waiting for you to go away so they can feed their almost independent youngster. So, go away! However, if the neighbor's cat is crouched nearby, see if you can get the youngster to perch on a tree branch.

Featherless young bird on ground
Try to return it to its nest. Retired wildlife biologist Art Anderson said that if the young are about the same age or size, just about any nest will do.

Damaged nest
If the nest has broken or can't be set back up, make one from a basket or bucket filled with dry leaves and grass. Attach it to the original location, if it is safe, or nearby. Place the remains of the old nest and the young birds in the container and the parent birds will find them.

Ground nesting birds
During prime nesting season, May through mid-July, refrain from mowing the prairie or allowing dogs and cats off leash. Planting trees also adversely affects the survival of ground nesting birds such as killdeer and meadowlarks. Predators – hawks and eagles – will use the trees for perches while they scan for small bird prey.

Habitat improvements
Tree-nesting birds benefit from the planting of more shrubs and trees for food and cover. Cover is the vegetation into which they can disappear to avoid predators or bad weather. Think about adding a water source too. And eliminate pesticides. Check the National Audubon Society's "Audubon at Home" website at www.audubon.org/bird/at_home.

Keep cats indoors
Cats don't need to be allowed to run free, killing small birds and animals, in order to have a full and happy life. Just ask any contented kitty lying on a cushy pillow in a sunny window. Plus, indoor cats have longer and healthier lives. For help in turning your mini-tiger into a real house cat, visit the American Bird Conservancy site at www.abcbirds.org/cats or get information from the Cheyenne Pet Clinic.

Wild bird rehabilitator permit
The first requirement is 100 hours of experience. Check other qualifications at www.fws.gov. Look under Permits, then Applications, then "MBTA," short for Migratory Bird Treaty Act. Or call the U.S. Fish and Wildlife Service's Migratory Bird Permit Office, 303-236-8171.

98 Professor sheds light on crossbills
Wednesday, May 16, 2007, Outdoors, page C2

Research points to more than one species of red crossbill in North America

Crossbills are species of birds that eat seeds from the cones of spruce, pine and other evergreens. Over time they've evolved mandibles that cross at the tips. These odd beaks can be slipped between the scales of cones to pry them apart far enough for the crossbills to reach seeds with their sticky tongues.

Both the white-winged and red crossbills can do this. However, the red crossbill was the star of the program given by Craig Benkman last month for the Cheyenne Audubon chapter.

Craig is a professor at the University of Wyoming, in the Zoology and Physiology Department, and is well recognized internationally for his crossbill studies. He has determined that there may be as many as nine types of red crossbills that are candidates for designation as separate species. Red crossbills are found in North America and Europe.

To be considered a species means the members of it either don't breed outside the group or crossbreeding produces no successful young.

Types of red crossbills are different in size and in the calls they make. They also have different tastes in cones.

While Craig can show you really cool 3-D graphics of his statistics at www.uwyo.edu/benkman, let's cut to the chase here.

Over the last 5,000 to 7,000 years, red crossbills have evolved their seed extraction methods to such an efficiency that the bills of different populations match seeds of particular conifer tree species. For instance, the red crossbills that work over lodgepole pine have different sized bills than those that specialize in spruces.

Watch a crossbill husk a seed (see the video on Craig's web page), and you will see it uses the same side of its bill each time. It has a sharp ridge in the upper mandible that acts as a wedge or hammer and in the lower mandible there is a groove that is perfectly sized for the preferred seed.

Using its tongue to hold the seed in the groove, the crossbill bites down and breaks the seed husk and then removes it. It's a very efficient system if the bird and the seed are perfectly matched.

Serendipitously, Craig discovered that instead of "collecting" birds, he could use dental impression material on live birds to measure their palates, the inside of their mandibles. He can statistically prove that crossbills with a particular seed preference have a particular groove measurement.

While a crossbill with a pinecone bill can get seeds out of a spruce cone and husk them, it isn't as fast and it can't eat as much per minute as the right type crossbill. In this case, time is food is life.

Craig can show that those birds forced to make do with the wrong seed are less likely to survive and less likely to produce young, even if they are in the same forest as the type of crossbill that matches the cones available.

Crossbill breeding is very dependent on having enough seeds. They breed any time of year, except perhaps late fall, so if a spruce-beaked bird can't find a good spruce cone crop, it won't breed until it does.

Craig has studied the crossbills of the South Hills range in Idaho extensively. The lodgepole pinecone crop is quite dependable, and the type of crossbill found there has been able to settle down over several thousand years and evolve to match its food source closely.

While individuals of other types of crossbills can be found in the South Hills, in among this resident type, Craig has found that they are unlikely to breed or crossbreed.

If mating should occur between crossbill types, the young might be inefficient at eating seed from all cone types and be doomed to never getting enough seed to be in condition to breed.

The evolution of crossbill beaks continues because trees continue to evolve tougher cones. The trees with the toughest cones will have seeds that survive to grow and produce more seed and trees.

On the other hand, crossbills with the best beaks for the toughest cones will produce more young. Craig calls this the co-evolutionary arms race. However, in many locations squirrels throw a monkey wrench in the works, which is another story.

If red crossbills really are nine separate species, birdwatchers will have to differentiate them by calls. That seems to be how the birds do it themselves.

As a flock, they travel nomadically across the northern forests. They land on a tree and begin sampling cones, calling out their results, so to speak, and attracting others of their type.

Within a few minutes a flock can decide a tree doesn't have enough seeds per cone to make it worth their expenditure of energy. Craig has been able to determine that the flock is more efficient at this than a lone bird. Remember, time is food is life, so it is better to be part of the flock.

And once in the flock of one type of crossbill, individual birds are unlikely to meet individuals of another type.

Craig and his graduate students continue to research answers to red crossbill questions.

The next question is how much data will it take to prove to the American Ornithologist's Union, the arbiter of North American bird species designation, that there is more than one species of red crossbill on this continent?

A note in the June 2007 issue of the national magazine, Birder's World, mentioned Craig's study and that the South Hills type is currently under review.

Stay tuned!

99 'Prairie Ghost'

Wednesday, June 13, 2007, Outdoors, page C1

The 'Where's Waldo' of the wilderness

The mountain plover has its disappearing act perfected – so much so that some people were convinced it was an endangered species.

If you stare really hard at the rocky soil, you may see a ghost of a bird, the "prairie ghost," but only if it moves.

If you are good at it, you can distinguish its white belly from a pale-colored rock. But if it turns its light brown back to you, it is indistinguishable from the surrounding tilled earth.

The nickname for the mountain plover is apt. Its disappearing act may be partly responsible for people thinking there were so few of them that the species would be a good candidate for listing as threatened or endangered.

On a damp morning in late May, just 50 miles east of Cheyenne and a few miles north of Bushnell, Nebraska, mountain plovers were present, right in the middle of alternating, mile-long strips of winter wheat, millet and fallow ground.

Not only were they present, but the plovers were nesting on the stony ridges of the fallow strips. A nest is harder to find than the birds though, because the eggs are on bare ground between the stones and they don't move. It's like playing "Where's Waldo?"

A mountain plover nest is a mere scrape made by the male with his feet. He makes several. The female lays three eggs in one and three eggs in another and then each parent incubates a nest. The parents will flick small pebbles at the eggs occasionally, but that's as far as nest building goes here.

Larry Snyder is good at seeing ghosts. His first encounter was about six years ago. While working one of his own fields, an odd-looking killdeer, one without the usual double neck band markings, flew up in front of him. He was able to find its nest and avoid driving over it.

A short time later, on a fishing trip with his daughters, he bumped into Chris Carnine of the Bird Conservancy of the Rockies. She was setting up the Nebraska Prairie Partners program, which was to include mountain plover nest surveys.

Chris identified the mystery bird. Its nest in Larry's field became the first documented mountain plover nest in the NPP program and also for Nebraska Game and Parks.

Chris found that Larry had a good eye for plovers, and he was hired to find more.

He still farms, but weekdays he works for RMBO.

In the spring he rides his neighbors' fields searching for nests.

He also does burrowing owl and raptor surveys.

The first farmer to sign up for the plover program was Larry's friend and neighbor, Bernie Culek.

As the third generation of his family on his farm south of Kimball, Nebraska, Bernie is always looking for better ways to make farming pay.

In 1992, when he came back to the farm, he changed it to a certified organic operation producing wheat, millet and several other grains.

Funding of the NPP program from a Nebraska Environmental Trust grant and Nebraska Game and Parks makes each mountain plover nest on his place worth $100.

He allows RMBO to find and mark nests and then he plows around them. He feels he should take some responsibility for wildlife.

Signing up for the program is a risk

some of Bernie's farming neighbors have not been willing to take, he said. The reluctant think the federal government might get too interested in plovers found on their land, even though the petition to list them was rejected in 2003 because there were more plovers than originally thought.

Bart Bly, currently in charge of the NPP program, said the long-term goal is to turn the program over to the landowners. They found a fifth of the nests last year.

But, said Bernie, for farmers like him, spring is very busy, and it is unlikely that spending hours to find a nest would be a good use of his time.

It can take two days – the longest interval Larry and summer field technician Cameron Shelton have had between nests this spring.

However, the morning of my visit we found two nests.

Larry put out an invitation for volunteers a couple months ago. I thought it would be a good chance to see another mountain plover, my first being last summer on a field trip with Larry and the folks from the Wildcat Audubon Society of Scottsbluff, Nebraska. Five other volunteers have been or will be out this spring.

The catch was learning how to drive a four-wheeler. It rates right up there with snowmobiles in obnoxiousness in my book. But it's a tool, a modern-day mule.

We rode half the length of the mile-long fallow strip at 6 miles per hour, three abreast, about 30 feet apart from each other, Larry, me, then Cameron. Then we rode back and out again, eventually sweeping the whole width of the strip.

I was watching the ground for rocks and hills instead of birds when a plover flew across in front of me, like a deer in the headlights.

Larry said "she" seemed to have shot out from under his front tire. It is impossible to tell the sex of a mountain plover sitting on a nest, but Larry and Cameron refer to them as "she" anyway. The only time in the field one can be certain of gender, Larry said, is when birds are copulating or the male is performing a courtship display or scraping a nest site.

Larry carefully examined the ground to make sure he hadn't run over the nest and wasn't going to step on it.

At a short distance he found three pale olive eggs with black splotches, each about an inch and a half long. He marked the nest with florescent orange stakes set 40 feet out in four directions.

Meanwhile, Cameron brought over a plastic jar of water for a float test. He examined each egg closely for any signs of pipping, where the hatchling might have picked a hole in the shell. If there was a hole, the float test could drown the chick. The test determines the age of the egg – the higher it floats in the water, the closer it is to hatching.

Incubation takes about 30 days, but the parents aren't tied to the nests. If it isn't too cold, they let solar energy work for them. But if it gets too hot, they stand, casting a shadow over the eggs, even holding out their wings sometimes, Larry said.

So temperature plays a big part in how successful nest hunting is on any given day. On a cold day or a hot day, where the adult flies up from is likely to be the nest. Otherwise, they might be out anywhere, stalking beetles, grasshoppers, crickets and ants – the extent of their food diversity.

After Larry took a location reading and filled out a nesting record form, he explained that we couldn't walk back from the nest to our four-wheelers the way we came. We must continue past the nest and circle back so that predators finding our scent later will also circle away.

A second plover flew, but when a little investigation didn't get a nest, we backed off and waited for the bird to return.

Larry is a patient person. He just hunkered down with his binoculars and waited. He said some birds have an attitude. While some are straightforward, others fly off over the hill and then sneak back.

Even though he sent Cameron around to the other side of the strip, neither of them could re-find the bird until Larry changed location. And then I saw a pale rock move. It was the bird again and the nest could be found. This one had only two eggs.

Larry said 13-lined ground squirrels are the most common nest predators, along with snakes.

Overall, Fritz Knopf, author of the Birds of North America Online account for mountain plover and the one who originated the "field clearing" idea in Colorado, told me the survival rate is very good, greater than 50 percent, sometimes even 90 percent, compared to maybe 25 percent for another ground nester, the mallard.

Last year the RMBO crews found 87 nests. This year, they are already up to 54. Larry hopes they break 100.

With his eye for prairie ghosts and the help of Cameron and the other two-man crew, they probably will.

A bird of contradictions

The mountain plover is a bird of the prairies. The naming mistake can be attributed to John James Audubon. The species was first collected by John Kirk Townsend along the Sweetwater River in Wyoming in 1832, said retired plover researcher Fritz Knopf.

Townsend shipped the specimen back to Audubon who thought that Townsend's description of the bird's location near the Continental Divide must mean it was found among mountain peaks. But the divide in Wyoming often runs through desert and wide-open prairie.

Also, even though classified as a shorebird, it doesn't spend time at the shore.

Historically, mountain plover breeding habitat is the short-grass prairie of the Great Plains, from Montana to New Mexico, but today populations can be found on tilled fields.

Even on the prairie, the mountain plover prefers disturbed ground, such as burns or areas overgrazed by cattle or trimmed by prairie dogs. Thus, what may be considered good ranching practice in Wyoming, which Fritz considers the major breeding landscape for plovers, may not be compatible with the plover's bare ground nesting requirements.

Researchers are also looking into the effects of pesticides on mountain plovers, not only on their breeding grounds, but in California's Imperial Valley where most of them winter.

Fritz said mountain plover populations were decimated by an outbreak of plague in prairie dogs in the late 1800s, but they prospered during the Dust Bowl of the 1930s. Bare ground to a mountain plover means no predator ambushes. The hordes of grasshoppers must have been like manna from heaven.

100 The early birder gets the bird in hand

Wednesday, July 18, 2007, Outdoors, page C2

Taking part in a banding provides one with a rare and incredible experience

A songbird in the hand is such an incredible thing, yet insignificant, a bit of tiny feathered flutter against your fingers – or a painful pinch of a beak.

Bird banding allows one to hold what normally can only be held from a distance with optics. It is a gift to hold these 1-ounce wonders and contemplate just how far they might have flown to nest in Wyoming, possibly from as far as South America.

The morning of July 1, friends and I volunteered to help with the MAPS banding station west of Laramie.

MAPS, the Monitoring Avian Productivity and Survivorship Program of the Institute for Bird Populations, has over 500 banding stations across the country. While there is an internship program that provides some of the labor, for 80 percent of the stations trained volunteers are essential.

At this station, even the site has been volunteered, by landowners Fred and Stephanie Lindzey. Ten 12-meter long mist nets have been set up in the same locations deep in the riparian zone along the Little Laramie River each year beginning in 2000.

The nets are unfurled six or seven times during the breeding season, late May through early August, from sunrise to noon each banding day.

This is also mosquito breeding season, and they were whining as I followed volunteer Larry Keffer across a soggy hay meadow and into thick willows and cottonwoods to check nets.

164   The Best of Cheyenne Bird Banter

Larry is a retired welder from Casper and got into banding three years ago there, up at the Audubon Center at Garden Creek.

The center is currently managed by his nephew, Ken, who, along with Larry's wife, also was working with us. Larry never thought he could do more than record data since his hands are crippled with arthritis, but he found he had plenty of dexterity with the fine crochet hook used to extract the birds from the nets.

Mist nets are made from very fine black threads. Set up in thick vegetation, the nets are invisible, and birds fly into them. Feisty species like the black-capped chickadee can manage to wrap several threads around their necks and feet in the 30-40 minutes between net runs.

Retrieving birds from a mist net is not for the squeamish. Kim Check, the Audubon Wyoming Community Naturalist now responsible for this MAPS site under the guidance of a master bander, took on a chickadee so deeply embedded, she was afraid it would die from stress.

At one point in the 15-minute ordeal, she asked me to lift one of the tiny threads hung up on the bird's emerging pin feathers. That's when I realized I hadn't brought my reading glasses. For bird outings I usually think binoculars.

Since the chickadee's life was more important than having to repair a hole in the net, the minute it quit fighting and seemed to go into a stupor, Kim didn't hesitate to start snipping. She decided not to take it back to the processing table which would stress it even more.

However, since this bird already had a band, we copied the numbers before Kim let it go. The chickadee flew into the bushes and disappeared with only one backward glance.

Most of the morning's other species – yellow warbler, house wren, veery, red-naped sapsucker, gray catbird, various sparrows – were much easier to extract.

Back at the picnic table, the birds, transported in white cloth bags, were identified by species, sex and age.

It is surprisingly difficult to identify some birds in the hand. Behavior and song are so much help in field identification.

Aging songbirds is particularly difficult. Two fat handbooks, "Identification Guide to North American Birds, Part 1 and 2," by Peter Pyle, help. But when you get right down to the nitty gritty, sometimes it just says, "more study is needed to tell the difference," Kim quoted.

The females, and the males of some species, have a brood patch on their belly, a big, bare patch of skin so that they can more directly transfer their body heat to incubating eggs. The condition of the brood patch skin, especially any sign of feather re-growth, tells how long ago the eggs hatched.

When a female cowbird was checked, she had no brood patch. But then we realized she wouldn't since cowbirds are parasitic nesters—dropping their eggs in other birds' nests for them to incubate, hatch and feed.

All kinds of information are recorded and eventually get into the hands of scientists.

Data for this MAPS station has been entered for 2000-2003 and some is published at www.birdpop.org. It shows 79 species have been banded or observed, of which 33 have been classified as breeding.

Another page shows that, as of 2003 (I think they must need data entry volunteers also) there have been 11 other MAPS sites in Wyoming.

You can wade through scientific discourse and learn the value of the data collected and how it is used to inform management decisions to combat what seemed to be a drastic drop in songbird populations around 1989 when the program began.

101 Rosy-finch survey provides bird's eye view

Wednesday, August 8, 2007, Outdoors, page C2

A bird's eye view is not for the faint of heart – or the faint of leg or lung. I found myself seated at the edge of a precipice at Schoolhouse Rock, about 11,500 feet, in the middle of July. We had just hiked up the Medicine Bow Peak trail in the Snowy Range.

While not actually dangling my feet over, I was close enough to the edge to touch it and appreciate Lake Marie 1,000 feet straight below.

To my left was the Diamond, another 500 feet higher.

No guard rails, no ropes and thankfully, no wind.

Five of us staunch members of the Audubon Society were looking for brown-capped rosy-finches (not to be confused with the other two species, black and gray-crowned) for the fourth year of a citizen science nesting survey.

You may remember me discussing it here the summer of 2004, when a University of Wyoming graduate student was seriously injured while using technical climbing equipment to reach one of the known nests hidden in a crack on the side of a cliff.

The three rosy-finch species breed at the highest altitude of any species in North America north of Mexico.

The brown-capped is the southernmost breeding of the three, found mostly in Colorado. The nests in the Snowy Range, in southeastern Wyoming, mark the northern limits of its known breeding range.

If you want to add all three rosy-finch species to your life list at one time, visit the top of Sandia Crest outside of Albuquerque, New Mexico, between November and March. You can take the tram up instead of navigating the road that rises 5,000 feet in elevation. Check www.rosyfinch.com for more information.

While white-crowned sparrows accompanied us on this hike up, they seemed to be birds of terra firma. It was the juncos that were willing to explore bits of vegetation clinging to rocky cliffs. The violet-green swallows shot out over the edge into empty space, following flying insects.

One junco, exploring the face of our rocky observation point, flitted right over me as if my shoulder was a geologic continuation. Its wings nearly brushed my ear. We spooked each other, I think.

While our survey party did hear the distinctive monotone call of the brown-capped rosy-finch, we were never able to pinpoint one of the milk-chocolate brown birds with raspberry tints, much less watch one slip into a crack.

The rosy-finch nest is inserted in rocky and inaccessible places, under large rocks in rock slides and moraines and on the walls of caves, abandoned mines and railroad tunnels, as well as cliff faces protected by overhangs. The nest itself is a cup shaped of woven grasses.

What was disturbing was that there were very few snowfields left in the vicinity. In summer, rosy-finches feed on the frozen insects exposed on melting snowfields and seeds surfacing along their margins.

There was lots of chittering noise from the swallows, making it tough to listen for finches. And then there was a human voice relaying information from across the lake, something about a broken leg.

With our binoculars and spotting scope (if your hiking party includes someone with younger legs and lungs like our son Bryan accompanying us this day, handicap them with equipment – they usually enjoy showing off their superior fitness), we found the harbinger of bad news heading for the Mirror Lake Picnic Area, just a glacial moraine beyond the far side of Lake Marie.

We watched vehicles of various agencies gather. Ant-sized rescuers wearing bright red and yellow hardhats scaled the boulders of the talus slopes and began climbing a smooth-faced peak.

I heard later that an experienced climber had fallen only 12 feet but landed hard on a rock ledge, breaking his leg. At the time we were pretty sure it wasn't another rosy-finch survey member since none of the 20 of us divided into the four parties had had enough time to get that high up. I wonder if the victim distracted himself while waiting for rescue by watching birds, some of which may have been rosy-finches.

Summer is so short at 10,000 feet. That's why rosy-finches can't wait for the snow to completely melt.

Back on June 23, though Lake Marie was ice-free, Lookout Lake, two lakes up and also part of the rosy-finch survey, was still mostly ice-encrusted and the trail along it snow-drifted. Bright yellow glacier lilies bloomed profusely wherever the snow had just melted.

By July 18, three days before the rosy-finch survey, the same hillsides the length of Lookout Lake were covered in columbine and there was no snow left to melt. The columbine were pale looking and probably past their prime, but other flowers were brilliant rose, yellow, blue, purple or white.

Looking closely at the emerald green carpet of vegetation, I could find the seed heads of previous blooms.

Every bird on the ground we saw seemed to be a white-crowned sparrow busy harvesting seeds. Every flock in a tree seemed to be mostly pine siskins. Also working the conifer crop were jays and pine grosbeaks.

I hope to make another pilgrimage to the high country yet this season, barring nasty weather. It isn't too soon to see snow falling up there.

I'm like a junco visiting the mountains in the summer, though I'm ingesting mountain scenery instead of mountain seeds. We're both storing up for spending the long winter back in town.

102 Going by the book doesn't prove bird's existence

Wednesday, October 3, 2007, Outdoors, page C2

If a bird flies through the forest and there is no one to see it, does it exist?

Conversely, if the annual conference of the American Ornithologists' Union is held in your state, will birds be found never before seen there?

Yes and yes. Several of the 500 attendees of the conference held in Laramie in early August observed what may be the first two records of lesser black-backed gull for Wyoming, if accepted by the Wyoming Rare Bird Records Committee.

One of the gulls was hanging out at Lake Hattie on the Laramie Plains and the other at North Gap Lake high in the Snowy Range.

Wyoming does not have a huge number of resident ornithologists or expert birders to cover our vast plains and mountain ranges so one has to wonder how many lesser black-backeds have visited previously.

The lesser black-backed is essentially a European species, but gulls are likely to travel long distances scouting new territory. North American birders started seeing this species in the winter along the Atlantic coast in the early 1970s.

Field guide range maps indicate at least a single record up to a few sightings every year for states in the eastern half of the U.S., but with a heavy concentration along the Front Range of Colorado.

This makes me smile. Several years ago, I went on a late fall field trip led by Tony Leukering and Doug Faulkner to look for gulls at the reservoirs around Fort Collins. We saw several rarities.

Are these guys gull magnets? Or do they have more knowledge of how to recognize species that aren't expected?

So I asked Doug about the new gull in Wyoming. He wrote back:

"You should look at Sibley's Lesser Black-backed range map. That one is pretty accurate, although as with most publications, it was already out-of-date before it hit the printers.

"LBBG is annual in winter in Colorado in small numbers (about 8-12 per winter; I often see 6 or more). In fact, it is regular enough that the Colorado Bird Records Committee no longer requests documentation.

"Colorado's first record is from 1976.

It wasn't until the 1990s, though, that the species really took off and started to occur annually, then in the early 2000s in relatively high numbers for an inland state.

"The Wyoming Bird Records Committee is reviewing documentation of one at Casper from winter 2004. If accepted, that would be the first state record.

"LBBG has been slowly expanding, geographically, westward as evidenced not only by Colorado's records, but also those from other states. More interestingly, the species has broken out of its "rut" of only occurring in winter inland. It is now being found more often in summer (Wyoming's two birds this year, plus several for Colorado and Nebraska in recent years), as well as earlier in the fall and later in the spring."

How many observations does it take before the field guide maps are altered? Last winter a lesser goldfinch, easily distinguished from our usual American goldfinch, was seen at a Cheyenne feeder almost daily, for months. The Sibley Guide to Birds shows a couple green dots meaning that there were already a few records for Wyoming.

But then came this summer. We had one visit our feeder. And so did people from Green River, Casper, Buford and Newcastle who posted their observations on Wyobirds, the e-list for learning about birds in Wyoming. Doug posted a report of small flocks around Guernsey when he birded the area.

Is this the beginning of a trend, an expansion of the lesser goldfinch range north or a one-time phenomenon? Time will tell.

Wyoming is woefully short of qualified observers, though not short of people interested in watching birds. I take a lot of bird identification questions over the phone from people who want to know more about the birds in their yards.

On the other hand, I've also taken calls from visiting birders, who, having looked at the Atlas of Birds, Mammals, Amphibians and Reptiles of Wyoming edited by the Wyoming Game and Fish Department, are positive that they have seen a first Wyoming record for a species they are very familiar with back home.

Are these visitors making a familiar species out of one of our similar local species, or have we locals not recognized an unusual species because we aren't familiar with it?

The Wyoming Bird Records Committee judges the credibility of all rare bird records for the state. A few folks looking to bag state records have been deeply disappointed at the slow speed of our committee, but it is staffed by volunteer experts with full-time jobs, and they do the best they can.

Us average birdwatchers are as important as the expert in documenting changes in the ranges of species. So how do we make our observations useful?

Study birds. Participate in data collection efforts like Project FeederWatch and eBird. Learn when and how to file a rare bird form. To request one, call the Lander Game and Fish regional office, 307-332-2688. And keep looking.

After all, as birdwatchers are fond of pointing out, the birds don't read the books.

2008

103 Birds stay warm, despite cold

Diving into snow drifts just one strategy used to deal with winter

Wool, fleece and down clothes; insulated rubber boots; vigorous shoveling and skiing; hot chocolate and soup; lap cat and household thermostat; quilts and down comforters; and maybe a trip to Albuquerque - that's how I survive winter.

Birds have similar strategies. The chief one is migration, whether down from the mountains or down to South America. It's about balancing food-as-fuel availability with air temperature. The colder the air, the more food birds must find to turn into calories to burn.

Insect eaters depart, except for the gleaners, like the brown creepers which are willing to eat frozen bug bodies found in bark crevices.

Seed, berry and bud eaters stay behind, as well as predatory species. Water birds stay as long as ice doesn't prevent them from getting to the pond weeds and animals.

Migration is a matter of following the food. Snowy owls are perfectly happy wintering in the Arctic unless there aren't enough lemmings to go around. Then they head south.

About 50 species out of a total of 325 on the Cheyenne bird checklist are observed regularly on the Christmas Bird Count. How do they survive?

First, there's fat. Songbirds will put on enough on average to weather three days of storm. More fat than that and they would be too overloaded to evade predators. Sea ducks pack on as much as 10 days' worth. That's how long they can go without being able to eat before they run out of fuel and die.

Then there's shivering. When the pectoral (breast) muscles contract and relax quickly, they produce heat.

That heat warms air trapped by feathers which work better as insulation than mammal hair. Most birds have some down feathers and birds of cold climates have especially good down. Think of eider down, which comes from eider ducks. But the more archaic species, ostrich, emu and kiwi, have none.

A cold bird's other feathers will lift away from its skin and trap more warm air, making the bird a completely different shape in cold than in hot weather. Others, like the common redpoll, have more feathers in winter than summer. Some north country birds have feathers on their legs, like the rough-legged hawk.

Otherwise, birds keep their bare parts warm by burying their beaks under their wings or hunkering down, fluffing feathers over their feet. But you've seen the silly Canada geese at Holliday Park, the ones refusing to migrate because people in the past fed them. They walk on the ice. How do they stand it?

Cold adapted birds have a sophisticated heat exchange system. Warm, arterial blood, traveling from the heart to the feet, passes cooled venal blood returning from the feet and warms it before it is pumped back through the heart. Basically, birds have cold feet so we don't have to worry about them getting stuck on cold metal perches on bird feeders.

Sometimes a sleeping bird's core temperature will drop 20 degrees from 108 degrees (chickadee body temperature) for a fuel savings akin to turning down our thermostats at night. However, if we humans let our body temperatures drop from 98.6 to 78.6 degrees, we'd die. Somehow birds can pull it off and wake up for another day of foraging.

A few birds even manage to enter a deeper state of torpor for months. A study in the 1930s of a poor-will over 85 days showed its body temperature fluctuating with air temperatures in the 60s.

Birds search out warm microhabitats. Grouse dive into snow drifts and stay as toasty as any Boy Scout in a snow cave – unless the surface gets iced over and then they are toast – the birds, that is, not the boys.

Starlings standing around chimneys are smart – until the fumes knock them out and they topple over.

The higher a perching type of bird is in the flock's pecking order, the closer to the trunk of an evergreen tree or the middle of a thicket it can roost and the more protected it will be from winter storms. So the more dominant a bird is, the more likely it is to survive. Besides, dominant birds eat better too and may have more fat going into a storm.

And then there's the "dog pile" effect. A researcher in Maryland cut the top of a hollow wooden fence post where eastern bluebirds had nested so he could remove it from time to time over the winter. Once he found 13 bluebirds packed inside, and another time found more, but two of those were dead from suffocation.

Hawks and owls prefer winter solitude since they are in competition with every other raptor for the limited supply of prey animals.

But for some species, especially the songbirds, sociability is the key to survival. Secretive during the summer nesting season, in winter small birds – chickadees, nuthatches, sparrows – form what is referred to as "mixed species flocks." It means more eyes watching for predators and potential food sources.

I think sociability is a good way for people to survive the winter, too. On January 5, members and friends of Cheyenne - High Plains Audubon Society will be gathering for the annual Christmas Bird Count and the tally party afterwards.

The more of us there are, the warmer we'll be!

104 Doves continue territory expansion, including here

I don't know about your neighborhood, but mine has a gang of doves loafing around on the street corners and they all sport the distinctive gang insignia: black marks tattooed on their necks. They also wear their tails squared off.

I've witnessed a gathering of as many as 28 of these large, pale gray birds raiding my neighbor's juniper hedge for berries.

I just hope the berries don't ferment, causing gang members to fly drunk. It's bad enough that they defecate in my driveway after every berrying spree!

The Eurasian collared-dove (the American Ornithologists' Union code is "EUCD") has been taking over neighborhoods for centuries. It is thought to have started as a native species in India, Sri-Lanka and present-day Myanmar (formerly Burma). In the 1600s it expanded to Turkey and the Balkans.

Next, EUCD flew through Europe: Yugoslavia, 1912; Hungary, 1930; Germany, 1945; Norway, 1954; Britain, 1955; and Portugal, 1974.

Invasion of northern China and Korea is thought to have come through India. Japan was invaded via China in the 18th or 19th century.

In the mid-1970s, a breeder brought EUCD to the Bahamas where a few escaped and 50 were released.

They were seen in Florida in the late 70s and verified there in 1986, quickly followed by sightings in Georgia and Arkansas. The invasion of the U.S. continued: Alabama, 1991; Texas, 1995; South Dakota, 1996; Iowa and Montana, 1997; Minnesota and Wyoming 1998; and Oregon, 1999.

By the time the species account was published in 2002 for Birds of North America Online, EUCD had also been documented in Colorado, Illinois, Kansas, Nebraska and Oklahoma. There is evidence that some birds were intentionally released in California, Missouri and Texas.

The most up-to-date map available on www.ebird.org shows New Hampshire, Vermont and Maine are the only states where birders have yet to report EUCD to that data base.

Some birds introduced to North America, such as house sparrows, thrive at the expense of native species or, in the instance of European starlings, at the expense of agriculture. In Pakistan, EUCD is considered an agricultural pest. Other released species, such as the ringed-turtle dove (now to be known officially as the African Collared-dove), fail to thrive.

EUCD appears to be prospering and enjoying our winters. There are no studies yet showing impacts on mourning doves returning in the spring looking for similar nesting habitat.

EUCD likes nesting in trees, preferably in urban areas. They hang out at bird feeders and at agricultural operations where spilled grain is available. And they will eat berries, as they do in my neighborhood. They roost on utility lines and in trees and other high places. They have a distinctively unmusical coo.

The federal government has classified EUCD as an unprotected species, just like house sparrows and starlings. In 2006, the Wyoming Game and Fish Department announced that EUCD can be hunted any season, anywhere, any method. Of course, with their fondness for urban landscapes, finding EUCD where the discharge of firearms is permitted could be a challenge.

And then pity the poor hunter in Nebraska. Jeff Obrecht, of the Wyoming Game and Fish Department, told me Nebraska's regulations refer only to "doves" and so any EUCD taken has to be counted towards a hunter's bag limit. I'm sure Nebraska never figured on anything but mourning doves when its rules were written.

Even though the first three EUCD in Wyoming were documented outside Cheyenne at the Wyoming Herford Ranch between May 16 and Oct. 9, 1998, someone in the Cody area stole a march on us, submitting the first breeding record in 2001. Since then, a second breeding record has been submitted for the Sheridan area for 2005.

Cheyenne birders, we must unite! Burns, Pine Bluffs, Albin, Carpenter, Meridan – please join us. The glory of the 28th Latilong is at stake! I'm sure EUCD is procreating in our latilong, defined by one degree of latitude and one degree of longitude, but we need to document it. We need evidence. Even though spring is a couple months away, we don't have research to tell us how early EUCD will breed in Wyoming.

Here's your chance.

In winter EUCD is comfortable flocking. A pair from the previous year may still be bonded. But later, the doves get territorial. The male will give an advertising coo and then from his high perch he will fly up at a steep angle with a lot of wing-clapping (just like pigeons) before descending in a spiral, tail spread. The account in Birds of North America Online says he then gives the "excitement" call.

The males bring the females twigs, stems, roots, grasses and urban litter and in one to three days the female has a nest built in a tree, or sometimes, on a building. Two eggs are laid, one after the other, and the parents take turns incubating for about two weeks. The young need around two-and-a-half weeks to fledge but aren't fully independent for another two or three weeks.

In friendly climates, EUCD may start nesting as early as February and produce up to six broods. No one has documented what happens in Cheyenne.

If you observe Eurasian collared-doves sitting on a nest or feeding young, let me know and I'll help you fill out the official paperwork. Who knows, those avian invaders could make you famous, at least in Latilong 28.

105 On tail of secretive goshawk

Wednesday, March 5, 2008, Outdoors, page C2

Twice it's been denied endangered listing because too little is known

The northern goshawk is not a bird on my life list despite my having lived all of my life within its North American range, roughly north of Interstate 80 or in the Rockies and west.

However, I have never lived within its habitat, the forest. Years of forest recreation and birding with experts has never led me to a glimpse of the gray-with-white-bellied hawk, even though it is a large bird: 2 pounds, 21 inches long with 41-inch wingspan.

The Sibley Guide to Birds describes the goshawk and the other two accipiter species, Cooper's and sharp-shinned hawks, as difficult to identify – though I'm pretty sure it is the sharp-shinned terrorizing my feeder birds. Accipiter species have the short, rounded wings and long tails that allow them to navigate in the trees. Other hawk species prefer the wide open spaces.

The goshawk is listed as a sensitive species in six of the eight U.S. Forest Service regions, including Region 2 which includes most of Wyoming.

It is a "management indicator species" which means it is potentially sensitive to habitat changes, especially since it requires large trees for nesting.

Twice the goshawk has been denied listing as a threatened or endangered species because it was ruled that there was not enough information to support either status.

How does one study a bird a field guide describes as secretive? How does one find a set of needle-like talons within a forest of needle-leaved trees?

Jeff Beck and two colleagues came up with a system a couple years ago based on a suggested national protocol. He was the local Audubon chapter's guest speaker last month and is assistant professor of Wildlife Restoration Ecology in the Department of Renewable Resources at the University of Wyoming.

He said traditionally biologists monitored any known goshawk nests for activity each spring. But over time this method shows a downward trend as, I would presume, even with a thriving population, preference for a particular pine tree nesting site might wane as the health of the tree declines over time.

Beck's team's job was to design a more statistically satisfying sampling method for the forest bioregion in Wyoming and Colorado.

First they studied 58 known goshawk territories and statistically analyzed them to see what they had in common.

Was it slope, the steepness of the mountain side? Or aspect, the direction the slope faced? Or elevation? The predicting factor turned out to be vegetation.

Nesting territories were 4.6 times more likely to be in lodgepole pine than spruce/fir forest.

This may not be news to falconers who prize goshawks and are also looking for nests – from which they are licensed to pluck young to train for their sport.

Next, knowing from research that a goshawk nesting territory averages 688 hectares, or 1,700 acres (and may contain several nests per pair over the years), Beck and his team laid a grid of 1,700-acre sampling units on Forest Service land and chose 51 units for a pilot monitoring program.

Finally, field biologists hit the ground twice, once during the time studies showed would coincide with nesting and once during fledging.

In each 1,700-acre study unit, the field biologists played a tape of goshawk calls to elicit a reaction from one if it was present. But because the auditory range was only 150 meters (492 feet), there were a lot of acoustical sampling points to cover in each unit.

It's one thing to draw dots on a map, but it's another to get to them, to overcome thick timber, steep slopes, swamps, bad weather and bears. Also, goshawks deal with intruders by slamming into them, so everyone had to wear hardhats. Next time you see field biology statistics, imagine all the sweat and stories that go into them.

What Beck and his colleagues found was a 65 to 75 percent probability of detecting goshawks. Also, 33 percent of the samples had goshawks. And goshawks were 6.5 times more likely to be seen in their primary pine habitat than their secondary spruce/fir habitat.

Using statistics, the team was able

to determine how many sampling units would be required to detect a 20 percent change in goshawk population. And they were able to determine that sampling sites closer to Forest Service offices produced nearly the same results as sampling remote sites and so monitoring costs could be reduced.

A long-term monitoring program like this could show if the goshawk population rises and falls in a natural cycle. It could show the effects of timber harvesting or recreation pressure, including that of falconers.

But with the pine beetle infestation launching itself throughout Colorado and Wyoming, it will undoubtedly document the goshawks' reaction to a much larger natural cycle in which, at this moment, their preferred nesting trees are dying.

Will it be easier for goshawks to find prey (rabbits, grouse and squirrels) when the trees are mere skeletons? If so, will that advantage be offset by the ease with which their main adversary, the great horned owl, devours their young?

Goshawks are also found in Britain, Scandinavia, northern Russia and Siberia and south to the Mediterranean region, Asia Minor, Iran, the Himalayas, eastern China and Japan. So, we can look for answers from biologists there and share our findings with them.

Meanwhile, I'll take a closer look at piles of sticks in large pine trees. Perhaps I should wear a hardhat, so I don't risk my head while adding to my life list.

106 How to get energy and save our sage grouse

Wednesday, April 2, 2008, Outdoors, page C2

Difficult task lies ahead to keep both resources valuable in Cowboy State

Is geology destiny? Geology is rocks. A particular weathered rock makes a particular kind of soil which, with water, grows particular vegetation. Particular vegetation feeds and shelters particular animals.

Thus, a geologic formation rich in oil and gas can be associated with certain wildlife species.

Using overlays last month at the Cheyenne – High Plains Audubon Society meeting, Alison Lyon-Holloran, conservation program manager for Audubon Wyoming, showed Wyoming's oil, gas and coalbed methane fields almost perfectly align with greater sage-grouse habitat.

The sagebrush ecosystem, on which the grouse is entirely dependent, stretches across Wyoming in a wide swath from the northeast to the southwest, avoiding the mountains in the northwest and the grasslands of the southeast.

If you have not driven across the state, it may be hard to believe that so many acres of sagebrush exist, from the ankle-high species on the dry hills to the small forests along riparian (stream) corridors.

It's hard to believe sage-grouse are so dependent on sage, from hiding their nests in a straggly old stand to grazing on the buds while keeping an eye out for predatory golden eagles.

It's hard to believe a chicken-like 6-pound male or 3-pound female is so shy and easily distracted that the U.S. Bureau of Land Management's drilling stipulations provide, on average, a 2-mile buffer zone around a lek during breeding season.

Those leks are collections of as many as 50-150 males each spreading spikey tail feathers, popping white-feathered neck sacs and defending small territories. The females stroll through, looking for the best genetic material, which, Alison said, may be the same one or two males for all of them.

Someone in the audience asked how sage-grouse are doing. Fine, Alison said, away from the energy development areas. Two wet years have really made a difference in what was a general decline during drought years. However, despite the moisture, they are not doing well in energy areas. It's too crowded and noisy.

Several energy companies have committed millions of dollars to provide offsite mitigation for wildlife and other land users who have lost the use of lands now in oil and gas production.

It would be nice to think that people could enhance sagebrush habitat away from all the wells to produce more grouse, but Alison, who studied sage-grouse for her master's thesis and has been immersed in the research and issues for the last 10 years, said there are no studies showing how to produce scraggly 100-year-old sagebrush stands.

The millions of dollars in mitigation money cannot be used to study why some sagebrush is not attractive to sage-grouse and what can be done to improve it.

It is conceivable, said Alison, that the few remaining healthy sage-grouse leks in Wyoming could be compromised, forcing the birds to be listed as either threatened or endangered – something neither energy companies nor environmentalists want to see happen.

If sage-grouse become threatened or endangered, it would mean more development restrictions for energy companies and much more work for the environmental community.

Of Wyoming's total 62 million acres, the federal government owns, and BLM manages, 41 million acres of minerals below the surface (and 18 million acres of the surface).

So far, 14 million acres of federal minerals have been leased for oil and gas. Don't forget state and private oil and gas leasing because 45 percent of Wyoming's total oil and 37 percent of its natural gas production comes from them. See BLM's 2007 annual report at www.blm.gov/wy.

In the old days, environmental groups would be preparing lawsuits. Instead, Alison and Audubon Wyoming executive director Brian Rutledge came up with the Greater Sage-grouse Species Survival Plan. They have hired Kevin Doherty, who studied sage-grouse for his PhD, to give the issue the necessary rigorous, scientific statistical scrutiny.

The National Audubon Society has taken notice also and has made sagebrush one of its top conservation concerns.

Key players from federal and state government have been working with energy and environmental groups to figure out how, during fluid mineral development, we can have our energy and our grouse, too, here in the state with the most grouse habitat of any in the country. And there are other sagebrush species that will benefit.

The highlight of Alison's presentation was the Steve Chindgren film, "It's Just Sagebrush," a half hour un-narrated look at wildlife in the sage over a year's time. It was filmed mostly between Farson and Pinedale.

If you haven't yet traveled a two-track, sagebrush tickling the belly of your pickup, pungent sage smell (not the garden variety) wafting through your open window along with a fine wind of dust as you bump over badger holes and glimpse heavy-bodied sage-grouse taking flight like lumbering World War II bombers, you should see the film.

So, is geology destiny? Yes, I think so. While geology (and climate) makes some states suitable for farming, geology has made Wyoming rich in fossil fuels and sagebrush. We just have to choose how to keep both resources valuable.

107

Wednesday, April 30, 2008, Outdoors, page C2

12 practical ways you can help keep birds safe

All winter our relationship to wild birds is confined to observation and, perhaps, feeding them. But now with migration and breeding seasons intersecting with an increase in human outdoor activity, we need to think about bird safety.

1. Litter – The cigarette stubbed out in the driveway disappears, but probably blew onto the neighbor's lawn where, if it isn't picked up, it will, like other loose trash, break down and its unnatural components will pollute soil and water. Before that is able to happen, litter could end up in the digestive system of curious babies, puppies and other animals. And remember all those photos of birds hampered by fishing line and other plastic debris.

2. Windows – If you are dreading the annual cleaning chores, skip your windows and tell people dirty ones are not as dangerous for birds. If you do wash your windows and find that one is particularly prone to getting messed up by birds thumping into it, you need to put some stickers on the outside. Cornell Lab of Ornithology, Student Conservation Association and Wyoming Public Radio send me those nice static cling type stickers every year so I can advertise my affiliations at the same time.

3. Cats – Nasty winter weather made it easy to keep your cat indoors. Just continue to keep it in and buy a harness and leash for little excursions, or build an outdoor pen with a screened roof. If you put a bird feeder outside a window, your indoor cat will be very happy. Just make sure the window screen is strong enough to withstand your cat's aborted bird attacks. If you don't have a cat and are tired of the neighbor's eating the birds that come to your feeder, borrow a cat trap from the animal shelter or get a dog to scare it off.

4. Feeders – Cold winters are marvelous for keeping bacteria in check around feeders. Don't quit feeding now in warm weather when migrating birds will make feeder watching even more interesting. But be sure to clean your feeders and feeding areas with a mild bleach solution every few weeks. If you see any lethargic house finches, perhaps with warty growths around their eyes, quit feeding for at least a week so the healthy birds don't come in and get infected.

5. Water – If you provide a bird bath, make sure it has sloping sides or a sloping rock in the middle so birds can wade in. Brush the scum out every day when you refill it. Think about disinfecting it periodically. If you have tanks for watering livestock, make sure they have bird ramps to avoid drownings.

6. Pesticides – If toxic chemicals

are sprayed on your lawn, you can keep small children and pets off for the necessary period of time, but birds can't read those cute little signs. Plus, pesticides wash into ground and surface water used by people and wildlife. Instead, try non-toxic lawn and garden care. Talk to Master Gardeners at the Laramie County Cooperative Extension Service, 633-4383.

7. Mowing – So you bought the house with five acres of prairie, and a riding mower, and you can't wait to get out there. Please relax, take a hike or go fishing instead, and let the ground nesting birds, including the meadowlarks everyone enjoys, get the next generation started. Give them till at least mid-July.

8. Dogs – During the crucial season for ground nesting birds, late April to mid-July, keep dogs on a leash so they don't raid nests.

9. Nest Boxes – A birdhouse that is meant to be safely used by birds will have certain crucial features. The opening will be sized precisely for the intended cavity-nesting species: house wren, mountain bluebird, tree swallow, flicker, etc. There's no perch sticking out below, where starlings can stand while reaching in to raid the nest. Some kind of latch allows the nest box to be opened for cleaning. The box is the right dimensions, has proper ventilation, is not painted a dark color and is situated at the right height. Check the library for a book with particulars.

10. Baby Birds – Short of a catastrophe killing their parents, baby birds seldom need our help. It is best to leave them alone. If you watch long enough, you'll probably see parents bringing food to the grounded fledgling until it gets up the gumption to fly. You can try setting featherless nestlings back in their nest or in a small bucket with twigs and grass hung somewhere safe near where you found them (but not if they are a ground-nesting species). Trying to feed baby birds yourself is usually not successful and deprives other wildlife species that depend on baby birds for their own food supply.

11. Shrubs and Trees – Cheyenne is in the midst of the grasslands, and if we are to promote the welfare of the beleaguered grassland bird species which have lost habitat due to plowing and development, we shouldn't promote planting trees and shrubs away from creeks and lakes. But right around our homes natural shade and windbreaks conserve energy, shelter migrating birds and attract birds we wouldn't see otherwise out here on the plains. Choose native fruit and seed producing vegetation.

12. Energy – There is no energy source yet that doesn't have some negative impact on wildlife. Remember, stuff you buy takes energy to produce so recycle and reuse, of course. And if you reduce the size of the house you need to heat and maintain and reduce the amount of stuff you buy that always seems to take additional energy and maintenance, guess what? You'll save money and have more time to enjoy life and watch birds!

108 Birding naked

It's not nearly as fun as it sounds

Birding naked is all the rage in southeastern Arizona. That's what Gloria Lawrence of Casper told me May 17 while she and five other Casper birders helped local Audubon members with the Cheyenne Big Day Bird Count.

Gloria was not enthusiastic about the birding naked field trips. Actually, going au natural is what most people do when they look at birds without optics. Birding without binoculars and scopes means using your naked eye – eye glasses and contacts excepted.

The morning of the count I put on my binoculars. With the elastic strap harness so many of us birders use, it really is like getting dressed.

And getting dressed the last two weeks has been complicated by having my right hand in a splint. After 23 years, I opted to have pregnancy-induced carpel tunnel syndrome repairs.

You know what? Binoculars, in addition to being made for two eyes, are made for two hands. While my left hand is pretty adept at many things, it couldn't hold the binocs up and focus them too. I'd like to find a skinnier and lighter pair anyway.

When there was a blackpoll warbler directly overhead in a willow at Lions Park, I was able to lay the binocs on my upturned face and use the focus barrel more easily. But every time the bird flitted, I had to lift them off and locate the bird again.

My usual technique of staring at the bird and then putting the binocs between me and the bird didn't seem to be working.

At least the western tanager was close enough to be identifiable naked. Bright yellow body, black wings and red-orange head, there's no mistaking it for anything else. But I soon gave up on any birds that had to be differentiated by spots and streaks. I just couldn't get my binocs focused on them fast enough.

Finally, I found my useful niche and pointed out bird blurs to other people in the group, "I saw a flash of orange head up into that tree." "Oh yes," someone replied, "a Bullock's oriole."

I said, "A sparrow went into those reeds." "Ah, a Savannah sparrow," they said. Of course, I've never been able to tell that species apart from any of the other obscure sparrows anyway, so no loss.

A boss I had years ago was blind in one eye and bought himself a monocular. Imagine – you could afford twice the optical quality if you were buying only half a pair of binocs.

I looked forward to our stop at Wyoming Hereford Ranch Reservoir #1 where we'd set up spotting scopes to look for water birds. Once they are set up, it takes only one hand to use them though often the focus knob is on the right side.

For years Mark and I didn't own a scope and pretty much bypassed checking out reservoirs on our own. The birds are always on the far side, and it takes more imagination than I have to make blurs into birds. But the cheap scope (now selling for $300) we finally bought really made a difference. I can see the field marks and appreciate the variety of species.

There are still many birds to be enjoyed even if you are birding naked. As long as your ears are working, a spring morning is full of different birds, starting with robins at 3 a.m.

Many birds are large and unique. I can tell a turkey vulture (leading edge of the underside of wing is black, trailing edge is silver) from a Swainson's hawk (trailing edge is dark, leading edge is light) from a red-tailed hawk (tail is "red", reddish brown) even at 75 mph with sunglasses on providing the birds aren't soaring too high.

Then there was the red-winged blackbird strolling toward me on the walk around Sloans Lake the morning of the count. I'd fallen behind the rest of the group and decided I might as well enjoy a bird close up if I could.

We stopped about two feet from each other, our eyes locking as if we were characters in a Harlequin romance. His black feathers were glossy and his fire-engine red epaulets were puffed out. His black eyes glinted in the sunshine. I hated to break our rapport, but I knew there was a female in stripy plumage who would appreciate him even more.

By evening Mark and I hit the lakes at F.E. Warren Air Force Base. I was tired of not really seeing birds and having to depend on everyone else to identify the blurs. It was such a good birding day otherwise – little wind, warm, sunny, trees hardly leafed out, the crabapples at their peak and the appearance of a mourning warbler that almost everyone else saw.

And then I saw them, a whole raft of sleeping pelicans. The lake was small enough that they were close enough to enjoy.

All together I'd say birding naked is just about as frustrating as birding without clothes would be uncomfortable – imagine sunburn, bugs, and thorns. What I didn't miss was my usual role as note taker for the group. But I missed having a close look at all my favorite little migrating feather balls and learning to identify new ones.

Remind me to avoid scheduling surgery on my left hand too close to the Christmas Bird Count. It would be kind of cold for birding naked.

Cheyenne Big Day Count May 17, 2008

123 species overall
L – Lions Park Wyoming Important Bird Area, 48 species
W – Wyoming Hereford Ranch Wyoming Important Bird Area, 81 species
R – High Plains Grasslands Research Station, 28 species
B – F.E. Warren Air Force Base, 34 species
O – Other observations, 39 species

Species	L	W	R	B	O	Species	L	W	R	B	O
Canada Goose	L	W		B	O	Ruddy Duck		W		B	
Gadwall		W		B		Pied-billed Grebe			R	B	
American Wigeon		W				Eared Grebe		W		B	
Mallard	L	W	R	B		Western Grebe	L	W			O
Blue-winged Teal	L	W	R	B	O	American White Pelican				B	O
Cinnamon Teal		W			O	Double-crested Cormorant	L	W			O
Northern Shoveler		W			O	Great Blue Heron					O
Northern Pintail		W				Black-crowned Night Heron	L				O
Green-winged Teal		W			O	White-faced Ibis		W			O
Redhead		W		B	O	Turkey Vulture	L				
Ring-necled Duck		W				Cooper's Hawk	L				
Greater Scaup		W				Broad-winged Hawk					O
Lesser Scaup	L	W		B		Swainson's Hawk		W	R	B	
Bufflehead		W				Red-tailed Hawk		W	R		

Species	L	W	R	B	O
American Kestrel		W			
Prairie Falcon		W			
Sora	L	W			
American Coot		W			O
Killdeer		W	R		
American Avocet		W			
Lesser Yellowlegs		W			
Willet		W			O
Spotted Sandpiper	L	W		B	
Marbled Godwit					O
Baird's Sandpiper					O
Stilt Sandpiper		W			
Wilson's Snipe		W			
Wilson's Phalarope		W			
Red-necked Phalarope		W			
Ring-billed Gull				B	O
Black Tern					O
Rock Pigeon	L			B	
Eurasian Collared-Dove	L	W	R	B	O
Mourning Dove	L	W	R	B	O
Great Horned Owl		W	R		
Chimney Swift	L				
Belted Kingfisher		W			
Downy Woodpecker	L		R		
Hairy Woodpecker			R		
Northern Flicker	L				
Olive-sided Flycatcher			R		
Least Flycatcher		W			
Dusky Flycatcher	L				
Say's Phoebe		W			
Cassin's Kingbird			R		
Western Kingbird		W			
Eastern Kingbird		W			
Plumbeous Vireo	L	W			
Blue Jay					O
Black-billed Magpie			R		
American Crow	L			B	O
Horned Lark		W			
Tree Swallow		W			
Violet-green swallow		W			
N. Rough-winged Swallow		W	R		
Bank Swallow		W	R		
Cliff Swallow		W			
Barn Swallow		W			
Black-capped Chickadee			R		
Mountain Chickadee					O
Red-breasted Nuthatch			R		
House Wren	L	W			
Ruby-crowned Kinglet	L	W			
Blue-gray Gnatcatcher		W	R	B	
Eastern Bluebird			R		
Townsend's Solitaire			R		
Veery		W			
Swainson's Thrush	L	W		B	
American Robin	L	W		B	O
Gray Catbird	L				
Northern Mockingbird	L				
Brown Thrasher			R		
European Starling	L	W		B	O
Orange-crowned Warbler	L	W		B	
Virginia's Warbler		W			
Yellow Warbler	L	W		B	O
Black-throated Blue Warbler	L				
Yellow-rumped Warbler	L	W	R		
Blackpoll Warbler	L	W	R	B	
American Redstart		W			
Ovenbird		W			
Northern Waterthrush	L				
Mourning Warbler		W			
Common Yellowthroat	L	W			O
Wilson's Warbler		W			
Western Tanager	L	W			
Spotted Towhee		W			
Chipping Sparrow	L	W		B	O
Clay-colored Sparrow			R		
Field Sparrow				B	
Lark Sparrow	L		R		O
Lark Bunting		W			
Savannah Sparrow			R		O
Song Sparrow	L	W		B	
Lincoln's Sparrow	L	W			
White-throated Sparrow		W			
White-crowned Sparrow	L	W			
Lazuli Bunting					O
Red-winged Blackbird	L	W	R	B	
Western Meadowlark		W		B	
Yellow-headed Blackbird	L			B	O
Common Grackle	L	W		B	O
Great-tailed Grackle					O
Brown-headed Cowbird		W		B	
Bullock's Oriole	L	W			
House Finch	L			B	O
Pine Siskin	L				O
American Goldfinch	L	W			O
House Sparrow	L			B	O

109

Nesting season a time for activity

Nesting season means a variety of building activities.

Nesting season means the dawn chorus of birdsong quiets down as the business of assuring the continuation of species gets underway.

Great horned owls get an early start. By mid-May a stick nest in a cottonwood west of town sported two owlets that with all their fluff seemed as large as their parents. But, apparently, owlets in the same nest don't hatch at the same time. Jana Ginter told me this spring she rescued two after a windstorm blew down their nest near Carpenter.

The rehabilitators at the Rocky Mountain Raptor Center in Fort Collins, Colorado, suspected, based on the size difference between the owlets, that there must have been a third that hatched in between. Detective work by Jana showed the third owlet was rescued and taken to rehabbers in Nebraska.

The big stick messes in the cottonwoods, along the shores of Lake Minnehaha at Holliday Park, belong to a colony of black-crowned night herons. It's hard to see the large birds on the nests once the trees leaf out, so many park users have no idea what's going on overhead.

Gulls are fond of nesting in colonies too, but on the ground, preferably on an inaccessible island.

May 31: Mark and I were in Casper for the 8th annual Wyoming Audubon Chapters campout and visited Soda Lake as part of a group of guests of Murie Audubon Society. The reservoir is not publicly accessible, and the birds seemed less skittish there than other reservoirs.

Double-crested cormorants and California gulls were shoulder to shoulder on a bit of sand, many quietly sitting on nests which were merely scraped-together mounds of natural debris. Then someone with a spotting scope called out, "Look, chicks!"

Sure enough, around the standing adult gulls were little gray fluff balls, hardly different from chicken chicks. Even though gulls quickly attain adult size, this species will go through five plumage variations in the first four years before getting complete adult coloration.

Walking along the North Platte River at Edness Kimball Wilkins State Park earlier in the day we were surrounded by noisy yellow warblers (the species is also named "Yellow Warbler") high up in the cottonwoods. Every distinctive call was easy to match up with another bright, daffodil-yellow bird. We were surprised when one flitted closer, to eye-level branches of a small tree. Then we spotted the cup-shaped nest in a junction of branches.

Robins build similar, but bigger, cup-shaped nests since they are nearly twice the length of a warbler, but they don't always build in trees. Every year, I get calls about them nesting on front porch light fixtures and dive-bombing homeowners.

We've had robins nest in the bushes under our window where we could look out and watch the nestlings develop. This year, when the male kept zooming past the window with his beak full of nesting material, the trajectory didn't seem right. I realized finally he was building on an exposed beam under the roof overhang, free from disturbance by squirrels, cats and human onlookers.

Canada geese will nest on manmade platforms, but so far, I've never seen them use the upended concrete culverts at North Crow Reservoir. Unlike a Christo landscape art project, these spoil an otherwise beautiful setting and I hope the state parks people will remove them. Most years I've found evidence of geese nesting on the far shore and observed at least two families of goslings per year.

As for other nesting strategies, I didn't stumble over any killdeer or meadowlark ground nests out on the prairie this spring, but I did see tree swallows flitting in and out of nest boxes probably meant for mountain bluebirds.

If you have been watching a nest this season, consider sharing your information through Cornell Lab of Ornithology's NestWatch citizen science program. Unlike Project FeederWatch, participation in this project is free. It is funded by the National Science Foundation and developed in collaboration with the Smithsonian Migratory Bird Center.

Go to www.nestwatch.org and learn how to monitor nesting birds so that the data collected can be of scientific importance. Even if you don't join, you can explore the data. Or learn best nest box construction and maintenance practices and other things at www.nestinginfo.org.

June 16: My robin fledglings left the safety of the nest. The one that insisted on sitting in the middle of the lawn was soon discovered by crows and could not be saved by half a dozen angry adult robins and my belated approach. Crows have to eat too, I guess.

But I glimpsed two other, smarter, fledglings deep in the bushes. They've already learned two things: it's a bird-eat-bird world out there and, you can't go home again – at least until you build your own nest.

110 Should a landfill go here?

Monday, August 11, 2008, ToDo, page C1

Public can chime in on plans for Belvoir Ranch

The city-owned ranch, which has tee-pee rings and other historic features, could soon be home to wind turbines and a garbage dump.

Where wildlife and pre-historic people once discovered an easy travel route, it isn't surprising that everyone from stagecoach drivers to fiber optic companies have followed.

And that route passes through the Belvoir Ranch, bought by the City of Cheyenne in 2003.

It begins five miles west of Cheyenne and stretches for 15 miles farther west, with Interstate Highway 80 as its northern boundary.

While some residents see the 18,000-acre purchase as a boondoggle, others see it as acquiring water rights and sites for a landfill, wind turbine farm and recreation. It is also a chance to preserve a microcosm of western cultural history.

Chuck Lanham of the Cheyenne Historic Preservation Board, the guide for a recent ranch tour, pointed out tepee rings at least 140 years old and other archeological features that will be studied.

Arapaho tribal elders have visited recently, sharing their knowledge of the land. Eastern Shoshone, Northern Cheyenne and Lakota tribes also have ties.

Ruts across the rolling, shortgrass prairie show the route of the Denver to Fort Laramie stage line. Other ruts are thought to be Camp Carlin supply wagon tracks to frontier forts. There are vestiges, too, of the old Lincoln Highway, precursor to U.S. Highway 30 and Interstate 80.

When the Union Pacific Railroad came, it built water tanks and "columns" to fill its steam-powered engines. Today, the ranch is crisscrossed by three sets of rails.

Eventually, the early homesteads became part of the huge Warren Livestock Company holdings. F.E. Warren called the main ranch house his "cabin," complete with tennis courts, pool and professional horse racing track. Remains are barely visible today.

Because of the 1962 Cuban Missile Crisis, Atlas missiles were installed on what soon became known as the Belvoir Ranch. The above-ground launching facilities were deactivated in 1965, but the concrete structures can be seen south of I-80 at exit 348.

Currently, the 1,800-acre Big Hole area is under a conservation easement with The Nature Conservancy. Local ranchers hold grazing and haying leases on the rest. The fees they pay cover most of the ranch's operating expenses.

A utility corridor provides easement for a power transmission line, four pipelines and two fiber optic lines. The Borie oil field continues operations, but mineral rights are not owned by the city.

A contract with Wyoming Game and Fish Department through their Hunter Management Area program allows some hunter access, the only legal public access to the Belvoir Ranch at present.

2009

Tuesday, January 13, 2009, Outdoors, Commentary, page B5

111 It's possible that wolves in Yellowstone are having a positive effect on songbirds

Back in the early 1990s, the National Audubon Society lobbied for the reintroduction of wolves in the Yellowstone ecosystem.

Why, some folks wondered, would an organization with a name equated with bird conservation be interested in wolves?

An Audubon member myself, I agreed with the ecologists who were saying it was important to have all the pieces of an ecosystem, from top dog predator on down to burying beetle and I lobbied for wolves on ecological principles.

There were a couple people who thought wolves shouldn't be reintroduced because, based on a few anecdotes, wolves might already be present.

If there were wolves in Yellowstone immediately before reintroduction, and not just casual stragglers or hybrids and captives dumped by people, they were nearly invisible, awfully quiet, well behaved and unproductive.

Today, commercial enterprises will take you on a wolf tour (www.wolftracker.com). Reintroduced wolves multiplied so quickly, they also became a noticeable nuisance to livestock operators.

Wolves are apparently having an effect on the Yellowstone ecosystem that their predator stand-ins, the coyotes, were not able to achieve between early 20th century wolf eradication programs and wolf reintroduction in 1995. The willows are increasing, which means increasing numbers of songbirds.

Doug Smith, leader of the Yellowstone Wolf Project for Yellowstone National Park, in a reply to my email query, was quick to point out that studies are still ongoing and that some people believe there is more than the wolf at work in the growth of willow shrubs. Papers are in the process of being written and Smith said, "As far as wolf impacts on songbirds, we are on our way to establishing the link that goes through willow and elk."

Willow grows in riparian zones, the areas along creeks and rivers. A healthy riparian zone, with lots of vegetation, absorbs rainfall and snowmelt like a sponge and releases it slowly into creeks. In an unhealthy situation, with little vegetation present, water runs off quickly, eroding the surface, depositing sediment in the stream where it suffocates fish eggs and the invertebrates that feed fish.

In a healthy riparian zone, vegetation slows the runoff water. Slow water can't carry as much sediment and organic matter, and so it drops it on the plants adjacent to the stream, rather than in the stream. Riparian plants, such as willow, thrive on and grow through the sediment deposits, eventually providing more and more vegetation.

If the lack of vegetation in a riparian zone is from overgrazing by wildlife or livestock, managers can reverse the trend by either fencing the animals out for a period of time or reducing the number of animals grazing and/or the time and amount they graze.

National park managers have restrictions that prevent them from removing elk which have kept the willows trimmed too well while the wolves were out of the picture.

However, the willows seem to be recovering and expanding. One theory is that climate change is providing a longer growing season. Another theory is that the Yellowstone fires of 1988 provided a huge increase in forbs (non-woody plants including wildflowers) which elk like better than shrubs, and they grazed the willows less.

A third theory is that elk no longer get to graze willows at their leisure since wolves are constantly nipping at their heels and running them off.

Range management scientists have spent years conducting studies of the effects of various grazing schemes and could probably make some predictions, but every ecosystem has its quirks.

Whether the wolves are totally or partly responsible for the regeneration of Yellowstone willows, we can reasonably predict healthier riparian zones.

From my birdwatcher's perspective, this means more and greater diversity of songbirds which are attracted to the insects associated with the willows and the shelter provided. Smith listed willow flycatcher, yellow warbler, common yellowthroat, Lincoln's sparrow and song sparrow in particular.

Improved riparian habitat means improved fisheries. It also means ephemeral and intermittent streams will flow a little longer each year.

The increase in vegetation can support more critters (even livestock outside the park). Wyoming's riparian zones are important to something like 70 percent of wildlife species.

Bureaucracy and politics will continue to plague the Yellowstone wolves, but if studies show wolves have helped repair an important part of their ecosystem, reintroduction has been worthwhile.

112 Wyoming has 48 places that are important to birds

Sunday, April 5, 2009, Outdoors, page E2

Spring means a birder's thoughts turn to migration and those hotspots where birds will be thickest.

Some spring hotspots are on a national list of Important Bird Areas. Two of those IBAs are right here in Cheyenne. No entrance fees required.

BirdLife International has identified places important to birds on every

continent, in 100 countries and territories. Places like Fiji, Romania and Peru. They work with local agencies to help implement conservation and education plans.

In 1995, the National Audubon Society became the sponsoring organization for the IBA program in the U.S. While some places are rated as globally important, such as Yellowstone National Park, others are recognized as important at the national and state level.

Audubon Wyoming has recognized 48 places as important to birds in our state so far. Coordinator Alison Lyon-Holloran is still taking nominations. Contact her in Laramie at 307-745-4848 or at aholloran@audubon.org. Check www.AudubonWyoming.org to see which sites are already in the program.

What makes a place important to birds? It is important to birds during migration, and/or breeding and/or wintering seasons for one or more species, meaning birds can find food, shelter and water and whatever else they require during a particular season. Alison also requires approval from the landowner before reviewing the nomination.

Nominating Lions Park was a no-brainer for my local chapter, Cheyenne – High Plains Audubon Society (CHPAS). We have people traveling to Cheyenne from a 200-mile radius because the park's trees, shrubs and lake attract so many species during spring migration. At the mid-May peak one year, I counted 60 species in two hours.

The nomination stalled at first when the ornithologists on the technical committee countered that we only saw a lot of birds at the park because a lot of people birded there. Yes, but we could probably find the same diversity and abundance of songbirds, if not the waterfowl, in all of the old neighborhoods. We couldn't very well walk through everyone's yard.

CHPAS continues to monitor the park's bird life through seasonal surveys and evaluates the impacts of new park developments.

The Wyoming Hereford Ranch has had a long and friendly relationship with the local birding community. Anna Marie and Sloan Hales welcome inspection by binocular, as long as no one disturbs the livestock, hops the fences, or intrudes on the residents of the ranch.

Again, I'd venture to say that other properties along cottonwood-filled creeks in southeastern Wyoming might have similar abundance and diversity. The difference is the Hales.

Not only have they welcomed birders, but they were thrilled to be part of the nomination process. They've worked with the Laramie County Conservation District to improve wildlife habitat and in cooperation with Audubon Wyoming to install signs this spring educating visitors about why their ranch is an IBA. The Hales have also created a little nature trail.

The ranch, as an oasis of wildness on the edge of Cheyenne, will only become more and more important a refuge as high-density housing and commercial enterprises continue to move into their neighborhood. Who knew over 100 years ago, when the ranch was established, people would want to build houses in cow pastures 10 miles from the State Capitol building?

IBA designation doesn't bind any landowner to any course of action. But it does make people aware that their actions will have an impact on birds. It makes us stop and think about beings besides ourselves and we get back to the original question: Does a bird have any value if you aren't a birdwatcher?

Sometimes it has an obvious usefulness, such as keeping pests under control. If nothing else, birds are a part of nature, and contact with nature is being scientifically proven to improve our mental health.

With the onset of spring, many of us are looking for an excuse to get outside. Here in Cheyenne we don't have to travel to Important Bird Areas, even our local ones, to see special birds. We just need to keep our eyes and ears open in our own backyards.

113 Young birds stage a summer drama series

Late summer is late to be hatching ducklings. Mama Mallard either lost her first brood or having raised them, thought she could slip in another before fall.

I saw her swimming with her very young family in a corner of Lake Minnehaha at Holliday Park early on a mid-August morning. Two ducklings suddenly propelled themselves forward, as if they were trying to catch flying insects. There was a flurry of peeps and I realized Mama was having a hissy fit, launching herself at a specific spot of water and then another and another while all five ducklings suddenly crowded together near shore.

That's when I saw the snakelike head of a young double-crested cormorant emerge. I doubt its underwater intentions were merely to tickle the ducklings' toes. I didn't stay long enough to see if getting beat up by a mad mom discouraged it or if it was finally successful in grabbing a snack. Sometimes the final act of the play is just too sad to stay and watch.

A tragedy played out at the park earlier, but I missed the coup de grace. The four big white domestic geese are prominent park citizens. Back in July, I counted four goslings in their midst, still in their fluffy grayish down. Considering the number of dogs being walked every day, I thought it brave of them to stand around on the mainland rather than on the island. But any dog with a brain would recognize their malevolent gaze and the damage their wedge-shaped bills can do to intruders.

So, I was surprised the day I counted only two goslings. And no, the white birds sleeping down by the water's edge are domestic ducks, not geese. You can tell because they have, umm, duck-shaped bills.

This brings up the latest chapter in an ongoing daytime drama. Since white domestic ducks are descendants of mallards and the mallards at Holliday Park act domesticated, not bothering to migrate anymore since they learned people will feed them illegally, it wasn't surprising that proximity would breed, well, hybrids.

Like a litter of stray kittens, no two of these hybrids seem to look the same. There's been more than one beginning birder who has flipped through their new field guide in frustration. Some hybrids come out as giants with perfect mallard coloring. Some are almost black. Currently, one has a big white spot on the back of its head that gives it a daffy look as it stands around with the other young ducks.

Not all gawky teenagers want to hang out with the others. For several weeks, I could depend on seeing one of the young black-crowned night-herons patrolling the lawn on the east side of the park, like a gargantuan sparrow. It didn't budge an inch as long as I didn't approach it directly and stayed on the sidewalk, even though I had a 125-pound dog walking beside me.

I don't know what our unflinching hero was finding in the grass, but four or five of its cohorts, also born in the colony of nests overhead and wearing identical stripy brown plumage, could be found stooped over at the edge of the island waiting to stab fish. Where are their parents? Sleeping days, I expect, now that they don't have to feed their young every minute.

It isn't unusual to see small birds harassing large birds. But a couple days ago, the David and Goliath story was a bit different. In front of Henderson Elementary School, I saw a Eurasian collared-dove flying after a Swainson's hawk. The hawk landed on the top of a utility pole and the dove on the attached streetlight, less than two feet away.

As I passed by, I could see the hawk was ignoring the live bird in favor of the meat under its talons. I can't imagine what would drive the dove to want to watch a hawk eat. Was it feeding on another dove or some other animal? I couldn't tell.

Thousands of coming-of-age stories are playing out in our backyards in late summer. Every time you see a speckled-breasted young robin on its own, somewhere there's a parent getting down to the business of finding enough to eat to prepare itself for migration. Or notice the grackle being pursued by a youngster thinking it is entitled to a few more free meals.

Just this morning I heard, but didn't see, two red-breasted nuthatches. Back from their summer in the mountains already? Were these the birds which visited my feeders all last winter, or their kids?

So many stories, so many conjectures, so little time.

114   To feed or not to feed?

Sunday, November 29, 2009, Outdoors, page E2

Local birdwatcher battles with whether her bird feeder is a good idea.

To feed or not to feed, that is the question this time of year.

On one side are the purists who say bird feeders are an unnatural source of food for birds. They blame the invasion of the East Coast by a western bird species, the house finch, on feeding. They'll point to avian diseases transmitted when unnaturally high numbers of birds congregate in the same location day after day.

The purists will mention birds die when they fly into windows near feeders or when they are attacked by loose cats. They argue that some birds may decide not to migrate if they have a ready food source. That is true for the Canada geese in Holliday Park and Lions Park.

But let's keep this discussion centered on the songbirds fond of sunflower seeds.

The purists are right: A bird in its native habitat does not need supplemental feed to survive the winter. If its preferred seed crop had poor production or becomes covered in snow, it will fly. Grosbeaks, redpolls, waxwings, crossbills and siskins are all noted for travelling when they need food, sometimes hundreds of miles from their expected wintering grounds.

Yes, the backyard feeding station can be hazardous to small birds, but probably not any more so than natural predators and hazards.

So why feed birds? Do it for your own enjoyment. Do it for the cheerful chatter, the bright colors, the bustle and hustle. If watching fish swim in a bowl relieves stress, as I've heard, then watching birds out the window not only relieves stress but is life affirming. It is for me.

Wildlife is elusive enough that most

people have little contact with it unless they hunt or fish or have spotting scopes or long lenses on their cameras. Without some other kind of personal relationship, how can we expect the general population to begin to buy into any kind of conservation ethic? Most wild animals are too dangerous to approach or feed. Chickadees seldom are.

Is it important to have a conservation ethic? Yes. What makes wildlife and land healthy makes people healthy. If you want the footnotes and scientific references, read one of Michael Pollan's recent books on food.

Meanwhile, let's talk about ethical bird feeding. For more information see the American Bird Conservancy, www.abcbirds.org.

Grow diversity in your yard by providing native flowers, shrubs and trees for shelter and habitat, and even food. Reduce or eliminate pesticide use. Pesticides are toxic to birds and can kill insects beneficial to them. Even seed eating birds feed their young insects.

Provide water and keep it clean and fresh. If you don't offer food, water will attract birds. Get one of those little heaters meant for bird baths or dog water dishes or use a portable pan or plastic dog food dish you can bring inside to thaw the ice.

Feed the good stuff, black oil sunflower seed – and thistle seed if you can afford it. Forget the mixes with red and white milo which tend to attract the non-native house sparrows and Eurasian collared-doves. They compete well enough with our native birds already.

You don't need to run a soup kitchen. A couple of feeders are enough. If the birds empty them in the morning, then wait until mid-afternoon or the next morning to refill them. We don't want to upset the natural balance too much.

Keep feeders clean. At our house,

we no longer use the feeders with the little saucers at the bottom—those get really gross. Our feeders are hung over the concrete patio so we can sweep up the debris regularly. If the weather gets warm, it is important to wash the feeders weekly before organisms can grow. If you notice sick birds, stop feeding for a week and clean everything.

Keep feeders within three feet of the window, so birds will be aiming for the perches instead of the glass or at least won't hit the glass so hard. Leave the window screen on so birds will bounce off or put decals on the outside of the window to break up the reflection. If feeding birds is for your enjoyment, there's no point in putting the feeders where you can't see them easily.

Keep your cat indoors—they look better if they haven't lost the tips of their ears to frostbite. If it isn't your cat lying in wait under the feeder, then send the dog out for a while to clear the area.

If you won't keep your cat indoors, make sure it doesn't have a place to hide in ambush within 25 feet of your feeder. And if you can't do that, don't feed birds.

If you have trouble with deer horning in, either don't feed the birds or put the feeders where troublesome wildlife can't reach them.

If sharp-shinned hawks start picking off seed-eaters at your feeder, congratulate yourself on attracting the next level in the food chain. Life in the wild is about death as well.

Get a field guide from the bookstore or the library and find out what birds are visiting. Take a close look at the LBJs and LGBs (little brown jobs and little gray birds) and you might be surprised how many kinds you've attracted. Many are just here for the winter, so enjoy them while you can.

2010

115 Meditation on pine beetles

Sunday, January 31, 2010, Outdoors, page E3

Is there life after tree death?

For anyone who doesn't regularly recreate in or travel through the forests of southcentral Wyoming and north central Colorado, the photos of pine beetle damage shown at January's Cheyenne-High Plains Audubon Society meeting might have been a shock. Especially the photos of grown trees blown down like straws, and campgrounds denuded by the removal of hazardous trees.

Many of the 75 people in the audience, however, judging by their questions and comments, have mountain property and are in the midst of the battlefield.

The largest mountain landowner, the U.S. Forest Service, was represented by the evening's speaker, Steve Carrey, director of renewable resources for the Medicine Bow-Routt National Forest. One irate audience member demanded to know why the Forest Service hadn't headed this epidemic off when it started.

The simple explanation is that pine beetles are always with us but were at a high point in their cycle when drought was weakening trees of an age beetles prefer, and warm winters didn't freeze any beetles dead following the initial outbreak in 1996 west of Denver. It created, as Steve said, a perfect storm. Lack of funding hasn't helped either.

Even with limitless funds, one cannot spray every pine tree in the forest or change the climate quickly.

One can only clean up the mess, clearing dead trees before they fall across roads, trails, power lines and campgrounds and before they begin to burn.

No one seems to want the dead trees – the price of timber is still too low to reopen more than one of the local sawmills. Some are being turned into pellets for pellet stoves, and there is talk of building a plant that uses wood to generate electricity.

Lodgepole pine is the main tree being killed. The stands we are used to seeing on the Medicine Bow are 80 to 150 years old, the re-growth after initial logging. Most of us in the audience will not be around to see this second re-growth reach maturity.

In fact, many people in the audience looked old enough to have been recreating on the forest more than 50 years (30 for me) and may not be around in 10-15 years when the trees are finished falling over and are no longer hazardous except as fuel in wildfires. Even then, a stroll off the trail will entail climbing over the deadfall.

Downed trees may, happily, slow illegal off-road driving.

It tears at my heart to see ponderosa pines turning red between Cheyenne and Laramie, along my favorite Pole Mountain trails, knowing that soon it will be unsafe to roam there – for a while. But I don't feel the same about the mountain sides of lodgepole monoculture over west of Laramie and have never yearned for a cabin in that dense forest.

Having, on quests for elk, tramped through the endless monotony of tree trunks as far as the eye can see, with no underbrush, no bird song, only squirrel chatter and the occasional break for a birdy, spruce-lined creek and beaver pond or rocky outcropping with a view of soaring hawks, I'm ready for a change.

Having driven endless miles of roads lined with future telephone poles right down to the shoulder, wondering when a deer will spring out to meet my bumper, I'll appreciate the change.

A connoisseur of cloud formations and sunsets, I look forward to vistas opening up. Let's just hope that all the mountain cabins and structures that come into view are picturesque.

There may be a lack of shade, but the forecast is that the sunny slopes will produce lots of grass and shrubs, even aspen, before the pines shade them out again, not unlike a clearcut or burn.

Just exactly which wildlife species will disappear, and which will appreciate the change, is ripe for research by a generation or two of grad students.

Doesn't this remind you of the 1988 Yellowstone fires?

The difference is that the Medicine Bow isn't quite done with the epidemic. For a few more years, each year's generation of beetles will fly to new trees mid-summer, where they'll burrow under the bark and lay eggs that hatch into larva that eat the trees' cambium layer, girdling and killing the trees over the winter, with the red needles showing the following summer as the next generation of adults flies off.

The year the new beetles can't find any live trees to bore into and lay eggs will be the year their population plummets.

If you want to see how our forest will soon look, visit central Colorado. Visit the website www.fs.fed.us/r2/bark-beetle .

Losing the forest we know and love is like losing our old dog, the one whose body language we know so well, he doesn't even have to ask to be let outside. The new forest will be as dynamic as a puppy, full of surprises and excitement, anxious to grow.

116 Listening for birds doesn't get easier with age

A couple months ago, our field trip reverberated with a bit of icy snow crunching underfoot, a tiny breeze rattling dry leaves and the murmur of bird watchers. When we stood perfectly still, straining our ears for a sound of bird life in the trees along Crow Creek, I finally heard the faintest whisper from a brown creeper, found the bird and pointed it out.

The creeper cooperated and everyone had a good look as it flitted to the base of a tree, spiraled up the trunk looking for dead and slumbering insects in the bark, and started over on the next tree.

Creepers have a very distinct but

faint call as they work and I wanted everyone to hear it, but almost no one else could, even though the 5-inch-long bird was close enough to see without binoculars – if you could pick out the bark-colored feathers from the bark.

I realized finally that nearly everyone on this field trip was older than me and perhaps they couldn't physically hear the creeper.

A fact of aging is losing the ability to hear high-frequency sounds. It isn't uncommon for an older birder to think that the population of kinglets in his favorite birding spot has decreased over time, only to discover it was his decreased hearing that diminished the number of the tiny, high-pitched voices he could hear.

Binoculars and spotting scopes are expected paraphernalia for bird-watchers. But if the birds aren't out in the open, or if you don't catch their movements flitting in the branches 50 feet overhead, hearing is the only way you'll know which direction to point your binoculars.

Acute hearing partly explains the extraordinary abilities of hotshot young birders, especially if they have been too busy birding to ruin their hearing with loud music.

Unfortunately, many people pick up birding in mid-life. Optics make up for failing sight, and field guides and all kinds of handheld devices make up for failing memory.

For failing hearing there are a few choices. I don't have any experience with any of these and if you do, tell me more about them.

The first step is to visit an audiologist and make sure the dearth of high-frequency birdsong can't be attributed to a dearth of birds. Depending on the type of hearing loss, there are kinds of hearing aids that will help birdwatchers.

There are lots of ads in birding magazines for binoculars, but not for aids to hearing. One I came across is the Songfinder (see at www.nselec.com). It is a little case on your belt connected to slim headphones. It picks up sound and translates it to your ears at a lower frequency. You choose from three settings how much lower.

Songfinder presupposes the user can hear the frequency of the human voice well. At $750, it is cheaper than the audiologist's special hearing aids mentioned by blogging birdwatchers. The drawback would be, if you've been birding for years, to suddenly hear a brown creeper sing alto, tenor, or even bass, relatively speaking.

The old-fashioned option is to get a parabolic microphone. You've seen photos of the scientist holding a big dish with a microphone in the middle connected to earphones. You can also connect it to a recorder so you can tell people you are recording birdsong, and they will think you are a science nerd instead of hard of hearing.

The Cornell Lab of Ornithology is offering an eight-day course in wild-life sound recording in June out in California, but I found only one small advertisement for this kind of listening equipment in my birding magazines, www.stithrecording.com.

The problems with fancy micro-phones are you have to lug them around, and they only amplify sound. You'll get a lot of other amplified noise. But you'll be in the same boat as the rest of us trying to pick out birdsong over traffic noise and wind.

There are bird sounds to be heard in winter. Some other soft, high frequency calls are Bohemian and cedar wax-wings communicating as they search for another berry-full tree, the gold-en-crowned and ruby-crowned kinglets scampering high in evergreen treetops, and horned larks, blowing to and fro over country roads and fields.

When birds start thinking spring, they, mostly the males, bring out their songs for some practice. They need to be in top form if they are going to keep other males from invading their territory and also attract the attention of the best females.

Luckily for us, the birds still sing even after a spring snowstorm. Also lucky for us is when Wyoming's state bird, the western meadowlark, projects its loud arias from roadside fences, it will be hard to miss no matter how old our ears get.

117 Spotting nests isn't easy, but here's an idea of where to look

Sunday, July 25, 2010, Outdoors, page E3

Back in the dark ages of bird appreciation, people collected wild bird eggs and nests to display them. It's illegal now unless you have a permit. But what I've always wondered is how they found the nests.

Or how about the researchers that measure eggs and nests? How do they find enough to make statistically valid statements?

And then I started counting the number of nests I've seen this season – without really trying.

First, there were two different great horned owl nests. You can't miss the big bulky affairs, though you could miss the bit of feathered head sticking up above the rim. Don't get any closer or you could get a talon in the face.

Then there was the face-off between a robin and a squirrel on the roof of the house next door. Robins have nested between the houses before, but it wasn't until early June that I saw the bulky cup balanced on the rafter up under the roof overhang and got the hairy eyeball from one of the parents.

The island in the middle of the lake at Holliday Park was so crowded this spring that some of the 60-70 Canada geese were perching in the trees and on the picnic shelter, trying to figure out how to balance eggs on a branch or roof

ridge. By the end of May, abandoned eggs littered the island and three families hatched two, seven and 17 goslings respectively.

One pair of mallards hatched seven ducklings, but after about a week there were only five. Another pair hatched eight and lost only one the first week. Ducklings are bite-sized compared to goslings.

Interestingly, it took the 15 white domestic geese until July to hatch four goslings.

The nests of the black-crowned night-herons became invisible as soon as the park's trees leafed out. The occasional squawk during the nesting season didn't begin to match the 49 birds counted earlier.

What about all the birds chirping around town? House sparrow nests are easy to spot – look for messy stick piles stuck into the letters of three-dimensional signs or anywhere they can squeeze themselves.

But what about interesting songbirds? Keep your eyes open. Memorial Day weekend, Mark and I birded along Crow Creek just as the trees were finally getting fully leafed out. We were staring into a clump of willows, trying to identify small songsters. Familiar, noisy birds were flying in – a yellow warbler, a robin and a western kingbird. They distracted me, and as I let my gaze follow them, I discovered their three nests, all in one spacious tree. What a treat.

A month later in similar habitat – mosquito infested – I saw an oriole's nest freshly woven and heard household murmurings from a nest plastered under a deck by a pair of Say's phoebes.

I might have to start a life nest list.

Nests aren't always the quintessential robin's cup of mud and twigs. Besides the oriole's woven sack hanging from a tree branch, burrowing owls and belted kingfishers use burrows, many shorebirds barely scrape out a depression on the ground, flickers peck out holes in trees (and house siding), loons float their nests, herons build tree top rookeries and peregrines nest on cliffs and building facades.

Nests are used only temporarily. As soon as the young fledge, which may be before they even learn to fly, the nest is abandoned. Some species may fix it up and start a second clutch right away. Big sturdy hawk nests may be used again the next year – by owls. Songbird nests disappear, broken down by wind and weather. Other birds and animals may steal the building materials for their own nests.

The nest is not a permanent home. Home is where a bird can find food, water and shelter. And for migratory birds, is home where they spend the winter, or where they spend the short few months reproducing?

If you want to know more about how and where your favorite birds nest, go to www.AllAboutBirds.org.

118 New order, new names and new species of birds dictated by AOU

Sunday, August 8, 2010, Outdoors, page E3

The American Ornithologists' Union has come out with the 10th supplement to the seventh edition (1998) of the Checklist of North American Birds, which means you can start penciling in changes in your current field guide or buy a new edition next year.

It can also mean that, like one subscriber to the Wyobirds e-list, you may be able to add two species to your life list without even looking out the window.

In the AOU's first days in 1883, birds were classified by appearance and habit. With study, a fine distinction could be made between similar birds that together never produced fertile young – separate species – and similar birds that were variations within a species.

Similar species were grouped into a

genus and similar genera were grouped into a family. It all made sense to birdwatchers in the field.

Then, as we became more globally aware, we tried to align the common and scientific names of birds with their counterparts overseas. Thus, our "sparrow hawk" became the "American Kestrel" some years ago.

Now DNA testing has come into common use, and ornithologists are making discoveries and adjustments regularly to reflect the evolutionary relationship of species to each other.

The latest changes are documented in The Auk, the AOU's journal, and they are meaningless to the casual birder who may have, like me, not learned the scientific bird names in Latin.

However, the American Birding

Association has done somewhat of a translation that shows a lot of the changes are a shuffling of species between different genera and a shuffling of the order of species and genera. For instance, green-tailed and spotted towhees will still be in the genus "Pipilo," but other towhees will be in "Melozone."

The AOU goes through cycles of splitting and lumping species. This time the whip-poor-will has been split. This isn't a big deal for us in Wyoming since we don't get them here (we have poorwills), but if you saw one in the southwest and one in the eastern U.S., you can now amend your life list and have "Eastern Whip-poor-will" and "Mexican Whip-poor-will" instead.

The winter wren got both global and continental splits. Now there will be the Eurasian Wren and in North America, there will be the Pacific Wren and the Winter Wren.

Luckily, "Birds of Wyoming," by Doug Faulkner, refers to the now former subspecies by nearly the same name as the Pacific wren, so we won't be too confused. In Peterson's field guides, it is noted that west of the Rockies winter wrens sound different than in the east,

which is part of the AOU's justification for the split as well as DNA differences.

This latest catalog of changes is all of the AOU's decisions only between January 1, 2009, and March 31, 2010. I'm sure more will continue to come.

What is the point to being picky about bird names? For ornithologists, it's scientifically precise labels in English and Latin. For the ABA listers, it's an accurate count of species on their life list.

But for us backyard birdwatchers, it's being able to communicate with each other, and with the scientists who want our observations for citizen science projects.

So my advice is to make it your priority to keep track of common names and the species getting split and lumped. Learning genera and families is secondary.

After a while, when you talk to someone new about birds, you'll be able to tell how old their field guide is by what common bird names they use. That means in addition to learning the new names, you can't forget any of the old names!

119

Bird IDs can be tricky, so a photo is always welcomed

Spring and early summer are when I get the most bird calls, questions about woodpecker damage, inconvenient robins' nests, but mostly bird identification.

Unless they can email me a defining photo, I usually give callers a few possibilities to look up and let them decide for themselves.

For instance, in spring Cheyenne regularly gets six species with dark or black heads, backs and wings, and

orange breasts, the most obvious being American robin, which we compare everything to.

The others are orchard oriole, Bullock's oriole, black-headed grosbeak, spotted towhee and the American redstart.

In early May, a friend mentioned having a flock of painted redstarts at her house. Was she misnaming American redstarts? She insisted on painted redstart.

At home I looked both up. They are both small (American is 5.25 inches and the painted is 5.75 inches) black-headed birds with red markings. The American has a white belly and red patches on its black wings and tail. The painted has a red belly and white patches on its black wings and tail. I saw it once in 1996 in southeastern Arizona.

There are no documented records for painteds in Wyoming as of 2008. Sibley's shows them in Arizona and New Mexico, in oak and pine canyons, with records of sightings in north-central Colorado.

There are two possible scenarios here. One is familiarity breeds complacency on my friend's part. She may have spent some time in the Southwest where she identified painted redstarts. When a similar bird showed up in her yard in Cheyenne, she assumed it was a species she knew and loved seeing previously. Who needs to look closely and look it up in the field guide again?

Me. I've been known to look through binoculars to enjoy common birds 15 feet outside my window, but I wouldn't expect everyone does that, so a general impression of small bird flashing black, white and red could remain misidentified, causing no harm until the observer talks about it to someone with too many field guides, like me.

The second scenario is familiarity breeding complacency on my part. Although I see maybe one American redstart every other spring, I page past the entry every time I look up other warblers in my field guide. The Cheyenne bird checklist (compiled by more knowledgeable people than me) says they are uncommon migrants. They normally hang out around riparian (stream) areas, so it would be unlikely for them to be on high prairie where my friend lives.

There is of course, a third scenario. The bird in question is not a redstart at all.

The future scenario I'd like is my friend gets a close look at and takes a photo of her visiting birds, double-checks her field guide, and based on her previous familiarity, is quite convinced she sees painted redstarts – and based on the species range map in her field guide, she realizes it is a rare species for Wyoming.

Next, she convinces the Wyoming Bird Records Committee she saw painted redstarts. It's a challenge. Observer credibility is as essential as good digital photos.

How does she get credibility? She becomes an active part of the birding community. By joining other birders on field trips, they will get a feel for her birding ability, and her ability to say, "Gosh, I guess that cerulean warbler was something else," which is what one of Wyoming's best birders said last month after some additional study.

There are advantages to birding with others. If everyone can see the same rare bird at the same time, they can confirm the identification. The records committee likes those kinds of reports, especially if a detailed description of the bird's look and behavior is submitted, along with justification for not identifying it as a similar species.

The field guide is sort of a birder's Bible – but with one main difference: the birds don't read it. They have wings and travel intentionally, looking for new habitat, or unintentionally, caught by wind. The range maps are just a measure of likelihood.

Birdwatching as a hobby shares something with gambling and fishing. We go out hoping for the next big thing, the next rare bird, even while we enjoy all the other birds we see.

So, next time painted redstarts show up, take a photo and then give me a call, and I'll be right out.

120 Holliday Park summer bird counts total 43 species

Between the last week in April and end of September, I counted 43 species of birds at Cheyenne's Holliday Park while walking a friend's dog about three times a week.

I recorded my observations at the free website, www.eBird.org, so now I can look back and tell you that there were 60-70 geese at the end of April, a high of 180 mid-July, including a crop of about 25 goslings, and in September there were around 130. I hope some more will migrate and not eat all the grass in the park.

Yes, there were the other usual urbanites: mallard, European starling, house sparrow and pigeon, but there were surprises.

From late April until the first week in August, I could count on up to a dozen double-crested cormorants each visit and maybe around five American white pelicans, both species trolling the lake for fish.

I caught glimpses of wood ducks and turkey vultures during spring and fall migration. Warblers passed through too, but identification is difficult because I don't take binoculars. It takes two hands to walk a 125-pound dog known to sometimes walk me when she sees other dogs, squirrels or her park friends.

Holliday Park has had a colony of black-crowned night-herons for more than 20 years. May 29, before the cottonwoods completely leafed out, Mark, my professional wildlife biologist husband, counted 49 adults working on their treetop nests. Two days later, they were invisible except for the occasional adult collecting another branch for repairs. But they were noisy.

And then August 2 I saw 20 brown-striped youngsters strung out along the edges of the lake, perched on rocks and branches, waiting to pounce on passing fish. This was not all the young that hatched. Park caretakers told me earlier they picked up a lot of dead young herons under the trees after a windstorm.

I noticed the chimney swifts sporadically June through August. They really do look like flying cigars compared to swallows. I wonder if I was too busy counting ducks to look up and see them more often.

There was a lull in the number of crows I counted mid-July. That could have been while they were protecting their eggs and nestlings by not drawing attention to themselves.

I think the flickers successfully fledged their young. I was used to hearing or seeing around two per visit, and then Aug. 24 there was a family of four together on the ground.

Common grackles weren't seen after Sept. 4 and red-winged blackbirds after Sept. 10, reducing the park's noise level.

The verdant lawns of the park look like perfect robin habitat. I was surprised not to see more hunting for worms. Perhaps regularly applied pesticides have reduced the food that lawn-loving species can find, or there is too much human and dog activity.

Of species not already mentioned, the spring and fall migrants on my Holliday Park list were: northern shoveler, redhead, lesser scaup, spotted sandpiper, western wood-pewee, yellow warbler, yellow-rumped warbler, common yellowthroat, Wilson's warbler, chipping sparrow and Brewer's sparrow.

The species that flew over only once were osprey, sharp-shinned hawk, Swainson's hawk, Franklin's gull, ring-billed gull, common nighthawk, belted kingfisher, downy woodpecker and black-capped chickadee.

The summer regulars were Eurasian collared dove, mourning dove, blue jay, cliff swallow, and American goldfinch.

Of the winter birds that should be returning from the mountains, I first heard the red-breasted nuthatch in late July – perhaps they nested in town instead – and the first junco flashed by me Sept. 27.

Who knows what else will drop by during the rest of fall migration?

2011

121 Patchwork birding benefits birds

Patchwork. The word draws my eye the way "quilt" does because both describe my indoor hobby the way "bird" describes my outdoor hobby.

But why was Ted Floyd, editor of "Birding," the American Birding Association magazine, making an obscure reference to patchwork in a recent issue? I emailed him, and he sent a link to a blog post he'd written about it and how it relates to green, environmentally friendly, birding.

Patchwork birding refers to birding in your own patch – your yard or a local park where you go often, versus jumping in the car or on a jet to see a rare bird.

Ted is concerned that birding has evolved into the hobby of the affluent who indulge in expensive travel and equipment, as has quilting, I would add, leaving huge carbon footprints right across great bird habitat. Of course, extreme birders wouldn't know about most rarities if local birders weren't regularly examining their local patches.

Just the week before reading Ted's patch reference, I finished reading "Life List" by Olivia Gentile, a biography of Phoebe Snetsinger. Phoebe was the woman determined to see as many of the world's bird species as possible.

She started birdwatching in 1965 but became obsessive about it after being diagnosed with terminal melanoma in 1981. Aided by an inheritance from her father, she went on multiple foreign bird tours every year. She valiantly endured bad weather, bad trails, and bad men, finally dying in a vehicular accident in 1999 in Madagascar, leaving a worldwide record of nearly 8,400 bird species, the most anyone had seen at that time.

We can charitably say Phoebe was birding before carbon footprints were in our vocabulary, and that extreme birding kept her sane and kept professional bird guides and tour operators employed. I hope someone has transferred her carefully kept note cards to eBird, the digital archive where scientists can make use of our personal birding observations.

Soon after Ted's reply, I got an email from the Cornell Lab of Ornithology describing a new eBird feature: patch and yard birding record keeping set up to allow for friendly competition within one's county. It will also give ornithologists more intensive information about birds. I imagine Ted knew all about this when he wrote his blog post – the world of professionals in birding is very small.

So now there is a name for the kind of birding most of us do. Most of us who begin to keep notes on the birds in our own backyards are already patchwork birding. I highly recommend www.

---

eBird.org as a record keeping alternative to notebooks and scraps of paper.

Ted thinks patchwork birding is the responsible, green way to bird – no great amounts of fuel are wasted in long distance travel.

It's amazing how many species of birds pass through my favorite patches: 50 in my backyard and a different 50 in Holliday Park here in Cheyenne since April 2010, when I began recording

sightings on eBird. That's not a lot of species among obsessed birders. However, frequently birding those areas helped me know exactly where to find an American kestrel for the Cheyenne Christmas Bird Count.

I've been thinking about how to control the size of my patchwork quilt making carbon footprint. Maybe I should spend less time quilting and more time walking around town watching birds.

122 Bird feeder quarantine was good for the birds, hard on the observer

Sunday, February 27, 2011, Outdoors, page E3

There he was, the lone house finch on the tube feeder, contentedly pulling black oil sunflower seeds out and munching them thoughtfully, left behind when the rest of the flock scattered.

I took a closer look and just as I feared, he showed outward signs that he was not a well bird, despite his glowing red head and chest. Eye disease. One eye was encircled in rings of crusty featherless wrinkles.

Sick birds conserve their strength. They don't fly off with the flock for every little perceived threat. When they get really sick, I've seen them huddle on my windowsill.

There isn't anything anyone can do for them, but I can protect the rest of the birds by taking down my feeders which will get the house finches to disperse and be less likely to pass diseases to each other or to other finch species.

This winter, I've had quite a regular crew showing up every day: two Eurasian collared-doves, two mountain chickadees, two red-breasted nuthatches, a downy woodpecker, 10 or so house finches and a few juncos with occasional appearances by pine siskins

and goldfinches. I really hated to disappoint them.

After I took the feeders down, dumped out the birdbath and swept all the seed debris off the patio, I watched later as the gang sat on the powerline while one or two individuals would sally forth and fly a circle around the last known location of the sunflower seed feeder. Then they left.

In a week, after Mark scrubbed the bird poop off the railing and patio and washed out the feeders with a mild bleach solution, he refilled the feeders, and nearly all the previous birds began to reappear within a day. The chickadees took five days.

I don't know where the sick house finch contracted his disease, but I do know that we had gotten behind in cleaning up our feeders and the area around them.

Feeding birds is something we do because we enjoy watching birds up close. The birds usually don't depend on feeding – they have plenty of naturally occurring seeds to forage, but they sure enjoy the convenience.

Songbirds can get a pox that affects

their eyes. But there is also house finch eye disease, mycoplasmal conjunctivitis, caused by a bacterium common to domestic turkeys and chickens, according to the Cornell Lab of Ornithology. It was first noticed in house finches in 1993 on the east coast, where house finches were introduced 50 years earlier.

The Lab has been studying the spread of the disease for the last 15 years using observations provided by birdwatching citizen scientists. After a major outbreak on the east coast a few years ago, the disease is no longer quite as prevalent. Some sick individual birds actually survive but apparently do not become immune to the disease.

The eastern house finches seem to be more susceptible, and one reason might be that most of them are thought to be inbred descendants of a small group that was introduced in the east in the 1940s from western North America where they are native. Inbreeding can cause susceptibility to disease.

The good news is, this is one avian disease that does not pose a health risk to people, except that quarantining our feeders and losing "our" birds for a week felt like a mental hardship. But then again, perhaps I accomplished more in that time because I wasn't distracted by the comings and goings I like to watch out the window above my laptop screen.

Some people watch fish swim in a bowl to reduce stress. Watching birds outside my window works for me. I'm glad the gang came back.

123

Sunday, June 5, 2011, Outdoors, page E3

Pelicans at Holliday Park: Why do they stop here?

The "American White Pelican," with its fantastic orange bill, seems more akin to a unicorn than any bird. My first sighting, above a river on the dry plains of eastern Montana, seemed out of place. But to see a flock at Holliday Park, in the middle of Cheyenne, seems miraculous.

Last year I tracked my sightings of pelicans in the park on Lake Minnehaha between April and July. On the three or four mornings a week I was there, I could almost always see a few.

I didn't observe any of the courtship antics like the kind the geese go through. The pelicans were either clumped together on the north side of the island, like a forgotten snowbank, ignoring the ruckus of nesting geese a few feet away, or they were out elegantly sailing on the water, dipping their bills in and catching fish, or just loafing. A few times I saw them sail into thermals overhead, wing flapping hardly a necessity.

Why do we see pelicans at Holliday Park? In April, some may be migrating. They winter along the Gulf of Mexico and head for the western states, Colorado, Wyoming, Montana, the Dakotas and western Canada, to breed. Pelicans on the other side of the Continental Divide spend winter in coastal California.

They look for big lakes in isolated places that have islands for breeding safely, such as the Great Salt Lake. In Wyoming there are three colonies: Bamforth National Wildlife Refuge, Pathfinder Reservoir and Yellowstone Lake. Any disturbance will cause them to abandon their nests.

Each breeding pair looks for a sub

colony where everyone else is at about the same stage in the breeding cycle. The nest is whatever a sitting pelican can pull up around itself with its bill. A parent keeps the two eggs warm under-foot and every day or two, for 30 days, swaps places with its mate and goes out as far as 30 miles to forage.

Three weeks after hatching, the chicks are all out of their nests and hud-dle at night in a group called a crech. Ten weeks after hatching, they are in the air, exploring everywhere until it's time to head south. By September, most pelicans have left Wyoming.

It takes three years before pelicans are old enough to breed so these imma-ture birds spend their summers hanging out. Apparently, Holliday Park, with its shallow water, is perfect despite the bur-geoning flock of domestic and Canada geese and all the people walking dogs.

I sometimes wonder what the unin-formed observer thinks pelicans are. Mutant swans or domestic white geese? At 16 pounds, they are much bigger than most geese and a little smaller than trumpeter swans. But at 108 inches, or nine feet, their wingspan is much longer than a swan's.

The brown pelican found on the coasts dives for fish, but the white pel-ican merely dips its pouched bill while swimming. These are the pelicans that are famous for synchronicity, forming a line and forcing small fish into the shal-lows of rivers, lakes or marshes where they can be scooped up. They also fish at night, by feel, rather than by sight.

Down around the Mississippi Delta, they are the bane of aquaculture, feed-ing at fish farms, but out here, they eat the rough fish and are generally not in competition for sport fish.

In the early 20th century, their popu-lations decreased, but in the 1960s they began to make a comeback. So, your chances of seeing a pelican, compared to a unicorn, are pretty good, especially if you stop by Holliday Park on sum-mer mornings.

124 Killer kitchen window adds to national bird death toll

Sunday, August 7, 2011, Outdoors, page E3

It became an almost daily occurrence this past May: a soft thump on the glass as another visitor to our backyard and bird feeders hit the kitchen window.

I tried putting up big stripes of blue painter's tape and that helped a little. Mainly, we needed to remember to check the yard for dazed birds before letting our bird dog out. Luckily, the couple we saw her take seemed to be the only window fatalities – that we knew about.

Migration seemed to be over after the first week in June. With just the regulars now, including the house finch with the white head and her friends, there have been no more collisions.

It's the visiting birds, 25 other species in our yard, mostly during spring migra-tion and not so much in the fall, which get confused by a window that reflects the trees. At least with the feeders with-in only a few feet of the window, they didn't have a lot of momentum when they hit. But it wasn't always feeder birds, and it wasn't always that window. In fact, it is windows everywhere.

Audubon Minnesota, a state office of the National Audubon Society, came out with a booklet available online for free,

Bird-Safe Building Guidelines, that explains the problem and solutions at the architectural level.

People love buildings with lots of natural light. If they are well-insulated, windows can save energy on lighting. But those glass-sided high-rises, and even residential windows, are calculated to kill hundreds of millions of birds per year in the U.S. Spring and fall migration are the most problematic times of year.

Anything that breaks up the glass expanse, like my painter's tape (engineered to peel off easily), or screening, helps. It has to be applied to the outside surface, though. Waiting to clean the dust off the outside of your windows until after migration might help, too, as can drawing drapes and shades to prevent birds from seeing straight through your house to a window on the other side.

Scaring the birds away with items hanging in front of the window, things that move in the breeze, like flagging, or that move and shine, like old CDs, might do the trick.

At the architectural level, Bird-Safe Building Guidelines discusses ideas for new buildings and retrofitted buildings:

netting, fritted glass, films applied to glass, etched glass designs, glass sloping to reflect the ground, taking into account proximity to habitat and feeding sites, and special glass making use of birds' ability to see ultraviolet patterns we can't. Problems occur mostly at the ground level and first few stories of buildings.

Then there is the problem of lit-up buildings attracting night-flying migrants, especially during bad weather, and all the ill effects of light pollution in general. Turning off interior building lights at night saves money and birds, and so does making sure outdoor lights are not needlessly lighting the sky.

Our killer kitchen window, a six-foot wide replacement with sliding halves, currently is only half screened. The track is still there for the full screen, so we should order one and put it in place from early April to mid-June. All the glass will be less reflective then, and birds still colliding may bounce off the screen.

But next spring, before we let Sally out, we'll check the area below the window for dazed birds. No need to increase the dog's "life list."

125 Crows come home to roost, bringing entertainment and fertilizer

Sunday, September 18, 2011, Outdoors, page E3

This summer, our street became the unwilling host to loud and raucous juveniles coming by at dusk and leaving messes in our driveways. They were young crows, coming home to roost in our neighborhood's big trees.

Since they settled down shortly after sunset, I could live with the noise, but they were back at it at 5 a.m., as

good as an alarm clock through our open windows.

Mid-spring this year, I noticed crows flying with sticks. I think they built a nest in a neighbor's spruce tree. It wasn't too surprising in early July to hear inexpert cawing.

One evening three young crows put on a performance for us. Up on the cross arms of the utility pole they restlessly moved about, one having to flutter its wings every time it wanted to step over an obstacle. Another one, on the high wire, kept flapping crazily to keep its balance. All three kept up a conversation with inflections of babies learning their mother tongue.

With binoculars it was easy to see the young crows' feathers weren't fully grown out, but otherwise, their plain awkwardness gave them away. For a week or two, I could find four of them in our trees or somewhere on our street, walking together, inspecting lawns.

Walking out one day while an adult was with them, I was suddenly the focus of a tirade of abusive adult language. What was the backstory? One should not daydream while walking the dog.

Last summer, my bird dog quietly picked up a young crow out of tall grass on the side of the road while I wasn't looking. It probably had been hit by a car. A study of banded nestlings in Illinois shows that the mortality rate within a crow's first year is 57 percent.

The dog proudly carried the limp bird home and was all smiles all the way, even though the parent birds followed us, yelling. Was this current, irate parent one of the birds that followed me and the dog home last year?

At a recent meeting of the Cheyenne – High Plains Audubon Society, we'd watched a documentary, "A Murder of Crows," about researchers proving that crows recognize faces and will convey to their young who to watch out for. I guess I am a marked woman, except it wasn't me that killed the young crow last year. I only provided it with a decent burial so it wasn't left on the side of the road for the foxes to find.

Crows don't migrate seasonally in the middle latitudes of North America, so I'm wondering if the family now roosting in our neighborhood will continue to noisily welcome the day an hour before sunrise, or if they will make friends with the flock I noticed last winter at the VA hospital. I sure hope they aren't so hospitable that they bring home friends, especially ones coming down from Canada for the winter.

Twenty years ago, crows were hard to find in Cheyenne. And then, like so many other immigrants to our fair city, they've decided it's a good place to raise a family.

We've planted trees on the prairie and made it inviting for crows, just as we've planted oil and gas machinery in sage grouse habitat, giving ravens, close cousins to crows, hunting perches and greater success preying on sage grouse eggs. But that's a story for another day.

I hope our crows only provide entertainment and a little extra fertilizer for our neighborhood.

126 Deliberate littering leaves local citizens wondering

Sunday, November 6, 2011, Outdoors, page E2

We enjoyed our summer Sunday mornings. They were golden. The low angle of the early light filtered through the leaves along the creek and a few birds sang.

The air was so still, we could hear every note, yet mosquitoes were absent. It is a perfect time for bird watching along a country road.

From week to week, we noticed changes. One week it was vociferous western kingbird families everywhere, another week it was tiny grasshopper sparrows on the barbed wire.

Once, a middle-aged pickup passed us and we waved to the old guy driving. He towed a light trailer with mesh sides, carrying a little mound of dried plant material and a garden hose.

I briefly wondered where a man would be going at 7 a.m., coming from town, hauling a trailer. Twenty minutes later we found out.

The hose and the dried weeds, plus some soiled paper towels, were on the side of the road. It was a well-watered spot where the weed seeds will easily sprout.

I am sure it is the same weeds and hose, because years of distinguishing birds and their various shades of color has sharpened my eye. No, the hose didn't fall out accidently. It was poorly tucked into the roadside vegetation – just the way you'd expect a slob to try to hide something quickly.

Public lands near towns are always victims of hit and run littering. My sister, who works for the U.S. Forest Service, tells me tales of contractors dumping building debris – and there is some along this local road – as well as an assortment of tires and furniture.

But here the land is privately owned. Perhaps this dumping is a personal statement to the owners, but more likely, the slob doesn't know to whom the land belongs.

I wonder if he's the one who, just this year, left evergreen branches, fireworks trash, a chair, a love seat, a mattress and box spring, an old computer and porn magazines.

Perhaps the litterer doesn't know that the Cheyenne compost facility takes any vegetation for free. It is open 10 a.m. to 5 p.m., closed on Tuesdays and Sundays (from March through October, it's open every day but Tuesday.).

Anyone in the county can dump anything for free at the Cheyenne waste transfer facility, 200 N. College, on the middle Saturday of May. If you can't wait, they'll take your old tires the rest of the year for $1.55 apiece, more if they are still on their rims. [In 2011]

Useable furniture and other things should be donated to charities, but whatever items are beyond repair only cost $10 per pickup load to take them to the transfer station – if you live in the city – more if you live outside city limits. For a small fee, the sanitation department will pick up things that don't fit in your regular bin.

Call the sanitation department at 637-6440 for particular costs and hours.

The city does its best to make it easy to dispose of trash properly. The recycling businesses even make it profitable, in some cases.

But teaching personal responsibility is the best way to control deliberate litter. In a state like Wyoming, where its citizens worship private property rights, you'd think there would be zero tolerance for making a mess of someone else's land, if only to preserve your own.

However, my husband Mark and I do have something in common with the litterer: We like having an excuse to enjoy a Sunday morning in the country. If that old guy reforms, he'll need a new reason for a drive. You see, we have this extra pair of binoculars....

127

Sunday, December 11, 2011, Outdoors, page E2

Plan to refresh Lake Minnehaha would benefit park visitors, including birds

What stinks at Holliday Park in the summer?

The waters of Lake Minnehaha, 6.5 surface acres in the middle of the park, are stagnant. There isn't enough movement of water and so it provides a perfect habitat for blue-green algae. In hot weather, it dies and produces the putrid smell.

This particular algal species can at times be toxic, killing dogs that drink it or sickening people coming in contact with it. It spreads on the water surface and blocks sunlight that would otherwise encourage growth of healthy organisms. Storm water runoff brings in more gunk and debris.

Teresa Moore, planning manager for the Cheyenne Parks and Recreation Department, invited me to read the recently compiled report from Ayres Associates proposing how to clarify the water.

1. Deepen the lake, from 3 feet to 8 or 9, with gradual slopes where there are now eroded banks. The island would not be rebuilt.

2. Instead of aerators, which have been tried before, install a SolarBee. The 300 already installed nationwide show they are effective in circulating water which creates surface turbulence that keeps blue-green algae from growing. It would be in the middle of the lake and powered by attached solar cells.

3. At the storm water inlets, put in SNOUTS, ingenious technology that collects gunk in an underground vault before it can go into the lake. Vacuuming the vault once a year would be easier than the maintenance department's current methods.

4. Develop wetlands-- cattails and rushes--by the inlets to catch remaining sediment so it doesn't fill in the lake over time.

5. Route "reuse" (treated waste) water through the lake. Cheyenne has plumbed itself to use it for irrigating other parks, cemeteries and athletic fields. The water would constantly flow through new inlets and out through a new automatic outlet (the current one has to be adjusted by hand), helping prevent blue-green algae growth. Reuse water would also irrigate Holliday Park.

From my birdwatching observations at the park, blue-green algae doesn't affect the Canada geese. By the middle of last June, I was counting 200 of them, including 40 goslings.

The adults were molting and unable to fly. By fall, wing feathers grown back in again, daily numbers (between 8-9 a.m.) were running 100-150. They spend time in the water, but mostly they graze the grass.

There are also a few dozen mallards and domestic ducks, three dozen white or gray domestic geese and occasional wild visitors: wood ducks, redheads and shovelers.

Removing the island would make me sad, but it would take with it the major location for goose nesting. By all standards – especially the standards of people trying not to step in goose poop – there are too many geese.

By clean water standards, there is too much nitrogen in the water, some of it from goose poop. Removing the island hatchery could encourage wild geese to disburse and nest elsewhere. The island is not used as a refuge from potential predators. When the geese feel threatened, they, and their goslings, head for the water, not the island.

The black-crowned night-herons used to nest in the island's trees, but when the big trees disappeared, they moved to the big cottonwoods to the north. Pelicans sometimes rest on the island in spring and summer, but I've seen them enjoy island-free lakes on F.E. Warren Air Force Base and they like a thick stand of cattails just as well.

What attracts the non-water birds are the trees. If willows are added to the shoreline, as suggested in the plan, over time, they will make up for the loss of the scrubby foliage on the island.

All of the improvements would clarify the water, allowing other organisms to grow, including the food chain that leads to fish. We might see more of the fish-eating bird species that we see at Lions Park, like the grebes.

Altogether, the proposed improvements would have a positive impact on birds – and other park users.

So, when can the digging begin? As soon as $1.5 million can be found. The city does not have a budget line for construction in the parks, though there are many repair and improvement projects needed.

Park damage just doesn't get the same respect a pothole does.

Because the Holliday Park project involves water and engineering, Moore said there are some funding options. She's an expert when it comes to writing grants.

128 A hawk ate my songbird!

Sunday, December 25, 2011, Outdoors, page E3

Bird feeder or bird feedlot, it's all a part of the food chain

Coming home from errands recently, I let the dog in and glanced out the window. What was that on the grass in the backyard? It was a sharp-shinned hawk sitting on its prey – a sparrow, perhaps. How exciting!

Mark and I have fed wild birds for years, and though we've seen plenty of sharp-shinneds patrol our yard, this was the first time one of us saw one be successful.

Most people think of small songbirds when they think about bird feeding, so watching hawks feed on feeder birds can come as an unwelcome surprise.

I've had callers who ask me how to protect "their" birds from hawks. They aren't always happy to hear me explain how wonderful it is that they are witnessing the next step in the food chain.

For a small hawk like the sharp-shinned, which has the aerodynamics to navigate the urban forest easily, our birdfeeders must seem like feedlots. But when the feeders/feedlots are right outside our windows and we welcome the same cheerful chickadees day after day, I think we forget their role in the food chain.

Mark and I are on a first-name basis with several farmers and ranchers who raise our meat, if not with the actual animals, plus we hunt and fish, commiserating with predator species. But even if we were vegetarian, we would be wrong to transfer that ideology to wild, meat-eating animals. Carnivorous, omnivorous and carrion-eating animals need animal protein to stay healthy.

Most of the little songbirds, including

our seed-eating feeder visitors, prey on insects and spiders when they are feeding their young and need lots of protein. No humans complain.

Conversely, some of the birds that we would consider meat eaters occasionally pick up the odd seeds or berries.

But, looking through my copy of Kenn Kaufman's "Lives of North American Birds," I found plenty of birds that eat only non-plant material: some of the grebes, all of the seabirds, pelicans, herons, cormorants, egrets, osprey, hawks, falcons, eagles, some shorebirds, many gulls, all of the terns, owls, nighthawks, swifts, most of the swallows and wrens, the dipper, both shrike species and some of the warblers – and warblers are the quintessential songbird!

Granted, warblers are eating insects and although insects are animals, their deaths don't seem to bother many people.

The day after I wrote the rough draft of this column, the dog and I, leaving for a walk around the neighborhood, witnessed a sharp-shinned hawk doing acrobatics a few feet over the driveway, fighting to hang on to a starling. There are so many of those invasive starlings that this seemed like a good thing, except that our feeders remained unvisited for the next six hours due to hawk fright. Oh well.

We, who feed birds, do so for our own enjoyment, to bring wild birds in close to us. I think if we are very lucky, we feed a hawk or two.

Since all of us feeding birds don't put out the same seed, I wonder if the hawks notice what their prey species have been eating. I can hear it now. "Ah, I just enjoyed a Gorges free-range, sunflower seed-fed sparrow!"

2012

129
Robins take up year-round residence

Spoiler alert: I'm about to disclose to you that one of the time-honored symbols of spring never entirely left last fall.

I'm talking about robins. I grew up in Wisconsin where the robin is the state bird and the prime grade-school example of avian seasonal migration. Imagine my surprise years later when I found my first wintering robin on a zero-degree day in December in southeastern Montana.

Wyoming has robins in winter, too, as does every one of the lower 48 states, with the greatest density in the southern states – where we imagine robins should be in winter.

Range maps in bird field guides plainly show robins all across the lower 48, year round, with the exception of parts of the Gulf Coast, Florida and the Southwest being winter-only. Conversely, Canadians and Alaskans should see robins only during the spring/summer breeding season.

Do robins breeding in Wyoming migrate? After reading the species accounts in "Birds of Wyoming" by Doug Faulkner and "The Birds of North America Online," I found no one has a definitive answer. Doug's assessment: "Movements of American robins in fall are highly complex and poorly understood in Wyoming."

During September and October, we see large flocks of robins, but these may be northern robins passing through. We don't know if some of the northern robins spend the winter here, thinking it's balmier than Canada, or if they gather up some of our local robins and take them along to Florida.

It seems robins are fickle about where they spend their winters. Berries and other fruits are acceptable substitutes for their favorite warm-season food, earthworms, and so they will only stick around where there is fruit, and only while it lasts.

This winter, my neighbors' junipers have a good crop of berries, and just about every January afternoon I saw one or two robins over there snacking. In rural areas of the west, wintering robins are most likely to find food along rivers and creeks full of fruit-bearing shrubs or up in the junipers. The more fruit, the more robins.

So, why do we consider the robin a sign of spring? I think most people aren't outside enough in winter, in the right place – near the fruit – to see the few robins around.

When spring comes, robins flocking during their migration peak in April are much more noticeable. People are spending more time outside then, or

The Best of Cheyenne Bird Banter

they might have the window open and hear the robins beginning to sing to establish territories and attract mates.

I'd like to suggest a different bird, and one just as noticeable, as a better sign of spring in Wyoming. We need a sign of hope since winter weather spans as many as eight or nine months and February, the shortest month, drags on forever, especially this year being Leap Year.

Mountain bluebirds could work, except they fly past town. They cross our southern state border as early as the beginning of February, with migration picking up in March. The bright blue males are easiest to see. I see them west of town usually, flashing around fence posts as we go out for one last ice fishing trip to North Crow Reservoir or an early hike dodging snow drifts at Curt Gowdy State Park.

Interestingly, mountain bluebirds and robins are in the same family, the thrushes. Like robins, bluebirds concentrate on animals (invertebrates) for food during the breeding season and fruits in the winter.

If you check your field guide range map, you'll see that there are mountain bluebirds wintering just south of Wyoming. With predicted climate changes, we could easily end up with bluebirds all winter too. Well, geez, that would leave the warblers as the only reliable, easy to see, true sign of spring. But they don't show up until mid-April and May. That's just too long a wait. I'll stick with looking for bluebirds.

Sunday, March 25, 2012, Outdoors, page E3

130 Snowy owls' visit a sight to behold

Thanks to Hedwig, millions of children may recognize a snowy owl.

She was Harry Potter's companion in the books and movies. How many of those children, some now adult, have caught a glimpse of these nearly snow-white owls during this winter's invasion?

Snowy owls in North America usually leave their summer breeding grounds by the Arctic Ocean and head south. Adult females travel the shortest distance before establishing winter territories, with males and juvenile females continuing on. Juvenile males travel farthest, especially if prey becomes scarce.

Cold is not a problem. All snowies stay warm with feathers covering their toes and nearly engulfing the tips of their beaks.

There are migrant snowies to be seen every winter, according to Christmas Bird Count data, in southcentral Canada, Montana, the Dakotas and New England. They will fan out a little further 50 percent of the time, to the Pacific Northwest and the upper Midwest and east through eastern Canada. They make it as far south as Wyoming and the central Great Plains 30 percent of winters. Experts admit they don't know entirely what drives this species' nomadic migration.

This year has been note-worthy for the number of sightings in 31 states as far south as Texas. It could be that birdwatchers are better connected than ever before, thanks to the internet. Observations aren't just scribbled in someone's notebook – they are shared and mapped.

But there are also a lot of birds, sometimes in groups. The thought is that the lemmings were particularly fertile last summer and provided enough prey that a bumper crop of young snowy owls fledged. Each pair can raise up to 12 young, compared to the two or three chicks our resident, similarly sized, great horned owls raise per year.

It's most likely that it was juvenile snowy owls that people observed and photographed this winter. They have the brown barring – horizontal stripes – across their bodies, though adult females have some also. The adult males are pure white.

In the February issue of Prairie Fire, an alternative Nebraskan newspaper, Paul Johnsgard reports that in the previous 35 years, a total of 21 snowy owls had been brought into the Raptor Recovery Nebraska facilities in Lincoln. However, between December and mid-January, 10 more snowy owls were picked up. Nine were emaciated and didn't survive.

It makes me wonder how well the snowies compete with local hawks. Do they prey on the same species of rodents?

Or maybe the problem is their hunting techniques. Unless a landscape is totally snow-covered, snowies really stand out. I saw my first one in a spruce tree by Old Main on the University of Wyoming campus winter of 1980-81, but more typically people see them in the grasslands, perched on a rise, a fence post or a utility pole.

They sit motionless, waiting for prey, or walk about looking rather than flying. Unlike most owls, they are diurnal – active in the daytime. Their hearing is sharp. They can locate potential prey under the snow. They also take ducks and shorebirds.

Snowy owls are circumpolar, meaning they breed in the polar region from Alaska through Canada, Greenland, Scandinavia, Russia and Siberia. "The Birds of North America Online" species account reports their conservation status – whether populations are increasing or decreasing – is unknown. Apparently, no one has spent enough time in the polar region to find out, though one scientist who went found snowy owls can seriously wound humans too close to their nests.

Visit http://www.allaboutbirds.org, another free CLO resource, to read about snowy owl natural history and hear one calling.

If you are willing to register, at no cost, you can access www.eBird.org and its huge database to look at maps and compare sightings from year to year.

131 Sunday, April 15, 2012, Outdoors, page E3
It's quite clear – birds losing war on the windows

Wyoming is a tourist destination. We love statistics on how many visitors come from how many other states and countries. We also try to keep visitors safe, reminding them to stay hydrated at our high, dry elevation, to stay away from dangerous wildlife and to avoid summer lightning storms.

Spring migration is like the beginning of tourist season for birds. On May 19, members of Cheyenne – High Plains Audubon Society and friends will again hit the local birding hotspots, hopefully at the peak of migration, to see how many different species of birds can be counted.

Some years we hit the shorebird migration just right, and others it's the flycatchers. But every year we hope for a warbler year. We scour the tree branches for those smaller-than-sparrow-sized, color-coded birds which are scouring the same branches for insects to devour.

Over the previous 18 years, we have had 31 of North America's 50 warbler species visit. Only four have made it every year: yellow warbler, yellow-rumped warbler, common yellowthroat and Wilson's warbler – probably because they are part of the 12 warblers breeding in Wyoming, and because they are abundant species.

Others we've seen only once because they breed in eastern North America and, for some reason, they take the scenic route through Cheyenne. They include golden-winged warbler, black-throated blue warbler, worm-eating warbler, prothonotary warbler, and six others.

Almost all of these were observed at one of Cheyenne's two Wyoming Important Bird Areas, Lions Park and Wyoming Hereford Ranch. But there is reason to believe that all of Cheyenne, wherever there are trees and shrubs hosting insects, is hosting common and rare warblers, if only people look.

Casual observation of Mark's and my yard has turned up nine species including regular appearances of Wilson's and yellow-rumpeds, sometimes a MacGillivray's and once, a chestnut-sided warbler.

Between mid-April and mid-June, who knows how many warblers pass through our yard? Maybe our retriever knows. Last year I caught her eating at least two after they were injured flying into our window.

While I'm fine with continuing to keep our remaining cat indoors year round (the other passed on last month at nearly 14 years old), we need the dog on squirrel offense duty. But even if we

didn't, there would still be injured birds.

Short of plywood over this one deadly window, how can we keep birds from hitting the glass? I tried a small sticker in the middle, but over the winter we collected a wreath all around it of lovely imprints of Eurasian collared-dove wings and tails, outlined in feather dust on the glass where they tried to avoid the sticker.

Hanging dangly, shiny objects in front of the window probably wouldn't work with the caliber of breezes we get – the objects would end up stuck in the gutter or perhaps banging on – and breaking – the window.

The American Bird Conservancy has come out with a new product this spring, BirdTape, which we are going to try. It sticks to the outside of the glass, breaks up the reflective surface that fools the birds, and is translucent – like frosted glass.

The strips of ¾-inch-wide BirdTape can be applied vertically four inches apart, or horizontally two inches apart. Studies show that our backyard birds will try to zoom between obstacles spaced any greater distance. It obviously takes less tape to do the vertical arrangement.

The tape also comes in rolls three inches wide. These can be cut into squares placed in a pattern leaving spaces between them four inches horizontally and two inches vertically.

I didn't do the math to see which tape size's pattern is more economical. Your choice might have more to do with whether you prefer bars or floating squares.

I'm not sure I like the idea of anything impeding my view of our backyard, but with up to a billion birds hitting home windows each year, according to ABC, I want to give this product a try. It's the least I can do to protect avian tourists on their annual spring and fall visits to Wyoming.

132 Peregrines back with a little help from friends

Sunday, May 13, 2012, Outdoors, page E3

Peregrine falcons were listed as endangered in the U.S. two years before I opened my first bird field guide in 1972.

The guide, "The Birds of North America," published by Golden Press in 1966, did not allude to the peregrine's diminishing population. It only said it was "a rare local falcon."

However, in the era of an awakening environmental consciousness, we all heard about the peregrine, a very handsome poster child for the drive to ban DDT, one of the pesticides responsible for poisoning birds of prey and causing their eggshells to be too thin for unhatched young to survive.

One doesn't expect to meet an endangered species in the wild, especially when ornithologists had declared it extirpated in the eastern U.S. by 1970 and in trouble in other parts of the world (peregrines are found everywhere except the Sahara, the Amazon and Antarctica). But I had another encounter with a peregrine last month, just outside Cheyenne.

My six peregrine observations, all since 2003, have been around Cheyenne, at either Wyoming Hereford Ranch or Lions Park. All but one was in spring.

I remember the first sightings, on Audubon field trips, for which I was relying on more experienced birders for identification. Once, at WHR Reservoir No. 1, we saw a peregrine in one of those legendary dives – once clocked by a scientist at 200 mph.

It slammed into an unsuspecting duck standing on a sandbar. The peregrine's former common name was "duck hawk" – ducks being a favorite among the many kinds of birds they eat.

Last month, my husband Mark and I saw a bird sitting in a cottonwood below the same reservoir, watching us. It had all the peregrine field marks, including the dark cheek patches, which must have been the inspiration for those cheek pieces for first-century Roman centurions' helmets.

Peregrines have been favorites of falconers for 3,000 years. While the young can be taken from wild nests and raised by humans, they are also bred in captivity. In 1970, the founder of The Peregrine Fund, Tom Cade, began breeding them in earnest, as did Bill Burnham of Fort Collins, future president of TPF, beginning in 1974.

By 1984, TPF had opened the World Center for Birds of Prey in Boise, Idaho. By 1997, 4,000 peregrines had been bred and released into the wild. By 1999, the peregrine was off the Endangered Species list. The fund continues to work to conserve raptor species around the world.

It isn't quite the same as the old days for the peregrines. Someone thought of also introducing – or hacking – them into cities that have plentiful pigeon prey and tall buildings that would imitate their cliff-face nesting habitat. Urbanites could be seeing peregrines much more often than we do.

While peregrines went missing in the eastern U.S., what happened to them in Wyoming? I asked Bob Dorn, co-author with his wife, Jane Dorn, of the book, "Wyoming Birds." From his research, he was able to give me a list of more than a dozen observation dates going back to 1929.

In 1939, Bob said O. C. McCreary

categorized the peregrine as "a rather rare summer resident," usually indicating that they are breeding, and "an uncommon migrant," meaning not quite so rare during migration. As Bob put it, "When you're at the top of the food chain, you are in scarce numbers." (Somehow, that isn't true of humans.)

The Wyoming Game and Fish Department's species account states that by 1970, Wyoming had no viable breeding population. They formed a partnership with TPF and over 15 years, 1980-1995, introduced 384 captive-bred peregrines. It was successful. There were 90 breeding pairs recorded in 2009, the most recent information available.

Today, breeding peregrines tend to be found in the northwest part of the state. Down here in the southeast, we have the potential to see migrants from April through May.

The most recently published field guide I have, "Peterson Field Guide to Birds of North America" (2009), does mention the peregrine was endangered – small concession to the idea that the hobby of bird identification can no longer be divorced from bird conservation.

The new Peterson range map shows there is still a big empty area in the middle of the country where the Golden guide had indicated wintering peregrines nearly 50 years before. But it also shows summer range, presumably breeding range, where the Golden guide did not.

Unfortunately, many threatened or endangered birds are not as charismatic as the peregrine. Experience with captive breeding may be nonexistent and the reason for a species' plummeting population may not be as simple as a particular pesticide. The commonality, however, is that human experiments with new technology often produce unexpected, bad consequences for some birds, while accidently promoting the unwanted reproduction of others – think starlings.

Meanwhile, birders continue to collect and share observations, causing range maps to continually be redrawn. Mark's and my single peregrine sighting on April 8 becomes part of the larger story.

Keep your eyes open, too.

133 Gardener reports from backyard: Bird life, death, and allegiance

Sunday, July 22, 2012, Outdo ors, page E3

What I know about the birds in our backyard I've mostly learned from watching from the window.

It's different being out there with them. This spring and summer, I've spent more time than usual out in the yard, working on my new vegetable garden.

We've always had robins, but now I've learned they recognize that a person digging is not only non-threatening, it can also be a source of earthworms.

The male of our local pair waited just a few feet behind me, not even flinching when I turned to look at him.

A couple weeks later, our robins brought their speckle-breasted youngsters to show them how to wash up in the birdbath, how to find earthworms and how to pick the ripening Nanking cherries from our hedge.

This year we have a huge cherry crop, but it seems that only the local robin family is picking. It would be nice to think they are defending their territory and our cherries from other hungry wildlife. Whatever the reason, we are harvesting plenty since a flock hasn't come in to eat them all in one day.

I've been trying to listen to "what the robin knows" ever since reading the book by that title. That means when I heard a robin squawking without ceasing very early one morning, I went out to investigate, finding a long-haired black cat – a potential nest robber – waiting under the bushes.

In return for food, water and cat eviction, our robins are not only defending the cherries, they perch on the garden fence posts, adding fertilizer and planting cherry pits.

We saw blue jays often in May and by early June, I observed one fly into the vegetable garden with something white in its bill. It hopped up to one of the tomatoes and carefully inserted the white object next to it, under the leaf mulch. It was a fecal sac, collected from one of its nestlings, removed to keep the nest clean, and buried so predators wouldn't track down the nest. But it was also tomato fertilizer.

But I don't think the blue jays were successful.

One evening, while working outside, Mark and I heard a plaintive blue jay call high overhead in one of the big green ash trees. And then, several times, we could see a blue jay attack something in a clump of leaves, creating a ruckus.

After about the third attack, four crows left the clump one at a time. I'm pretty sure the blue jay got the raw end of the deal, losing nestlings. I try not to have favorites in the bird world – perhaps the crows were teaching their offspring how to feed themselves.

And then there was the incessant twittering one weekend. It's a familiar background sound, but I finally connected it to downy woodpeckers.

Hour after hour, as we worked out in the yard, I could hear this calling between three or four downies. It must have been the young fledging. A month before, we'd seen a lot of one pair picking over the bark of our tree limbs for bugs, the male announcing his presence by hammering on some metallic part of the utility pole.

We sent the house finches and Eurasian collared-doves packing when we took down the sunflower seed feeder at the end of May. The doves had already produced one brood. You can tell the youngsters even though they are the same size as their parents – their black neck markings are a bit indistinct and they gaze around at the world wide-eyed.

But the thistle feeder is still up, and we can count at least two pairs of goldfinches visiting multiple times a day. They nest later than other songbirds, waiting until the source of food for their nestlings, seed, especially wild thistle seed, is available.

Did you know that goldfinches are the only songbirds that feed mashed seed to their nestlings? Other seed eaters switch to insects – more protein for building bones. It makes one wonder how goldfinches manage without that source of protein?

On June 30, I saw my first hummingbird of the year in our neighborhood – two weeks early. It was time to do the hummers a favor and hang their feeder – our tubular-type red garden flowers weren't blooming yet.

And the flickers came and worked on the ant invasion on the front lawn.

Isn't it nice when we and the birds can help each other? It's what it's like to be part of a healthy ecosystem.

---

134 Colorado black swift wintering grounds are found in Brazil

Imagine that in 2009 there was still one bird species whose wintering location was still unknown. And imagine that for that same bird species, few of its nesting colonies had even been found until the late 1990s.

Let me introduce the black swift, the North American subspecies (not that the southern subspecies is better known).

At 7.5 inches long, the black swift is longer than our local chimney swift by 2 inches and its wingspan is an 18-inch curve. Swifts are perpetual bug-eating flying machines that might be mistaken for swallows but look more like flying cigars with wings.

The first black swift was documented in 1857 on Puget Sound in Washington State, and the first nests in 1901 in California sea caves where ocean spray kept them moist. By 1919, intrepid egg collectors found their nests behind mountain waterfalls.

In the 1950s, Owen A. Knorr made the black swift his master's thesis at Colorado University in Boulder, making a concerted effort to look for nests in Colorado by learning mountain climbing skills and developing a system for predicting which waterfalls would be nest locations. He found 25 colonies, each with a handful of mossy nests stuck to tiny rocky ledges, each one holding one nestling.

In 1997, Kim Potter was one of two biologists beginning a new search for swifts. A year later, Rich Levad got hooked on looking for them and joined her in organizing surveys through the Rocky Mountain Bird Observatory (now Bird Conservancy of the Rockies), infecting others with swift enthusiasm along the way.

I met Levad and Potter in 2005 when Wyoming Audubon members helped them find flammulated owls in Wyoming's Sierra Madre range. Already one year into a diagnosis of Lou Gehring's disease, Levad was soldiering on impressively.

When he had to cut back on field work, Levad started writing "The Coolest Bird: A Natural History of the Black Swift and Those Who Have Pursued It," still making edits the day before his death in 2008. You can find the 152-page, free edition provided by the American Birding Association online at www.aba.org/thecoolestbird.pdf.

It's a great read about an exciting bird and many memorable characters – check out the scathing exchange between Knorr and a dignitary in Arizona who believed a bird species only existed if he could hold the collected specimen – the dead body, in other words.

I spoke recently with one of Levad's protégés, Jason Beason, director of special projects at the Rocky Mountain Bird Observatory and lead author of an article about a black swift breakthrough published in the Wilson Journal of Ornithology this past March about finally discovering the black swift's wintering grounds.

Every August, black swift adults leave each morning to collect food and later at twilight they slip back to feed the young. This is when researchers hope to see them.

Levad learned that training field observers increased their abilities to find swifts, upping known Colorado colonies from 27, including Knorr's found in the 1950s, to 86, but it wasn't until mist netting was tried in a couple of narrow canyons that it became apparent how many swifts were eluding detection.

Banding the captured swifts and recapturing many of them the following years showed how loyal they are to nest sites.

Beason, Potter, and another of the paper's authors, Carolyn Gunn, wanted to strap recorders on the birds to find out where they go in winter, but most equipment is designed to attach to a bird's leg and swifts hardly have a leg. They never walk. If they land at all, they cling to vertical surfaces. It's thought that for some swift species, non-breeders stay aloft for a year or two.

Enter the British Antarctic Survey, which had developed a micro geolocator that works off day length to determine location and archives the data every 10 minutes for a year. One was strapped on the back of each of four black swifts about to leave Colorado in September 2009.

Beason and his team were able to recapture three of the four swifts in the fall of 2010 and download and process the data.

Beyond doubt, at least these black swifts, from two colonies in Colorado, winter in the Amazon basin of western Brazil. Next summer, Beason plans to outfit a few swifts from Idaho to see if they winter there, too.

There are also a few other documented black swift colonies in the West, including Montana and Utah, and of course, the gazillion in Colorado, but none in Wyoming, probably "just because nobody's gotten out and looked up there," Jason told me.

So I asked him how we could help, thinking of that flammulated owl survey, but also realizing that few of those same people are capable of climbing up to waterfalls off the beaten track, much less hiking out in the dark after the swifts come home.

Beason said to let him know of any small grants he could apply for. It wouldn't take much, maybe $1,000, to add a stop next summer on his way to Idaho, to check out where Knorr thought he once saw a black swift flying at Grand Teton National Park. Grants, schmantz. I have a better idea: crowd sourcing, or the Tinkerbelle solution. If all of us made a small contribution, we might add a breeding bird species to the Wyoming records.

135 Celebrity field guide author visits Cheyenne

In September, Ted Floyd was a guest of the Cheyenne – High Plains Audubon Society. He is the editor of the American Birding Association's magazine, the author of the Smithsonian Field Guide to the Birds of North America, and a really sharp birder.

On the field trip along Crow Creek, he was able to identify a first-of-the-year female chestnut-sided warbler (rare in Cheyenne), in a treetop. It didn't look very distinctive, but behavior and voice helped him identify it.

Ted has a rather humble attitude towards his birding and literary talents, as evidenced by the following interview.

Question. What was your first field guide when you started birding in 7th grade?

Answer. The fourth edition of Roger

Tory Peterson's "Eastern Birds." It was brand-new at the time.

Q. How many bird field guides do you have in your collection?

A. Hundreds. Literally.

Q. When did you start dreaming about writing your own bird field guide?

A. I've been thinking about writing a field guide almost from the very beginning. When I was in the eighth grade, I created my own "checklist sequence" – I thought it was better than Peterson's.

Q. How did you get to be the author of the Smithsonian Field Guide to the Birds of North America?

A. Honestly, I'm not entirely sure. The folks at Scott & Nix contacted me; then we had a long series of informal chats; and, eventually, we all agreed that we'd do the field guide. My name is on the front cover, but it's been a collaborative effort.

Q. How did Charles Nix and George Scott think this field guide could be different and better than all the North American guides currently available?

A. The Smithsonian Guide is holistic. It encourages birders to employ a "whole-bird" approach to bird identification: Look at the bird, listen to the bird, pay attention to molt and behavior, take note of ecology and the environmental context – and do that all at once. It's a very natural approach for beginners. For more experienced birders, who can be very rigid and compartmentalized about bird identification, some amount of reprogramming may be required.

Q. How long was it after signing the contract before the books were on store shelves? How much of that time did it take you to actually write the field guide?

A. The guys at Scott & Nix are slavedrivers, and I mean that in a good way. They were excellent at keeping the project on schedule. I would say

the project took about a year of organization, and then it took me a year to write the book.

Q. When you were writing the 28-page introduction to birdwatching and the species accounts, what kind of birdwatcher did you have in mind?

A. Anybody who's interested in nature and open-minded about new ways to engage the natural world.

Q. In your research for this guide, what was the most surprising thing you learned about a bird you thought you knew?

A. As I listened to recordings of duck vocalizations, I was enthralled by how beautiful they are. I have come to believe that the Redhead has one of the most arrestingly beautiful songs of any North American bird species – right up there with the Hermit Thrush or Winter Wren. I wonder how many birders even know that Redheads say anything at all!

Q. If Paul Lehman is the go-to guy for range maps for North American field guides, including this, plus National Geographic's and the Sibley Guide, was your personal knowledge of bird ranges added to any of the maps?

A. Yes, but it's not as if I "overruled" Paul Lehman on anything. Rather, the folks involved with map production (including me) had conversations about range limits for certain species. We also had conversations about the best color scheme to use.

Q. On pages where more than one species account appears, they are often laid out side by side, but when they are laid out one over the other, it is easy to miss the lower one when rapidly flipping pages to identify a bird from a large group such as warblers or shore birds. Am I the only one who has problems with that?

A. You need to slow down when you read, Barb...No, seriously, layout is a huge issue with this or any field guide. I can't begin to convey to you how much time all of us labored over where to place the species. In the linear format of a book--you go from page 1 to page 2 to page 3 – it's impossible to present the multi-dimensional problem of comparing species. I think we got it right in most instances.

I'm grateful for comments like yours. That's because a second edition is in the offing, and we'll be tweaking the formatting in places. If you or anybody has suggestions, please tell me about it (tfloyd@aba.org). You'll make a difference.

Q. What other kinds of changes will you be making in the second edition?

A. New taxonomy, a few new names even, and some changes to range maps. We'll also correct the single typo from the first edition.... On a substantive note, look for some new photos. There will be more photos showing distinctive geographic variation and more photos showing cool bird behaviors.

136 Goose population success is messy problem for parks

Sunday, November 25, 2012, Outdoors, page E2

As your resident bird lady, it's time for me to bring science to the issue of too many geese in Cheyenne parks.

The domestic geese that Teddie Spier mentioned in her letter to the editor Nov. 6 are not a problem. The city can round them up any time, which they did this summer at Holliday Park, leaving behind four whites and a gray.

Mallards are common park ducks, but here they are a fraction of park waterfowl. Mid-winter, the large flock of ducks on the open water at Lions Park is made up of species eating aquatic invertebrates, not mallards begging for handouts.

It's the wild geese, properly known as Canada geese. (If one of them hails from Canada, you could refer to it as a Canadian Canada goose.)

Over the last three years, I have been counting the birds at Holliday Park around 8 a.m., 10 days per month on average, recording the results at www. eBird.org. In the spring of 2010, Canada geese were numbering 60-100 per day. This spring they were running over 200. You can access my data for free by setting up your own login and password at the website.

Cheyenne geese move between the parks, golf courses, F.E. Warren Air Force Base and rural fields, so to get the big picture, look at the Cheyenne Christmas Bird Count, which strives to count geese all over town at the same time. The data is available for free at: http://netapp.audubon.org/cbcobservation/Historical/SpeciesData.aspx.

I found eight Canadas were recorded in 1974, then none until 50 in 1983. In the 1990s, numbers jumped into the hundreds, and by 2000, to over 2,000. Last year's count was 1,332, probably not a sign of a downward trend but instead some geese may have been in fields outside the count circle.

The increase in geese, and geese that aren't migrating, is nationwide over the last 50 years. Hunting (2 million harvested in 2002) hasn't held back the Canadas. Plus, the birds in most parks, including ours, are safe by law. No one can hunt within city limits.

So yes, there is more goose poop in our parks than before. Because it is recycled grass, I don't find it as objectionable as dog droppings.

At Holliday Park, goose nesting was confined to the island, but this year there were three pairs nesting off-island – three ganders hissing at park visitors trying to walk the sidewalks – for four weeks of incubation. I worry geese beaks are about eye-level with small children.

Because Canada geese and other migratory waterfowl are protected by international treaty and congressional acts, the city can't touch them without permission from the U.S. Fish and Wildlife Service. Before the city could try addling eggs to slow population growth, FWS asked the city to have a ban on feeding birds in the parks.

According to Birds of North America Online, which is summaries of scientific bird studies available to the public for an annual subscription fee, Canada geese eat grass-type plants almost exclusively, adding berries and seeds in the winter, though they've learned to find waste grain in farm fields.

People objecting to the city's feeding ban, saying it's bad for the geese especially in winter, need to keep several things in mind:

--People often feed the geese junk food rather than dried whole corn, which is what farmers have determined works for domestic geese.

--Handouts represent very little of the total diet of the 1,500-plus Cheyenne geese – most of which are too busy grazing far from the parking lots.

--According to research, urban geese have adapted to a year-round diet of grass.

--Our geese often fly to nearby fields for grain.

The urban Canada goose is looking for lawns next to ponds, say the studies referenced by BNAO. I don't foresee the city draining lakes and paving parks since people like grass and water as much as the geese do.

Where it is imperative to keep geese away, such as airport runways, harassment by dogs has some effect. But don't try this yourself since it's illegal to harass a federally protected species. It probably isn't realistic to fence Holliday Park and turn it into a dog park, either.

I haven't seen much evidence of predation except for the cormorants eyeing goslings. What we need is a way to harvest Canada geese within the city without using firearms, and to be practical, feed them to the hungry. Wild geese are very nutritious, especially when park employees work hard to grow the grass they eat.

Instead, we have to wait and see if a feeding ban and egg addling will limit the goose population. If not, we'll be stepping around more droppings and territorial ganders.

2013

137
Winter is good time to spot unusual birds

Last winter, snowy owls irrupted. Meaning, there were sightings all across the northern tier of the lower 48 states. Apparently, more owls fledged than usual, and there weren't enough small rodents to go around in their Arctic winter territories so, they headed for more productive habitat.

This year in Cheyenne, it's the seedeaters that are irrupting, or at least coming down from the mountains.

My first inkling was the Steller's jays I saw at a friend's, up on the north edge of Cheyenne, enjoying the pine-juniper windbreak and the birdfeeders. They are dark blue with black heads, unlike the usual blue and white blue jay. Five made an appearance for the Cheyenne Christmas Bird Count on Dec. 22, as they have eight out of the last 38 years.

Named for Georg Steller, the first to find this bird and describe it for science while serving as the naturalist travelling with Vitus Bering in 1740-42 to what became Alaska, Steller's jay is found in western mountains down to Central America.

Both its usual plant (seeds, nuts, fruits) and animal (small vertebrates) foods must be in short supply in nearby mountains. Even if the Birds of North America lists cookies and other picnic provisions as preferred food,

don't be tempted. Give them black-oil sunflower seed.

Making its first-ever appearance on the Cheyenne bird count was the pygmy nuthatch. A flock was noted several weeks before on the west side of town, and we were able to re-find it. The five individuals were mixed in with white-breasted and red-breasted nuthatches and mountain chickadees, all in the same pine tree.

The pygmy nuthatch is another mountain species, but it seldom comes down. It needs dead or partially dead trees with cavities, not just for nesting, but also to stay warm. Studies show families, even whole flocks, will pile into a cavity when it's cold. The birds at the bottom are the warmest, but the entire space will be several degrees warmer than it is outside.

There must be empty food caches and a dire lack of frozen insects to pick out of the bark of mountain pine trees for pygmies to leave their known hollow trees for an urban area where we keep dead wood to a minimum.

I was thrilled to see evening grosbeaks on the Guernsey-Ft. Laramie Christmas Bird Count on Dec. 29. They were at a feeder between Guernsey and Hartville, looking like over-sized goldfinches. Another mountain species, they expanded their range east from the Rockies in the mid-1800s. It's thought that the planting of box elder (their favorite seeds) and ornamental fruit-bearing trees, and the invasion of spruce budworms, led them on.

Today, they are not quite so common back east – the reason they were brought to attention as the 2012 American Birding Association Bird of the Year. They are well known for their irruptive behavior, usually every other winter. We've had a handful of them on each of nine Cheyenne Christmas Bird Counts over the last 38 years.

The range map for common redpolls in Douglas Faulkner's "Birds of Wyoming," shows that every winter they will show up in the northeast corner of Wyoming. They breed in the Arctic. This year, they are all over the state, according to multiple reports on the Wyobirds elist, with 24 present for the Cheyenne Christmas Bird Count.

Redpolls, too, seem to show up at bird feeders on alternate winters. If you are familiar with house finches at your feeder, scan them closely for redpolls, slightly smaller, streaky brown birds with a small red spot on the forehead and sometimes a wash of pale pink on the breast.

On their home turf, redpolls eat the very small spruce and birch seeds. At your feeder, small seeds like white millet would be a good replacement.

In his report of the Cheyenne Christmas Bird Count, compiler Greg Johnson said the rarest sighting was a red-bellied woodpecker, a species of the eastern U.S., particularly the southeast. The first ever recorded sighting of one in Wyoming was in Cheyenne in 1992. Then there were two other sightings of single birds in eastern Wyoming in 1993 and 2002, followed by three sightings at the Wyoming Hereford Ranch outside Cheyenne in 2002, 2006 and 2008.

Irruptive is not the explanation for the appearance of this woodpecker in Cheyenne. Lost is more like it, though lost seems to be coming a regular habit. Officially, the term is "vagrant." This individual may have been caught in some weather in October and was lucky enough to find Mike Schilling's feeding station, where it has been since.

There is only one way to see species uncommon for Cheyenne, and that is to look. A well-stocked feeder helps, but the best way is to get outside and keep your eyes open. And when you see some unusual bird, tell someone.

138 Game and Fish needs our help

Sunday, February 10, 2013, Outdoors, page E3

It's easy to support the work the Wyoming Game and Fish Department does. Just buy a hunting license. Or show up at the Capitol during the state legislative session to testify on the merits of license fee increases.

The department gets 80 percent of its funding from license fees, but it is the legislature that approves any fee changes every six or seven years. By this session, the fees approved in 2007 had

20 percent less buying power, thanks to inflation, but the legislation did not pass.

Yet, there are more expenses. There are more people coming to work here who need wildlife education. And there's more baseline data collection and monitoring work to be done in the face of more energy development.

Surprisingly, at the committee meeting Feb. 1 to hear testimony on the second bill proposing increasing hunting fees, there was a lobbyist for a minor sportsmen's group opposed. His board members begrudge having to pay more to hunt, even when it is apparent that the cost of everyday agency work gets more expensive.

In my testimony, I mentioned that my husband and I hunt and fish, we enjoy nongame wildlife, and we made an investment to support the Game and Fish by buying lifetime fishing licenses for our family. Later, the lobbyist told me we birdwatchers ought to be paying something, too.

He is right. There are more people in Wyoming enjoying looking at non-game wildlife, including birds in their backyards, than are hunting it. We are indirectly benefiting from the 6 percent of hunting license fees spent on nongame species work.

However, grants and legislative funding cover most of the $9.5 million (14.5 percent of the total Game and Fish budget) spent on nongame species: programs to prevent aquatic invasive species invading; programs to prevent "sensitive species" from requiring listing as threatened or endangered; programs for wolves and sage-grouse; and work on brucellosis and chronic wasting disease.

There is also one biologist who tracks all the bird species not hunted.

How can a non-hunter support Game and Fish?

First, we need better terminology. Rather than "non-hunter," say "wildlife watcher." Rather than "nongame," I like "watchable wildlife," a term the department already uses, even if it does seem to include the huntable megafauna.

Some states sell special vehicle license plates to support wildlife. That was suggested here a few years ago, but apparently, the University of Wyoming is going to be the only entity with the sacred right to raise funds that way.

Some states have a check-off on their income tax forms to give people an easy option to contribute a few dollars, but it will be decades before any Wyoming legislator wants to prematurely end her career by suggesting instituting state income tax.

Colorado uses the majority of its lottery income to support its wildlife programs. Wyoming considers legislation to join one of the national lotteries every year. If it ever passes, could funds be earmarked for wildlife?

In other places, a special license allows a person access to special state land. With so much federal land available for recreation, that probably wouldn't work in Wyoming, either.

The federal government once proposed a minor tax on outdoor gear that would be shared with states, but the gear companies nixed that.

Game and Fish does have a nice selection of items available in their gift shop here in Cheyenne and online, but seriously, who needs another mug or T-shirt if you already belong to one wildlife organization or another?

What we really need is a voluntary wildlife watching license: Something on the order of $25 per family, with the option of contributing more and being listed in the back of Wyoming Wildlife magazine, as supporters of other organizations are in their publications.

Besides being listed in the magazine, one's support could be shown with a small sticker on the car window, maybe pasted right next to the annual state parks entrance pass. We could also charge visitors non-resident fees if they also wanted a wildlife watching license.

And then, as sometimes happens, maybe third parties would offer perks for license holders – perhaps a discount from local purveyors of outdoor gear. Or maybe each year, license holders would be put in a drawing for a pair of super-duper binoculars or a spotting scope.

But really, for some of us, just knowing we are contributing to the well-being of all the wildlife in Wyoming – and there are a lot more kinds of critters out there than the ones sportsmen hunt – would be worth it.

If you have any other ideas, please contact Wyoming Game and Fish Department Deputy Director John Emmerich, 777-4501.

139 Wyoming Birding Bonanza strikes again

Sunday, April 7, 2013, Outdoors, page E2

Are you ready for the second annual Wyoming Birding Bonanza? Polish your binoculars because you can be a winner.

The competition was dreamed up last year by James Maley and Matt Carling, both from the University of Wyoming's Department of Zoology and Physiology. James is collections manager of the Museum of Vertebrates and Matt is an assistant professor.

Their goal is to increase the number of bird observations for Wyoming during spring migration that are recorded in the eBird.org database and to get birders into the habit of submitting information. The data is used by scientists.

Last year, the contest ran from mid-April to mid-June, but this year, it is being pared back to May 1-31, concentrating on the peak weeks.

And again, thanks to sponsors like last year's, Cheyenne - High Plains, Laramie and Meadowlark Audubon societies, as well as UW's Biodiversity Institute, Audubon Wyoming and eBird, there are prizes.

Registered contestants who enter at least 15 checklists will receive a WBB T-shirt. A checklist is a list of bird species and number of individuals of each, seen in a particular location during a period of time. James promises this year's T-shirt will be a work of art. Everyone who turns in at least 10 checklists will be entered in a grand prize drawing.

Also, for each Wyoming county, the participant reporting the most species will win a prize. Last year, I was the Laramie County winner and received the latest edition of the National Geographic field guide. This year, our county is up for grabs since I'm going to be out less often.

For better odds, try birding Big Horn, Converse and Sublette counties, where no checklists were turned in last year, James said.

"April, May, and June of 2012 are now the top three months of all time for number of checklists statewide," he said. There were 1,282 turned in, compared to 424 for the same months in 2010. A total of 266 species was observed in 2012.

I know I paid closer attention to the birds around me because of the competition. I found a summer tanager in our backyard May 11, considered rare for Wyoming.

James passed on a list of other rare bird sightings from 2012:

--1 Glossy Ibis at Meeboer Lake (west of Laramie) on April 17

--1 Lesser Black-backed Gull also at Meeboer Lake on April 17

--1 Black-and-white Warbler at Holliday Park on April 21

--1 Juniper Titmouse at Guernsey State Park on April 22

--1 Long-tailed Jaeger at Hutton Lake NWR on May 3

--1 Northern Cardinal in Laramie on May 4

--5 Short-billed Dowitchers at Hutton on May 5

--1 Snowy Owl at Keyhole State Park on May 15

--1 Blackpoll Warbler at Hereford on May 15

--1 Cattle Egret in Rock River on May 17

--1 White-eyed Vireo near Lander on May 28.

So, are you ready to earn that WBB T-shirt? You can do it by simply counting the birds in your backyard for a few minutes at least 15 different times. Here's what you need to do.

First, sign up at www.eBird.org, if you haven't already. It's free. Click on the "About eBird" link, and then the "eBird Quick Start Guide," the first link on that page.

When setting up your observation locations, select a hotspot marker if there is one at one of your locations already, such as Wyoming Hereford Ranch or Lions Park. Otherwise, on the map your personal marker may be hidden underneath the hotspot's. You can view your data for a hotspot alone or collated with everyone else's. It's also free.

Here are the rules.

Counting:

--Participants will count only full species as defined by the current American Birding Association checklist.

--Birds identified to a taxonomic level above species may be counted if no other member of the taxonomic level is on the checklist. For example, duck sp. can be counted if no other ducks are seen.

--Birds counted must be alive and unrestrained. Sick and injured birds are countable. Nests and eggs do not count.

--Electronic devices are allowed but see ABA's Code of Ethics for guidelines.

Time: We will extract final eBird data for the Bonanza on 30 June 2013.

Area: Anywhere in Wyoming.

Conduct:

--Participants must only count birds unquestionably identified. If in doubt, leave it out.

--Know and abide by the rules.

--Share information with other birders – they'll thank you.

Good birding to all!

140

Sunday, May 5, 2013, Outdoors, page E3 and Southeast Wyoming Extra

Early birds yield clues

First birds of the season can tell us about climate change

The great joy of springtime, if you are a birdwatcher of any sort, is seeing your first robin, first bluebird or first mourning dove of the year.

There is sometimes a friendly bit of competition where serious birders gather – to see who is first to report their "FOYs," first of the year observations, especially of more obscure migratory species, say "Greater Yellowlegs," a long-legged shorebird.

Those of us in southeastern Wyoming have the advantage over the birders in the rest of the state posting on the Wyobirds elist, as many spring migrants often funnel up against Colorado's Front Range and across Cheyenne before spreading out over the rest of Wyoming.

At eBird.org, where ordinary folks file their bird observations for free, for their own record-keeping and for use by scientists, FOY data is constantly updated and can be found in the Explore Data section under "Arrivals and Departures."

A check of the Wyoming statistics shows that Del Nelson got the jump on all of us this year by birding January 1 near Crowheart, Wyoming, and reporting 28 species – mostly birds we expect to see mid-winter.

However, Del's list included a single western meadowlark. On occasion, individuals of migratory species like that miss the bus south in the fall and sometimes find a perfect pocket of habitat that allows them to survive the winter. Insectivorous birds like meadowlarks usually prefer live insects, not the foods of wintering birds: frozen bugs picked out by flickers, seeds preferred by finches, or warm-blooded creatures preyed on by hawks.

A few days later, Del reported a mountain bluebird, another bird uncommon in winter, which I always thought of as a sign of impending spring. Even robins aren't reliable – one was listed for Wyoming January 2.

Studying the "Birds of Wyoming" compendium by Doug Faulkner, I found that many migratory bird species often have a few individuals observed in Wyoming during Faulkner's designated winter months of December through February. If you don't count those species, the first true spring migrant (no over-wintering records so far), the 97th species listed by eBird for 2013 in Wyoming, is the group of sandhill cranes seen February 12 in Riverton – by Del Nelson, the birder who must be spending more time afield than anyone else in the state.

Here in Laramie County, our signs of spring, our FOYs, were observed more seasonally:

Killdeer – March 5
Robin – March 6
Mountain bluebird – March 7

Meadowlark – March 16
Turkey vulture – March 29
Mourning dove – March 30
American avocet and Swainson's hawk – April 7.

Granted, in a state like Wyoming with a sparse population of birdwatchers, it is quite possible the first flock of anything to flit over the county line goes unnoticed. Sometimes we are hiding at home during snowstorms.

Brian Kimberling, a columnist writing for the New York Times, recently posed the idea that FOYs might help us track climate change the way tracking plants has. There is a website, www.BudBurst.org, asking citizen scientists (you and me) to track when particular perennial species bloom. Changes are already noticeable when historic records of eccentric gardeners and naturalists are examined, showing blooming times advancing as much as a week over a few decades.

I'm not sure the migrations of birds are as useful as the bloom times of plants. After all, plants sit in one place and accumulate degrees of heat necessary to bloom, while birds will push the envelope in their quest for food, sometimes losing their gamble when, after a pleasant spring weather spell, disaster hits. Many dead birds were reported after our April 15-17 snowstorm.

The opposite of FOY, what I think of as LOS, "Last of the Season," might be more accurate a measure. Sometime in April, just when I think I've seen the last of the juncos until fall, another bout of cold blows in and they reappear briefly, pushed back into town from their summer homes in nearby mountains.

But there are whole groups of birds, mostly the insectivorous species, which have never been reported in winter in Wyoming: hummingbirds, vireos, most of the shorebirds, flycatchers, swallows, swifts, terns, dickcissels, bobolinks, and most warbler species.

When those birds begin to show up earlier and earlier, establishing a trend over the years, it will be one way we'll know that global climate trends apply to us, too, right here in the Magic City.

141

Encourage birding as a lifelong addiction

Ask a simple question of a man pulling weeds in a public garden in Juneau, Alaska. It is always possible you will discover you both know the same people.

Alaskans, like Wyomingites, are always interested in where visitors are from. They, like us, often are from somewhere else themselves.

This summer, when I told Merrill Jensen, manager of the Jensen-Olson Arboretum (the co-founder is no relation of his), that I was from Cheyenne, he said he graduated from Cheyenne's East High.

We both graduated in 1974. But I graduated from an altogether different East High, 1,000 miles east of Cheyenne. So, the only person I could think of that might have graduated with him is actually one of Merrill's old buddies – and the husband of the friend I walk with every morning.

As my husband, Mark, called our attention to a nearby pair of harlequin ducks in the bay just yards from the edge of the gardens, Merrill remarked that he is also an avid birder.

So that precipitated discovery of another mutual acquaintance, May Hanesworth.

May was the "Bird Lady" of Cheyenne when Mark and I moved here. We went to the 1989-90 Christmas Bird Count tally party held at her elegant apartment, and the next thing I knew, I'd been recruited to type bird lists from Christmas and spring counts for

submission to the newspaper, which I still do.

May, born in 1900, was of the generation that believed real ladies didn't type. But she had elegant hand-writing. And she must have been an elegant music teacher in the Cheyenne school district.

Merrill remembers going to Audubon meetings in her living room in the 1960s. His parents discovered he had led his first-grade classmates on a "bird field trip" around his elementary school playground, so they indulged his interest in birds by tracking down local Audubon folks.

In a recent email, Merrill remembered those early days:

"(May) gave me a lot of encouragement and was able to persuade my parents to install a bird feeder/bath in the back yard. It was one of my kid duties to keep it filled in the winter. I remember we didn't have much diversity coming through to the feeder; lots of house sparrows, house finches and juncos.

"I don't remember going on any actual birding trips with May, just going to her home in the winter for meetings and watching birds out her window. I was the youngest member of the group by a long shot!" Merrill wrote.

By the time I met May, she was entering her 90s. Though she no longer went out birding, she continued to compile the bird count lists, calling all her local contacts. She was the go-to person for bird questions, remembering where to find the regular species and the particulars of the rare bird sightings.

May was in her late 90s before she was willing to become "Bird Compiler Emeritus," finally passing on in 1999 at age 99. But her influence lives on for Merrill.

"As I went through junior high and high school, there were too many other demands on my time, and I didn't go to any more meetings past probably 1968. I have continued to be an avid birder and take my binoculars everywhere.

"As to my further Auduboning, I participated in the Christmas Bird Counts while I was at Washington State with the head of the zoology department and in the Boise area with staff from Deer Flat National Wildlife Refuge.

"Here in Alaska, I've led several bird walks, do the CBC and I've just rotated off of the Juneau Audubon Society's board where I served for 4 1/2 years. Even though I'm the resident plant geek, birds still play a large part of my outdoor experiences and will continue as long as I'm able to."

Here it is, about 45 years after Merrill last sat in May's living room, and her example of the birding volunteer spirit lives on.

But let's not forget those parents who recognized, indulged and enabled their son's life-long birding addiction.

Do you know children who notice birds? Indulge them today. It will add a layer of richness to their lives, wherever they go.

142 Fall migration kicks up kites, but not the kind found on strings

Sunday, October 6, 2013, Outdoors, page E2

Recently, we've discovered some new kids on the block – well, over the block to be precise.

Three Mississippi kites were soaring, fluttering, soaring, fluttering high up above our house on September 2. This is a type of hawk rarely recorded in Wyoming.

I'm not sure Mark and I would have run outside with binoculars as the crow-like birds soared overhead if our friend, Chuck Seniawski, failed to mention seeing them on his way home just a day earlier, a mile away.

About three years ago, Wayne McNicholas told me about seeing one of these kites hanging around College and South Greeley Highway. He's seen them elsewhere and was familiar with them.

The Birds of North America Online describes the Mississippi kite as a "sleek, acrobatic, crow-sized raptor,"

so I wonder how many others we might have just shrugged off as odd-behaving crows, especially since they don't look pale gray with the sky's light behind them.

The BNA account describes the kite's range as central and southern Great Plains, but I also checked www.eBird.org.

In Greeley, Colorado, in July 2012, seven birds were documented with photos, and in August 2013, two birds. Our only previous local sighting recorded was James Maley's in August 2012, at the Cheyenne Airport Golf Course.

A number of other sightings in the last 10 years have been along the North and South Platte rivers in western Nebraska and northeastern Colorado. It's no accident kites are seen along rivers – big trees are favorite nesting habitat.

As the kites expand their range,

nesting in colonies in groves as well as in urban areas, more people have learned they eat insects on the wing, as well as small animals such as mice and snakes. That's good. But kites also defend their nests when people get too close, and that has been a problem in some urban areas.

We don't know where exactly in South America they go in the winter, but the number of birdwatchers there is increasing.

The other excitement was my identifying a great crested flycatcher, an eastern species, in our backyard September 17. That day, after a week of rain, the backyard was suddenly full of birds.

There were several kinds of nearly identical gray flycatchers I'm not comfortable identifying. However, around 11 a.m., I noticed something larger than a warbler but not as hefty as a robin.

The bird had a bright yellow belly and a rufous (birder-talk for the color of an Irish setter) tail. The breast was a plain gray and the back was darker. I paged through my field guide but then had to get on an Audubon conference call.

Mid-way through the call, the bird came back, a mere 15 feet from my window. When I looked through the field guide again, I came up with a perfect match. Two days later, I spotted it again, briefly – and Mark missed it again.

Like the Mississippi kite, great crested flycatchers are seen regularly in western Nebraska and northeastern Colorado but hardly in Wyoming. Doug Faulkner's "Birds of Wyoming," published in 2010, lists no reports for spring, a few for summer (including one in Cheyenne in 1967) and four reports for fall, but all in the northern part of our state.

Doug's summary of great crested flycatcher distribution is, "They are most likely to occur at wooded migrant traps and along river systems characterized by a mature cottonwood overstory."

That's a good description of the Wyoming Hereford Ranch, on the edge of Cheyenne, where Ted Floyd also saw a great crested flycatcher a couple weeks earlier, and why the ranch was designated an Important Bird Area in the state. Thousands of migrating birds appreciate the big old trees along the creek as a place to rest and refuel on insects.

I don't have Crow Creek running through my yard, but I am in a 50-year-old neighborhood where the first homeowners planted many trees, though not always in the right place. Lately, some have had to be removed.

There are many neighborhoods like ours that if more people were paying attention during spring and fall migration, we could prove my contention that Cheyenne is one big migrant trap.

So, keep planting trees and shrubs (but not over sewer lines or under utility lines or too close to buildings and fences), and keep your eyes open for the next rare bird.

143 Curiosity, generosity rewarded by UW's Biodiversity Institute

Sunday, November 10, 2013, Outdoors, page E2

It's wonderful when friends are recognized for a lifetime of work they enjoy.

Last month, the Biodiversity Institute recognized Chris Madson of Cheyenne, and Jane and Robert Dorn, formerly of

Cheyenne, now residing near Lingle.

The Biodiversity Institute, established in 2012, is a division of the University of Wyoming's Haub School of Environment and Natural Resources. It "seeks to promote research, education, and outreach concerning the study of living organisms in Wyoming and beyond (www.wyomingbiodiversity.org)." This was the first year for what will be biannual awards.

Chris's award for "Contributions to Wyoming Biodiversity Conservation" highlights his 30 years as editor of Wyoming Wildlife, the magazine published by the Wyoming Game and Fish Department. The week before the awards ceremony, he retired.

Each issue has been a compilation of the work of the best nature and outdoor photographers and writers who were attracted to the prize-winning magazine. Judith Hosafros, longtime assistant editor, should also be credited for her attention to graphic details and proofreading that made it easy to read all these years.

Most subscribers turned to page 4 first, to read Chris's monthly elucidation of issues or hosannas to nature, and then they looked for any articles he authored.

Getting in touch with Chris for what might have been a minute could turn into a conversation exploring a topic in nearly any field – not surprising for a man with degrees in biology, English, anthropology and wildlife.

Chris's dad was also a writer and conservationist in Chris's native state of Iowa. He remembers his dad interpreting the scenery on long car trips. When I spoke to two of Chris and Kathy's three daughters at the awards, Erin and Ceara, they both mentioned long drives as favorite times with their dad.

Chris made Wyoming Wildlife much more inclusive than the typical hook and bullet publication – for instance, the October issue had three major non-game bird articles. Illuminating the conservation ethic was always uppermost for Chris, and that's why he was nominated for this biodiversity award.

The Dorns received the Contributions to Biodiversity Science Award. Both Bob and Jane trained as scientists: Bob with a doctorate in botany, and Jane with a masters in zoology. They met in 1969 at UW, he coming from Minnesota and she from Rawlins. They have been a productive partnership ever since.

When Bob first started his studies at UW that year, he realized there was no single good plant guide for Wyoming, and he set out to correct that, publishing "Vascular Plants of Wyoming" in 1977. It's essentially a key he made for identifying hundreds of plants, based on his and many others' research, and Jane has provided scientific illustrations for it. The third edition, still with a humble, plain brown paper cover, is available through UW's Rocky Mountain Herbarium. It's considered the bible by anyone working in botany in Wyoming.

Bob has had his own biological consulting business, working on clearances and inventories for threatened and endangered species, reclamation evaluations and wetland determinations. But he has continued to have scientific papers published and other books. Many of his contracts called for inspecting remote areas, and at this point, out of the 448 units he divided the state into back in 1969, he has botanically surveyed 445.

Jane is no slouch, botanically. Growing up, she spent a lot of time on her grandparents' ranch, and her parents impressed on her that everything has a name. I'm not sure it is possible to divide Bob and Jane's joint interests in botany and birds, but when researching in the nation's great scientific libraries, Jane tends to find the birds.

Having met them through the local Audubon chapter, Bob and Jane became my mentors when I first started writing this bird column in 1999. They put their research into two editions of their book, "Wyoming Birds." Doug Faulkner continually credits them throughout his 2010 book, "Birds of Wyoming." Jane wrote the chapter for him on the history of Wyoming ornithology, and Bob wrote the chapter on landforms and vegetation.

While both books often save me from having to make phone calls, the Dorns' book also has 70 pages of Wyoming birding hotspots and directions on how to get to them.

What Jane, Bob and Chris have in common is not only intelligence and education, but insatiable curiosity that has and will keep them going long after any official retirement; the afternoon before the awards ceremony on campus, I found Bob doing research in the herbarium.

And they also share a huge spirit of generosity, making all of us, maybe unknowingly for many people, beneficiaries of their scientific and conservation passions.

2014

144 Owls are among us

Sunday, January 5, 2014, Outdoors, page E2

Here's how to tell if the elusive bird is lurking in your Cheyenne neighborhood.

In late November, Mark and I became aware that a flock of crows, also known as a murder of crows, was convening just before sunset in a neighbor's big spruce tree.

They were very loud, very raucous, as if they were a lynch mob yelling for noose justice.

Our double-paned windows are somewhat of a sound barrier, but when we let the dog out, we were bombarded with enough noise to overwhelm a backyard cookout.

Was there an owl roosting in the spruce? It's a big tree, probably planted when the neighborhood was new 50-60 years ago, so you can't easily see inside, even when standing beneath it.

Or had the crows decided to establish a roost in our neighborhood? That was an unbearable thought.

Thanksgiving morning, while I was out sweeping up sunflower seed hulls from under our bird feeder and throwing the ball for the dog, the crows sounded even more agitated – gathered in a spruce even closer to our house. "There must be an owl within those thickly-needled branches," I thought. "And he isn't getting any sleep after a night of hunting."

The next morning, just before sunrise, I lifted the window shade and saw a lump on the bare branch of our big green ash tree. Yep, a great horned owl. I told the dog she would have to wait a few minutes before she could go out.

The owl was perched about a foot away from a small squirrel nest made of dry leaves stuffed into a vortex of small branches. Leaving the kitchen lights off, I pulled out my binoculars and there was just enough light to see which way the owl was facing. It wasn't surprising that it was facing the squirrel nest, bobbing its head up and down in a circular way, to get a better fix on a squirrel probably trying desperately not to be heard breathing.

There's a bigger nest, or drey, on the other side of the alley. Ours looks like it is barely big enough for one squirrel, much less the three scampering around our yard every day, teasing the dog.

I was surprised that the owl didn't just poke a taloned foot or sharp beak into that pile of leaves. But great horned owls prefer to feed in openings where they can perch and then wing after prey they hear or see, and pounce, pinning it to the ground. Eventually, this owl spread its wings and flew off.

No more mobbing crows here, however, owls have come up in recent conversations with two women I know, one living east of town and one on the northwest edge of Cheyenne. Both women were pretty sure their local owls were knocking off rabbits, the great horned's favorite food. And both women seemed fine with that, noting that there seemed to be bunny abundance this year.

I've talked to my share of folks who complain when an avian predator grabs a meal, especially if the prey is a cute songbird or furry animal. So, in addition to getting reports on owl activity, it was gratifying to hear people appreciate owls, even for their feeding habits.

If you are connected to any sources of birding news, you know that this winter there is another irruption of snowy owls, but in the Northeast and upper Midwest rather than the Great Plains, as it was two years ago. Another shortage of lemmings in the Arctic, forcing them south, I guess.

Snowy owls like to be out in the open, being birds of the tundra, even if it's the middle of the day, making them relatively easy to pick out when there isn't too much snow acting as camouflage.

So how many great horned owls are among us, shrouded in a cloak of nocturnal invisibility or daytime coniferous cover? What about the smaller, less common owls of southeastern Wyoming: eastern screech-owl, long-eared owl, short-eared owl?

Is there a great horned owl in your neighborhood? Look for the signs: angry crows, the odd rabbit leg on the sidewalk, a large bird flashing through the beam of your headlights, and even the chunky silhouette, the size of Harry Potter's snowy owl, in a tree or on a fencepost at dawn or dusk.

Don't begrudge your dog's request to be let out on a winter's evening or just before dawn. Follow and take a look around.

145 The great migration

Sunday, February 9, 2014, Journey, page E1

Head east this spring to meet the famous sandhill cranes

One of the great annual events of the natural world, especially for North America, happens just down the road from Cheyenne every spring. Yet it isn't as well-known, much less well-attended, by Wyomingites as it is by people from all over the country, even the world.

I'm talking about the spring migration of sandhill cranes.

Yes, there are millions of migrating birds, but most don't stand nearly 4 feet tall in flocks of thousands, out in the open, making such a racket that they can't be missed.

More than 500,000 birds, representing 80 percent of the entire sandhill population, come in for a landing along a stretch of the Platte River, between wintering in New Mexico and Texas and breeding in Canada and Alaska.

The peak time for Nebraska is the month of March into the first week in April, about when I get my annual spring urge to travel.

Driving Interstate 80 five hours east (and don't forget to account for the lost hour entering the Central time zone), to an elevation 4,000 feet lower, is to meet spring a couple weeks early. Central Nebraska has a Midwestern flavor with birds to match, so it's even more like getting out of Dodge for a vacation.

When Mark and I first went to see the cranes, our boys were younger than 12, too young to be allowed in the blinds at the Rowe Audubon Sanctuary. Can you imagine how quickly the cranes would leave if small children staged a temper tantrum, echoing through the plywood construction? So, we left them with a friend in Kearney for a few hours. We've been back a couple times since.

I love the openness. The only trees are in the river valley. But those trees are exactly what the cranes don't want.

The Rowe Audubon Sanctuary, since its establishment in 1974, has worked diligently to remove trees from its stretch of the river, leaving unvegetated sandbars for the cranes to roost on at night, with no place for predators to skulk unseen. Damming the river upstream has eliminated spring floods that would normally clear the channels regularly.

The blinds at Rowe, near Gibbon, 20 minutes from Kearney, and at The Crane Trust Nature and Visitors Center further east, near Grand Island, allow people to view cranes at sunrise and sunset.

While the cranes (even the occasional whooping crane) are scattered in the local fields and wetlands feeding on corn and invertebrates all day, great for photo ops, it's the blinds that allow you to see the concentration of birds where they roost for the night.

If you want to get closer, sign up to stay overnight in the special photographers' blinds – no heat or light allowed – and pay $200-$300 for the privilege.

It is a privilege to watch these magnificent birds from the blinds, but it may not seem like it if you don't bring your warmest boots and layers of clothing. That's the downside of being further east – the cold is damp.

Once you enter the blind, at 5 p.m. (6 p.m. after daylight saving time starts March 9), you aren't allowed to leave for two to three hours, until it's dark enough to sneak away. Alternatively, if you enter at 5 a.m., 6 a.m. DST, you must wait until after the birds have left before you can leave. The blinds do have adjacent chemical toilets now, but the guides discourage their use.

Not only do you want to wear dark clothes to keep from spooking the birds, but regular flashlights are not allowed, and bright LCD screens are frowned on.

And for heaven's sake, leave your flash at home, and make sure you deactivate the flash on your point-and-shoot or smart phone. If your flash triggers a mass bird departure, everyone in the blind, up to 31 other people, will hate you, because there won't be a second chance to see sandhills that morning or evening.

Blaine McCartney, a photographer at the WTE, recommends a 400mm lens to get close enough to the birds, along with a monopod. Though everyone gets their own little window, there isn't really room for tripods.

Judy Myer, a Cheyenne photographer, went on a shoot with the Fort Collins camera club last year. The club members used the Rowe blinds one morning and the Crane Trust blinds in the evening.

"The evening viewing was dark, but we could hear them," she said. "Is one place better than the other? I can't really answer that except to say I wouldn't do (those blinds) again in the evening."

Instead, she said, she would head to the bridge at the trust, where, for $15, you can watch the cranes fly overhead in the evening to their roosts.

But that just goes to show everyone's experience can be different. I'm not familiar with The Crane Trust blinds. We've had pretty good luck at Rowe, and it's closer.

The Trust exists because of the settlement in 1978 from a lawsuit contending that the Grey Rocks Dam, built on the North Platte in Wyoming, had a negative impact on whooping cranes and other wildlife in Nebraska downstream on the Platte. Like Rowe, they do a lot of work to clear vegetation from the river channels and offer educational opportunities.

Yes, it's half a day's drive each way. Yes, it can be cold.

But no nature film can take the place of being surrounded by a crowd of birds continuing a ritual that's tens of thousands, maybe millions of years old, that's partly instinctual and partly learned from their parents.

Their calling fills your ears with a roar you never forget.

Sunday, February 16, 2014, Outdoors, page E2

146 Let's rethink mega windfarm on behalf of birds, efficiency

David Yarnold is not happy.

The president of the National Audubon Society writes in the January/February issue of Audubon magazine that our country's wind farms kill 573,000 birds a year, including 83,000 raptors.

The Migratory Bird Treaty Act and the Bald and Golden Eagle Protection Act should be protecting most of those birds, he says.

It's illegal to kill them without a permit, but the Interior Department has only enforced the law once, he says. Apparently, wind farms don't have permits for all the birds killed.

A new federal rule allows wind companies to get 30-year permits. But to Yarnold, that represents too many birds, with no incentives to cut the number of deaths.

Wind energy is a great idea. It's been used for centuries to propel boats, grind grain, pump water.

A structure for catching the wind can be erected wherever the power is needed, though a backup system is essential for windless days. People are working on more efficient battery systems.

But leave it to American ingenuity to take a simple idea and enlarge it, making it industrial-sized, much like family farming morphed into industrial agriculture.

Wind energy is clean, producing no pollution except whatever manufacturing the components entails and maintenance requires. We need cleaner energy sources like wind since the traditional fuel-burning, power-producing businesses are reluctant to make their energy production cleaner. Never mind the climate change debate – we all have to breathe.

But wind energy has an Achilles heel. Developers want to site numerous turbines in the windiest places, which also attract birds. Collisions with the blades, the towers and the transmission lines kill birds and bats. Wind farms have mazes of roads running over habitat, forcing out wildlife.

Audubon suggests targeting development for areas that are already disturbed or developed, avoiding areas known to be dense with birds, such as the Prairie Pothole region, the Texas Gulf Coast, and the northeast's raptor migration bottlenecks.

If you don't care about birds, I suppose you wouldn't see any of this as a problem. But you should care. To sum up Basic Ecology 101, every living thing, including you, is connected to every other living thing. It's hard to predict how a loss of birds may affect you. It could be as simple as insect populations getting out of control and decimating crops.

But there are other reasons to rethink the concept of the mega wind farm.

I am a fan of dispersed power production, placing it among the structures where we live and work. For instance, solar panels over every roof, providing extra roof insulation and hail protection. Solar panels over parking lots would keep cars and asphalt cool. Small windmills could be placed along every highway where power lines are already strung. What if we were to place constellations of pinwheels on the outer walls of a skyscraper to produce power for that building?

The advantage of disbursed power production is we don't lose the power consumed by transporting it over long distances. Plus, any power outages would affect fewer people at a time.

OK, so every location in the country isn't terribly windy, but as a descendent, and mother, of engineers, I think we can engineer our way to more efficient turbines. It's happening already.

Last month, a story in this paper mentioned in passing that Ogin Inc. has invented a wind turbine with cowling, or shrouding as they are calling it. I went online to www.oginenergy.com to see what it was about.

Compare the old-style propeller-driven plane with the more efficient, more powerful jet engine enclosed by cowling. This new wind turbine design is the same thing. According to their information, "energy output is increased up to three times per unit of swept area."

Ogin turbines are smaller, at 200 feet versus the current 500-foot-tall turbines, so they can fit into already developed landscapes more easily. Because they are shorter and the tips of the blades are outlined by the shrouding, it is believed fewer birds would be killed.

Testing of this new design will be happening at the infamous Altamont Pass in California, where some years ago, biologists helped engineers change turbine tower designs from open lattice work into the smooth cylinders we know today – taking away perches for raptors which were otherwise unwittingly launching themselves into the blades.

There are vertical axis wind turbines, identical to the one in Cheyenne at the Children's Village, which, at only 30 feet tall, have far less impact visually and environmentally.

Vertical turbines would even be a good replacement in wind farms, says California Institute of Technology professor John Dabiri. Placing them close together improves their efficiency by a factor of 10, using a much smaller footprint per kilowatt of production than current, giant horizontal axis turbines we see. [http://www.caltech.edu/content/caltechs-unique-wind-projects-move-forward]

Ever since we first felt the wind pushing at our backs, we have been refining ways for it to aid us. The challenge is to make our design choices work for other species as well.

147 The bird migration picture gets animation

Sunday, March 23, 2014, Outdoors, page E2

This year, Feb. 19 marked the first sighting of mountain bluebirds in Cheyenne. This is early, but not unusual. I can't help thinking the next batch of February snowstorms drove them back south again.

Recently, I discovered I can watch animated maps of bird migration. These maps on www.eBird.org take the data of 60 selected bird species and show their journeys across the country, week by week.

The data in these maps come from bird sightings that citizen scientists – you and me – have submitted over the years.

In a field guide, the mountain bluebird's yearly movements are difficult to depict on a static range map that accompanies their descriptions.

They are settled mostly over the Rocky Mountain West, avoiding the Pacific Coast. But in winter, they leave the northern Rockies and mountains and leak out over the Great Plains (eastern Colorado, Kansas, Texas panhandle), in addition to the interior of California and Oregon, the southwest and Mexico. Some even winter in southern Idaho.

To watch the animation of our sightings of them is fascinating. As you watch, you'll see a spectrum of fire colors flicker across the map. These colors indicate their rate of occurrence, which is the probability of detection.

Areas with slight possibility of occurrence are a cold, ashy gray. As the possibility increases, the color warms to orange, finally heating up through yellow to white-hot—where the species is thickest.

As the animation cycles from week to week, the "flames" flicker across the land. As someone who was asked to drop statistics before the professor was forced to flunk me, this visualization of numbers, statistical modeling, is magic.

Watching the screen is like watching flocks of mountain bluebirds roaming the prairie. And I notice that even in January, there is a faint haze of orange in Wyoming. It means someone was outside, or at least looking out the window, noticing bluebirds in the depths of winter.

Other species are completely absent from the U.S. for six months.

In mid-April, the western tanager explodes over the Mexican border in a hurry to find the best breeding locations. Then it spreads out into little islands – islands of preferred breeding habitat scattered over western mountain ranges. Then it seems to drift slowly south beginning in mid-July as young birds explore. It is entirely gone – from the U.S. at least – by October.

Our state bird, the western meadowlark, a short-range migratory species, apparently overwinters in low numbers in southern Wyoming. I'm glad we picked a bird that doesn't completely abandon us.

For each species with a map, there are notes that describe what is going on, and admission that sometimes the numbers have biases. One of those biases is detectability.

In the spring, birds, mostly the males, are often singing during migration. But by the time they head south, they can be rather quiet. The note for grasshopper sparrow, a small, drab, brown bird says, "it appears that the species just disappears when in fact thousands are passing southward.... Ideally, future versions of these maps will be able to incorporate species-specific detectability variables and will start measuring abundance, not just occurrence."

Another bias is caused by birders themselves, and their propensity to flock to where the most birds are. In the discussion of the blackpoll warbler map, the note says, "...there are biases in how birders sample the landscape. For this reason, we have tried to promote the use of random counts so that widespread habitats (with less rare bird potential) are sampled in a proportion that more closely resembles their percentage 'on the ground.'"

Good luck with that!

Where would you prefer to spend a spring morning birdwatching? Along Crow Creek, among the cottonwoods where interesting warblers are known to show up? Or out on some treeless, nameless, numbered gravel road in the hinterlands of Laramie County? It could be worth a look, though.

Don't forget to take your notebook and pencil (or your eBird reporting app) with you everywhere this spring and submit all your bird observations to www.eBird.org.

You may be helping to re-write – and re-visualize – what we know about bird migration.

148   Owl family draws visitors to Lions Park

Sunday, May 11, 2014, Outdoors, page E2

There's been quite the parade of admirers trekking to Lions Park to see the pair of owls that nested there this spring, and their three owlets.

By mid-April, they became widely known within the Cheyenne birding community and among regulars at the park. Generally speaking, they can be found in the trees north of Sloans Lake and the Cheyenne-Kiwanis Community House.

I suspect someone aiming a long-lens camera at the top of a tree will have passersby surreptitiously looking in the same direction to figure out what they are shooting. Or, being Cheyenne-friendly, they'll simply ask. Then they, too, become converted to the owl-watching cult.

The day I went to see them, my husband, Mark, and I could only find one adult and one young, but I'd heard that one of the owlets had been seen on the ground, toddling, like a Furby toy, to another tree – and climbing it. It takes a few weeks before owlets are strong enough to fly much.

The owlets will stay with their parents for the summer, so we hope everyone keeps their dogs leashed while in the park. The neighborhood red foxes present enough of a challenge.

When it comes to breeding, great horned owls get an early start in the year. The male can be heard hooting in February to establish his territory. Chances are, his mate from last year is still around. Other than courtship, they don't roost together during the year. They don't build a nest. Instead, they use a tree cavity or an available nest in a tree made by a hawk, crow, heron or squirrel.

The female is the one who incubates the (typically) two eggs. She'll lay more if food – prey animals – is very abundant. For more than 30 days between February and March, she can successfully incubate through winter conditions, even -27 degrees.

The male keeps her fed. Food found in our park could include rabbits, mice, waterfowl and other birds. This was not a good winter to find ducks, since Sloans Lake stayed completely frozen until mid-March.

Research shows owls occasionally take squirrels, and with the overabundance available in the park, that would be my guess as to what they are eating. If anyone finds owl pellets – the compacted balls of bones that are regurgitate by the owls – we could find out for sure.

At 6 weeks old, and nearly equal to

their 22-inch-tall parents, young owls climb out of the nest and take a stroll onto nearby branches. Over the next four weeks, they practice flying short distances and may be found at times roosting on the ground.

The siblings hang out together, but the parents, except for occasionally dropping off food, prefer to roost away from the kids, to avoid hearing their incessant begging that starts up whenever the parents come near.

The owlets start out catching insects and eventually learn to catch mammals and birds by the perch and pounce method. By October, they are ready to fend for themselves.

Typically, young owls are 2 years old before they breed. But it really depends on the amount of prey available. If pickings are slim, many can't find a big enough territory to support a family because there are probably more dominant owls in the area chasing them off. The researchers call the unpaired birds "floaters."

Great horned owls don't migrate seasonally. But the young disperse to find new territory, looking for some place that has an abundance of prey. Studies cited in Birds of North America Online show they moved a mean distance of 46 miles. Otherwise, they would have a long wait before they could take the place of their parents' generation – this species has been documented to live more than 20 years. So, for the young, it's about waiting for those years when rabbit reproduction is up.

Whether the current pair nests in the park again next winter depends on the nest they used still being in good shape – or if a replacement is found. But more importantly, is there still enough food?

Great horned owls across North America, the only continent where they are found, work out answers to these questions every year.

It seems, despite people feeding the park squirrels (even though they shouldn't, and the over-abundant population is chewing up and damaging park trees), the owls are here to bring balance. It's another step in making a manmade landscape more natural.

149 Wyoming refuge is a treasure hidden in plain sight

Sunday, June 22, 2014, Outdoors, page E3

In early June, Hutton Lake National Wildlife Refuge birds are busy reproducing. They barely notice birders.

The refuge is southwest of Laramie. It's small by national refuge standards, just under 2,000 acres, and relatively unknown compared to others in Wyoming like Seedskadee or the National Elk Refuge.

Hutton Lake has little to offer people: no visitor center, no restrooms, no picnic tables, no fishing, no hunting, no camping, no off-road vehicles, horses or dogs allowed anywhere, no trees, no dramatic landscape, and no decent road – until recently.

Instead, it caters to wildlife, attracting 29 mammal species, six amphibian and reptile species and 146 kinds of birds, including 60 species that have been known to nest there.

What do avian visitors find at Hutton Lake?

Five small lakes, including namesake Hutton, have a variety of wet habitats – shallow water for puddle ducks and wading birds, deeper water for diving ducks, muddy shores for shorebirds and thick reed beds for nesting. On land, there are greasewood thickets perfect for nesting songbirds like the sage thrashers. The short grass of the surrounding plains, as green as a golf course this spring, will have its share of bird nests on the ground – grassland species do without trees.

The comparatively flat (the Snowy Range glimmers in the distance) and nearly featureless topography of the Laramie River Valley does have a few rocky outcrops and ridges. The astute birder will find eagles and hawks perched on them or soaring overhead.

Hutton is part of a complex

Ann Timberman is the project manager for the Arapaho National Wildlife Refuge Complex, which includes Hutton Lake and two other small refuges nearby, but which are closed to the public because of endangered species work. There's also Pathfinder near Casper, and Arapaho, the main refuge, is where the complex's headquarters are located, outside Walden, Colo.

In some ways, Ann's job, which she's had for 10 years now, is easy. The National Wildlife Refuge System doesn't have to manage for multiple, and often conflicting, uses like the Bureau of Land Management or the Forest Service. Its mission is to benefit wildlife. Hutton Lake was established in 1932 "to provide resting and breeding habitat." Livestock grazing permits are available only in years when it's been determined it will benefit wildlife.

Ann and I toured Hutton Lake together June 2 on a wonderfully windless day. Bringing along the spotting scope did not make for the most efficient interview – we kept losing our conversational focus while focusing on the differences in field marks for immature

bald and golden eagles and other bird-watching matters.

Improvements welcomed

The tour was to show off improvements made last year, the biggest being the roadwork, tons of gravel filling the deep ruts I remembered from my last visit. The road improvement also extends to the two-track across state land between Sand Creek Road, which is the closest county road, and the boundary of the refuge.

Even a small car with minimal clearance can navigate the single lane road, as we found when we saw one at the new gravel parking lot at the end of the road.

One improvement was unglamorous, but very expensive – replacing the infrastructure that regulates the flow of water from one of the lakes to another.

This summer, an interpretive trail and observation platform will be built at one of the lakes.

There's a birdwatching blind now, too, built last year by an Eagle Scout candidate, with funding for materials provided by Laramie Audubon Society.

I went out again to Hutton five days later with some of the chapter members on a field trip. As much as they appreciate the improved road, they are a little sad to lose vehicle access to some of the roads that are now for pedestrians only. Tim Banks, trip leader, pointed out that some of their older chapter members are not going to be hiking in to regain closer views of the lakes.

Laramie Audubon members are just about the only regular visitors and the only interest group which keeps tabs on the refuge. They worked to have it designated as a Wyoming Important Bird Area.

Partnerships benefit wildlife

In fact, two bird lovers, Gere and Barbara Kruse, were responsible for the recent improvements. In their memory, their daughter, Babs, brought $42,000 to Bob Budd, executive director of the Wyoming Wildlife and Natural Resource Trust, asking for help finding an appropriate wildlife/public use habitat project in Albany County.

The Trust matched the donation. Laramie Rivers Conservation District's Martin Curry, resource specialist, wrote the grant and oversaw most of the work. Other cooperators were the Wyoming Game and Fish Department and the refuge, as well as its parent agency, the U.S. Fish and Wildlife Service. A total of $111,000 will have been spent when the improvements are finished.

There are drawbacks to having a better road. Back in January, kids started a fire even though fires are not allowed, and it got out of control. Thankfully, the refuge is on local law enforcement's beat, and Albany County firefighters put it out. Ann decided to lock the gate for the winter, allowing only walk-in access.

With only 3.5 staff members for the whole Arapaho refuge complex, locals become Ann's eyes and ears at Hutton Lake. There are few birds and few people on the windswept plains in winter. But, for instance, deciding when in spring to open the gate will depend on local birders apprising her of conditions. Visitors can also report suspicious or illegal activities – impossible to hide on the open plains.

For Ann, from a management perspective, making the refuge more accessible is a double-edged sword of sorts, allowing in vandals as well as visitors. But, she said, in the long run, it pays to make friends and develop partnerships. In this case, sharing Hutton Lake with people who appreciate it benefits the wildlife. And that fits the refuge's mission.

If you go

The refuge is open to driving on established roads as conditions permit and to hiking on roads and trails year-round. Wildlife watching and photography are the recreational activities allowed. Spring, especially April, is a great time for birdwatching.

There is no drinking water and no restroom. Please pack out trash. Hunting, shooting, fishing, fires and camping are not permitted.

How to get there

From Laramie, drive south on U.S. 287. When the huge cement plant comes up on your right less than two miles south of I-80, aim for the plant's front office using one of the crossroads, but instead of entering the plant, veer left (south) and you will be on Sand Creek Road. After about 8 miles, you will see a brown sign for Hutton Lake pointing to the right. Turn and follow the gravel trail to the refuge entrance, which is marked by a large sign and a small parking area.

More information is available at http://www.fws.gov/refuge/hutton_lake/.

150 Mind your manners to reduce bird stress

Sunday, August 17, 2014, Outdoors, page E3

I'm sure your parents taught you, as mine did me, that it is impolite to stare.

Does this rule apply, in some way, to birds? After all, the point of birdwatching is to watch them.

Know that whenever you enter a

bird's environment, it can bother a bird. For instance, even when you are on the other side of a window, it may react to your presence.

I recently heard an anecdote about a hawk nest so close to a public road that it was well known. Birdwatchers regularly showed up to watch and photograph the chicks as they grew.

What these folks apparently missed was that the parents were agitated. The presence of the birdwatchers bothered them. The situation could easily have caused the parents to abandon the chicks. And even though it apparently didn't, stress on the birds could cause some unintended consequences down the road – just as it does for people.

There is a new field guide that came out this spring, one that offers something a bit different from the rest.

The New Birder's Field Guide to Birds of North America, by Bill Thompson III, is recommended if you are a casual backyard birdwatcher who wants to know more.

It explains the hobby of birdwatching, why it's fun, how to get into it, what to wear to be comfortable, how to adjust binoculars. What follows is a page per species with helpful information for identifying each one.

But one brief chapter bears on this column's subject, titled "Birding Manners."

Some of it pertains to birding with others: keep your voice down, treat others as you'd like to be treated, stay with the group, share the spotting scope, help beginners, pish in moderation.

What is pishing? It's an attempt to get a better look at a bird by getting it to come out of the vegetation by making a noise that sounds like "pish," which happens to sound like a bird alarm call. The birds come out to see what's wrong. Playing recorded bird songs to attract a bird that thinks he's hearing a rival is another method to bring it out of hiding.

As Thompson asks new birders to use these techniques in moderation, he explains, "We owe it to the birds we love so much to respect their privacy."

This is the beginning birdwatcher's version of the American Birding Association's Birding Code of Ethics. The part that pertains to the nesting hawks' situation reads:

"1(b) To avoid stressing birds or exposing them to danger, exercise restraint and caution during observation, photography, sound recording, or filming....

"Keep well back from nests and nesting colonies, roosts, display areas, and important feeding sites. In such sensitive areas, if there is a need for extended observation, photography, filming, or recording, try to use a blind or hide, and take advantage of natural cover."

If the ABA members, vying to see as many bird species as possible, can restrain themselves, I think the rest of us can as well.

Given today's optics and cameras, it might have been quite possible to observe the activity in the hawk nest from a less intimidating distance, since building a blind on the side of a public road probably isn't feasible. Contacting the adjacent landowner for permission to erect a temporary blind might have been a solution.

But on the other hand, if we are observing the hawks for our own enjoyment and not as a part of scientific study, two minutes from inside our car would be quite enough, rather than hour after hour, day after day. Try to make part of your enjoyment of birds knowing that your actions haven't endangered or distressed them.

There is so much interesting bird behavior to watch unobserved by the birds if you walk carefully, and stop and stand still often, being the proverbial fly on the wall. If you don't make noise or make sudden movements, birds in the bushes will continue to flit about feeding. If you sit as still as a rock at the shore, the shorebirds may pass close by.

And should a bird look you in the eye, acknowledge it as you would a person, with a nod.

And then look away, so it can continue with its important business of living.

151 6 Reasons why you should go to "Bird-day"

Thursday, September 11, 2014, page B4

To mark 40 years since the hatching of the Cheyenne – High Plains Audubon Society, you are invited to the "Bird-day" celebration Sept. 26-28.

While the Wyoming Audubon Society was established in 1950, local Audubon members decided to form their own chapter, achieving their goal in 1974.

Judging by the newspaper clippings preserved in the chapter's scrapbook, this was a coming together of environmental activists who enjoyed bird watching, and serious birdwatchers concerned for the future of birds.

Today, the chapter still offers a mix of educational activities, environmental advocacy, citizen science and birdwatching.

So how do Bird-day festivities apply to you? We've come up with at least six possibilities:

1 You use eBird. You can hear more about the citizen science programs offered by the Cornell Lab of Ornithology from its director, John W. Fitzpatrick, at the Sept. 27 banquet.

2 You are a gardener. This free presentation, "Be a Habitat Hero," talks about a program and its benefits to all the pollinators: birds, bats, butterflies and bees. Connie Holsinger's talk is Sept. 26, 7 p.m. at Laramie County Community College. It's free and open to the public.

3 You've always wanted to visit the legendary Wyoming Hereford Ranch. And it happens to be a designated Wyoming Important Bird Area, as it attracts unusual migrants. To help you find and identify them, Ted Floyd, editor of American Birding Association's magazine is leading a field trip Sept. 27. Meet at 7 a.m. at the parking lot at LCCC's Center for Conferences and Institutes.

4 You have or know kids in kindergarten through eighth-grade. Take them to the "Adventures with Audubon" programs led by educators from Audubon Rockies and Cheyenne Botanic Gardens Children's Village on Sept. 27, with sessions at 10 a.m. and from 2-4 p.m. at LCCC.

5 You simply want to know more about birds. You'll definitely want to attend the talks on Saturday (see schedule).

6 You like birthday cake and want to help John Cornelison, founding president of the Cheyenne – High Plains Audubon Society, celebrate 40 years of bird education and conservation in southeast Wyoming.

152 Can birds save the world?

Sunday, October 26, 2014, Outdoors, page E2

Last month, the National Audubon Society publicized the result of a seven-year study to determine what would happen to North American birds if the change in climate continues as predicted.

The startling conclusion is that by 2080, nearly half our bird species, 314 (588 were studied), would have a hard time finding the food and habitat they need. They probably would not adapt, since evolution normally needs more than 65 years. So, they could become extinct.

"OK," some people say, "big deal, I've never seen more than three kinds of birds anyway."

That attitude was prevalent in the 1960s when eagles began producing eggs with shells so thin, the weight of the incubating parent crushed them.

"So what?" people said back then, especially if eagles made them and their lambs nervous.

The culprit was discovered to be DDT. And it was discovered to do nasty things to people as well. So, you might say that birds saved the world from DDT (except it continues to be produced to control malaria).

Last month, the Cheyenne – High Plains Audubon Society celebrated its 40th anniversary. John Fitzpatrick, director of the Cornell Lab of Ornithology, was keynote speaker at the banquet: "How Birds Can Save the World."

Fitzpatrick's premise is birds are so many species of canaries in the coal mine. Or, to localize the analogy, so many sage-grouse in the oil patch. We should pay attention to what they are trying to tell us before we hurt ourselves.

The Audubon report makes predictions based on two long-term, continent-wide citizen science efforts: the Christmas Bird Count (begun in 1900) and the Breeding Bird Survey (begun in 1966).

The Cornell Lab of Ornithology itself is well-known for citizen science projects, such as Project FeederWatch and the Great Backyard Bird Count. But the one that has mushroomed into a global phenomenon is eBird (www.eBird.org).

People who enjoy birdwatching have learned over the last 10 years to put just a little extra effort into it by counting birds they see and entering their notes online. Scientists can now see where bird species go and when, as if they have radar running year round. The more people enter observations, the clearer the picture emerges. And population changes are clearer, too.

When bird numbers change, or populations move, it's due to one or more changes in the species' environment. Some can be directly attributed to people, such as building a subdivision over a burrowing owl colony, and some indirectly, like climate change causing nectar-producing flowers to bloom too early for migrating hummingbirds.

Back in the 1970s, saving the environment always seemed to mean doing without, like hippies living off the grid. To some extent, curbing our desire for items built with planned obsolescence, like the latest smartphone, would preserve a little more landscape.

But Fitzpatrick's contention is that we can live smarter, rather than poorer, have our cake and eat it too, have our lifestyle and our birds.

We need creative people. For instance, I read 400,000 acres of California cropland is barren for lack of water this year. Yet power companies are stripping vegetation in the Mohave Desert to build arrays of solar panels. What if farmers rented out those barren fields for temporary solar installations?

There's work being done on solar paving. Imagine a sunny city like Los Angeles being able to power itself from all its lesser used streets, rather than depending on the transmission of electricity across hundreds of miles.

What if we put as much effort as we put into getting man on the moon into finding ways for every part of the country to produce energy in a way that keeps birds happy and us healthy?

I'm not an engineer, and probably neither are you. There is a shortage of them in this country. How can we raise more engineers and research scientists?

Take kids birdwatching. No, this isn't exactly one of Fitzpatrick's fixes. It's mine.

What are your kids doing on Saturday mornings? Watching cartoons and competing in athletics are all well and good. But what birdwatching does for children, and the rest of us, is to make us ask questions about the birds and their behaviors, to research, to communicate with others, and now, to search the eBird database.

When children develop curiosity through birdwatching – or other disciplines – they begin to see themselves in the sciences, in engineering, in technology, in all those "hard" subjects. And we will have the creative minds we need.

Our local Audubon chapter, now age 40, will continue with its traditional field trips (open to accompanied children and recorded for eBird, of course), educational meetings and projects, habitat improvements, and conservation advocacy. But watch for those special opportunities to introduce your children, grandchildren or neighbor children to birds. Because birds can save the world.

153 Feral cat policy will fail

Wednesday, December 10, 2014, Opinion, page C9

Last month, the Cheyenne City Council passed an ordinance allowing the Cheyenne Animal Shelter to implement a "trap, neuter, vaccinate and release" program for feral cats in the city.

The shelter staff is tired of euthanizing cats – 84 last month alone, many more in spring months – and sees this as a proactive measure.

The Community Cat Initiative allows "community cat caregivers" to bring in feral cats and pay $30 to sterilize and vaccinate, then release them, their ears tipped so they can easily be recognized as neutered.

Normally, unwanted cats, if not adoptable (and there is a barn cat adoption program for the less sociable), are euthanized.

I object to the TNR program, as it is referred to, for several reasons.

One is, I love cats. Our current feline, an indoor cat, is pushing 16 and is curled up on my shoulder as I write this.

I think more inhumane than euthanizing them is leaving cats outdoors. Feral cats as well as roaming family pets encounter life-threatening dangers: vehicles, predators – including other cats, not to mention inhospitable weather.

Conversely, feral cats untrapped – and unvaccinated – are public, human health concerns.

Why tolerate cats running loose, but not dogs?

It's also inhumane to leave wildlife at

the mercy of a non-native predator like the cat. Many of our native birds here on the prairie are ground nesters, easy prey, as are small mammals.

In the U.S., free-roaming domestic cats kill an estimated 1.4 billion to 3.7 billion birds and 6.9 to 20.7 billion mammals each year, according to a U.S. Fish and Wildlife Service study. More recent studies show it could be more.

Nowhere in the literature has "trap, neuter, vaccinate and release" been shown to be successful in controlling feral cat populations.

On paper, the program sounds good, and I wish it worked.

Simply put, if you have a colony of cats and neuter all of them, the colony will die out when the last cat dies. Problem solved in the space of a feral cat's lifetime – probably less than five years.

In real life, no agency practicing "trap, neuter, vaccinate and release" has been able to trap enough cats to substantially lower the population.

Cheyenne's policy, waiting for the public to bring feral cats in, is doomed to fail even more rapidly.

Trapping cats is a bit like herding them. Plus, do the soft-hearted have deep enough pockets?

A staff member at the shelter said they are pursuing grants that would allow for a more aggressive "trap, neuter, vaccinate and release" program.

Meanwhile, we'll have an ever-increasing feral cat population (think about lying awake at night listening to cat fights) until nature finally deals with it – probably an ugly new and deadly disease. Not very humane.

Here are some more humane suggestions.

Hunt for nests of kittens and bring them in to be neutered and adopted at the age they can be socialized and become happy indoor cats. But don't allow them to be released outdoors.

Also, instead of charging people to bring in feral cats for neutering and vaccination, pay them $30. Putting a price on a species sent the passenger pigeon to extinction and nearly did the same for the buffalo.

Next, release adult, neutered feral cats, if they cannot be socialized, in a cattery, a place where they are safe and wildlife is safe from them.

Those options I've mentioned take money. Meanwhile, the problem grows.

I don't think it is fair to ask people charged with sheltering animals to do what really needs to be done from the wildlife and public health standpoint.

The wildlife agencies need to step in, as they have in Hawaii, another place where non-native predators, including feral cats, are decimating the wildlife.

Removing feral cats, euthanizing them, is not a happy proposition. Each one looks just like our own cat.

We need the fortitude to take actions to insure the well-being of cats. Releasing them to fend for themselves is not good for them nor for wildlife.

154 Risking nice Wyoming weather, grebes, loons get caught

Sunday, December 21, 2014, Outdoors, page E2

You probably recognize that sinking feeling I had the morning of Nov. 10 when we cleared Denver traffic and a solid wall of cloud was suddenly visible 50-60 miles away, between us and home.

The rain, predicted for afternoon, started around 9 a.m. at Fort Collins, Colorado. In a few miles it turned to flakes. The road surface quickly iced as we climbed in elevation.

Northbound traffic slowed to a crawl, but only because there was a traffic jam of emergency vehicles gathered near the Colorado-Wyoming state line, where vehicles slid off the interstate earlier. One was lying on its roof.

No matter how slowly, we were happy to still be creeping toward home.

Some birds, however, were not as lucky with the weather.

One would think that migratory birds would be tuned into changes, but even they can be caught unawares.

If you remember that week, along with the snow, the temperatures dropped into negative numbers at night. My husband was contemplating an early start to the ice fishing season.

On Nov. 14, I had a bird call – people wondering how to help a Western grebe found at the plant west of town. They took it to the Cheyenne Pet Clinic, which is licensed to handle wild birds.

The bird had to be euthanized because a wing joint was broken and couldn't be repaired. Veterinarian Christopher Church said two other grebes were rescued and brought in that week, and staff were able to release them at the Wyoming Hereford Ranch. Later that day, a Wyobirds report came in about a loon stuck in a small bit of open water, unable to take off. Someone in the Riverton area reported eared grebes, I think it was, also getting stuck.

Grebes and loons have bodies evolved for swimming underwater, not walking. Their legs are at the back of their bodies, like an outboard motor, and not under their center of gravity like a normal bird.

Because their feet do all the work when underwater, their wings are small. And their bones are not light and hollow like a songbird's, but dense, making it easier to dive. Flying is difficult for them.

Ornithologist Joel Carl Welty calculated a loon's wing-load, square centimeters of wing area to bird weight in grams, as 0.6. On the other hand, a black-capped chickadee is 6.1--comparatively buoyant. A Leach's petrel, an ocean-going bird, finds flying extremely easy at 9.5.

So, these heavy loons and grebes, hardly ever trying to move around on land, can only take to the air by flapping while pattering their feet against the water surface, Loons need as much as 650 feet for takeoff, according to Arthur Cleveland Bent, another ornithologist.

You can see where this is going. The grebe tucks its head under its wing one night and the next morning looks around at new ice hemming it in. "Oh crud."

The loon in the Wyobirds report kept busy diving for fish, and even tried walking a bit on the ice, but the next day, when the little bit of open water had frozen over, and the same observer went back, she saw no trace of the loon – not a feather or drop of blood, despite the bald eagles hanging around. It's quite unlikely that it flew. Perhaps the ice was finally thick enough for someone to walk out and rescue it, or for a predator to carry it off.

Ducks, which are better-balanced, need little space to take off, but have managed to become trapped in ice also.

What happened to the grebe with the broken wing? Grebe species migrate at night. Apparently, they can get disoriented in snowstorms or fog or get confused by the sight of a wet parking lot shining in reflected lights and hit it hard, thinking it's water.

The common loon migrates through Wyoming, as do three species of grebes we see most often: pied-billed, eared and Western. Doug Faulkner, in "Birds of Wyoming," describes their fall migration patterns, always mentioning that a few individual birds don't leave until the reservoirs freeze up.

For these risk takers, the later they stay, the fewer birds they have to share the food source with. Some years, the bet pays off, and they are better fed when they arrive on the wintering grounds, reaping the benefits, such as better reproduction. But then again, maybe they don't make it.

After surviving this latest, unexpectedly dicey road trip, our weather forecasting being not much better than the lingerers', I'm wondering if we should have taken a lesson from all the smart loons and grebes that headed out by October for their ice-free wintering grounds.

2015

155 Archiving bird columns shows changes

Sunday, January 11, 2015, Outdoors, page E3

I'm afraid to mention this, lest the editor of the Wyoming Tribune Eagle think I've been doing this too long, but next month is the beginning of my 17th year writing this bird column.

It started because Bill Gruber, the Outdoors editor in 1999, asked me if I'd be interested.

I protested that there were people in town more knowledgeable – and there still are. But I had the time. And I could always research and ask the experts.

Besides Bill, I've worked with these other editors: Ty Stockton, Cara Eastwood Baldwin, Shauna Stephenson, Kevin Wingert and now Jodi Rogstad. All have been kind in their editing, catching style and grammatical errors.

A year ago, I had this great idea to archive all of my past columns as blog posts. I'd taken an online course in blogging as part of my teaching recertification, and I was intrigued. For one thing, I could add a widget that allows me to search all my past posts. So I could find out how many times I'd written about say, the Christmas Bird Count (about a dozen times).

I decided to make it a publicly accessible blog, www.CheyenneBirdBanter. wordpress.com. So far, I have 86 followers from all over the world without actively publicizing it.

Because bird topics are seasonal, and because there might be followers, strict chronological order wouldn't be best. So I used chronological order within each month, starting with February. The first post was the column I wrote that month, in 1999, followed by the one from February 2000, and so on.

Then I realized that these old columns could be outdated. So each one is accompanied not only by the date it originally was published, but by a short update on the topic.

There are some things that just don't change in the bird world, but technology has. I can now find an incredible amount of information online, and I can ask experts questions without having to call them long distance or mail a letter to them.

The most dramatic change in the bird world has been the advent of eBird, of course. The first column mentioning it was in 2003. It seems like every six months they come up with a new way for all of us citizen scientists to explore the eBird database – and more easily contribute to it. Amazing scientific studies are generated by it too.

The birds themselves continue to change. Mostly, it's population numbers and distribution.

For instance, there are more crows

in Cheyenne today. There are way too many more Eurasian collared-doves now than there were in 1999, a year after the first one in Wyoming was identified in Cheyenne.

Do we have fewer numbers of any species? Evening grosbeaks don't seem to be visiting anymore. But a few years ago, lesser goldfinches started becoming regular, if still uncommon, visitors.

There is never a lack of topics to explore in the bird world. Feedback shows that many WTE readers are willing to come along on these sometimes intellectual excursions with me.

Hearing from readers is what makes writing these columns better than merely writing in a diary or notebook.

Information from readers has driven me to investigate topics, especially when there are several calls about the same thing. What to do about flickers drilling holes in wood siding is a column I've forwarded often since writing it.

Interestingly, for a while if you googled my name, the column that seemed to come up most often – because a friend in Colorado reposts my columns to his blog – is the one I wrote about the University of Wyoming graduate student studying hummingbird metabolism. In fact, it has been included in some online science anthology I can't access without buying a subscription.

There are now more than 300 Bird Banter columns posted. It has been fun looking back at them, seeing how, between the lines, they reflect my family's life. And I'm happy to have become the community bird lady, a responsibility which I appreciate.

More conventionally, I can be classified as a science writer. Actually, that isn't too far off from my course of study in college – and what one of my professors thought I should be.

Well, thanks, WTE editors and readers, for this monthly privilege. What's up at your bird feeders these days?

156 Sunday, February 8, 2015, Outdoors, page E2
"Habitat Heroes" wanted to grow native plants

Sometimes, wildlife issues seem to be out of the hands of ordinary people, people like those of us who are not wildlife biologists, land managers or politicians. Often, it seems futile to write a letter or email stating my opinion.

Connie Holsinger has devised a way for us to do something for wildlife right in our own backyards - literally.

Connie is the founder of the Habitat Hero program, which shows people in the Rocky Mountain area how to turn all or part of their yards, no matter what size, even a container or an apartment balcony, into wildlife habitat for birds, bees, butterflies and, may I

add, even bats.

A popular term for this is "wildscaping." Add to that the term "waterwise" and Connie immediately grabs the attention of everyone who pays an increasing amount for watering their lawns as well as those who recently read the articles in the paper about Laramie County's finite water supply.

Connie is a native of Maine, in a zone that enjoys 50 inches of precipitation each year, compared to Cheyenne's 10-15 inches. When she moved to Massachusetts, she discovered birds, as well as the fact she can plant what would attract them to her yard. She volunteered with

Massachusetts Audubon's Ipswich River Wildlife Sanctuary on habitat improvements.

Next, at her home on Sanibel Island, Florida, she discovered if she ripped out all the invasive vegetation and planted natives, her once-quiet yard was suddenly full of birds.

Relocating to the Front Range of Colorado in 1998, she learned what semi-arid means, especially when a major drought was just getting started. And she also learned that some native plants like the semi-arid life – after she killed her plantings of native penstemons two years in a row because she was rotting their roots with too much water.

It's no surprise that a smart woman like Connie then put "waterwise" with "wildscaping," a natural fit here in the arid West.

Also, the decline in the numbers of bees and butterflies documented in recent years makes even more important the idea of converting conventional urban/suburban landscapes into nectar and pollen havens, in addition to providing seeds and berries and cover for birds. Not to mention that native plants can take less work and water (read money) than a lawn.

With funding from the Terra Foundation, her private foundation that supports projects restoring the Colorado River Basin, Connie launched the "Be a Habitat Hero" campaign in 2013.

Anyone who would like to pursue the designation of "Habitat Hero" can apply through the website, www.HabHero.org, in September to see if their yard measures up. Last fall, 28 people, including Laramie County master gardener Michelle Bohanan, earned the designation.

While most of Cheyenne's homeowners and renters have mastered the basics of lawn care and keeping shrubs and trees alive, and many have a flair

for flowers and vegetables, wildscaping requires a little change in horticultural practices, and a little change in mindset.

Explaining exactly how to transform all or part of a conventional yard or commercial landscape into a wildscape will be the topic of a Habitat Hero workshop scheduled March 28 at Laramie County Community College, 9 a.m. – 4:30 p.m. The $15 registration fee covers lunch, handouts and a tote bag for each participant full of donated items.

The three speakers will be Susan Tweit, plant biologist and author of "Rocky Mountain Garden Survival Guide;" Jane Dorn, co-author of "Growing Native Plants of the Rocky Mountain Area" (a digital version will be given to each participant); and Clint Basset, Cheyenne Board of Public Utilities water conservation specialist.

The major sponsors are Laramie County Master Gardeners, Cheyenne – High Plains Audubon Society, Audubon Rockies (which now administers the Habitat Hero program), Cheyenne Botanic Gardens and the Laramie County Conservation District.

One of the fun parts of the day will be the panel discussion, when the three speakers take a look at selected yards submitted by participants in advance and make recommendations on how to transform them into wildlife destinations.

"Plant it and they will come," Connie has said often.

This approach to landscaping benefits wildlife, but Connie said it speaks to her soul too when she sees the birds, bees and butterflies.

Her biggest aha moment came when she realized, "I can create a habitat in my yard, and take it beyond looking pretty" – making a difference in the world – in her own backyard.

.

157 Are you a bird expert?

Raise your hand if you've been reading my bird column for the 16 years I've been writing for the Wyoming Tribune Eagle.

Good for you!

And even if you haven't been reading it that long, here's a quiz to see what you've learned so far. All the birds mentioned are listed on the Cheyenne Bird Checklist posted at the Cheyenne-High Plains Audubon Society website.

Ready?

1. What "sign of spring" shows up most often on Cheyenne Christmas Bird Counts?
a. Western Meadowlark
b. Red-winged Blackbird
c. Mountain Bluebird
d. American Robin

Answer: (d) The robin has been seen on almost every Cheyenne Christmas Bird Count since our first, 60 years ago, and the red-winged blackbird about half as often. Meadowlarks have been seen six times, and bluebirds never.

2. Which large white birds visit Cheyenne in small flocks each spring to go fishing?
a. Snow Goose
b. American White Pelican
c. Tundra Swan
d. Great Egret

Answer: (b) While lone great egrets are seen occasionally, flocks of pelicans show up regularly. Snow geese and swans don't eat fish.

3. Which is the only blue bird that would have been seen here in pioneer times?
a. Mountain Bluebird
b. Blue Jay
c. Blue Grosbeak
d. Indigo Bunting

Answer: (a) Pioneers would have seen mountain bluebirds. Farmers planting windbreaks made our high plains friendly to blue jays which were noticeably present by 1939. Indigo buntings were recorded by the 1950s and blue grosbeaks by the 1960s.

4. Which black-colored bird seen around Cheyenne never raises its own offspring?
a. Common Grackle
b. Red-winged Blackbird
c. Yellow-headed Blackbird
d. Brown-headed Cowbird

Answer: (d) Brown-headed cowbirds always leave their eggs in nests of other birds. Historically, they needed to be off right away to follow the buffalo.

5. Which woodpecker is more often seen pecking Cheyenne lawns instead of trees?
a. Downy Woodpecker
b. Hairy Woodpecker
c. Northern Flicker
d. Red-headed Woodpecker

Answer: (c) I get more calls about strange, polka-dotted birds digging for grubs in people's front lawns, but yes, the flicker is a woodpecker. Just ask anyone whose wood siding has been pecked.

6. Which bird only nests on the ground?
a. Western Meadowlark
b. Wood Duck
c. Black-crowned Night-Heron
d. Great Blue Heron

Answer: (a) Wood ducks nest in tree cavities or nest boxes. Great blue herons and black-crowned night-herons almost always nest in colonies in trees. But the meadowlark, like many grassland birds, always nests on the ground. Don't mow your prairie until July, after nesting season.

7. Several species can be seen in both southeastern Wyoming and the Middle East. Which one didn't require human help to get here?
a. Caspian Tern
b. Rock Pigeon
c. Ring-necked Pheasant
d. Eurasian Collared-Dove
Answer: (a) The Caspian tern, a rare visitor here, occurs naturally on all continents except Antarctica. Pigeons, pheasants and collared-doves started out as Eurasian (including the Middle East) species.

8. Which big hawk likes the Magic City so well it flies from Argentina to nest in our neighborhoods?
a. Red-tailed Hawk
b. American Kestrel
c. Swainson's Hawk
d. Northern Harrier
Answer: (c) The Swainson's hawk winters in Argentina. The other three may get as far south as Panama.

9. Besides Wyoming, what other states claim the Western Meadowlark as their state bird?
a. Kansas
b. Nebraska
c. Montana
d. North Dakota
e. Oregon
Answer: (a, b, c, d, e) All claim the western meadowlark.

10. How many warbler species have been observed since 1993 on the Cheyenne Big Day Bird Count, at the height of spring migration?
a. 23
b. 27
c. 31
d. 35
Answer: (c or d) There have been 31 warbler species on our Big Days, by my count. However, there are 35 listed on the Cheyenne checklist. Take credit for either answer.

11. What sandpiper likes nesting on our prairie, and even on football fields?
a. Killdeer
b. Greater Yellowlegs
c. Lesser Yellowlegs
d. Wilson's Snipe
Answer: (a) Killdeer. Both yellowlegs pass through on their way to nest in Canada. Snipe nest here, but only on the edge of water.

12. Three of these species spend only the winter in Cheyenne. Which one leaves instead?
a. American Tree Sparrow
b. Dark-eyed Junco
c. Rough-legged Hawk
d. Lark Bunting
Answer: (d) Lark buntings leave Wyoming to winter in the southwest and Mexico. The others arrive: juncos after nesting in the mountains, tree sparrows from Alaska and Canada, and rough-leggeds from the Arctic.

How did you do?

Whatever your score, by taking part in the quiz, you show you are part of the community of inquisitive birdwatchers.

Remember, whatever local wisdom about birds is cited here, your careful observation could turn it on its head. Birds never stop teaching us new things.

158 Birds are always around to fascinate the young

Sunday, May 24, 2015, Outdoors, page E2

I've been invited to visit with a group of mothers to share with them a few tips on birdwatching with young children.

It's been more than 20 years since our kids were preschoolers and I'm trying to remember just what my husband, Mark, and I did. We must have done something right: One son recently bought his own binoculars, and the other reports interesting birds from his travels.

I doubt we were very different from other parents who have a serious interest in a field or outdoor pursuit: You just take the kids with you. We took ours birdwatching, fishing, hunting, camping and hiking.

Of course, it isn't necessary to be the child's parent in order to mentor them – just more convenient.

Babies are as mobile as the distance you are willing to carry them – as long as diapers and milk hold out.

When kids start walking, you are suddenly limited to how far they are willing to go. They are a lot more willing if they are comfortable: warm and dry – or cool in the summer, protected from sunburn and bites, not averse to outhouses or bushes, with plenty of food and water, and naptime far in the distance.

How do you make a child interested in birds? Like so many other traits, you model it. No guarantee it will take.

The great thing about fostering an interest in birds is there are always birds around. And they have color, movement and sound. All you have to do is point. You don't have to know much at first.

As kids get older, it isn't hard to introduce them to a field guide full of colorful illustrations, then working together to figure out the names of bird species or going online some place like www.allaboutbirds.org.

Toy binoculars are perfect for imitating adult birdwatchers. By grade school, kids might be able to appreciate what they are seeing through higher quality binoculars.

Don't make up stuff when you don't know the answer. It's OK to say "I don't know." Look it up...or call me.

It's OK if your child doesn't become an ornithological know-it-all by age 7. Perhaps you observe your child is often distracted by rocks, weeds, sticks or worms instead. There's a lot of nature to enjoy out there besides birds.

It doesn't hurt to point out a pretty flower (try not to pick it) or insect or an animal track. Birders often learn something about a bird by observing its whole environment – food sources, nesting materials, perches, predators.

It's OK if your kids find other ways to entertain (or distract) themselves while you bird. Maybe they would like to take along a sketchbook, a camera, or a butterfly net. But sometimes kids just have to dig in the dirt or chase around and be silly.

Every child is different so it is up to you to figure out what will keep yours interested in coming outdoors with you again.

If you want philosophical guidance, look for a new book called "How to Raise a Wild Child, The Art and Science of Falling in Love with Nature," by Scott D. Sampson, known for his appearances on the PBS Kids show "Dinosaur Train."

His worry is if more kids don't get

outside and learn to love it, nature will lose her constituency and the Earth will be ravaged until it can no longer support human life.

He wants to see more "hummingbird" parents rather than helicopter parenting, allowing kids to make discoveries. He wants to see school playgrounds filled with natural landscapes and objects, not asphalt and gravel. He wants kids to get dirty. He has a bibliography listing studies proving why spending time in nature is good for kids – and the rest of us.

Sampson's book is a direct descendent of Richard Louv's "Last Child in the Woods" (www.ChildrenandNature. org), but it has "Nature Mentoring Basics" and lists of things you can do at different age levels.

If you need more local ideas, check out WY Outside, http://www.wyoutside. com. This year they are holding the WY Outside Challenge.

My family camped a lot when my sister and I were kids, but I don't remember either of our parents doing anything much, beyond sending us to Girl Scouts, to guide both of us into our love of the outdoors, except supporting us as we began to seek the outdoors on our own.

Not every child delighting in a wild bird is going to become an ornithologist. That's OK. It is their appreciation for birds and the rest of nature we are after, hoping that it will foster good stewardship and a healthy life.

159 Many mountain birds mean summer of no regrets

Sunday, September 27, 2015, Outdoors, page E3

This fall I have no summer regrets. I made it to the mountains several times.

For me, the best reason for living in the West is access to mountains – living within commuting distance of timberline.

From Cheyenne, the alpine tundra along Trail Ridge Road in Rocky Mountain National Park is about two hours away, as are the trailheads for the Snowy Range in the Medicine Bow National Forest.

The national park was my introduction to mountains when I was 6 years old. I had traveled from Wisconsin with my parents and grandparents on the occasion of my uncle's graduation from Colorado University. This year, the occasion was his memorial, and I was helping introduce his 6- and 3-year-old grandchildren to mountains.

The Snowies, on the other hand, I found on my own, when the lotto game that is federal seasonal work brought me to Wyoming. I was lucky this summer to visit three times, twice above 10,000 feet.

On Father's Day afternoon it was rather appalling to see the traffic on Rocky Mountain's Trail Ridge Road, amplified by the park's 100th anniversary celebration.

It's a pilgrimage. At every comfort station, one parks and walks a trail out into the landscape. But other than a selfie with magnificent mountains in the background, I'm not sure if many of the pilgrims know what they are seeking as the stiff wind makes them shiver in their tank tops, short shorts and flip flops.

A few weeks later in mid-July, all of us on the Audubon field trip at least knew exactly what miracles to look for as pilgrims hurried past us.

We wanted to see the sparrow-like American pipits. It's hard to pick them out from the litter of rocks and plethora of wildflowers. But soon we recognized their calls and realized they were all around us.

Our other goal was the white-tailed ptarmigan – high-altitude relative of sage-grouse – which turns white in winter and brown in summer. Except that in July, the birds are really just a mottled/speckled brown and white, matching perfectly those lichen-encrusted rocks scattered all around.

We found the location of the previous e-Bird sighting of a ptarmigan and resigned ourselves to examining every rock along the way, knowing that unless the wind ruffled the bird's feathers or it decided to move, we might never see it. But we were joined by a birding tour leader on her day off, as well as two other hikers who were lucky enough to find a hen taking a stroll and who pointed it out. There are some advantages to crowds.

A week later in the Snowies, Mark and I took one of the trails starting at Brooklyn Lake, expecting many fewer people.

But a file of at least 40 teenagers from a Midwestern church passed us, toting serious backpacking equipment. I like to think that, like the crowds in Rocky Mountain, these people will become supporters for preserving this country's wild lands.

The wonderful wildflower displays made up for a lack of birds on this first Snowies trip, but three weeks later, on an Audubon chapter hike, things were reversed. The wildflowers were waning, but the birds were gathering, and we were the big group, 15 people between the ages of 10 months and 75 years old.

We never hit tree line, only getting as far as the trees growing in isolated islands. Gobs of ruby-crowned kinglets flitted in and out of the branches of Engelmann spruce. Three mountain chickadees carried their conversation to the outer branches where we could see them clearly. Pine grosbeaks, larger versions of our house finches in town, were busy grooming their feathers in plain sight. Young spotted sandpipers, their bodies mere halos of stiff white fuzz perched on impossibly long legs, scrabbled after their parent, negotiating the rubble at the foot of a snowfield still melting and providing the watery habitat they needed.

Juncos were flashing their white outer-tail feathers everywhere. Soon, we will see them down in town.

Not only did the 10,000-foot elevation offer its usual respite from summer heat, but puffy clouds, dead ringers for snow clouds, sailed by on cold wind, keeping us in our winter jackets, which we were experienced enough to bring. Birdwatchers just don't hike hard enough to warm up, and this day there were 17 species of birds making the 3-mile round trip take more than four hours.

Back at the parking lot, the fall feeling, stirred by the wind and the gathering birds, was amplified by realizing the meadow grasses had gone to seed and turned brown – in early August.

Now fall is finally here at lower elevations.

Summer is such a fleeting season at high altitude, but at least this year, I didn't let it pass me by.

160 Feed winter birds for fun

Feeding birds in your backyard is a time-honored tradition. It makes a great gateway to building your interest in birds. But there are a few things you should keep in mind if you decide to put up a feeder.

Birds don't need our food. They are good at finding natural food. Don't worry if you don't have food out for them every day, although being consistent means you are more likely to see interesting birds.

Bird feeding is really about enjoying the birds, so put your feeders close to windows you look out of often. Be sure to put them close so that birds won't hit your windows at high speed when leaving your feeder.

Keep your feeding operation affordable. I've had people complain bird seed is expensive. But it's up to you how much seed to put out and how often. Fill feeders at the time of day you can enjoy watching the birds.

Never put out more feeders than you can keep clean or clean up after. Feeders can get gunky and can spread diseases. Every couple weeks, clean them with soap and water, maybe a little bleach, and rinse well. If you see a sick bird, don't put the feeders back up for a week. We usually don't feed in the summer because even more disgusting stuff grows in feeder debris.

Be sure to keep the seed hulls swept up every few days or think about feeding hulled sunflower seeds.

Don't be cheap. Rather than the bags of mixed seed, go for the black-oil sunflower seed. Seed mixes often contain filler seed – or at least seed that birds around here won't eat – and you'll just be sweeping it up anyway. Black oil sunflower seed attracts a wide variety of seed-eating birds. Buy the 40-pound sack at the feed store for a better price per pound. If it still seems too expensive, feed only the amount you can afford each day.

Leave the cats indoors. There are many reasons cats should live indoors fulltime, including their health and safety, but really, is it fair to invite birds to your yard where a predator lurks? The feeder may be on a pole or hanging above the cat, but certain birds prefer to feed on the spilled seed on the ground.

On the other hand, if a neighbor cat stakes out your yard, you can make sure the area around the feeder has no place for a cat to hide. I've also heard of putting up a 2-foot high wire fence around the feeder, maybe at a radius of about 6 feet. The time it takes the predator to jump the fence gives the birds enough advanced warning to get out of the way.

Offer variety. Some birds like tube-style and hopper feeders. Others that prefer feeding on the ground can learn to use a shelf feeder. Consider nyjer thistle, which is expensive, but use a special feeder for it designed with smaller seed ports or ports that are below the perches, something goldfinches and chickadees can handle but others can't. Add a suet or seed cake. It may help draw in woodpeckers and chickadees. Offer peanuts and you may get blue jays – and squirrels.

Don't clean up your flowerbeds in the fall. The seed-eating birds attracted to your feeders will enjoy the seed heads. Plus, tree leaves, while providing mulch, may also provide a variety of eggs of insects (many beneficial) that the birds enjoy picking over.

On a frigid day, have open water in a birdbath. It is almost more attractive than food. Find some kind of shallow bowl, preferably with sloping sides, which won't break if the water freezes. It should be easy to bring in the house to thaw out. Or get an electric heater designed for birdbaths or dog water dishes.

For more detailed feeding information, go to my archives at www.CheyenneBirdBanter.wordpress.com. Look for "Bird feeding" in the list of topics.

Study your visitors. From your feeder-watching window, scan your trees and shrubs and garden beds to see if you can get a glimpse of more than house finches and house sparrows, especially in the spring. Of the 85 species I've seen in or above our yard, I've recorded 27 from November through March, prime feeder season.

Share your bird sightings at www.eBird.org, or for $18, this winter you can take part in Project FeederWatch, www.feederwatch.org. It isn't too late to sign up. You get a nifty bird calendar poster and a handbook. Even if you don't participate, the website is full of information about bird feeding and feeder birds.

Have fun. However, if you find it isn't fun, take down the feeders. Reduce your stress by going for a walk and enjoy the birds along the way.

2016

161

New camera technology can help birders get perfect shot

I have often wished the view through my binoculars could become a photograph of that colorful warbler high in the tree, the distant hawk or the swimming phalarope.

Then digiscoping was invented – a digital version of trying to take a photo through a scope. The idea is that you don't need a camera with a big lens if you can use your scope instead.

But who wants to carry around the heavy tripod and scope, plus a camera to attach to it? Not me.

But a couple years ago, the Cheyenne Audubon chapter had members Greg Johnson and Robin Kepple give a talk on their birding trip to Australia. The bird photos were fabulous. What camera was used? Canon PowerShot SX50 HS.

The PowerShot series of cameras is really a collection of point and shoots – I have an early one, but it doesn't zoom like the SX50. They all have lots of manual and partially manual ways to adjust speed, aperture and color. You can do a surprising number of things, including macro and video. Some will even connect to your smart phone to transmit photos.

The SX50 (and now there is an SX60 and rumors of an SX70, not to mention Nikon's cameras in this class) is moderately priced, between $300 and $600.

That price might get you another lens for a digital single lens reflex camera, the type the professionals use.

And the SX50 weighs only 1 pound 6 ounces, whereas my Brunton 8 x 42 binocs weigh 4 ounces more. A recent publication of the American Birding Association, "Birder's Guide to Gear," features four men who did a photographic Big Day. They could only count bird species they photographed. All of them carried multiple camera bodies and lenses. Imagine the weight.

Among our birding friends, my husband, Mark, was the first to follow Greg and Robin's lead by buying an SX50 in the fall of 2014. By spring of 2015, there were three or four people carrying these cameras on a local field trip. Even our friend, ABA magazine editor Ted Floyd, has one now. It makes his Facebook posts even more entertaining.

Ted mentioned that young birders seem to be forsaking binoculars for these "compact ultra-zooms" as they've been referred to. They have one big advantage over binocs. If you snap a photo of an unusual bird, you can then show it to your birding companions using the 2.8-inch screen on the back, beginning a good half hour or more's discussion of the finer points of feathers.

And it is really handy to have a photo

when you submit your field trip checklist to the eBird database where the experts want proof of the rare bird you saw.

Are Mark and his friends practicing the art of photography? I'm not sure. They all seem to be using the camera on the automatic setting. Their goal is to get the bird. They don't worry about whether the background contrasts nicely.

Often, the camera's automatic setting determination is matched by the location's lighting for a really nice shot. Fixing the framing of the subject can be accomplished back on the computer with cropping. Putting the camera on a tripod would probably improve the number of well-focused shots. Though these cameras come with image stabilization technology, it is sorely tested by flighty birds.

Mark has taken 7,500 photos so far. I asked him if he thought about bringing just the camera on birding trips, since it zooms farther than our scope. It's kind of a pain carrying camera, scope and binocs.

No, he said, the camera lacks a wide field of view. It makes it difficult to refind that speck of distant movement you saw with your naked eye.

With the steady advancement of technology in my lifetime alone, computers have gone from room-sized to hand-sized. Cameras have gone from the wooden box my grandmother used in 1916 to who-knows-what in the next 10 years.

Equally amazing is how birders take the latest technology and use it for learning more about birds. We've learned so much from eBird, for instance – all those observations from birdwatchers being sent in via internet from all over the world.

And how about geolocators? Attached to birds, they allow scientists to track them during migration.

But let's not forget the thrill of photography itself. Like artist John James Audubon, you can see the bird you shot today displayed for posterity on your computer screen.

162 UW songbird brain studies shed light

Sunday, February 28, 2016, Outdoors, page E2

We are used to thinking about many animals standing in for humans in studies that will benefit us: rats, chimps, rabbits. But should we add songbirds to that list? They apparently work well for studying how we learn to speak.

At the February Cheyenne Audubon meeting, Karagh Murphy, a University of Wyoming doctoral candidate in the Zoology and Physiology Department, explained how Bengalese finches help her study how brains learn.

Learning by example, whether bird or human, takes place in two parts. First the student observes, or in the case of

male birds learning to sing so they can defend their territory and attract mates, they listen. Then they attempt imitation, practicing by listening to themselves and getting feedback.

What Karagh wanted to know is if Higher Vocal Center neurons in the birds' brains are active at both stages – hearing and doing. It's just a simple matter of plugging a computer into the right place in a bird's brain.

First though, you have to wrangle your subjects, capturing them in the walk-in-sized aviary, then over time, get them used to having the wispiest of cables attached to the tiny instrument on their heads. Otherwise, they are too stressed to sing.

Karagh recorded the firing pattern of the HVC neurons, producing something like the electrocardiogram that shows heart beats and compared it to the spectrogram, another linear graph of peaks and valleys that visualizes the frequencies of the song she played for the bird to hear, and then the song the bird sang. Both spectrograms matched the peaks and valleys of the HVC neuron pattern, essentially showing the neurons are used for both auditory and motor output – the action of singing.

Recently, something very similar has been found in humans, called mirror neurons.

The second speaker was Jonathan Prather, an associate professor in the department's neuroscience program. While Karagh has been studying males learning to sing, Jonathan has been figuring out what the female Bengalese finches want to hear.

Female birds don't sing. At most, they produce call notes to communicate. But they enjoy listening to males sing, and they judge them by their song to determine which one is the fittest potential mate, which will give them the fittest young.

Jonathan thought there might be a "sexy syllable," some part of the song that would get the females excited, measured by how often the females call in response. He measured their responses as he played back songs he had manipulated.

Or maybe it was tempo, so he manipulated the recording to go faster in some trials, then slower in others. Or maybe the female birds would react differently to songs at different pitches. That would be similar to human women who, studies have shown, are attracted to men with deeper voices (connected to higher testosterone levels).

Apparently, female finches are looking for quantity and complexity, for males who sing in the most physically (neuromuscular-wise) demanding way.

That means sweeping from high to low notes a lot, and really fast. Think how opera stars singing the most demanding repertoire get the biggest applause. A bird that can sing well is well-fed, healthy and of good breeding – perfect father material.

The field of neurobiology is more about figuring out human brains, but when birds are used as models, birdwatchers find it intriguing. The questions from the Audubon audience reflected their familiarity with birds.

Our songbirds in Wyoming are only seasonal singers, so birds from equatorial locations that sing year round are used to make trials more efficient. Would there be a difference?

Are female bird brains different from the male brains? Yes, because learning songs increases one part of the male brain, however, females have other roles that increase the size of other parts of their brain.

If a young bird never hears another bird sing, will it eventually sing? Not really, it will only babble in an unformed way, as human babies do when they start out.

If a young bird hears only the singing of a different species, will it learn that song instead? Yes, although not completely perfectly – there is some genetic influence on bird song.

And what about the mimics? What about birds like starlings and mockingbirds that learn to imitate lots of other birds' songs and even some human vocalizations and mechanical noises? Karagh broke out in a grin. That line of study could keep her busy for her entire career.

163 Bird count day gives us big picture

Sunday, May 22, 2016, Opinion, page C9

May Hanesworth was ahead of her time. An active Cheyenne birder as early as the 1940s, she made sure the results of the local spring bird counts were published every year in the Cheyenne paper. She recruited me in the 1990s to type the lists for her. She felt that someday there would be a place for that data, and she was right.

A few years ago, members of the Cheyenne-High Plains Audubon Society collected and uploaded that data to eBird.org, a global database for bird observations. The oldest record we found was for 1956.

We refer to the count we make at the height of spring migration as the Big Day Bird Count. Elsewhere in the world, competitive birders will, as a small team or solo, do a big day to see how many species they can find in a specified area. But the idea of a group of unlimited size like ours going out and scouring an area is unusual, though closer to what the originator, Lynds Jones, an Oberlin College ornithology professor, had in mind back in 1895.

Now eBird has started a new tradition as of last year, the Global Big Day. This year, it was scheduled for May 14, the same day as ours. Results show 15,642 people around the world saw 6,227 bird species. For our local count, 20 people looked for birds around Cheyenne, and 107 species were counted (see the results on page E3 of today's edition).

Finding our favorite birds in the company of friends is a good incentive for taking part, but there is the science too. Back in the spring of 1956, May saw 85 species. And when Mark and I started in the 1990s, 150 seemed to be the norm – perhaps because Cheyenne had more trees by then. However, the last 10 years, the average is lower, 118.

Maybe we aren't as sharp as earlier birders. Or we are missing the peak of migration. Or we have lost prime habitat for migrating birds as the surrounding prairie gets built over and elderly trees are removed in town. Or it's caused by deteriorating habitat in southern wintering grounds or northern breeding grounds.

But imagine where we would be without the Migratory Bird Treaty.

This year marks the 100th anniversary of the first agreement in 1916, between the U.S. and Great Britain (signing for Canada), followed by other agreements and updates. In summary: "It is illegal to take, possess, import, export, transport, sell, purchase, barter, offer for sale, purchase or barter any migratory bird, or parts, nests or eggs."

Even migrating songbirds, like our Wyoming state bird, the western meadowlark, are protected.

But who would want to hurt a meadowlark?

Look at the Mediterranean flyway. Birdlife International reports 25 million birds of all kinds along that flyway are shot or trapped every year for fun, food and the cage bird trade. Perpetrators think the supply of birds is endless. But we can point to the millions of passenger pigeons in North America prior to the death of the last one in 1914, to show what can happen.

The city of Eliat, Israel, is the funnel between Africa and Europe/Asia on the Mediterranean flyway, and to bring attention to the slaughter, the annual

Champions of the Flyway bird race is based there. A Big Day event, this year it attracted 40 teams, Israeli and international, which counted a combined total of 243 species during 24 hours.

This year, funds raised by the teams are going to Greece to support education and enforcement – killing migratory birds is already illegal. Some of the worst-hit areas are in forests above beaches popular with tourists. Attracting birdwatching tourists could pay better than killing and trapping birds, a kind of change that has been beneficial elsewhere.

Many factors affect how many birds we see in Cheyenne on our big day, but we do have control over one aspect: habitat. If you live in the city, plant more trees and shrubs in appropriate places. If you live on acreage, protect the prairie and its ground-nesting grassland birds. And then join us on future Cheyenne Big Day Bird Counts and contribute to the global big picture of birds.

164 New bird singing, maybe breeding

Sunday, June 19, 2016, Outdoors, page E3

There is a new bird on our block. It's a loud bird. That's how I know it is here, even though it is tiny – only 4.25 inches long – and prefers to hang out unseen around the tops of mature spruce trees while gleaning insects and spiders.

The ruby-crowned kinglet, despite its name, is not a brightly colored bird. It is mostly an olive-gray-green, with one white wing-bar. Only the male has the red crown patch, and he may show it when singing, but the red feathers really stand up like a clown's fright wig when he's around other male ruby-crowneds.

We get a variety of small migrating songbirds in our Cheyenne yard. In May, we had a lazuli bunting, pine siskin, clay-colored sparrow and even our first ever yellow-breasted chat.

This isn't the first time for a ruby-crowned kinglet in our yard. I recorded one at www.eBird.org on April 25, 2012, and another April 24, 2015. They are usually on their way to the mountains to nest in the coniferous forest of spruce, pine and fir trees.

The difference this year is that beginning May 8, I've been hearing one every day. My hopes are up. Maybe it is going to nest. My neighborhood has the requisite mature spruce trees.

I talked to Bob Dorn May 27, but he thought that it was still too early to suspect breeding. They might have been waiting out cold spring weather before heading to the mountains. Bob is the co-author of "Wyoming Birds" with his wife, Jane Dorn. Their map for the ruby-crowned kinglet shows an "R" for the Cheyenne area, "Resident" – observed in winter and summer with breeding confirmed.

The Dorns' breeding record is from the cemetery, where they saw kinglet nestlings being fed July 18, 1993. They also suspected breeding was taking place at the High Plains Grasslands Research Station just west of the city June 2, 1989 and June 15, 1990.

For more recent summer observations that could indicate breeding in Cheyenne, I looked at eBird, finding three records between July 3 and July 7 in the last five years, including Lions Park. There were also a couple late June observations at the Wyoming Hereford

Ranch and Lions Park in 2014.

I first learned the ruby-crowned kinglet's distinctive song in Wyoming's mountains. You've probably heard it too. Listen at www.allaboutbirds.org. It has two parts, starting with three hard-to-hear notes, "tee-tee-tee", as ornithologist C.A. Bent explained it in the 1940s, followed by five or six lower "tu or "tur" notes. The second half is the loudest, and sometimes given alone, "tee-da-leet, tee-da-leet, te-da-leet."

Those who have studied the song say it can be heard for more than half a mile. The females sing a version during incubation and when nestlings are young. The males can sing while gleaning insects from trees and while eating them. Neighboring kinglets have distinctive signature second halves of the song, and males can apparently establish their territories well enough by singing that they can avoid physical border skirmishes.

Actual nesting behavior is not well documented because it is hard to find an open cup nest that measures only 4 inches wide by 5 to 6 inches deep when it is camouflaged in moss, feathers, lichens, spider webs, and pieces of bark, twigs and rootlets – and located 40 feet up a spruce tree.

The female kinglet builds the nest in five days, lining it with more feathers, plant down, fine grass, lichens and fur. She may lay as many as eight eggs. The nest stretches as both parents feed the growing nestlings tiny caterpillars, crickets, moths, butterflies and ant pupae.

Ruby-crowned kinglets winter in the Pacific coast states and southern states but breed throughout the Rockies and Black Hills and in a swath from Maine to Alaska. If my neighborhood kinglet stays to breed, it will be one more data point expanding the breeding range further out onto the prairie.

While kinglets are not picky about habitat during migration, for breeding they demand mature spruce-fir or similar forest. Some communities of kinglets decrease in the wake of beetle epidemics, salvage logging and fires. However, the 2016 State of the Birds report shows them in good shape overall – scoring a 6 on a scale from 4 to 20. High scores would indicate trouble due to small or downward trending population, or threats to the species and its habitats during breeding and non-breeding seasons.

As of June 19, the kinglet is still singing – all day long. If it is nesting on my block this summer, I must thank the residents who planted spruce trees here 50 years ago. What a nice legacy. We should plant some more.

165 Kids explore nature of the Belvoir Ranch

Sunday, July 17, 2016, Outdoors, page E2

I was delighted to recognize my neighbor at the Belvoir Ranch Bioblitz last month. She is going to be a senior at Cheyenne East High in the fall and was there with two friends. All three were planning to spend the weekend looking for birds, mammals, herps (reptiles and amphibians), pollinators, macroinvertebrates and plants to fulfill hours required for their Congressional Award gold medals.

The weekend could have served for all four award areas: volunteer public service (we were all volunteer citizen scientists collecting data), personal development (the staff taught us a lot of new things), physical fitness (hiking up and down Lone Tree Creek in the heat was arduous), and expedition/exploration (many of us, including my neighbor and her friends, camped out and cooked meals despite being only 20 miles from Cheyenne).

Mark and I have attended other bioblitzes around the state, but this was the first one close to Cheyenne. With all the publicity from the four sponsoring groups, Audubon Rockies, The Nature Conservancy, University of Wyoming Biodiversity Institute and the Wyoming Geographic Alliance, a record 100 people attended, plus the staff of 50 from various natural science disciplines.

When I asked my neighbor why she and her friends had come, she said, "We're science nerds." That was exciting to hear.

There were a lot of junior science nerds in attendance with their families. Small children enjoyed wading into the pond along the creek to scoop up dragonfly and damselfly larvae – and even crayfish.

A surprising number of children were up at 6 a.m. Saturday for the bird survey. The highlight was the raven nest in a crevice on the canyon wall, with three young ravens crowding the opening, ready to fledge.

Sunday morning's bird mist netting along the creek was very popular as well. Several birds that had been hard to see with binoculars were suddenly in hand.

Because it wasn't at an official bird banding site, the mist netting was strictly educational and the birds were soon released. Several young children had the opportunity to hold a bird and release it, feeling how light it was, how fast its heart beat and feeling the little whoosh of air as it took flight. What I wouldn't

give to know if any of the children grow up to be bird biologists or birdwatchers.

The Belvoir Ranch is owned by the city of Cheyenne and stretches miles to the west between Interstate 80 and the Colorado-Wyoming state line. The city bought it in 2003 and 2005 to protect our upstream aquifer, or groundwater, as well as the surface water.

While limited grazing and hunting continues as it did under private ownership, other parts of the master plan have yet to come to fruition, including construction of a wind farm, landfill, golf course or general recreation development. It is normally closed to the public. However, progress is being made on trails to connect the ranch to Colorado's Soapstone Prairie Natural Area and/or Red Mountain Open Space.

A good landowner takes stock of his property. The city has some idea of what's out there, including archeological sites. But with budgets tightening, there won't be funding to hire consultants for a closer look. But there are a lot of citizen scientists available.

The data from the Bioblitz weekend went into the Wyobio database, www.wyobio.org, a place where data from all over Wyoming can be entered. The bird data also went into eBird.org.

The data began to paint a picture of the Belvoir: 62 species of animals including 50 birds, eight mammals, four herps, plus 13 taxa of macroinvertebrates (not easily identified to species) and 12 taxa of pollinators (bees and other insects), plus many species of plants. All that diversity was from exploring half a mile of one creek within the ranch's total 18,800 acres – about 30 square miles.

The members of the City Council who approved the ranch purchase are to be congratulated on making it public land in addition to protecting our watershed. Sometimes we don't have to wait for the federal and state governments to do the right thing. The essence of Wyoming is its big natural landscapes, and we are lucky to have one on the west edge of Wyoming's largest city.

Let's also congratulate the parents who encouraged their children to examine the critters in the muddy pond and pick up mammal scat (while wearing plastic gloves) on the trails among other activities.

Someday, these kids will grow up to be like my high school neighbor and her friends. Someday they could be the graduate students, professors and land use professionals. No matter what they become, they can always contribute scientific data by being citizen scientists.

166 Pondering how much eagles can take in life

Just when we thought eagles were safe (bald eagles were taken off the threatened and endangered species list in 2007) we discover that golden eagle numbers are still down. And there are plans to build a massive wind farm in Wyoming which will take the lives of both bald and golden eagles.

I should have written a column about this earlier so you could send your comments to the U.S. Fish and Wildlife Service, but I was sidetracked by spring migration.

However, staff at Audubon Rockies and their counterparts at the Natural Resources Defense Council and the Wilderness Society have written extensive comments backed by science and experience.

The Power Company of Wyoming (PCW) is developing the 1,000-turbine Chokecherry/Sierra Madre Wind Energy Project. It is located on 500 square miles in Carbon County, southcentral Wyoming, where there is some of the best wind in the country. It will be the largest onshore wind farm in the U.S.

PCW is working with the Fish and Wildlife Service on improving the locations for turbines and has reduced the projected take to 10-14 golden eagles and 1-2 bald eagles per year. The definition of "take" is death incidental to industry activities.

The projected take numbers also account for the eagles that will live because PCW will retrofit 1,500-3,000 power poles per year for eagle safety. Eagles' large wingspans can cause their electrocution when they perch on poles, and then they touch two electrical hotspots at the same time and cause a completed circuit.

PCW is applying for an eagle take permit for the first half of the development. It is voluntary but good insurance. PCW saw a competitor without a permit get hit with a $1 million fine for killing eagles.

The Fish and Wildlife Service is in the process of updating the eagle take rule. It will probably apply to the second half of PCW's development, the other 500 turbines.

The update would give wind power companies across the country 30-year permits, to cover the expected lifespan of a windfarm, rather than the current five years. However, Fish and Wildlife proposes a review every five years.

Audubon Rockies concedes that PCW needs some assurance that they can operate for a longer length of time that will make the investment worthwhile – they can't get investors if there is a possibility eagle deaths will shut down part of the development after the first five years.

However, there are concerns. In the proposed rule update, any monitoring done by the company would be considered proprietary and not be required to be available to public scrutiny. Audubon feels more transparency is needed on what is happening with our eagles.

And there needs to be more flexibility to manage the windfarm/eagle interactions as more eagle research is done. We don't know yet how eagles will deal with the Chokecherry/Sierra Madre development. It's not just the spinning windmill blades, the tips of which can travel 150 mph. Eagles also collide with the transmission lines and towers.

Because it takes eagles five years to reach sexual maturity, we know their populations can't quickly bounce back like rabbits.

The site of PCW's Chokecherry/Sierra Madre wind project is gorgeous. The thought of developing it is heartbreaking. But the company has done a lot of work and spent a lot of money studying the wildlife problems. They deserve clear answers from the federal government on what they can and can't do.

Eagles are just one of the items addressed in the draft environmental impact statement for the wind farm. Other wildlife, including bats and songbirds, are affected too.

By the end of the year, we will find out how Fish and Wildlife will react to public comments, not only on Chokecherry/Sierra Madre but also the proposed update of the eagle take rule.

Does clean energy have to come down to this? Do we have to fill Wyoming's open spaces (they are not empty spaces) with industrial clutter? Why didn't the coal companies spend millions on cleaner power plant emissions research instead of on litigation at every turn?

Why does alternative energy, specifically wind and solar, have to follow the old centralized, mega-production model? I still think disbursed ["distributed" is the frequently used term] power production would be better, safer – less of a target for troublemakers.

In comparison, look at how Mother Nature spreads oxygen-producing plants everywhere. Even where natural or man-made catastrophes have stripped the vegetation, it doesn't take long for another little oxygen-producing factory to take hold.

Plus, wouldn't you like to park in the shade of a solar panel while shopping at the mall? Adding solar panels to our rooftops and choosing energy efficient appliances will not only cut our personal utility bills, but in a way, save eagles in the future.

167 Collaboration could keep eagles safe

Sunday, September 4, 2016, Outdoors, page E3

Last month, while researching the wind energy/eagle issue, I learned about new technology that could help eagles survive encounters with wind farms.

IdentiFlight uses stereoscopic cameras to detect and identify eagles in flight far enough out to shut down a turbine, preventing a deadly collision.

The idea that cameras hooked up to a computer can learn to "see" eagles, using machine vision technology, is as remarkable as the collaboration behind it.

It starts with Renewable Energy Systems, started in 1982, and now a global company in the business of designing and installing as well as developing wind energy projects.

I spoke with Tom Hiester, vice president of strategy for RES Americas, whose office is in Broomfield, Colorado.

He said RES is funding the development of IdentiFlight and will own the rights to the technology and sell equipment. Other wind companies concerned with avoiding the fines for killing eagles will be the customers.

RES is working with Boulder Imaging, a Boulder, Colorado, tech company specializing in industrial precision applications.

Initial testing of the IdentiFlight system was done through the U.S. Department of Energy's National Renewable Energy Laboratory. Its testing facility, the National Wind Technology Center, is south of Boulder on 300 acres up against the foothills where the wind can be ferocious. Companies, universities and government agencies come to test their turbines for reliability and performance.

Machine vision requires training the computer. In this case, it needed to see how real eagles fly. A golden eagle and a bald eagle were brought in from the Southeastern Raptor Center where birds of prey are rehabilitated. They also happened to be the mascots for Auburn University, Auburn, Alabama. You can see a video at www.energy.gov/eagles.

Hiester told me they have found that eagles are more susceptible to collisions when hunting. Their heads are down, eyes concentrating on the ground. Machine vision has to identify a moving object as an eagle at 1,000 meters to give the appropriate turbine the 30 seconds needed to shut down.

This summer, IdentiFlight is getting tested by a third party selected by the American Wind Wildlife Institute (now the Renewable Energy Wildlife Institute). AWWI was organized about eight years ago. Half its partners are a who's who of wind energy companies. The other half are national environmental organizations such as Audubon and the National Wildlife Federation, as well as wildlife managers represented by the Association of Fish and Wildlife Agencies and scientists represented by the Union of Concerned Scientists.

One of AWWI's interests is minimizing eagle deaths. They expect to publish and share what they learn. Besides detecting and deterring eagles from wind turbine collisions, they are also looking at lead abatement (lead shot in carcasses left by hunters will poison eagles because eagles often eat dead animals), reducing vehicle strikes (by removing dead animals along roads), and improving the habitat of eagle prey species.

AWWI science advisors include Dale Strickland of Cheyenne. His environmental consulting firm, Western EcoSystems Technology, has studied wind and wildlife interactions across the country for years.

AWWI selected the Peregrine Fund to conduct the testing. The Peregrine Fund, established in Idaho in 1970 to protect and reestablish peregrine falcon populations, also works now with other raptors around the world.

The test site is Duke Energy's Top of the World wind farm outside Casper. In general, Wyoming has more eagles than other states, and some of our topographic features that cause strong wind also concentrate eagles.

For the test, IdentiFlight cameras have been set up on a tower with a 360-degree view. When motion is identified as an eagle, and velocity and proximity figured, human researchers in an observation tower confirm it. In the future, the system would be totally automated, and the identification of an eagle would trigger the shutdown of the turbine in the eagle's path. IdentiFlight can also be used to survey for eagles on prospective wind sites.

Hiester said the number of eagles actually killed by wind turbines is minor. There are more deaths from other causes. But, as more and more wind projects are built, that could change, especially in Wyoming where there is a lot of wind and a lot of eagles.

Most other bird species flying through wind farms don't have the federal protections that eagles do. IdentiFlight won't do much for them unless they fly alongside the eagles. Hiester said that thermal imaging techniques could help identify them and bats.

168 Winter raptor marvels, mystery show up in southeast Wyoming

Sunday, December 4, 2016, Outdoors, page E4

Mark and I drove over to join the Laramie Audubon Society on their mid-November raptor field trip on the Laramie Plains.

It was a beautiful day that makes you forget all the previous white-knuckle drives over the pass. However, what's good weather for driving isn't always good for finding raptors.

Trip leader Tim Banks checked his intended route the day before and found nary a hawk, falcon, owl or eagle. So instead, we drove across the Laramie Plains on a route his chapter frequently takes for general birding.

The reason for our first stop was a mystery, but then the broken branch stub of a lone cottonwood across the road became a great horned owl. However, a rough-legged hawk and a northern harrier were too distant to enjoy.

Finally, at Hutton Lake, out of the birdless sky, the wind picked up and kicked out a golden eagle, two bald eagles, and a ferruginous hawk.

Three weeks before, on a Cheyenne Audubon field trip at Curt Gowdy, we saw two bald eagles in the canyon. Another day at the park, Mark spotted three checking out his stringer of fish.

Bald eagles are marvelous looking, but I also marvel at their history, from endangered species to birds seen three times in three weeks.

Bald eagles were first federally protected in 1940. Later, they were classified as endangered. Banning the pesticide DDT and educating people not to shoot them allowed their numbers to increase. In 1995, they were reclassified as merely threatened. They were completely delisted in 2007, though they are still protected by the Bald and Golden Eagle Protection Act.

While bald eagles do breed in Wyoming, there are more here in the winter, migrating from farther north. Fish are their favorite food (carrion is second choice), so looking for them around reservoirs and Wyoming's larger rivers is good strategy, especially if there are big cottonwoods for them to roost in.

We all recognize the adult bald eagle, dark brown with white head and white tail, but until they are about 4 or 5 years old, they are dark with splotchy white markings like those of young golden eagles.

Golden eagles never came quite as

close to extinction as bald eagles, but they were targeted by stock growers. In 1971, one man confessed to killing many of the 700 found shot or poisoned near Casper.

Golden eagles live in Wyoming's grasslands and shrublands year round. They might choose to nest on cliffs. And they prefer eating rabbits, ground squirrels, prairie dogs and the occasional new lamb if the rancher isn't watching.

If you see a massive raptor flying in Wyoming in the winter, it is probably an eagle. Balds and goldens have wingspans about 80 inches long.

But if it is a smaller dark bird, wingspan only 50-plus inches, with a neater black and white pattern under the wing, it might be a rough-legged hawk.

Every winter they come down from their Arctic breeding grounds, sometimes right into Cheyenne, wherever there's a power pole perch, open land, and mice, voles or shrews. It's a break from eating lemmings all summer.

They were also shot at, but like all migratory birds, they are now protected by the Migratory Bird Treaty Act.

For me, the most fascinating raptor we saw on the Laramie Plains is less common: a ferruginous hawk. Its name refers to the color of rusted iron because its top side is a reddish brown. Its belly is a creamy white, slightly spotted, compared to the streaky rough-legged's. Both have feathers all the way down their legs.

However, some sources say the ferruginous shouldn't have been in Wyoming in November. They are almost all supposed to migrate south in October and return in March.

Some field guides show the Colorado and Wyoming border as the north boundary of their winter range. I think that winter range boundary at the state line may have more to do with the greater number of birders in Colorado in the past who could distinguish between ferruginous and rough-legged. But there are now a dozen Laramie Plains and Cheyenne-area eBird records for ferruginous from November through February within the past three years.

Guess I can no longer assume in winter any large dark hawk that isn't a red-tailed hawk is a rough-legged. It might be a ferruginous.

Meanwhile, we can all brush up on our hawk identification skills or download the free Merlin Bird ID app for help. It will make winter more interesting.

2017

169 Birding by app: New adventures in tech

Mark and I finally made the jump to smart phones last month. Our children are applauding.

What I was really looking forward to once I was in possession of a smart phone was eBird Mobile. My daughter-in-law, Jessie, was using it when we birded together over the holidays. It means that you can note the birds you see on your phone while you are in the field and then submit them as an eBird checklist.

The second day I had my phone, I went to eBird.org to find out how to download it (in the Help section search for "eBird Mobile"). It's free. If you aren't signed up for eBird already, it will help you do that for free also. Then I prepared for a trial run birding out at F.E. Warren Air Force Base with Mark.

Because we are rather miserly with our monthly data allotment, I chose to use the app offline while in the field. But because I was establishing a new birding location for the mobile version, I did that while I was at home and could use our Wi-Fi.

The preparation for offline means you are downloading an appropriate checklist of birds possible for the area. Otherwise eBird Mobile will give you the world list, 10,414 species, to scroll through.

As we birded, I scrolled through the much shorter list of local possibilities and added the numbers of each species seen as I observed them. At the end of the trip, I hit the submit button.

However, on my next eBird Mobile attempt it was bitterly cold. Recording birds while holding a pencil in a mittened hand works, but it was too cold to risk a bare hand to manipulate the touch screen, though I have since invested in "touch screen" gloves.

The mobile app can't do everything the regular checklist submission process does, like attach photos. But that upgrade may be coming soon. Meanwhile, you can edit your mobile-produced checklists on the eBird website whenever it's convenient.

I've also downloaded the free Merlin Bird ID App and tried it. I told Merlin where I was, what day it was, how big and what color the bird was and where it was (ground, bush, tree, sky) and up popped a photo of the most likely candidate, other possible species, general information and bird song recordings.

Both apps are Cornell Lab of Ornithology projects and are designed to get more people excited about birds. More data collected means more understanding, and more understanding means better conservation of birds.

The lab has even more up its sleeve. At a recent meeting, staff from far-flung places gathered to discuss making animated migration maps that will allow zooming in on particular locations. Recently, Audubon and CLO announced eBird Mobile is available on the dashboard of select Subaru models. That's an update I wouldn't mind seeing the dealer for.

CLO employs a lot of tech people. Job openings on the eBird website list required technical qualifications. Preferred qualifications include "An interest in birds, nature, biology, science, and/or conservation helpful."

So maybe it doesn't surprise you that our son, Bryan, with a degree from the University of Wyoming in software engineering – and exposed to birdwatching from birth – has become not only a birder, but in October moved to Ithaca, New York, to work for CLO.

He can bird to and from work, walking through the famous Sapsucker Woods. He tells us the winter regulars include many of the same species we see in Cheyenne. However, he says he sees four kinds of woodpeckers: downy and hairy, which we see, but also red-bellied woodpecker and pileated woodpecker, eastern birds.

Surrounded by serious birdwatchers all week, perhaps on weekends you would be forgiven for picking up a different hobby. But no, on the Martin Luther King holiday, everyone from Bryan's office went up near Seneca Falls and found snowy owls, a gyrfalcon, northern shrike and thousands of snow geese.

The next weekend, Bryan and Jessie went back and found two more snowy owls and three kinds of swans.

The full eBird website can help me predict the height of spring migration in Ithaca, and I hope to time Mark's and my visit accordingly. But we must fit in one last trip to Texas to visit our younger son, Jeffrey, before he and his wife move to Seattle for new jobs.

If your children aren't moving back to Cheyenne, at least let them live in interesting places.

170 Citizen science meets the test of making a difference

Sunday, May 14, 2017, Outdoors, page E4

Birdwatchers have been at the forefront of citizen science for a long time, starting with the Christmas Bird Count in 1900.

Today, the Cornell Lab of Ornithology is leading the way in using technology to expand bird counting around the globe. Meanwhile, other citizen science projects collect information on a variety of phenomena.

But is citizen science really science? This question was asked last December at the first Wyoming Citizen Science Conference.

The way science works is a scientist poses a question in the form of a hypothesis. For instance, do robins lay more eggs at lower elevations than at higher elevations? The scientist and his assistants can go out and find nests and count eggs to get an answer.

However, there are hypotheses that would be more difficult to prove without a reservoir of data that was collected without a research question in mind. For instance, Elizabeth Wommack, curator and collections manager of vertebrates at the University of Wyoming Museum of Vertebrates, studied the variation in the number of white markings on the outer tail feathers of male kestrels. She visited collections of bird specimens at museums all over the country to gather data.

Some kestrels have lots of white spots, some have none. Are the differences caused by geography? Many animal traits are selected for (meaning because of the trait, the animal survives and passes on the trait to more offspring) on a continuum. It could be north to south or dry to wet habitat or some other geographic feature.

Or perhaps it was sexual selection – females preferred spottier male tail feathers. Or did the amount of spotting lead directly to improved survival?

Wommack discovered none of her hypotheses could show statistical significance, information just as important as proving the hypotheses true. But at least Wommack learned something without having to "collect" or kill more kestrels.

Some citizen science projects collect data to test specific hypotheses. However, others, like eBird and iNaturalist, collect data without a hypothesis in mind, akin to putting specimens in museum drawers like those kestrels. The data is just waiting for someone to ask a question.

I know I've gone to eBird with my own questions such as when and where sandhill cranes are seen in Wyoming. Or when the last time was that I reported blue jays in our yard.

To some scientists, data like eBird's, collected by the public, might be suspect. How can they trust lay people to report accurately? At this point though, so many people are reporting the birds they see to eBird that statistical credibility is high. (However, eBird still does not know a lot about birds in Wyoming and we need more of you to report your sightings at http://ebird.org.)

Are scientists using eBird data? They are, and papers are being published. The Cornell Lab of Ornithology itself recently published a study in Biological Conservation, an international journal. Their study tracked requests for raw data from eBird for 22 months, 2012 through 2014.

They found that the data was used in 159 direct conservation actions. That means no waiting years for papers to be published before identifying problems like downturns in population. These actions affected birds through management of habitat, siting of disturbances like power plants, decisions about listing as threatened or endangered for example. CLO also discovered citizens were using the data to discuss development and land use issues in their own neighborhoods.

CLO's eBird data is what is called open access data. No one pays to access it and none of us get paid to contribute it. Our payment is the knowledge that we are helping land and wildlife managers make better decisions. There's a lot "crowd sourced" abundance and distribution numbers can tell them.

Citizen science isn't often couched in terms of staving off extinction. Recently I read "Citizen Scientist, Searching for Heroes and Hope in an Age of Extinction," by Mary Ellen Hannibal, published in 2016. In it, she gave me a new view.

Based in California, Hannibal uses examples of citizen science projects there that have made a difference. She looks back at the early non-scientists like Ed Ricketts and John Steinbeck who sampled the Pacific Coast, leaving a trail of data collection sites that were re-sampled 85 years later. She also looks to Pulitzer Prize-winning biologist E.O. Wilson, who gives citizen science his blessing. At age 87, he continues to share his message that we should leave half the biosphere to nature – for our own good.

Enjoy spring bird migration and share your bird observations. The species you save may be the one to visit you in your own backyard again.

171 Bird by ear to identify the unseen

Sunday, July 16, 2017, Outdoors, page E5

Here on the western edge of the Great Plains, our trees don't grow so thick that you can't walk all the way around one to see the bird that's singing. But it is still useful to be able to identify birds by sound.

I'm a visually-oriented person, so over time I've learned to identify our local birds well enough to often figure out who they are as they flash by. I can only identify bird voices of the most common or unique sounding species.

At the big box stores in town, in the garden departments, there is almost always an incessant cheeping overhead from invading house sparrows.

If you get up at oh-dark-thirty on a spring or summer morning in town, you are likely to hear the cheerful "cheer-io" of a robin.

Putting up a bird feeder may bring in house finches with their different chatter. I especially like hearing the goldfinches around the thistle feeder which sound as if they are small children calling questions to each other.

Birding by ear becomes a more important skill in the mountains where the forest is thicker. The Cheyenne – High Plains Audubon Society's mid-June field trip was to the Vedauwoo recreation area on the Medicine Bow National Forest. We planned to hike the Turtle Rock trail. Since most of Wyoming's birds are found near water, we focused on the beaver ponds.

Some birds, like the flocks of tree swallows flitting across the water, are never hidden away.

But one warbling bird was. It didn't sound quite like a robin. I went through a mental list of birds that like riparian, or streamside, habitats and casually remarked, "Maybe it's a warbling vireo."

Then I realized I could check the free Merlin app on my phone and play a recording of a warbling vireo. Amazingly, it matched.

Yellow warblers are almost always somewhere around in the brush around water at upper elevations too, and we could hear one. It has a very loud, unique call. Being bright yellow, it isn't hard to spot singing in the willows.

There are species of birds that resemble each other so closely - the empidonax flycatchers – that it is necessary to hear them sing to tell them apart. On the other hand, there are species that sound so much like each other, it causes the problem people used to have telling me and my mom apart on the phone.

For example, robin and black-headed grosbeak songs have a clear, babbling quality, but if you listen a lot while the grosbeaks are here during migration, you can tell who is the real robin.

On the Turtle Rock trail, chapter member Don Edington picked out a bird at the tip top of an evergreen, singing away. It was yellow, with black and white wings, like an over-sized goldfinch. Its head had the lightest wash of orangey-red. It was another robin voice impersonator, the western tanager.

Visually, the sparrows are mostly a large brown cloud in my mind. The same can be said for distinguishing, much less remembering, many bird songs. I like birds with easy to remember songs, like the ruby-crowned kinglet, another bird to expect in the forest. It is so tiny, your chances are slim for seeing it on its favorite perches in large spruce trees.

After being inundated by Swainson's thrushes this spring (all completely mute while they inspected our backyard), it was a pleasure to catch the trill of one on the trail. But then I checked it against a recording on Merlin and realized we had the thrush that doesn't trill upwards, but the other, trilling downwards, the hermit thrush.

It does help to study the field guides in advance of seeing a bird species for the first time – just knowing which ones to expect in a certain habitat is helpful. Studying bird songs before venturing into the woods again would be as useful.

I need to crack open that new book by Nathan Pieplow, "Peterson Field Guide to Bird Sounds of Eastern North America," and the corresponding recordings at www.petersonbirdsounds.com.

Except, we'll only find the species we share with eastern North America. We won't find our strictly western bird species until he finishes the western edition. But I could work on his technique for distinguishing songs before I spend too much more time in the woods.

172 Bird-finding betters from generation to generation

When your interest in birds takes you beyond your backyard, you need a guide beyond your bird identification book. That help can come in many forms – from apps and websites to a trail guidebook or local expert.

Noah Strycker needed a bird-finding guide for the whole world for his record-breaking Big Year in 2015. His book, "Birding without Borders," due out Oct. 10, documents his travels to the seven continents to find 6,042 species, more than half the world total.

In it, he thoughtfully considers many bird-related topics, including how technology made his record possible, specifically www.eBird.org. In addition to being a place where you can share your birding records, its "Explore Data" function helps you find birding hotspots, certain birds and even find out who found them. Strycker credits its enormous global data base with his Big Year success.

Another piece of technology equally important was http://birdingpal.org/, a way to connect with fellow enthusiasts who could show him around their own "backyards." Every species he saw during his Big Year was verified by his various travelling companions.

Back in 1968, there was no global data base to help Peter Alden set the world Big Year record. But he only needed to break just over 2,000 species. He helped pioneer international birding tourism through the trips he ran for Massachusetts Audubon. By 1981, he and British birder John Gooders could write "Finding Birds Around the World." Four pages of the nearly 700 are devoted to our own Yellowstone National Park.

When I bumped into Alden at the Mount Auburn Cemetery in Cambridge, Massachusetts, (a birding hotspot) in 2011, he offered to send me an autographed copy for $5. I accepted. However, until I read Strycker's book, I had no idea how famous a birder he was.

As Strycker explains it, interest in international birding, especially since World War II, has kept growing, right along with improved transportation to and within developing countries, which usually have the highest bird diversity. However, some of his cliff-hanging road descriptions would indicate that perhaps sometimes the birders have exceeded the bounds of safe travel.

For the U.S., the Buteo Books website will show you a multitude of American Birding Association "Birdfinding" titles for many states. Oliver Scott authored "A Birder's Guide to Wyoming" for the association in 1992. Robert and Jane Dorn included bird finding notes in the 1999 edition of their book, "Wyoming Birds." Both books are the result of decades of experience.

A variation on the birdfinding book is "the birding trail." The first was in Texas. The book, "Finding Birds on the Great Texas Coastal Birding Trail," enumerates a collection of routes connecting birding sites and includes information like park entrance fees, what amenities are nearby, and what interesting birds you are likely to see. Now you can find bird and wildlife viewing "trails" on the Texas Parks and Wildlife website. Many states are following their example.

People in Wyoming have talked about putting together a birding trail for some years, but it took a birding enthusiast like Zach Hutchinson, a Casper-based community naturalist for Audubon Rockies, to finally get it off the ground.

The good news is that by waiting this long, there are now software companies that have designed birding trail apps. No one needs to print books that soon need updates.

The other good news is that to make it a free app, Hutchinson found sponsors including the Cheyenne–High Plains Audubon Society, Murie Audubon Society (Casper), Wyoming State Parks, and WY Outside – a group of nonprofits and government agencies working to encourage youth and families in Wyoming to spend more time outdoors.

Look for "Wyoming Bird Trail" app on either iTunes or Google Play to install it on your smart phone.

Hutchinson has made a good start. The wonderful thing about the app technology is that not only does it borrow Google Maps so directions don't need to be written, the app information can be easily updated. Users are invited to help.

There is one other way enterprising U.S. birders research birding trips. They contact the local Audubon chapter, perhaps finding a member, like me, who loves an excuse to get out for another birding trip and who will show them around – and make a recommendation for where to have lunch.

173 Kitchen window like a TV peering into lives of birds

Sunday, September 17, 2017, Outdoors, page E4

The view out of our 4-by-6-foot kitchen window is the equivalent of an 85-inch, high-definition television screen.

The daytime programming over the summer has been exceptional this year. Not many murder mysteries, thank goodness, and instead, mostly family dramas.

The robins always seem to get on screen first. Walking flat-footed through our vegetables and flowers, the speckle-breasted young, unlike some human teenagers, kept looking towards the adults for instruction and moral support.

Young birds have this gawky look about them. They have balance issues when they land on the utility line. Or they make a hard landing on a branch. They look around, tilting their heads this way and that. Maybe they are learning to focus.

The first hummingbird of the season showed up July 10, nearly a week earlier than last year. Luckily, their favorite red flower, the Jacob Cline variety of monarda, or beebalm, was blooming two weeks ahead of schedule.

We immediately put the hummingbird feeder up (4 parts water to 1 part white sugar – don't substitute other sugars – boiled together, no red dye, please, but maybe a red ribbon on the feeder). Within a few days we had a hummingbird showing up regularly at breakfast, lunch and dinner – which is when we watch our window TV.

Sometimes we saw three at a time, often two, though by August 25 sightings dropped off. It is difficult to distinguish between rufous and broad-tailed females and juveniles that come. Kind of like trying to keep track of all the characters in a PBS historical drama.

My favorite series this summer was "Father Knows Best." Beginning July 1, a lesser goldfinch male, and sometimes a second one and females, started joining the American goldfinches at our thistle tube feeder.

The lesser goldfinch is the American goldfinch's counterpart in the southwestern U.S., and they are being seen more regularly in southeast Wyoming. They are smaller. Like the American, they are bright yellow with a black cap and black wings, but they also have a black back, although some have greenish backs.

Every day the lesser males showed up, pulling thistle seed from the feeder for minutes at a time. Unlike other seed-eating songbirds which feed their young insects, goldfinches feed their young seeds they've chewed to a pulp. After a couple weeks, we began to wonder if one of them had a nest somewhere.

August 4, the lesser fledglings made their TV debut. The three pestered their dad at the same time. My husband, Mark, got a wonderful photo of the male feeding one of the young. However, within five days the show was over, the young having dispersed.

Year round we have Eurasian collared-doves. I've noticed one has a droopy wing, the tip of which nearly drags on the ground. She and her mate are responsible for the only X-rated content shown on our backyard nature TV – that's how I know the droopy-winged bird is female.

One morning outside I noticed a scattering of thin sticks on the grass and looked up. I saw the sketchy (as in a drawing of a few lines) nest on a branch of one of our green ash trees, with the dove sitting on it. Every time I went out, I would check and there she was, suspended over our heads, listening in on all our conversations, watching us mow and garden.

Then one day I heard a frantic banging around where Mark had stacked the hail guards for our garden. It was a young dove. It had blown out of the nest during the night's rainstorm. The sketchy (as in unreliable) nest had failed.

The presence of the trapped squab, half the size of an adult, would explain the behavior of the mother nearby who had been so agitated that she attracted our dog's attention.

I put the dog in the house and went to extract the young bird. It didn't move as I approached and scooped it up. There is something magical about holding a wild bird, even one belonging to a species that has invaded our neighborhoods, sometimes at the expense of the native mourning dove. So soft, so plump. I set it down inside the fenced-off flower garden. Later, I checked and it was gone.

Within a few days, Droopy-wing and her mate were involved in another X-rated performance. Then I noticed one of them fly by with a slender stick. Sure enough, two days later she was back on her rehabbed throne, incubating the next generation.

174

Sunday, October 15, 2017, Outdoors, page E4

Project FeederWatch tells us a lot about juncos and our backyard birds

Despite snow on the ground and pea soup fog at South Gap Lake in the Snowy Range (11,120 feet elevation), on Sept. 27 I saw a flock of dark-eyed juncos. They like snow. I should see the first ones down in my yard mid-October, when alpine winter conditions get too rough.

Juncos are those little gray birds that come in five subspecies and multiple hybrid colorations in Cheyenne, but they all have white outer tail feathers. They are my sign of the start of the winter bird feeding season – and the Project FeederWatch bird counting season.

Project FeederWatch is a citizen science opportunity for people with bird feeders to count the birds they attract as often as once a week (or less) between November and early April. Begun in Canada in 1976 and in the U.S. in 1987, more than 20,000 people participated last year. The data is used in scientific studies, many of which are summarized on the project's website.

Participation costs $18. You receive a research kit, bird identification poster, the digital version of Living Bird magazine and the year-end report.

If you feed wild birds or are considering it, you must visit the Project FeederWatch site, whether you register for the program or not. It is now beautifully designed and packed with information.

For instance, in the "Learn" section, I find juncos prefer black-oil sunflower seeds – and seven other kinds. I stick with black-oil because it's popular with many species in Cheyenne. I also learn juncos prefer hopper-style feeders, platform feeders or feeding on the ground.

Seventy-one species are listed as potential feeder birds in the Northwest region, which stretches from British Columbia to Wyoming. However, about 17 of those species have yet to be seen in Cheyenne, so click on the "All About Birds" link to check a species' actual range.

The Project FeederWatch website addresses every question I can think of regarding wild bird feeding:

--Grit and water provision

--Feeder cleaning

--Predator avoidance

--Squirrel exclusion

--Window strike reduction

--Sick birds

--Tricky identification, like hairy vs downy woodpecker.

In "Community" section you'll find the results of last season's photo contest, participants' other photos, featured participants, tips, FAQs, the blog, and the FeederWatch cam.

I find the "Explore" section

fascinating. This is where you can investigate the data yourself. The "Map Room" shows where juncos like to winter best.

Based on last season's data, in the far north region of Canada, juncos were number 12 in abundance at feeders. In the southeastern U.S., they were number 13. However, in the southwest, which has a lot of cold high elevations, they were number two, as they were in the northeast region, and number three in the central region, the northern Great Plains. Here in the northwest region, they were number one. We have perfect junco winter conditions, not too cold, not too warm.

However, looking at the top 25 species for Wyoming in the same 2016-2017 season (based on percent of sites visited and the average flock size), juncos came in fifth, after house sparrow, house finch, goldfinch and black-capped chickadee. Other years, especially between the seasons beginning in 2007 and 2013, they have been number one.

I looked at my own Project Feeder-Watch data to see if I could spot any dark-eyed junco trends.

I get in 18-20 weekly counts per year. In the past 18 years, there were three years when the juncos missed none or only one of the weeks, in 2001, 2005 and 2008. Those seasons also happened to be the largest average flock sizes, 8.65 to 9.72 birds per flock.

Later, there were three seasons in which juncos came up missing six or seven weeks, 2011, 2013 and 2016. Two of those were the seasons of the smallest average flock sizes, 1.6 to 2.5 birds per flock.

It appears my local junco population was in a downward trend between 2008 and 2016. Let's hope it's a cycle. Or maybe our yard's habitat has changed or there are more hawks or cats scaring the juncos away. Or some weeks it's too warm in town and they go back to the mountains.

One yard does not make a city-wide trend, but we won't know what the trend is unless more people in Cheyenne participate.

How many FeederWatchers are there in Cheyenne? We've had as many as four, back in 1999-2004, but lately there's only been one or two of us. Statewide, Wyoming averages 25 participants per year.

If you sign up, you'll have your own red dot on the map (but your identity won't be publicized). I hope you'll become a FeederWatcher this season.

175

Sunday, November 12, 2017, Outdoors, page E4

Wyoming's greater sage-grouse conservation plan is in jeopardy

Wyoming successfully addressed the sage grouse issue through a collaboration of state and local government, sportsmen, conservationists, the oil and gas industry, and agricultural interests.

Over six years, the state was able to draw up a plan to establish protected core areas of habitat. Good habitat is the best protection for this species which has declined 30 percent across the west since 1985.

The plan leaves a large majority of Wyoming open to oil and gas and other development.

In 2015, the U.S. Fish and Wildlife Service said state plans across the west were good enough that it wouldn't start proceedings to list the sage grouse as threatened or endangered.

Here in Wyoming, the Sage-Grouse Implementation Team, headed by Bob Budd, is working hard. The team represents all the previous collaborators.

However, the new federal administration is intent on dismantling anything that happened under the previous president. It tasked new U.S. Department of Interior secretary Ryan Zinke with reviewing all state sage grouse plans to either toss them or amend them.

None of the collaborators on Wyoming's plan are happy with this – including the oil and gas people who desire certainty for their business plans. Wyoming Governor Matt Mead is not happy either.

I went to the Bureau of Land Management's public meeting November 6 in Cheyenne to find out more about the proposed amendments to Wyoming's plan.

I heard these criticisms:

--Switching to using sage grouse population numbers to determine an oil and gas producer's ability to drill and plan for mitigation (more sage grouse, more leniency) would leave companies with a lot of unwanted uncertainty. Sage grouse numbers vary enormously from year to year due to weather and other natural effects.

--Basing conservation plans on sage grouse population numbers rather than habitat would discount the 350-plus other species that depend on the sagebrush ecosystem, including 22 "species of conservation concern."

--Messing around with the plan could cause U.S. Fish and Wildlife to decide the sage grouse warrants listing after all. That would close much more land to oil and gas drilling, as well as coal mining and other mineral extraction.

--The current Republican administration thinks states should have more say in issues like this, and the six years of collaboration Wyoming went through is a perfect example of how it can happen. Ironically, it's the Republicans in Washington who now decree they know what is best for us.

--Wyoming's conservation plan has been in effect for only two years, which is not enough time to gauge success. Instituting major changes now would cost a lot of taxpayer money that could be better spent in the field.

BLM invites us to comment during their scoping process. They want to know if we think they should amend the management plans that were developed by the states to protect sage grouse.

They don't make it easy, says my husband, a retired BLM wildlife biologist.

Go to http://bit.ly/GRSGplanning (case-sensitive). Click on "Documents and Reports." This will give you a list of documents. Only "GRSG Notice of Intent" is available for commenting. "GRSG" is ornithological shorthand using initial letters of the parts of the bird's common name.

After you read the document, click on "Comment on Document." You'll have to fill in the title of the document you are commenting on: "GRSG Notice of Intent." And then you have 60 minutes to finish the procedure or everything you've written disappears. You may want to compose your comments elsewhere and then paste them in.

The deadline for comments is either Nov. 27 or Nov. 30 – there's a discrepancy in BLM's handouts from the public meeting. Go with the earlier date if you can.

To educate yourself before commenting, you can visit the Wyoming State BLM office in Cheyenne, 5353 Yellowstone Road, or contact them at 307-775-6259.

But if you are most interested in what is best for sage grouse, it may be easier to jump to the analysis provided by conservation groups like the National Audubon Society, www.audubon.org/sage-grouse. The former Audubon Wyoming executive director Brian Rutledge was instrumental in the Wyoming collaboration and is still involved as NAS's director of the Sagebrush Ecosystem Initiative.

Two other interested groups are Wyoming Wildlife Federation, http://wyomingwildlife.org/, and the Wyoming Outdoor Council, https://wyomingoutdoorcouncil.org/.

All three organizations offer simple digital form letters that can be personalized, and they will send them to BLM. However, BLM says it gives more credence to comments sent via their own online form.

I hope you can take a few minutes to put in a good word for the bird that maybe should be our state mascot.

Next month I'll look at what the Wyoming State Legislature did last session that may also negatively affect sage grouse.

2018

176 How well do birds tolerate people?

Every soaring bird I saw in early February along 1,300 miles of interstate highway between Nashville, Tennessee, and Fort Lauderdale, Florida, was a black vulture or turkey vulture.

However, near Vero Beach, Florida, where we were visiting Cheyenne snowbirds Karen and Fred Pannell, there was a black bird of a different shape, a magnificent frigatebird, a life bird for both me and my husband, Mark.

But about those vultures. Were they really more abundant along the interstate than away from it? Were they waiting for roadkill? We passed a couple landfill "mountains" that were big vulture magnets, too.

We think wild birds go about their lives oblivious to people, or at least avoiding us. Except for birds coming to feeders. Or ducks at the park looking for handouts. Or Canada geese that enjoy eating the grass on park lawns and the leftover grain in farmers' fields.

We know that some human activities are detrimental to birds. But how many are beneficial to them? Chimney swifts have experienced both. We took down the old hollow trees they used to build their nests in, and they moved into our chimneys.

The speaker at February's Cheyenne – High Plains Audubon Society meeting, Cameron Nordell, relayed interesting research results on nesting ferruginous hawks and their reactions to people that could answer some of those questions. Nordell, Raptor Fellow at the University of Wyoming Biodiversity Institute, is with the Wyoming Raptor Initiative.

In his previous work in southern Alberta, Canada, Nordell and his colleagues experimented in part to see at what distance hawks would flush from their nests as researchers approached by vehicle or on foot to check the nests for other aspects of the study.

Southern Alberta is a mix of agriculture, oil and gas and other development. The farmers and homeowners have planted trees on the prairie and the ferruginous hawks have found them to be great for nesting – they are a ground-nesting hawk otherwise. The trees give them better protection from predators.

However, along with people came another species that climbs trees and raids nests: racoons. Barns and other structures have helped increase the population of great horned owls and they too prey on the nestlings.

Ferruginous hawks nesting near the busiest roads were more tolerant than birds that had not seen as much traffic.

Approaching vehicles were tolerated better than approaching people.

Raptors have been shown to hang out by roads, looking for injured prey species. The problem is that they risk getting hit by vehicles, too.

The Wyoming Raptor Initiative (see https://wyomingbiodiversity.org/Initiatives-Programs) wants to understand the state's raptors better, including the road problem. It has two goals:

"To synthesize our scientific understanding of raptors in Wyoming so that the public, scientists, land managers and energy companies will be better informed in developing and implementing future conservation strategies and land mitigation efforts.

"To foster appreciation of raptors in Wyoming and the world through education and outreach efforts."

Nordell and his colleagues will be looking at previous studies of raptors in Wyoming, gathering more data, talking to all kinds of people to get more information, and then they'll relay what they learn.

What will they discover about Wyoming's ferruginous hawks, for instance?

What human activities help them or harm them?

Nordell also studied arctic peregrine falcons near Hudson Bay, where there were few direct human impacts. However, the weather was ferocious. Too much rain, and a young bird, poorly nourished, could succumb to the cold rainwater collecting in the cliff-face nest. Better-fed youngsters had better survival rates.

The next questions: What affects the availability of peregrine prey species and the peregrine parents' ability to bring food back to the nest? Is there any human influence on their success? Are humans linked in any way to that Arctic location getting demonstrably rainier?

What will be discovered about peregrines in Wyoming? I watched one nail a duck on a ranch reservoir just outside Cheyenne once. The human-made lake attracted the peregrine's food target – southeastern Wyoming doesn't have many natural water bodies.

I look forward to answers from the Wyoming Raptor Initiative. I'm sure they will also discover many more questions.

177 Keep birds safe this time of year

Sunday, May 6, 2018, Outdoors, page E6

It's that time of year that we need to think about bird safety – migration and nesting season.

The peak of spring migration in Cheyenne is around mid-May. If you have a clean window that reflects sky, trees and other greenery, you'll get a few avian visitors bumping into it. Consider applying translucent stickers to the outside of the window or search online for American Bird Conservancy's Bird Tape.

If a bird hits your window, make sure your cat is not out there picking it up.

The bird may only be stunned. If necessary, put the bird somewhere safe where it can fly off when it recovers.

How efficient is your outdoor lighting? In addition to wasting money, excessive light confuses birds that migrate at night. Cheyenne keeps getting brighter and brighter at night because people, especially businesses with parking lots, install lighting that shines up as well as down. It is also unhealthy for trees and other vegetation, not to mention people trying to get a good night's sleep.

Do you have nest boxes? Get them

cleaned out before new families move in. Once the birds move in or you find a nest elsewhere, do you know the proper protocol for observing it?

If not, you might be interested in NestWatch, https://nestwatch.org/, a Cornell Lab of Ornithology citizen science program for reporting nesting success.

Their Nest Monitoring Manual says to avoid checking the nest in the morning when the birds are busy, or at dusk when predators are out. Wait until afternoon. Walk past the nest rather than up to it and back, leaving a scent trail pointing predators straight to the nest. And avoid bird nests when the young are close to fledging (when they have most of their feathers). We don't want them to get agitated and leave the nest prematurely.

Some birds are "flightier" than others. Typically, birds nesting alongside human activity – like the robins that built the nest on top of your porch light – are not going to abandon the nest if you come by. Rather, they will be attacking you. But a hawk in a more remote setting will not tolerate people. Back off and get out your spotting scope or your big camera lenses.

If your presence causes a young songbird to jump out of the nest, you can try putting it back in. NestWatch says to hold your hand or a light piece of fabric over the top of the nest until the young bird calms down so it doesn't jump again. Often though, the parents will take care of young that leave the nest prematurely.

Loose cats and dogs should also be controlled on the prairie between April and July – and mowing avoided. That is because we have ground-nesting birds here on the edge of the Great Plains such as western meadowlark, horned lark and sometimes the ferruginous hawk.

There will always be young birds that run into trouble, either natural or human-aided. Every wild animal eventually ends up being somebody else's dinner. But if you decide to help an injured animal, be sure the animal won't injure you. For instance, black-crowned night-herons will try to stab your eyes. It is also illegal to possess wild animals without a permit so call a licensed wildlife rehabilitator like the Cheyenne Pet Clinic or the Wyoming Game and Fish Department, 307-777-4600.

Avoid treating your landscape with pesticides. The insect pest dying from toxic chemicals you spread could poison the bird that eats it. Instead, think of pest species as bird food. Or at least check with the University of Wyoming Extension office, 307-633-4383, for other ways to protect your lawn and vegetables.

Are you still feeding birds? We take our seed feeders down in the summer because otherwise the heat and moisture make dangerous stuff grow in them if you don't clean them every few days. Most seed-eating birds are looking for insects to feed their young anyway. Keep your birdbaths clean, too.

However, we put up our hummingbird feeder when we see the first fall migrants show up in our yard mid-July, though they prefer my red beebalm and other bright tubular flowers.

Make sure your hummingbird feeder has bright red on it. Don't add red dye to the nectar, though. The only formula that is good for hummingbirds is one part white sugar to four parts water boiled together. Don't substitute any other sweeteners as they will harm the birds. If the nectar in the feeder gets cloudy after a few days, replace it with a fresh batch.

And finally, think about planting for birds. Check out the Habitat Hero information at Audubon Rockies.

Enjoy the bird-full season!

178 Bird counting

The Cheyenne – High Plains Audubon Society has been holding an annual Big Day Bird Count at the height of spring migration since at least 1956 (see more at https://cheyennebirdbanter. wordpress.com). But this year we essentially did two counts five days apart.

It started with birder and author Noah Strycker visiting mid-May to give a talk at the library about his 2015 record-breaking global Big Year (6,042 species) and his book, "Birding Without Borders." He had the next day free, May 15, before heading for another speaking engagement. Naturally, we volunteered to take him birding.

He said since he'd never been to Wyoming before, he wanted to see 100 species. I enlisted the help of Bob and Jane Dorn, authors of "Wyoming Birds," and Greg Johnson, also a chapter member, whose global bird life list is just over 3,000 species.

An ambitious route was mapped out, starting at 6 a.m. with a couple of hours at the Wyoming Hereford Ranch, then Lions Park, onto Pole Mountain and over to Hutton Lake National Wildlife Refuge and the other Laramie Plains lakes. This would be followed by a drive down Sybille Canyon over to the state wildlife areas and reservoirs on the North Platte.

Thirty-six people signed up in advance for the field trip. Most couldn't come for the whole day, including the two birders from Jackson, three from Lander, one from Gillette and four from Colorado. By dinnertime, there were only 10 of us left.

After the Laramie Plains Lakes, we'd only made it to Laramie and Strycker had seen 118 species, so we had dinner there and returned to Cheyenne by 8

p.m. The day before he saw a life bird in Colorado on the way up from the airport – the lark bunting, Colorado's state bird. The day after the field trip, Johnson took him to see another life bird, the sharp-tailed grouse, on the way back.

Somehow the carpooling worked out – ten vehicles at the most. Strycker rode at the front of the caravan with the Dorns and saw birds the rest of us didn't. That's the way it is with road birding. But even on foot at the ranch, 30-some people didn't see all the same birds.

It was a beautiful day – not much wind – and we dodged all the rain showers. Strycker is welcome back anytime.

The following Saturday lived up to its terrible forecast so Johnson rescheduled our regular Cheyenne Big Day Bird Count for the next day, May 20, when it finally warmed up a bit and stopped raining.

Only eight of us showed up at 6:30 a.m. and represented a wide spectrum of birding experience. We searched Lions Park thoroughly, then the Wyoming Hereford Ranch and the High Plains Grasslands Research Station (permit required) – very little driving. I think we had about 80 species by 3 p.m. Four other people were birding the local area as well.

The final Big Day tally was 113. Not bad, considering we stayed within a 15-mile-diameter circle centered on the Capitol – essentially our Christmas Bird Count circle. That's consistent with recent years.

Ted Floyd, the American Birding Association's magazine editor (who birded at the ranch with Strycker, his associate editor) and I have discussed whether a birder will see more birds on their own or with a group.

Floyd birds by ear, so not having a lot of people-noise works for him. For me, I appreciate the greater number of eyeballs a group has – often looking in multiple directions – and the willingness of people to point out what they are seeing. Presumably, a group of 30 birders sees more than a group of eight.

However, the larger group may be looking at several interesting birds simultaneously, making it hard to keep up.

But there's nothing much more enjoyable in spring than joining gatherings of birds and birders, or any time of year. Look for Cheyenne Audubon's field trip schedule at https://cheyenneaudubon.wordpress.com/.

Cheyenne Big Days compared

The 119 birds with an "N" before their name were seen by Noah Strycker in southeastern Wyoming May 15. Additional birds he saw are marked *. The 113 birds with a "B" were counted in the Cheyenne area on the Cheyenne Big Day Bird Count May 20. The combined list has 145 species.

N B	Canada Goose	
N B	Wood Duck	
N B	Blue-winged Teal	
N B	Cinnamon Teal	
N B	Northern Shoveler	
N B	Gadwall	
N	American Wigeon	
N B	Mallard	
B	Northern Pintail	
N	Green-winged Teal	
N	Canvasback	
N B	Redhead	
N	Ring-necked Duck	
N B	Lesser Scaup	
N B	Ruddy Duck	
N*	Sharp-tailed Grouse	
N B	Pied-billed Grebe	
N B	Eared Grebe	
N B	Western Grebe	
B	Clark's Grebe	
N B	Double-crested Cormorant	
N B	American White Pelican	
N B	Great Blue Heron	
B	Great Egret	
N B	Black-crowned Night-Heron	
N B	White-faced Ibis	
N B	Turkey Vulture	
B	Osprey	
N B	Golden Eagle	
N	Northern Harrier	
N	Sharp-shinned Hawk	
N B	Cooper's Hawk	

N B	Bald Eagle	
N B	Swainson's Hawk	
N B	Red-tailed Hawk	
N	Ferruginous Hawk	
N	Sora	
N B	American Coot	
N	Sandhill Crane	
N	Black-necked Stilt	
N B	American Avocet	
N B	Killdeer	
N	Least Sandpiper	
N	Long-billed Dowitcher	
B	Wilson's Snipe	
N B	Wilson's Phalarope	
N B	Spotted Sandpiper	
N	Willet	
N	Lesser Yellowlegs	
N B	Ring-billed Gull	
N	California Gull	
N B	Black Tern	
N B	Forster's Tern	
N B	Rock Pigeon	
N B	Eurasian Collared-Dove	
N*	White-winged Dove	
N B	Mourning Dove	
N B	Eastern Screech-Owl	
N B	Great Horned Owl	
B	Chimney Swift	
B	Broad-tailed Hummingbird	
N B	Belted Kingfisher	
B	Red-headed Woodpecker	
N B	Downy Woodpecker	

N Hairy Woodpecker
B Northern Flicker
N B American Kestrel
N B Western Wood Pewee
N Least Flycatcher
N Dusky Flycatcher
N B Cordilleran Flycatcher
N B Say's Phoebe
N B Western Kingbird
N B Eastern Kingbird
B Warbling Vireo
N B Blue Jay
N B Black-billed Magpie
N B American Crow
N B Common Raven
N B Horned Lark
N B Northern Rough-winged Swallow
N B Tree Swallow
B Violet-green Swallow
N B Bank Swallow
N B Barn Swallow
N B Cliff Swallow
B Black-capped Chickadee
N B Mountain Chickadee
N B Red-breasted Nuthatch
N B House Wren
N Marsh Wren
B Blue-gray Gnatcatcher
N B Ruby-crowned Kinglet
N Mountain Bluebird
B Townsend's Solitaire
N B Swainson's Thrush
B Hermit Thrush
N B American Robin
N B Gray Catbird
B Brown Thrasher
N B Sage Thrasher
N B European Starling
N McCown's Longspur
N* Ovenbird
N* Tennessee Warbler

N B Orange-crowned Warbler
B MacGillivray's Warbler
N B Common Yellowthroat
N B American Redstart
N Northern Parula
N B Yellow Warbler
B Chestnut-sided Warbler
N Blackpoll Warbler
N B Yellow-rumped Warbler
B Wilson's Warbler
N Grasshopper Sparrow
N B Chipping Sparrow
N B Clay-colored Sparrow
N B Brewer's Sparrow
N B Lark Sparrow
N B Lark Bunting
N Dark-eyed Junco
N B White-crowned Sparrow
N B Vesper Sparrow
N B Savannah Sparrow
N B Song Sparrow
N Lincoln's Sparrow
N Green-tailed Towhee
B Western Tanager
N Black-headed Grosbeak
B Lazuli Bunting
N B Yellow-headed Blackbird
N B Western Meadowlark
B Orchard Oriole
N B Bullock's Oriole
N B Red-winged Blackbird
N B Brown-headed Cowbird
N B Brewer's Blackbird
N B Common Grackle
B Great-tailed Grackle
B Evening Grosbeak
N B House Finch
N B Pine Siskin
N B American Goldfinch
N B House Sparrow

179

Burrowing owls materialize on SE Wyoming grasslands

Burrowing owls were like avian unicorns for me until this spring. Mark, my husband, and I searched prairie dog towns in southeastern Wyoming to no avail.

It wasn't always like that. Fifteen years ago, there was a spot on the east edge of Cheyenne guaranteed to produce a sighting for the Cheyenne Audubon Big Day Bird Count. But the area around it got more and more built up.

I did some research through my subscription to Birds of North America, https://birdsna.org, and discovered burrowing owls don't require complete wilderness.

These owls are diurnal – they are active during the day, most active at dawn and dusk. However, when the males have young to feed, they hunt 24/7.

The eggs are laid in old animal burrows, primarily those of prairie dogs. Because prairie dogs live in colonies, the burrowing owls tend to appear in groups, too, though much smaller. Besides nesting burrows, they have roosting burrows for protection from predators. They stockpile prey in both kinds of burrows in anticipation of feeding young. One cache described in a Saskatchewan study had 210 meadow voles and two deer mice.

Western burrowing owls, from southwestern Canada to southwestern U.S., winter in Central and South America. However, there are year-round populations in parts of California, southernmost Arizona and New Mexico and western Texas and on south. But there is also a subspecies of the owl that lives in Florida and the Caribbean year round. They excavate their own burrows.

Burrowing owls breed in the open, treeless grasslands. No one is sure why, but they like to line their nesting burrows with dung from livestock. They, along with their prairie dog neighbors, appreciate how grazing animals keep the grass short. It's easier to see approaching predators.

The owls' biggest natural nest predator is the badger. Both young and adults can scare predators away from their burrows by giving a call that imitates a rattlesnake's rattle.

Short grass means it's easier to catch prey by walking or hopping on the ground as well as flying. Burrowing owls also like being near agricultural fields.

The fields attract their primary prey species: grasshoppers, crickets, moths, beetles, in addition to small mammals like mice, voles and shrews.

You would think these owls are ranchers' and farmers' best friends. However, in the Birds of North America's human impacts list are wind turbines, barbed wire, vehicle collisions, pesticides and shooting. I'm surprised by shooting.

Since western burrowing owls can't be blamed for making the holes in pastures (they only renovate and maintain burrows by kicking out dirt), I can only surmise that varmint hunters have bad eyesight and can't tell an owl from a prairie dog. It could be an easy mistake: Owls are nearly the color and size of prairie dogs and have similar round heads. Except the owls stand on long skinny legs. From a distance the owls look like prairie dogs hovering over the burrow's mound – and then if you watch long enough, they fly.

Burrowing owls have been in sharp decline since the 1960s despite laying 6 to 12 eggs per nest. The Burrowing Owl Conservation Network, http://burrowingowlconservation.org, reports the U.S. Fish and Wildlife Service lists them as "a Bird of Conservation Concern at the national level, in three USFWS regions, and in nine Bird Conservation Regions. At the state level, burrowing owls are listed as endangered in Minnesota, threatened in Colorado, and as a Species of Concern in Arizona, California, Florida, Montana, Oklahoma, Oregon, Utah, Washington, and Wyoming."

In our state, Grant Frost, Wyoming Game and Fish Department wildlife biologist, said "(burrowing owls) are what we classify as a species of greatest conservation need (SGCN), but mostly due to a lack of information, their status is unknown. That is why these surveys were started three years ago. There are 15 surveys being done throughout the state in potential habitat ... each survey route is done three times each year during set times to occur during each of the three nesting stages – pre-incubation, incubation/hatching, and nestling."

When Grant said he could lead an Audubon field trip to see the owls and other prairie birds, 15 of us jumped at the chance.

As might be predicted from the BNA summary of the literature, the owls were in the middle of an agricultural setting of fields and pastures. We watched them hunt around a flock of sheep and enjoy the view from the tops of fence posts along an irrigation canal.

The first sightings of the morning were distant – hard to see even with a spotting scope. But as we departed for home, driving a little farther down the road, two burrowing owls appeared much closer, and we all felt finally that we could say we'd seen them and not just flying brown smudges.

180 Condor visits Wyoming. Next one needs to find steel instead of lead

Sunday, August 19, 2018, Outdoors, page E2

Exciting news in the Wyoming bird-watching community: A California condor, North America's largest raptor with 9 ½-foot wingspan, was sighted July 7 west of Laramie perched on Medicine Bow Peak. The reporting birder was Nathan Pieplow. He is the author of the Peterson guide to bird sounds. Maybe he recorded it.

Wing tags printed with a big T2 declared this was a female condor hatched and raised in 2016 at the Portland, Oregon, zoo and released in March at the Vermilion Cliffs National Monument in northern Arizona.

Several people from the Laramie Audubon chapter climbed up to see the condor. Brian Waitkus got excellent photos.

Medicine Bow Peak, elevation 12,014 feet, is a popular destination for hikers who want a challenge including lightning and boulder fields. As many as a dozen hikers were congregating near the condor July 9. The condor didn't mind people but was flushed by three dogs off leash, observed Murie Audubon president Zach Hutchinson.

T2 was one of many condors released into the wild by the Peregrine Fund working to re-establish the population of this officially endangered species. In 1982, there were only 22 birds left. Today there are 500, half flying free in Arizona, Utah, California and Baja Mexico. Some are now breeding in the wild. For more, read "Condors in Canyon Country" by Sophie A. H. Osborn and https://www.peregrinefund.org/.

The distance between the Arizona release site and the peak is only 440 miles as the condor flies, not difficult for a bird that can travel 200 miles per day. T2 was spotted earlier, on June 28, near Roosevelt, Utah.

The closest previous Wyoming condor sighting was 1998, in Utah at Flaming Gorge Reservoir, which spans the Utah-Wyoming line.

T2's visit was brief. A Peregrine Fund researcher following the condor using telemetry later got the signal 30 miles away indicating the bird was not moving. By the time he arrived, the bird was dead. It's been sent to the U.S. Fish and Wildlife Service for autopsy. Foul play was not suspected.

Serendipitously, soon after the first news broke about T2, Chris Parish, director of global conservation for the Peregrine Fund, was about to drop his daughter off in Laramie. He offered to give a talk on condors sponsored by the Laramie Audubon Society and the University of Wyoming Biodiversity Institute.

In his presentation, Chris touched briefly on the history of restoring the condor population.

Condors are tough. They survived the large mammal extinction 10,000 years ago. However, they are slow to reproduce, only one chick every two years. At propagation centers, experts can get a pair to lay an extra egg to put in an incubator.

Condors live 50-60 years by avoiding predators and finding new habitat. A few are still being shot, despite condors being as harmless as turkey vultures, eating only carrion – already dead animals. They fly into powerlines and get hit by vehicles, too.

The biggest problem for condors is poisoning from lead ammunition, Chris said. When a deer is shot, the bullet disintegrates into hundreds of fragments. Often, the fragments are in the gut pile, or offal, that hunters leave in the field. Offal is the condor's main dish.

All those little lead fragments add up and eventually cause lead poisoning. Some of those lead fragments also find their way into game meat people eat. Researchers try to check the blood lead levels of all free-flying condors once a year and treat them, if necessary, before releasing them again.

Our national symbol, the bald eagle, also feeds on carcasses. In 1991, lead shot for waterfowl hunting was banned, but upland animals – and birds like the eagle – are not protected.

A few years ago, the Arizona Game and Fish Department asked hunters on the Kaibab Plateau, where condors are released, to voluntarily use steel ammunition or to remove offal. They offered each participant two free boxes of steel ammunition. Participation is now at 87 percent. A similar program is nearly as successful in Utah. California has banned lead ammunition since 2008, said Chris.

The Peregrine Fund holds shooting trials and gives away steel ammunition for hunters to test. Chris, a lifelong hunter, spouts ballistic statistics with ease.

The bottom line is lead and steel ammunition of comparable quality are nearly the same cost. However, manufacturers need encouragement to offer more variety.

Chris also said, yes, steel ammunition takes a little practice for the hunter to become proficient with it, but practice is required any time a hunter switches to the same caliber ammunition made by a different manufacturer.

Steel bullets aren't silver bullets for all wildlife problems. But maybe Wyoming can join the steel states.

That way we'll make it safer here when more condors show up.

181 Can you ID that bird?

Sunday, October 14, 2018, Outdoors, page E2

Cheyenne bird book coming in late October

I'm very good at procrastinating. How about you? But I've discovered there are some advantages.

From 2008-10, I wrote "Bird of the Week" blurbs for the Wyoming Tribune Eagle to run in those sky boxes at the top of the To Do section pages. But they needed photos.

I asked one of the Wyobirds e-list subscribers from Cheyenne, Pete Arnold. Pete invites people to join his own e-list, where he shares his amazing bird photos. He generously agreed.

Using the checklist of local birds prepared by Jane Dorn and Greg Johnson for the Cheyenne - High Plains Audubon Society, I chose 104 of the most common species and set to work figuring out which weeks to assign them to. Pete perused his photos and was able to match about 90 percent.

We eventually met in person – at Holliday Park. Pete stopped on his way to work one morning to snap waterfowl photos and I was walking a friend's dog and counting birds. We discovered we have several mutual friends.

By the time our two-year project was over, I'd heard about making print-on-demand books, uploading files via internet for a company to make into a book. I rashly promised Pete I'd make a book of our collaboration. After the paper published BOW, I had all the rest of the rights to the text. And I've had college courses in editing and publishing.

Here's where my procrastination comes in. Over the next six years, my family had three graduations, three weddings, three funerals and two households to disassemble, not to mention my husband Mark retired and wanted to travel more.

Finally, a couple years ago, I gave print-on-demand a trial run through Amazon, designing my small book about quilt care. I realized then the bird book would be beyond my talents and software. I considered learning InDesign but also started looking for a professional.

I discovered, through the social media site LinkedIn, that Tina Worthman designed books in her spare time. We'd started talking when she got the job as director of the Cheyenne Botanic Gardens. No more spare time.

However, Tina recommended Chris Hoffmeister and her company, Western Sky Design. What a great match – she's a birder! I didn't have to worry about her mismatching photo and text. And she could speak to Pete about image properties and other technicalities.

The book features a 6 x 6-inch image of each bird. Chris asked Pete to provide bigger image sizes, since the small ones he'd used for the paper would be fuzzy. He also had to approve all the cropping into the square format. But the upside of my procrastination is he had more photos to choose from.

There were still a few species Pete didn't have and so we put out a call on Wyobirds. We got help from Elizabeth Boehm, Jan Backstrom and Mark Gorges.

Meanwhile, even though the WTE features editor at the time, Kevin Wingert, had originally edited BOW, I sent my text for each species and all the other parts of the book (introduction, acknowledgements, word from the photographer, bird checklist, resources list) to Jane Dorn, co-author of the book "Wyoming Birds." Another friend, Jeananne Wright, a former technical writer and editor, and non-birder, caught a few ambiguities and pointed out where I'd left non-birders wondering what I meant.

The title of the book was the last step. Instead of naming it Bird of the Week, two years' worth of bird images and written bird impressions/trivia are organized differently. The title is "Cheyenne Birds by the Month, 104 Species of Southeastern Wyoming's Resident and Visiting Birds."

The book is being printed by local company PBR Printing – print-on-demand is too expensive for multiple copies.

While the book will be available late October at the Wyoming State Museum and other local outlets, our major marketing partner is the Cheyenne Botanic Gardens, a natural fit since it is in the middle of Lions Park, a state Important Bird Area.

The Gardens will have the book available at their gift shop and at two book signings they are hosting: Tuesday, Nov. 20, 11:30 a.m. – 1 p.m. and Sunday, Dec. 9, 1 – 3 p.m., 710 S. Lions Park Dr.

You can get a sneak peak, and Pete's behind the camera stories, at our presentation for Cheyenne Audubon at 7 p.m. Oct. 16, in the Cottonwood Room at the Laramie County Library, 2200 Pioneer Ave.

For more information about the book and updates on where to find it, see Yucca Road Press, https://yucca-roadpress.com/.

It took part of a village to make this book and we are hoping the whole village will enjoy reading it.

2019

182 Careful what you wish for

Wind development on the Belvoir Ranch has its downsides

This month marks the 20th anniversary of my first Bird Banter column for the Wyoming Tribune Eagle. I wrote about cool birds seen on the ponds at the Rawhide coal-powered plant 20 miles south of Cheyenne.

This month's topic is also connected to Rawhide. It's NextEra's 120-turbine Roundhouse Wind Energy Center slated partly for the City of Cheyenne's Belvoir Ranch.

Roundhouse will stretch between I-80 south to the Wyoming border and from a couple miles west of I-25 and on west 12 miles to Harriman Road. The Belvoir is within. It's roughly a 2- to 3-mile-wide frame on the north and west sides. All the power will go to Rawhide and tie into Front Range utilities.

The 2008 Belvoir masterplan designated an area for wind turbines. In the last 10 years, I've learned about wind energy drawbacks. I wish the coal industry had spent millions developing clean air technology instead of fighting clean air regulations.

We know modern wind turbines are tough on birds. Duke Energy has a robotic system that shuts down turbines when raptors approach. Roundhouse needs one – a raptor migration corridor exists along the north-south escarpment along its west edge.

But in Kenn Kaufman's new book, "A Season on the Wind," he discovers that a windfarm far from known migration hot spots still killed at least 40 species of birds. Directly south of the Belvoir, 125 bird species have been documented through eBird at Soapstone Prairie Natural Area and 95 at Red Mountain Open Space. Both are in Colorado, butting against the state line.

Only a few miles to the east, Cheyenne hotspots vary from 198 species at Lions Park to 266 at Wyoming Hereford Ranch, with as many as 150 species overall observed on single days in May. With little public access to the Belvoir since the city bought it in 2003 (I've been there on two tours and the 2016 Bioblitz), only NextEra has significant bird data, from its consultants.

There are migrating bats to consider, plus mule deer who won't stomach areas close to turbines – even if it is their favorite mountain mahogany habitat on the ridges. The Wyoming Game and Fish Department can only suggest mitigation and monitoring measures.

There are human safety and liability issues. The Friends of the Belvoir wants a trailhead on the west edge with trails connecting to Red Mountain and Soapstone. Wind turbines don't bother them.

However, during certain atmospheric conditions, large sheets of ice fly off the blades – "ice throw." Our area, the hail capital, could have those conditions develop nearly any month of the year.

The noise will impact neighbors (and wildlife too) when turbines a mile away interfere with sleep. Disrupted sleep is implicated in many diseases.

Low frequency pulses felt 6 miles away (the distance between the east end of the windfarm and city limits) or more cause dizziness, tinnitus, heart palpitations and pressure sensations in the head and chest. The Belvoir will have bigger turbines than those on Happy Jack Road, reaching 499 feet high, 99 feet higher.

A minor issue is the viewshed. In Colorado, the public and officials worked to place the transmission line from the Belvoir to Rawhide so that it wouldn't impact Soapstone or Red Mountain. What will they think watching Roundhouse blades on the horizon?

Because this wind development is not on federal land, it isn't going through the familiar Environmental Impact Statement process. I'd assume the city has turbine placement control written into the lease.

The first opportunity for the public to comment at the county level is Feb. 19. And in advance, the public can request to "be a party" when the Wyoming Industrial Siting Council meets to consider NextEra's permit in March.

NextEra held an open house in Cheyenne on Nov. 28. They expect to get their permits and then break ground almost immediately. This speedy schedule is so the windfarm is operational by December 2020, before federal tax incentives end.

It doesn't seem to me that we – Cheyenne residents – have adequate time to consider the drawbacks of new era wind turbines – for people or wildlife. Look at the 2008 Master Plan, http://belvoirranch.org. Is it upheld by spreading wind turbines over the entire 20,000 acres, more than originally planned? People possibly, and wildlife certainly, will be experiencing low frequency noise for 30 years.

At the very least, I'd like to see NextEra move turbines back from the western boundary two miles, for the good of raptors, other birds, mule deer, trail users, and the neighbors living near Harriman Road. The two southernmost sections are already protected with The Nature Conservancy's conservation easement.

What I'd really like to see instead is more solar development on rooftops and over parking lots in Cheyenne. Or a new style of Wyoming snow fence that turns wind into energy while protecting highways.

Sunday, March 17, 2019, Outdoors, page E2

183 BirdCast improving birding – and bird safety

Last year, the folks at Cornell Lab of Ornithology improved and enhanced BirdCast, http://birdcast.info/. You can now get a three-night forecast of bird migration movement for the continental U.S.

This not only helps avid birders figure out where to see lots of birds but helps operators of wind turbines know when to shut down and managers of tall buildings and structures when to shut the lights off (birds are attracted to lights and collide), resulting in the fewest bird deaths.

The forecasts are built on 23 years of data that relate weather trends and other factors to migration timing.

Songbird migration is predominately at night. Ornithologists discovered that radar, used to detect aircraft during World War II and then adapted for tracking weather events in the 1950s, was also detecting clouds of migrating birds.

There is a network of 143 radar stations across the country, including the one by the Cheyenne airport. You can explore the data archive online and download maps for free.

CLO's Adriaan Doktor sent me an animation of the data collected from the Cheyenne station for May 7, 2018, one of last spring's largest local waves of migration. He is one of the authors of a paper, "Seasonal abundance and survival of North America's migratory avifauna," based on radar information.

At the BirdCast website, you can pull up the animation for the night of May 6-7 and see where the migrating birds were thickest across the country. The brightest white clouds indicate a density of as many as 50,000 birds per kilometer per hour – that's a rate of 80,500 birds passing over a mile-long line per hour. Our flight was not that bright, maybe 16,000 birds crossing a mile-long line per hour. A strong flight often translates into a lot of birds coming to earth in the morning – very good birdwatching conditions. Although if flying conditions are excellent, some birds fly on.

I also looked at the night of May 18-19, 2018, the night before last year's Cheyenne Big Day Bird Count – hardly any activity. The weather was so nasty that Saturday, our bird compiler rescheduled for Sunday, which was not a big improvement. We saw only 113 species.

Twenty-five years ago, the third Saturday of May could yield 130 to 150 species. Part of the difference is the greater number of expert Audubon birders who helped count back then. Birding expertise seems to go in generational waves.

But we also know that songbird numbers are down. I read in Scott Weidensaul's book, "Living on the Wind," published in 1999, about Sidney Gauthreaux's 1989 talk at a symposium on neotropical migrants. He used radar records to show that the frequency of spring migrant waves across the Gulf of Mexico was down by 50 percent over 30 years. Radar can't count individual birds or identify species, but we know destruction or degradation of breeding and wintering habitat has continued as people develop rural areas.

But I also wonder if, along with plants blooming earlier due to climate change, the peak of spring migration is earlier. A paper by scientists from the University of Helsinki, due to be published in June in the journal "Ecological Indicators," shows that 195 species of birds in Europe and Canada are migrating on average a week earlier than 50 years ago, due to climate change.

Would we have been better off holding last year's Big Day on either of the previous two Saturdays? I looked at the radar animations for the preceding nights in 2018, and yes, there was a lot more migration activity in our area than on the night before the 19th. Both dates also had better weather.

As much fun as our Big Day is – a large group of birders of all skill levels combing the Cheyenne area for birds from dawn to dusk (and even in the dark) – and as much effort as is put into it, there has never been a guarantee the Saturday we pick will be the height of spring migration.

The good news is that in addition to our Big Day, we have half a dozen die-hard local birders out nearly every day from the end of April to the end of May adding spring migration information to the eBird.org database. It's a kind of addiction, rather like fishing, wondering what you'll see if you cast your eyes up into the trees and out across the prairie.

I recommend you explore BirdCast. info (and eBird.org) and sign up to join Cheyenne Audubon members for all or part of this year's Big Day on May 18. See the chapter's website and/or sign up for the free e-newsletter, https:// cheyenneaudubon.wordpress.com/ newsletters/.

184 Giving away the ranch: What the Roundhouse Wind Energy Project application tells us

May 2019, Cheyenne – High Plains Audubon Society "Flyer"

My friends and I are amateurs at tilting at windmills on behalf of wildlife and recreation. We are concerned about NextEra's Roundhouse Wind Energy Project slated to begin construction in August at the Belvoir Ranch, owned by the City of Cheyenne, and on adjoining private and state land.

The 120 499-foot-tall turbines will be scattered over 49,000 acres a few miles west of Cheyenne, from I-80 south to the state line and nearly from I-25 to Harriman Road (Wyoming Highway 218).

The friends I've met with are the representatives from The Nature Conservancy, Granite Canon Environmental Committee, Wyoming Pathways and Cheyenne Mountain Bike Association. I represent Cheyenne Audubon.

We've missed opportunities to voice our concerns due to inexperience but met several times with Roundhouse project director Ryan Fitzpatrick, Cheyenne native (I knew his 4th grade teacher) and Fort Collins resident. He's charming. But he works for NextEra. He told us to present our "asks" on behalf of wildlife and recreation but few were accommodated in the Roundhouse application to the Wyoming Industrial

Siting Council, http://deq.wyoming. gov/isd/application-permits/resources/ roundhouse-wind-energy-project/. The hearing is scheduled for June 13-14.

Audubon and the other groups are recommending relocating six turbines in the southwest corner, to benefit wildlife, recreation and safeguard adjacent protected areas: TNC's Big Hole conservation easement, Red Mountain Open Space and Soapstone Prairie Natural Area (the last two in Colorado). NextEra is relocating one, T8, at the city's request.

Birds, along with bats, are the wildlife killed directly by turbine blades. Hundreds of hours of wildlife studies for the application show WEST consultants found 34 bird species in the western part of the Belvoir and AECOM found 67 species in the southeastern private/state land area. AECOM included extra survey locations in riparian areas where songbirds hang out.

No studies were done in the northeastern part of the Belvoir since that was leased only a few months ago, in December 2018. Ironically, that's the part of the Belvoir where Audubon, TNC and the University of Wyoming Biodiversity Institute found 24 species

June 11 and 12 during the 2016 Bioblitz.

The eBird.org bird species list for adjacent Red Mountain and Soapstone Prairie combined is 144. Laramie County, where the Belvoir is located, has a list of 319 species. Why are the application's species numbers so low?

For every weekly survey of 60 minutes looking for eagles and other raptors, only an additional 10 minutes was devoted to songbirds. Eagles have major federal protection including substantial fines. Songbirds have less protection, even before the teeth were taken out of the Migratory Bird Treaty Act by the current federal administration.

Low species counts mean consultants are not giving us the picture of migration diversity that eBird.org records indicate, or the clouds of migrating birds from radar records found at BirdCast. org. I think WEST's estimate of 300 dead birds per year is low.

Methodology for counting dead birds after turbines begin operation was not ready at the time the application was submitted. The bird surveys are not complete either. How can Audubon, an

official party at the ISC hearing, make informed requests for changes?

Cheyenne Audubon will ask NextEra to have the project operator consult BirdCast.org and determine what nights clouds of migrating birds are thickest funneling up the Front Range and shut down the turbines for a few hours.

There's no room here to discuss the whole hawk and eagle situation, but I trust the U.S. Fish and Wildlife Service to take that on.

The 2008 Belvoir master plan, developed with public input, called for limited wind development. Without that same extensive public involvement, the city chose to let NextEra's turbines be spread across the entire ranch. The economic benefits will come at the expense of recreation and wildlife – even though those two, when handled properly, could provide economic benefits themselves in perpetuity, compared to the wind development's 30 years.

It would be so much easier to convince the powers that be of the economic value of birds and recreation if I had deep pockets.

185 Participating at the Roundhouse hearing was an intense venture

Friday, July 5, 2019, Opinion, page A7

The Cheyenne-High Plains Audubon Society agrees clean energy is needed. However, wind energy is deadly for birds when they are struck by turbine blades.

Beginning last December, CH-PAS discussed its concerns about the Roundhouse Wind Energy development with company, city and county officials. The 120-turbine windfarm will extend from Interstate 80 south to the Colorado state line and from I-25 west to Harriman Road.

The Wyoming Industrial Siting Council hearing for the approval of Roundhouse Wind Energy's application was held June 13 in a quasi-legal format.

Cheyenne-High Plains Audubon Society filed as a party, preparing a pre-hearing statement. The other parties were the Wyoming Department of Environmental Quality's Industrial Siting Division, Roundhouse and Laramie County, also acting on behalf of the city of Cheyenne.

We all presented our opening

statements. Then the Roundhouse lawyer presented her expert witnesses, asking them leading questions. Then I, acting in the same capacity for CHPAS as the lawyer for Roundhouse, cross-examined her witnesses. One was a viewshed analysis expert from Los Angeles, the other a biologist from Western EcoSystems Technology, the Cheyenne consulting firm that does contract biological studies for wind energy companies across the country.

Then CHPAS presented our expert witness, Daly Edmunds, Audubon Rockies' policy and outreach director. Wind farm issues are a big part of her work. She is also a wildlife biologist with a master's degree from the University of Wyoming.

We were rushed getting our testimony in before the 5 p.m. cutoff for the first day because I was not available the next day. I asked permission to allow Mark Gorges to read our closing statement the next day, after the applicant had a chance to rebut all the conditions we asked for.

The seven council members chose not to debate our conditions. Some conditions were echoed by DEQ. But it was a hard sell, since Wyoming Game and Fish Department had already signed off on the application.

Here are the conditions we asked for:

1) Some of the recommended wildlife studies will be one and a half years away from completion when turbine-building starts in September. Complete the studies first to make better turbine placement decisions.

2) Do viewshed analysis from the south and share it with adjacent Colorado open space and natural area agencies.

3) Get a "take permit" to avoid expensive trouble with the U.S. Fish and Wildlife Service if dead eagles are found.

4) Use the Aircraft Detection Lighting System so tower lights, which can confuse night-migrating birds, will be turned on as little as possible. This was on DEQ's list as well.

5) Use weather radar to predict the best times to shut down turbines during bird migration.

6) Be transparent about the plans for and results of avian monitoring after the turbines start.

7) Relocate six of the southernmost turbine locations because of their impact on wildlife and the integrity of adjacent areas set aside for their conservation value.

The second half of the hearing dealt with county/city requests for economic impact funds from the state. The expected costs are from a couple hundred workers temporarily descending on Cheyenne requiring health and emergency services.

At the June CHPAS board meeting, members approved staying involved in the Roundhouse issue. The Roundhouse folks have a little mitigation money we could direct toward a study to benefit birds at this and other windfarms. There is a Technical Advisory Committee we need to keep track of. And we need to lobby to give Game and Fish's recommendations more legal standing so they can't be ignored.

It's too bad I don't watch courtroom dramas. The hearing would have been easier to navigate. But everyone – DEQ employees, the Roundhouse team, council members, hearing examiner, court reporter – was very supportive of CHPAS's participation. They rarely see the public as a party at these hearings. I just wish we could have had one or more conditions accepted on behalf of the birds.

186 Bird families expand in summer

Early summer exploded with babies. In addition to our family adding the first baby of the new generation (do wild animals relate to their grand-offspring?), I noticed a lot of other baby activity.

Driving past Holliday Park at twilight at the end of June I caught a glimpse of what looked like three loose dogs. They were a mother racoon and two young scampering across the lawn.

Walking our dog around the field by our house, I saw a ground squirrel mother herd a youngster out of the street and back to the safety of the grass. There's also an explosion of baby rabbits in that field driving everyone's dogs crazy.

We have a pair of Swainson's hawks nesting in our neighborhood, and they are using the field as their grocery store. I'm not sure exactly where they are nesting, but I'm guessing it is one of the large spruce trees. Whenever I'm at the field, I catch a glimpse of at least one hunting. But I also glimpse them from my kitchen window soaring, meaning I can add them to my eBird.org yard list. The yard list is all the species I've seen from the window or while out in the yard. The Swainson's have put me at 99 species so far – over about 12 years.

When it warmed up, we spent more time in our backyard and I noticed other signs of family life. We always have a raucous community of tree squirrels, one generation indistinguishable from the next, chasing each other round and round in our big trees.

This year I've been hearing a mountain chickadee sing. No, not the "chick-a-dee-dee-dee" call—that's their alarm call—but a sweet three-note song (listen at https://www.allaboutbirds.org/).

I'm also learning the various phrases American goldfinches use while they spend the summer with us. We've left our nyger thistle seed feeder up for them (no, nyger thistle is not our noxious weed and it is treated not to sprout). They sometimes come as a group of four, including two males and two females, and sometimes a younger one.

The downy woodpeckers have been visiting as well. They go for one of those blocks of seed "glued" together that you buy at the store. You would think they would go for bugs hiding in the furrowed bark of the tree trunks. Maybe they do, in addition to the seed block.

The robins have been busy. I observed a youngster walking through my garden as it tried to imitate the foraging action of the nearby adult, but it finally resorted to begging to be fed.

Within the space of a couple days, I was contacted about two problem robins attempting to build nests on the tops of porch lights. Porch lights, because they usually provide a shelf-like surface under the safety of the roof overhang, are quite popular. But not everyone trying to use the adjacent door likes getting dive-bombed by the angry robin parents.

In the first situation, Deb, our former neighbor, said the robin was trying to build a nest on a porch light with a pyramidal top. The bird could not make her nest stick and all the materials from all her attempts slid off and accumulated on the porch floor. Providing another ledge nearby might not have worked for such a determined bird. Instead, Deb opted for screening off the top of the light. Hopefully Mama Robin found a better location in Deb's spruce trees.

Our current neighbor, Dorothy, texted me the next day, wondering what she and her family were going to do about being attacked by the robin which had built a nest on her (flat-topped) front porch light. Maybe avoid walking out the front door and walk out through the garage instead, I said. I asked her if she had a selfie stick so she could take pictures of the inside of the nest to show her two young boys.

Down at Lions Park a new colony of black-crowned night-herons has been established. Listen for them behind the conservatory. The colony at Holliday Park is still going strong.

In the far corner of Curt Gowdy State Park, I caught a glimpse of a bird family I hadn't seen together before. Way up on the nasty El Alto trail, I saw a brown songbird I couldn't identify readily. And then the parent came to feed it, a western tanager. The youngster has a long way to go before attaining either the look of its mother, if female, or if male, the bright yellow body with black and white wings and the orange head like its father.

187 Audubon Photography Awards feature Pinedale photographer

Sunday, August 11, 2019, Outdoors, page E2

Last month, a familiar name appeared on my screen, "Elizabeth Boehm."

I was reading an email from the National Audubon Society listing the winners of the 2019 Audubon Photography Awards.

I have never met Elizabeth in person. But she was one of the people who replied when I put out a request on the Wyobirds e-list for photos of the few bird species we didn't have for photographer Pete Arnold's and my book published last year, "Cheyenne Birds by the Month." She generously shared six images.

With my similar request on Wyobirds back in 2008 for "Birds by the Week" for the Wyoming Tribune Eagle, Pete supplied most of the 104 photos (the others were stock), and he contributed 93 for the book. Here's the small world connection: Pete is Elizabeth's neighbor whenever he and his wife visit his wife's childhood home in Pinedale.

Now here is the big world connection: Elizabeth won the 2019 Audubon Photography Awards in the professional category. To qualify as a professional, you must make a certain amount of money from photography the previous year.

A week later, Audubon magazine arrived and there, printed over a two-page spread, like the grand prize winner, was Elizabeth's winning photo: two male sage grouse fighting on an entirely white background of snow.

I decided it was time to get to know Elizabeth better and interviewed her by phone about her prize-winning photography. Elizabeth won the Wyoming Wildlife magazine grand prize a couple years ago and one year she was in the top 10 for the North American Nature Photography Association. Her photos have been published in Audubon magazine. "I was totally surprised," she said of her latest win.

More than 8,000 images were submitted by 2,253 U.S. and Canadian photographers. Categories included professional, amateur, youth (13-17 years old), Plants for Birds (bird and a plant native to the area photographed together) and the Fisher Prize (for originality and technical expertise).

Elizabeth started shooting landscapes

and wildflowers 25 years ago, then started selling images 10 years later, adding wildlife to her subjects. Now she works her day job only two days a week.

Of her winning image she said, "I usually go out in the spring. I know the local leks. I like snow to clean up the background. The hard part of photographing fights is they are spontaneous. It's kind of a fast, quick thing."

The males fight in the pre-dawn light for the right to be the one that mates with all the willing females. "I set up the night before or in the middle of the night. It's better waiting and being patient," she said.

Elizabeth visits leks one or two times a week March through April. This past spring was too wet for driving the back roads. Even the grouse weren't on the leks until late. They don't like snow because there is nowhere to hide from the eagles that prey on them.

This winning photo is from three or four years ago. Elizabeth came across it while searching her files for another project and realized it could be special with a little work.

Audubon allows nothing other than cropping and a few kinds of lighting and color adjustments. At one point, Audubon requested Elizabeth's untouched RAW image. See the 2019 rules, and 2019's winning photos, at https://www.audubon.org/photoawards-entry. Her camera is a Canon EOS 6D with a Canon 500 mm EF f/4L IS USM lens. The photo was taken at 1/1500 second at f/5.6, ISO 800.

In September, National Audubon will finalize the schedule for the traveling exhibit of APA winners.

Elizabeth sells prints at the Art of the Winds, a 10-artist gallery on Pinedale's Main Street. You can also purchase images directly from her at http://elizabethboehm.com. She offers guided local birding tours and is also the organizer for the local Christmas Bird Count.

Photographers are a dime a dozen in the Yellowstone – Grand Teton neighborhood where Elizabeth shoots. She works hard to have her work stand out. She also donates her work to conservation causes like Pete's and my book, which is meant to get more people excited about local birds and birdwatching.

Look on the copyright page of "Cheyenne Birds by the Month" for the list of Elizabeth's contributions. You can find the book online through the University of Wyoming bookstore, the Wyoming Game and Fish store and Amazon, etc.

In Cheyenne it's at the Wyoming Game and Fish Department, the Cheyenne Depot Museum, Wyoming State Museum, Cheyenne Botanic Gardens, Riverbend Nursery, Cheyenne Pet Clinic, Cheyenne Regional Medical Center's Pink Boutique, Barnes and Noble, PBR Printing and out at Curt Gowdy State Park.

188 Nestling ID benefits from crowd sourced help

Sunday, September 15, 2019, Outdoors, page E2

Cheyenne resident Priscilla Gill emailed me a bird photo that her son, Matthew Gill, took Aug. 6. Could I identify the birds?

Digital technology is wonderful. Thirty years ago, I would get phone calls asking for ID help (and I still do) but it can be difficult to draw a mental picture. I must figure out how familiar with birds the callers are so I can interpret the size and color comparisons they make.

At least with an emailed photo, the ease of identifying the bird is only dependent on the clearness and how much of the bird is showing. In this case, the photo clearly showed two little nestlings so ungainly they were cute. They were black-skinned, but all a-prickle with yellow pin feathers and had large, lumpy black bills. They were nestled on top of a platform of sticks balanced high up on the pipe infrastructure at a well pad.

Those bills first made me think ravens. However, the nest was near Greeley, Colorado, where ravens are rarely seen.

Digital photos are easy to share. I forwarded the photo to Greg Johnson, my local go-to birder who enjoys ID challenges. But after a couple days without a reply, I figured he was somewhere beyond internet contact, so I sent the photo on to Ted Floyd, Colorado birder and editor of the American Birding Association magazine.

He had no idea. No one has ever put together a field guide for nestlings. Julie Zickefoose comes close with her book, "Baby Birds: An Artist Looks into the Nest", where she sketched nestlings of 17 species at regular intervals.

Ted suggested I post the photo to the ABA's Facebook group, "What's this bird?"

Meanwhile, Greg was finally able to reply: mourning dove. They only have two young per nest, and they build stick nests.

By this time, I had joined the Facebook group and was starting to get replies. It's a little intimidating – there are 39,000 people in the group. There were 13 replies and 37 other people "liked" some of those replies, essentially voting on their ID choice.

I was surprised to see a reply from someone I knew, my Seattle birding friend, Acacia. Except for the person who suggested pelicans (based on the enormous bills), the replies were split between mourning dove and rock pigeon. I was most confidant about the reply from the woman who had pigeons nest on her fire escape.

On reflection, "pigeon" seemed to make more sense, and Greg agreed. Pigeons are known for adapting to cities because the buildings remind them of cliffs they nest on in their native range in Europe and Asia. It seems odd to think of them nesting in the wild, but there's a flock around the cliffs on Table Mountain at the Woodhouse Public Access Area near Cheyenne. Mourning doves and Eurasian collared-doves, on the other hand, are more likely to hide their nests in trees.

But birds can sometimes adapt to what we humans present them with. Short of following the nestlings until they can be identified via adult plumage or comparing them to photos of nestlings that were then followed to adulthood, we can't say for sure which species they were.

Out there in the open, did these two make it to maturity? I wonder how easy it would be for hawks to pick off both the parents and young.

Here in Cheyenne at the end of August, I've noticed the field by my house has gotten very quiet at ground level – virtually no squeaking ground squirrels anymore. However, many mornings I'm hearing the keening of the two young Swainson's hawks probably responsible for thinning that rodent population. The youngsters and parents sit on the power poles and watch as my friend Mary and I walk our dogs past.

The two kids have even been over to visit at Mark's and my house. One evening while out in the backyard, I happened to look up and see the two sitting on opposite ends of the old TV antenna that still sways atop its two-story tower. That gives new meaning to the term "hawk watching." They leave white calling card splats on the patio, so I know when I've missed one of their visits.

Another day, as I did backyard chores accompanied by the dog, one of them sat in one of our big green ash trees, sounding like it was crying its heart out – maybe it was filled with teenage angst, knowing how soon it needed to grow up and fly to the ancestral winter homeland in the Argentinian grasslands.

189

How 3 billion breeding birds disappeared in past 48 years

"Decline of the North American avifauna" is the title of the report published online by the journal Science on Sept. 19.

The bird conservation groups I belong to summed it up as "3 billion birds lost."

In a nutshell (eggshell?), there are three billion (aka 29%) fewer breeding birds of 529 species in North America than in 1970.

The losses are spread across common birds such as western meadowlark, as well as less common birds in all biomes. While the grasslands, where we live, lost only 720 million breeding birds, that's 53% – the highest percentage of the biomes. And 74% of grassland species are declining. Easy-to-understand infographics are available at https://www.3billionbirds.org/.

Two categories of birds have increased in numbers: raptors and waterfowl. Their numbers were very low in 1970 due to pesticides and wetland degradation, respectively. Eliminating DDT and restoring wetlands, among other actions, allowed them to prosper.

The 11 U.S. and Canadian scientists crunched data from ongoing bird surveys including the North American Breeding Bird Survey, the Christmas Bird Count, the International Shorebird Survey and the Partners in Flight Avian Conservation Database.

Weather radar, which shows migrating birds simply as biomass, shows a 14% decrease from 2007 to 2017.

Two of the contributors to the study are scientists I've talked to and whose work I respect. Adriaan Dokter of Cornell Lab of Ornithology is working with me, Audubon Rockies and the Roundhouse developers. We want to see if weather radar can predict the best nights to shut down wind turbines for the safety of migratory birds passing through the wind farm they are building at the southwest corner of I-80 and I-25.

I've met Arvind Panjabi with Bird Conservancy of the Rockies headquartered in Fort Collins, Colorado, on several occasions. BCR does bird studies primarily in the west as well as educational programs.

How does the number of birds make a difference to you and me? Birds are the easiest animals to count and serve as indicators of ecological health. If bird numbers are down, we can presume other fauna numbers are out of whack too - either, for instance, too many insects devouring crops or too few predators keeping pest numbers down. Ecological changes affect our food, water and health.

The decline of common bird species is troubling because you would think they would be taking advantage of the decline of species less resilient to change. But even invasive species like European starling and house sparrow are declining.

The biggest reasons for avian population loss are habitat loss, agricultural intensification (no "weedy" areas left), coastal disturbance and human activities. Climate change amplifies all the problems.

A coalition including Audubon, American Bird Conservancy, Cornell Lab of Ornithology, Environment and Climate Change Canada, Bird Conservancy of the Rockies and Georgetown University have an action plan.

There are seven steps we can all take. The steps, with details, are at https://www.3billionbirds.org/. Most of them I've written about over the past 20 years so you can also search my archives, https://cheyennebirdbanter.wordpress.com/.

1. Make windows safer. Turn off lights at night inside and outside large buildings like the Herschler Building and the Cheyenne Botanic Gardens during migration. Break up the reflections of vegetation birds see in our home windows during the day.

2. Keep cats indoors. Work on the problem of feral cats. They are responsible for more than two-thirds of the 2.6 billion birds per year cats kill.

3. Use native plants. There are 63,000 square miles of lawn in the U.S. currently that are only attractive to birds if they have pests or weeds.

4. Avoid pesticides. They are toxic to birds and the insects they eat. Go organic. Support U.S. bill H.R. 1337, Saving America's Pollinators Act. Contact Wyoming's Representative Liz Cheney and ask that registration of neonicotinoids be suspended. Birds eating seeds with traces of neonics are not as successful surviving and breeding.

5. Drink shade-grown coffee. It helps 42 species of migratory North American birds and is economically beneficial to farmers.

6. Reduce plastic use. Even here, mid-continent rather than the ocean, plastic can be a problem for birds. Few companies are interested in recycling plastic anymore.

7. Do citizen science. Help count birds through volunteer surveys like eBird, Project FeederWatch (new count season begins Nov. 9), the Christmas Bird Count (Cheyenne's is Dec. 28), and if you are a good birder, take on a Breeding Bird Survey route next spring.

To aid grasslands in particular, support Audubon's conservation ranching initiative, https://www.audubon.org/conservation/ranching.

In a related Science article, Ken Rosenberg, the report's lead author, says, "I am not saying we can stop the decline of every bird species, but I am weirdly hopeful."

190 Conservation ranching is for the birds – and for the cows

Sunday, December 15, 2019, Outdoors, page E2

You'll run across arguments saying our farmlands would be put to better use raising food crops for people instead of forage crops for cattle. Maybe so – back east.

But Wyoming's remaining rangeland, its prairie grasslands and shrublands, is not suited to raising crops. We don't have the water or the soils. But we do grow excellent native forage, originally for buffalo, now for cattle.

And what a great system it is – no fossil fuels required to harvest that forage – the animals do it for you! On top of that, good range management is good for birds.

However, grassland birds were identified as the group having declined the most in the past 48 years, according to https://www.3billionbirds.org/.

At a recent Cheyenne Audubon meeting, Dusty Downey, Audubon Rockies' lead for the organization's Conservation Ranching Initiative, explained part of the problem is grassland conversion. When ranchers can't make enough on cattle, they might try converting rangeland to cropland or to houses and other infrastructure. With hard work, cropland can be restored someday, but houses are a permanent conversion and wildlife suffers habitat loss.

Eighty-five percent of grasslands and sagebrush steppe is privately owned. So Dusty, raised on, and still living on, a ranch by Devils Tower, and his boss, Alison Holloran, a wildlife biologist, thought reaching out to ranchers about enhancing their operations could benefit both birds and cattle. Offering a financial incentive makes it attractive and might keep land in ranching.

National Audubon picked up the idea and made it a national program. The "Grazed on Audubon Certified Bird Friendly Land" logo can help ranchers get anywhere from 10 to 40 cents per pound more, depending on the market.

Conservation ranching is now popular in Dusty's Thunder Basin neighborhood where ranchers know him and his family. Through the program, ranchers learn techniques for maximizing production over the long term that also benefit birds and they get help finding funding for ranch improvements. With

third-party certification, they earn the privilege of selling their meat at a premium price to people like me who value their commitment.

We also value meat free of hormones and antibiotics, so that is part of the certification. And we appreciate that cows eating grass produce less methane, part of the climate change problem, than if they eat corn.

Dusty said in the past 15 years, grass-fed beef sales have grown 400 percent, from $5 million a year to $2 billion.

Audubon-certified beef is available at Big Hollow Food Coop in Laramie, the Reed Ranch in Douglas, in Colorado, other western states and online. See https://www.audubon.org/where-buy-products-raised-audubon-certified-land#.

Grazing prairie looks simple. But grazing management is both art and science.

What does the vegetation need? How is it interacting with weather and grazers? Grassland vegetation needs grazing to stay healthy. Dusty cited a four-year study that showed an ungrazed pasture was not as productive or as diverse as one that had been grazed properly. Grazed plots showed five times more birds, two times more arthropods (food for chicks) and five times more dung beetles (the compost experts) than ungrazed plots.

Grazing grasslands down to bare ground like the buffalo did looks bad, but in the right context it allows highly nutritious plants to grow that can't compete otherwise. It also aids bird species that require bare ground or very short grass somewhere in their lifecycle, between courtship and fledging.

My experience with prairie plants in the Habitat Hero demonstration garden at the Cheyenne Botanic Gardens showed plants grazed down to ground level by rabbits rebounded the next spring. But you can't let the rabbits in year-round or the same season year after year.

The gold standard when I was studying range management at the University of Wyoming was rest-rotation grazing. Now it's producing a changing mosaic of plants by adjusting grazing timing on a multi-year cycle for any given pasture, tailored to the plants there and the rancher's goals. Laramie County Conservation District helps local landowners figure it out.

For an elegant explanation of the dance between animal and prairie plant, read a recent blog post by Chris Helzer, https://prairieecologist.com/2019/11/13/ what-does-habitat-look-like-on-a-ranch/. He is the director of science for The Nature Conservancy-Nebraska.

Chris talks about growing a shifting mosaic of plants that will be more resilient through drought and other extremes. He also said, "Chronic overgrazing can degrade plant communities and reduce habitat quality, but a well-managed ranch can foster healthy wildlife populations while optimizing livestock production."

Next time you meet a rancher, restaurant owner or grocery store manager, ask them if they've heard about Audubon-certified meat. Tell them it's good for birds – and cows.

2020

191 Be a Citizen Scientist in your backyard

Sunday, January 19, 2020, Outdoors, page E2

Along with the news last fall that there are 3 billion fewer birds in North America than in 1970, conservation organizations came out with a list of seven actions people can take.

No. 7 on the list is "Watch birds, share what you see." In fact, citizen science efforts, like the 120th annual Christmas Bird Count season that finished up Jan. 5, provided part of the data for the study that showed the bird decline.

There aren't enough scientists to collect data everywhere, so they depend on us informed lay people to help them.

There's another organized opportunity coming up for you to count birds Feb. 14-17: the Great Backyard Bird Count.

GBBC history

Begun in 1998 by the National Audubon Society and Cornell Lab of Ornithology, the GBBC dates always coincide with Presidents' Day weekend. Scientists wanted to get a snapshot of where the birds are late winter, before spring migration begins.

The difference between this public participation bird count and the others at the time, is data reporting is entirely online. Some results are nearly real time on the website, like watching the participant map light up sporadically every few seconds as someone else hits "Send."

In 2002, Cornell started another online citizen science project, eBird, which collects data year-round from citizen scientists. In 2013, the GBBC was integrated with eBird. And now both have global participation from birdwatchers in 100 countries.

At the GBBC website you can find all kinds of interesting information about last year's count and prepare for this year.

2019 broke records

There were 209,944 checklists submitted in 2019. A checklist is the list of birds seen by one person or a group birding together. GBBC asks participants to bird for a minimum of 15 minutes and to not travel more than 5 miles for one checklist. Originally, the emphasis was on watching the birds in your backyard, but you can bird anywhere now.

There were 32 million birds counted, of 6,849 species. Columbia counted 1,095 species, the most of any country, even though only 1,046 checklists were submitted (there were 136,000 checklists for the U.S.). This time of year, a lot of our North American summer birds are in Columbia and other Central and

South American countries.

The list of top 10 species most frequently reported starts with the cardinal, not native to Cheyenne, and the junco, common at our feeders, made second place. All the birds on this list were North American because the majority of 224,781 participants last year were from our continent. Birders in India are getting excited, though, and that might change someday.

California made the top of the list of states for most checklists submitted, 10,000. All the top 10 states were coastal, either Great Lakes or ocean. That's where the most people live.

Trends in North America showed up during the 2019 count, such as a high number of evening grosbeaks in the east. Canada had fewer finches because of a bad seed crop, and apparently the finches went south because there were higher numbers of finch species – red crossbills, common redpolls, and pine grosbeaks – in the northern states.

You can prepare ahead

The GBBC website has links to other sites to help you identify birds (if you don't have a copy of my "Cheyenne Birds by the Month" already!):

--Merlin (also available as a free phone app) will ask you questions about the comparative size of the bird, color, activity, habitat, and give you a list of possibilities.

--All About Birds and the Audubon Bird Guide are both helpful.

--And if the weekend finds you in Central or South America, check out the link for Neotropical Birds Online.

Take photos

Don't forget to take photos – there's a contest with these categories:

--Birds in their habitat

--Birds in action

--Birds in a group

--Composition—pleasing arrangement of all features

--People watching birds.

How to get involved

Participate in the Great Backyard Bird Count Feb. 14-17

Count with CHPAS locally

Join Cheyenne–High Plains Audubon Society members from 10 a.m. to noon Feb. 15, for free at the Children's Village at the Cheyenne Botanic Gardens, 710 S. Lions Park Road. We'll bird a little around the park and then come back and enter our data. All ages are welcome. And we have binoculars to share. Contact bgorges4@msn.com if you have questions.

If you are new to GBBC and want to participate on your own, participation is free. Instructions are at https://gbbc.birdcount.org/.

If you already eBird, submit checklists (15-minute minimum) to your account at http://ebird.org.

192

Sunday, February 16, 2020, Outdoors, page E2

Wyobirds gets tech update and Wyoming Master Naturalists gets initial discussion

Technology drives changes in the birding community as it does for the rest of the world. We always wonder how hard it will be to adapt to the inevitable.

In January, the folks at Murie Audubon, the National Audubon Society chapter in Casper, announced that they would no longer pay the fees required for hosting the Wyobirds elist. There have been plenty of donations over the years to offset the $500 per year cost but, they reasoned, now that there is a no-cost alternative, why not spend the money on say, bird habitat protection or improvement? Also, the new option allows photos and the old one didn't.

But the new outlet for chatting about birds in Wyoming works a little differently, and everyone will have to get used to it. We've changed before. We had the Wyoming Bird Hotline until 2006 for publicizing rare bird alerts only. No one called in about their less than rare backyard birds, their birding questions and birding related events like they do now on Wyobirds.

The only problem with leaving the listserv is figuring out what to do with the digital archives. They may go back to 2004, the first time Wyobirds was mentioned in Cheyenne Audubon's newsletter.

Now the Wyoming birding community, and all the travelers interested in coming to see Wyoming birds, can subscribe to Wyobirds (no donations necessary) by going to Google Groups, groups.google.com, and searching for "Wyobirds." Follow the directions for how to join the group so that you can post and get emails when other group members post. I opted to get one email per day listing all the postings. That will be nice when spring migration begins and there are multiple posts each day.

Google Groups, a free service from Google, is one way the giant company gives back, and we might as well take advantage of it.

Wyoming Master Naturalists

Wyoming is one of only five states that does not have a Master Naturalist program, however, it's in the discussion stage.

What is a Master Naturalist and what do they do? Jacelyn Downey, education programs manager for Audubon Rockies who is based near Gillette, explained at the January Cheyenne Audubon meeting that programs are different in each state.

Most are like the Master Gardener program, offering training and certification. Master naturalists serve by taking on interpretive or educational roles or helping with conservation projects or collecting scientific data. The training requires a certain number of hours, and keeping up certification requires hours of continuing education and service. But it's not a chore if you love nature.

Master Gardeners is organized in the U.S. through the university extension program. Some Master Naturalist programs are too, as well as through state game and fish or parks departments or Audubon offices or other conservation organizations or partnerships of organizations and agencies.

Colorado has at least two programs, one through Denver Audubon and another in Ft. Collins to aid users of the city's extensive natural areas.

Dorothy Tuthill also spoke. She is associate director and education coordinator for the University of Wyoming Biodiversity Institute. She pointed out that several of its programs, like the Moose Day surveys in which "community scientists" (another term for people participating in citizen science) gather data, are the kinds of activities a Master Naturalist program could aid.

Audubon and the institute already collaborate every year with other organizations and agencies on the annual Wyoming Bioblitz. It's one day during which scientists, volunteers, teachers, families and kids together gather data on flora and fauna in a designated area. This year's Bioblitz will be July 17-19 near Sheridan on the Quarter Circle A Ranch, the grounds of the Brinton Museum.

With a Wyoming Master Naturalist program, a trained corps of naturalists could be available to help agencies and organizations by visiting classrooms, leading hikes, giving programs and helping to plan and participating in projects and surveys.

Audubon chapter volunteers are already involved in these kinds of things: adult and child education, data collection on field trips and conservation projects. Many of us might broaden our nature expertise beyond birds and learn more about connecting people to nature. But it would be nice to wear a badge that guarantees for the public that we know what we are talking about.

Just how a Wyoming Naturalist Program would be set up is being discussed right now. Maybe a Google Group needs to be formed.

193 High capacity water wells can negatively affect birds, other wildlife

Sunday, March 8, 2020, Outdoors, page E2

The relationship between groundwater and surface water is important to birds and other wildlife – and people.

Some surface water is merely runoff from rain and snow that hasn't yet soaked in and recharged the groundwater. Other surface water, like wetlands, is the result of high groundwater levels. Springs along a creek also depend on an adequate amount of groundwater.

Groundwater and surface water along streams and in wetlands grow vegetation wildlife depends on for shelter and food. Seventy percent of Wyoming's bird species require these wetter areas.

Precipitation can vary from year to year, but on average, it recharges the groundwater – the aquifer. Aquifers are geologically complicated, but mostly water flows through permeable layers much the same way surface water drains. In Laramie County, both surface and groundwater flow somewhat west to east.

If someone puts in a well and starts pumping, it will lower the water table – the top of the groundwater – for some distance from the well. If the water is for domestic use, it is filtered through a septic system and mostly returned to the groundwater. However, if it is used for irrigating lawns and gardens, much of it evaporates and is lost. If too many wells are sipping from the same aquifer, the water table drops, and people are forced to drill deeper wells.

Another side effect of the water table dropping is wetlands and streams dry up, affecting wildlife.

Wyoming has complex water laws for allocating surface water. The first person to homestead on a creek got the senior water rights. In a drought year, he might be the only one allowed to remove water from the creek.

Groundwater rights are not as clear-cut, as far as I can tell. More than 25 years ago, I remember being in eastern Laramie County putting on an Audubon presentation for the Young Farmers club. It was on the negative effects of human population growth. The farmers were already complaining then about the growing number of developments and the wells causing the water table to drop.

In 2015, the Laramie County Control Area Order was established in eastern Laramie County to keep an eye on the situation.

Before that, 2010 to 2014, the Natural Resources Conservation Service, under the Agricultural Water Enhancement Program, spent taxpayer funds to buy out 24 irrigation wells at $200,000 each within this same area, saving 1 billion gallons annually. The farmers could grow dryland wheat instead.

And now, in the same area, the Lerwick family is asking for a permit to drill eight high-capacity wells for maximum production of 1.5 billion gallons per year for agricultural purposes. We assume it's for irrigation, and that irrigation water will not be recharging the aquifer much. I don't get it. Permitting new high-capacity wells after paying to retire others in the same area makes no sense at all.

Neighboring farmers and ranchers are alarmed. Professional hydrologists can predict how it will negatively impact their water supplies. Creeks and wetlands, the few out there, will dry up and the neighbor's wells will have to be re-drilled.

Beginning March 4 and for 30 days, the state engineer is asking for comments about the effectiveness of the 2015 Laramie County Control Area Order which guides groundwater development in the area of the proposed wells.

On March 18, the state engineer will hold a hearing regarding the Lerwick permits and will hear from the affected neighboring farmers and ranchers – 17 of them.

Is it fair for someone to get a new well permit that will cause all his neighbors the expense of drilling deeper? Instead, can a community, through governmental agencies, come to an agreement that an area is no longer suitable for irrigated agriculture?

The Ogallala Aquifer, of which this High Plains Aquifer is part, extends under parts of Wyoming, South Dakota, Nebraska, Kansas, Colorado, New Mexico and Texas. For several generations, farmers have been mining it. We can call it mining because more water is extracted than returned. It is not a sustainable situation for anyone.

Cheyenne – High Plains Audubon Society is speaking up for the birds and other wildlife, but it's doubtful wildlife will be considered much in the calculation of acre-feet and gallons per minute and other details of water rights. We already know that in the last 50 years grassland birds have lost the most population of any North American habitat type. Unsustainable mining of water in Laramie County, should the new high-capacity wells be permitted, won't help.

194

Saturday, May 2, 2020, ToDo, page B2

How to become a birdwatcher

I am living under the flight path of major construction. A Swainson's hawk is plucking cottonwood branches from one neighbor's tree and taking them over my house to another neighbor's tree to build a nest.

Lately, a gang of 60 or 70, puffed up and strutting around in shiny black feather jackets, shows up along our back wall – no motorcycles for them – they're common grackles. They even scare away the bully robin that keeps the house finches from the black oil sunflower seed we've put out.

A pair of northern flickers has been visiting the seed cake feeder. We know they are male and female – he has the red mustache. The black and white pair of downy woodpeckers are visiting regularly. The male has the red neck spots.

One small, yellow-breasted stranger shows up every day at the nyger thistle seed feeder. It's a female lesser goldfinch, not a regular species here. We recognize that her yellow, black and white feather scheme is arranged differently from the American goldfinch's.

I look forward to the springtime antics of birds in my backyard, but this year, millions of people are discovering them for the first time in their own yards and neighborhoods. Suddenly, it's cool to notice birds and nature. It's almost cool to be called a birdwatcher.

Would you like to be a birdwatcher, or a birder? Here's how.

Step 1 – Notice birds

Watch for bird-like shapes in the trees and bushes and on lawns. Watch for movement. This time of year, birds are making a lot of noise and song. See if you can trace the song to the bird with his beak uplifted and open.

Step 2 – Watch the birds for a while

Are they looking for food like the red-breasted nuthatches climbing tree trunks and branches?

Are they performing a mating ritual like the Eurasian collared-dove males that launch themselves from the top of a tree or utility pole, winging high only to sail down again in spirals?

Are they picking through the grass like common grackles do, looking for grubs to eat? Are they flying by with a beak full of long wispy dead grasses for nest building like the house sparrows do?

Step 3 – Make notes about what you see

Or sketches, if you are inclined.

Step 4 – Bird ID

But if you want to talk to other birdwatchers, you need to do a little studying.

You are in luck if you live in the Cheyenne area. In 2018, Pete Arnold and I put together a picture book of 104 of our most common birds, "Cheyenne Birds by the Month." You'd be surprised how many birds you probably already know. Go to www.yuccaroadpress.com/books to examine current purchasing options.

You can also go to www.allaboutbirds. org. You can type in a bird name or queries like "birds with red breasts" (which covers all shades from pink and purple to orange and russet). If you click on "Get instant ID help," it will prompt you to download the free Merlin app. It will give you size comparison, color, behavior and habitat choices and then produce an illustrated list of possibilities – nearly as good as sending a photo to your local birder.

The best way to learn birds is to go birdwatching with someone who knows more than you. But since that probably isn't possible this spring, settle for a pair of binoculars and hone your eye for noticing field marks – the colors and shapes that distinguish one bird species' appearance from another's.

Keep in mind that even expert birders can't identify every bird – sometimes the light is bad and sometimes, and often for a species as variable as the red-tailed hawk, it doesn't look exactly like its picture in the field guides by Peterson, Kaufman or Sibley.

Step 5 – Go where the birds are

In Wyoming, that is generally wherever there is water – and trees and shrubs. At least that's where you'll find the most bird species per hour of birding. But the grasslands are special. Drive down a rural road, like nearby Chalk Bluffs Road, and watch to see what birds flock along the shoulders and collect on the barbwire fence: meadowlarks, lark buntings, horned larks. Watch out for traffic.

Step 6 – Invite the birds to visit you

Plant trees and shrubs and flowers and use no pesticides. Put out a bird bath, put out a feeder. Keep them clean. Keep cats indoors. I have more detailed advice on bringing birds to your backyard here: https://cheyennebirdbanter.wordpress.com/2018/11/01/basic-wild-bird-feeding/.

Step 7 – Join other birdwatchers

Some of the nerdiest birders I know will say they prefer to bird alone, but they still join their local Audubon chapter. In Cheyenne, that's the Cheyenne-High Plains Audubon Society. People of all levels of birding expertise are welcome. Sign up for free email newsletters today and join when you are ready.

Step 8 – Give back to the birds

People do not make life easy for birds. Our activities can affect birds directly and indirectly. Today, I read that the popular neonicotinoid pesticides affect birds' abilities to successfully migrate if they eat even a small amount of treated seed, or an insect that has eaten treated plant material.

Writing letters to lawmakers is one option, but so is planting native plants, and so is recording your bird observations through citizen or community science projects like www.eBird.org and taking part in other conservation activities.

Step 9 – Call yourself a birdwatcher or a birder

You can do this as soon as you start Step 1, noticing birds. Not everyone does. Welcome to the world of birdwatching!

195

Friday, June 5, 2020, ToDo, page B2

2020 Big Day Bird Count best in 18 years

Cheyenne Audubon's 61st Big Day Bird Count May 16 was the best in 18 years: 141 species, with 39 people contributing observations. In those 18 years, the total number of bird species counted ranged from only 104 to 132.

Thinking about the decline in North American birds over the past 50 years, it isn't surprising that the average count for 1992-2002 is 147 species (range: 123 – 169) and the average count for 2009-2019 is 114 (range: 104 – 128).

In a way, I think the pandemic made a difference this year, plus a lucky break offset not being able to access F.E. Warren Air Force Base and part of the High Plains Grasslands Research Station.

The Cheyenne Big Day is held the third Saturday in May, as early as May 13 and as late as May 21, hopefully catching the peak of spring migration.

Sometimes migration runs late, as it apparently did in 1993 (record high total count 169 species), when wintering species like dark-eyed junco and Townsend's solitaire were counted – but we also aren't clear how far from the center of Cheyenne people were birding back then – some of our winter birds go only as far as the mountains 30 miles to the west.

Sometimes, like 1993, we get interesting shorebirds, usually heading north earlier than songbirds. Or, if the reservoirs are full, we don't have any "shore" and thus few shorebirds.

1993 and 2020 have some other interesting comparisons. Great-tailed grackles, birds of the southwest, were first reported breeding in Wyoming in 1998, and now their Cheyenne presence is spreading. Eurasian collared-doves, escaped from the caged bird trade and now nesting in our neighborhoods, were not recorded here before 1998.

But in 1993, we knew where to find burrowing owls. Now that location is full of houses.

The number of observers might matter, especially their expertise. Traditionally, we meet as a large group and hit the hotspots one at a time, Lions Park, Wyoming Hereford Ranch, the research station. The experienced birders might zero in on a vireo's chirp buried in the greenery while the bored novice birder notices American white pelicans flying overhead at the same time.

But this year might be proof that birding on our own (at least by household) as we did, ultimate physical distancing, could be more productive. All the birding hotspots were birded first thing in the morning, when birds are most active and most easily detected.

In addition, it was a magnificent spring migration day. While home for breakfast, lunch and dinner between outings, Mark and I observed a total of 23 species in our backyard, more than any of the days before or after May 16, more than any day in the last 30 years.

Now that we have lots of local birders reporting to eBird, it is easy to see May 16 was the best birding day of May 2020 in Cheyenne. However, the next day we found species we missed, the pelicans and the American redstart.

The thrill of seeing colorful migrants and welcoming back locally breeding birds was as wonderful as every year. But I missed the gathering of birders.

To see the 2020 species list broken out by location (Lions Park, Wyoming Hereford Ranch, High Plains Grasslands Research Station and others) and the comparison with 1993, go to www.cheyennebirdbanter.wordpress.com.

Cheyenne Big Day Bird Count, May 16, 2020

Canada Goose
Wood Duck
Blue-winged Teal
Cinnamon Teal
Northern Shoveler
Gadwall
American Wigeon
Mallard
Redhead
Ring-necked Duck
Lesser Scaup
Common Merganser
Ruddy Duck

Chukar
Pied-billed Grebe
Eared Grebe
Western Grebe
Clark's Grebe
Rock Pigeon (Feral Pigeon)
Eurasian Collared-Dove
White-winged Dove
Mourning Dove
Common Poorwill
Chimney Swift
Broad-tailed Hummingbird
Sora

American Coot
American Avocet
Killdeer
Baird's Sandpiper
Wilson's Snipe
Wilson's Phalarope
Spotted Sandpiper
Lesser Yellowlegs
Ring-billed Gull
Forster's Tern
Double-crested Cormorant
Great Blue Heron
Black-crowned Night-Heron
Turkey Vulture
Osprey
Northern Harrier
Sharp-shinned Hawk
Cooper's Hawk
Swainson's Hawk
Red-tailed Hawk
Ferruginous Hawk
Eastern Screech-Owl
Great Horned Owl
Belted Kingfisher
Red-headed Woodpecker
Downy Woodpecker
Hairy Woodpecker
Northern Flicker
American Kestrel
Peregrine Falcon
Prairie Falcon
Olive-sided Flycatcher
Western Wood-Pewee
Least Flycatcher
Gray Flycatcher
Cordilleran Flycatcher
Say's Phoebe
Ash-throated Flycatcher
Great Crested Flycatcher
Western Kingbird
Eastern Kingbird
Loggerhead Shrike
Blue Jay
Black-billed Magpie
American Crow
Common Raven
Mountain Chickadee
Horned Lark

Northern Rough-winged Swallow
Tree Swallow
Violet-green Swallow
Bank Swallow
Barn Swallow
Cliff Swallow
Ruby-crowned Kinglet
Red-breasted Nuthatch
White-breasted Nuthatch
Blue-gray Gnatcatcher
Rock Wren
House Wren
European Starling
Gray Catbird
Brown Thrasher
Northern Mockingbird
Eastern Bluebird
Mountain Bluebird
Veery
Swainson's Thrush
Hermit Thrush
American Robin
House Sparrow
House Finch
Red Crossbill
Pine Siskin
Lesser Goldfinch
American Goldfinch
Chestnut-collared Longspur
Chipping Sparrow
Clay-colored Sparrow
Lark Sparrow
Lark Bunting
White-crowned Sparrow
White-throated Sparrow
Vesper Sparrow
Savannah Sparrow
Song Sparrow
Lincoln's Sparrow
Green-tailed Towhee
Spotted Towhee
Yellow-headed Blackbird
Western Meadowlark
Orchard Oriole
Bullock's Oriole
Baltimore Oriole
Red-winged Blackbird
Brown-headed Cowbird

Brewer's Blackbird
Common Grackle
Great-tailed Grackle
Yellow-breasted Chat
Northern Waterthrush
Black-and-white Warbler
Orange-crowned Warbler
MacGillivray's Warbler
Common Yellowthroat
Northern Parula

Yellow Warbler
Blackpoll Warbler
Palm Warbler
Yellow-rumped Warbler
Wilson's Warbler
Western Tanager
Rose-breasted Grosbeak
Black-headed Grosbeak
Lazuli Bunting

196 Cheyenne Audubon tries a new field trip strategy

Friday, July 10, 2020, ToDo, page A8

The Cheyenne – High Plains Audubon Society has been adapting to pandemic life. We now Zoom for our board meetings, and our fall lectures will probably also be via Zoom.

Field trips are harder to adapt. Our field trip chairman, Grant Frost, suggested a survey of the Cheyenne Greenway birds in late April, and many of us signed up to individually bird a section. Our May Big Day Bird Count was arranged similarly. At the end of June, we tried "separate but simultaneous" at Curt Gowdy State Park – choosing different trails.

This time, there was some pairing up – but it is much easier to keep two arms' lengths away from one person than a group. However, the trails between the visitor center and Hidden Falls were practically a traffic jam of heavy-breathing bicyclists, reported the birders who headed that way. They had to continually step off the trail to allow bikes to pass.

One of our Laramie Audubon friends took the trail from Crystal Reservoir towards Granite Reservoir and met up with the many participants of a footrace.

Mark and I were lucky. We chose a trail with little shade, not very conducive to a summer stroll. But the trail passes along the lake shore and creek, through ponderosa pine parkland, grasslands (sad to say, much of it has gone over to cheatgrass in the last five years), mountain mahogany shrubland, cottonwood draws and across a cliff face in the stretch of about two miles.

We saw 29 species: gulls over the lake, a belted kingfisher along the creek, chickadee in the pines, meadowlarks in the grassland, green-tailed towhees in the shrubs, a lazuli bunting in the cottonwoods and rock wrens in the rocky cliff. The total for the morning, including what the other eight participants hiking in the forest saw, was 71 species.

While we could see the runners on the trail across the water, Mark and I met only two people on our trail, a friendly father and son on their bikes. So, it was a little disconcerting to come back to the trailhead three hours later and find in addition to the two vehicles there when we started, 10 more. One was the park ranger's truck, one from Colorado, one from Oregon and the rest from Laramie County, like us. They must have all gone the other way.

A normal Audubon field trip serves at least two purposes besides recreation.

One is to find birds and to report them, now that there is a global database, www.eBird.org. But the other is to learn from each other. Our local bird experts are happy to share their knowledge with newcomers. Even the experts discuss with each other their favorite field marks for identifying obscure birds.

This time, we did have someone new to birding show up, and one of our members graciously allowed her to accompany her. As we finished our hikes, we reported back by the visitor center where we gathered with our lunches under a pine – spaced as required. There was general conversation about birds we'd seen and other topics dear to birdwatcher hearts. I almost canceled the Zoom tally party I'd suggested for the evening but decided to go ahead with it anyway.

Five of us signed on, including our new birder – now a new chapter member. I'd invited people to share photos from the day and showed landscape shots of where Mark and I hiked. Mark shared his shots of a yellow warbler and a mountain bluebird. Someone photographed a nest of house wrens, and Greg Johnson shared two photos we could use to compare the beaks of hairy and downy woodpeckers – the best field mark for telling them apart (the hairy's is proportionately longer).

Then it occurred to me, maybe we should have a tally party via Zoom after more field trips and not just during pandemics. It could be a way for bird photographers to show off their pictures and for all of us to learn more about identifying the birds we see. It's a chance for birders to flock together, something we like to do as much as the birds.

Our next socially distant field trip will be July 18. We'll meet at the Pine Bluffs rest area to explore the natural area behind it and document what we find for the annual Audubon Rockies Wyoming Bioblitz. Check for details soon at www.cheyenneaudubon.wordpress.com.

197 Summertime is family time for birds

Sunday, August 2, 2020, ToDo, page B1

I asked one of our sons if he'd done any interesting birdwatching lately. He said no, it isn't as exciting as during spring migration.

I would disagree. Return migration starts up in mid-July. Migrating shorebirds were at the Wyoming Hereford Ranch Reservoir No. 1 then, while low water levels made their favorite mudflats.

One sure sign of impending autumn is the hummingbirds coming into town. My red beebalm's first flower was in bloom for about two days when it attracted the first broad-tailed hummingbird July 11. It was finished nesting in the high country and it, or other broadtails, made daily visits for 10 days. Then, a male rufous hummingbird returning from breeding – maybe in northwest Canada – came by. As the beebalm reached its peak, we had a hummingbird buzzing in every daylight hour or so, checking the flowers' recharge of nectar and mostly ignoring the hummingbird feeder.

However, birdwatching in my neighborhood in July and August is more about family drama.

Kids are naturally noisy, and the Swainson's hawks in the nest two yards down are no exception. One of the young took a tumble and landed on a branch several feet below the nest, which is set in the top of a spruce. It cried all day, but I think it climbed back up because it looked like there were two young back on the nest July 24.

One day, I thought one of the young Swainson's had fledged and was sitting in our tree. I could hear a slightly off rendition of the call, maybe like a young bird still practicing, but couldn't spot it at all. Later, I realized it was a blue jay doing imitations. And then there were the three blue jays flitting through our backyard that didn't sound like full-fledged blue jays. They weren't. Husband Mark's photo showed one still had puffy baby feathers on its rump.

July and August are when many plants bear fruit here. Whole extended families of robins strip our chokecherries even though I don't think the fruit is ripe yet.

In the neglected front yard around the corner, there's a wonderful crop of thistle. Usually, it's the American goldfinches helping themselves, but the other day there was a lesser goldfinch, which is not as common. Both are species that nest later than other songbirds because they are waiting to feed their young chewed up thistle seed instead of insects, like the other songbird parents.

If you keep your eyes open, you may see parents feeding young, even after they've fledged, like the yellow warblers we saw along Crow Creek. And, when you see five house wrens hanging around the same willow tree, you know they are siblings who haven't dispersed yet.

Young crows take longer to mature. One of the smarter species of birds, not everything they need to know is hard-wired in their brain. They must learn it. After my cleaning the other day, my dental hygienist and I peered out the window wondering just why the young crow was rolling a rock-like object around

– sorry, didn't think to bring binocs to my appointment.

One surprise this summer has been the number of mourning doves. Within a few years of the first sighting of Eurasian collared-doves in Wyoming, here in Laramie County in 1998, we quit seeing mourning doves breeding in our neighborhood. But this summer, if we look closely at the doves on the wires, many have the mourning dove's pointy-tailed silhouette. Perhaps they've finally learned to compete with the collared-doves for nest sites.

For some species, their parental duties are already finished, and they are free to flock around Cheyenne with their pals. The other morning, I estimated there were 150 common grackles carrying on boisterously in treetops and on lawns. Eventually, they will head south.

If bird behavior interests you, read Jennifer Ackerman's new book, "The Bird Way: A New Look at How Birds Talk, Work, Play, Parent and Think." Ackerman writes, in a very readable way, about the latest science that is discovering that birds approach those five kinds of behaviors in myriad ways.

I flipped to the section on parenting. From egg shape to nest shape to who feeds the young and how they are protected, birds have evolved strategies to suit their environment.

But it isn't always an eons-long process. If they aren't successful with a nest in one location one year, they may move to a different location the next.

Or they knock people on the head if they suspect they've harmed their chicks, like the Australian magpie does.

And those birds can remember people for 20 years. Yikes.

Thankfully, our birds are easier to live with, especially when we preserve prairie habitat and enhance the city forest, letting them enrich our lives.

198 Migratory Bird Treaty Act back in full force

Canada is happy again. It was not happy in December 2017 when the solicitor of the U.S. Department of the Interior reinterpreted the U.S. Migratory Bird Treaty Act so that it allowed industry to accidentally kill birds without any penalty – including birds that spend summers in Canada.

In August this year, the National Audubon Society, American Bird Conservancy, other conservation organizations and eight states successfully sued to get that reinterpretation reversed by U.S. District Court Judge Valerie Caproni.

It was the hat-making industry that early on ran afoul (afowl?) of people who value birds. Wading birds that grow luxurious plumes during the breeding season and other birds were being slaughtered so that the feathers could adorn women's hats – and sometimes whole birds were stuffed and perched on women's heads.

In 1896, Harriet Hemenway and Minna B. Hall, no slaves to fashion, organized the Massachusetts Audubon Society for the Protection of Birds to save the birds from decimation. Ten years before, George Bird Grinnell organized a group he called the Audubon Society in New York City.

By 1898, 16 more state Audubon societies were formed, leading to the founding of the National Audubon Society for the Protection of Birds in 1905.

In 1916, the U.S. and Great Britain, on behalf of Canada, signed the Migratory Bird Treaty. In 1918, the U.S. enacted the Migratory Bird Treaty Act to implement it. In later years, with bipartisan support, the treaty and the act were expanded to include agreements with Mexico, Japan and what is now Russia.

The U.S. Fish and Wildlife Service is the agency setting the MBTA policies and enforcing them.

Unless permitted by regulation, there's a prohibition to "pursue, hunt, take, capture, kill, attempt to take, capture or kill, possess, offer for sale, sell, offer to purchase, purchase, deliver for shipment, ship, cause to be shipped, deliver for transportation, transport, cause to be transported, carry or cause to be carried by any means whatever, receive for shipment, transportation or carriage, or export, at any time, or in any manner, any migratory bird...or any part, nest, or egg of any such bird."

Technically, teachers should not display abandoned robins' nests or migratory bird feathers in their classrooms without license from the U.S. Fish and Wildlife Service.

Without the MBTA, BP (British Petroleum) would not have paid $100 million in penalties for killing an estimated one million birds in the Deepwater Horizon oil spill. The fine went to wetland and migratory bird conservation as compensation.

Without the full protection of the MBTA between December 2017 and this August, snowy owls were electrocuted in four states, oil spills happened in three states, and there were other examples of avoidable bird deaths that the U.S. Fish and Wildlife Service investigated but could not penalize anyone for.

The potential for hefty fines has led to industry innovation, such as covering oil field waste pits and protecting birds from electrocution. There's still work to be done. Recent numbers show up to 64 million birds per year are still killed by powerlines, seven million by communication towers, half to one million by oil waste pits, and oil spills still happen.

It's hard for industry leaders to understand why birds should matter more than their profits. Birds are not just pretty faces. They work. They perform ecological services, which means they do things like keep other species in balance that can become pests to humans otherwise.

According to the study published in September 2019, "Decline of the North American Avifauna," by Cornell Lab of Ornithology, American Bird Conservancy, Environment and Climate Change Canada, U.S. Geological Survey, Bird Conservatory of the Rockies, Smithsonian Migratory Bird Center and Georgetown University, North America has 3 billion fewer birds today than in 1970 due to loss of habitat and other human-caused problems. What if they were all still with us? Would one advantage be that we would need fewer chemical pesticides and have fewer of their side effects?

We have a lot in common with birds. Birds are more like us than we ever expected. They learn, they plot, they communicate – even with other species. Jennifer Ackerman's latest book, "The Bird Way," explores what scientists are learning.

Environmental protection regulations have taken a hit in the last four years. As people who breathe air and drink water, more of us should be more concerned. At least the bird protections regained by the recent MBTA verdict will help people as well, if somewhat indirectly.

Next, the National Audubon Society is going to court to defend the National Environmental Policy Act. The birds will appreciate that.

199 Project FeederWatch brightens winter with backyard birds

Saturday, November 7, 2020, ToDo, page B2

Nov. 14 marks the beginning of Mark's and my 22nd season participating in Project FeederWatch. It's a community/citizen science winter bird count endeavor started by Cornell Lab of Ornithology and Birds Canada back in 1987.

It's open to people of any age and any expertise level who are willing to put up a feeder and count the birds that visit and report them 1 to 21 times during the 21-week season. This year's season ends April 9. Even if you don't participate, there's a wealth of free data, bird I.D. help and information about feeding birds available at www.feederwatch. org (and fun stuff like the participants' photo contests).

Here's how Mark and I do it. Every year, we update the description of our backyard – size doesn't change but how many trees and shrubs might. We describe our birdbath and three bird feeders: sunflower seed tube, nyjer thistle seed tube and the cage that holds a block of pressed-together seed.

For the two-day count period, we choose Saturday and Sunday each week, even now that Mark is retired. There must be a minimum of 5 days between counts, so we stick with the same days each week – it's easier to remember.

We could print out an official tally sheet for each week, but we just use a scrap sheet of paper on the kitchen table. All our feeders, and the ground under them, are visible from the kitchen window.

During the count, we are looking for the largest number that can be seen at one time of each species – at the feeders and in our bushes and trees. We estimate snow depth and amount of time we watch. We don't spend hours at the window. We spend less than one hour over the two days and just check as we walk by.

By Sunday evening, we can enter the count data online – including any comments on bird interactions and observations of disease – and upload bird photos. There's now a phone app for reporting counts too.

It's fun looking at our own data. CLO makes cool charts. I can see how the number of species and number of individuals changes during a season. I can compare all 21 seasons by species – back in 1999-2000, we were seeing goldfinches nearly every week, much less often in 2019-2000.

Our yard's landscaping has changed and matured. Over the 1999-2000 season, we saw 12 species total. Over 2019-20, it was 21 species, though one week only one bird, a junco, was seen during the two-day count period.

There were 20,000 participants last year, but only 27 in Wyoming, urban and rural. We could use more data to give scientists a more accurate view of our birds. Consider joining.

The participation fee of $18 ($15 for CLO members) funds nearly the entire endeavor, including mailing a research kit to first timers: instructions and bird i.d. poster. We all can opt for the calendar, 16-page annual report and a digital subscription to Living Bird, a 70-page, full-color quarterly magazine normally available for the minimum $39 CLO membership fee.

What will you see at your feeders? Here's the list of the top 25 species based on the percentage of Wyoming participants reporting them last season:

Eurasian collared-dove: 77
House finch: 74
House sparrow: 66
American goldfinch: 66
Dark-eyed junco: 66
Black-capped chickadee: 66
American robin: 59
European starling: 55
Northern flicker: 55
Red-breasted nuthatch: 55
Downy woodpecker: 48
Black-billed magpie: 44
Blue jay: 37
Mountain chickadee: 37
Red-winged blackbird: 33
American crow: 33
Pine siskin: 33
Rosy finch species: 25
Hairy woodpecker: 25
Common raven: 22
White-breasted nuthatch: 22
Common grackle: 22
Sharp-shinned hawk: 22
Wild turkey: 18
Song sparrow: 18

There's an irruption of pine siskins this year because there isn't a good seed crop in Canada. You may see more of them at your feeders.

Here in Cheyenne, we are unlikely to see wild turkeys or rosy finches, but the other species, and more, are all possible. If you go to Project FeederWatch's "Common Feeder Birds Interactive," set it for "Northwest" and "Black oil sunflower seed" and you'll find photos of most of our species. Click on each photo and discover what other kinds of food and feeders that species prefers.

CLO has the free Merlin phone app for identifying birds. You answer simple questions about location, size, color, behavior and habitat for your unknown bird and it shows you photos of possible birds.

For each species, CLO's All About Birds website, www.allaboutbirds.org, will give you multiple photos, sound recordings, range map, habitat, food, nesting, behavior information, conservation status, cool facts, backyard tips and their names in both Spanish and French.

I hope you'll join Project Feeder-Watch this winter with me and Mark. It is one of the things I like about winter.

200 First Cassin's finch visits Gorges backyard

Saturday, December 5, 2020, ToDo, page B2

By early November, our winter feeder birds are back.

House finches are the most abundant and show up every day. Juncos come when the weather's bad. This year, we are regularly hosting two red-breasted nuthatches and two mountain chickadees.

Occasionally, a downy woodpecker, flicker or collared-doves fly in. The goldfinches are unreliable, but their close cousins, the pine siskins, are showing up every day. That's unusual for them, but they are part of the flock pushed south this year due to a bad seed crop in the north.

I was gazing out the window at the birds busily flitting about the feeders and patio paving below, then realized I was seeing an odd bird in the mix.

House finches are the faded brown birds with faded stripes down their breasts. The males have pale pink heads that get redder in the spring. Pine siskins have stripes too but are smaller and their stripes are very dark - plus, on their wings they have a white bar and a flash of yellow.

The odd bird had the pine siskins' dark breast stripes, but it was the size of the house finch. It couldn't be dismissed as an aberrant house finch because there were light-colored markings on its head that house finches don't have, and the back of the top of its head was, well, kind of a pointy topknot. Time to get out the Sibley Field Guide to Birds: "Female Cassin's Finch," the 103rd species to fly over or into our yard.

The males have pink/red heads like house finches, but with the topknot being the brightest. Unlike the female, their breast stripes are very faint, fainter than the house finch's.

To get an overview of everything known about a bird species, I go online to Cornell Lab of Ornithology's "Birds of North America Online," but it doesn't exist anymore. It's been rolled into "Birds of the World" at www.birdsoftheworld.org, where my subscription is still good ($49 per year, or by the month or discounted for three years).

When I pulled up the Cassin's finch page, I was surprised to find a notation that I'd recorded this species in eBird seven times. Clicking on that link showed my two current observations, August last year in the Snowy Range, April 2014 and December 2013 in Hartville, June 2013 in a canyon in Washington State and July 2011 at Upper North Crow Reservoir.

This is a finch that breeds in coniferous forests of the Rocky Mountains, from just over the Canadian border to northern New Mexico and Arizona.

It can migrate altitudinally, spending

the winter at lower elevations (Hartville, in Platte County, is at only 4,600 feet and Cheyenne at 6,100, compared to 10,000 feet in the Snowies) or latitudinally, flying as far south as central Mexico. Sometimes they just hang out if the seed crop is good. The one that visited us must have lost her flock.

Cassin's finch's closest relative is the purple finch, an eastern species, diverging from it genetically 3 million years ago. It diverged from the house finch 9 million years ago.

Ornithologists have classified Cassin's as a "cardueline" finch, a subfamily of finches of 184 species worldwide, including the Hawaiian honeycreeper species. In North America, it includes the redpoll, pine and evening grosbeaks, pine siskins, goldfinches, rosy finches, crossbills and our "rosefinches"—house, purple and Cassin's.

Besides sharing similar skull formation, cardueline species feed their young regurgitated seeds. Other perching birds feed theirs' insects. Cardueline species can grip a plant stem and extract seeds from flower heads. I see house finches and goldfinches do that in my wildflower garden all the time.

Sparrows wait until the seeds fall to the ground – I've never seen a junco, a species of sparrow, pluck seeds from plants or feeders, though one was experimenting last year.

I was curious if "cardueline" came from the same origins as "card" in cardinals, named for the religious figures in red robes, but red wouldn't hold for all the sub family species.

It's from "carduus," meaning wild thistle or artichoke. Artichoke is a giant thistle-type plant in the aster/sunflower family. And this makes perfect sense. These finches like to pluck seeds from flower heads, including thistle, coneflower, sunflower and aster.

I'm glad my cardueline finches can also pluck black oil sunflower seed out of our hanging tube feeder since it doesn't take long to clean out the seeds in our garden.

We look forward to hosting the birds during a winter we can't host people.

2021

201 Mullen Fire changes forest habitats

Saturday, May 1, 2021, ToDo, page B2

It isn't good, it isn't bad. We can't make moral judgements. It just is. This is the message Jesse McCarty had for us about the Mullen Fire.

McCarty is a wildlife biologist and on the natural resources staff of the Medicine Bow – Routt National Forest's Laramie Ranger District. The Mullen Fire started Sept. 17, 2020, on the forest in the Savage Run Wilderness Area. The source of ignition is still under investigation.

From there, firefighters were able to keep it from burning an area around Lake Owen critical to the safety of Cheyenne's water supply. But on Sept. 26, the wind pushed the fire down and around on a one-day, 30,000 acre-run to the east. That's a swath 6 miles wide and 8 miles long.

That was the day Cheyenne's skies turned orange, even though we were 70 miles downwind of the fire. That is the day that if you breathed that orange air, your lungs didn't feel right for a couple months afterwards.

(To see the extent of the fire, go to the website that tracks wildland fires, https://tinyurl.com/mullen-wildfire.)

The Cheyenne – High Plains Audubon Society invited McCarty to talk about what the effects of the fire were and will be on wildlife, especially birds, and what restoration work is planned.

This forest has been using certain bird species as indicators of habitat. Not all bird species specialize in a narrowly described habitat, but each species monitored is tied to a particular one. For instance, the Lincoln's sparrow is found around wet mountain meadows. As the meadow fills in with trees over time, there will be more forest species such as the brown creeper.

After a fire, the American three-toed woodpecker moves in. A species of the spruce-fir habitat, it is most numerous where insects are taking advantage of dying trees. When the flush of those insects is over and low growth is sprouting, another bird species will move in. On it goes until the spruce-fir forest is re-established and golden-crowned kinglets are at home again.

The Forest Service is continuing its bird surveys this summer. It also keeps an eye on threatened and endangered species and others in special, protective categories.

Field biologist Don Jones of Laramie asked an important question. In view of the warming climate (the forest was experiencing another drought year in 2020), will areas that were once spruce-fir come back, or will the vegetation of a drier climate prevail, like pine-juniper?

Jones is young enough that he may see the answer in his lifetime.

The more than 55 people (not counting instances of more than one person per screen) around the state and beyond who were participating in the Zoom meeting were also concerned about other wildlife, such as the large mammals. McCarty said that there didn't appear to be large mammal carcasses in the wake of the fire. The new vegetative growth after the fire will attract big game.

The insect life will have taken a hit where it couldn't find moist places to hide, McCarty said, but there is not much fire science related to insects.

When McCarty visited the forest in December, he found green growth. Sometimes, he said, this is from the caches of seeds squirrels and other small animals make. Also, the heat of the fire will have opened the serotinous cones of lodgepole pine, releasing seed. Aspen growth is also stimulated by fire.

The spread of cheatgrass is a concern and so the forest is using applications of Rejuvra, an herbicide that keeps it from germinating. There will also be grass seeding and tree planting in critical areas such as steep slopes.

Burned areas in the Savage Run Wilderness Area will not be repaired – the definition of a wilderness area is that people do not interfere with ecological processes there.

For most of us in the audience, the Medicine Bow is our forest, and we want to know how we can volunteer to help it recover. This year, the forest is not allowing volunteers within the burn area, but you can find other volunteer needs by contacting Aaron Voos, aaron. voos@usda.gov.

As the summer recreation season gets started, we will find trails and campgrounds in the fire area that are closed. Please honor the forest's directives for your own safety until hazardous trees have been dropped and burnt slopes are stabilized.

And make sure you don't cause the next forest fire.

202 Close encounters of the robin kind found in backyard

Saturday, July 10, 2021, ToDo, page B2

You could say that the robins in our backyard are benefitting from global warming this summer.

After 32 years managing without it, Mark and I had air conditioning installed, and the robins discovered it offered a good nesting location.

We normally can keep things comfortable by closing windows before the outside temperatures get hotter than the inside, plus the basement stays chilly. But with warmer and sometimes smokier summers, it seemed like the right time to invest in heat pump technology, referred to as a mini-split. It also provides heat and can be hooked up to a solar electric system someday.

The robins built their whole nest before we were aware. It is on top of the new conduit in the corner by the back door we don't use much. With the roof overhang, it is well protected.

I've heard about robins building nests on porch lights and attacking anyone who goes in and out the associated door. Gardening takes us back and forth below this nest location, but neither robin parent divebombed us or the dog. Mark even put up our 8-foot stepladder once to take a photo and there were no complaints.

Every time I glanced at the nest when a parent was on it, incubating the eggs, staring at me, I'd apologize for another disruption.

Finally, the day came when I noticed, looking out the kitchen window, that one of the parents was pausing on one of our fence posts with a big juicy, bright green caterpillar in its beak. There were many more treats for the nestlings, but caterpillars seemed the most popular.

It takes a lot of herbivorous prey to raise baby robins and I wondered what plant damage the robins were averting this summer. Gosh, it might have been the right year for growing cabbages. My last efforts were aborted by caterpillars.

By June 19, there was one large nestling left in the nest, almost filling it. By June 20, the nest was empty. I didn't see any speckle-breasted baby robins anywhere.

I went to the corner of the yard by the compost bins to re-pot houseplants. As I approached, a robin flew in, perching on a branch eye level with me. I stopped, and we looked each other in the eye. I murmured congratulations in case it was one of our parent robins. Then it flew to a new perch a few feet away and I turned, and we locked eyes again.

Most wild animals are interested in staying away from people unless we are handing out food. Otherwise, they don't encourage our attention because that is often dangerous.

The robin shifted position again, caught my eye, and then flew off around the upright junipers. I could hear again the quiet call it had been making on the other side of the bushes, plus another odd one. So, I circled the junipers and when I got to the point where I could see into the interior, there was the fledgling.

Unlike a killdeer which tries to draw you away from its nest, I felt like the robin had led me to the fledgling. Minutes later, the fledgling flashed away to another shrub, but I didn't go in pursuit.

Within a week, June 26, I saw a robin sitting on the nest again. Less than three feet away, a male house sparrow with a beak full of dry grass waited patiently for the robin to take a break. His mate waited behind him. I know we have a housing shortage in Cheyenne, but does the robin have a spare room, or what?

We still have a feeder hanging over the patio, under the clear corrugated plastic roof. It's one of those cage types that uses the blocks of seed that seem to be glued together. The red-breasted nuthatches visit it multiple times a day, pecking away.

A pair of these birds nested in a rotten stub on a tree across the street. We think these are the birds flying over our low house to our feeder. On June 25, I saw five nuthatches on the feeder, probably the whole family dining together. They are completely at home. In fact, as I walk back and forth doing chores, I sometimes remember to look up to where, two or three feet over my head, a nuthatch is completely unconcerned by my presence, or that I've stopped so close.

Maybe, like the geese in the park, they read body language and distinguish between danger and safety.

203 Neighborhood Swainson's hawks fledge three; fall migration underway

Just as they did last year, a pair of Swainson's hawks nested in the neighbors' spruce tree two houses down.

Thanks to some tree pruning in between, Mark and I had a perfect view of the nest from our bathroom window.

I'm sure the hawks were a little put out this spring to discover after their long migratory haul from Argentina that the field adjacent now sports a three-story apartment building under construction. But about a quarter mile away is the Greenway and the railroad right of way, still plenty of open space and tasty ground squirrels.

By July 7 we could see two fuzzy white heads in the nest. Nearly three weeks later, they were mostly brown. And then the youngsters started climbing out of the nest and onto the tree branches. That's when we realized there were three of them.

We think the day one of the juveniles left the nest for the first time was July 25. At 6 a.m., it was sitting on a bare branch just over our back wall, looking straight back at us through the kitchen window.

There were a few days the youngsters cried a lot for parental attention. One day they landed in our tree and then all three circled low over our block. It's become quieter, but they are still spending time in the neighborhood, sometimes on the nest tree.

It amazes me that a large hawk, best suited for flying grasslands in search of rodents (summer) and large insects (winter), would choose to nest in a residential neighborhood. I'm glad we can provide the big trees they require to successfully breed.

Hummingbirds

The hummingbirds are a mystery this year. Their favorite red beebalm was halfway through blooming the last week in July and I hadn't seen them yet.

I checked my records on eBird.org and saw since 2013 they have arrived for a three-week stay starting the last week of July or the first week of August. My beebalm is blooming ahead of schedule and they may miss it. I caught a glimpse of one hummingbird July 30 as it flitted quickly over other flowers.

Maybe the red beebalm is early this year because of all our earlier hot weather and moisture. Maybe the broadtailed hummingbirds are later because our mountains, where they nest, have been unusually full of nectar-filled flowers and they are staying longer.

Maybe we should all put up our hummingbird feeders anyway. Remember, use a little heat to dissolve 1 part white sugar in 4 parts water. Use no other sugar types, use no red dye, and replace any nectar that gets cloudy-looking.

Weidensaul's new book

Mark and I are reading "A World on the Wing: The Global Odyssey of Migratory Birds" by Scott Weidensaul. A whole chapter is devoted to Swainson's hawks and unraveling the mysteries of their breeding and migration using new tracking technology.

The book also discusses the number of ways migrating birds are killed by human actions, directly and indirectly, that are preventable.

For instance, because many songbirds

migrate at night, one of their navigational aids is starlight. Unfortunately, the glow from cities is attracting them and studies show more migrants in cities than there used to be. But when the small birds land in the mornings, do they find the trees and shrubbery full of insects they need to eat to recharge? Sometimes, they find well-lit skyscrapers and become disoriented, circling until exhausted, falling to the ground, discovered dead on the sidewalk in the morning.

City night light is detrimental to other life too, including plants and people without room-darkening shades. It increases with each porch and parking lot light left on. But it can also be decreased by one resident, one business owner and one municipality at a time.

For your home security lighting, see if you can use motion detection technology. You'll save money on your electric bill. For parking lot lights and streetlights, choose those that are hooded, lighting only what's below and not the sky. You'll save money, too.

Without our own astronomical observatory, like Flagstaff, Arizona, I don't think we will become an International Dark Sky City, asking Cheyennites to drive with only parking lights on, but it would be neat.

Fall migration has already begun. The Swainson's hawk family will head south sometime after the middle of September. Only six or eight weeks after fledging, the young Swainson's all over western North America make a journey of as much as 7,000 miles to the Argentine pampas. I imagine it looks something like Wyoming grasslands there. Safe travels, kids and parents.

204 Dry Creek restoration to improve hydrology, habitat

Saturday, September 4, 2021, ToDo, page B2

Jeff Geyer is fixing Cheyenne's Dry Creek.

First, how did it get its name? Jeff, Laramie County Conservation District water specialist, told me that unlike Crow Creek, our other stream that starts in the mountains, Dry Creek starts somewhere on the F.E. Warren Air Force Base. He said it never had much of a channel, with the water frequently spreading out in flat, temporarily marshy areas and percolating into the water table below as it flowed after a rain or snow event.

Fast-forward 160 years. The Greenway now follows Dry Creek as it crosses northern Cheyenne west to east, parallel to Dell Range Boulevard. At North College Drive it heads southeast to the new East Park and crosses under Interstate 80. It joins Crow Creek near where the sewage treatment plant is today on Campstool Road.

What's changed is the Dry Creek watershed, which drains two-thirds of Cheyenne. More land surfaces surrounding the creek have been paved and built on over the last 30 to 40 years as Cheyenne expands. Jeff says you can see the change on Google Earth (use the free Pro version you can download).

Snowmelt and rainfall aren't absorbed by pavement and roofs, so they run off into Dry Creek, making much higher flows. Higher flows are faster. Faster flows are straighter. Straighter flows have more energy to erode the soil. Between Campstool and I-80, that energy cut 5-foot-deep banks and sent good soil into Crow Creek where it gets deposited in the downstream reservoirs - not good for reservoirs, or the fish in Crow Creek.

In 2019, Jeff started to fix a small section of Dry Creek that will make a difference. The idea is to slow the creek down by increasing its sinuosity which will reduce the energy of the water. The water flow needs to look more like a traveling snake – looping to one side and then to the other, rather than a straight stick.

Mathematically, a straight stream has a sinuosity of 1 – the ratio of the distance the water travels is 1 to 1 with the length of the valley. Jeff would like to see a sinuosity of 1.2 or 1.4, meaning that in a 100 feet of valley length, the water would loop an extra 20 to 40 feet.

The banks of a sinuous stream will still erode a bit, but much of the dirt will be deposited in the next curve – slow moving streams can't carry as much soil suspended in the water.

While some earth work was required to reduce the 5-foot cutbank in places to give Dry Creek access to the flood plain during rainfall or snowmelt events, much of the sinuosity building is being done with willow stems, logs, posts and stakes.

At just the right location and angle in the stream bottom, Jeff and volunteers pounded in stakes in a line and then wove willow stems, forming a "Beaver Dam Analog." The willows were from a nearby location where they die back and new willows continue growing.

The woven willows are like snow fence that slows the wind, making the snow drop out into drifts. This structure slows water carrying dirt so the dirt will drop and form a bar where willows will grow, and their roots will stabilize the stream bed. There is already a nice stand of coyote willows in one spot.

Up on the flood plain are "Post Assisted Log Structures." Logs are pinned to the flood plain to make a rough passage that will also slow water down.

Long term, slower stream flow will allow more water around the creek to be absorbed and stored. That underground water flows like surface water and will eventually resurface in the creek, recharging it. Jeff is hoping for a little water to be always in Dry Creek – maybe it will need a new name.

Changing Dry Creek's hydrology, Jeff also expects to provide the moisture needed for more diverse vegetation for wildlife habitat. Mule deer and ermine have been seen. Cheyenne Audubon members have been making bird observations. Lorie Chesnut, a member, was instrumental in obtaining a $3,000 grant through the National Audubon Society's Western Water Network Grants this year that paid for the stakes and native plants.

As Jeff surveyed the conservation district-managed pasture that surrounds the first phase of the hydrology project (and a second phase that has just begun to the south), he frowned at all the 6-foot-tall mullein stalks and the other non-native weeds. Much more work will be required to transform the pasture into prairie more useful to ground-nesting birds and other wildlife, bringing it back to its formerly lush and flower-filled self.

205

Fall reservoir birding is a leisurely affair, mostly black and white

Birds and birders are in a rush during the spring.

The birds are hurrying to get from their wintering grounds to their breeding grounds. But fall birding is as leisurely as that of the birds' migration south.

On the fourth Saturday in October, the Cheyenne Audubon field trip was to Fossil Creek Reservoir Natural Area, Fort Collins, Colorado, about 45 miles south of Cheyenne.

A reservoir during migration seasons is the avian equivalent of a truck stop, a crossroads with each species having its own itinerary. Birders are looking for the most interesting birds, the most exotic license plates.

Since ducks, geese and other water birds placidly rest or feed (unless a bald eagle passes by), every birder gets a chance to look through a spotting scope at them. We had five scopes on this trip.

We were dismayed to see the low water level. Much of the reservoir was mudflats with Fossil Creek trickling from pond to pond. Then we realized there were four kinds of shorebirds probing in the mud.

American avocets, shorebirds, waded in shallow water. These birds of the western Great Plains are ghostly white with black wings by the time they head south for a winter mostly on beaches, including those in southern U.S. and Mexico. In spring they have cinnamon-pink heads and necks.

No need for special optics to enjoy the many American white pelicans we saw, also white with black wing markings. With wingspans of 90 to 120 inches, they fly in lines, like geese, and sometimes spiral with thermals. Another bird of the Great Plains and Intermountain West, they head south to water that stays open so they can fish.

There were rafts of gulls, almost all ring-billed, also the most common gull around Cheyenne. It prefers to nest inland in the northern states and Canada and winter inland in the south and along the Pacific and Atlantic coasts.

We also found a lesser black-backed gull. In winter they are most common along the Atlantic and Gulf coasts, less common inland in the eastern half of the U.S. But the latest range map shows an influx into eastern Colorado. Perhaps the state tourism department invited them to make the trip from their summer homes located anywhere from Iceland to Siberia.

A raft of American coots, each bird the darkest slate gray accented with a bright white bill, was enjoying a day of rest in their migratory trip – or maybe not. Their range map (www.AllAbout-Birds.org) shows some can be found year-round in a narrow strip along the east edge of the Rockies from Montana through Wyoming and Colorado.

Western grebes, dark gray from the top of their heads and down the back of their thin necks, but white from their chins to their breasts, were busy diving for small fish. They were stopping over, heading for the Pacific Coast, anywhere from Vancouver Island to Mexico. The range map shows them year-round inland in central Mexico too, but I don't know if that's a population of birds that doesn't migrate or if some northern birds join the locals.

Buffleheads, small black and white ducks, were bobbing around, playing a game of one-upmanship, furiously beating their wings, "standing" on their toes to look large and menacing, while raising their crests of white, then diving. They breed up in western Canada and think much of the U.S., including Cheyenne, is a lovely place to spend the winter.

There was a handful of lesser scaup, another black and white duck, but with a pale blue bill. Breeding from Alaska down to Wyoming, they head south either for the Pacific Coast or the southern states, or even the southernmost tip of Central America, or the Caribbean. Definitely not as cold tolerant as the buffleheads.

Common mergansers, the females sporting their shaggy red-feather crests, mixed with other, sleeker, redheaded ducks, including those known as redheads, plus a few canvasbacks, distinguishable by combined forehead and bill silhouettes forming straight diagonals.

In Wyoming, common mergansers may be seen year-round. Whether the same individuals stick around all year, or the ones from farther north move down for the winter, I don't know.

Redheads breed in Wyoming, but this western species likes to go at least as far south as New Mexico.

Canvasbacks breed in central Colorado and north into Alaska, but they head south for winter, some only as far as southern Colorado.

Finally, yes, there were Canada geese and mallards, the most recognizable waterbirds. You will see their permanent flocks and the winter ducks like buffleheads – and birdwatchers – around Cheyenne reservoirs if there's open water this winter.

206 Saturday, December 11, 2021, ToDo, page A12
Bird feeding safety: clean feeders, cat fencing, glass obstruction

Winter is the most popular season for feeding birds.

Watching birds from your window is an entertaining and affordable, even educational hobby to lighten long winters. But please keep safety in mind as you apply these tips.

Cleanliness

Whether you choose a tube feeder, hopper feeder (looks like a little house), cage (for blocks of seed or suet) or platform feeder, make sure it is scrubbable.

The Cornell Lab of Ornithology recommends every two weeks taking feeders apart and brushing out all the detritus and washing them in a diluted bleach solution. You can use your dishwasher instead. Rinse feeders well and let dry thoroughly before refilling.

Wear gloves when handling dirty feeders or wash your hands afterwards.

Seed that gets wet can harbor mold and bird diseases. If you notice any finches with disfigured faces, it's time to take down all your feeders for a week to temporarily disburse (social distance) the flock while you get them clean.

The one best seed – most nutritious and most popular – for our local seed-eaters is black oil sunflower seed. But unless you can afford to buy hull-less, you will have moldering hulls below the feeder. If you feed one of the bird seed mixes, there are a lot of seeds in it our birds won't eat, and they also end up making a kind of mat you'll want to rake up regularly. At our house we hang the feeders over the patio and sweep often.

Finches like nyjer ("thistle" that doesn't sprout) seed. It is very fine, requiring tube feeders with smaller holes or a fabric "sock." The hulls are tiny and blow away. If you put out suet, make sure the weather is cold to keep it from going rancid – or dripping.

Window strikes

Birds have a hard time identifying glass. They see the reflection of sky and vegetation, smack into your window and die or are severely injured, becoming a snack for other animals. Or if two of your windows on opposite sides of your house line up, they may think they can fly through.

Your regular window screens can break the reflection and soften the impact. There are other strategies and stickers that can be stuck to the outside of the glass (see https://abcbirds. org/glass-collisions/stop-birds-hitting-windows/).

The easy strategy is to place your feeders within three feet of your favorite bird-watching window—or even stick a suction-cup feeder on the window itself. That way, when the sharp-shinned hawk startles your flock, none of them will be moving fast enough to hurt themselves bumping into the window.

Cats

Our cats love bird-feeding season. They sit on the windowsill for hours, entranced. But if you haven't made your felines into indoor cats yet like Lark and Lewis, please don't feed the birds.

What about the neighbors' cats? That's tricky. You might be able to convince neighbors that indoor cats are safer, healthier and more fun, and that they could then take up bird feeding like you.

Realistically, you are going to have to cat-proof your bird feeding station. While it is good to have cover, shrubs and trees, near your feeder so seed-eating birds can escape hawks, you don't want it so close cats can pounce on birds feeding on the ground.

You might try encompassing the area under the feeder, where the birds feed on the ground, with a short fence – one you can step over. The idea is that while a cat can sneak up on a flock unobserved, having to leap the fence will give the birds the visual warning they need to escape.

Water

Water is another way to attract birds – if you can keep your winter birdbath clean. It also has to stand up to freezing and thawing (unless you add a heater) and it needs to be easy to remove ice from or clean, like a flexible plastic trash can lid.

Birds should be able to reach the water when perched on the rim. If there is a sloping edge or sloping rock, birds will also be able to walk in for a bath.

Squirrels

Our fox squirrels are entertaining, but they can destroy birdfeeders and scarf down all your birdseed. We have a tube feeder that shuts down when any animal heavier than a finch sits on it.

Funnel-shaped barriers can be mounted on the pole below a feeder and/or placed over the top of a feeder, especially one that is hanging. Our feeders hang from the underside of our patio roof.

You can also distract squirrels by feeding them peanuts nearby.

Timing

Decide how much seed you can afford. Put seed out at the times of day you are most likely to enjoy watching your feeder. Being consistent will bring the most visitors, but if your seed isn't available, the flock will move on to one of their other regular daily stops.

More information

The Feederwatch.org website is a fantastic free resource. You can find out what birds are seen in our area, each species' favorite foods and the best types of feeders for each.

The Project Feederwatch season runs early November into April. See feederwatch.org to join anytime and add your sightings.

The Christmas Bird Count has a feeder-watching component too. See cheyenneaudubon.org to find out how to take part.

2022

Saturday, January 8, 2022, ToDo, page A10

207 Ghosts of Christmas Bird Counts past visit local birdwatcher

Christmas 1989 was Mark's and my first Cheyenne Christmas Bird Count and the first time we met most of the people attending the tally party afterwards.

May Hanesworth, then in her mid-80s, was the count compiler and we met at her apartment. It was a scary place for me, the mother of two boys, ages 1 and 4, because it was filled with breakable figurines of birds. But May, a retired music teacher, was not concerned, and the boys and I often visited on Cheyenne – High Plains Audubon Society business after that. Later, I learned that she and her husband, Bob, secretary of the Cheyenne Frontier Days Committee for 25 years, had had a gracious home on 8th Avenue.

When May could no longer handle the job of compiler, Jane Dorn took over. She and her husband, Robert, are the authors of "Wyoming Birds." When Jane retired, they moved to Lingle and started the Guernsey – Fort Laramie CBC. We were planning to drive over to help this year, but both of our vehicles developed unroadworthy symptoms the day before.

Our next compiler was Greg Johnson, but he's moved on to bigger things – he's the CBC editor for our region. Grant Frost has the Cheyenne job now.

As the business end of the 1989 tally party got going, the Lebsack girls, maybe middle school age, took our boys into the kitchen to play. Their dad, Fred, was one of those birders who loved to geek out on subjects like the finer points of feather coloration. He died prematurely in 2011, and his widow, Judy, and his daughters now live in California.

The one person we had met previous to the tally party was Nels Sostrum, thanks to the regional Audubon director whom we knew through our old chapter in Miles City, Montana.

We always thought we would see more of Nels when he retired from the state, but he jumped straight into his other hobby, painting. And then he met Anne, and through her he acquired stepchildren and step-grandchildren. I hadn't seen him for a long time when his obituary showed up in the paper this fall. Nels's painting of Battle Creek in the Sierra Madre Range hangs on our wall and will always remind me of birding with him.

John Cornelison was at that tally party, too. After tallying the birds, the discussion turned to electing a new chapter president. John volunteered. Mark volunteered to be vice president and I, program chair. Later, we learned that John was the founding president back in 1974.

For many years, John and his wife, Joanne, invited the chapter to hold the tally party at the Westgate community building where there is a large living room with plenty of space for tables and chairs and laying out potluck contributions. Mark and I saw John and Joanne at an event last fall and were saddened to learn of John's death in December. The family asked that our chapter be one of two organizations receiving memorial donations.

I'm guessing that Jim and Carol Hecker were also at our first Cheyenne tally party. Jim was one of the pediatricians our boys saw at the Cheyenne Children's Clinic. He encouraged me to drop the "Dr." when addressing him outside the office and it took a while to do so.

When the boys were young, we had a CBC tradition to stop by mid-morning at their house to warm up, eat Christmas cookies and drink hot chocolate - and count the birds at their feeders. We still enjoy their hospitality.

In 1989, Mark and I were younger than the usual Audubon demographic. People with children spend most of their organized social time in kid-related groups. But there is something to be said for hanging out with people old enough to be your kids' grandparents and great-grandparents, especially when the real relatives live far away. And yes, we raised two sons who are assets to the Cheyenne CBC, whenever their families' Christmas travel schedules coincide with the date (not this year).

This Christmas, our toddler-aged granddaughter received her first pair of binoculars – from her maternal grandfather. This birding thing can be infectious!

Whatever your age and birding ability, look up www.CheyenneAudubon. org. Join us for hybrid programs, field trips and other activities such as the 8th Annual Cheyenne Habitat Hero Workshop Jan. 29 at Laramie County Community College, also available virtually.

Cheyenne Christmas Bird Count

Dec. 18, 2021, 15 participants, 36 species observed count day and 5 count week. List compiled by Grant Frost.

CW – count week: species observed on one of the three days before or after, but not on the count day.

Snow Goose CW	Red-tailed Hawk 7
Cackling Goose 781	Rough-legged Hawk 4
Canada Goose 1512	Ferruginous Hawk 1
Northern Shoveler CW	Eastern Screech-owl 1
Mallard 226	Great Horned Owl 3
Northern Pintail 2	Belted Kingfisher 1
Ring-necked Duck CW	Downy Woodpecker 1
Common Goldeneye 19	Northern Flicker 14
Common Merganser CW	Northern Shrike 2
Rock Pigeon 230	Blue Jay 11
Eurasian Collared-Dove 162	Blacked-billed Magpie 53
Wilson's Snipe 1	American Crow 87
Cooper's Hawk CW	Common Raven 8
Northern Goshawk 1	Mountain Chickadee 8
Bald Eagle 2	Horned Lark 13

Red-breasted Nuthatch 5
White-breasted Nuthatch 2
European Starling 233
Townsend's Solitaire 14
American Robin 8
House Sparrow 170

House Finch 75
American Tree Sparrow 26
Dark-eyed Junco 53
Song Sparrow 2
Red-winged Blackbird 24

208 How to keep prairie birds, and us, safe

Saturday, February 5, 2022, ToDo, page A10

"Nurturing the Prairie" was the theme of this year's Cheyenne Habitat Heroes workshop held last month. For me, that includes the plants, animals and people.

Cheyenne sits in the middle of the shortgrass prairie so what we "townies" do matters as well.

Zach Hutchinson, workshop presenter and community science coordinator for Audubon Rockies, reminded us of the study showing North America has lost 2.9 billion birds, including 53% of grassland birds, since 1970. This means that for every 100 birds you could count along a certain distance of our county roads then, today you would only count 47.

One of the biggest causes is loss of habitat, including the conversion of undeveloped land into subdivisions, commercial property or cropland. Cheyenne is going through a terrific building phase. The landscaping in new high density residential neighborhoods will soon draw in birds, but not the grassland birds. It is the ring of small-acreage landowners around the city who can make a difference.

First, what shape is the acreage in? Is it full of native prairie grasses and what range managers call forbs, which the rest of us call wildflowers? Or was it overgrazed and is now full of invasive weeds like toadflax and needs renewal?

Another workshop speaker, Aaron Maier, range ecologist for Audubon Rockies, talked at length about regenerative agriculture and how farmers are changing their practices, so they spend less on fertilizers and trips with the tractor yet sequester more carbon, capture more moisture and accumulate more beneficial soil microbes.

Aaron also talked about healthy grassland grazing practices benefiting wildlife as well, as laid out by the Audubon Conservation Ranching Initiative. Ranchers following Audubon's guidelines for best practices for land, wildlife and livestock management are guaranteed premium prices for their product marked as "Audubon Certified."

But the small acreage owner is probably not going to be grazing cattle. In fact, without 30-36 acres and a seasonal rotation plan, they can't even graze one horse for one year (without supplemental feed) but must keep them much of the year in a corral to avoid making their entire property into a dust bowl.

Not to say that there aren't grassland birds that sometimes enjoy bare ground – after all, they evolved alongside the buffalo, famous for creating mosaics of bare ground in their migrations.

A lot of small acreage owners don't have livestock, but they do have cats and dogs that can be very detrimental to grassland birds. It's easy to see how, once you realize grassland birds nest on the ground.

Horned larks, western meadowlarks, vesper sparrows, savannah sparrows and other grassland bird species have come up with various ruses and camouflages to avoid native predators. However, they haven't evolved yet to deal with what the American Bird Conservancy considers to be an invasive species: cats.

Cats kill more than a billion birds a year in the U.S. Zach pointed out that popular "trap, neuter and release" programs have a flaw – they allow cats to go back outside and kill more native birds and small mammals. It's a touchy subject. I admit to having been the owner of an indoor/outdoor cat up until 1990, when I started keeping my cat indoors. Four cats later, I'm a proponent of catios – screened outdoor areas – and taking leashed cats for walks.

Grassland birds nest sometime between April and July. That's a good time to keep dogs on a leash so they won't find and eat bird eggs. And it's an excellent time to abstain from mowing both the previous year's and current year's growth. If you value wildlife, mow only after consulting the professionals over at the Laramie County Conservation District.

However, you may want to forgo much vegetation around your house and outbuildings. The national Firewise program, firewise.org, has guidelines for protecting property from fire on the forest edges as well as in the grasslands.

And what can we townies do for grassland birds? Use less energy. Buy less new stuff. Every energy source I can think of has been detrimental to wildlife: harvesting whale oil, excavating peat, cutting firewood as well as producing the climate-changing fumes of coal, oil and natural gas and the toxic residue of nuclear, and building the cleaner but often habitat- and migration-disrupting installments of hydro, wind and solar power.

It seems as soon as we come up with energy saving changes – like families having fewer children and more efficient appliances, someone invents something like the new energy-intensive game of cryptocurrency mining. Don't mind me, I'm a trifle depressed after watching a new movie, the very dark comedy, "Don't Look Up."

But I plan to look up – spring bird migration will commence any day now.

209 Raptors entice birdwatchers to follow the "The Nunn Guy" in cold early start

Saturday, March 19, 2022, ToDo, page A10

A Cheyenne Audubon field trip in mid-February, starting at a frosty 8 a.m., usually attracts only a handful of diehards. But throw the word "raptor" into the publicity and suddenly there are 20-some people milling around in the parking lot at Lions Park, anxious to go see eagles, hawks, falcons and owls.

Or maybe it was the thought of travelling south to a balmier climate. Our destination, "Raptor Alley," starts in Nunn, Colorado, 30 miles south of Cheyenne. And it was balmy – 50 degrees, sunny, no wind and dry gravel roads.

We met our tour guide, Gary Lefko, "The Nunn Guy," at the Soaring V Fuels gas station/store. A seasoned trip leader knows how important it is to start a birding trip with empty bladders, especially in the nearly treeless farm fields of eastern Colorado.

Gary was also prepared with raptor identification handouts. Good thinking, because Mark and I discovered just before we left Cheyenne that many in the group considered themselves novice bird watchers.

Caravanning is not the ideal way to introduce people to birds. With carpooling, we pared down the number of vehicles to nine. When we joined Gary, he used handheld radios to tell our car what he was seeing, and then I texted a message to one person in each vehicle, such as "Red-tailed on the pole on the right up ahead."

Our end point was Pierce, Colorado, 5 miles south on U.S. Highway 85, but 30 miles as we shuttled back and forth along the county roads spaced on a 1-mile grid.

Gary later sent me his bird list from the trip, and even though Mark and I were only two cars behind him, he counted more raptors than we did:

Northern Harrier: 2
Bald Eagle: 2
Red-tailed Hawk: 6
Rough-legged Hawk: 4
Ferruginous Hawk: 3
Great Horned Owl: 4
American Kestrel: 2
Prairie Falcon: 3

We also documented rock pigeon, Eurasian collared-dove, black-billed magpie, horned lark, European starling and western meadowlark – 14 of them!

Gary frequently pulled over and jumped out of his trusty Subaru to train his spotting scope on a raptor in a lone treetop, on top of a utility pole or floating in the sky, giving everyone a chance to take a look. We may not have walked any miles, but we had plenty of exercise climbing in and out of our vehicles.

Raptor Alley is Gary's invention, and the genesis can be traced back to his wife giving him a bird feeder nearly 25 years ago. He bought 14 more feeders, but what hooked him and made him go buy binoculars and a field guide, was seven Monk parakeets visiting his feeders. The feral, bright green, tropical birds made themselves at home in Colorado Springs for a while.

Relocating to the outskirts of Nunn (current population 586) in 2002, Gary has now identified 135 bird species around his house. He's also just a couple miles from the western border of Pawnee National Grassland, a 30- by 60-mile tract administered by the U.S. Forest Service that is famous in international birding circles.

In some ways, Gary fits the stereotype of the birding loner, patrolling Weld County roads in search of avian rarities, but he also wants to spread the joy of birdwatching. When his mother told him years ago about the Florida birding trail, his first thought was, "Colorado needs one!"

Birding trails, routes like Raptor Alley, are mapped with notes about accessibility, conditions and birding highlights. Modern versions are on the internet and who better than Gary, an IT professional and web designer, to provide it? He started out with a five-county area he called the Great Pikes Peak Birding Trail. I have a t-shirt from that iteration.

It evolved into the Colorado Birding Trail, https://coloradobirdingtrail.com/, run by Colorado Parks and Wildlife. You can find "Raptor Alley" on the map, click on the link and get mile-by-mile directions and helpful hints like, "Be careful pulling onto the shoulder of roads, as many are soft and you could get stuck."

Gary has identified 23 raptor species hanging out there in the winter.

Why there? Good prey base – lots of rodents, and lots of perches for watching for them.

Along the way, Gary picked up graduate courses from Colorado State University in conservation communication and a certificate in non-profit administration. Gary's project for his certificate involved a whole new venture, setting up the Friends of the Pawnee National Grassland, https://www. friendsofthepawneegrassland.org/.

Part of that is an iNaturalist project to document the plants and wildlife, https://www.inaturalist.org/projects/birds-and-more-of-the-pawnee-national-grassland. iNaturalist is global, community-based science, a perfect fit for a man with a personal mission to bring people to nature.

Thanks, Gary, for taking us to visit your birding "patch."

210
WGFD bird farm pheasants recruit hunters; sage grouse farming appeases developers

It's a matter of degrees when you are in charge of raising thousands of ring-necked pheasants.

Ben Milner, bird farm coordinator for Wyoming Game and Fish Department's Downar Bird Farm near Yoder, is also scrupulous about cleanliness, especially with the storm clouds of avian flu gathering on the eastern horizon.

Ben gave the Cheyenne – High Plains Audubon Society a tour in mid-March, before the eggs start rolling in. Before we could enter the facility, we had to step onto a soapy mat and squelch around a bit to kill any germs. Inside, it looked clean enough to perform surgery.

Each year, 18,000 pheasants are produced here and another 16,000 at Game and Fish's bird farm in Sheridan. Sheridan started in 1938 and Downar in 1963.

Each fall, Ben holds back 135 roosters and 1,350 hens for breeding, while the rest are released for hunting. The breeders make their home in nine acres of enormous pens secured against predators.

When the spring breeding season kicks in, each hen would normally stop laying after filling a nest with 12 to 15 eggs. But because employees go out every day to collect eggs, and hens have access to nutritious food, each averages 40 to 50.

The eggs are sorted, cleaned and stored in racks sized for pheasant eggs, smaller than chicken eggs, at 55 degrees, which suspends development of the embryos. When there are 6,700 eggs, they move to the giant incubator and 99.7 degrees. The racks tip every one to three hours to imitate the hen turning the eggs in her nest, keeping the embryos from sticking to the shells.

After 19 days, the eggs are placed in the hatcher, in chick-sized trays where they can hatch. After that, chicks move into brooder houses, where heaters set at 100 degrees substitute for brooding hens. They are soon pecking at waterers and feed.

After two weeks, the chicks are allowed to walk in and out of small outside pens and then eventually into the larger pens. These pens are so large that they are farmed. The crop is kochia – an invasive weed in everyone's garden, but it provides good cover and food in addition to the purchased feed.

The old brood stock is released in May at Springer and Table Mountain Wildlife Habitat Management Areas as well as several walk-in areas.

Wyoming has not allowed raising exotic or native game animals privately, except exotic birds. At Downar, Game and Fish settled on ring-necked pheasants, natives of Asian jungles. Private bird farms order eggs and raise pheasants and other exotic gamebird species. Very few escape and reproduce because they are hunted by sportspeople and predatory animals.

Why does Game and Fish continue to produce an artificial population of pheasants, basically for put-and-take hunting? Ben sees pheasants as a way to introduce hunting to kids and adults, including women who have traditionally made up a small percentage of hunters. Game and Fish sponsors three kids-only hunt days each season on the Springer Wildlife Habitat Management Area and four in November at Glendo State Park to help recruit the next generation of sportsmen and women.

Historically, it was hunters who raised funds through licenses and tags and lobbied for wildlife so that it wouldn't be extirpated by other interests such as farming, ranching, mining and energy extraction. So, thank those early hunters when you enjoy watching Wyoming wildlife.

Unfortunately, a few developers, alarmed by decreasing populations,

think the bird farm method will make up for the loss of sage grouse habitat due to development. I'm discouraged that somehow influential people were able to convince the Wyoming legislature that this could be done by a private company.

Legislation gave Diamond Wings Upland Game Birds five years to give it a try, but this session they had to ask for and received another five, despite a large turnout against.

It turns out raising sage grouse is not like raising chickens – or pheasants.

First, there are no captive flocks to gather eggs from. Diamond Wings is allowed to steal up to 250 eggs per year from hens in the wild. So much for calling this captive "breeding." Sage grouse hens do not lay more eggs when they lose them, like the pheasants do. Plus, sage grouse chicks apparently need more instruction from the hens to succeed, unlike the pheasants.

Studies in Utah and Colorado concluded that captive breeding is not a viable way to increase sage grouse populations. Wildlife biologists say protecting sagebrush habitat is best. And what's good for sage grouse is good for other sagebrush-dependent wildlife.

People from many areas of expertise agreed on a Wyoming sage grouse management plan back in 2015 to keep them from being listed as threatened or endangered, avoiding a host of public land use restrictions.

211

Saturday, May 14, 2022, Outdoors (online version because newsprint version misplaced)

How power production underlies bird problems and other bird news

Last month, you may have read that a subsidiary of NextEra Energy will be paying a hefty fine for killing eagles at its wind developments, including Roundhouse, on the southwest edge of Cheyenne.

The company took a big gamble by not applying for an eagle "take" permit. The permit would have required expenditures, but now the company will have to spend money on remediation plus the fines.

Three years ago, I signed up to be party to the Wyoming Department of Environmental Quality's hearing on Roundhouse, representing Cheyenne Audubon. I still get the occasional registered letter with news about changes to the Roundhouse development plan.

I wasn't surprised to get a call from Ryan Fitzpatrick, my main Roundhouse contact. It sounds like the company may be installing a system to sense raptors approaching wind turbines so the turbines can be shut down before slicing an eagle. That's the system at the Top of the World wind farm. Ironically, bald eagles are increasing in number, however golden eagles are not faring as well.

Avian influenza reached Wyoming last month in poultry and wild birds. I've been following the story day by day through my favorite birding institutions, including the National Audubon Society and Cornell Lab of Ornithology. It seems to be travelling with migrating waterfowl and possibly affecting songbirds. It might be a good idea to put away the bird feeders for a while, instead of having to scrub them frequently. We usually take ours down for the summer anyway.

If you find any dead birds, report them to the Wyoming Game and Fish Department. Pick them up the same way you do dog droppings: grasp the bird with your hand gloved in a plastic bag. Then pull the bag carefully inside out over the bird and seal the bag shut.

I don't know if bird flu is transmissible to cats, but this would be a good time to start keeping your cats indoors so they won't eat dead birds.

Good news for sage grouse and the diverse group of people who in 2015 worked so hard to come to an agreement on the policies to protect primary habitat areas in Wyoming. The number of oil and gas parcels offered for lease has been reduced on critical sage grouse habitat for the Bureau of Land Management's next sale. There are scads of current leases that are not being drilled, so don't blame sage grouse for high gas prices.

But we really need to drop the conventional use of fossil fuels as soon as possible, and that isn't just because it is getting too warm for cute little pikas living on our mountain tops.

Let's consider the cost of air pollution to humans. It isn't healthy to breathe emissions from tailpipes and smokestacks or smoke from the increasingly frequent wildfires attributed to warming climate.

There's wildfire destruction itself. I saw concrete examples recently while driving to Louisville, Colorado. On one side of four-lane-wide Dillon Road, there is a very nice residential area that burned down to the concrete foundations that are now shaded by dead black trees. The houses on the other side of the street are safe, so far.

Mark's and my sons are doing their part for fighting climate change. Both drive electric cars. We plan to follow suit as soon as we need to replace a car.

Going electric is only going to help birds if the source of the power doesn't produce climate-warming pollution, slice them with turbine blades or cover grasslands and deserts with solar panels. To me, it looks like the most harmless alternative is solar panels on existing infrastructure. There's a million square feet of roof on our Lowe's distribution center. There's a nearly quarter-mile-long south-facing wall on the new eastside Microsoft installation. Could Cheyenne be forward thinking enough to write building codes that require buildings to produce power?

These are my daydreams this spring as I watch my first flock of white-crowned sparrows flit from shrub to shrub along Crow Creek on its way to the mountains to nest.

May 21 is the Cheyenne Big Day Bird Count, and once again, Cheyenne Audubon, www.CheyenneAudubon.org, will document the diversity of avian migration for the scientific record. Think about joining us. Someday, someone will examine our records, hopefully documenting increasing diversity here on out as we get a handle on our power problem.

212 Cheyenne Big Day Bird Count catches Arctic visitor

Saturday, June 4, 2022, ToDo, page A10

I'm sure our Cheyenne Big Day Bird Count compiler for Cheyenne Audubon, Grant Frost, was thinking to avoid cold, nasty weather when he picked May 21 instead of the 14 for the count, but it snowed the day before anyway. Our total of 125 species is not too shabby considering the weather was chilly, but luckily not windy.

We had several highlights during the bird count:

Red-throated loon juvenile was seen at Sloans Lake for several days before and on the count. It is considered rare in Wyoming, wintering on either coast and nesting in the Arctic.

Common loon juvenile, same place.

Broad-tailed hummingbird was trying to get nectar out of frozen crabapple blossoms at the Cheyenne Botanic Gardens.

Harris's sparrow may winter next door in Nebraska but is seldom seen here.

Red-headed woodpeckers showed up in two locations, including a pair in one.

Baltimore oriole, the eastern counterpart to our Bullock's, came by with a female.

No eagles were seen.

I came across the scan of a "Tribune Eagle" article about the 1982 Big Day, which was held a week earlier than this year's, where 40 people contributed to the count. The total number of species seen was nearly the same – 124.

The difference between species seen in 1982 and 2022 was 29, a figure close to how many were spotted in 2021, but not this year, 27. But if you look at eBird for the first three weeks of May this year in Laramie County, 185 species are listed. Some species passed through before our count day and may have still been present in smaller numbers, leading us to miss any sightings.

Aside from all the species name changes in the last 40 years, the most interesting assessment is in what species were not logged on the 1982 list but were in 2022:

--Cackling goose was split from Canada goose in 2004.

--Eurasian collared-dove was first observed in Wyoming here in Cheyenne in 1998.

--Great-tailed grackle in 2003 was my first Cheyenne observation.

--Common raven, though they have always been reliably seen starting about 10 or 15 miles west of town, my first Cheyenne observation wasn't until 2010.

The 1982 count lists five winter species we didn't see this count: bufflehead (duck), rough-legged hawk, northern shrike and at the time, what are now subspecies of dark-eyed junco listed as two species, Oregon junco and gray-headed junco. Maybe they migrated earlier this year thanks to weather or climate change.

Evening grosbeak made the 1982 list, but it is hard to find them anywhere these days. They are listed as a globally threatened species.

Black-bellied plover and mountain plover, grassland species recorded in 1982, rarely make our count anymore, but eBird has sightings recorded for April 2020 – when everyone was out birding more than usual.

Our Big Day count area is essentially the same as our Christmas Bird Count, a 7.5-mile diameter circle centered on the state Capitol building. There are more trees to attract birds than in 1982, or in 1956, when only 85 species were counted, according to early compiler May Hanesworth. But as the surrounding grasslands are built upon, mowed and invaded by free-roaming dogs and cats, the grassland birds will be harder to find.

Cheyenne Big Day Bird Count, May 21, 2022

125 species, 19 participants

Cackling Goose
Canada Goose
Wood Duck
Blue-winged Teal
Cinnamon Teal
Northern Shoveler
Gadwall
American Wigeon
Mallard
Northern Pintail
Green-winged Teal
Redhead
Ring-necked Duck
Lesser Scaup
Common Goldeneye
Ruddy Duck
Pied-billed Grebe
Eared Grebe
Western Grebe
Clark's Grebe
Rock Pigeon
Eurasian Collared-Dove
Mourning Dove
Broad-tailed Hummingbird
American Coot
American Avocet
Killdeer
Marbled Godwit
Least Sandpiper
Semipalmated Sandpiper
Western Sandpiper
Wilson's Phalarope
Red-necked Phalarope
Spotted Sandpiper
Solitary Sandpiper
Greater Yellowlegs
Willet

Ring-billed Gull
California Gull
Common Loon
Red-throated Loon
Double-crested Cormorant
American White Pelican
Great Blue Heron
Black-crowned Night-Heron
Turkey Vulture
Osprey
Northern Harrier
Cooper's Hawk
Swainson's Hawk
Red-tailed Hawk
Great Horned Owl
Belted Kingfisher
Red-headed Woodpecker
Downy Woodpecker
Northern Flicker
American Kestrel
Olive-sided Flycatcher
Western Wood-Pewee
Willow Flycatcher
Dusky Flycatcher
Say's Phoebe
Western Kingbird
Eastern Kingbird
Warbling Vireo
Blue Jay
Black-billed Magpie
American Crow
Common Raven
Black-capped Chickadee
Mountain Chickadee
Horned Lark
Northern Rough-winged Swallow
Tree Swallow
Violet-green Swallow
Bank Swallow
Barn Swallow
Cliff Swallow
Ruby-crowned Kinglet
Red-breasted Nuthatch
Blue-gray Gnatcatcher

Rock Wren
House Wren
European Starling
Gray Catbird
Northern Mockingbird
Townsend's Solitaire
Swainson's Thrush
Hermit Thrush
American Robin
House Sparrow
House Finch
Pine Siskin
American Goldfinch
Chipping Sparrow
Lark Sparrow
Lark Bunting
White-crowned Sparrow
Harris's Sparrow
Vesper Sparrow
Savannah Sparrow
Song Sparrow
Lincoln's Sparrow
Green-tailed Towhee
Spotted Towhee
Yellow-breasted Chat
Yellow-headed Blackbird
Western Meadowlark
Bullock's Oriole
Baltimore Oriole
Red-winged Blackbird
Brown-headed Cowbird
Brewer's Blackbird
Common Grackle
Great-tailed Grackle
Orange-crowned Warbler
MacGillivary's Warbler
Common Yellowthroat
Yellow Warbler
Yellow-rumped Warbler
Wilson's Warbler
Western Tanager
Black-headed Grosbeak
Lazuli Bunting
Indigo Bunting

213

Fledge week observations entertain local birdwatcher

This summer, I miss the company of our dog of 16 years, Sally, while gardening in the backyard.

One day at the end of May, I stopped to take a flower photo, crouching down at eye level, a little glad that she wasn't around to photobomb my efforts. When I glanced off to the side, I realized I was also eye level with one of our robins, three feet away. He was watching me intently. I took his picture, and he didn't even blink.

At least once a spring, I hear from folks who are being strafed by furious robins every time they try to use their front or back door because the robins have built their nest on the porch light and are very territorial about anyone coming near.

This is the second year we've had robins nesting above our back door, and where I was crouching was only a few feet away from it. We more often use the attached garage's back door, but still, early June chores took me back and forth a lot, and the robins were courteous. I tried to return the favor, stopping whenever our paths were about to cross so as not to delay their delivery of worm meat to the young in the nest.

Serendipitously, my garden digging coincided with the robins' hunt for food – I brought lots of tiny critters closer to the surface, and watering transplants brought out the worms. Mark saw the young minutes after they fledged, and I saw one just once. I hope the neighbor's cat didn't get them. Sally, the bird dog, would have tried. As of June 20, the robins were incubating another set of eggs.

The week before, two avian families arrived at our feeders. The only food out, besides the thistle in case a goldfinch comes by, is a chunk of suet-type stuff we stuck in one of those hanging cage feeders. A plain dark brown bird landed on the cage and stabbed at the brown stuff. There was something familiar about it, the bill, the shape – oh, baby starling! And then its two siblings and a parent showed up, and it was like watching a human family with small children visit the ice cream shop. A lot of shuffling and bumping and to-ing and fro-ing.

Millions of starlings must go through this feeding performance every year – how else could there be millions of starlings out there to perform those "murmurations," clouds of birds performing sky-high arabesques captured on videos playing on the internet?

A few minutes later, a small, plump, light brown bird landed on the cage, fluttering its wings. Its parent quickly followed, a male house sparrow – they are the ones with the black goatees. He pecked the suet stuff and fed the slightly smaller bird. Soon, he was besieged by two more young, all three rapidly fluttering their wings, apparently the "feed me" signal. Nearly as amusing to watch was both families navigating our bird bath at the same time. Sparrow and starling shoulders bumped together.

The Swainson's hawk pair nested again in the neighbor's spruce tree. Every time I walk the neighborhood, I see at least one adult flying. We think the pile of sticks and whitewash in our driveway in May and early June was the adults searching one of our overhanging silver maples for the perfect nesting materials, breaking off green sticks and dropping rejects.

I was concerned that the new apartment building in the field adjacent to our neighborhood would be a problem for the hawks' hunting, but this year, the church's gravel parking lot is home to a new colony of ground squirrels.

On June 16, one of the young hawks was trying to perch in our trees and was getting mobbed by blue jays.

The red-breasted nuthatches returned to the nesting cavity in the mountain ash tree across the street. The mountain chickadee seems to have nested somewhere else this year – but can sometimes be heard singing.

Before our shrubs leafed out, I saw a house wren checking out a tree cavity across the alley. Now he sings nonstop all day.

It's hard to make myself take a walk without Sally, but there are plenty of friends and neighbors I meet when I do, including the wild animals.

214 Friday, August 5, 2922, ToDo, page A10
Merlin's "Sound ID" uncovers hidden birds

Learning to identify birds by sight is simple – page through the field guide until you see a bird that matches or go birdwatching with someone who knows more than you.

One shortcut to the process is the Cornell Lab of Ornithology's free Merlin app.

You give it the bird's specs – relative size, color, behavior/habitat – and it gives you a short, illustrated list of possibilities. You can also give it a bird photo from your phone (including a photo of the screen on the back of a camera) and hit "Get Photo ID."

Learning to identify a bird by song or call is easy here on the edge of the Great Plains. Our most common birds vocalize while walking on lawns and prairie, sitting on bare branches and fence posts, swimming on water or soaring above. I can see robins chirping, crows cawing, house finches singing, collared-doves moaning and house sparrows cheeping.

It turns out I'm missing the birds that like to hide in vegetation but can still be heard. I've always thought that some winter I would sit down with a compilation of western bird song recordings and

memorize them – hasn't happened in the last 30 years.

But now Merlin has a new feature, "Sound ID." It came out last summer as part of the free app, but it's this summer people are talking about it, even our Airbnb host, for whom it sounded like his gateway drug to birdwatching addiction.

The first step is to download the Merlin app for Android or iOS. Then open the menu (those three little lines stacked up) and choose Bird Packs. Install the one for "US: Rocky Mountains." This helps Merlin give you better choices. You can change it if you visit elsewhere.

Choose "Sound ID" from the home screen. Tap the microphone icon and hold out your phone towards the bird sound you hear. Closer is better, but start recording where you are first, in case moving closer scares the bird away. I found that Merlin doesn't hear everything I hear.

Merlin creates a spectrogram of what it hears, and it scrolls across the top of your screen. Eventually, it creates a list of the birds it is hearing, including a photo of each. Each time Merlin hears a species, it highlights the name so you can connect sound and name. Also, if you click on the bird, you'll get a list of other recorded sounds you can compare for that species, to double check Merlin's accuracy.

Early one morning recently, I stood on a corner in my neighborhood, recording and watching as half a dozen bird names filled my screen. But wait – great-tailed grackle? We have them in Cheyenne, usually at the country club and the air base, but I have not heard their loud, raucous calls on my side of town. How do I tell Merlin I heard common grackles instead? But I will still give every shiny blackbird's tail a closer look.

On the other hand, while I was hiking the Headquarters Trail at the end of July, Merlin told me I was hearing a warbling vireo. I hardly ever see them, so I have never perfected identifying them by sight, but now that musical warbling in trees along a creek will have me considering them when I hear it again.

And there's more. You can add these sound recordings to your eBird checklists. You can see if it's a bird already on your life list. Or Merlin will generate lists of birds where you plan to travel. It can sort them by most common at the top of the list. And for the most competitive birders, it can generate a list of birds they haven't seen in that area – their target species.

The Cornell Lab of Ornithology can tell you how all this magic happens. Mostly, it is from the crowd-sourced data from its community scientists all over the world – us birdwatchers.

Some 30 years ago, Beauford Thompson, a sixth-grade teacher at Davis Elementary School, told me we would have handheld devices that would help us do all kinds of things. I was imagining typing notes, maybe a digital day planner. Now, I use my smart phone for video calls, photographing and identifying flowers, reading books, tracking hikes, finding recipes and cafes, and counting birds.

Recording birds could become another time-eater, but learning bird songs and calls and contributing to the global avian knowledge is worthwhile. But let's not forget to sometimes go outside and enjoy the world empty-handed again.

215

Friday, November 4, 2022, ToDo, page A10

Audubon Rockies' Hutchinson discusses community science

Zach Hutchinson is Audubon Rockies' community science coordinator. He is currently located in Casper, although he plans to relocate to Cheyenne as soon as local real estate prices are realistic.

He spoke at Cheyenne Audubon's October meeting about community science, which started out being called "citizen science." The new name is more inclusive – you don't have to be a U.S. citizen to participate – or be a college-educated scientist.

Zach said community science contributed to Bird Migration Explorer, https://explorer.audubon.org/. I'll have more about this new endeavor in a future column.

Community science has also contributed data to the State of the Birds 2022 report, www.stateofthebirds.org/2022.

Most groups of birds, including our grassland birds, are still losing population, while others increased during the last couple decades. For instance, waterfowl increased because they benefitted from concentrated efforts by sporting groups, although you don't have to be a hunter to buy a Federal Duck Stamp to contribute.

This year's report highlights North American species that are at the "tipping point," which means, after having lost 50% or more of their population since 1970, the report said, "These 70 species are on a trajectory to lose another 50% of their remnant populations in the next 50 years if nothing changes."

Thirteen of those tipping point species occur in Wyoming regularly, either as residents or migrants, some considered common and others uncommon on this scale: abundant, common, uncommon, rare.

I didn't include the species that are rare in our state in this list of 13:

--Greater Sage-Grouse
--Western Grebe
--Rufous Hummingbird
--Mountain Plover
--Long-billed Dowitcher
--Lesser Yellowlegs
--Red-headed Woodpecker
--Olive-sided Flycatcher
--Pinyon Jay
--Evening Grosbeak
--Black Rosy-Finch
--Chestnut-collared Longspur
--Bobolink

The primary causes of downward population trends are:

1. Habitat loss.
2. Cats (2.6 billion birds a year).
3. Windows, (624 million).
4. Vehicle collisions (214 million).
5. Industrial collisions, including wind turbines (64 million).

Zach went over the seven ways we can help birds:

1. Make windows safer day and night.
2. Keep cats indoors.
3. Reduce lawn, plant natives.
4. Avoid pesticides.

5. Drink shade-grown coffee.
6. Protect our planet from plastic (Think of waterbirds mistaking floating plastic for food.).
7. Watch birds, share what you see.

For more about each point, see www.birds.cornell.edu/home/seven-simple-actions-to-help-birds/.

"Watch birds, share what you see," means taking part in community science. Zach said this is how we find out about population trends, range expansion, and if there are losses, we can see where in the life cycle it happens so that action can be focused.

You've probably heard me talk about www.eBird.org before. Birdwatchers submit lists of birds they've seen, anywhere and anytime, using smart phones or computers.

I can delve into the data on the website and discover 272 species have been observed at the Wyoming Hereford Ranch headquarters, 216 at Lions Park and 151 at the High Plains Grasslands Research Station where the Cheyenne Arboretum is located.

The Christmas Bird Count is the most famous annual community science project, with this year's being the 123rd.

Two years ago, Zach said, 80,000 people took part, counted 2,355 species (worldwide), and traveled 500,000 miles on foot, by skis and by other means. Check https://cheyenneaudubon.org/ to find out about participating in the Cheyenne count in December.

The Great Backyard Bird Count, a snapshot of where birds are in late winter, celebrated its 24th anniversary last February. In 192 countries, 384,641 people participated and 7,099 species were counted on 359,479 checklists submitted. It's held over Presidents' Day weekend.

Zach runs bird banding stations every summer and people sign up to help (https://rockies.audubon.org/). Birds are caught in fine "mist nets" and then are measured and banded.

Bird banding provides data on demographics, productivity, recruitment (adding individuals to the population) and survival – when a bird previously banded is recaptured, or a band is recovered from a dead bird.

This year, 54 species were netted at Zach's stations. Usually, 500 new birds are banded but this summer it was only 340, probably because the drought has affected breeding and recruitment, Zach said.

Audubon Rockies launched a new community science project last summer on the Yampa River in Colorado. People on commercial float trips, including Zach, counted birds: 55 species and 732 individual birds. Stopping for a few minutes in a calm eddy in otherwise inaccessible places to count birds will add richness to the tourists' experiences and give science a new perspective.

There are other community science endeavors, such as iNaturalist, which is interested in plants as well as animals. Some have been very specific, such as The Lost Ladybug Project.

Consider becoming a community science participant in one or more ways.

216 Unusual birds "on the road" this fall in southeastern Wyoming

Friday, December 23, 2022, ToDo, page A10

On Nov. 9, a friend called to tell me she heard a story on KUWR, Wyoming's National Public Radio affiliate, about a Blackburnian warbler that blew across the Atlantic to an island off the southwest British coast, exciting birdwatchers.

It's ironic that this eastern North American bird was named by a German zoologist for an English naturalist, Anna Blackburne (1726-1793). She never saw a live specimen, but her name seems appropriate because the 5-inch-long male burns with a flaming orange throat and head on a body that is otherwise black and white.

We've had a few Blackburnians accidentally find their way to Wyoming. Under the Explore tab on eBird.org, you'll find that my husband, Mark Gorges, was the last to record one in Wyoming, a female, on May 28 at Wyoming Hereford Ranch.

Warblers typically eat insects, so the lost warbler Mark saw could find them in late May. Warblers leave the north in September and October, when cold weather limits their food supply.

However, beginning Nov. 11, Chuck Seniawski has had a pine warbler visiting his Cheyenne feeder nearly every day through Nov. 27, so far. This is another lost eastern North American species – and it is way late for an insect eater.

Pine warblers, according to Doug Faulkner's "Birds of Wyoming," published in 2010, are "vagrants." Their normal migration, breeding and winter ranges in the Eastern U.S. and southeastern Canada are nowhere near Wyoming.

However, Doug wrote, every fall there is at least one reported in Wyoming, usually between mid-August and mid-September. Doug's only winter report was a pine warbler that spent five days in December 1988 eating peanut butter at a feeder in Gillette.

Chuck says his pine warbler pecks

at his sunflower feeders, hunts on the ground underneath and uses the birdbath. He isn't sure if the bird is eating seed bits or finding something else. When he posted a photo, Don Jones, eBird regional data reviewer in Laramie, who spent four years back East, agreed with his identification. Also, Chuck had just seen one in Central Park in New York City.

Pine warblers look a little like a female or a winter-plumage male American goldfinch, yellowish with dark wings with two white wingbars, so maybe we should all examine our feeder birds more closely.

Serious birders stake out reservoirs during fall migration, including the Laramie Plains Lakes. Jonathan Lautenbach was rewarded with being the first to record two king eiders, sea ducks, on Nov. 12 through 18 at Lake Hattie. He reported they were a female and a juvenile male, plain brown. The adult male, not seen, would be half white and half black, with a bright yellow-orange "bill-shield" on its forehead.

eBird shows these king eiders as the first to be recorded in Wyoming. Doug Faulkner does not list them at all in his 2010 book, which is a comprehensive review of bird sightings up until that point.

King eiders breed in the Arctic, across northern-most Canada. They winter around coastal Alaska and northeastern Canada, but there are frequent winter sightings in lower 48 states, most often coastal. They are also usually female and juvenile birds.

Cheyenne birder Grant Frost was probably checking Sloans Lake in Lions Park for interesting ducks and other waterbirds when he came across a small flock of bushtits Nov. 3 and again Nov. 27. "Peterson's Field Guide to Birds of North America," published in 2020, describes their habitat as brushy woodlands and pine-oak forests of the southwest.

But if you look closely at Peterson's range map, it shows this thin line of purple (meaning year-round resident) drawn up the Front Range of Colorado, practically pointing to Cheyenne. More bushtits may be in our future. Look for pale brown and gray, 4.5-inch-long birds building sack-like hanging nests.

Grant also found a blue-headed vireo at Lions Park on Nov. 1, and it was last seen there Nov. 3 by Vicki Herren.

Vireos are much like warblers – eating insects – but also fruit in winter. This species breeds across Canada, through New England and down through the Appalachians. It winters along the southeast coasts of the U.S.

It's possible that the birds from western Canada would head south through Wyoming to get to the Texas Gulf Coast. They are just hard to pick out from other vireos and warblers bouncing around in the trees.

Unusual bird observations submitted to eBird automatically get flagged. You are asked to write a description of your observation and submit a photo, if you can. Someone appointed by eBird for that area will decide whether your record becomes public.

These days, eBird and the Wyoming Bird Records Committee work together. Find out more about the committee at https://wybirdrecordscommittee. wordpress.com/.

2023

217 Habitat leasing to provide new tool for Wyoming conservation

Friday, February 3, 2023, ToDo, page A10

Bob Budd dropped the name of a new conservation tool during his book talk for the Cheyenne–High Plains Audubon Society last month. So, I asked Bob for more details a few days later.

The new habitat leasing program Bob mentioned is like conservation easements, but short term and with a lower price per acre.

First, let's look at what a conservation easement is. Wikipedia has an extensive definition showing it dates back to the 1950s or earlier, but to summarize, an interested landowner finds willing partners to pay him or her not to use their land for certain purposes.

Those certain purposes are most often development or subdivision, especially on farm and ranch land. Because the acreage can no longer be subdivided under a conservation easement, the property loses the value associated with subdivision.

The consenting landowner (it's always a voluntary agreement) is paid for conserving the land. Who pays the landowner? In Bob's experience as executive director of the Wyoming Wildlife and Natural Resource Trust, a state agency, in setting up some of these, it can be a mix of money from a non-profit organization like The Nature Conservancy, a farm or ranch organization, and government agencies, including the U.S. Department of Agriculture's Natural Resource and Conservation Service (NRCS).

The conservation easement becomes part of the property, passed along to the next owner.

The landowner may recognize the conservation value of their land and seek the easement. The buyers of the easement confirm the conservation value and the financial value through an extensive appraisal process.

The land could be valuable for wildlife. Or maybe for other ecological services such as absorbing precipitation to decrease flooding downstream, instead of increasing impervious pavement.

Around here, raising beef cattle doesn't pay as well as selling land for homesites. A rancher may be lucky enough to improve their bottom line by leasing some of their property for windfarms, solar farms or oil and gas development. Up until now, a conservation easement was one of few ways to be paid for providing wildlife habitat. But they are a hard sell because they are forever.

Well, now we will have habitat leasing. The details are still being ironed out, but Wyoming will be piloting the concept this spring. Simply, a landowner can sign a contract for a period of years, maybe 10 or 15, and receive an annual payment in return for maintaining their acreage to benefit habitat, migration routes and/or other ecological services.

It could be habitat for a species of concern, with an agency contacting the landowner to see if they want to sign up.

For this pilot program, Bob has been working with NRCS and the Wyoming Game and Fish Department. The habitat they are interested in is the seasonal migration corridors that have caught the public's attention.

The Wyoming Migration Initiative has identified routes that are used by deer and antelope year after year as they move north from their wintering grounds to higher-elevation breeding grounds and back again in the fall.

These routes have to provide forage for the travelers, or they will fail to breed successfully. The animals don't seem to find new routes when there are obstacles.

So, protecting the historic migration routes with habitat leasing seems like a fair transaction for both the rancher and the wildlife.

Forty years ago, when I was in college studying natural resources and then range management, environmentalists and ranchers seemed to be on opposite sides of the fence, especially on topics like wolf reintroduction. But the wildlife folks and the ranchers have found they have much in common. Here in

Wyoming, for instance, they have been successful in collaborating on how to help sage-grouse.

Bob has been there on the sage-grouse work. He's the ranch-raised kid who, as he explains in his new book, "Otters Dance," used to run feral through the willows, watching the birds and frogs.

In his previous job as the ranch manager for The Nature Conservancy's Red Canyon Ranch near Lander, Bob worked out ways to keep cows and wildlife happy simultaneously. He knew his stream restoration worked when a family of otters moved in.

The ranchers Bob knows are knowledgeable about the wildlife on their places and always interested in learning more.

I remember Bob saying one time when Mark and I visited Red Canyon Ranch that when the environmentalists visited, they wanted to see the cows and find out how many there were. Visiting ranchers wanted to see the endangered plants.

Bob, himself, is a special kind of person. Pick up his book at the Wyoming State Museum, Game and Fish headquarters, the Cheyenne Frontier Days museum or online and see what I mean. He can take the fence down between two opposing camps. With him riding herd on this habitat leasing pilot, I'm pretty sure it can be successful.

218

Friday, March 3, 2023, ToDo, page A7

Birders get look behind the scenes, find more eBird perks

eBird has come a long way since its debut in 2002.

As a means of collecting scientific bird data by offering birders a place to save their bird lists, Cornell Lab of Ornithology invented an ingenious bit of community (or citizen) science, and it just keeps getting better.

Anyone can go to eBird.org and sign up for free. The website, under the Help tab, has tutorials on how to enter your bird sightings.

Don Jones, University of Wyoming graduate student studying sagebrush songbirds, and Cheyenne Audubon's February guest speaker, said that for Wyoming, 15,000 different birdwatchers have submitted 200,000 checklists so far. Wyoming eBird data was recently added to the Wyoming Natural Diversity Database.

Globally, as of the 20th anniversary May 2022, 820,000 eBirders contributed 1.3 billion observations.

Since scientists are expected to use eBird data, there is a review process. Once, I received a polite email from the regional reviewer asking if I had indeed seen 49 black-crowned night-herons at Holliday Park, and if so, could I send more information.

When I explained that it was a breeding colony that has been there for years (and is still there, but a bit diminished as the park loses the big cottonwoods), my report was accepted. Today, I can look up that night-heron sighting on eBird and tell you it started May 29 at 7:45 a.m. and I saw 220 birds of 15 species while walking 1.5 miles in an hour.

Don, a volunteer eBird reviewer for 10 years, explained that if the reviewer doesn't think you have enough information to verify the entry, the entry can stay on your list, but it won't be publicly available. Don's been in that boat, especially when birding abroad when he's discovered he's made identification mistakes. But then he was able to fix them.

The globe is divided into review areas. We are in the Laramie/Goshen counties area. Volunteer reviewers familiar with bird life here, like Don, set a filter for each species, specifying which months it might be seen and maximum number seen at one time. The number is higher for a migratory species during migration months than during breeding months when birds spread out and become secretive.

Filters do change over time. Perhaps an invasive species like the Eurasian collared-dove has moved in or another species, like the dickcissel, is becoming rarer.

In the last few years, eBird has added new perks for birdwatchers. One is signing up for notices for birds you'd like to see.

For instance, I can generate a list of species I haven't seen in Laramie County but others have – target species. My 87 target species seem to be a lot of rarities – species unlikely to be seen here, but maybe common elsewhere. For instance, eBird has only three reports of prairie warbler, an eastern species, in Cheyenne, in 2000 and 2001. I have a much better chance of finding native burrowing owls last reported in 2022.

Once you know what birds you want to see, you can sign up for alerts. There are two kinds. Rare Bird Alerts are for species the American Birding Association considers rare for your area of interest. If I sign up for Needs Alerts for Laramie County, I'll be alerted whenever someone reports a species I haven't seen here yet.

Note: When eBird says "Laramie," they mean our county, not our neighboring town to the west.

eBird is handy for preparing for a birding trip to an area you aren't familiar with by showing where publicly accessible hotspots are and generating a list of species for you. You can see the latest observations.

You can even generate a multiple-choice species identification quiz for a location at a particular time of year, either with photos or bird sounds.

After your trip, you can pull together all the checklists you submitted and add notes and photos to make a "Trip Report" to save and share.

Under the Science tab are all sorts of wonderous interpretations of eBird data: Visualizations of bird abundance, abundance trends, migratory route animations plus improved range maps showing breeding, wintering and migration areas for each species.

There's the list of published studies using eBird data. There were 160 peer-reviewed publications in 2022, like this one: "Bai, J. P., Hou, D. Jin, J. Zhai, Y. Ma, and J. Zhao (2022) "Habitat Suitability Assessment of Black-Necked Crane (Grus nigricollis) in the Zoige Grassland Wetland Ecological Function Zone on the Eastern Tibetan Plateau." Diversity 14(7)."

It's incredible to think we birdwatchers, while having fun watching birds all over the world, with just a little extra effort, maybe using the mobile app, can contribute knowledge that helps birds.

For questions about eBird in Wyoming, contact Don at djones46@uwyo.edu.

219 Longspurs animate local shortgrass prairie

Friday, May 5, 2023, ToDo, page A7

Eastern Laramie County has no mountains, but it is not flat.

We were looking for birds north of Hillsdale (a town name indicating the varied topography), walking across the shortgrass prairie on a very fine morning (meaning no wind) in late April. We were surrounded by small birds popping up, circling us and then upon landing, becoming invisible.

A nearby windbreak was full of robins and red-winged blackbirds, but up the hill, where the grass was well-grazed, barely an inch tall, it was full of grassland birds like western meadowlarks and horned larks. And lots of longspurs.

Your field guide, if not brand new, will show them as McCown's longspurs. While John P. McCown was stationed with the U.S. Army in Texas along the Rio Grande, he collected several bird specimens. Presumably it was winter, when these longspurs are wintering there and in southern New Mexico and due south in Mexico.

McCown sent the specimens back east and the ornithologists determined his longspur was a new-to-them species. In 1851, they named it in honor of McCown.

However, by 2020, a closer examination of McCown's career showed that he'd served on the frontier with less than perfect integrity and then joined the Confederate army. Altogether, he became someone the North American Classification Committee of the American Ornithological Society did not want to honor, and the bird's name was changed to thick-billed longspur. The committee is considering removing people's names from all bird names, which in North America would affect 150 species. You will need a new field guide when that happens.

But out on the prairie, the birds have no nametags, only their markings. The thick-billed longspur has a heavy, seed-cracking bill. It is closely related to sparrows and eats seeds all winter. However, in spring it eats insects and invertebrates and will feed them to its young.

As we walked, the longspurs kept popping up and circling us. Perhaps we were kicking up insects as we walked, just like cows or buffalo. It's also time for the males to do their aerial territorial mating display. They are marked with distinctive black bibs this time of year, and with their tails fanned out, white with dark center stripe and black lower edge, they are, after seeing so many, easy to separate from the more numerous horned larks, which have much blacker tails.

Over the last 50 years, the thick-billed longspur population is down 94%, mostly due to changes in their habitat. They are on Wyoming Game and Fish Department's "Species of Greatest Conservation Need" list which includes 80 bird species: https://wgfd.wyo.gov/Habitat/Habitat-Plans.

Wyoming has about 27% of the world's thick-billed longspurs. Their breeding range is primarily eastern Wyoming, much of Montana and small extensions into Colorado, Nebraska, Saskatchewan and Alberta.

Game and Fish attributes population declines to prairie fragmentation by agriculture (plowing), urbanization (subdivisions) and fire suppression. Stressors include energy development (including wind energy), invasive species (like cheatgrass), off-road recreation, altered fire and grazing regimes (longspurs prefer heavily grazed areas), drought and climate change.

Maybe the academics can study how many houses per square mile can be built on the prairie before longspurs decamp. But not all homeowners take care of their property in the same way.

First, to protect ground-nesting birds like longspurs, meadowlarks and horned larks, people are keeping their dogs off the prairie, or at least on a leash, April through July.

Second, people who value grassland species of all kinds refrain from mowing too often, especially April through July to protect the nesting birds, but also to reduce extreme fire risk.

It seems counterintuitive. If the short-grass prairie grasses are repeatedly cut back (some people erroneously believe they need to mow more than once every couple years), the grasses begin to struggle. The less-shaded soil gets too hot, and heat-loving species move in, such as the more combustible, non-native cheatgrass.

Prairie grasses are so cool. They have deep roots so they can make a comeback from drought and grazing. Wanda Manley, who lives out on the prairie and has a master's degree in range management, told me that even after a (normal) grass fire, the growing point of each grass plant stays green and recovery is rapid. But where the prairie has been abused, fires are so hot, the soil burns, and recovery will take much longer.

If you are someone who owns a patch of prairie and a riding mower and who enjoys a reason to get out there on a nice day, why not leave the mower parked and grab your binoculars? Walk out, maybe to the top of one of the hills, and listen for the music of the longspurs, these small birds that have been visiting our prairie every spring for thousands of years.

220

House sparrow effect demonstrated in backyard

I blame the puppy.

When she joined our family last September, I thought it would be a good idea to feed the birds hulled sunflower seeds so that there wouldn't be hulls under the feeder for her to chew.

I noticed over the winter that we had more house sparrows visiting us than usual. Normally, few ever bothered to crack open our usual black oil sunflower seeds. They might look around under the feeder for scraps, but they don't usually sit on the feeder pulling out seeds.

Turns out they really like sunflower seeds – if they don't have to deal with the hulls. And with more hanging around, more of them thought about nesting here, but not for the first time.

Last year, after the robins fledged one batch of young and laid one or two eggs for the next, the house sparrows started building their nest on top. They completely covered the robin eggs with a hollow ball of dry grass stems. The robins left. We took the whole mess down. House sparrows are one of three non-native bird species in the U.S. that are legal to disturb or kill without a permit, the others being starlings and pigeons, probably for agricultural reasons originally.

This year we were happy to see the robins return to the ledge over our back door. It looked like the eggs hatched mid-May, about the time we left on a trip. The puppy left, too, so I didn't worry about her picking up any fledglings falling out of the nest.

When we came home, the nest was empty. Mark took it down so the house sparrows wouldn't take it over – the world does not need more house sparrows. Originally native to Europe and Asia, they have done a wonderful job of colonizing the globe, except for Antarctica.

I was surprised that the robins didn't want to nest on our ledge a second time. They seemed to have abandoned our yard. On the other hand, every time I stood at the kitchen sink and looked out the window, there would be a male house sparrow on the wire, sometimes with dry grass in his beak. He would fly off somewhere to the left, out of sight.

Late June, Mark and I were standing not far from the robins' favorite inner corner of our house exterior. We were discussing exactly where to set up a kennel to keep the puppy (and garden) safe when we aren't outside with her.

Barely 6 feet as the spider crawls from the robins' favorite ledge are various electrical boxes hanging on the wall. I noticed one had a long piece of dead grass sticking out from the bottom. We opened the box and found it half full of dry grass and a dozen feathers, and four tiny eggs. House sparrow eggs.

Dry grass and electrical connections are not a good combination. We cleaned out the box and put duct tape over the hole in the bottom where the wires, and house sparrows, entered it.

Within hours, we had robins in the yard again. They were our robins, the ones that don't spook or attack us when we cross paths in the backyard. Within two days there was most of a robin nest rebuilt on the ledge.

Some of the dry grass the robins collected, they pulled from the spots where puppy pee has killed the lawn, so we have the puppy to thank for making building materials so accessible.

For years I've heard that as cute as invasive house sparrows are, they steal nesting cavities from native birds like bluebirds, or the red-breasted nuthatches that nested across the street in a tree hollow the last two years. This year, house sparrows have it.

Otherwise, I've never seen a house sparrow nest in the wild, except for the old hollow trees in one corner of Lions Park. Mostly I've seen their messy nests sticking out of large commercial signs and other cavities of the human-built environment.

This recent experience shows that house sparrows can interfere with nesting of birds that don't use cavities, like robins.

On to the next mystery: Why am I seeing gulls in Cheyenne this summer? Usually, they don't get any closer to town than the landfill. There must be a new source of food around here, either trash or fish.

Oh, and I saw a hummingbird in Lions Park at the back of the amphitheater. It was inspecting the railings, maybe for spider webs for making a nest? It's about four weeks earlier than we see hummingbirds in town when they return from nesting in the mountains.

221

Friday, September 8, 2023, ToDo, page A11

Crow loses life but aids researchers for years to come

When you invite friends for dinner, you don't expect them to greet you and then say, "By the way, you have a dead crow on your front lawn."

After dinner I took a plastic trash bag with me and went out to investigate. It was still there. A sleek black pile of feathers.

Because Highly Pathogenic Avian Influenza (HPAI) is still going around, as well as West Nile Virus, I decided I didn't want to look closely at this bird. I used the poop bag technique, putting the bag over my hand, grasping the bird and then pulling the bag over it and tightly tying it shut. And I put the first bag into a second. Then, on the outside, I wrote the date.

If you know me, you know that dead birds go into the freezer. Next, I emailed Elizabeth Wommack, curator and collections manager at the University of Wyoming Museum of Vertebrates. She collects dead animals with spines, like birds, mammals, fish, reptiles and amphibians.

The day I was headed over to Laramie, I was packing the crow into a lunch-sized cooler with re-freezable blocks of ice when Mark said, "Take the other birds, too."

"What other birds?" I asked.

He went to the freezer and brought back three small birds, each in their own plastic, sealable sandwich bag.

"There are no notes on these," I said. "Where did they come from? And when?"

"I don't know."

This is why I always write the information down, usually on a scrap of paper I stick in the bag with the bird. It's been at least four years since the last time we dropped off any dead birds and apparently, our dead bird memories don't go back even that far. They are most likely birds we found in our yard, perhaps window strike fatalities.

I found Elizabeth on campus at the Biodiversity Institute. In the intake room I filled out a simple form while she took the crow out to examine it.

The bird was molting and she pointed out the new feathers coming in and how worn the edges of the old feathers were. There were tiny ants around the crow's face. Their first target is the eyes, but I had frozen them before they could do any damage. When the bird is taxidermied, the stomach contents will be recorded. Sometimes crows eat inedible things like foil, Elizabeth said.

She said it's a hard time of year for the adults now. Molting takes lots of energy and they also have their adult-sized children harassing them, begging for food. Plus, crows and other corvids like ravens and magpies are more susceptible to West Nile than other bird species.

The museum makes tissue samples available to researchers in the future who may determine the cause of death. The crow is a more valuable specimen than the other three birds because the location and date of collection and death are known.

One of the other birds was a Townsend's solitaire. In (a gloved) hand, you realize how slender it is compared to its cousin, the robin. The second was an orange-crowned warbler. Elizabeth gently pushed back the grayish, yellowish feathers on its head, and you could barely see a smudge of orange.

The third bird was much easier to i.d., a red crossbill. The crossed tips of the upper and lower parts of the bill are unmistakable.

But the best that can be said about these three birds is that they died in Cheyenne sometime before the day they were donated.

Elizabeth is glad to have more specimens, including game animals – or parts of them. Contact her, ewommack@uwyo.edu, to find out exactly which parts she needs.

Bird flu is still out there. On the U.S. Department of Agriculture's Animal and Plant Health Inspection Service, you can find a map showing how many cases have been detected by state and data for each case. As of the end of August, Wyoming had 137 cases reported while surrounding states ranged from 35 (Nebraska) to 231 (Colorado). Wyoming's most recent case listed was from Park County July 31.

There's more information from the U.S. Fish and Wildlife Service and the U.S. Centers for Disease Control and Prevention. Only one human case of bird flu has been found so far.

To report diseased wildlife, contact the Wyoming Game and Fish Department. Their website, https://wgfd.wyo.gov/, has more information about HPAI. Search "bird flu" and look for the news article, "Game and Fish asks public for help with HPAI."

222 Newcomers: Not all of Wyoming's birds have been here forever

Friday, October 6, 2023, ToDo, page A11

Just as many of us living here today didn't have family in Wyoming at the turn of the last century or earlier, many bird species didn't either.

I was perusing "Birds of Wyoming" by Douglas W. Faulkner, published in 2010, where I found records of first observations and population explosions of species in the state. Keep in mind that in the early days, there weren't many people recording bird species.

First, there are the familiar species introduced to North America from Europe, but it took some of them a while to make it to Wyoming.

Rock pigeons were introduced in eastern North America in the early 1600s and it's unknown when they made it here.

House sparrows were released for the first time in New York City in 1851, but it was the ones introduced in Salt Lake City that made it to Evanston in 1874. Birds released in Denver in 1877 expanded their population and were settled in Cheyenne by the 1890s.

First reports of European starlings in Wyoming were in Laramie and Laramie County in 1937. Starlings made Jackson Hole by 1941. Large counts, over 1000 birds, didn't become routine until 1990.

Eurasian collared-doves were first sighted in Florida in the 1980s, but the first Wyoming state record was in 1998 here in Cheyenne at the Wyoming Hereford Ranch. I remember being with the group there trying to distinguish them from ring-turtle doves, pet birds that escaped from time to time.

Sometimes bird species are native elsewhere in North America and eventually get to Wyoming: Chimney swift, 1924; blue jay, 1958 (dramatically increasing in the 1970s) and eastern bluebird, 1901, near Cheyenne but as of 2010 most breeding was seen along a bluebird trail in Crook County in northeastern Wyoming.

The indigo bunting, the eastern equivalent of our lazuli bunting, started infiltrating Crook County and was documented in 1949. Another was documented in southwestern Wyoming by 1959.

A blue grosbeak was first reported in 1962 in Torrington and is now considered a regular breeder in the state, especially along the North Platte.

There are species that were already in Wyoming when ornithologists started looking, but the distribution and numbers have increased. American white pelicans were up in Yellowstone National Park but colonized Pathfinder Reservoir near Casper by 1984. Double-crested cormorants were also up in Yellowstone and also flocked to the new reservoirs in the eastern part of the state.

The American crow barely showed up on Christmas Bird Counts around Wyoming in early years. Faulkner wrote, "Fewer than 4% of the CBCs reporting crows had totals exceeding 300 individuals from 1951-2004. Roughly around year 2000, many CBCs experienced up to a ninefold increase...." Certainly Cheyenne did and they are still here.

Common ravens were always seen a few miles west of town, but they have increased their numbers statewide and have been seen in Cheyenne sporadically the last 10 years.

Bobolinks, fancy-looking songbirds of the grasslands, were spotted this year in eastern Laramie County where Darrel and Marilyn Repshire's wetland pasture was undergoing restoration. Historically, they were common around Cheyenne, but more recently breeding birds were concentrated in irrigated meadows in northeast Wyoming.

The common grackle was documented in Wyoming in 1858 but was rare here in the southeast. Then it had a population explosion in the 1970s. The first record of the similar great-tailed grackle was 1989, near Cheyenne, now slowly spreading across the state.

Interestingly, one of our most common backyard birds, the house finch, was only present along Wyoming's southern border, including Cheyenne, in the first half of the twentieth century. Faulkner wrote that they expanded in the late 50s, with Casper's first nest record in 1984 and Jackson Hole's in the mid-90s.

Game birds from beyond North America are a group that often gets released for hunting. They don't often naturalize widely and so new birds are constantly released, like the popular ring-necked pheasants of China and East Asia. Sometimes you'll see escapees from bird farms like the chukar of Europe and Asia. Also from that region are gray partridges which sometimes can make a go of it around grain crops.

The wild turkey was introduced in Wyoming in western Platte County in 1935 in a trade with New Mexico for some sage-grouse.

The Canada goose, by the early 20th century, could be found in the river basins in Eastern Wyoming, but that wasn't enough for hunters and introductions of all kinds of subspecies were made.

Northern Bobwhite is only native to southeastern Wyoming. If you see it elsewhere in the state, those birds are from introduced populations.

Whether they immigrate with help from people or move in on their own, birds are constantly testing new locations for suitability—for living and raising young.

223 Bird strikes, bird movements interest UW students

Friday, November 3, 2023, ToDo, page A8

Cheyenne Audubon's October meeting attendees heard from two University of Wyoming students about their bird studies, and about WYOBIRD, the Wyoming Bird Initiative for Resilience and Diversity.

Katie Shabron is an undergraduate who is already involved in bird studies, measuring the number of birds killed by colliding with windows on campus. Window collisions are the second worst human-caused hazard for birds in the U.S.—the first is loose cats.

This fall there was a terrible slaughter of migrating songbirds in one day caused by the perfect reflection of sky by the all-glass façade of the giant McCormick convention center on the edge of Lake Michigan in downtown Chicago. It's been a hazard for years.

On the UW campus, trees and building facades have been mapped and a phone app made available to students allows them to record instances of dead birds as well as no dead birds.

Katie said the first year's data didn't pick up many dead birds, creating more questions such as, are campus building layout and design not conducive to bird strikes? Are birds hitting windows but fluttering away and dying elsewhere?

Katie said the most effective defense against window strikes, if it's too late to install the special glass, is sheets of tiny dots that stick to the outside of windows. They are only visible from outside. Turning out lights at night, which UW does, and especially on tall buildings in big cities, reduces strikes, too.

PhD candidate Emily Shertzer is focused on tracking birds across their full annual cycle as she studies the effect of gas field development on birds near Pinedale.

Traditionally, bird studies have taken place during breeding season, when birds are returning to their breeding grounds and sticking around their nests. That was partly due to the tracking methods available, like banding.

Emily bands birds with the traditional metal leg band with the unique number that can be looked up through the national Bird Banding Laboratory if the bird is recaptured. Her birds also have three colored bands in unique combinations so that they can be identified by sight, without having to capture them.

Radio telemetry has been around for a while for large animals, but now that radio tags can be small enough for birds to wear, it's possible to track the bird's location every 30 seconds. It's much easier to figure out what kills birds on the breeding grounds where fledgling mortality is high.

Through the MOTUS system of stationary antenna towers being set up around the world by different entities, a bird's more extensive travels can be tracked as they fly by and ping an antenna. Each passing bird can be identified and the owner of the tracking device on it is notified.

Emily has set up a similar, but small system to track her study birds around their breeding territory after she finds a nest of a Brewer's sparrow, sage sparrow or sage thrasher. Being able to track the young birds means she can find them quickly if they die and discover the reason such as hail or other bad weather or predators. If birds can make it past the fledgling stage and all the predators and accidents waiting to happen, they might live seven or eight years.

The condition of the parent birds predicts the condition of the young and their ability to survive those early days.

Apparently, human development within their breeding area does negatively affect fledgling survival.

Do these attached radio devices make a bird more likely to die? No, they don't seem to. The tags have to be less than 3% of the bird's weight.

Emily's subjects are migratory birds, and their routes can be traced by equipping them with geolocators. These don't send signals but instead, they record light levels, showing the timing of sunrise and sunset where the bird is. Turns out this is a way to tell the bird's migratory route and where it spends the winter. But you must recapture that bird when it returns in the spring to get the data. Good thing males are fairly faithful to their breeding site.

Finding out where birds die is a step towards improving conditions. Emily cited the example of two populations of one songbird species that breed hundreds of miles apart in southeastern U.S. One population was doing well, the other was rapidly declining. A study showed the population doing well spent the winter spread out in Central and northern South America. The declining group all spent the winter together in a comparatively small area where their habitat was rapidly being destroyed.

We need lots more ornithologists studying birds to understand their many characteristics and behaviors. UW's WYOBIRD program gives students more field experience and builds interest in bird studies. Check out the opportunities for involvement and support, https://wyobird.org/.

Emily is also looking for funding for her continuing studies. Contact her at eshertze@uwyo.edu.

224 Biologist attends meeting of flyway council protecting migratory birds

Do you know what North American flyway you live in? I was born in the Atlantic, grew up in the Mississippi, live in the Central and visit my granddaughter in the Pacific.

Birds don't usually change flyways like that, but they can be blown off-course. And some prefer to migrate east-west, like harlequin ducks. They winter off the Pacific coast, from Alaska down to Oregon, and head east, inland, to breed, including in northwestern Wyoming.

Wyoming is split between the Central and Pacific flyways, right down the Continental Divide, and although he lives in Cheyenne, Wyoming Game and Fish Department biologist Grant Frost represented Wyoming at a meeting of the Pacific Flyway Council last year. He shared his experience at the November Cheyenne Audubon meeting.

The flyway councils are the people who gather all the data they can get their hands on, looking at academic studies as well as non-governmental and governmental wildlife data (including eBird more and more) in August or early September. There are also reports from Canada and Mexico and a second meeting in the spring.

The health of populations of migratory game birds like ducks, geese, mourning doves and sandhill cranes is considered. Non-migratory gamebirds like pheasants are not. Then the council conveys hunt limits for each species to the states which translate them into limits for hunting regulations that come out in fall.

While the councils can tell each state the maximum number of a species that can be killed, the states can choose to be more conservative.

The Pacific Flyway Council and the other councils were established in 1952. In 2006, the flyways established non-game bird technical committees. Grant was assigned to the one for the Pacific. He's been a bird nerd for a long time, but the meeting gave him new perspectives on birds and bird management.

With the Pacific Flyway extending from a corner of New Mexico on up to Alaska, there are a wide variety of concerns and cultural ways of relating to birds.

For instance, Utah has a swan hunting season, but not Wyoming.

Bald eagles were protected nationally in 1940, but back then Alaska offered a bounty on them because they were competing for salmon. Then Alaska became the 49th state in 1959 and began protecting bald eagles.

Sometimes, managing one species to increase their population has the secondary effect of depleting another species of concern. Grant mentioned the population of common ravens, arguably one of the smartest birds, which has become more successful by adopting the habit of shopping for groceries/roadkill along the highways. But more ravens mean more of them finding and eating the eggs of species of concern like sage grouse and desert tortoises.

Sometimes three species are involved: eagles fly over Caspian tern nesting colonies, causing the terns to flush. While their nests are unprotected, gulls gobble the eggs and young.

Then there are the Indigenous people who have always hunted birds and collected eggs, especially in a tough environment like Alaska. Grant heard gull eggs are particularly prized. Bird pelts go into traditional crafts.

The 2023 Alaska Subsistence Spring/Summer Migratory Bird Harvest was April 2 through August 31, when eggs are most plentiful, and feathers are brightest. Thirty species are listed: waterfowl, waterbirds, shorebirds, seabirds, cranes and owls. Owls? They are big, but here in Wyoming they are not considered game. Perhaps in Alaska they are not considered food either but harvested for feathers.

Grant also sat on the raptor subcommittee which was addressing the number of peregrine falcons being taken by falconers. Who knew we'd finally have this problem when for years we thought peregrines might become extinct? Then there are the protected golden eagles, much more numerous than bald eagles,

killing sheep. And there's discussion about the effects of climate change.

Next year the Pacific Flyway Council will be meeting in Wyoming. The meeting Grant attended was in Juneau, Alaska.

There are new ways of studying migration every year and new knowledge gained from them, influencing the work of all the councils.

Recently I checked out a new book from the Laramie County Library, "Flight Paths: How a Passionate and Quirky Group of Pioneering Scientists Solved the Mystery of Bird Migration," by Rebecca Heisman. It's not too technical for most readers, especially people who read my bird columns.

I noticed a bookplate inside said that the book was added to the library's collection on the advice of a library patron. Thank you, whoever you are! I'll try to return the book as soon as I can so someone else can read it!

2024

225 Latest Cheyenne Christmas Bird Count looks a bit different from 1956's

Recently, Bob Dorn shared the results of the Cheyenne Christmas Bird Count from the December 1955-January 1956 count season, the 56th CBC (overall).

It's interesting to compare the differences over 68 years:

--Then, the 7.5-mile-diameter count circle was centered on the KFBC radio station when it was on East Lincolnway, where Channel 5 is now, Dave Montgomery told me. Now it's the Capitol.

--The percentage of open country was higher. Laramie County had only 60,000 people, today 100,000.

--The Cheyenne Audubon Club became the Cheyenne – High Plains Audubon Society in 1974.

--Married women now get to use their own first names. I first met Mrs. Robert Hanesworth, May, in 1989, when she was the Cheyenne count compiler.

--Lt. Col. Charles H. Snyder could have been with F.E. Warren Air Force Base, giving count participants access to that part of the count circle. Today we have retired Col. Charles Seniawski birding the base for us.

Seven bird names have changed:

--Some Canada geese are now cackling geese.

--Marsh hawk is now northern harrier.

--Red-shafted and yellow-shafted flickers are now northern flicker.

--American magpie is now black-billed magpie.

--Gray shrike is now northern shrike.

--Common starling is now European starling.

--The white-winged, Oregon and pink-sided juncos were combined with other juncos as the dark-eyed junco.

Participation has changed, too. We had 24 people help this time compared to only seven in 1956. So naturally we traveled more hours and more miles by foot and vehicle. And back in the 50s, apparently the hours put into watching bird feeders weren't separated.

For our Dec. 16 count we had similar weather – not too windy, no snow – but warmer, around 50 instead of 40.

As for the birds themselves, we counted more species and more geese, crows and starlings. Interestingly, we reported a greater variety of ducks, hawks and falcons, too.

But it's been a long time since we've seen evening grosbeaks. This may be the result of the decline in their population overall.

This year's highlights were the

northern goshawk in Western Hills seen during count week (CW), the three days before and after count day, and the lone snow goose at Lions Park.

Audubon Field Notes – 56th CBC

Published by the National Audubon Society in Collaboration with the U.S. Fish and Wildlife Service

56th Christmas Bird Count; Vol. 10, No.2; two dollars per copy; April 1956

436. Cheyenne, Wyo. (7 ½-mile radius centering from radio station KFBC on east edge of town; city parks and cemeteries 30%, open prairie, deciduous & evergreen trees 20%, prairie roadside 10%, open meadows, reservoirs and creek bottoms 40%).

Jan. 2, 8 a.m. to 4:30 p.m. Clear; temp. 31 degrees to 46 degrees; wind W, 15-35 m.p.h.; no snow. Seven observers in 3 parties. Total party-hour, 56 (6 on foot, 50 by car); total party-miles, 148 (8 on foot, 140 by car).

Canada Goose 12
Mallard 20
Rough-legged Hawk 5
Golden Eagle 1
Marsh Hawk 1
Red-shafted Flicker 13
Hairy Woodpecker 1
Downy Woodpecker 1
Horned Lark 2029 (4 Northern)
American Magpie 25
American Robin 3
Bohemian Waxwing 2
Gray Shrike 1
Common Starling 98
House Sparrow 138
Evening Grosbeak 25
House Finch 4
Pine Grosbeak 4
Pine Siskin 2
White-winged Junco 1
Oregon Junco 86 (pink-sided 84)
American Tree Sparrow 18
Lapland Longspur 22

Total, 23 species (2 additional subsp.), about 2512 individuals. (Observed in area count period: American Goldeneye, Ring-necked Pheasant, Mountain Chickadee, Mockingbird, Townsend's Solitaire, Common Redpoll, Slate-colored Junco).

Charles Brown, Mrs. Charles Brown, Mr. & Mrs. Robert Hanesworth, Wilhelmina Miller, Lt. Col. and Mrs. Charles H. Snyder (compiler) (Cheyenne Audubon Club).

Cheyenne Christmas Bird Count – 124th CBC

Dec. 16, 2023; 24 participants

Feeder watch time: 11 hours, 36 minutes; Walking: 12 hours, 25 minutes, 19.56 miles; Driving: 4 hours 19 minutes, 87.3 miles

Compiler: Grant Frost

Cackling Goose 183
Canada Goose 1686
Snow Goose 1
Mallard 207
Northern Shoveler 18
Green-winged Teal 3
Lesser Scaup CW
Common Goldeneye 2
Rock Dove (pigeon) 479
Eurasian Collared-Dove 107
Mourning Dove 3
Ring-billed Gull CW
Golden Eagle 1
Northern Harrier 9
Sharp-shinned Hawk CW
Cooper's Hawk 1
American Goshawk CW
Bald Eagle 2
Red-tailed Hawk 6
Rough-legged Hawk CW
Ferruginous Hawk 1
Eastern Screech-Owl CW
Great Horned Owl 1
Belted Kingfisher 2
Downy Woodpecker 3
Hairy Woodpecker 1
Northern Flicker 21

American Kestrel 2
Merlin 2
Northern Shrike 1
Blue Jay 2
Black-billed Magpie 84
American Crow 108
Common Raven 12
Black-capped Chickadee 1
Mountain Chickadee 9
Horned Lark 270
White-breasted Nuthatch 1
Red-breasted Nuthatch 2
Brown Creeper 1
Winter Wren 1
European Starling 221
Townsend's Solitaire 5
American Robin 2
House Sparrow 205
House Finch 63
Pine Siskin 1
American Goldfinch 9
American Tree Sparrow 13
Chipping Sparrow 1
Dark-eyed Junco 61
White-crowned Sparrow 6
Song Sparrow 2
Red-winged Blackbird 50

Acknowledgements

Writing Bird Banter columns for the Wyoming Tribune Eagle's readers for 25 years has been a privilege and I've enjoyed working with various editors.

Outdoors section editor Bill Gruber's invitation to write a monthly (or twice a month for a while) column in 1999 came about because I was the one writing news releases about Audubon chapter events. They included my name and phone number, so Bill started calling me when he needed the local angle on bird news. I'm forever in his debt for giving me this role in the community.

Bill left for a new career culminating in becoming a Florida state parks superintendent. The Outdoors section continued under Ty Stockton who now works for state government.

Cara Easton Baldwin was next. I still have the wool ski socks she gave me for Christmas. She's gone on to work for the governor's office and for other publications and organizations.

You can recognize Shauna Stephenson's era because of the many sub-headlines she used. She went on to work for Trout Unlimited and last I checked, she is a market gardener in Montana and serves on the board of the Mountain Mamas, an environmental group.

Kevin Wingert was more of a temporary Outdoors editor. However, he oversaw the "Bird of the Week" project that I did with photographer Pete Arnold from mid-2008 to mid-2010. Those short essays and photos (not included here) became the book, "Cheyenne Birds by the Month," which has sold more than 1,500 copies locally (and more through print-on-demand – including 14 copies in Italy, inexplicably).

Around 2010, the Outdoors section was placed in the E section, the Features section, starting on page E2 in full color. Page E1 was reserved for colorful feature stories, sometimes my column. I reported to Jodi Rogstad, the Features editor. She sold the managing editor on the idea of me adding a monthly garden column in 2012. Often, she would shoot me column ideas, suggesting localizing a topic she had seen on the national wire service.

Ellen Fike stepped in for a little while. In the confusion, a couple columns did not appear in the WTE, only through Dave Lerner's digital news service. I've included them in this collection anyway.

Niki Kottmann took over as Features editor in the fall of 2019, just in time for the pandemic, and was followed by Will Carpenter, who left the paper in 2024.

Of course, my columns do not get in the paper without the approval of the managing editor. When I started, she was Mary Woolsey, followed by Reed Eckhardt and currently Brian Martin.

For this iteration of Bird Banter, I'd like to thank graphic designer Chris Hoffmeister for her patience and great ideas. Elizabeth Sampson and Ursula Vigil, thank you for reading through and cleaning up typos and missing words and grammatical mistakes.

Thank you, readers. Once my picture started showing up alongside each column back in 1999, readers seeing me at the grocery store began to stop and tell me their bird stories. It's been a way to hear what birds are up to around town. And get invited to give bird talks to local clubs. These days readers are more likely to text or email me a bird photo with their question.

Besides editors and readers, I'd like to thank all the people sharing information, most of whom are named in the columns. From backyard birdwatchers to the staff of the University of Wyoming Biodiversity Institute, the UW Department of Zoology and Physiology and staff members of government agencies and environmental non-profits, it's been a pleasure meeting you. In particular, Jane and Robert Dorn, authors of "Wyoming Birds," have always been readily available authorities.

For this "Best of" edition I asked for volunteers to vote on their favorite columns. Thank you, Jane Dorn, Beth Dykstra, Bill Gruber, Jeff Hackett, Yoma Ullman and Ursula Vigil.

And finally, to Audubon and all the members of the Cheyenne – High Plains Audubon Society, the staff of Wyoming Audubon, now rolled into the regional office of Audubon Rockies, and the staff and members of the National Audubon Society, all of whom continue to battle for the birds: thank you.

INDEX OF TOPICS

Numbers correspond to article numbers, not page numbers.

Belvoir Ranch, 110

Big Day Bird Count, 4, 108, 163, 178, 195, 212

BioBlitz, 165

Bird atlas, 2

Bird banding, 100

Bird Banter archives, 155

Bird baths, 35

Bird behavior, 176, 186

Bird checklist, 84

Bird conservation, 152, 189, 190, 217

Bird counts, 4, 13, 14, 37, 50, 61, 74, 108, 163, 165, 174, 178, 191, 195, 199, 207, 212

Bird diseases, 5

Bird feeding, 9, 114, 122, 128, 160, 206

Bird finding, 172

Bird flu, 87

Bird gardening, 30, 32

Bird habitat, 126, 127, 201, 204

Bird i.d., 6, 33, 45, 46, 67, 102, 119, 188

Bird i.d.: ducks, 53, 96

Bird i.d.: sound, 116

Bird irruptions, 137

Bird names, 118

Bird nests, 48

Bird news, 211

Bird people, 143

Bird photography, 161, 187

Bird quiz, 157

Bird records, 47

Bird reports, 28, 29

Bird rescue, 36

Bird safety, 107, 124, 131, 177, 208

Bird science, 218, 223

Bird song, 19

Bird taxonomy, 8

Bird trails, 209

Bird watching, 1, 12, 15, 18

Bird species
    Bluebirds, 44
    Burrowing Owl, 179

Cassin's finch, 200

Cedar Waxwing, 95

Chickadee, 66

Condor, 79, 180

Cranes, 42

Crossbills, 98

Crow, 125, 221

Dipper, 57

Doves, 80, 104

Ducks, 73

Eagles, 166

Flammulated Owl, 85

Geese, 136

Goshawk, 105

Grebes, 154

Gulls, 75

House Sparrow, 220

Hummingbirds, 24, 83

Juncos, 11

Kinglet, 104

Kite, 142

Loons, 154

Mountain Plover, 99

Owls, 38, 81, 144, 148

Pelican, 123

Peregrine, 132

Raptors, 168, 209

Red-bellied Woodpecker, 39

Ring-necked pheasant, 210

Robin, 129

Rosy-finches, 101

Sage-Grouse, 93, 175

Sandhill Crane, 145

Sharp-tailed Grouse, 82

Snowy Owl, 130

Starling, 63

Swifts, 134

Thick-billed Longspur, 219

Trumpeter Swan, 59

Turkey Vulture, 94

Warblers, 54, 92

Woodpeckers, 86, 90

BirdCast, 183

Birding, backyard, 17, 18, 55, 89, 113, 133, 173

Birding, beginning, 62

Birding, by ear, 171

Birding, kids, 141, 158

Birding Cheyenne, 88, 120, 121, 181

Birding ethics, 150

Birding hotspot, 40

Birding naked, 108

Birding publications, 60

Birding Wyoming, 22, 27

Birds & climate change, 140

Birds & energy, 106

Birds & energy, wind, 146, 167

Birds & energy, wind, Roundhouse, 182, 183, 184, 185

Birds & water wells, 193

Birds, baby, 48, 97

Birds in winter, 103

Birds in Yellowstone, 111

Birdwatching, 21, 194, 205

Birdwatching, Merlin, 214

Breeding Bird Survey, 23

Cats indoors, 3, 52, 153

Cheyenne Audubon, 151

Christmas Bird Count, 13, 37, 61, 207, 225

Citizen science, 170, 215

eBird, 139, 169

Field trips, 196

Fledging, 31

Flyways, 224

Great Backyard Bird Count, 14, 191

Habitat Hero, 156

Habitat: backyard, 43

Hanesworth, May, 10

Numbers correspond to article numbers, not page numbers.

Hazard: windmills, 71
Hunting, 26

_____

Important Bird Area, 49, 112

_____

Migration, 34, 72, 147, 224
Migration, fall, 25, 58, 203, 216
Migration, spring, 16, 64
Migratory Bird Treaty
    Act, 198, 224

_____

Nesting, 109, 117, 197,
    202, 203, 213

_____

Pine beetle, 115
Project FeederWatch, 12,
    74, 174, 199

_____

Ranching, conservation, 190
Range management, 51
Rocky Mountain Bird
    Observatory, 65
Roundhouse wind, 182,
    183, 184, 185

_____

Songbird brains, 162
Squirrels, 77, 78

_____

Thanksgiving Bird Count, 50
Travel,
Mountains, 159
    Wyoming, 69, 70, 76, 91, 149

_____

University of Wyoming
    Vertebrate Museum, 221

_____

West Nile Virus, 56, 68
Wildlife watching license, 138
Window hazards, 20
Wyobirds, 41, 192
Wyoming birds, 222

INDEX OF PEOPLE, PLACES, BOOKS, AGENCIES, ORGANIZATIONS, ETC.

Numbers correspond to article numbers, not page numbers.

1838 Rendezvous Historic Site 320

2016 State of the Birds report, 164

3BillionBirds.org, 189

———

A Birder's Guide to Wyoming, 172

A Murder of Crows documentary film, 125

A Season on the Wind, 182

A World on the Wing: The Global Odyssey of Migratory Birds, 203

Access to Wyoming's Wildlife, 76

Ackerman, Jennifer, 197

Acopian Center for Conservation Learning, 94

AECOM, 184

Agricultural Water Enhancement Program, 193

Aircraft Detection Lighting System, 185

Alaska Subsistence Spring/ Summer Migratory Bird Harvest, 224

Alcova Reservoir, 76, 79

Alden, Peter, 172

AllAboutBirds.org, 158, 164, 168, 174, 194, 199

Allyn, Lela, 77

American Bird Conservancy, 114, 131, 177, 198, 206

American Birding Association, 60, 72, 118, 121, 135, 137, 172, 178, 188, 189

American Ornithologists' Union, 8, 102, 103, 118

American Wind Energy Association, 71

American Wind Wildlife Institute, 167

Amundson, Marta and Larry, 22

Anderson, Stan, 34, 49

Apache-Sitgreaves National Forest, 81

Arapaho National Wildlife Refuge Complex, 149

Arapaho tribe, 110

Arnold, Pete, 181, 187, 194

Art of the Winds, 187

Atlas missiles, 110

Atlas of Birds, Mammals, Reptiles and Amphibians in Wyoming, 47, 79, 102

Audubon Center at Garden Creek, 100

Audubon Conservation Ranching Initiative, 189, 208

Audubon Minnesota, 124

Audubon Photography Awards, 187

Audubon Rockies, 151, 156, 165, 166, 172, 185, 189, 190, 208, 215

Audubon Wyoming, 51, 106, 112, 139, 175

Audubon Wyoming Community Naturalist, 100

Auk, The 118

———

Baby Birds: An Artist Looks into the Nest, 188

Backstrom, Jan, 181

Bakken, Bradley Hartman, 83

Bald and Golden Eagle Protection Act, 168

Baldwin, Cara Eastwood, 155

Banks, Tim, 168

Barber, Brian, 151

Barnes and Noble, 187

Barr Lake State Park, Colorado, 72

Basset, Clint, 156

Battle Creek, 76, 85

Bauldry, Vincent, 44

Beason, Jason, 134

Beaver Dam Analog, 204

Beck, Jeff, 105

Belvoir Ranch, 110, 165, 182, 184

Benkman, Craig, 98

Bent, Arthur Cleveland, 154, 164

Berquist, Francis, 68

Big Hole, 110

Bildstein, Keith, 94

Bioblitz, 165, 184

Biological Conservation journal, 170

Bird banding, 215

Bird Banter, 155

Bird Conservancy of the Rockies (See also Rocky Mountain Bird Observatory), 189, 198

Bird flu, 87, 221

Bird Migration Explorer, 215

Bird of Conservation Concern, 179

Bird of the Week, 181

Bird Tape for windows, 177

BirdCast, 20, 183

Birder's World, 60

Birdhouse Network, 90

Birding magazine, 121

Birding Without Borders, 172

BirdingPal.org, 172

BirdLife International, 163

Birds Canada, 199

Birds of North America Online, 86, 92, 99, 129, 136, 142, 179, 200

Birds of Wyoming, 129, 137, 140, 142, 143, 154, 216, 222

Bird-Safe Building Guidelines, 124

BirdSource, 60

———

BirdTape (for windows), 131

Birek, Jeff, 151

Black Hills, Wyoming, 86, 91

Black Mountain fire lookout, 69

Blackburne, Anna, 216

Blog posts, 155

Bly, Bart, 99

Boehm, Elizabeth, 181, 187

Borie oil field, 110

Boulder Imaging, 167

Bowers, Jennifer, 81

Breeding Bird Survey, 23

Budd, Bob, 51, 149, 175, 217

Bureau of Land Management, 106, 175, 211

Burrowing Owl Conservation Network, 179

Buteo Books, 172

———

Cade, Tom, 132

Camp Carlin, 110

Canadian Wildlife Service, 34

Canon PowerShot camera, 161

Caproni, Valerie, U.S. District Court Judge, 198

Carleton, Scott, 83

Carling, Matt, 139

Carrey, Steve, 115

Cats Indoors, 3

Cerovski, Andrea (see also Orabona), 8, 17, 23, 45, 49

Champions of the Flyway, 163

Check, Kim, 100

Checklist of North American Birds, 118

Checklist of the Birds of Cheyenne, Wyoming and Vicinity, 84

Chesnut, Lorie, 204

Cheyenne - High Plains Audubon Society (see also Cheyenne Audubon), 1, 9, 33, 42, 62, 73, 76, 81, 88, 91, 92, 93, 106, 115, 125, 131, 135, 139, 151, 152, 156, 163, 171, 172, 176, 178, 181, 185, 196, 210, 217, 225

Cheyenne Animal Shelter, 153

Cheyenne Audubon (see also Cheyenne - High Plains), 84, 162, 184, 190, 192, 195, 204, 205, 207, 211, 215, 223, 224

Cheyenne Audubon Club, 225

Cheyenne Big Day Bird Count, 195, 211

Cheyenne Bird Checklist, 103, 157

Cheyenne Birds by the Month, 187, 194

Cheyenne Board of Public Utilities, 156

Cheyenne Botanic Gardens, 43, 88, 151, 156, 181, 187, 212

Cheyenne City Council, 153

Cheyenne Compost Facility, 126

Cheyenne Depot Museum, 187

Cheyenne Greenway, 196, 203

Cheyenne Habitat Hero Workshop, 208

Cheyenne Mountain Bike Association, 184

Cheyenne Pet Clinic, 48, 97, 154, 177, 187

Cheyenne Regional Medical Center Pink Boutique, 187

CheyenneBirdBanter. com, 160, 194

Chindgren, Steve, 106

Christmas Bird Count, 189, 207, 215

Church, Christopher, DVM, 154

Citizen science, 170

Citizen Scientist, Searching for Heroes and Hope in an Age of Extinction, 170

City of Cheyenne, 184

Cobirds, 80

Code of Birding Ethics, 81

Colorado Birding Trail, 209

Colorado Breeding Bird Atlas, 2

Colorado State University Cooperative Extension, 90

Community Cat Initiative, 153

Community science, 215

Condors in Canyon Country, 180

Congressional Award, 165

Conn, Laura, 97

Conservation Ranching Initiative, 190

Conservation Reserve Program, 82

Contributions to Biodiversity Science Award, 143

Contributions to Wyoming Biodiversity Conservation, 143

Cornelison, John, 151, 207

Cornell Lab of Ornithology (other than bird counts), 43, 60, 90, 109, 121, 122, 130, 152, 109, 170, 183, 189, 198, 199, 211, 214, 218

Costopolous, Barbara, 61

Crane Trust Nature and Visitors Center, 145

Creekmore, Terry, 168

Crow Creek, 142, 204, 211

Culek, Bernie, 99

Curry, Martin, 149

Curt Gowdy State Park, 57, 64, 168, 186, 187, 196

———

Decline of the North American Avifauna study, 189, 198

Denver Audubon, 192

Denver to Fort Laramie stage line, 110

Diamond Wings Upland Game Birds, 210

Digiscope, 161

Doherty, Kevin, 106

Doktor, Aadrian, 183, 189

Domenici, Dominic, 79

Dorn, Jane and Robert, 6, 8, 21, 24, 25, 33, 34, 37, 39, 40, 47, 61, 69, 79, 84, 86, 132, 143, 156, 164, 172, 178, 181, 207, 225

Downar Bird Farm, 210

Downey, Dusty, 190

Downey, Jacelyn, 192

Droll Yankee bird feeders, 77

Dry Creek, 204

Duke Energy, 167, 182

Duncraft bird feeders, 77

Dunne, Pete, 92

———

Eagle take permit, 211

East Park (see also Kiwanis Park), 204

Eastern Shoshone tribe, 110

Easton, Beth, 28

eBird, 103, 120, 121, 129, 139, 140, 147, 151, 155, 160, 163, 164, 170, 172, 183, 186, 196, 203, 215, 216, 218

eBird Mobile, 169

Edmunds, Daly, 185

Edness Kimball-Wilkins State Park, 109

Environment and Climate Change Canada, 189, 198

Numbers correspond to article numbers, not page numbers.

Erwin, Kathleen, 82
Esterbrook Campground, 69

———

F. E. Warren Air Force Base, 108, 136, 169, 204
Farr, Robert, DVM, 97
Fatal Light Awareness Program, 20
Faulkner, Doug, 58, 75, 85, 102, 118, 127, 137, 140, 143, 154, 216, 222
Felley, Dave, 23, 28
Feral Cats and Their Management, 153
Finding Birds Around the World, 172
Fitzpatrick, John, 151, 152
Fitzpatrick, Ryan, 184, 211
Flamm Fest, 85
Flaspohler, Dave, 92
Flicker, John, 64
Flight Paths: How a Passionate and Quirky Group of Pioneering Scientists Solved the Mystery of Bird Migration, 224
Floyd, Ted, 72, 121, 135, 142, 151, 161, 178, 188
Fort Collins, 75
Fort Collins Audubon Society, 62
Fort Laramie National Historic Site, 61
Fossil Creek Reservoir Natural Area, Colorado, 75, 205
Fox squirrel, 77, 78
FOY, First of Year species observations, 140
Friend Park Campground, 69
Friends of the Belvoir, 182
Frost, Grant, 179, 196, 207, 212, 216, 224

———

Gammon, Dave, 66
Garden Creek, 27
Gauthreaux, Sidney, 183
Gentile, Olivia, 121
Georgetown University, 189, 198
Gerhart, Bill, 82
Geyer, Jeff, 204

Gibbons, Euell, 89
Gill, Matthew, 188
Gill, Priscilla, 188
Ginter, Jana, 109
Global Big Day, 163
Gooders, John, 172
Gorges, Bryan and Jessie, 169
Goshen Hole, 76
GPS, 79
Gramm fire, 86
Granite Canon Environmental Committee, 184
Grayrocks Reservoir, 61
Great Backyard Bird Count, 215
Great Pikes Peak Birding Trail, 209
Greyrocks Reservoir, 145
Growing Native Plants of the Rocky Mountain Area, 156
Gruber, Bill, 155
Guernsey, 61, 137
Guernsey State Park, 61
Gunn, Carolyn, 134

———

Habitat Hero, 151, 156, 190
Hall, Minna B., 198
Hanesworth, May, 10, 141, 163, 207, 225
Hannibal, Mary Ellen, 170
Hanson, Dave, 29
Hartville, 137, 200
Hawk Mountain Sanctuary, 94
Hawk Springs Reservoir, 76
Headquarters Trail, Medicine Bow National Forest, 214
Hecker, Jim and Carol, 12, 207
Heisman, Rebecca, 224
Helzer, Chris, 190
Hemenway, Harriet, 198
Hensel fire, 69
Hicks, Martin, 17
Hiester, Tom, 167
High Plains Aquifer, 193
High Plains Grasslands Research Station, USDA (High Plains Arboretum), 88, 164, 178, 195, 215
Highly Pathogenic Avian Influenza, 221

Hillsdale, Laramie County, 219
Hoffmeister, Chris, 181
Holliday Park, 59, 109, 117, 120, 121, 123, 127, 136, 181, 186
Holloran, Alison (see also Lyon, Alison), 151, 190
Holloran, Matt, 93
Holsinger, Connie, 151, 156
Hosafros, Judith, 143
How to Raise a Wild Child, 158
Hutchinson, Zach, 172, 180, 208, 215
Hutton Lake National Wildlife Refuge, 73, 76, 149, 168, 178

———

Identiflight, 167
Important Bird Area, 76, 112, 131
iNaturalist, 209, 215
Ingelfinger, Franz, 19
International Shorebird Survey, 189
Interstate 80, 110

———

Jensen, Merrill, 141
Johnsgard, Paul, 130
Johnson, Greg, 71, 79, 84, 137, 161, 178, 181, 188, 207
Jones, Don, 216, 218
Jones, Lynds, 163
Juneau Audubon Society, 141

———

Kaufman, Kenn, 35, 80, 128, 182
Keffer, Ken, 100
Keffer, Larry, 100
Ketcham, Jeff, 88
Keto, Ruth, 56, 77
Kimberling, Brian, 140
Knopf, Fritz, 99
Knorr, Owen A., 134
Kozlowski, Steve, 86
Kroodsma, Donald, 134
Kruse, Gere and Barbara, 149

———

Lake Hattie, 102, 216
Lakota tribe, 110
Lanham, Chuck, 110

Laramie Audubon Society, 73, 139, 149, 168, 180

Laramie County, 185, 193

Laramie County Community College, 84

Laramie County Conservation District, 43, 156, 204, 208

Laramie County Control Area Order, water, 193

Laramie County Library, 43

Laramie County Master Gardeners, 156

Laramie Plains lakes, 102, 108, 178, 216

Laramie Range, 73, 91

Laramie Rivers Conservation District, 149

Lautenbach, Jonathan, 216

Lawrence, Gloria and Jim, 21, 41, 49, 108

Lebsack, Fred, 10, 25, 28, 207

Lee, Bob, 63

Lefko, Gary, 58, 209

Lek, 82

Lerwick family, 193

Leukering, Tony, 75, 102

Levad, Rich, 85, 134

Life List, biography, 121

Lincoln Highway, 110

Lindzey, Fred and Stephanie, 100

Lions Park, 4, 6, 12, 40, 49, 54, 62, 73, 76, 96, 108, 112, 131, 132, 136, 148, 164, 178, 181, 186, 195, 215, 216

Lives of North American Birds, 128

Living on the Wind, 183

Lone Tree Creek, 165

Lopez, Gus, 68

Luce, Bob, 37

Lyon, Alison (see also Holloran), 44, 49, 70, 106

Lyon-Holloran, Alison, 112

Madson, Chris, 143

Maier, Aaron, 208

Maley, James, 139

Mammoth Hot Springs, 91

Manley, Wanda, 219

Martinez del Rio, Carlos, 83

Mason, Joanne, 28

Massachusetts Audubon, 172

Massachusetts Audubon Society for the Protection of Birds, 198

Master Gardeners, 192

McCartney, Blaine, 145

McCown, John P., 219

McCreary, O.C., 132

McDonald, Dave, 70

McEneaney, Terry, 49, 91

McNamee, Stan, 63

McNicholas, Wayne, 142

Mead, Matt, Wyoming Governor, 175

Meadowlark Audubon Society, 139

Medicine Bow National Forest, 69, 159, 171

Medicine Bow Peak, 180

Medicine Bow Range, 70, 73

Medicine Bow-Routt National Forest, 115, 285

Merlin Bird I.D. app, 169, 171, 194, 199

Merlin Sound I.D., 214

Michelson, Chris, 91

Migratory Bird Treaty Act, 146, 163, 168, 198

Milner, Ben, 210

Moench, Belinda and Don, 28

Monitoring for Avian Productivity, 100, 215

Moon, Deb, 186

Moore, Teresa, 127

Moose Day, 192

MOTUS, 223

Munro, Bill, 69

Murie Audubon Society: 27, 109, 172, 192

Murphy, Karagh, 162

Myer, Judy, 145

Naked birding, 108

National Audubon Society, 43, 111, 112, 124, 146, 152, 175, 187, 189, 190, 192, 204, 211

National Bird Banding Laboratory, 223

National Environmental Policy Act, 198

National Renewable Energy Laboratory, 167

National Wildlife Federation, 43

National Wildlife Health Center, 87

National Wind Technology Center, 167

Natural Resources Conservation Service, 193, 217

Natural Resources Defense Council, 166

Nebraska Crane Festival, 145

Nebraska Prairie Partners program, 99

Nelson, Del, 140

NestWatch, 109, 177

New Birder's Field Guide to Birds of North America, 150

NextEra energy company, 182, 184, 211

Nordell, Cameron, 176

North American Bluebird Society, 44

North American Breeding Bird Survey, 189

North American Nature Photography Association, 187

North Crow Reservoir, 109

Northern Cheyenne tribe, 110

Nunn Guy, The, 209

Obrecht, Jeff, 103

Ogallala Aquifer, 193

Ogin Inc., 146

Orabona, Andrea (see also Cerovski), 151

Oregon Trail Ruts State Historic Site, 61

Osborn, Sophie A.H., 180

Otters Dance book, 217

Pacific Flyway Council, 224

Panjabi, Arvind, 72, 86, 189

Pannell, Karen and Fred, 176

Parish, Chris, 180

Partners in Flight Avian Conservation Database, 189

Patchwork birding, 121

Pathfinder Reservoir, 76

Patrick, Sue, 38

Pawnee National
Grasslands, 76, 209

PBR Printing, 181, 187

Peregrine Fund, 79, 132, 167, 180

Perky-Pet bird feeders, 77

Peterson Field Guide to Birds of
North America, 2008, 132

Peterson Field Guide to the
Bird Sounds of Eastern North
America, 171

Pieplow, Nathan, 180

Pine beetle, 115

Point Reyes Bird Observatory, 65

Pole Mountain, Medicine Bow
National Forest, 115

Post Assisted Log Structures, 204

Potter, Kim, 85, 134

Power Company of
Wyoming, 166

Prairie Fire newspaper, 130

Prairie Ghost, 99

Prairie Partners program, 65, 99

PrairieEcologist.com, 190

Prather, Jonathan, 169

———

Raptor Alley, Colorado, 209

Raptor Recovery Nebraska, 130

Rawhide coal power plant, 182

Rawhide Reservoir, 1

Red Mountain Open Space,
Colorado, 165, 182, 184

Renewable Energy Systems, 167

Repshire, Darrel and Marilyn, 222

Riverbend Nursery, 187

Robin nest, 31

Rocky Mountain Bird
Observatory (see also Bird
Conservancy of the Rockies),
58, 65, 72, 85, 86, 99, 134, 151

Rocky Mountain Garden
Survival Guide, 156

Rocky Mountain
National Park, 159

Rocky Mountain
Raptor Center, 109

Rogstad, Jodi, 155

Rogstad, Lucy, 27

Romero, Dave, 49

Rosenberg, Ken, 189

Rothwell, Reg, 17, 43

Roundhouse Wind, 182, 184, 185

Roundhouse Wind Energy
Project, 182, 184, 185

Rowe Audubon
Sanctuary, 42, 145

Rutledge, Brian, 106, 175

Ryder, Ron, 1, 8, 80

———

Sagebrush Ecosystem
Initiative, 175

Sage-Grouse
Implementation Team, 175

Sampson, Scott D., 158

Sandia Crest, 101

Saratoga Lake public
access area, 76

Schmoker, Bill, 72

Scott & Nix field guide
publishers, 135

Scott, Oliver, 21, 40, 54, 172

Scouts, 69

Seagraves, Tom, 88

Seminoe Reservoir, 76

Seniawski, Chuck and Sue, 43, 90,
142, 216, 225

Senner, Stan, 64

Shabron, Katie, 223

Shea, Ruth, 59

Sherman Mountains, 91

Shertzer, Emily, 223

Shirley Basin, 26

Sibley Field Guide to Birds, 200

Sibley Guide to Birds, 105

Sierra Madre Range, 76

Simkins, Velma, 80

Smith, Doug, 111

Smith, Shane, 18, 43

Smithsonian Field Guide to the
Birds of North America, 135

Smithsonian Migratory
Bird Center, 198

Snetsinger, Phoebe, 121

Snowy Range, 70, 76,
101, 159, 200

Snyder, Larry, 99

Soapstone Prairie Natural Area,
Colorado, 165, 182, 184

Society for Range
Management, 51

Soda Lake, 109

Songfinder, 116

Sostrum, Nels, 207

South Gap Lake,
Snowy Range, 174

Southeastern Raptor Center, 167

Species of Greatest Conservation
Need, WGFD, 219

Spiker, Mayor Jack, 88

Springer-Bump Sullivan Wildlife
Habitat Management Area, 76

Squirrel, fox, 77, 78

Stephenson, Shauna, 155

Stockton, Ty, 155

Strickland, Dale, 167

Strycker, Noah, 172, 178

Symchych, Catherine, 15

———

Table Mountain Wildlife Habitat
Management Area, 76

Terra Foundation, 156

Tessman, Steve, 63

The Bird Way: A New Look at
How Birds Talk, Work, Play,
Parent and Think, 197, 198

The Birds of North America,
Golden Press, 132

The Coolest Bird: A Natural
History of the Black Swift, 134

The Nature Conservancy –
Nebraska, 190

The Nature Conservancy,
165, 184, 217

Thompson III, Bill, 24, 36, 150

Thompson, Beauford, 214

Timberman, Ann, 149

Top of the World wind
farm, 167, 211

Townsend, John Kirk, 99

Trail Ridge Road, Colorado, 159

Treasure Island public
access area, 76

Tuthill, Dorothy, 192

Tweit, Susan, 156

Numbers correspond to article numbers, not page numbers.

U.S. Centers for Disease Control, 87, 221

U.S. Fish and Wildlife Service, 43, 79, 82, 136, 166, 175, 179, 180, 198, 221

U.S. Forest Service, 86, 115

U.S. Geological Survey, 198

U.S. Highway 30, 110

Union Pacific Railroad, 110

University of Wisconsin - Stevens Point, 44

University of Wyoming, 93, 130, 218

University of Wyoming Biodiversity Institute, 139, 143, 165, 176, 180, 184, 192

University of Wyoming Extension office, 177

University of Wyoming Haub School of Environment and Natural Resources, 202

University of Wyoming Museum of Vertebrates, 170, 221

University of Wyoming Zoology and Physiology Department, 83, 98, 139, 162

Upper North Crow Reservoir, 200

Vascular Plants of Wyoming, 143

Vedauwoo Recreation Area, 171

VerCauteren, Tammy, 65

Warren Livestock Company, 110

Warren Peak, 91

Weidensaul, Scott, 34, 183, 203

Welch, Ken, 83

Welty, Joel Carl, 154

WEST (see also Western EcoSystems Technology), 184

West Nile Virus, 56, 68, 221

Western EcoSystems Technology Inc., 71, 167, 185

Western Sky Design, 181

Western Water Network Grant, 204

What's This Bird? 188

Wildcat Audubon Society, 99

Wilderness Society, 166

Wildscaping, 156

Wilson Journal of Ornithology, 134

Wingert, Kevin, 155, 181

Wissner, Catherine, 43, 107

Witcosky, Jeff, 86

Wommack, Elizabeth, 170, 221

Woodhouse, Gay, 88

World Center for Birds of Prey, 132

Worthman, Tina, 181

Wright, Jeananne, 181

WY Outside, 172

Wyobio database, 165

WYOBIRD, 223

Wyobirds, 41, 130, 154, 192

Wyoming Audubon Chapters Campout, 109

Wyoming Audubon Society, 151

Wyoming Bioblitz (see also Bioblitz), 192

Wyoming Bird Hotline, 192

Wyoming Bird Initiative for Resilience and Diversity, 223

Wyoming Bird Records Committee, 47, 79, 102, 119, 216

Wyoming Bird Trail app, 172

Wyoming Birding Bonanza, 139

Wyoming Birds book, 24, 132, 143, 164, 172, 178

Wyoming Citizen Science Conference, 170

Wyoming Department of Environmental Quality, 185, 211

Wyoming Department of Health, 68

Wyoming Game and Fish Department, 40, 43, 47, 82, 103, 110, 132, 138, 143, 149, 177, 182, 185, 187, 210, 211, 217, 219, 221, 224

Wyoming Geographic Alliance, 165

Wyoming Hereford Ranch, 58, 62, 76, 112, 131, 132, 142, 151, 178, 195, 215, 216, 222

Wyoming Hereford Ranch Reservoir No. 1, 67, 197

Wyoming Important Bird Area, 151, 181

Wyoming Industrial Siting Council, 182, 184, 185

Wyoming Master Naturalists, 192

Wyoming Migration Initiative, 217

Wyoming Native Plant Society, 69

Wyoming Outdoor Council, 175

Wyoming Pathways, 184

Wyoming Raptor Initiative, 176

Wyoming State Office Bureau of Land Management, 175

Wyoming State Engineer, 193

Wyoming State Museum, 181, 187

Wyoming State Parks, 172

Wyoming Tribune Eagle, 155, 181, 182

Wyoming Wildlife and Natural Resources Trust, 149, 217

Wyoming Wildlife Consultants, 93

Wyoming Wildlife Federation, 175

Wyoming Wildlife magazine, 143, 187

Yarnold, David, 146

Yellowstone National Park, 91, 111

Yellowstone Wolf Project, 111

Young Farmers club, 193

Zickefoose, Julie, 188

Zinke, Ryan, U.S. Department of Interior, 175

Zoom, 196